D0712981

DATE DUE

AP 2'05			

HISTORICAL DICTIONARIES OF RELIGIONS, PHILOSOPHIES, AND MOVEMENTS
Edited by Jon Woronoff

Historical Dictionary of Reformed Churches

Robert Benedetto
Darrell L. Guder
Donald K. McKim

*Historical Dictionaries of Religions,
Philosophies, and Movements, No. 24*

The Scarecrow Press, Inc.
Lanham, Maryland, and London
1999

SCARECROW PRESS, INC.

Published in the United States of America
by Scarecrow Press, Inc.
4720 Boston Way
Lanham, Maryland 20706
http://www.scarecrowpress.com

4 Pleydell Gardens, Folkestone
Kent CT20 2DN, England

Copyright ©1999 by Robert Benedetto, Darrell L. Guder, and Donald K.
McKim

British Library Cataloguing in Publication Information Available

Library of Congress Cataloging-in-Publication Data

Benedetto, Robert, 1950–
    Historical dictionary of Reformed Churches / Robert Benedetto, Darrell
L. Guder, Donald K. McKim.
        p. cm. — (Historical dictionaries of religions, philosophies, and
    movements ; no. 24)
        Includes bibliographical references.
        ISBN 0-8108-3628-9 (hardcover : alk. paper)
        1. Reformed Church—History—Dictionaries. I. Guder, Darrell L.,
    1939–   . II. McKim, Donald K. III. Title. IV. Series.
    BX9415.B46   1999   98-50486
    284'.2'09—dc21   CIP

⊚™ The paper used in this publication meets the minimum requirements of
American National Standard for Information Sciences—Permanence of
Paper for Printed Library Materials, ANSI/NISO Z39.48–1992.
Manufactured in the United States of America.

In memory of Robert S. Paul,
a churchman in the Reformed tradition
whose scholarship, piety, and witness
have instructed and inspired us

Contents

Editor's Foreword

As is evident from its name, the Reformed church tradition was born of the Protestant Reformation in Europe. To many, this segment of Christianity is also known by the name of a reformer (e.g., Calvinist or Zwinglian) or a form of church government (e.g., Presbyterian or Congregational) or even a locality (e.g., Bohemian Brethren or Waldensian). The variety of names reveals a certain diversity within a family of churches. This diversity, which sometimes impedes greater unity, has created a wealth of theological and literary expressions and an extraordinary ability to reach out to communities around the world. From Europe, the Reformed churches have spread to Africa, Asia, the Americas, and the Pacific Islands, and their numbers are still growing.

This *Historical Dictionary of Reformed Churches* covers a broad span of activities, from theology and government to education and social activism. It presents a detailed chronology followed by specific entries on the geographical regions in which the Reformed faith has become rooted. Other entries are devoted to outstanding figures, men and women of many different places and times, from the Reformation to the present day, who in different ways have nurtured and shaped the Reformed tradition. As with other volumes in this series, the book contains a comprehensive bibliography and other supplemental materials given in appendixes.

Weaving together the varied threads of the Reformed tradition to create this historical dictionary required a team of three authors and an international panel of consultants. Robert Benedetto, who coordinated the project, is associate librarian and associate professor of bibliography at Union Theological Seminary and the Presbyterian School of Christian Education in Richmond, Virginia. Darrell L. Guder is professor of evangelism and church growth at Columbia Theological Seminary in Decatur, Georgia. Donald K. McKim is academic dean and professor of theology at Memphis Theological Seminary in Memphis, Tennessee. All three have written books and articles on the Reformed tradition. Together, and with consultation from nearly four dozen experts, they have compiled this comprehensive volume documenting the historical tradition of the Reformed churches they serve.

Jon Woronoff
Series Editor

Preface

This dictionary includes biographical, historical, and theological articles arranged in alphabetical order. Although it covers the period from the Reformation to the end of the twentieth century, its focus is the modern world Reformed tradition. The aim of the dictionary format is to present information about the Reformed churches of the world in a concise form that is accessible to the modern reader.

Biographical articles cover Reformed theologians, Bible translators and scholars, educators, ecumenical and denominational leaders, and others who have made important contributions to the life of the Reformed churches. These articles recognize the contribution made by Western missionaries to the global spread of the Reformed churches during the nineteenth and twentieth centuries. The contribution of an ever growing number of indigenous church leaders in Africa, Asia, and Latin America is also noted. Biographical articles are limited to deceased persons. A few biographies lack reliable birth and death dates, which is noted by the use of a question mark (1839?) or the term "flourished" (fl.).

Historical articles identify important movements, events, documents, and institutions that have shaped the world Reformed tradition. In addition to these concise historical articles, the volume features twenty-six longer regional articles that survey the history of the Reformed churches around the world. Many, but not all, of the Reformed churches in these regions are members of the World Alliance of Reformed Churches. Appendix 3 is a complete list of the member churches of WARC. Statistical information regarding the number of Christian, Protestant, and Reformed adherents in many countries can vary widely and should be used with caution. In most cases, the statistics presented in the dictionary are derived from the *Information Please Almanac* (1998), David B. Barrett's *World Christian Encyclopedia,* and information supplied by the World Alliance of Reformed Churches.

The dictionary includes major theological terms used by Reformed churches, as well as related terms that may have a social, cultural, political, or economic relation to the Reformed tradition. Some terms have universal importance, whereas others are important in specific regions of the world. All of the articles are cross-referenced by the use of boldface formatting.

The book concludes with an extensive bibliography and several appendixes that are meant to enhance the usefulness of the volume and point the reader to further avenues of study.

Acknowledgments

We would like to express our appreciation to H. McKennie Goodpasture, professor emeritus of missions, and Syngman Rhee, visiting professor of evangelism and mission at Union Theological Seminary and Presbyterian School of Christian Education in Richmond, Virginia, who helped establish the parameters of the project and assemble our team of consultants. Alan P. F. Sell of United Theological College in Wales reviewed the dictionary at several stages and offered advice and criticism. Milan Opocenský of the World Alliance of Reformed Churches graciously responded to our inquiries about world Reformed churches, and I. John Hessalink supplied helpful information about Reformed churches in Japan.

The project would have been impossible without the input and encouragement of our team of consultants from around the world. These colleagues suggested biographical entries for the dictionary and prepared biographical sketches, sent materials on the history of the Reformed churches in their regions and wrote histories of these churches, provided bibliographies, and communicated valuable perspectives and insights that have been incorporated into the dictionary. Their labors, which were the foundation of the project, are recognized in the list of consultants that follows.

Several staff members at Union Theological Seminary and Presbyterian School of Christian Education made important contributions to the dictionary. Kathleen DuVall, managing editor of *Interpretation,* provided editorial help and proofread the manuscript. Reference librarian Patsy Verreault arranged for interlibrary loans and conducted on-line bibliographical searches. Acquisitions librarian Hobbie Carlson translated several French documents that were used to prepare articles. Student assistant Kathryn J. Addo performed a variety of bibliographical and other tasks. The authors are also grateful to Christa R. Benedetto, who prepared translations of Spanish documents. The labors of these and other colleagues made the project possible.

The book is dedicated to the memory of Robert S. Paul (1918–1992). A graduate of St. Catherine's College and Mansfield College of Oxford

University, Paul was ordained in the Congregational Church of England and Wales and served as associate director of the Ecumenical Institute (World Council of Churches) in Bossey, Switzerland (1954–1958). During a long academic career he was professor at Hartford Seminary Foundation (1958–1967), Pittsburgh Theological Seminary (1967–1977), and Austin Presbyterian Theological Seminary (1977–1987). His books include *The Assembly of the Lord: Politics and Religion in the Westminster Assembly and the Grand Debate* (1985), *The Church in Search of Its Self* (1972), *Ministry* (1965), *The Atonement and the Sacraments* (1960), and *Cromwell: The Lord Protector* (1955). Robert S. Paul was our teacher, mentor, friend, and colleague, and we are deeply grateful for his life and ministry.

Consultants

CONSULTING INSTITUTIONS AND ORGANIZATIONS

World Alliance of Reformed Churches
Geneva, Switzerland

GENERAL CONSULTANTS

H. McKennie Goodpasture
Union Theological Seminary and Presbyterian School of Christian Education
Richmond, Virginia

Alan P. F. Sell
The United Theological College
Aberystwyth, Cardiganshire
Wales

REGIONAL CONSULTANTS

Africa

Simão Chamango
Seminário Unido de Ricatla
Maputo, Mozambique
(Mozambique)

F. Maritz
Dutch Reformed Church in Zimbabwe
Harare, Zimbabwe
(Zimbabwe)

John W. de Gruchy
University of Cape Town
South Africa
(South Africa)

Steve de Gruchy
Kuruman Moffat Mission
Northern Cape
South Africa
(South Africa)

Micheal Chot Lul
Nile Theological College
Khartoum North, Sudan
(Sudan)

Abwenzoh William Membong
Presbyterian Church in Cameroon
South West Province
Cameroon, West Africa
(Cameroon)

Isaiah Wahome Muita
Presbyterian Church of East Africa
Nairobi, Kenya
(East Africa)

Edmond Razafimahefa
Church of Jesus Christ in Madagascar
Antananarivo, Madagascar
(Madagascar)

Enyi B. Udoh
University of Calabar
Calabar, Nigeria
(Nigeria)

Asia

Franklyn J. Balasundaram
The United Theological College
Bangalore, South India
(India)

L. R. Bawla
The Presbyterian Church of Myanmar
Tahan-Kalemyo, Myanmar
(Myanmar)

Maksal Hynniewta
Khasi Jaintia Presbyterian Synod
Meghalaya, India
(India)

Arthur James
Gujranwala Theological Seminary
Gujranwala, Pakistan
(Pakistan)

In Soo Kim
Presbyterian College and Theological Seminary
Seoul, Korea
(Korea)

Martha L. Moore-Keish
Emory University
Atlanta, Georgia
(India)

Paul Chun Chi NG
The Hong Kong Council of the Church of Christ in China
Hong Kong
(Hong Kong)

Edward L. Senner
The Presbyterian Church in Taiwan
Taipei, Taiwan
(Taiwan)

Kihyoung Shin
Union Theological Seminary and Presbyterian School of Christian Education
Richmond, Virginia
(Korea)

Stephen Suleeman
Sekolah Tinggi Theologia
Jakarta, Indonesia
(Indonesia)

Yugo Suzuki
Minato-ku, Tokyo
Japan
(Japan)

Kikuko Yamamoto
Aoba-ku, Sendai
Japan
(Japan)

Yeow Choo Lak
Association for Theological Education in South East Asia
Republic of Singapore
(Southeast Asia)

Suee Yan Yu
United Bible Societies Translation Center
Malang, Indonesia
(Malaysia)

Franklin J. Woo
National Council of Churches in the U.S.A.
New York
(China)

Europe

Bruno Corsani
The Waldensian Church
Pinerolo, Italy
(Italy)

Leo J. Koffeman
Reformed Churches in the Netherlands
Leusden, Netherlands
(Netherlands)

Milan Opocenský
World Alliance of Reformed Churches
Geneva, Switzerland
(Central and Eastern Europe)

Jerzy Stahl
The Evangelical-Reformed Church in Poland
Warsaw, Poland
(Poland)

Iain R. Torrance
Kings College
University of Aberdeen
Aberdeen, Scotland
(Scotland)

Daniel Vanescote
United Protestant Church of Belgium
Brussels, Belgium
(Belgium)

Mesoamerica and South America

Paulo Bronzeli
Seminário Presbiteriano do Sul
Campinas, Brazil
(Brazil)

Guidoberto Mahecha
La Paz, Bolivia
(Bolivia)

Sidney H. Rooy
San José, Costa Rica
(Argentina, Uruguay)

Edgar Moros-Ruano
Universidad de los Andes
Mérida, Venezuela
(Colombia, Venezuela)

José Luís Velazco
Toluca, Mexico
(Mexico)

Middle East

Raafat Girgis
Union Theological Seminary and Presbyterian School of Christian Education
Richmond, Virginia
(Egypt)

Stanley H. Skreslet
Union Theological Seminary and Presbyterian School of Christian Education
Richmond, Virginia
(Middle East)

North America and Caribbean

Everson T. Sieunarine
San Fernando, Trinidad
West Indies
(Trinidad)

Peter Wyatt
The United Church of Canada
Etobicoke, Ontario
Canada
(Canada)

Oceania

Tauira Marama Gaston
Hermon Theological College
Papeete, Tahiti
(French Polynesia)

Hilary Christie-Johnston
The Uniting Church in Australia
Sydney, Australia
(Australia)

Peter Matheson
Knox College
Dunedin, New Zealand
(New Zealand)

Fiama Rakau
Presbyterian Church of Vanuatu
Port Vila, Republic of Vanuatu
(Vanuatu)

Acronyms and Abbreviations

ABCFM	American Board of Commissioners for Foreign Missions
ABM	Australian Board of Missions
AHMS	American Home Missionary Society
AIM	Australian Inland Mission
AIPRAL	Association of Presbyterian and Reformed Churches in Latin America (Asociación de Iglesias Presbiterianas y Reformadas en América Latina)
APC	Asian Presbyterian Council
CAM	Central American Mission (Costa Rica, Nicaragua, etc.)
CANAAC	Caribbean and North American Area Council (WARC)
CARC	Caribbean Association of Reformed Churches
CCAP	Church of Central Africa Presbyterian (Malawi, Zambia and Zimbabwe)
CCC	Church of Christ in China
CCWM	Congregational Council for World Mission
CEPAD	Evangelical Committee for Relief and Development (Nicaragua)
CISRS	Christian Institute for the Study of Religion and Society (Bangalore, India)
CMS	Colonial Missionary Society (Canada); Commonwealth Missionary Society (Great Britain)
CNI	Church of North India
COCU	Consultation On Church Union (USA)
COS	Church of Scotland
CPC	Christian Peace Conference
CSI	Church of South India
CS	Church of Scotland Mission
CUEW	Congregational Union of England and Wales
CUS	Congregational Union of Scotland
CUSA	Congregational Union of South Africa
EATWOT	Ecumenical Association of Third World Theologians

EFCC   Evangelical Fellowship of Congregational Churches (South
            Africa)
EKD   Evangelical Church in Germany (Evangelische Kirche in
            Deutschland)
FAIE   Argentine Federation of Evangelical Churches (Federación
            Argentina de Iglesias Evangélicas)
FEM   Evangelical Federation of Mexico (Federación Evangélica
            de Mexico)
FEMEC   Federation of Protestant Churches and Missions in Cameroon
            (Fédération des Eglises et Missions Evangéliques du
            Cameroon)
FEPS   Federation of Swiss Protestant Churches (Fédération des
            Eglises Protestantes de la Suisse)
FFKM   Christian Council of Churches in Madagascar
FFPM   Federation of the Protestant Churches in Madagascar
FIEU   Federation of Evangelical Churches of Uruguay (Federación
            de Iglesias Evangélicas del Uruguay)
FPF   Protestant Federation of France (Fédération Protestante de
            France)
GA   General Assembly
GK   Dutch Reformed Church (Gereformeerde Kirk)
GMS   Glasgow Missionary Society (Scotland); Gospel Missionary
            Society (Kenya)
HKCCCC   Hong Kong Council of the Church of Christ in China
ICC   International Congregational Council
IMC   International Missionary Council
IPB   Presbyterian Church of Brazil (Igreja Presbiteriana do Brasil)
IPC   Presbyterian Church of Colombia (Iglesia Presbiteriana de
            Colombia)
IPIB   Independent Presbyterian Church of Brazil (Igreja
            Presbiteriana Independente do Brasil)
IPRC   Presbyterian Reformed Church of Cuba (Iglesia Presbiteriana
            Reformada de Cuba)
IPU   United Presbyterian Church of Brazil (Igreja Presbiteriana
            Unida do Brasil)
JEMM   Jamaica Ecumenical Mutual Mission
LAM   Latin American Mission (Costa Rica)
LMS   London Missionary Society
MECC   Middle East Council of Churches
MEDH   Ecumenical Movement for Human Rights (Argentina)
            (Movimiento Ecuménico por los Derechos Humanos)

NAPARC	North American Presbyterian and Reformed Council
NCRMS	Netherlands Christian Reformed Missionary Society
NGK	Dutch Reformed Church (Nederduitse Gereformeerde Kerk)
NGSSA	Dutch Reformed Mission Church in South Africa (Nederduitse Gereformeerde Sendingkerk in Suid Afrika)
NHK	Dutch Reformed Church (Nederduitse Hervormde Kerk)
NZG	Netherlands Missionary Society (Nederlandsch Zendeling-Genootschap)
PCUS	Presbyterian Church in the United States (1861–1983)
PCUSA	Presbyterian Church in the United States of America
PC(USA)	Presbyterian Church (U.S.A.)
PEMS	Paris Evangelical Missionary Society
PFB	Presbyterian Fellowship in Bangladesh
RB	Reformed Alliance (Reformierter Bund), Germany
RCA	Reformed Church in Africa; Reformed Church in America
RCZ	Reformed Church in Zimbabwe
RPS	Reformed Press Service
TEE	Theological Education by Extension
TSF	Three-Self Formula
TSPM	Three-Self Patriotic Movement (China)
UCA	Uniting Church in Australia
UCBWM	United Church Board for World Ministries
UCC	United Church of Canada; United Church of Christ (USA)
UCCJ	United Church of Christ in Japan (Nihon Kirisuto Kyodan)
UCCP	United Church of Christ in the Philippines
UCCSA	United Congregational Church of South Africa
UCCZ	United Church of Christ in Zimbabwe
UCJGC	United Church of Jamaica and Grand Cayman
UPCNA	United Presbyterian Church of North America
UPCUSA	United Presbyterian Church in the U.S.A.
URC	United Reformed Church (United Kingdom); Uniting Reformed Church (South Africa)
WARC	World Alliance of Reformed Churches (Presbyterian and Congregational)
WCC	World Council of Churches
WSCF	World Student Christian Federation
YMCA	Young Men's Christian Association
YWCA	Young Women's Christian Association

Chronology

1500 Christians constitute 19 percent of the world's population. Printing presses in Europe number about 40, with 8 million volumes printed, a large proportion being Christian works.

1505 Martin Luther enters Augustinian monastery at Erfurt. John Colet is appointed Dean of St. Paul's, London. John Knox, Scottish reformer, born (d. 1572).

1509 John Calvin, Swiss reformer, born (d. 1564). Erasmus lectures at Cambridge (–1514); dedicates his *Praise of Folly* to Thomas More.

1516 Erasmus publishes the first Greek New Testament with his own Latin translation.

1517 Martin Luther, in protest against sale of indulgences, posts his 95 Theses on the door of Castle Church in Wittenberg (Oct. 31); Protestant Reformation begins.

1519 Huldrych Zwingli (1484–1531) installed as minister in Zurich. Reformation spreads across Switzerland.

1522 Luther translates the New Testament into German.

1524 Zwingli abolishes Roman Catholic Mass in Zurich.

1525 William Tyndale's translation of the New Testament into English is printed by Peter Schoeffer at Worms.

1528 Ten Conclusions of Berne debated with Roman Catholic adversaries in Berne, Switzerland. Reformation begins in Scotland.

1529 Zwingli and Luther debate at Marburg Colloquy.

1531 Zwingli is killed at the Battle of Kappel attempting to impose Zurich Protestantism on Roman Catholic cantons. First complete edition of Aristotle's works published by Erasmus.

1532 Reformed movement begins in France under the influence of John Calvin.

1533 Thomas Cranmer appointed archbishop of Canterbury.

1534 England under Henry VIII breaks with the Vatican. Confession of Basel drafted by Oswald Myconius. Luther completes translation of Bible into German.

1535 First printed English Bible, translated by Myles Coverdale.

1536 John Calvin joins the reform movement in Geneva and publishes the first edition of his *Institutes of the Christian Religion.*

1538 Calvin banished from Geneva and settles in Strasbourg (–1541). Act of Supremacy declares the authority of the pope void in England. Desiderius Erasmus (b. 1465) dies. Tyndale (b. 1494) burned at stake near Brussels.

1539 Calvin's *Commentary on the Epistle to the Romans.*

1541 Calvin returns to Geneva, making it the center of Reformed faith and life. John Knox leads Calvinist Reformation in Scotland.

1545 Council of Trent first convened (–1563), 19th Ecumenical Council. Counter-Reformation begins.

1546 Martin Luther dies (b. 1483).

1547 Severe persecution of Protestants in France (72,000 executed); English Reformation strengthened under Edward VI.

1549 Consensus Tigurinus agreement on the Lord's Supper closely allied Calvinism and Zwinglianism.

1552 *Book of Common Prayer* published in England (2d ed.).

1555 In England: Hugh Latimer and Nicholas Ridley burned at the stake for their Protestant views. John Knox returns to Scotland for 10 months (–1556); then exiled to Geneva. First Protestant congregation organized from a growing Protestant movement in France.

1556 First Reformed missionary party of 18 French Huguenots sent from Geneva to an area near Rio de Janeiro, Brazil; despite the coming of a second group, the work collapses. Thomas Cranmer burned at the stake in England.

1557 France: 35 percent of population reputed to be Protestants (Huguenots).

1559 University of Geneva (then, Geneva Academy) founded for the training of Protestant ministers. Calvin publishes the final edition of his *Institutes* *of the Christian Religion*. Huguenots create French Reformed Church (72 congregations, 400,000 adherents) at first national synod. John Knox returns to Scotland after 12 years in exile.

1560 Church of Scotland adopts Calvinism; drafts the Scots Confession. The Geneva version of the English Bible is published.

1561 St Helena: first Christians (Dutch). First Calvinist refugees from Flanders settle in England. Ministers in Scotland draw up the Confessions of Faith, mainly the work of John Knox. Thomas Norton translates Calvin's *Institutes of the Christian Religion* into English.

1562 French Wars of Religion (–1594); 3,000 French Protestants (Huguenots) massacred at Toulouse and 1,200 slain at Massacre of Vassy.

1563 Heidelberg Catechism. John Foxe's *Book of Martyrs*. The term "Puritan" first used in England.

1564 Index Tridentinus of prohibited books. John Calvin dies (b. 1509). Scots Psalter.

1566 Philip II of Spain gives orders to suppress the Calvinist movement in the Low Countries; Second Helvetic Confession unites Calvinism and Zwinglianism.

1567 Second Helvetic Confession adopted by Hungarian Reformed Church.

1568 Europeans discover Polynesia (the island of Nui in Tuvalu).

1570 Consensus of Sendomir: Calvinists, Lutherans, and Moravian Brothers of Poland ally against Jesuits.

1572 Saint Bartholomew's Day Massacres; 3,000 Huguenots killed in France. John Knox dies (b. 1505). English "Admonition to Parliament," advocating Presbyterian principles, marks the beginning of a Puritan movement in England (–1660).

1574 Hubert Languet's *Vindiciae contra tyrannos*, political theories of the Huguenots.

1580 Surinam: first Christians (Dutch). Francois de la Noue's *24 Discours politiques et militaires*, Huguenot point of view on France's Wars of Religion.

1581 James VI of Scotland signs Second Confession of Faith.

1582 Robert Browne's statement on Congregational principles. University of Edinburgh founded.

1584 John Cotton, American religious controversialist, born (d. 1652).

1587 John Knox's *History of the Reformation in Scotland* published posthumously.

1588 Publication of the Geneva Bible in French based on 40 years of scholarship at the Genevan Academy. King Philip II of Spain sends Spanish Armada to invade England; its defeat saves England and the Netherlands from possible incorporation into the Spanish Empire.

1593 Henry Barrow and John Greenwood martyred in England.

1594 Richard Hooker's *Laws of Ecclesiastical Polity*.

1598 Edict of Nantes ends French Wars of Religion by granting religious liberty and civil equality to Huguenots in France. Mauritius: first Christians (Dutch).

1599 James VI of Scotland: "Basilikon doron," on divine right of kings.

1600 Christians constitute 20.7 percent of the world's population.

1602 Dutch government sends missionaries to evangelize Malays in the East Indies.

1603 Roger Williams, American religious controversialist, born (d. 1683).

1605 Dutch expel Roman Catholic missionaries from Indonesia and replace them with Dutch Reformed chaplains of the Dutch East India Company.

1611 King James Version (KJV), or Authorized Version (AV), of English Bible published.

1617 John Calvin's collected works posthumously published in Geneva.

1618 Synod of Dort (–1619) condemns Arminianism. European Thirty Years War (–1648).

1619 Dutch colonize Indonesia.

1620 English Pilgrims sail to America on the *Mayflower*, draft and sign Mayflower Compact, and found Plymouth Plantation in Massachusetts. Bohemia forcibly made Roman Catholic by Austrian armies; 30,000 Protestants expelled, others massacred.

1628 Dutch in New York organize first Christian Reformed Church on Manhattan Island.

1630 Puritans migrate to the New World under the leadership of John Winthrop (–1642); found Massachusetts Bay Colony.

1633 John Cotton, leading Puritan and defender of Congregationalist polity, arrives in Boston.

1634 Anne Hutchinson, religious controversialist (d. 1643), migrates to Massachusetts.

1636 Welsh Puritan Roger Williams (1603–1683) banished from Massachusetts; founds Providence, Rhode Island; proclaims complete religious freedom. Harvard College, the first college in America, founded to train ministers.

1638 Anne Hutchinson in Rhode Island. Scottish Covenant drawn up and signed; Charles I abandons liturgy and canons in Scotland; flourishing of Covenant, or Federal Theology.

1639 Increase Mather, American Congregationalist, born (d. 1723).

1640 Ninety-six editions of Calvin's works were printed in England by this date; surpassed only by the printed works of William Perkins. John Milton's *Of Reformation Touching Church Discipline in England.*

1641 Massacre of thousands of Protestants in Ulster by Irish Roman Catholics; Scotland sends 10,000 troops to suppress the insurrection. General Court of Massachusetts Bay Company codifies 100 laws.

1642 Civil War in England (–52).

1643 Westminster Assembly is convened and adopts Presbyterianism (–1653); produces the *Westminster Confession*, the *Larger Catechism*, the *Shorter Catechism*, the *Form of Presbyterial Church Government* and the *Directory of Public Worship*. The Solemn League and Covenant, Scottish hope for a Presbyterian England. Roger Williams's *Key into the Language of America.*

1644 Samuel Rutherford's *Lex Rex,* on constitutional government.

1646 A meeting of Cambridge Synod (–1648) produces the Cambridge Platform, summarizing American Congregational beliefs; John Eliot (1604–1690) begins preaching to Native Americans in Massachusetts; eventually 4,000 baptized in 14 "praying towns."

1648 Treaty of Westphalia ends Thirty Years War. British Virgin Islands: first Christians (Dutch). *The Book of the General Lawes and Libertyes of Massachusetts.*

1649 Society for the Propagation of the Gospel in New England chartered by the Puritan-controlled parliament.

1650 James Ussher's *Annales Veteris et Novi Testamenti*, giving beginning of world as 4004 B.C.

1651 Dutch establish Cape Colony, South Africa.

1653 Cromwell's Protectorate (–1658). Brian Walton edits *The London Polyglot Bible* containing 10 languages (–1657).

1655 Cromwell forbids Anglican services of worship.

1656 Richard Baxter's *The Reformed Pastor.*

1657 American Congregationalists adopt the Half-Way Covenant (–1662), easing requirements for baptism, and effectively ending strict Congregationalist polity.

1658 English Congregationalists draft Savoy Declaration. Ceylon: Dutch finally drive out Portuguese and ban Roman Catholicism.

1661 Rise of English Nonconformity (–1666). John Eliot translates the New Testament into Algonquin; complete Bible by 1663.

1663 Cotton Mather, of Massachusetts, born (d. 1772).

1666 John Bunyan's *Grace Abounding to the Chief of Sinners.*

1675 The Helvetic Consensus Formula of Zurich, Protestant scholastic creed known for its contention that the Hebrew vowel points in scripture are divinely inspired. King Philip's War (–76) in New England: hostilities between Native Americans and Puritan settlers led to the bloodiest conflict in seventeenth century New England.

1677 Increase Mather's *The Troubles That Have Happened in New England.*

1678 John Bunyan's *Pilgrim's Progress.*

1679 Reforming Synod in Massachusetts bemoans the secularization of New England.

1681 Religious toleration accorded to Hungarian Protestants.

1682   Forced conversion of 58,000 French Huguenots to Roman Catholicism.

1684   Increase Mather's *Remarkable Providences.*

1685   Edict of Nantes revoked by Louis XIV; more than 250,000 Huguenots flee from France to England, Prussia, Holland, and America. Increase Mather becomes president of Harvard College (–1701).

1689   English Toleration Act grants toleration to Dissenters; a step toward religious freedom.

1692   Witchcraft trials held in Salem, Massachusetts; nineteen people executed.

1693   Cotton Mather's *Wonders of the Invisible World.*

1700   Christians constitute 21.7 percent of the world's population. Indonesia (then Dutch East Indies): 100,000 Protestants on Java, 40,000 on Ambon.

1702   Cotton Mather's *Magnalia Christi Americana*, ecclesiastical history of New England.

1703   Jonathan Edwards, American theologian and president of the College of New Jersey (later Princeton University), born (d. 1758).

1706   Francis Makemie and seven other ministers organize the first American presbytery, founding the Presbyterian Church in the United States of America.

1707   Isaac Watts's *Hymns and Spiritual Songs.*

1710   Cotton Mather's *Essay to Do Good.* Thomas Reid, Scottish philosopher born (d. 1796).

1716   William Tennent evangelizes in American colonies. Christian religious teaching prohibited in China.

1722   In Ceylon, Protestants number 424,392 (21% of the population) through forced conversion by the Dutch Reformed Church.

1723   Zinzendorf founds Moravian colony in Herrnhut, Saxony (southeast of Berlin).

1726   Beginning of Great Awakening in America.

1727   Jonathan Edwards preaching in America (–1758). William Tennent

Sr. begins his Log College (later Princeton University). Beginning of higher criticism of the Bible.

1728 William Law's *A Serious Call to Devout and Holy Life.*

1729 "Adopting Act" requires Presbyterian ministers in America to agree with the Westminster Confession of Faith on "essential articles" but leaves room for disagreement on "non-essentials."

1731 Protestants expelled from Austria by the archbishop of Salzburg.

1734 Revival in the Connecticut River Valley led by Jonathan Edwards.

1735 Revival in Wales under Howel Harris. George Whitefield's conversion; begins evangelistic travels in 1736.

1737 Jonathan Edwards's *A Faithful Narrative of the Surprising Work of God* concerning revivalism in the Connecticut River Valley.

1738 George Whitefield's evangelistic campaigns in North America (1738–1770); heard by 80 percent of the entire population.

1739 First evangelistic open-air sermon in England for centuries preached by George Whitefield.

1740 Gilbert Tennent's "The Danger of An Unconverted Ministry," sermon delivered at Nottingham, Pennsylvania.

1741 The "Old Side"/"New Side" division of the American Presbyterian Church. Jonathan Edwards's "Sinners in the Hands of an Angry God" sermon delivered at Enfield, Massachusetts; a Great Awakening spreads throughout the thirteen American colonies (–1742), bringing mass conversions of the population.

1746 Jonathan Edwards's *A Treatise Concerning Religious Affections.*

1749 Protestants in England include 15,000 Congregationalists and 50,000 nonconformists.

1750 The thirteen American colonies (white population) consist of 95 percent professing Christians (50% Congregationalist, 30% Anglicans, and 10% Presbyterians), though only 5 percent affiliated as church members.

1752 Timothy Dwight, U.S. educator, born (d. 1817).

1754 Jonathan Edwards's *Inquiry into Freedom of the Will.*

1763 American Roman Catholics number 24,000; growing to 35,000 by 1789; 1.5 million by 1800; and 6 million by 1890.

1766 Planters from Scotland begin Presbytery of British Guyana.

1768 Friedrich Schleiermacher, German theologian, born (d. 1834). John Witherspoon assumes presidency of Princeton University.

1769 British Captain James Cook visits Tahiti; is killed in Hawaii (1779).

1770 Death of George Whitefield (b. 1714).

1780 Sunday schools popularized by Robert Raikes of Gloucester: 200,000 children enrolled in England in 1786; movement spreads to Wales in 1798; and then to Scotland, Ireland, and America.

1781 Act of Toleration by Austro-Hungarian Emperor Joseph II.

1787 Tolerance in France.

1789 French Revolution: church/state separation and religious liberty proclaimed in France.

1791 American Bill of Rights goes into effect.

1792 Second Great Awakening begins in America among Congregationalist and other New England churches (–1820s).

1795 London Missionary Society (LMS) founded (interdenominational, later Congregationalist).

1796 First LMS missionaries sent to South Pacific (Tahiti). Glasgow Missionary Society, Edinburgh Tract Society, and Edinburgh Missionary Society organized in Scotland. Ceylon: British drive out Dutch forces, find 67,000 Ceylonese still Roman Catholics despite 140 years' ban.

1797 Protestant missionaries from the London Missionary Society arrive in Tahiti, Tonga, and Marquesas. Netherlands Missionary Society (NZG) founded in Rotterdam.

1799 Church Missionary Society founded in London. Schleiermacher's *On Religion: Speeches to Its Cultured Despisers.*

1800 Christians constitute 23.1 percent of the world's population. Widespread evangelistic camp meetings begin in America: Kentucky Revival awakening, with crowds of up to 25,000, sweeps through Kentucky, Tennessee, and the Carolinas. Beginning of local revivals in Scotland: Lewis, Harris, Perthshire.

1801 Dutch Reformed Protestants in Ceylon number 342,000, or 14 percent of the population; many convert to Buddhism by 1830. Plan of Union adopted between American Congregationalists and Presbyterians (–1852).

1802   The Synod of Pittsburgh of the Presbyterian Church, U.S.A. organizes itself into "the Western Missionary Society" to reach frontier whites, Indians, and Negro slaves.

1805   Namibia (Southwest Africa): receives first mission (LMS) in South Africa.

1807   Britain bans slave trade. Robert Morrison (LMS), first Protestant missionary to China, arrives in Macao.

1810   American Board of Commissioners for Foreign Missions (ABCFM) organized (interdenominational, later Congregationalist). Evangelical awakenings (revivals) in Switzerland (Robert Haldane), France, Low Countries, Germany. The Cumberland Presbytery of Kentucky, U.S., excluded from Presbyterian Church. Société des Amis formed in Geneva by Protestant revivalists.

1815   Basel Evangelical Missionary Society founded in Switzerland.

1816   Botswana (then, Bechuanaland): receives first mission (LMS).

1817   Proposal by Hall and Newell of ABCFM to evangelize millions throughout the world by sending 30,000 Protestant missionaries from the U.S. and Europe in 21 years. Robert Moffat begins 50-year ministry among Tswana of Southern Africa. King of Prussia directs Reformed and Lutheran Churches in Prussia to form an Evangelical Union.

1820   Hiram Bingham and the first company of ABCFM missionaries arrive in Hawaii (then, the Sandwich Islands).

1821   Schleiermacher's *Christian Faith* (–1822). ABCFM missionaries arrive in the Cook Islands.

1822   Paris Evangelical Missionary Society founded (France).

1823   Cook Islands: receives first mission (LMS).

1824   American Sunday School Union formed.

1825   Bombay Missionary Union formed in India with Congregationalist and Presbyterian missionaries. Church of Scotland Mission (Presbyterian) organized in Edinburgh.

1827   Celebes: Netherlands Missionary Society begins work.

1830   LMS missionaries arrive in Samoa.

1832   Iran (then, Persia) entered by the ABCFM under the name Mission to the Nestorians.

1833   Lesotho (then, Basutoland): receives first mission (Paris Mission, PEMS). English Congregationalists draft Declaration of Faith.

1834   Friedrich Schleiermacher dies (b. 1768).

1835   Lyman Abbott, American preacher, born (d. 1922). American evangelist Charles G. Finney's *Lectures on Revivals of Religion.*

1836   ABCFM sends Marcus and Narcissa Whitman and Henry and Eliza Spalding to work among Native Americans in the Oregon Territory. Booklet: "The Duty of the Present Generation to Evangelize the World: An Appeal from the Missionaries at the Sandwich Islands to their Friends in the United States."

1837   Great Awakening in Hawaii: 27,000 adults (20% of population) convert to Protestant Christianity (–1842). American Presbyterians split into two denominations, the "Old School" and the "New School." The Old School General Assembly establishes a foreign mission board.

1839   Scottish Highlands Awakening: Oban vicinity, the nearby islands, and parts of the Lowlands (–1843).

1839   Opium War (–1842); Britain defeats China and forcibly opens the door for commerce and missionaries.

1840   David Livingstone (d. 1874) begins missionary work and explorations in southern Africa.

1841   Edinburgh Medical Missionary Society founded in Scotland.

1842   Treaty of Nanking allows Christian missionaries into China.

1843   Disruption of the Scottish Church.

1847   American theologian Horace Bushnell (1802–1876) publishes *Christian Nurture*, stressing education rather than conversion as a means of entry into the church. American preacher Henry Ward Beecher (d. 1887) minister at Plymouth Congregational Church, Brooklyn.

1849   Charles G. Finney's (1792–1875) evangelistic campaigns in Britain, 1849–1851 and 1859–1861.

1851   England and Wales: state Census of Religious Worship: 61 percent of entire population attend church every Sunday.

1852   Harriet Beecher Stowe publishes *Uncle Tom's Cabin.*

1853   David Livingstone (1813–1873) (LMS) passes through Zambia (then Northern Rhodesia) on way to Luanda, Angola. Johann Herzog's *Encyclopedia of Protestant Theology* (–1868).

1854 International missionary conference in New York inspired and guided by Alexander Duff.

1857 Evangelical Awakening in America under Charles G. Finney and others (one million converts in two years); spreads to Europe, India (1859), and China (1860).

1858 David Livingstone begins exploration of Zambezi and Shire rivers; others begin missionary work in Malawi (then Nyasaland). Townsend treaty between USA and Japan opens Japan to Christian missionaries. Philip Schaff's *History of the Christian Church* (–1892).

1859 Second Evangelical Awakening in Britain, reaching over 3 million with 1.1 million converts: 100,000 in Wales, 300,000 in Scotland, 100,000 in Ulster, and over 500,000 in England. Darwin's *Origin of the Species*.

1860 Revival in South Africa erupts under Andrew Murray (Dutch Reformed), sweeps the Afrikaner churches.

1861 U.S. Civil War (–1865): Presbyterian Church in the United States of America supports the U.S. government, forcing southern Presbyterian churches to withdraw; these churches organize the Presbyterian Church in the Confederate States of America, later renamed the Presbyterian Church in the United States. LMS Samoan pastors arrived in Tuvalu (Ellice Island) and Tokelau Island.

1869 First Vatican Council held in Rome: papal infallibility defined, widening gulf between Roman Catholicism and other Christian churches.

1870 British evangelists reach the height of their influence. Punjab: beginning of mass movement of 50 percent of Hindu Chuhras in Sialkot to American Presbyterian mission; continuing revival up to 1912.

1873 American evangelist Dwight L. Moody conducts revivals in the United Kingdom and the United States (–1891).

1875 Alliance of Reformed Churches (Presbyterian) organized in London; merges with the International Congregational Council in 1970 to become part of the World Alliance of Reformed Churches (Presbyterian and Congregational). Union of four Presbyterian denominations creates the Presbyterian Church in Canada. American Bible Conference movement begins.

1882 India: Anglicans and Protestants number 500,000. Korean treaty with U.S. ensures religious freedom in Korea; Presbyterian and Methodist missionaries enter two years later.

1884   American Presbyterian evangelist J. Wilbur Chapman rallies urban areas. Protestant missionaries in Korea.

1885   Zambia (then, Northern Rhodesia): receives first mission (Paris Mission, PEMS).

1886   Himalayan region of Sikkim receives first mission (Church of Scotland). Washington Gladden's *Applied Christianity: Moral Aspects of Social Questions* states the position of the American Social Gospel movement.

1888   Student Volunteer Movement for Foreign Missions organized in the U.S., with the slogan "The Evangelization of the World in this Generation." The Pacific island of Nauru receives first mission (LMS).

1890   Shanghai: foreign mission conference, with 1,295 missionaries present.

1891   International Congregational Council organized in London; merges with Alliance of Reformed Churches (Presbyterian) in 1970 to become part of the World Alliance of Reformed Churches (Presbyterian and Congregational).

1892   Ecclesiastical heresy trial of Charles A. Briggs (1841–1913) of Union Theological Seminary in New York leads to theological controversy in the Presbyterian Church, U.S.A.

1893   World Parliament of Religions, directed by Presbyterian minister John Henry Barrows, meets in Chicago.

1894   Madagascar: first indigenous church, Malagasy Protestant Church (ex LMS); Soatanana Revival begins among LMS churches in Madagascar, lasting 80 years (Fifohazana, Revivalists).

1895   Christian Endeavour movement numbers 38,000 societies worldwide, with 2,225,000 members.

1900   Christians constitute 34.4 percent of the world's population. Boxer Rebellion in China kills 47,000 Roman Catholics and 2,000 Protestants, with 186 missionaries and children. In Hawaii, catastrophic decline of native population through disease from 200,000 (1775) to 70,000 (1850) to 35,000 (1900). New York Ecumenical Missionary Conference held with 25,000 members and 200,000 attenders. John R. Mott's *The Evangelization of the World in This Generation.* Sigmund Freud's psychoanalysis.

1904   Max Weber's *The Protestant Ethic and the Spirit of Capitalism.*

1907   Massive revival in Korea; growth of churches spreads to Manchuria and China.

1908   Union of Presbyterians, Congregationalists, and Dutch Reformed in South India. Nyasaland: Elliott Kamwana baptizes 10,000 in Tonga. Organization of the Federal Council of Churches in the United States.

1909   Trial of American Presbyterian missionaries William M. Morrison and William H. Sheppard, who fought economic and social exploitation in the Congo.

1910   World Missionary Conference, Edinburgh, Scotland: 1,355 delegates; beginning of the 20th century ecumenical movement. Protestant and Anglican missionaries worldwide number 45,000. American evangelists (–1930) Billy Sunday and Homer Rodeheaver preach to 100 million, with 1 million converts (–1930).

1912   Church of Scotland revised *Prayer Book*.

1914   World War I begins (–1918). Foreign missionaries in Africa: more than 4,000 Protestants and almost 6,000 Roman Catholics. Protestants in Japan grow to 103,000 from only 10 in 1872. China: Protestant and Anglican missionaries number more than 5,400.

1916   Kenya: mass movement begins into all churches.

1917   Bolshevik Revolution in Russia.

1918   Global influenza pandemic, the most deadly in history, sweeps the world in three waves over two years, killing approximately 40 million. Movement into churches in the Belgian Congo takes on massive proportions. Fundamentalism/modernism controversy erupts within American Protestantism (–1931), splitting every major denomination.

1919   Karl Barth's (b. 1886) *Commentary on Romans*, the beginning of Protestant dialectical theology.

1920   League of Nations gives mandate to colonial powers to control Pacific Islands.

1921   International Missionary Council (IMC) organized at Lake Mohonk, New York. Church of Scotland Act.

1924   First international Christian radio station, NCRV, organized by Dutch Protestants in the Netherlands. Karl Barth's *The Word of God and the Word of Man*. A group of American Presbyterians publish the "Auburn Affirmation."

1925   United Church of Canada organized from the union of Presbyterians, Congregationalists, and Methodists. Scopes Monkey Trial held in Dayton, Tennessee. Life and Work movement started in Stockholm.

1927 Faith and Order movement founded at Lausanne. Anti-Christian movement in China: 5,000 of the 8,000 Protestant missionaries depart. Church of Christ in China founded, uniting seven Protestant denominations.

1928 Ecumenical Missionary Conference held in Jerusalem.

1929 The Presbyterian Churches in Scotland unite to form the Church of Scotland. H. Richard Niebuhr's *The Social Sources of Denominationalism*.

1930 Japan: Kingdom of God Movement begun under evangelist Toyohiko Kagawa, reaching over one million (75% non-Christian) in a two year period (–1934).

1932 Karl Barth's *Church Dogmatics* (–1967). Indonesia (then, Dutch East Indies): conversion of 30,000 Muslims around Modjowarno, East Java. *Re-thinking Missions* published in America as a result of the Laymen's Foreign Missions Inquiry. Reinhold Niebuhr's (1892–1971) *Moral Man and Immoral Society*.

1933 German Protestant Church organized, an amalgamation of all Protestant Churches in Germany.

1934 USSR: Stalin attempts to liquidate the entire Christian church. Barmen Synod in Germany organizes the Confessing Church; drafts Theological Declaration of Barmen.

1935 Karl Barth leaves Germany for Basel; writes *Credo*.

1936 Japan: Nationwide United Evangelistic Movement launched by Toyohiko Kagawa.

1937 Martin Niemoeller, German pastor and leader of the Confessing Church, interned in a concentration camp by Hitler (–1945). K. S. Latourette's seven-volume *A History of the Expansion of Christianity* (–1945).

1938 Scotland: Iona Community founded by George F. MacLeod and members of the Church of Scotland. Muscat and Oman: Reformed Church in America mission reports five conversions in 50 years.

1939 World War II (–1945); the Holocaust.

1941 Gemeinde für Evangelisation und Erweckung organized in Zurich, Switzerland. Reinhold Niebuhr, *The Nature and Destiny of Man* (–1943).

1946   Revised Standard Version of the New Testament published in the USA.

1947   Church of South India is organized by the union of Methodists and Anglicans with previously united Reformed and Congregationalist bodies.

1948   World Council of Churches is organized in Amsterdam. Communists in China expel Western missionaries (–1951). La Violencia, civil war in Colombia; 100,000 killed, Protestants persecuted during a period known as "The Violence" (–1958).

1950   Christians constitute 34.1 percent of the world's population. Korean War (–1953). Twenty-five Protestant and four Eastern Orthodox denominations, with 32 million members, organize the National Council of the Churches of Christ in the U.S.A.

1951   Three-Self Reform Movement in China, to eradicate foreign influence in the churches.

1952   H. Richard Niebuhr's *Christ and Culture*. The Revised Standard Version of the Bible published in the U.S.A. for Protestants.

1954   United Church of Christ in Japan (Nippon Kirisuto Kyodan) adopts a Confession of Faith. Beginnings of American civil rights movement with Supreme Court decision in *Brown v. Board of Education.*

1956   Presbyterian Church in the U.S.A. (PCUSA) affirms the ordination of women; Presbyterian Church in the United States (PCUS) follows in 1964.

1957   U.S. Congregational Christian Churches unite with the Evangelical and Reformed Church to form the United Church of Christ; adopt a Statement of Faith (1959).

1958   Christian peace movement begins in Prague. Church of Jesus Christ in Madagascar adopts a Statement of Faith.

1959   Karl Barth's *Dogmatics in Outline*.

1961   Decision to form Pacific Conference of Churches (PCC) made at Malua, Samoa.

1962   Vatican Council II (–1965). Consultation on Church Union (COCU) organized in the United States. Western Samoa becomes first Pacific Island nation to become independent.

1964   Western missionaries expelled from Sudan. Fiji Council of Churches organized.

1965   Cameroon: world mission and evangelism consultation held in Yaounde, "The Evangelization of West Africa Today." Indonesia: Communist coup thwarted; 250,000 massacred; mass revivals begin. Moltmann's *Theology of Hope.*

1966   Burma expels 250 Protestant and Anglican foreign missionaries. Great Proletarian Cultural Revolution in China destroys churches and forbids Christian worship. First Assembly of Pacific Conference of Churches in Lifou, Loyalty Islands.

1967   Western missionaries expelled from Guinea. Solomon Islands Christian Association (SICA) founded. The Council of Churches in Indonesia drafts A Common Comprehension of Faith. United Church of Christ in Japan adopts a Confession on the Responsibility during World War II. Congregational Church of England and Wales drafts a Declaration of Faith. United Presbyterian Church in the U.S.A. adopts the Confession of 1967.

1968   Major schisms occur in Pakistan among Presbyterians, Methodists, and Anglicans. Ulster civil rights campaign leads to fighting between Protestants and Roman Catholics. Karl Barth dies (b. 1886).

1970   World Alliance of Reformed Churches (Congregational and Presbyterian) organized from the merger of separate Presbyterian and Congregational bodies. Church of North India organized by union of Anglican, Baptist, Brethren, Disciples, Methodist, and United churches.

1971   Over 500 indigenous churches in the Congo deprived of legal recognition as official recognition is given to three churches only: Roman Catholic Church, the Protestant Church of Christ in Zaire, and the indigenous Church of Jesus Christ on Earth through the Prophet Simon Kimbangu (Greek Orthodox added in 1972).

1972   Union of the Presbyterian Church of England with the majority of English and English-speaking Welsh congregations to form the United Reformed Church. Presbyterian Church in the Republic of Korea drafts a New Confession.

1973   Theological Declaration of Korean Christians drafted in opposition to actions of the South Korean government. Caribbean Conference of Churches (CCC) founded in Kingston, Jamaica.

1975   Civil war in Angola severely disrupts church life (–1991). Reformed Christians suffer persecution in Mozambique during years of civil war (–1992).

1977 Presbyterian-Reformed Church in Cuba adopts a Confession of Faith. Presbyterian Church in Taiwan drafts a Declaration on Human Rights.

1979 Churches in China opened for public worship. Broederkring of the Dutch Reformed Church in South Africa adopts a Theological Declaration against Apartheid. Karo-Batak Protestant Church in Indonesia adopts a Basic Confession. Presbyterian Church of Taiwan adopts a Confession of Faith.

1980 Christians constitute 32.8 percent of the world's population. United Church of Canada drafts a creed.

1981 The majority of the Churches of Christ in Britain unite with the United Reformed Church. Church of Toraja in Indonesia adopts a Confession.

1982 Dutch Reformed Church (NGK) in South Africa excluded from WARC for supporting apartheid; NGK formally withdraws its support of apartheid in 1986. Presbyterian Church in Bolivia begun by Korean missionary Chong Moo Park.

1983 United Presbyterian Church in the U.S.A. (UPCUSA) and the Presbyterian Church in the United States (PCUS) reunite to form the Presbyterian Church (U.S.A.), ending the American Civil War division of 1861; begins to draft "A Brief Statement of Faith" (1990).

1985 Uniting Aboriginal and Islander Christian Congress, a body that oversees all ministry with aboriginal people, approved by the Uniting Church of Australia. Christian Dalit Liberation Movement founded in India. Civil War in Sudan (continues strife that goes back to the mid-1950s). South African ministers draft Kairos Document.

1986 United Church of Canada apologizes to representatives of its native congregations.

1988 Collapse of communism liberates churches in former communist states (–1989). Reformed churches in Zimbabwe hold first meeting of Reformed Ecumenical Council in Harare.

1990 Legal end of apartheid in South Africa.

1991 The Protestant church in Madagascar acts as mediator between the government and strikers during a "national demonstration" for political reform.

1992 Persecution of the Protestant minority in Sudan begins.

1993   One hundredth anniversary Parliament of the World's Religions held in Chicago.

1994   Dutch Reformed Church in Africa and the Dutch Reformed Mission Church in South Africa unite to form the Uniting Reformed Church.

1997   The transfer of Hong Kong from Britain to China creates an uncertain future for Hong Kong's Protestant churches.

NOTES

Balmer, Randall, and John R. Fitzmier. *The Presbyterians*. Westport, Conn.: Greenwood Press, 1993.

Barrett, David B. *World Christian Encyclopedia*. New York: Oxford University Press, 1982.

González, Justo L. *The Story of Christianity*. 2 vols. San Francisco: Harper & Row, 1984.

Grun, Bernard. *The Timetables of History*. New York: Simon & Schuster, 1975.

Youngs, J., and T. William. *The Congregationalists*. Westport, Conn.: Greenwood Press, 1990.

Introduction

A leading scholar of Christian demographics tells us that in the year 1900, about 80 percent of the world's Christian population was white and lived mostly in Europe and North America.[1] This fact is reflected in the textbooks of church history and theology from that day to our own. However, as a result of many factors, including the remarkable success of nineteenth- and twentieth-century Christian mission and the parallel secularization of the West, about 60 percent of the world's Christians now live in the non-Western world. Africa, Asia, and Latin America are experiencing tremendous growth, and it is projected that before long 80 percent of the world's Christian population will live in the southern hemisphere, reversing the demographic picture that existed in 1900.

This shift in Christian demographics signals a change in the way Christianity will be understood and interpreted by the majority of Christians. As Andrew Walls notes, "The process is already beginning to produce changes in Christian priorities, and in the structure of Christian thought, practice, and government."[2] As the dynamic center of Christianity continues to move into the southern hemisphere, it will become more obvious that Christian theology is no longer an exclusive product of the European and North American churches and the issues that emerge in the postindustrial West. Lamin Sanneh tells us that

> Christianity has become a genuinely multicultural world religion, thriving profusely in the idioms of other languages and cultures, marked by a lively cross-cultural and interreligious sensibility, unburdened by the heavy artillery of doctors and councils, and otherwise undaunted by the scandalous paucity of money, trained leadership, infrastructure and resources.[3]

What is emerging in the southern hemisphere is a vibrant, non-Western Christianity that will require a rethinking and reordering of the Christian agenda. With such changes on the horizon, Christian historical and theological literature can no longer focus on the European and North American continents alone. The growth of new churches and non-Western expressions of faith means that a significant realignment of perspective is imperative.

When we consider the various "denominational" traditions within Christianity, including the Reformed tradition, the need for realignment is no less present. The major Reformed organization, the World Alliance of Reformed Churches (WARC), was founded in 1875. In that year 21 Presbyterian denominations, primarily from Europe and North America, affiliated into a "world organization." As recently as 1960 Europeans and North Americans in WARC represented almost 75 percent of the total membership. The international body remained primarily Presbyterian until 1970, when it merged with the International Congregational Council (founded in 1949). At that time WARC membership increased to 114 churches from seventy countries. By the late 1990s membership had grown to 211 churches in 104 nations, representing 70 million Reformed Christians and a growing number of churches from non-Western countries. By some estimates, WARC's 211 member churches represent about 70 percent of the world's Reformed Christians. This is the context in which the Reformed churches and their tradition are to be understood.

EUROPEAN ORIGINS OF THE REFORMED TRADITION

As its name implies, the *Reformed* tradition grew out of the sixteenth-century Protestant Reformation. The Reformed churches consider themselves to be the Catholic Church reformed. The movement is rooted in the Augustinian tradition and originated in the reform efforts of Huldrych Zwingli (1484–1531) of Zurich and John Calvin (1509–1546) of Geneva. Other Protestant reformers, including John Oecolampadius (1482–1531), Martin Bucer (1491–1551), Peter Martyr Vermigli (1500–1562), John Knox (c. 1513–1572), Heinrich Bullinger (1504–1575), Girolamo Zanchi (1516–1590), and Théodore Beza (1519–1605), also helped to shape the theology and organizational life of the Reformed tradition during the Reformation and post-Reformation period.

Major centers of Reformed influence were established in Zurich, where Zwingli preached, and later in Geneva, where Calvin was active. Zwingli's ideas were very influential in Germany and in German-speaking Switzerland, whereas Calvin's work took root in French-speaking Switzerland and in France. Following the death of Zwingli in 1531, Geneva gradually became the most important center of Reformed Protestantism. A haven for Protestant refugees, Geneva by 1557 included more foreigners than citizens. Many of these refugees later returned to their own countries where they helped to establish Reformed churches. Many Protestants also came to

Geneva to study at the Geneva Academy (1559), a primary school that also offered advanced course work in theology. The academy enrolled three hundred students at the time of Calvin's death and gradually developed into a major educational institution.

The Reformed churches spread through Europe in a primarily northwestern direction but also moved to the east, becoming established in the Central European countries of Hungary, Poland (prior to the Counter-Reformation), and the Czech Republic. In these lands Bohemian Brethren allied themselves with the movement. The Reformed movement was prevented from moving further eastward into Russia, however, by the entrenched Orthodox Church. It was also prevented from moving south and southwest by a dominant Catholicism in Italy, Spain, and Portugal. In Italy, however, groups of Waldensians maintained a Protestant faith. In the far north, its spread was checked by a firmly established Lutheranism. The Reformed churches moved from Switzerland, their country of origin, to parts of France, Germany, the Netherlands, and the British Isles.

Although the Reformed movement was dependent on many Protestant leaders, it was John Calvin's tireless work as a writer, preacher, teacher, and social and ecclesiastical reformer that provided a substantial body of literature and an ethos from which the Reformed tradition grew. Calvin's major work, the *Institutes of the Christian Religion* (Basel, 1536; Geneva, 1559), is modeled on the Apostles' Creed. The work discusses Father, Son, Spirit, and church in its four books. In addition to the *Institutes*, Calvin produced other important works, including the Genevan Catechism (1541), biblical commentaries, and sermons. This exegetical, theological, and sermonic literature laid the foundation of Reformed Protestantism.

Calvin's work also provided a basis for church organizational life and worship. His *Ecclesiastical Ordinances* (1541) provided a model for church organization with its description of four types of church officers: pastors, teachers, elders, and deacons. Reformed church life has generally been governed by pastors and elders meeting together in a "session" (Presbyterian) or "consistory" (Reformed). John Knox relied on Calvin's work to produce the Presbyterian Book of Discipline (1560), the basis for Presbyterian church organization. However, Reformed churches have not been limited to these organizational models. In the Congregationalist tradition church life is governed by the "church meeting," a completely democratic meeting at which the minister normally presides. Calvin's *Form of Church Prayers* (1540) became the basis of Reformed liturgy and worship. The work emphasized psalm singing and a service structured around word and sacrament. Calvin's influence in both the theological and organizational life of the Reformed churches has been so pervasive that the tradition of the Reformed churches is often referred to as "Calvinism."

Reformed Protestants distinguished themselves not only from Roman Catholicism but also from other emerging Protestant traditions, especially Lutheranism and the so-called left-wing groups of the Reformation, popularly known as "Anabaptists." Divisions with Lutherans arose over different understandings of the Lord's Supper, the nature of the church, liturgy, and the relationship between law and grace. The Anabaptists broke with Zwingli by insisting on more sweeping theological and social reforms, including the rejection of infant baptism and the strict separation of church and state. Many political and cultural factors also contributed to the fragmentation of the churches of the Reformation. In modern times, the various doctrines that have historically divided Protestants have been reexamined in light of scriptural teaching and the experience of the churches. As a result, the boundaries of fraternal relations have been enlarged and the number of church unions have greatly increased, especially during the twentieth century.

As the Reformed churches matured, their theology was expressed in various confessions and catechisms, including Huldrych Zwingli's Sixty-Seven Articles of Religion (1523), the First Confession of Basel (1534), the First Helvetic Confession (1536), the Lausanne Articles (1536), the Geneva Confession (1536), the Zurich Consensus (1549), the Confession of Faith of the English Congregation at Geneva (1566), the Gallican Confession of Faith (1559), the Scots Confession of Faith (1560), the Belgic Confession of Faith (1561), the Heidelberg Catechism (1563), the Second Helvetic Confession (1566), and later, the Westminster Confession of Faith (1647) and other confessions of the modern period. Reformed churches consider the Bible to be the sole authority for faith and life, but many churches are also guided by these confessions and catechisms that incorporate some of the major distinctives of Reformed theology.

THE THEOLOGY OF THE REFORMED TRADITION

Reformed theology is not easily defined. Lutherans have their Book of Concord, but the Reformed have no single document or collection of documents that permanently expresses their theology; in fact, churches that came out of the Congregationalist tradition have generally declined to subscribe to creedal statements. Reformed and Presbyterian churches have, with a few exceptions, also resisted creedal prescription. Instead, they have written and recognized multiple confessions as true expressions of the Reformed faith. In the Congregationalist, Presbyterian, and Reformed traditions there is an unwillingness to displace the Bible as *the* sole authority. Several years ago it was estimated that more than sixty creeds would qualify as Reformed.[4] The number is undoubtedly much higher today, and the perspectives much more varied as churches in the southern hemisphere and northeast Asia have come to maturity.

Despite the reluctance of the Reformed churches to draft a single document that might describe their theology, some have tried to equate the term "Reformed" with a specific set of "Calvinistic" doctrines drawn from one or more of the Reformed confessions. This approach is used, for example, by those who still speak of the "five points" of Calvinism—total depravity, unconditional election, limited atonement, irresistible grace, and the perseverance of the saints—as the heart of Reformed theology. In fact, these "five points" are not taken from Calvin but from the Canons of Dort, a Reformed statement drafted in the Netherlands some fifty years after Calvin's death, in answer to five Arminian points. Although Reformed Christians have such confessions and catechisms to guide them, there is no absolute agreement on the specific doctrines that constitute Reformed theology.

Reformed confessions and theological statements are seen as expressions of scriptural teachings. New confessional statements based on scripture arise as the interpretation of scriptural texts changes with new knowledge and as churches find themselves in changing social, cultural, and political contexts.[5] All Reformed confessions are to be compared and studied as genuine expressions of the tradition that nevertheless are not universally prescribed for all of the churches.

The common theological elements that unite the Reformed churches are best expressed in the Constitution of the World Alliance of Reformed Churches (revised 1982), which states that membership is open to

> any church which accepts Jesus Christ as Lord and Saviour; holds the Word of God given in the scriptures of the Old and New Testaments to be the supreme authority in matters of faith and life; acknowledges the need for continuing reformation of the church catholic; whose position in faith and evangelism is in general agreement with that of the historic Reformed confessions, recognizing that the Reformed tradition is a biblical, evangelical, and doctrinal ethos, rather than any narrow and exclusive definition of faith and order.[6]

The WARC statement stresses the evangelical, biblical, and doctrinal nature of the Reformed churches. The churches are evangelical in their confession of Christ as Lord and Savior; biblical in their reliance on the Bible as the authority of faith, life, and the continuing reform of the church; and doctrinal in their acceptance of Reformed confessions as summaries of biblical faith. Of the Reformed confessions, the Heidelberg Catechism is probably the most universally accepted creed now used by churches in Germany, Hungary, the Netherlands, Scotland, the United States, and elsewhere.

The various creeds, confessions, and books of church order used by Reformed churches represent a variety of perspectives but also share common elements. The Presbyterian Church (U.S.A.) *Book of Order,* for example, mentions several Reformed doctrines that its churches hold in high regard.[7] These doctrines include God's sovereignty over all of life, as the one who "creates, sustains, rules, and redeems the world"; the election (i.e., choosing) of the people of God for service as well as for salvation; covenant life marked by a disciplined concern for order in the church according to the Word of God; stewardship that shuns ostentation and seeks proper use of the gifts of God's creation; and recognition of the human tendency to idolatry and tyranny, which calls the people of God to work for the transformation of society by seeking justice and living in obedience to the Word of God. Although these Reformed doctrines may not be universally shared by all churches, the themes of God's sovereignty, election, the convenantal nature of the church, stewardship, human sinfulness, engagement with the world, and Christian obedience are doctrines that frequently appear in Reformed theology.

THE REFORMED TRADITION IN THE MODERN WORLD

As the Reformed churches spread around the world, they adopted different names. The European churches in France, Holland, Hungary, Switzerland, and other nations called themselves Reformed to distinguish the "Reformed" doctrine of these churches from Roman Catholicism and Lutheranism. Churches of Anglo-Saxon heritage, including those in the United Kingdom, the United States, and the British Commonwealth countries, have taken the name "Presbyterian" or "Congregational," which emphasize their governance structure. Many Reformed churches in the southern hemisphere use the name "Evangelical," emphasizing their Reformed Protestant heritage.

From the seventeenth through the nineteenth centuries the Dutch Reformed, Scots and American Presbyterians, and English and American

Congregationalists were successful in transplanting Reformed churches to various parts of the vast Dutch and British trading and colonial empires, as well as to areas of growing American influence, including Latin America, Asia, and the islands of the Pacific. Two great mission organizations, the American Board of Commissioners for Foreign Missions and the London Missionary Society, were especially effective in organizing new churches. The Evangelical Mission Society in Basel, the Paris Evangelical Mission Society, and the Scottish Missionary Society were also influential.

During the twentieth century, especially following World War II, non-Western churches experienced remarkable growth. Today there are large Presbyterian and Reformed churches in most regions of the southern hemisphere. On the continent of Africa, large Congregational, Presbyterian, and Reformed churches, containing about one-half of Africa's Reformed Christians, are located in South Africa. There is also a large Presbyterian church in central Africa's Democratic Republic of the Congo. Other African countries with significant Presbyterian and Reformed membership include Cameroon, Egypt, Ghana, Kenya, and Malawi. The island nation of Madagascar is host to an important Reformed outpost in the Indian Ocean.

Asia, Central America, and South America also have large numbers of Reformed churches. In Asia, the largest churches are found in Korea and Indonesia. Indonesia contains more than one-third of all Asian Reformed Christians, and there are now more Presbyterians in Korea than in the United States. Taiwan has a strong Presbyterian church, and there are growing churches in the southeast Asian region. In Central and South America, Brazil has the largest Reformed church membership. There are many small Reformed churches in Asia, Mesoamerica, and South America where Protestant communities are minorities.

Presbyterians, Congregationalists, and Reformed Christians have also joined with other Protestants in united churches. A strong Reformed element is present in the united churches of China, India, Japan, Philippines, Thailand, the islands of the Pacific, and in the united churches of Western countries such as Australia, Canada, Germany, the United Kingdom, and the United States.

Together with the Western Reformed churches of Europe and North America, the churches of Africa, Asia, and Latin America are reshaping the Reformed tradition into a multicultural, multiethnic, and multinational phenomenon. The Reformed churches of the twentieth century have become a worldwide movement.

NOTES

1. Barrett, David, ed., *World Christian Encyclopedia: A Comparative Study of Churches and Religions in the Modern World AD 1900–2000* (Oxford: Oxford University Press, 1982), 3, 29.

2. "The Christian Tradition in Today's World." In *Religion in Today's World: The Religious Situation of the World from 1945 to the Present Day*, ed. Frank Whaling (Edinburgh: T. & T. Clark, 1987), quoted in Lamin Sanneh, "Global Christianity and the Re-education of the West," *Christian Century*, July 19–26, 1995, 715.

3. Ibid., 717.

4. John H. Leith, ed., *Creeds of the Churches* (Chicago: Aldine, 1963), 127.

5. Lukas Vischer writes that "the Reformed family has never sought to express the faith of the church through one statement" but through multiple confessions that respond to changing circumstances. See Lukas Vischer, ed., *Reformed Witness Today: A Collection of Confessions and Statements of Faith Issued by Reformed Churches* (Bern: Evangelische Arbeitsstelle Oekumene Schweiz, 1982), 9.

6. Cited by Alan P.F. Sell, "The World Alliance of Reformed Churches," in *Encyclopedia of the Reformed Faith*, ed. Donald K. McKim (Louisville: Westminster/John Knox, 1992), 403.

7. *The Constitution of the Presbyterian Church (U.S.A.)*, pt. 2, *Book of Order* (Louisville: Office of the General Assembly), G-2.0500.

The Dictionary

- A -

ABEDNEGO, MARTINUS (1910–1976). Indonesian lay leader in the Reformed Church of Indonesia. Abednego was director of the office of Protestant Directorate General of the Ministry of Religious Affairs and a member of the Central Committee of the Indonesian Christian Party. As a young man he was a teacher and helped organize the first conference of the World Student Christian Federation (WSCF) in Asia (Citeureup 1933). As a church and political leader, Abednego played a role in the development of church–state relations in **Indonesia**, where the constitution guarantees freedom of religion but the majority of the population practices Islam, and the tendency is toward the establishment of Islam as the state religion. Abednego served as member and chair of several committees of the National Council of Churches in Indonesia, including the Committee for Spiritual Nurture of the Armed Forces, Committee on Church and Society, Committee for Scholarship, and Committee for Education.

ABISKHAIRUN, ALEXANDER (1865–1949). Egyptian Presbyterian elder and political and church leader. Born in Abnub, Abiskhairun graduated from the American College in Asyūt in 1882 and later studied law. He became a member of the Evangelical Church in 1880 and served as its head. In 1940 Abiskhairun was installed as an elder of the Qasr al-Dubara Evangelical Church, one of the largest Presbyterian congregations in Cairo. He was also elected to the Egyptian House of Representatives in 1936 and served for almost 10 years.

ABORIGINAL RELATIONS. The relations between the Reformed churches and the indigenous peoples of **Australia**, **New Zealand**, the **Pacific** Islands, the **Caribbean**, the Americas, and other areas of the world. Many Reformed churches have carried out evangelistic and benevolent work among indigenous peoples. Some work has been very

1

positive and has been well received over many years. Recently, however, churches have begun to recognize the sometimes destructive impact of Western culture (and a westernized gospel) on the lives of native peoples. In some cases, churches have offered a formal apology. For example, in 1986 the United Church of **Canada** carried its apology to representatives of native congregations. This action was an opportunity for healing, celebration, and renewed partnership in ministry.

ABU DHABI. *See* MIDDLE EAST

ACCOMMODATION (Latin *accommodatio*). Adaptation or adjusting by **God** of the divine message to fit the capacities of a human audience. Theologians such as Origen, Chrysostom, Augustine, and **John Calvin** used the term to explain God's method of communication with humanity. Images of God as parent, teacher, and physician are divine ways of accommodation by which God communicates in ways that humans can understand. It is as though the Creator lisps in order to "accommodate the knowledge [of God] to our slight capacity" (*Inst.* 1.13.1). All **knowledge of God** is accommodated **revelation**. This is the way God has chosen to communicate with human beings and is a genuine means of revelation despite human limitations and sinfulness. **Scripture** is one of the most important examples of accommodation; it is written by human authors in order to convey the divine message. Other avenues of accommodated revelation include God's law (*Inst.* 2.11.13), the Lord's Prayer (3.20.34), and the **sacraments** (4.1.1). The supreme example is Jesus Christ, in whom God is revealed as a human being. Calvin says, "In Christ God so to speak makes himself little, in order to lower himself to our capacity" *(Comm. 1 Pet. 1:20)*. Through such divine accommodation, human beings are able to understand and appreciate God's gracious desire to be revealed in ways commensurate with human capacity.

ADAMS, NEWTON (1804–1851). American Congregationalist medical and evangelistic missionary in **South Africa**. Sent out by the **American Board of Commissioners for Foreign Missions** in 1835, Adams received permission from the Zulu king to establish a **mission** home and school in Umlazi, near Durban. He educated Zulu children at the primary and high school levels and fostered development in the mechanical arts and trades. He became involved in colonial politics on behalf of Zulu interests and mediated intertribal and land conflicts. Although advocating cultural change in some areas (e.g., polygamy), Adams fought for Zulu land rights and served on the first Natal Land Commission; the Natalian system of native "locations" set the pattern for the "reserves" or "native areas" of the 20th century. Ordained by the Dutch Reformed Church in 1844, Adams combined **evangelism**, **education**, and medical care throughout his ministry.

AFRICA. *See* CENTRAL AFRICA; EAST AFRICA; NORTH AFRICA; SOUTH AFRICA; SOUTHERN AFRICA; WEST AFRICA

AHN, BYUNG-MU (1922–1996). Korean theologian. Born in Pyongannam Province in northeast **Korea**, Ahn graduated from Dajung College in **Japan** and Seoul National University in Korea. He studied New Testament at Heidelberg University, where he graduated in 1965. He taught at Kangnam University (formerly Chungang Theological Seminary), Yonsei University, and Hankuk Theological Seminary. Ahn was dismissed from two positions because of his involvement in the democratic movement in Korea, and he was imprisoned in 1976. He founded a theological journal, *The Theological Thought,* wrote 18 books, and was one of the founders of **Minjung theology.**

ALEXANDER, ARCHIBALD (1772–1851). American Presbyterian minister and founding professor of **Princeton Theological Seminary**. Born in Rockbridge County, Virginia, Alexander studied theology with William Graham at Liberty Hall Academy (later Washington and Lee University), Virginia. It was from Graham that Alexander learned the Scottish Common Sense philosophy that he would later bring to Princeton Seminary. Alexander served as president of Hampden-Sydney College (1796–1807) and pastor of Pine Street Presbyterian Church in Philadelphia (1807–1812). In 1812 he became the first professor at Princeton Seminary. Alexander's program at Princeton combined high academic standards with personal piety, and his influence on the school and its graduates was profound. His publications include *Evidences of the Authenticity, Inspiration, and Canonical Authority of the Holy Scriptures* (1830); *Thoughts on Religious Experience* (1844); *A Brief Compend of Bible Truth* (1846), on theology; and *Outlines of Moral Science* (1852), on ethics.

ALGERIA. *See* NORTH AFRICA

ALLAN, ALEXANDER M. (1880?–1946?). Scottish Presbyterian missionary and journalist in Colombia. Born in Ayrshire, **Scotland**, Allan went to sea at age 16 and spent several years traveling. He settled in **New Zealand**, where he attended seminary and worked as a colporteur for the British and Foreign Bible Society. He was appointed a missionary in Colombia with the Presbyterian Church in the U.S.A. and arrived in

Barranquilla in 1910, where he began colportage work. In 1911 he began work in Bogotá as an educator, evangelist, and journalist, founding the newspaper *El evangelista cristiano* (later *El evangelista colombiano*) in 1912. This paper had wide influence, strengthening the evangelistic and educational work of the church. He moved to Tolima in 1914 and continued evangelistic work, forming churches, schools, and mission stations throughout the region. In 1920 he founded the Colegio Americano of Girardot. His ministry played an important role in the expansion of the Presbyterian Church in Colombia.

AMAKU, E. N. (1898–1974). Nigerian teacher, author, and prominent member of the Reformed Church. He studied at Duke Town School and the Hope Waddell Training Institution in Calabar. Amaku pioneered written literature in the Efik language. He assisted in the production of an Efik-English dictionary and wrote books intended for Nigerian students (notably *Edikot Nwed Mbuk*). Amaku's works also include poetry, lyrical accounts of the Efik sons and daughters *(Nwed Enyin Mbo Ima),* proverbs, and stories of Jesus Christ *(Jesus Christ Ke Uto)* for Sunday school use. He translated over 140 hymns into Efik, wrote eight plays, and produced novels that won prizes at the International Institute for African Languages in London. Amaku's works are still used in primary and secondary schools in **Nigeria**.

AMERICA. *See* UNITED STATES OF AMERICA

AMERICAN BOARD OF COMMISSIONERS FOR FOREIGN MISSIONS (ABCFM). Organized in Massachusetts in 1810, the interdenominational ABCFM was the first American foreign missionary society. Primarily a Congregationalist body, the society was also supported by Presbyterian, Associate Reformed, and Dutch and German Reformed churches until these bodies organized their own missionary societies. Although the ABCFM conducted **mission** work in Tennessee and Georgia among the Cherokees (1817), and in Mississippi among the Choctaws (1818), it is primarily known for its vast international work. The ABCFM established mission work in many parts of the world, including **India** (1813), **Hawaii** (1820), **Syria** (Beirut, 1823), **China** (1830), **Greece** (1831), **Africa** (1834), and **Japan** (1869). By 1894, the society employed over 550 missionaries and operated over 400 congregations (with 41,522 members) and over 1,000 schools (with 50,000 students). Its personnel conducted scientific research, prepared **Bible translations**, founded schools and colleges, established printing presses, and provided medical services. In 1961 the ABCFM was merged into the United Church

Board of World Ministries (UCBWM), an arm of the newly created United Church of Christ.

AMERICAN HOME MISSIONARY SOCIETY (AHMS). Founded by New York Congregationalists, the American Home Missionary Society (1826–1893) was the most important Protestant society for new church development in the **United States** before the Civil War. The AHMS was an interdenominational organization supported by Presbyterian, Dutch Reformed, and Associate Reformed churches. These supporting churches withdrew by 1861, and in 1893 the society was renamed the Congregational Home Missionary Society. The work of the AHMS was carried out in New England and gradually extended to the western frontier. By 1893 the society employed workers in almost every state and territory, including 2,000 pastors and missionaries who served over 3,800 congregations. The society funded the construction of over 2,400 churches and over 400 parsonages, organized schools, provided grants for new church development, and ministered to immigrants.

AMERICAN SAMOA. *See* PACIFIC OCEAN ISLANDS

AMES, WILLIAM (1576–1633). English Puritan theologian whose theological and ethical writings influenced Protestant thought in 17th-century **England** and **America.** Ames was converted through the ministry of **William Perkins** at Cambridge, where he became a fellow (1601–1610). His strong **Nonconformist** views led to difficulties with the established church, and Ames moved to the **Netherlands**, becoming professor of theology (1622) and later rector (1626) at the University of Franeker. Ames's major theological work, *A Marrow of Sacred Theology* (1623), was constructed according to the method of Ramist logic and drew "faith" and "observance" (works) together as major branches of theology, which he defined as "the doctrine or teaching of living to God." For Ames, theology was not primarily speculative but practical. His *De Conscientia* (1622; 1630), translated as *Conscience with the Power and Cases Thereof* (1639), expanded the second part of Ames's *Marrow*. Ames's *Philosophemata* (1643) functioned as a prolegomena to theology.

ANALOGY. Literary/rhetorical device used in language to express similarities between elements otherwise unlike. The term is used theologically to indicate ways by which human language can describe **God.** Thus humans speak of the "justice" of God based on human experience of "justice," which may be similar to, but neither identical with nor totally different from, divine justice. John Calvin's doctrine of the **knowledge**

of God relies on the use of analogy when he speaks of the evidences of God in the created order (*Inst.* 1:5–6; see also Rom. 1:19ff.). Yet no saving knowledge of God is ultimately possible from the created order because of the sinful human condition, according to **Karl Barth.** True knowledge of God only comes through God's **revelation.** In opposition to **Emil Brunner,** Barth denied the validity of analogy as a way of understanding God, arguing that only the "analogy of faith" (Latin *analogia fidei*) rather than the "analogy of being" (Latin *analogia entis*) can produce true knowledge of God.

ANCESTOR WORSHIP. Theology and practice related to the spirits of the dead. Ancestor veneration is widespread in **Africa, Asia (India, China,** and **Japan),** and the **Pacific** region. The basis of appealing to ancestors is the belief in a spiritual state after **death.** Dead persons continue their existence as members of the family and nation. The living may appeal to their ancestral spirits to help the family, community, or nation. Elements of this practice are sometimes carried over into Christian worship, where the living presence of ancestors is acknowledged. In **East Africa,** for example, the extended family includes the unborn, the living, and the dead (i.e., the dead who are "alive" in Christ). All are part of the same community of saints, which spans time and space.

ANDEAN REPUBLICS AND GREATER COLOMBIA. Colombia and Venezuela, historically called *Gran Colombia,* along with Bolivia, Peru, and Ecuador, have many features in common. Their coastal regions are low-lying areas; the Andes Mountains are in their central regions; and, where they face Brazil, their rivers drain through tropical forests into the Amazon. The most common languages are Spanish, Aymara, and Quechua. The Roman Catholic Church has dominated the religious life of the region.

The Catholic Church came to South America with the Spanish conquerors in the 1500s. The first Protestant congregations appeared in the late 1800s through the work of missionaries from the **United States, Great Britain,** and **Canada.** Religious toleration was limited for the early *evangélicos,* but persecution such as occurred in Colombia during "the Violence" of 1949 to 1958 was rare. By the 1990s many Protestant churches were in the region, but they made up less than 5 percent of the population. The largest Protestant denominations were the Seventh Day Adventists and various Pentecostalists.

Colombia. The Reformed churches were established first in Colombia. Pioneer **Henry Barrington Pratt** arrived in 1856, sent by the

Presbyterian Church in the U.S.A. He and others who followed, including **Alexander M. Allan** and **Adam H. Erwin**, emphasized evangelization and **education**. In major cities the Presbyterian secondary schools, *Colegios Americanos,* became widely respected. The Presbyterian Church of Colombia established its first synod in 1937 and in 1959 celebrated its ecclesiastical independence from the home church in the United States. A theological school for indigenous pastors was organized in 1916. The first graduating class of 1919 included **Juan Libreros Camargo.** By 1982 the school had grown into the Presbyterian and Reformed Theological Seminary of Greater Colombia, located in Barranquilla. In the 1990s, the church counted two synods, 50 congregations, and about 10,000 members. During this period the two synods disagreed on matters of social justice. They avoided splitting apart but struggled with the ongoing Reformed issues of faithfulness to **God** and rejection of all idolatries. Also notable in Colombia is the Cumberland Presbyterian Church (CPC), begun in 1927 through the pioneering witness of Walter L. Swartz from the CPC in the **United States.** Congregations began in Cali and later spread to several cities in the Valle region. The principal activity of the Cumberland Church is a secondary school, the *Colegio Americano* in Cali, established in 1928.

Venezuela. The Presbyterian Church of Venezuela was established by missionaries coming by way of Colombia. At the invitation of Venezuela's president Andrade in 1896, a family of Presbyterian educators, Heraclio, Celia, and Julia Osuna, moved from Bogota to Caracas and started a Presbyterian school. The first steps toward forming a congregation were taken in 1897 by Theodore and Julia Pond, Presbyterian missionaries in Colombia who moved to Venezuela. Other Protestants joined with them in 1901 to form the first Presbyterian congregation, the Church of the Redeemer, in Caracas. Presbyterian ministries included a secondary school, the *Colegio Americano* in Caracas; the publication of religious literature; the training of evangelists, including **women**; and work in public **health** and the organization of cooperatives. The Presbytery of Venezuela was organized in 1943. By 1991 it had become an independent synod with two presbyteries. Pastors are educated at the seminary in Barranquilla, Colombia. The church counts about 700 members and applies its resources to social justice issues, ecumenical cooperation, and its own renewal.

Bolivia. The Aymara and Quechua people are important groups whose languages are still spoken along with Spanish. Though the country is rich in minerals and agricultural products, it ranks as one of the poorest in Latin

America. Even today the Protestant churches are small, the largest being the Seventh Day Adventists, Nazarenes, and Friends. The Presbyterian Church in Bolivia began in 1983 through the work of a Korean missionary, Chong Moo Park. Korean missionaries later established several centers for training pastors. The church is said to have congregations among the Aymara people in La Paz, Santa Cruz, and Cochabamba. The Presbytery of La Paz began in 1986 and soon established ecumenical contacts with other Reformed churches in Latin America. In 1989 Presbyterians established the Bolivian Union Evangelical University. In partnership with the Independent Presbyterian Church of Brazil and the Presbyterian Church (U.S.A.), the Bolivian Presbyterians, who numbered about 1,200 in 12 congregations in 1994, support service projects in nutrition, agriculture, livestock raising, and handicrafts.

Ecuador. The first permanent Protestant work in Ecuador began in 1896 and has been continued, since 1945, by the United Evangelical Church of Ecuador. The United Evangelical Church grew out of the United Andean Indian Mission, a joint venture among Quechua-speaking people by four churches in the United States: the Presbyterian Church, U.S.; the United Presbyterian Church, U.S.A.; the Evangelical and Reformed Church (later part of the United Church of Christ); and the Evangelical United Brethren Church. The United Church serves the region with programs in evangelization, education, health care, and agriculture. Today the church counts 15 congregations and about 500 members.

Peru. Two Reformed churches have ministered in Peru: the Evangelical Presbyterian Church of Peru, established in 1917 by missionaries from the Free Church of Scotland, and the National Presbyterian Church of Peru, established among the Quechua Indians in 1937 by an independent group of Presbyterians. Bible translation was promoted by James Thomson (1788–1854), who worked in Peru and in other countries of Latin America. In the 1980s a Maoist guerilla movement, *Sendero Luminoso* (Shining Light), killed many Presbyterians in the area of Ayacucho. One of the Presbyterian pastors, Pedro Arana, gained national prominence for his advocacy of **human rights.** By the 1990s both of these Reformed churches were connected to others in Latin America and also to the Presbyterian Church (U.S.A.), and they counted a total of 15,000 members. The two churches merged in 1995 to form the Evangelical Presbyterian and Reformed church in Peru. The church operates projects in health care, education, nutrition, programs for street children, and cooperatives for farmers. *See also* John A. Mackay

ANDERSON, RUFUS (1796–1880). Secretary of the **American Board of Commissioners for Foreign Missions** (ABCFM). Born in Yarmouth, Maine, Anderson was educated at Bowdoin College (1818) and **Andover Theological Seminary** (1822). He served as assistant secretary (1826–1831) and secretary (1832–1866) of the ABCFM. Under Anderson, the ABCFM developed a theory of mission work called the **Three-Self Formula**, explained in his *Outline of Missionary Policy* (1856). Anderson asserted that the goal of **mission** work was to establish self-governing, self-supporting, and self-propagating churches; to decentralize the mission enterprise by developing indigenous churches with ordained clergy from the local population, as well as local organizational structures, support, and outreach. Anderson also wrote pamphlets on the subject and a book, *Foreign Missions: Their Relations and Claims* (1869). In addition to writings on mission policy, he wrote works of mission history, including *History of the Sandwich Islands Mission* (1870).

ANDOVER NEWTON THEOLOGICAL SCHOOL. American theological seminary of Congregational heritage. Organized in 1808 at Andover Academy in Massachusetts, Andover Theological Seminary was founded as an alternative to Harvard, which had come under the influence of **Unitarianism.** The theology of the school was influenced by the New Divinity theology of **Samuel Hopkins.** It was a center of Calvinistic orthodoxy until the 1880s, when it embraced **liberalism**. In 1908 the school moved to Cambridge, Massachusetts, and affiliated with Harvard. When the board of visitors blocked a 1922 merger with Harvard Divinity School, the Andover faculty resigned in protest. The seminary did not resume operations until 1931, when it affiliated with the Baptist Newton Theological Institute. The school educates ministers for the United Church of Christ and other denominations.

ANDRIANAIVORAVELONA, JOSEPH (1877–1961). Protestant minister and educator in **Madagascar.** Andrianaivoravelona was a deacon and preacher at Anatirova Church (1895–1898) before devoting his energies to teaching and school administration. He taught at Ambositra (French Protestant Mission) and Ambatonakanga schools (1899–1918), and served as a director of Miaramirinda High School (1939–1947) and Mahitsy Regional School (1949–1953). He was ordained in 1909, helped to organize youth and women's groups in the Madagascar church, and wrote poetry and hymns. Eighteen of his hymns appear in the Protestant hymnbook of the Madagascar church.

ANET, LÉONARD JEAN FRANÇO HENRI (1812–1884). Belgian Reformed minister and secretary of the Belgian Christian Missionary Church. Born in Vaudois, Anet attended the Faculté de l'Oratoire in Geneva, where he studied with Merle d'Aubigné. Encouraged to work in Belgium, Anet was ordained in l'Église de l'Observatoire in Brussels. In 1837 ministers of the official church organized the Belgian Evangelical Society, which evolved into an independent church, free of state control. Anet served the society as secretary and helped organize the primary schools and evangelization programs of the denomination. Anet also led the effort to repatriate to Great Britain young girls who were exploited in the brothels of Brussels. He edited *History of the First Thirty Years of the Evangelical Society or Belgium Missionary Christian Church* (1875) and became an important spokesperson for Belgian Protestantism.

ANGOLA. *See* SOUTHERN AFRICA

ANTHROPOLOGY, CHRISTIAN. A Christian understanding of human beings drawn from God's **revelation** in **scripture.** The term first appears in Protestant works of the late 16th century. According to Christian anthropology, human beings are created in the image and likeness of **God** but have fallen into **sin.** Redemption comes by Jesus Christ through the power of the **Holy Spirit.** The redeemed are destined to be with God. Reformed anthropology emphasizes a **knowledge of God** implanted in all people (*sensus divinitatis*; "sense of divinity"; *Inst.* 1.3.3), the radical bondage of the human will to the power of sin, and the wholly regenerative power of the Holy Spirit who gives believers a new nature and new will that is free to obey God's will. Both Christian and Reformed anthropology consider human nature in its personal, social, sexual, and spiritual dimensions, and recognize the formative power of language, gender, culture, and social location in shaping the individual person.

APARTHEID. Afrikaner word for the political, social, and economic structures of racial separation developed in the Republic of **South Africa.** Apartheid legally ended in 1990. Rooted in colonial racism, the apartheid legislation of 1948 institutionalized the separate development of the races, setting aside about 11 percent of the land for the nonwhite population and limiting the employment and **education** available to nonwhites. The theology of the dominant Dutch Reformed churches supported apartheid as a divinely ordained social arrangement to avoid the mixing of races and keep black Africans under tutelage, although there was dissension within the church on this issue. The ecumenical community strongly criticized apartheid from its inception. In 1982 the **World Alliance of Reformed Churches** suspended South African churches whose membership supported apartheid. In 1990 the South African government set aside the enabling laws and began to dismantle apartheid; the major Dutch Reformed Church had by then repudiated its earlier justification of South Africa's racial policies.

APOLOGETICS. The defense of Christian faith, often through reasoned arguments. Reformed apologists have moved in different directions. Some have argued for the existence of **God** by following the theistic arguments articulated by St. Anselm, Thomas Aquinas, and others. The truth of Christianity is said to be established by internal and external arguments that prove the Bible is a **revelation** of God. These "proofs" include miracles, prophecy, and historical and archaeological evidence. This approach to Protestant apologetics was developed during the 17th and 18th centuries under pressure from enlightenment deism and rationalism, and it is still explored today by Protestant philosophers working in the field of **philosophy of religion.** Other Reformed apologists reject arguments based on human **reason** and appeal instead to the truth of God, which is known in Jesus Christ by the witness of the **Holy Spirit.** Following **John Calvin,** they argue that belief in **scripture** as God's revelation emerges from the Spirit's illumination rather than from the evidence of reason. Although evidence may enrich the faith of believers, it does not provide a basis for **faith. Karl Barth** proposes this line of argument, maintaining that the truth of God's revelation is beyond all means of human testing or criteria and thus is beyond apologetics.

ARCHITECTURE. The architecture of Reformed churches has been shaped by an emphasis on the proclamation of the **Word of God** and the **sacraments.** The pulpit is central and often is raised to emphasize the importance of preaching; seating is arranged to enable unobstructed hearing. Tables for the **Lord's Supper** replace altars; often these are placed at floor level to emphasize the equality and fellowship enjoyed by the congregation. The baptismal font is visibly integrated into corporate worship.

The international expansion of the Reformed churches has created many architectural challenges. Reformed pastors and missionaries have taken different approaches in the emerging churches: some transplanted the architecture of their home churches in **Europe** and **North America**; others paid minimal attention to architecture to avoid attaching sacred associations to human structures; still others sought to "baptize" indigenous architecture for the church's use, with mixed success. The functions of corporate worship (public assembly for praise, proclamation, and sacrament; space for fellowship and service; and hospitality) influence church architecture in a general way, but the Reformed churches worldwide have not embraced any one particular architectural tradition in the construction and use of church buildings.

ARGENTINA. *See* SOUTHERN CONE OF SOUTH AMERICA

ARMAND HUGON, AUGUSTO (1915–1980). Italian civic leader and Waldensian historian. Armand Hugon worked for many years as a teacher and principal at the secondary school of Torre Pellice. He served as mayor of Torre Pellice from 1949 to 1961 and was the first president of the Council of the Pellice Valley (1957). He is widely known as a Waldensian historian, having published a standard history of the **Waldensians**, *Storia dei Valdesi, II, dall'adesione alla Riforma all'Emancipazione (1532–1848)*, and a biography of Agostino Mainardo (1487–1563), an Augustinian monk who became a Protestant pastor in **Switzerland.** As president of the Society for Waldensian History, Armand Hugon organized its first annual meeting in 1957. These meetings have become important scholarly gatherings for historians from **Italy** and other European countries. Armand Hugon was also an elder and teacher in the Waldensian church and gave inspired leadership to its programs and mission.

ARMINIANISM. A theological movement that emerged from the teachings of **Jacob Arminius**, who opposed views held by **John Calvin** on **election, predestination,** and **grace**. The Arminian document known as the Five Remonstrant Articles (1610) was countered by the Calvinist "five points" formulated at the Synod of Dort (1618–1619). Arminianism teaches that despite **sin**, human beings are free to respond to the gospel and that election occurs after God's grace is given. **God** elects to **salvation** all whom God foresees will repent and believe in Jesus Christ. This is a "conditional election" in that it is dependent on God's **foreknowledge** of the human response. Human beings may resist grace and may at some point fall away from the gospel. In the process of salvation believers use their free will to cooperate with the grace of God extended to them. Arminianism spread throughout the world and was particularly evident in the theology of John Wesley (1703–1791).

ARMINIUS, JACOB (1560–1609). Dutch theologian who opposed the strict formulations on **predestination** associated with **Calvinism.** His followers came to be called Arminians. Arminius was educated at the Universities of Marburg (1575), Leiden (1576–1581), Basel (1582–1583), and Geneva (1582, 1584–1586). He served as a pastor in Amsterdam (1588–1603) and a professor of theology at Leiden from 1603. Arminius believed that Paul's letter to the Romans taught a "conditional predestination" in opposition to the "unconditional" views of contemporary Calvinists. He believed that God's predestination of individual destinies is based on divine **foreknowledge** of the way individuals will come to faith. God's "prevenient grace" is the work of the **Holy Spirit** in preparing individuals to choose to have faith in Jesus Christ. The views of Arminius were advocated by John Wesley and subsequently incorporated into the Methodism and the Holiness traditions.

ARTS, VISUAL. The expression of the biblical, theological, and historical dimensions of Reformed Christianity in painting, sculpture, stained glass, and other visual media. Reformed Protestantism has been ambivalent about the arts. Reformed churches took seriously the Old Testament prohibition against graven images, and Reformed communities were determined to avoid the representational excesses of medieval Catholicism. Protestant reformers **Huldrych Zwingli** and **John Calvin**, in their attempt to restore the books of **scripture** as the sole basis of **faith**, purged their churches of the "books of the unlearned": statuary, wall paintings, tapestry, stained glass, and other visual representations they considered idolatrous. In **Holland** the interior walls of churches were whitewashed. These unadorned walls were celebrated in the paintings of Dutch artist Pieter Saenredam (1597–1665). Reformed Christianity's emphasis on simplicity of life and lack of personal adornment also discouraged artistic expression.

Although austerity in worship and indifference to artistic expression persisted in many Reformed churches, a more tolerant attitude gradually emerged. Calvin welcomed depictions of scenes from the Bible in private homes and praised landscapes and historical subjects in secular art. Calvin's encouragement of Bible scenes and landscapes reached its height in the work of 17th-century Dutch painters **Rembrandt van Rijn**, Gerard Dou, and Jacob van Ruisdael, who gave artistic expression to Reformed ideas. Dutch naturalism portrayed the human condition in all its complexity, exhibiting a spiritual and emotional depth not found in earlier work. The use of stained glass windows, banners, paraments, and even statuary within Reformed churches has increased during the 20th century. This is especially true outside **Europe**, where the artistic depiction of biblical narratives is an important means of cultural expression. There have been attempts by Reformed scholars, including **P. T. Forsyth** (*Religion in Recent Art* [1905]) and **Hans R. Rookmaaker** (*Modern Art and the Death of a Culture* [2d ed., 1973]), at exposition and critique of artistic works.

ARUBA. *See* CARIBBEAN

ASIA. *See* EAST ASIA; NORTHEAST ASIA; SOUTHEAST ASIA; SOUTHERN ASIA

ATONEMENT. The means by which the relationship between **God** and humanity, broken by **sin**, is restored through the **death** of Jesus Christ. Several views have been advanced to explain the atonement, but no single view has the exclusive sanction of Christian theology or the Reformed tradition. Sacrificial and penal images are prominent in early Reformed **confessions** and **catechisms.** Some views of the atonement stress the "objective" or "divine" dimension; others the "subjective" or "human" dimension. One view emphasizes what Christ has done by virtue of who he was; the other view stresses the effects of Christ's work on those who believe in him. Reformed theology has spoken of the **threefold office** of Christ as prophet, priest, and king. These images also provide a framework for understanding the atonement. As prophet, Christ discloses and embodies truth to exemplify the way to life; as priest, he offers a vicarious sacrifice for sin; and as king, he embodies liberating power to conquer suffering and death. Contemporary understandings of atonement are shaped by cultural and biblical perspectives.

AUBURN AFFIRMATION (1924). An affirmation drafted by a group of American Presbyterian ministers who met in Auburn, New York. The document was circulated throughout the church and eventually signed by more than 1,200 ministers, many from New York. The Auburn Affirmation declared unconstitutional the action of the Presbyterian **General Assembly** of 1923, which required all ministerial candidates to affirm five "essential" doctrines. These five doctrines included the **inspiration** and inerrancy of **scripture**, the virgin birth, Christ's **death** as a sacrifice to satisfy divine justice, the physical **resurrection** of Jesus, and Christ's power to work miracles. The 1923 Assembly had followed actions taken by the 1910 and 1916 Assemblies, which also tried to secure doctrinal conformity. The signers of the Auburn Affirmation maintained that the Assembly's action elevated some doctrines over others and, in effect, amended the church's constitution without the approval of the church's presbyteries. The General Assembly of 1927 later agreed with this interpretation. The supporters of the Auburn Affirmation understood their protest as a plea for toleration and theological diversity, whereas opponents saw it as an indication of serious doctrinal erosion within the church.

AUSTRALIA. The people of Australia are predominantly Christian (Protestant, 50 percent, with 26 percent Anglican; and Roman Catholic, 26 percent).

Congregational Churches. Congregationalism was introduced to Australia by missionaries of the **London Missionary Society**, who founded the first Reformed church in Hobart, Tasmania, in 1830. Congregationalism was established through the efforts of **Henry Hopkins**, a wool merchant and philanthropist who helped bring the first Independent ministers to Australia and built several Congregational churches.

Congregational unions, beginning with the Congregational Union of Tasmania (1837), were formed throughout Australia in the 19th century as a means of mutual support in the vast expanse of Australia. In 1904 the national Congregational Union of Australasia was begun (New Zealand was a member but withdrew in 1960). In 1977 most Congregationalists joined the Uniting Church in Australia. The Fellowship of Congregational Churches, composed of about 20 churches in New South Wales, as well as the three congregations of the Queensland Congregational Fellowship, centered in the Brisbane-Ipswich area, declined to join the union. **Winifred Kiek** was an important church and ecumenical leader.

Presbyterian Churches. Presbyterianism was introduced to Australia by **John Dunmore Lang** and by Scots, Welsh, and English settlers who came to Australia during the 19th century. The first church was built at Ebenezer, New South Wales, in 1809. In the 20th century, settlers from the **Netherlands, Hungary, Czechoslovakia**, and **China** also contributed to the growth of the church. Divisions among Presbyterians in **Scotland** were reflected in the Australian churches. In 1865, however, various Presbyterian groups within each state united. In 1886 these state groups joined together in a federal union of churches. As a result of these church unions, the Presbyterian Church of Australia was organized in 1901, shortly after the inauguration of the Commonwealth of Australia. **John Flynn** is recognized as one of the early leaders of Australian Presbyterianism. In 1977 a large part of the Presbyterian Church (65–

70 percent) joined with the Congregational and Methodist Churches to form the Uniting Church. Presbyterian churches that remain outside the Uniting Church include the Presbyterian Church of Australia, a conservative denomination that continues the tradition of the original Australian Presbyterian Church of 1901; the Presbyterian Reformed Church of Australia; the Westminster Presbyterian Church; and the Presbyterian Church of Eastern Australia, established in 1846 by Scottish settlers who maintained connections with the Free Church rather than the Church of Scotland.

United Churches. In 1977 the Uniting Church in Australia was formed by Congregational, Presbyterian, and Methodist churches. The merger was a result of discussions that had taken place between 1957 and 1977. The name of the denomination reflected the hope that other denominations might join. About one-third of Australian Presbyterians and one-tenth of Congregationalists declined to enter the union. The Uniting Church became the third largest church in Australia behind the Anglican and Roman Catholic Church.

The doctrinal basis of the church is the Basis of Union, written by the Joint Commission on Church Union. Although it is not a detailed confession of faith, the declaration acknowledges the Apostles' and Nicene Creeds, the Reformation **confessions**, and later documents, including the **Westminster Confession** (1647), the **Savoy Declaration** (1658), and the Forty-Four Sermons of John Wesley (1793).

Both men and **women** serve as ordained clergy. The church is governed by a network of councils: the congregation, the council of elders, the parish council, the parish meeting, the **presbytery**, the synod, and the assembly. The assembly meets every three years and attends to doctrine, worship, and discipline. Nearly 3,000 congregations and 55 presbyteries constitute the church, which is affiliated with the **World Alliance of Reformed Churches.**

The Uniting Church features an increasing multiculturalism reflective of Australia's diverse population. More than 5 percent of its membership worships in languages other than English. The **Uniting Aboriginal and Islander Christian Congress**, established through the work of aboriginal minister Charles Enoch Edward Harris (1931–1993), oversees all ministry with aboriginal peoples. The church takes a strong ecumenical stance and is the largest nongovernmental provider of social services in Australia. It advocates aboriginal rights, disarmament, **human rights**, and economic and **social justice.** Six theological colleges, most associated with universities, serve the church.

Reformed Churches. Australian Reformed churches include the Free Reformed Churches of Australia; the Welsh Calvinistic Methodist Church; the Hungarian Reformed Church in Australia; and the Reformed Churches of Australia, organized by Dutch immigrants to Australia after World War II. The Dutch church subscribes to the Belgic Confession, the **Heidelberg Catechism**, the Canons of the Synod of Dort, and the Westminster Confession.

AUSTRALIAN INLAND MISSION (AIM). Presbyterian **mission** to the sparsely populated regions of northern and central **Australia**. Founded in 1912 by **John Flynn**, the mission sent ministers, nurses, doctors, and welfare workers to people in the Australian outback. Flynn established radio communication in remote regions of Australia, and in 1928 he began the Flying Doctor Service.

AUSTRIA. *See* CENTRAL AND EASTERN EUROPE

AUTHORITY. The criteria or sources for Christian **faith**, doctrine, and life. Traditionally, Christian authority is said to spring from four sources: **scripture, tradition, reason**, and experience. Reformed theology emphasizes the primacy of scripture; it is the sole authority, the "rule of faith and life" (**Westminster Confession**, chap. 1). Tradition, as expressed in church creeds and **confessions**, in the decisions of councils, and in the writings of commentators and theologians, is appropriated by Reformed theology only when its teachings are in accord with scripture. Reason, impaired by **sin** and by itself incapable of a saving knowledge of **God**, is by God's Spirit the means by which the biblical **revelation** is understood, the church's teachings are assessed, and the activities of the Spirit communicated. Experience, expressed as a living faith, is the fruit of the gospel, not a source of it; genuine Christian experience is always in accord with scripture. Although the various sources of authority can be harmoniously used in various combinations, each is subject to the revelation of God in scripture.

- B -

BAHRAIN. *See* MIDDLE EAST

BAILLIE, DONALD MACPHERSON (1887–1954). Scottish Presbyterian theologian and ecumenist and brother of **John Baillie.** He studied at **New College, Edinburgh**, and at Marburg and Heidelberg before or-

dination in the United Free Church (1918). From 1934 he was professor of theology at St. Andrews University and gained renown for his book *God Was in Christ* (1948), which sought to correct some older Christological views while also vigorously defending historic **Christology**, especially by rejecting docetism in Christology. His *Theology of the Sacraments* (1957) was also an important work. Baillie was active in promoting the Student Christian Movement, the **Iona Community**, and he participated in the Faith and Order Conferences in Edinburgh (1937) and Lund (1952).

BAILLIE, JOHN (1886–1960). Scottish Presbyterian theologian and writer and brother of **Donald Baillie.** He studied in **Scotland** and **Germany** before becoming professor of divinity at **New College, Edinburgh** (1934–1956). He was one of the Church of Scotland's greatest contemporary theologians and **moderator** of its **general assembly** (1943). Baillie is said to have combined the old liberal theology with the insights of **Karl Barth** while also holding a strong tendency toward the mystical. His major books included *And the Life Everlasting* (1933), *Our Knowledge of God* (1939), *The Belief in Progress* (1950), and his undelivered Gifford Lectures, *A Sense of the Presence of God* (1962). Baillie became widely known for the devotional works *A Diary of Private Prayer* (1936) and *Invitation to Pilgrimage* (1942). A strong supporter of the **ecumenical movement**, Baillie was a president of the **World Council of Churches** (WCC) and a leader at the WCC assemblies in Amsterdam (1948) and Evanston (1954).

BAINTON, ROLAND H. (1894–1984). American Congregationalist minister and Reformation historian. Born in **England**, Bainton emigrated with his parents to **Canada** in 1898 and to the **United States** in 1902. He graduated from Whitman College and Yale University, where he began to teach church history in the Divinity School in 1920. In 1927 he was ordained to the Congregationalist ministry. Bainton taught ecclesiastical history at Yale Divinity School for 42 years (1920–1962). He was an animated lecturer and the recipient of many honorary doctorates. Bainton's writings are wide-ranging. His works *The Travail of Religious Liberty* (1951) and *Christian Attitudes toward War and Peace* (1960) reveal a strong commitment to social involvement and ecumenics. He produced several scholarly studies of historic figures, including his award-winning, *Here I Stand: A Life of Martin Luther* (1950), *Bernardino Orchino* (1940), *Erasmus of Christendom* (1969), and *Hunted Heretic: The Life and Death of Michael Servetus, 1511–1553* (1953). His historical surveys include *The Horizon History of Christianity* (1964), *The Church of Our Fathers* (1941), written specifically for youth, *The Reformation of the Sixteenth Century* (1952), *The Age of the Reformation* (1956), and two studies of **women**, *Women of the Reformation in Germany and Italy* (1971) and *Women of the Reformation in France and England* (1973).

BANGLADESH. *See* SOUTHERN ASIA

BAPTISM. God's **covenant** sign administered with water and in the name of the triune **God**, baptism seals the promises of the gospel to those who are united with Jesus Christ by **faith.** Through the **sacrament** of baptism, one is "enrolled, entered, and received into the covenant" and into God's family (Second Helvetic Confession, chap. 20; cf. Westminster Shorter Catechism, question 94). Regeneration, forgiveness of **sin**, commitment to God in Jesus Christ, and the desire to "walk in newness of life" are dimensions of this action (**Westminster Confession**, chap. 28). Reformed theology recognizes the validity of both adult and infant baptism. Those who profess faith in Christ are baptized by the **church** as their entry into the covenantal family of God. The Reformed tradition understands baptism as the New Testament equivalent to the Old Testament practice of circumcision (Rom. 4:11). Infant children of believers are baptized to indicate their incorporation into the church. They are baptized on the basis of the covenant promises extended to them through their parents. Where infant baptism is practiced, **confirmation** is viewed as an opportunity for children to express publicly the faith into which they were baptized. Some Reformed churches have chosen not to baptize infants, practicing instead "believers' baptism."

BARCLAY, WILLIAM (1907–1978). Scottish Presbyterian minister, New Testament scholar, and a popular and effective biblical communicator. Barclay was born in Wick and attended Glasgow and Marburg Universities. He was ordained in the Church of Scotland in 1933 and served a parish in Renfrew. In 1947 he began to lecture in New Testament at Glasgow University and became a professor in 1964. Barclay wrote the 17-volume *Daily Study Bible,* which has enjoyed great success among both laity and clergy. He believed in **universalism** and held nontraditional views on such doctrines as the virgin birth, miracles, and the **authority** of scripture. Through his 70 publications, including a translation of the New Testament and television broadcasts, Barclay's ministry had worldwide influence.

BARLOW, ARTHUR RUFFLE (1888–1965). Church of Scotland missionary and Bible translator in **Kenya.** Barlow began an informal association with the **mission** at Kikuyu in 1903; three years later he became a full member of the Church of Scotland mission. Known for his linguistic skill, Barlow reduced the Kikuyu language to writing, prepared a grammar, and translated schoolbooks, hymns, and the Bible into the Gikuyu language. He collaborated with Harry Leakey of Kabete to produce a translation of the New Testament (1926). With Leakey, Leonard Beecher, Charles Muhoro, and other scholars, Barlow produced a Gikuyu-English Dictionary, eventually published in 1964. In addition to his language work, Barlow was superintendent of the mission at Tumutumu and secretary of the mission council. An authority on Kikuyu culture and an active participant in the Presbyterian Church of East Africa, Barlow served the mission for 35 years.

BARMEN DECLARATION. *See* THEOLOGICAL DECLARATION OF BARMEN

BARROW, HENRY (ca. 1550–1593). English Congregationalist minister and separatist. Barrow was educated in law at Clare Hall, Cambridge, and became a member of the bar at Gray's Inn in 1576. He was converted from a dissolute life around 1580 to strict Puritan views. He studied **scripture**, became a friend of **John Greenwood**, and came to respect the views of **Robert Browne**, who advocated the formation of churches separate from the Church of England. In Barrow's view, the **church** is "a company of faithful people separated from the unbelievers and . . . gathered in the name of Christ." Barrow set forth these views in his publications, including *A True Description of the Visible Congregation of the Saints* (1589) and *A Brief Discovery of the False Church* (1590). Because nonconformity to the established church was considered a threat to national security, Barrow was tried in 1590 for spreading seditious ideas through his books. He was hanged three years later. Barrow is sometimes considered to be the founder of modern **Congregationalism**, though he denied that he was a mere "sectary."

BARTH, KARL (1886–1968). Swiss Reformed theologian and pastor. Barth studied theology in Bern, Berlin, Tübingen, and Marburg under liberal theologians Wilhelm Herrmann and Adolf von Harnack. He served as assistant pastor and then pastor in Safenwil (1911–1921) and became an outspoken critic of his former teachers, who supported World War I. Barth's *Commentary on Romans* (1919; rev. 1922) departed from current scholarship by developing a theological interpretation of the epistle. The work also established his credentials as one of the most important theologians of the early 20th century. He accepted a chair of Reformed theology at Göttingen (1921) and established friendships with Eduard Thurneysen, Rudolf Bultmann, Friedrich Gogarten, and **Emil Brunner** as they developed a **dialectical theology.** In 1925 Barth moved to Münster and in 1930 to Bonn. Barth vigorously opposed a growing National Socialism. He was dismissed from his chair at Bonn in 1935 and then moved to Basel, where he taught for the rest of his career. He was a founder of the **Confessing Church** in opposition to the German Christians who supported Hitler. After World War II, Barth called for reconciliation with Germany, and he delivered the opening address at the first meeting of the **World Council of Churches** in 1948. Among Barth's many writings, his 13-volume *Church Dogmatics* (1936–1977) is a comprehensive expression of his thought and is regarded as a seminal work of theology. His dogmatics are thoroughly Christological, and this perspective forms the basis for Barth's recasting of major Reformed doctrines such as **creation, providence, sin, covenant,** and **election.** He rejected the validity of infant **baptism** and his thinking in some areas approached **universalism.** Barth's influence on Christian theology has been of enduring relevance.

BASEL MISSION. *See* EVANGELICAL MISSION SOCIETY IN BASEL

BATTLES, FORD LEWIS (1915–1979). American church historian and **Calvin** scholar. Born in Erie, Pennsylvania, Battles was educated at West Virginia University and Tufts University. He traveled as a Rhodes scholar to England and studied with C. S. Lewis at Oxford. Battles served as an intelligence officer during World War II. After the war he returned to West Virginia University to teach English (1945–1948) and then enrolled at Hartford Seminary, earning a doctorate in Old Testament (1950). He shifted his interests to church history and taught that subject at Hartford Seminary (1950–1968), **Pittsburgh Theological Seminary** (1968–1979), and Calvin Theological Seminary (1979). He served on his denomination's Commission on Hymnody (1966–1973), helping to produce the *Hymnal of the United Church of Christ* (1969). A widely known Calvin scholar, Battles translated the reformer's works into English and became a respected interpreter of Calvin's theology. His major works include translations of Calvin's *Institutes* (1559 ed., 1960; 1536 ed., 1975), *Calvin's Commentary on Seneca's 'De Clementia'* (1969),

Calvin's *Catechism 1538* (1972), and a collection titled *The Piety of John Calvin: An Anthology* (1978). He also produced *A Computerized Concordance to Institutio Christianae Religionis 1559* (1972) and *An Analysis of the Institutes of the Christian Religion of John Calvin* (1980). A collection of his interpretative articles was published as *Interpreting John Calvin* (1996).

BAVINCK, HERMAN (1854–1921). Dutch Reformed theologian. The son of a minister of the Dutch Reformed Secessed Church, Bavinck received his doctorate from the University of Leiden in 1880. He became professor of systematic theology at Kampen, where he served from 1882 to 1902, and then professor at the **Free University** from 1902. He worked within the Dutch Reformed Church to unite theologically opposed groups, to enhance its educational system, and to address social concerns. Bavinck's four-volume *Gereformeerde Dogmatiek* (1895–1901; *Reformed Dogmatics*) reflects his view that **God** is the object of theology and **scripture** its source of knowledge. His concept of the "organic **inspiration**" of scripture acknowledged the personalities of the biblical writers. Along with **Abraham Kuyper**, Bavinck helped to revive Dutch Reformed theology at the beginning of the 20th century. His work maintained continuity with historic Reformed theology, but he sought to bring the older theology into discussion with the thought of his time. His influence continues, particularly within the Dutch Calvinist **tradition** in America.

BAXTER, RICHARD (1615–1691). English Puritan pastor and theologian. Baxter was largely self-educated and was ordained in the Church of England in 1638. While serving at Kidderminster (1641–1660), he supported the Parliamentary side in the English Civil War and served briefly as a military chaplain. As a result of his **Nonconformist** leadership, he was expelled from the Church of England in 1662. Forbidden to serve as a pastor, Baxter continued to preach and was imprisoned in 1685 and 1686. He also participated in the overthrow of James II. A prolific writer, Baxter sought reconciliation of the differing factions in the English national church and a tolerance for religious diversity. Baxter also sought a middle ground between antinomianism and **Arminianism**. His pastoral labors are detailed in *The Reformed Pastor* (1656). He also wrote an extensive work, *The Saint's Everlasting Rest* (1650), which describes "the blessed state of the Saints in their enjoyment of God in glory." Both works are theological classics. His autobiography is entitled *Reliquiae Baxterianae* (1695).

BAYLY, ALBERT FREDERICK (1901–1984). English Congregational-ist minister and hymn writer. Born at Bexhill, Sussex, Bayly graduated from the University of London and Mansfield College, Oxford. He was ordained in 1929 and served various pastorates until 1972. He is con-sidered a leader in the revival of British hymn writing, which occurred during the 1960s and 1970s. Bayly's first hymn collection, *Rejoice, O People,* was published in 1950. Notable pieces include "O Lord of Ev-ery Shining Constellation" and "What Does the Lord Require of Thee?" Bayly produced three more publications: *Again I Say, Rejoice* (1967); *Rejoice Always* (1971); *Rejoice in God* (1977). Several recent denomi-national hymnals have included Bayly's hymns.

BEECHER, LYMAN (1775–1863). American Congregationalist, later Presbyterian minister and educator. Beecher was born in New Haven, Connecticut, and graduated from Yale in 1797. He was ordained in 1799 and served the East Hampton Presbyterian Church, New York (1799–1810), and then Congregational churches at Litchfield, Connecticut (1810–1826), and Hanover Street, Boston (1826–1832). For the next 10 years Beecher served as both pastor of the Second Presbyterian Church in Cincinnati and president of Lane Theological Seminary. Beecher was a founder of the American Bible Society and, like his daughter, **Harriet Beecher Stowe**, an antislavery activist. He preached a form of **Calvin-ism** that emphasized human ability to respond to God's **grace.** His di-vergence from **Reformed orthodoxy** led to accusations of heresy. In 1835, Beecher was acquitted in **presbytery** and synod trials held in Ohio. He later embraced **Charles G. Finney's** "new measures" revivalism and believed the millennium would begin in America.

BELGIUM. *See* NORTHERN EUROPE

BELIZE. *See* MESOAMERICA

BENNETT, M. KATHERINE JONES (1864–1950). American Presby-terian home mission leader and advocate of the **ordination** of **women.** Bennett was born in Englewood, New Jersey, and graduated from Elmira College in 1885. After working as a schoolteacher, Bennett assumed lead-ership roles within the Presbyterian Church in the U.S.A., where she served as president of the Woman's Board of Home Missions and be-came an active voice on behalf of Presbyterian women. She was the first woman to present a board report to the **General Assembly** (1916). In 1923 she was appointed vice president of the National Board of Home Missions. With co-author Margaret Hodge, Bennett produced a report entitled "Causes of Unrest among Women of the Church" (1927). Bennett served on several ecumenical bodies, including the Council of Women for Home Missions, the Federal Council of Churches, and the National Committee on the Cause and Cure of War.

BENSON, LOUIS (1855–1930). American Presbyterian minister, lawyer, and hymnologist. Born in Philadelphia, Benson studied at the University of Pennsylvania and **Princeton Theological Seminary.** He practiced law from 1877 to 1884 and was ordained in the Presbyterian Church in the U.S.A. in 1886. After a pastorate in Germantown, Pennsylvania, from 1888 to 1894, Benson became editor of several hymnals produced by the Presbyterian Church, including *The Hymnal* (1895). He was a member of the committee that prepared the *Book of Common Worship* (1905). Benson also lectured in liturgics at Auburn and Princeton seminaries. Among his books on hymnody are *The Best Church Hymns* (1898), *Studies of Familiar Hymns* (1903; 1923), *The English Hymn: Its Development and Use in Worship* (1915), and *The Hymnody of the Christian Church* (1927). Benson's personal hymnology library of some 9,000 works was donated to Princeton Theological Seminary.

BERKHOF, HENDRIKUS (1914–1995). Dutch Reformed theologian and ecumenical leader. Born in Appeltern, Gelderland, **Holland**, Berknof was educated in Amsterdam, Leiden, and Berlin. Following pastorates at Lemele (1938) and Zeist (1944), he joined the staff of the Church and World Institute at Driebergen (1950) and became professor of dogmatics and biblical theology at the University of Leiden (1960). In addition to his academic responsibilities, Berkhof was active in the **World Council of Churches** (WCC), serving on its Central Committee (1954–1975). He also participated in meetings of the **World Alliance of Reformed Churches** and was elected president of the Ecumenical Council of the Netherlands (1975). Influenced by the theology of **Karl Barth**, **Friedrich Schleiermacher**, and Hans Küng, Berkhof wrote more than 20 books, including *Christ and the Meaning of History* (rev. ed. 1979), *Christian Faith: An Introduction to the Study of the Faith* (rev. English ed. 1985), and *Two Hundred Years of Theology: Report of a Personal Journey* (English translation, 1989).

BERKOUWER, GERRIT CORNELIUS (1903–1996). Dutch Reformed minister and theologian. Berkouwer was educated at the Christian Gymnasium and the **Free University of Amsterdam**, where he studied the thought of **Abraham Kuyper** and **Herman Bavinck**. After serving churches in Oudehorne and Amsterdam, he joined the faculty of the Free University, teaching modern theology (1940–1945) and systematic theology (1945–1973). He was an observer at Vatican Council II (1962) and wrote *The Second Vatican Council and the New Catholicism* (1965). He also studied **neoorthodoxy** and summarized the theology of **Karl Barth** in *The Triumph of Grace in the Theology of Karl Barth* (1956). Berkouwer's own views are contained in 14 volumes, published under the title *Studies in Dogmatics* (1952–1976). As a confessional theologian, he tried to develop a theology that was faithful to **scripture**, sensitive to the insights of the Reformed **confessions**, and relevant to the needs of the **church.** He believed that theology was not an academic exercise alone but a primary means of informing the pulpit ministry of the church.

BERTHOUD, PAUL (1847–1929). Swiss Reformed missionary in Northern Transvaal, **South Africa**, and **Mozambique.** Trained as a doctor at Edinburgh, Berthoud went to Basutoland in 1872 under the auspices of the Free Church of Canton Vaud. The Free Church later sent him to found the **mission** of Valdezia at Spelonken in Northern Transvaal among the Tsonga people. When Berthoud lost his wife and five children to sickness, he returned to **Switzerland.** He remarried and returned to the mission field in 1886 under the Mission Society of the Free French Swiss Churches (Geneva, Neuchatel, and Vaud). He worked in Mozambique, first at Ricatla (1886) and then at Lourenço Marques (Maputo), where his second wife and three children died in 1900. Berthoud continued his mission well into his old age, seeing the Golden Jubilee of Valdezia in 1925. His publications include *Lettres missionnaires de M. & Mme Paul Berthoud de la mission romande, 1873–1879* (1900).

BEZA, THÉODORE (1519–1605). Reformed theologian and successor to **John Calvin** in Geneva. Born in Vézelay, **France**, Beza learned Greek from Calvin's teacher, Melchior Wolmar. He identified with the Reformation movement, taught Greek at the Academy of Lausanne from 1549 to 1558, and then was called to the newly opened Academy of Geneva. In 1559 he became rector and assumed an increasingly active role in representing Genevan Protestantism throughout Europe. After Calvin's death in 1564, Beza became head of the Academy and **moderator** of the Company of Pastors. His writings include a Greek text of the New Testament and a number of polemical works defending Reformed views of the **sacraments** and **predestination** (*Tabula praedestinationis* or *The Sum of All Christianity* [1555]; *Confession* and *Book(s) of Christian Questions and Answers* [1570; 1575]). His *Life of Calvin* appeared in

1564 and has been published in many editions. Contemporary scholars have criticized Beza for his scholastic tendencies in handling **scripture** and in his development of the doctrine of predestination. Yet his role in molding the Reformed tradition is clear: Beza solidified Calvin's work and strengthened the presbyterial system of **church government.** His view that inferior magistrates have the right to revolt against idolatrous governments (*De jure magistratum*; 1573) also became an important concept within the Reformed tradition.

BIBLE TRANSLATIONS. The increase in Bible translations since the 16th century is a result of the Reformation's concern that **scripture** be accessible to all people. The invention of the printing press and the expansion of knowledge associated with the Renaissance made possible Bible translations from Latin into the vernacular. European translations were produced in Italian (1471), French (New Testament, 1474), Dutch (Old Testament, 1477), Spanish (1478), and German (Luther's New Testament, 1522). In English, Tyndale's New Testament (1526) was of primary importance. More translations followed as a result of the growth of Christian **mission**: Persian (1546), Malay (1629), Tamil (1715), Ashanti (1764), and Bengali (1800). By 1804 Bible translations had appeared in 72 languages. During the 19th and 20th centuries, the work of the British and Foreign Bible Society (1804) and other Bible societies, together with the Protestant missionary movement, increased the number of translations to more than 2,000 (300 complete Bibles, 700 complete New Testaments, and scripture portions in 1,000 additional languages), representing almost 99 percent of the world's people. Roman Catholic translations in the vernacular also increased during the modern period. Prior to 1943 Catholic translations were based on the Latin Vulgate. During the last half of the 20th century many new Catholic translations, based on Hebrew and Greek texts, have appeared. In addition to its religious significance, Bible translation has had a profound cultural and social impact by contributing to literacy and the growth of literary traditions.

BIBLICAL CRITICISM. The study of **scripture** using textual, literary, and historical methods. These methods provide a basis on which to interpret the Bible. The Confession of 1967 states that the **church** has "an obligation to approach the scriptures with literary and historical understanding." This is predicated on the fact that the scriptures are human documents, "conditioned by the language, thought forms, and literary fashions of the places and times at which they were written." Biblical criticism seeks to answer questions about the preservation, transmission, and message of the biblical texts. Various fields of specialty have evolved, including textual, form, redaction, canonical, literary, feminist, and liberationist criticism. Reformed scholars have recognized that scripture contains a theological message and that the tools of biblical criticism can help that message to be heard. The **Holy Spirit** enables individual Christians and the church to hear the **Word of God** in and through scripture.

BIBLICAL EXEGESIS. The explanation or interpretation of biblical texts, especially an extended exposition of **scripture.** Exegesis deals with technical matters of reliability of text, meaning of words, and grammatical structure of passages. It uses the results of **biblical criticism** to place scripture in its proper historical, cultural, and literary context. The church's theological understanding is advanced by the work of biblical exegesis.

The Reformed churches have produced many outstanding biblical exegetes, including the early Protestant theologians **John Calvin, Martin Bucer,** and **Heinrich Bullinger.** Reformed exegetes including William Robertson Smith (1856–1894) and **Charles A. Briggs** were leading pioneers in the development of biblical criticism. **Adolf Schlatter** and **C. H. Dodd** wrote expositional works. **Karl Barth** wished to go beyond historical-critical methods to a "theological exegesis," seeking divine meaning behind the scriptural texts. Other Reformed scholars who contributed to biblical exegesis include **James Moffatt,** Oscar Cullmann (1902–1999), G. Ernest Wright (1909–1974), and Eduard Schweizer (1913–).

BINGHAM, HIRAM (1789–1869). American Congregationalist minister and missionary in **Hawaii.** Born in Bennington, Vermont, Bingham graduated from Middlebury College in 1816 and **Andover** Theological Seminary in 1819. Bingham went to Hawaii in 1820 with the **American Board of Commissioners for Foreign Missions.** He spent his first years of service learning the Hawaiian language and reducing it to writing. In the early 1820s he published elementary lessons in Hawaiian on the mission press. Other works followed, including the first book, *Na Himeni Hawaii* (1823), a 60-page hymnal prepared by Bingham and **William Ellis.** Bingham also translated **scripture** portions, books of the Bible, and books for children. In addition to serving as head of the Hawaiian **mission,** Bingham organized schools and was the first pastor of Kawaiahaʻo Church in Honolulu. Between 1823 and 1832, Queen **Kaʻahumanu** aided in the mission work by urging Christian faith upon her subjects. Bingham became a trusted adviser of Hawaiian royalty, who passed Christian laws proposed by the missionaries. The passage of these laws brought the mission into conflict with sailors, merchants, and others who did not share the Puritan morality of the missionaries. In 1840 Bingham returned to New Haven, Connecticut, where he preached and wrote his account of *Twenty-one Years in the Sandwich Islands; or The Civil, Religious, and Political History of Those Islands* (1847).

BLAKE, EUGENE CARSON (1906–1985). American Presbyterian minister, denominational leader, and ecumenist. Blake was born in St. Louis and took his first year of theological studies at **New College**, Edinburgh, before graduating from **Princeton Theological Seminary** in 1932. He served churches in Albany, New York (1935–1940), and Pasadena, California (1940–1951). In 1951 he was elected stated clerk of the United Presbyterian Church in the U.S.A. and served until 1966. With **John Mackay** of Princeton Seminary, Blake issued "A Letter to Presbyterians" (1954) denouncing the excesses of U.S. Senator Joseph McCarthy. Influenced by **Reinhold Niebuhr** and striving for an "ecumenical consensus theology," Blake called for the formation of a **church** that was "truly reformed, truly catholic, and truly **evangelical**" in a famous sermon at Grace Cathedral (Episcopal) in San Francisco (1960). His call for a merger of four mainstream Protestant denominations (Episcopal, Methodist, Presbyterian, and United Church of Christ) marked the beginning of the Consultation on Church Union (COCU), an effort that continued for several decades. In 1966 Blake became general secretary of the **World Council of Churches** (WCC) in Geneva and served until his retirement in 1972. Blake's active ministry as stated clerk and general secretary was marked by efforts to establish racial justice and the **ordination** of **women**, to end the Vietnam War, and to increase participation by third world churches in the WCC.

BOEGNER, MARC (1881–1970). French Reformed pastor, theologian, ecumenical leader, author, and resistance leader. Boegner studied law and theology in Paris and became a pastor in 1905. He participated in the **ecumenical movement** from the Edinburgh Conference (1910) to the Second Vatican Council (1962–1965). In 1911 he became professor at the Theological Seminary of the Reformed Mission Society. After medical service in World War I, he served as pastor of the Reformed congregation in Passy (1918–1953). Boegner was president of the Protestant Church Federation of France (1929–1961), and president of the National

Council of the French Reformed Church (Eglise Réformée de France, 1938–1950). He also served as one of the presidents of the **World Council of Churches** (Amsterdam, 1948–1954). After taking part in the French Resistance during World War II, Boegner chaired CIMADE, the aid agency of Protestant youth associations in France, and helped to rebuild the links between young French and German Christians. In his preaching and numerous publications, as well as his worldwide involvement in ecumenical endeavors, Boegner emphasized the **evangelical** call for church unity as a sign of the coming of God's Kingdom.

BOHEMIAN BRETHREN. A pre-Reformation Christian community in Bohemia that broke away from the Catholic Church and allied itself with the Protestant movement. Later known as Unitas Fratrum and Moravian Brethren, the movement originated in Prague in 1453 in reaction to the preaching of Archbishop Rokycana. In 1457 a group of Brethren settled in the town of Kunvald in east Bohemia to live according to the apostolic model found in the New Testament. The group grew within Bohemia and Moravia during the 16th and 17th centuries and suffered persecution. Presiding Bishop Lukas summarized Brethren doctrines and provided leadership for the group during its formative period from 1496 to 1528. In 1616 the Synod of Zeravic codified the doctrines of the church. The Brethren, who came largely from the common people, desired to live as obedient disciples of Jesus Christ. The community emphasized fidelity to **scripture**, Christian discipleship, and an ecumenical outlook. The Battle of White Mountain (1620) drove Protestants from Bohemia and Moravia, and the Brethren, including **Jan Amos Comenius**, were dispersed throughout Europe. A group of Brethren who survived this persecution went to the estate of Count Nikolaus Ludwig von Zinzendorf in 1722, when the church was reconstituted as the Moravian Church. The Brethren had a profound influence on the character and growth of Protestantism in **Central and Eastern Europe**.

BOLIVIA. *See* ANDEAN REPUBLICS AND GREATER COLOMBIA

BONAR, HORATIUS (1809–1889). Scottish minister and hymn writer. Bonar was educated at the University of Edinburgh. After **ordination** in 1837, he served in the Church of Scotland in Kelso, Roxburghshire, but left the church during the Disruption of 1843. He then became a leader in the Free Church in Kelso. Bonar received a D.D. degree from the University of Aberdeen in 1853. In 1866 he became pastor of the Chalmers Memorial Church, Edinburgh. He also became **moderator** of the Free Church General Assembly in 1883 and served as a joint editor of the church newspaper, *The Border Watch.* Through books and personal correspondence, Bonar gained great influence throughout **Scotland.** He composed hymns set to popular tunes to interest young people in his parish. He wrote over 600 hymns and published eight hymn collections. Of enduring popularity are "Blessing and Honor," "Here, O Our Lord, We See You Face to Face," and "Go, Labor On." Most of Bonar's hymns are marked by simplicity and devotional warmth.

BOOK OF COMMON ORDER. *See* COMMON ORDER, BOOK OF

BOOK OF COMMON PRAYER. *See* COMMON PRAYER, BOOK OF

BOOKS OF DISCIPLINE. *See* DISCIPLINE, BOOKS OF

BOTSWANA. *See* SOUTHERN AFRICA

BOTTOMAN, ADOLPHUS MKONDO (fl. 1920s–1980s). South African Presbyterian minister and **moderator** of the General Assembly of the Presbyterian Church of Africa. Born at Mount Ayliff Cape, Bottoman was educated as a teacher and graduated from Wright Theological College. He was ordained in 1942, served several churches, and was elected stated clerk of the **general assembly** (1970–1972). From 1973 to 1985 he served as moderator of the general assembly. During his tenure the church initiated many new programs and approved the **ordination** of **women** as **deacons, elders,** and ministers.

BRAGA, ERASMO DE CARVALHO (1877–1932). Brazilian Presbyterian minister, ecumenist, and leader of the Presbyterian Church of Brazil. Born in Rio Claro, Braga was educated at the Instituto Teológico and the Seminário Presbiteriano in São Paulo. He became pastor of the Presbyterian church in Niteroi and wrote for several publications, including the church press. In 1901 he began teaching at the Presbyterian seminary in Campinas and later taught in Rio de Janeiro. He also maintained an interest in **missions,** founding a mission among the Caiua Indians in Mato Grosso and, in 1910, initiating the Brazilian Presbyterian mission in Portugal. Braga devoted his life to ecumenical service, representing the Brazilian church at many world conferences sponsored by the Faith and Order and Life and Work movements, and also the mission-related assemblies in Panama (1916), Montevideo (1925), and Jerusalem (1928). He also served on the Executive Committee of the International Missionary Council. In 1924 he was elected **moderator** of the Presbyterian Church of Brazil (Igreja Presbiteriana do Brasil), and in 1931 he organized the Federation of Evangelical Churches of Brazil. A leading thinker in Brazilian Protestantism, Braga wrote a popular primer for elementary schools and published a Hebrew grammar, a Hebrew-Portuguese dictionary, biblical and scientific works, and articles on ecumenism and missions.

BRASH, THOMAS CUDDIE (1873–1957). Accountant, businessman, and elder in the Presbyterian Church of Aotearoa New Zealand. With only three years of primary education, Brash worked his way up from factory dairy hand to national secretary of the Dairy Board. He then became director of the Fruitgrowers Federation. A Presbyterian elder for 50 years, serving in five different congregations, Brash was president of the Bible Class Movement, chair of the Assembly Finance Committee, and **moderator** of the Presbyterian **general assembly** (1944). He was a strong ecumenist, chairing the National Missionary Council and attending the **World Council of Churches** meeting in Amsterdam in 1948. Brash's concern for **mission** prompted his enthusiastic participation in the New Life Movement, which reached out to nominal Presbyterians. Described as liberal and **evangelical**, Brash was also an advocate of the Student Christian Movement and **women elders.**

BRAZIL. The people of Brazil are primarily affiliated with the Roman Catholic Church (85 percent); there is also a growing Protestant minority. Reformed **church** affiliation is less than 200,000 in a country of 90 million people.

    Presbyterian Churches. In 1555 **John Calvin** sent missionaries to Brazil, as part of a French colonial venture, in an attempt to start a Reformed community there. The **mission** failed, but the Reformed tradition in Brazil dates from this effort.

    Protestant Christianity was not established in Brazil until the 19th century, after Brazil became an independent nation (1822). The country encouraged European and North American immigration, and Protestant churches were initially organized for the expatriates. American Presbyterian Ashbel G. Simonton (1859) brought the **Reformed orthodoxy** of **Charles Hodge** and the Presbyterian Old School to Brazil and firmly planted it in the emerging Presbyterian church; the Westminster Standards continue to define Brazilian **Presbyterianism.** Simonton organized the first Presbyterian congregation in Brazil (Rio de Janeiro, 1862) and the first **presbytery** (1865); he ordained the first Brazilian Protestant minister, the converted Catholic priest **José da Conceição**, and founded the first Protestant seminary (1867).

The first generation of American missionaries came from the southern Presbyterian church (PCUS), some in fact emigrating because of the outcome of the Civil War. Some of these Presbyterians held views compatible with the legacy of African slave importation sponsored by the Portuguese in Brazil and sanctioned by the Brazilian Catholic establishment. The northern church (PCUSA) followed the southern with missionary expansion from 1870. Presbyterians demonstrated their Reformed legacy by immediately starting schools; Campinas and São Paulo are considered the cradle of **education** in Brazil. The school systems started there would later be developed by the republic. Church and presbytery formation moved ahead, and by the 1880s the Presbyterian Church of Brazil (IPB; Igreja Presbiteriana do Brasil) was self-governing, although American missionary influence was strong and a continuing source of contention.

The political reshaping of Brazil as a constitutional republic (1889) disestablished Roman Catholicism and introduced the separation of **church** and state. This change presented Reformed churches with new opportunities; but the nationalism of the political process also exacerbated tensions between Brazilian and American missionary interests, especially over the control of the churches. Many Brazilians wanted to increase Brazilian leadership in their churches. The tensions, fueled by disagreements about doctrinal orthodoxy, led to division. **Eduardo Pereira** considered the synod's toleration of freemasonry (1900) a threat to Reformed orthodoxy and in 1903 led one-third of the church membership to form the Independent Presbyterian Church (IPIB; Igreja Presbiteriana Independente do Brasil). It is the oldest Brazilian church under indigenous leadership (the Presbyterian Church of Brazil did not form its **general assembly** until 1910).

The indigenization of the IPB moved ahead when the North American Presbyterian churches drafted the Brazil Plan of 1917. This was a comity arrangement that ended the IPB's dependency upon American Presbyterian agencies and redefined the latter's missionary responsibility, assigning southern Brazil (Rio, São Paulo, Parana, Santa Catarina) to the PCUSA, and the northern, eastern, and western Brazil missions to the PCUS. Thereafter, the expansion of the largest Brazilian church was managed by a committee made up of the PCUS, PCUSA, and IPB. Later, North American mission work in the IPB officially ended and the missionaries were integrated into the church as "fraternal workers."

The Reformed emphasis on theological **discipline** shaped Brazilian Presbyterianism through its seminaries. The schism of 1903 hurt the Presbyterian seminary in Rio de Janeiro, which moved to Campinas in 1907. With continuing support from the PCUSA, the school at Campinas maintained its commitment to Reformed learning and piety while increasing the role of Brazilians on the faculty. The PCUS expanded mission work in the north through evangelism, education, and literature distribution. The mission spread inland, and schools were organized in connection with new pastorates. In 1919 one such school in the state of Pernambuco was moved to Recife to become a seminary. From 1925 the seminary in Recife was a joint enterprise of the IPB, the IPIB, the Congregationalists, and both the PCUS and the PCUSA. In 1958 the Centennial Seminary was founded in Vitoria.

The linkage with North American Presbyterianism channeled U.S. problems to Brazil, including the **fundamentalist-modernist controversy.** Non-Brazilian fundamentalists targeted the emerging **ecumenical movement**, creating such mistrust that the major Brazilian Presbyterian denominations still remain distant from the **World Council of Churches**, although they are members of the **World Alliance of Reformed Churches.** Theologians and pastors who favored ecumenical ties and raised social issues, especially the injustices of Brazil's racial situation, were decried as "leftist" and "liberal." These theological controversies since the 1940s have resulted in further church division, the dismissal of seminary faculty, and tensions with North American partner churches. Many Presbyterian and Reformed Christians who were open to ecumenical linkages and concerned about the social implications of the gospel formed the United Presbyterian Church of Brazil (IPU; Igreja Presbiteriana Unida do Brasil) in 1983. The three Presbyterian churches (IPB, IPIB, IPU) form the largest contingent within a total of 15 Reformed denominations in Brazil.

Brazilian church leaders include **Erasmo Braga, Jerônimo Gueiros, Alvaro Reis, Guilherme Kerr**, and missionaries **Sarah Kalley** and **Robert Reid Kalley**, and **Edward Lane**.

Other Reformed Churches. Scottish Congregationalist Robert Kalley (1855) founded the first Sunday school in Brazil and the oldest continuing Protestant congregation. Several Free Churches joined together and the denomination was formally organized in 1942, taking the name Evangelical Congregational Church of Brazil. Until 1970 the church was under the United Church of Christ in the U.S.A.

Several Brazilian denominations are the result of immigration: the Christian Reformed Church (1932), a denomination with members of Hungarian descent; the Arab Evangelical Church (1954), originally Syrian Evangelical Church; the Evangelical Reformed Church (1933), begun by Dutch Reformed settlers; the Swiss Reformed Church; and the Armenian Evangelical church.

BRIDGMAN, ELIJAH COLEMAN (1801–1861). American Congregationalist missionary in **China.** Bridgman graduated from **Andover** Seminary in 1829 and was appointed one of the first American Protestant missionaries to China by the **American Board of Commissioners for Foreign Missions.** He became a scholar and interpreter of Chinese language and culture, publishing in English the *Chinese Repository*, an important periodical that documents the early history of the Chinese **mission.** He was an evangelist and pastor in Shanghai, supervised the production and distribution of the Cantonese-language Bible, and mediated between the British and Chinese after the Opium War. Bridgman tried to spread North American influence in China and promoted Western learning and development. He was respected by Chinese authorities who treated him favorably. Bridgman's publications were widely read and helped shape American attitudes toward China.

BRIEF STATEMENT OF FAITH (1991). Eleventh confessional document in the *Book of Confessions* of the Presbyterian Church (U.S.A.), which originated in the 1983 reunion of the Presbyterian Church in the United States and the United Presbyterian Church in the U.S.A. The 80-line statement, cast in short poetic lines, is structured in three parts corresponding to persons of the **Trinity.** The statement begins with the introductory phrase, "In life and in **death** we belong to **God**," and closes with a "Gloria Patri." The structure is ordered after the apostolic benediction of 2 Corinthians 13:14 and begins with the Second Person of the Trinity. Other features of the statement include its use of male and female images of God, gender-inclusive **language**, and the affirmation that both **women** and men are called to "all ministries of the Church." The Brief Statement recognizes human exploitation of neighbor and **nature.** The entire statement is designed for use in public **worship** and in the educational ministries of the church.

BRIGGS, CHARLES A. (1841–1913). American minister, biblical scholar, and ecumenist. Briggs was born in New York City and was educated at the University of Virginia, Union Theological Seminary (N.Y.), and the University of Berlin. After **ordination** in the Presbyterian Church in 1870, he served a New Jersey church before being called to Union Seminary as professor of Hebrew and Cognate Languages. In 1890 he accepted a newly created chair of biblical theology. In his inaugural address, "The Authority of Holy Scripture," Briggs promoted the use of **biblical criticism** and sharply criticized the doctrine of biblical inerrancy. His address led to a major controversy within the Presbyterian Church, and Briggs was tried for heresy by the Presbytery of New York. Though acquitted, he was suspended from the ministry by the **General Assembly** in 1893. The assembly's refusal to sustain his election to the biblical theology chair led the seminary to sever ties with the denomination. Briggs was later ordained in the Protestant Episcopal Church and from 1904 served as professor of theology at Union Seminary. During the last decade of his life Briggs worked on behalf of Christian unity. With S. R. Driver and Francis Brown, he prepared the *Hebrew and English Lexicon of the Old Testament* (1891–1896) and was an editor of the International Critical Commentary series to which he contributed the work on *Psalms* (1906). Among his other numerous publications are *The Bible, the Church and Reason* (1892), *The Higher Criticism of the Hexateuch* (1893), *General Introduction to the Study of Holy Scripture* (1899), and *The Incarnation of the Lord* (1902).

BRIGHT, JOHN (1908–1995). American Presbyterian minister and Old Testament scholar. Born in Chattanooga, Tennessee, Bright was educated at **Union Theological Seminary** in Virginia and Johns Hopkins University, where he became a disciple of archeologist W. F. Albright. Bright returned to Union Seminary, serving as professor of Old Testament from 1941 to 1975. He was a confident expositor of the Old Testament, arguing with Albright that the archeological record confirmed the basic historicity of the biblical accounts. His books include *The Kingdom of God* (1953), *The Authority of the Old Testament* (1967), and *A History of Israel* (3d ed. 1981).

BRITISH ISLES. *See* UNITED KINGDOM

BROADCASTING, RELIGIOUS. *See* RELIGIOUS BROADCASTING

BROTHER-SISTER. Terms of address among ministers and congregational members used in some Protestant denominations. According to the New Testament, early Christians addressed each other as "brother" and "sister," expressing the metaphoric familial relationship that results from submission to Christ and adoption into the family of God. As a general practice, the usage died out by the late third century, continuing only in clerical and monastic circles. Since the Reformation, "brother" and "sister" have reemerged as terms of address in some Latin American and North American churches. This usage is a constant reminder that in Jesus' formation of the apostolic community, hierarchical and patriarchal patterns of authority were to be radically reordered in structures of mutuality expressed as brother- and sisterhood. This radical reordering of human relationships is evidenced in many contemporary movements of spiritual vitality, including **house churches**, base ecclesial communities (Latin America), and the reemergence within Protestantism of intentional and even monastic communities (e.g., Taize).

BROWN, WILLIAM ADAMS (1865–1943). American Presbyterian minister, liberal theologian, and ecumenist. Brown was born in New York City, educated at Yale University, **Union Theological Seminary** (N.Y.), and the University of Berlin, where he studied under Adolf von Harnack. In 1892 he began to teach theology at Union Seminary, remaining on the faculty for 44 years. Brown worked with the Federal Council of Churches and was active in home missions and the **ecumenical movement.** His books, *The Church: Catholic and Protestant* (1935) and *Toward a United Church* (1946), pointed the way toward the **World Council of Churches.** Brown's work emphasized the life and teachings of the "historical Jesus" and did not share in the more traditional view of Christ. He had little interest in "dogmas to be received on **authority**" but instead tried to expound "living convictions, born of experience." His theology was Christocentric in the sense that he believed **God** was uniquely at work through Jesus to initiate a transformation in the lives of his followers. In turn, these followers would transform the social order into the ultimate reign of God. Brown's *Christian Theology in Outline* (1906) is one of the most important works of American theological **liberalism.**

BROWNE, ROBERT (ca. 1550–ca. 1633). English Puritan minister and separatist leader. Browne was educated at Corpus Christi College, Cambridge, where he was influenced by Presbyterian leader **Thomas Cartwright.** Following graduation, Browne declined to be ordained, charging that the church's hierarchy was incompetent. In 1579 he began preaching without the bishop's permission, and in 1581 he became the leader of a covenanted independent church. He was imprisoned for these actions; following his release, he immigrated with his congregation to Middleburg, in the Netherlands, where he published *A Book which sheweth the Life and Manner of all True Christians* (1582) and *A Treatise of Reformation without Tarying for Anie* (1582). In the latter work he argued that the Church of England was beyond all hope of reformation and that the true **church** should be established without "tarrying" for the magistrate. After disagreements with church members in the

Netherlands, Browne went to Scotland, where he again found fault with the church's order. He then reconciled with the Church of England and became master of St. Olave's School in 1586. In 1591 he was ordained rector of Achurch-cum-Thorpe, Northamptonshire, where he remained for 43 years. The quarrelsome Browne died in prison after a fight with a local constable. Browne's views of the church so influenced the development of **Congregationalism** that the early followers of the movement were called "Brownists." Browne declared that "the Church planted or gathered, is a company or number of Christians or believers, which by a willing **covenant** made with their **God**, are under the government of God and Christ, and keep his laws in one holy communion."

BROWNLEE, JOHN (1791–1871). Scottish Congregationalist missionary in **southern Africa**. With little formal education, Brownlee was sent to southern Africa by the **London Missionary Society** (LMS) in 1815. By 1820 he had resigned from the LMS and became a government-appointed missionary among the Xhosa people. He founded the Tyumie valley **mission** with William R. Thompson, which the government used as a colonial outpost. Uncomfortable with his government-supported status, in 1826 Brownlee rejoined the LMS and established a mission on the Buffalo River. His mission station, destroyed during a war between the Xhosa people and the colonial government, became the site of King William's Town. The congregations that grew from Brownlee's work eventually became part of the United Congregational Church of South Africa.

BRUNNER, H. EMIL (1889–1966). Swiss Reformed minister and theologian associated with **dialectical theology** and the **neoorthodox** movement. Brunner was born in Zurich and educated at the universities of Zurich and Berlin as well as **Union Theological Seminary** (N.Y.). He was pastor at Obstalden in **Switzerland** from 1916 to 1924 and then became professor of theology at Zurich, where he served from 1924 to 1953. He taught at Christian University, Mitaka, Tokyo, **Japan**, until 1955. Brunner's work became widely known as a result of his lecture tours and through translations of his books. He was initially associated with **Karl Barth** and the school of dialectical theology, which criticized theological **liberalism**, especially its optimistic assessment of human nature and identification of human progress with the will of **God**. Like Barth, he tried to bring the insights of the Reformation to the contemporary scene and thus was called "neoorthodox." The writings of Søren Kierkegaard (1813–1855) and Martin Buber (1878–1965) were important influences on Brunner. He eventually broke with Barth over the issue of the **revelation** of God. He maintained that revelation could be discerned outside **scripture** and that even sinful humanity has a "point of contact" with God in its ability to hear and respond to God's revelation. Brunner's *Nature and Grace: A Discussion with Karl Barth* (1934) was answered by Barth's angry *Nein!* Brunner's *The Mediator* (1927; English translation 1934) was the first presentation of **Christology** from the perspectives of dialectical theology. Other important writings include *The Divine Imperative* (1932; English translation 1937), *Man in Revolt* (1937; English translation 1939), *Our Faith* (1935; English translation 1936), *Revelation and Reason* (1941; English translation 1947), *Truth as Encounter* (English translation 1954), and his three-volume *Dogmatics* (1946–1960; English translation 1949–1962). Brunner was deeply concerned with the **church** and had a passion for ecumenical involvement.

BRYDEN, WALTER W. (1883–1952). Canadian Presbyterian minister and professor. Born near Galt, Ontario, Bryden graduated from the University of Toronto in 1906. He entered **Knox College** to study for the ministry and simultaneously completed a master's degree in psychology in 1907. He spent one year in **Scotland**, where he came under the influence of **James Denney.** Following graduation in 1909, Bryden studied in Strasbourg, was ordained, and became pastor of churches in Lethbridge (Alberta), Melfort (Saskatchewan), and Woodville (Ontario). In 1927 he was appointed professor of church history at Knox College. Upon the retirement of Thomas Eakin in 1945, Bryden was appointed principal and served the college for the rest of his life. A dominant force at Knox College, Bryden was influenced by the theology of **Karl Barth** and was a leader in the theological renewal of the Presbyterian Church of Canada. In his most important book, *The Christian's Knowledge of God* (1940), Bryden criticizes **natural theology** and emphasizes **revelation** as the starting point for theology. He tried to steer a middle course between "modernism" and what he called "rational orthodoxy."

BUCER, MARTIN (1491–1551). Protestant reformer in Strasbourg. Bucer was born in Sélestat in Alsace and joined the Dominican order. He was attracted to the work of Erasmus and became an adherent of Martin Luther. In 1521 Bucer left the Dominicans; he subsequently married and in 1522 went to Strasbourg, where he became an important Protestant leader. He was an international figure who frequently participated in colloquia and diets, beginning with the **Marburg Colloquy** in 1529. He worked diligently to try to overcome the Lutheran-Swiss controversies on the **Lord's Supper.** His mediating influence is found in the Tetrapolitan Confession of 1530. With Philip Melanchthon, he led the Protestant–Catholic colloquies of 1539 to 1541. Bucer also influenced **John Calvin** during his three-year stay in Strasbourg, especially on topics such as **predestination** and the Eucharist as well as **worship**, the offices of **ministry**, church order and **discipline**, and **education.** Bucer's vision of a reformed **church** and Christian society, while stifled at points by the city council in Strasbourg, gained recognition in Calvin's Geneva. Bucer also helped to establish **confirmation** as a Reformed rite. Bucer's opposition to the Augsburg Interim of 1548 led to his exile to **England**, where he became professor of divinity at Cambridge in 1549. His influence on Anglicanism is found in the *Ordinal* (1550) and the **Book of Common Prayer** (1552). Bucer's *The Kingdom of Christ* (1557), presented to King Edward VI, contained a plan for national reform to produce a Christian society. His sense of communion and community in Christ are lasting legacies to the Reformed tradition.

BULGARIA. *See* CENTRAL AND EASTERN EUROPE

BULLINGER, JOHANN HEINRICH (1504–1575). Swiss-German Protestant reformer. Born in Bremgarten, Canton Argau, **Switzerland**, Bullinger was educated at the School of the Brethren of the Common Life in Emmerich and then at the University of Cologne. At Cologne he read the works of Erasmus, Martin Luther, and Philip Melanchthon, which greatly influenced him. When he returned to Switzerland in 1523, he supported the reform in Zurich led by **Huldrych Zwingli** and participated in the Berne Disputation of 1528. After losing his inheritance in the destruction of the Second Kappel War (1531), Bullinger fled to Zurich. Following Zwingli's death on the battlefield, Bullinger became his successor in December 1531. In Zurich, Bullinger presided over the synod of the canton that he helped reorganize; he was also involved in the reform of the school system and in civic affairs. Bullinger was a prolific writer, having published more than 100 works and preached approximately 7,500 sermons. Over 12,000 manuscript letters also exist in Bullinger's hand. His major work, *The Decades* (1549), is a full theology in the form of 50 sermons. He was the principal author of the Second Helvetic Confession (1566), an extremely important Reformed confession. With **John Calvin**, he also authored the *Consensus Tigurinus* (*Agreement of Zurich,* 1549), which provided a common framework on the issue of the **Lord's Supper**, enabling the French and German Reformed traditions to remain united. His influence was felt throughout Europe, particularly in the state church form of government of Elizabethan **England**. His "One and Eternal Testament or Covenant" (1534) formed the basis for the subsequent development of **federal theology.**

BUNYAN, JOHN (1628–1688). English Puritan writer and preacher. Bunyan was born at Elstow, near Bedford, **England**. He was converted by reading A. Dent's *Plain Man's Pathway to Heaven* and Bishop L. Bayly's *Practice of Piety*. He became recognized as an Independent preacher (1657) and was well known for his skill. After the Restoration (1660), Bunyan was imprisoned for 12 years in the Bedford jail for preaching. Following his release, he continued to work among the Independents. He wrote more than 60 books during and after his imprisonment. His three major works are *Grace Abounding to the Chief of Sinners* (1666), *Pilgrim's Progress* (1678; 1684), and *The Holy War* (1682). *Pilgrim's Progress* is considered the greatest allegory of the Christian life in the English language. This work helped Puritan thought enter into the theological tradition of the English Reformation. Bunyan was influenced by Calvinistic ideas and had a strong sense of God's **grace** and **predestination.** He viewed the present world as the scene of spiritual warfare over the **salvation** of the soul.

BURKINA FASO. *See* WEST AFRICA

BURLEIGH, JOHN HENDERSON SEAFORTH (1894–1985). Scottish Presbyterian minister and church historian. Burleigh was born in Kelso and educated at the universities of Edinburgh, Paris, Strasbourg, Oxford, and Aberdeen (D.D., 1937). He served several churches before becoming professor of ecclesiastical history in Edinburgh, a position he held for 33 years. Burleigh convened the Church and Nation Committee (1949–1954) and was principal of **New College**, Edinburgh, from 1956 to 1964. He also served as **moderator** of the Church of Scotland in 1960. His publications include *The City of God: A Study of St. Augustine's Philosophy* (1944) and *A Church History of Scotland* (1960). Burleigh was editor of the *Evangelical Quarterly* (1943–1949) and *Augustine's Earlier Writings* (1953).

BURMA. *See* SOUTHERN ASIA

BUSHNELL, HORACE (1802–1876). American Congregationalist minister and theologian. Bushnell was born in Connecticut and graduated from Yale in 1827. After working as a journalist, he wanted to study for the ministry; however, during a period of doubt he decided to return to

Yale to study law. After his **conversion** at a Yale revival in 1831, Bushnell studied theology under **Nathaniel William Taylor.** He was also influenced by Samuel Taylor Coleridge. Bushnell was ordained to the Congregationalist ministry in 1833 and became pastor of the North Church of Hartford, Connecticut. He ministered there until ill health forced his resignation in 1859. Bushnell's work had a major impact on subsequent American theology. He believed that all language is poetic rather than literal at its fundamental level, and therefore language can only approximate the spiritual mysteries of which it speaks. The disciples of Bushnell later used his views to recast traditional Christian doctrines. Bushnell's major work is *God in Christ* (1849). His *Christian Nurture* (1847) was influential in the religious training of young people, arguing that Christian **education**, not revivalism, is the best way to convey the **faith.** Bushnell's *Nature and the Supernatural* (1858) teaches that both natural and supernatural things share a common spiritual reality. *The Vicarious Sacrifice* (1866) focuses on the work of Christ and concludes, in opposition to the substitutionary **atonement** view of scholastic **Calvinism**, that Christ's **death** was an ultimate expression of God's love and provides the example for humanity to follow in self-giving sacrifice. Bushnell's views helped lay the groundwork in America for the reception of the romanticism and **liberalism** of **Friedrich Schleiermacher.**

- C -

CALVIN, JOHN (1509–1564). French Protestant Reformer, pastor, and theologian in Geneva. Born in Noyon, in Picardy, **France**, Calvin's father obtained two ecclesiastical benefices for his son. At age 12, Calvin was sent to the Collège de la Marche to prepare for theological studies and the priesthood but quickly progressed to the Collège de Montaigu. After his father's controversy with the Bishop of Noyon, Calvin was directed to study law. He attended the universities at Orléans and Bourges and received his degree. When his father died in 1531, Calvin returned to literary studies and was influenced by the leading humanist teachers. It was as a humanist scholar himself that he published his first book, a commentary on Seneca's *De Clementia* (1531). However, Calvin experienced a "sudden **conversion**" and quickly became a leader of the Protestant movement in Paris. Forced to flee the city in 1533, he traveled through Europe and wrote his first theological work, *Psychopannychia* (1534), in which he attacked the doctrine of soul sleep.

In 1536 **William Farel**, the leader of the Protestant Reform in Geneva, prevailed upon Calvin to join him. After major difficulties with the town council, the two reformers left Geneva, with Farel going to Neuchatel and Calvin to Strasbourg. In Strasbourg, Calvin worked as a pastor and came under the influence of **Martin Bucer.** In 1541, when Geneva was under considerable pressure to revert to Roman Catholicism, Calvin was induced to return to the city and undertook sweeping ecclesiastical and civil reforms. Through his preaching, teaching, counseling, and international leadership, Calvin became the leading voice of Reformed Protestantism—a movement distinct from Lutheranism and the Anabaptist groups. Calvin's reform in Geneva helped to shape the institutional life of the Reformed churches as they spread throughout Europe and abroad.

Calvin published the first edition of his *Institutes of the Christian Religion* in March 1536. Through its successive editions until the definitive Latin edition of 1559 the work expanded in size and importance, becoming a monumental work of theology. His 1539 French translation of the book is known as a model of French prose. Although Calvin's *Institutes* quickly became a literary standard, it also became a standard of Reformed theology, with its four books structured around the Apostles' Creed: Father, Son, Spirit, and **church.** Calvin also taught Reformed fundamentals in a *Catechism* (1541) of 55 lessons that emphasizes the work of Christ and the nature of the church. Calvin's literary output, including letters, sermons, and biblical commentaries, was prodigious. His theology stresses God's gracious initiative in **salvation**, the believer's union with Jesus Christ who as true prophet, priest, and king is the only source for salvation, and the sanctifying work of the **Holy Spirit**, who draws the church and believers into service in the world until the final reign of **God** is realized.

CALVINISM. The theological perspectives that became systematized from the 17th century as expressions of the essential insights of **John Calvin.** Although many of the distinctives of Calvinism emerge from Calvin's own writings, other Reformed theologians including **Huldrych Zwingli, Théodore Beza, Heinrich Bullinger**, and **John Oecolampadius** also introduced important insights and helped to further the movement. Reformed **confessions** such as the Scots Confession (1560), **Heidelberg Catechism** (1563), Second Helvetic Confession (1566), and the **Westminster Confession** (1647) are important theological summaries of Calvinistic doctrine. Calvinism has taken a variety of forms throughout history, being influenced by the societies and cultures in which it has taken root. It has also been influenced by ideas that grew out of the Enlightenment, taking both scholastic and moderate forms. During its first 300 years Calvinism was primarily centered in **Europe** and **North America.** However, during the missionary movement of the 19th and 20th centuries, and especially during the post-World War II period, new churches were organized in **Africa, Asia**, and the Americas, and these churches have written Reformed creeds and **confessions** that reflect considerable diversity. Within this diversity, the principal insights of Calvinism include God's electing and initiating **grace**, the believer's union with Christ, and the **Holy Spirit's** sanctifying power to move the **church** into the world in **mission** and ministry until the reign of **God** is fully realized. Calvinism is now a worldwide movement, with many national Reformed churches having become members of the **World Alliance of Reformed Churches.**

CAMARGO, JUAN LIBREROS (fl. 1900–1960s). Colombian Presbyterian minister. In 1919 Camargo was among the first group to graduate from the newly organized theological school in Barranquilla (1916). He served churches in Medellin and Cereté and worked for many years in the coastal regions. Camargo was one of the founders of the Nazareth Presbyterian Church in Alto Sinú. He also served as teacher and chaplain of the Colegio Americano in Barranquilla.

CAMBRIDGE PLATFORM AND SYNOD (1646). Statement on **church government** by American Congregationalist ministers and **elders** who met in Cambridge, Massachusetts. The synod's Platform, drafted by representatives from 29 churches, advocates a Congregationalist polity. Although councils and synods would continue to serve a useful advisory role, they were to have no binding **authority.** The Platform also affirmed a church–state union. Under this union, Congregationalist polity would be preserved by the civil authority, which would maintain the power to **discipline** heresy and to preserve the church's unity.

CAMERON, ANDREW (1855–1925). Minister in the Presbyterian Church of Aotearoa **New Zealand.** Educated first at Theological Hall, Dunedin, and later in Europe at Edinburgh, Jena, and Leipzig, Cameron became minister at Anderson's Bay, Dunedin, in 1884. He was active in educational and social affairs, serving on the Otago High Schools Board. A strong supporter of the Theological Hall, Dunedin, Cameron was the founder of **Knox College**, Dunedin, and played an important role in the formation of the Presbyterian Social Service Association. Elected **moderator** of the **general assembly** in 1912, Cameron served as vice chancellor (1810) and chancellor (1812) of Otago University, and senator of the University of New Zealand.

CAMEROON. *See* WEST AFRICA

CAMPBELL, JOHN McLEOD (1800–1872). Scottish Presbyterian minister and theologian who developed a significant understanding of the **atonement.** The son of a minister, Campbell studied at Glasgow University (1811–1820) and became minister of the church in Row (Rhu) in Dunbartonshire. In 1830 Campbell was arraigned for heresy in the Dunbarton Presbytery for preaching "the doctrine of universal atonement and pardon through the **death** of Christ, and also the doctrine that assurance is of the essence of **faith** and necessary to **salvation.**" He was found guilty and deposed from the Church of Scotland ministry by the **General Assembly** in 1831. He later became pastor of a Congregational church in Glasgow (1834). Campbell's *The Nature of the Atonement* (1856) criticizes the legalistic framework in which he believed **Calvinism** had cast the atonement, and he argued that humanity's primary relation with **God** is as Father rather than as righteous Lord. The atonement is grounded in God's desire to provide salvation for erring children. Campbell interpreted Christ's suffering as the perfect repentance performed on behalf of impenitent humanity. The cross shows God's grief and hatred of **sin** while also portraying Jesus' obedient faith in the Father. Campbell's critique of the penal substitutionary view of the atonement and desire to see the atonement in light of the **incarnation** eventually gained acceptance among other theologians in the Reformed tradition, including **Karl Barth**, Jürgen Moltmann, and Thomas F. Torrance.

CANADA. The country is primarily Christian, with Roman Catholics (46 percent) the majority, and United Church Protestants (16 percent) and Anglicans (10 percent) minorities.

The Reformed tradition was brought to Canada by Presbyterians who immigrated from the American colonies and from the British Isles, by Congregationalists who arrived from New England, and by Congregationalist "Independents" who came from Great Britain. Although these Anglo-American settlers maintained some of the traditions of their home churches, they gradually created Reformed churches that are uniquely Canadian. Later Dutch Reformed immigrants from the Netherlands founded churches and schools while maintaining an expression of the Reformed tradition strongly influenced by their place of origin. Today the major expressions of the Reformed tradition in Canada are found in the United Church of Canada and the Presbyterian Church in Canada. Both bodies are members of the **World Alliance of Reformed Churches.** Smaller denominations representing the Reformed tradition include the Presbyterian Church in America (Canadian Section) and several Dutch Reformed churches.

Presbyterian Churches. During the last quarter of the 18th century Presbyterians arrived in Canada from Pennsylvania and upper New York. This American presence was soon eclipsed when, during the 19th century, many Scots and Irish immigrated to North America because of economic hardships at home. Although American influence would later be felt in the Canadian churches through **revival** movements, **temperance**, Sunday school **education**, and the **social gospel**, after the early 19th century Canadian **Presbyterianism** looked to Scotland rather than to America for its ministers and the growth of its churches through immigration.

Because of the great distance from **Scotland** and the isolated conditions of the Canadian settlements, the bonds between Scottish and Canadian Presbyterians were never formalized, so the Canadian churches functioned independently. The Scots who settled in the Maritime Provinces were primarily United Presbyterians, **Dissenters** from the Church of Scotland. This body would eventually absorb Scottish immigrants with Church of Scotland and Free Church backgrounds. In the vast expanses of Canada many of the differences that had divided the Presbyterian churches in Scotland were put aside to attend to more pressing needs: recruiting, training, and paying ministers, carrying out **mission** work, and finding a place in Canadian society alongside Catholics, Anglicans, and Methodists.

The Canadian churches were successful in overcoming divisions and unifying Canadian Presbyterianism. Three streams of Canadian Scottish churches merged during the period of the "Great Disruption" from 1844 to 1875. These were the Church of Scotland, the Free Church of Scotland, and the Secessionists. The first **general assembly** of the Presbyterian Church in Canada was held in Montreal in 1875, uniting these Scottish streams and giving Canada a national Presbyterian body. This unification of Canadian Presbyterianism occurred less than a decade after Canada had gained national political unity. When the United Church of Canada was formed, about 30 percent of Canadian Presbyterians elected not to join the union. They retained the name Presbyterian Church in Canada, and they considered themselves to be in "historical continuity with the Church of Scotland." Union with the United Church was opposed for many reasons, including the desire to retain specifically Presbyterian doctrine, polity, and practices; the belief that organic unity was not critical to Christian witness, but rather that each individual denomination had its own important witness, identity, and mission; and a fear that the uniting church would drift into theological **liberalism.**

The Presbyterian Church in Canada adheres to the **Westminster Confession** and the Larger and Shorter **Catechisms** as subordinate standards to **scripture.** It also recognizes the Second Helvetic, Belgic, and Gallican (Confession of La Rochelle) **confessions** and the **Heidelberg Catechism.** It supports cross-cultural mission in **Taiwan, Japan, Nigeria**, and other parts of the world. The church's major center for theological education is **Knox College**, Toronto (1844). **Women** have been ordained as ministers and elders in the church since 1966.

Canadian Presbyterianism produced missionaries **John Morton, Marion Fairweather, George Leslie Mackay**, and **Robert Baird McClure**; educators **Lydia Gruchy** and **Thomas McCulloch**; denominational leaders **James Ralph Mutchmor** and **George Campbell Pidgeon**; novelist **Charles William Gordon**; and historians **Walter W. Bryden** and **John T. McNeill**.

Congregational Churches. Congregational churches were founded in Nova Scotia by Independents from Britain and by thousands of New England Congregationalists who arrived between 1749 and 1760. Many American immigrants were spurred on by Governor Lawrence's Proclamation of 1758, which promised land and religious freedom to all Protestants. The new immigrants endured harsh living conditions; new Reformed churches had difficulty keeping ministers. Of the 11 congregations founded during the 17th century, nine dissolved or became Baptist churches under the influence of Henry Alline, an evangelist from New England who drew many Congregationalist members into his revivalist New Light churches.

Although **Congregationalism** declined in Nova Scotia, it gained new life during the 1830s when **Henry Wilkes** became pastor of the Congregational church in Montreal (1836). Wilkes was also appointed agent of the newly organized Colonial Missionary Society (CMS), a Canadian subsidiary of the **London Missionary Society.** In this capacity Wilkes recruited ministers from Britain, established more than 25 Congregational churches, and by 1841 had secured CMS funding for 30 Canadian ministers. The Congregational churches also received help from the **American Home Missionary Society.**

Congregational churches never spread to western Canada, where "union" or community churches had been established. These were independent, community-based Protestant churches that welcomed members of all denominations. Union churches had much in common with Congregational churches and their growth, to more than 3,000 at the formation of the United Church of Canada, minimized the need for westward expansion.

United Churches. In 1925 several Protestant denominations joined to form the United Church of Canada. The four major denominations were the Presbyterian Church in Canada, the Congregational Churches of Canada, the Methodist Church of Canada, and the General Council of Local Union Churches (earlier some 19 separate acts of union involving 40 distinct bodies had produced these churches). At the time of union the United Church became the largest Protestant church in Canada.

The United Church carries on a variety of ministries that serve the needs of the diverse population of Canada. Indigenization has been a major emphasis in cross-cultural mission. A strong social-ethical stance and prophetic critique of society are characteristic of the church. A commitment to ecumenism and ecumenical dialogue with bodies such as the Anglican Church and the Disciples of Christ has also been maintained. The church's doctrinal views were set forth in the Basis of Union, written between 1904 and 1910. Twenty articles of doctrine are found in the Basis, with neither Methodist nor Presbyterian influences dominating.

Church government of the United Church of Canada is conciliar, with a hierarchical series of church courts and legislative bodies. The local church is governed by an official board. Other courts include the **presbytery**, the conference, and the general council. Representation in these three bodies is half clergy and half laity. Congregations are free to choose their own ministers, though the denomination may contribute to the process. Women have been ordained to the ministry of the United Church since 1936.

Dutch Reformed Churches. The Christian Reformed Church in North America was established by Dutch immigrants to Canada prior to World War II. Characteristic of this church is a concern for participation in society on the basis of one's Christian confession in the tradition of **Abraham Kuyper**, and a strong interest in the relationship of church and culture. The church has founded three post-secondary schools: the Institute for Christian Studies in Toronto, Redeemer College in Burlington,

Ontario, and King's College in Edmonton, Alberta. Other Dutch churches include the Christian Reformed Churches in Canada, established after World War II by immigrants from the Netherlands, the Reformed Church in Canada, and the Canadian and American Reformed Churches.

CAPITALISM. The socioeconomic system of most of the industrialized West, which is based upon the free flow of goods and money as determined by the marketplace. Profit, the accumulation of wealth, and investment are the basic motivation of capitalism, and competition is its basic methodology. In his classic work, *The Protestant Ethic and the Spirit of Capitalism* (1904), Max Weber argued that **Calvinism** and **Puritanism**, through its **Protestant ethic**, laid the foundation for modern capitalism. Weber's view has been debated by economic historians; most now recognize a Protestant linkage but also stress the importance of social and political factors. The Reformed churches have valued the individual freedom and initiative of the capitalist system but have lamented the disparity of income and quality of life it engenders. The growing importance of the non-North Atlantic churches has intensified the debate about capitalism. These churches argue that because of an inequality in the distribution of income and wealth and the toleration of monopolies, capitalism victimizes their societies, deepens poverty, and fosters dependency on the industrialized nations. Some Reformed Christians have seen the answer in some adaptation of socialism. Others call for a Reformed witness of critical interaction with capitalism, stressing the priority of market reform according to Christian values of justice, peace, and the integrity of **creation.**

CAREY, WILLIAM (1761–1834). British Baptist missionary in **India** and a pioneer of modern Protestant **mission.** Born near Northampton, **England,** Carey worked as a shoemaker (1777–1789), and became a self-taught minister influenced by **Calvinism.** He became pastor of the Baptist church in Moulton (1786), after serving one year as its preacher. In 1792 his pamphlet, *An Enquiry into the Obligations of Christians to Use Means for the Conversion of the Heathens* and sermon, "Expect Great Things from God; Attempt Great Things for God" inspired the organization of the Baptist Missionary Society. As a member of the society he was the first British missionary sent to **India.** He mastered the Bengali language, and after five years of working on an indigo plantation near Calcutta, he went to the Danish colony at Serampore (north of Calcutta). In Serampore Carey worked as a teacher and evangelist; with a team of helpers translated the whole Bible (except Joshua to Job) into Bengali;

wrote grammars and dictionaries in five Indian languages; printed **scripture** portions in 36 languages; founded an Indian Baptist denomination and Serampore College (1819); organized the Agricultural and Historical Society of India; and was appointed professor at Fort William College, where he wrote an important work of Bengali prose, the *Bengali Colloquies.*

CARIBBEAN. The people of the Caribbean are predominantly Christian. Protestants are the majority in Jamaica (56 percent). In Guyana, Christian (52 percent) and Hindu (34 percent) religions are practiced; Protestants compose the majority of the Christian population. Trinidad and Tobago is divided between Catholic (33 percent), Protestant (29 percent), and Hindu (25 percent) religions. Catholic majorities are found in Grenada (64 percent), Cuba (nominally 85 percent), and the Netherlands Antilles.

Cuba. The island nation was a possession of **Spain** from the 16th century until its independence in 1899. In the postindependence period, Cuba has been ruled by dictators. In 1958 Fidel Castro led a popular but communist-influenced revolution. Cuba was closely allied with the Soviet Union from the 1960s until its breakup in 1989.

During the 1880s small Protestant churches were established in Cuba. One of the first Reformed congregations was begun in the home of lay leader Evaristo Collazo. In 1890 Collazo invited **Anthony Thomas Graybill** to help organize his fellowship into a church. During his visit, Graybill baptized more than 40 adults, helped the congregation elect two **elders**, and ordained Collazo as pastor. In 1899 **Robert L. Wharton** settled in Cárdeñas, where Graybill had worked. Wharton organized churches and schools in Caíbarién and Remédios and was appointed superintendent of the Presbyterian **mission** in 1904.

In 1914 the Central Presbytery was organized, and in 1918 the two American Presbyterian denominations working in Cuba combined their work, forming the Presbytery of Havana. The church continued to grow, becoming established in the provinces of Havana, Matanza, and Las Villas. After the Cuban Revolution, the Presbyterian schools were nationalized and lost their religious identity, but the Presbyterian-Reformed Church of Cuba (Iglesia Presbiteriana-Reformada en Cuba) continued to function. The church became autonomous in 1967 and 10 years later produced a Confession of Faith. Ministers are educated at the United Seminary of Matanzas.

Grenada. The island nation was a French possession from 1650 to 1762, when the British took control. Grenada became self-governing in

1967 and independent in 1974. During the early 1980s the government of Grenada became allied with Cuba and the Soviet Union; a U.S. invasion in 1983 restored democratic government by the end of 1984.

The Presbyterian Church of Grenada was established in 1800 by the **Scottish Missionary Society**; for more than a century the church was part of the Church of Scotland. During the 1950s the church was a **presbytery** of the Presbyterian Church of Trinidad and Grenada. In 1983 the church became autonomous; it adopted a constitution in 1986. The church works closely with the United Church of Canada.

Guyana. Located in northeastern South America, Guyana was settled by the Dutch in the early 17th century. It remained a Dutch colony until the 19th century, when it was taken over by the British and named British Guyana (1831). More than 100,000 slaves were brought to Guyana during the years of the slave trade. East Indians also worked the plantations and by the early 20th century more than 200,000 had immigrated to the British colony.

In 1808 the **London Missionary Society** (LMS) sent John Wray to Guyana. He and his successors established churches among the slave population, who were emancipated in 1834. Out of this work emerged the British Guyana Congregational Union (1883). When the LMS withdrew, the church was unable to sustain itself. During the 20th century the church received aid from the **Commonwealth Missionary Society** and the government of Guyana. With this support the church was able to minister to Arawak Indians and to bauxite miners. The Guyana Congregational Union trains its ministers at the United Theological College of Kingston, Jamaica.

The visit of **John Morton** in 1880 began the process that brought Canadian Presbyterian missionaries to Guyana. John Gibson (1885) and J. B. Cooper (1895) pioneered work among East Indians who labored on the sugar plantations. In 1930 the first Guyanese elders were ordained. In 1945 a presbytery was established and the church became autonomous, calling itself the Canadian Presbyterian Church. In 1961 the church changed its name to the Guyana Presbyterian Church. Schools established by the church were taken over by the government in 1966.

Scottish settlers in Guyana organized a church in 1815 and called their first minister, Archibald Browne, in 1816. A presbytery was organized in 1837, and a second presbytery in 1839; the two presbyteries united in 1855. The Presbytery of Guyana was supported by the government until 1899, when its subsidy was reduced; in 1945 the government ceased its support. The Presbyterian Church of Guyana became independent from the Church of Scotland in 1967.

Jamaica and Grand Cayman. Jamaica was a Spanish possession from the early 16th century until 1655, when the British took control. The abolition of **slavery** took place in the late 1830s, resulting in a decline of the Jamaican sugar plantations. In 1866 the island became a British colony. A constitution was produced in 1944, the island became self-governing in 1959, and independence was obtained in 1962.

The Presbyterian church of Jamaica and Grand Cayman began when the Scottish Missionary Society sent three missionaries to Kingston in 1800. Work was carried out among slaves on the sugar plantations. These slaves were emancipated in 1838 and in 1848 a synod was organized. The church also worked among the East Indian population of Jamaica. During the 1840s the church established missions in Calabar, **Nigeria**, and in the **Gold Coast**.

The Congregational church in Jamaica began when missionaries from the **London Missionary Society** arrived in 1834. The first congregation was organized in 1839 and by 1877 several congregations formed the Congregational Union of Jamaica. The church relied on the Congregational Union of England and Wales and other congregational bodies for financial support and ministers.

In 1965 the Presbyterian Church of Jamaica and Grand Cayman and the Congregational Union of Jamaica merged to form the United Church of Jamaica and Grand Cayman. The church is involved in urban ministry, **education**, youth work, and **mission.**

Netherlands Antilles and Aruba. The Netherlands Antilles are two groups of self-governing islands, separated by 500 miles of ocean; one group lies north of Venezuela, the other to the northeast. Aruba is also a self-governing island north of Venezuela. These islands were colonized by the Dutch.

The United Protestant Church includes the Protestant Church of Aruba, the United Protestant Church of Bonaire, and the United Protestant Church of Curaçao. The church's autonomous congregations carry out their own educational and evangelistic work, and they ordain their own ministers. Relations are maintained with the Netherlands Reformed Church in **Holland.**

Trinidad and Tobago. Trinidad was a Spanish possession from the time of its European discovery by Columbus (1498) until 1797, when the British took control. The French held the island for a brief time after 1781, developing plantations for the production of sugar. After slavery was abolished in the late 1830s, East Indian laborers were brought to the colony to work on the plantations. The government of British-controlled Tobago was combined with Trinidad in 1889. The country became independent in 1962.

John Morton, a Canadian Presbyterian minister, visited Trinidad in 1864. During his visit he became concerned for the 20,000 East Indians who worked the sugar plantations. Following his return to Canada, Morton lobbied the Presbyterian Church of the Maritime Provinces to begin a Trinidad mission among the East Indian people, and offered himself as a missionary. He arrived in 1868 and spent the rest of his life in Trinidad. He was joined in 1870 by Kenneth Grant, and thereafter by other Canadian missionaries. The missionaries organized primary and secondary schools and St. Andrews Theological College (1892) in San Fernando. One of the students to come out of these schools was **Lal Bihari**, pastor of the Susamachar Church. The educational and evangelistic work of Morton, Grant, and Lal Bihari laid the foundation of the Presbyterian Church in Trinidad and Tobago. A synod was organized in 1961 and in 1988 locally educated ministerial graduates began to assume positions in the church.

Other Countries. Small Reformed churches of Scottish origin are located in Antigua and Barbuda, the Bahamas, Bermuda, St. Vincent and the Grenadines, and other islands in the Caribbean. Puerto Rico is a self-governing island associated with the **United States.** The Presbyterian Church in Puerto Rico, founded in 1860, is concentrated in the western part of the island around Mayagüez, and is a synod of the Presbyterian Church (U.S.A.). Pastors for its 73 churches are educated at the Evangelical Seminary of Puerto Rico in Rio Piedras. The United Church of Puerto Rico, with a Congregationalist heritage, began in 1899. The Evangelical Church in the Dominican Republic is a union church. Organized in 1920, it has roots going back to 1834.

CARTWRIGHT, THOMAS (ca. 1535–1603). English Presbyterian minister and Puritan theologian. Cartwright was educated at Cambridge and became a Fellow of Trinity College in 1562. In 1570 he was named professor of divinity at Cambridge; the next year he was dismissed because of his vigorous opposition to the Anglican form of **church government** put in place by the Elizabethan Settlement. Cartwright engaged in a longstanding theological debate with Archbishop John Whitgift on the issue of church government. He argued for a church built on presbyterian polity established by the state. He also advocated severe penalties for breaking the Ten Commandments but wanted to keep temporal and spiritual jurisdictions separate. The church would administer **discipline.** In the Admonitions Controversy (1572–1574), Cartwright again opposed Whitgift. He went into exile in Heidelberg and Antwerp, where he ministered to the English congregations. Upon his return to England in 1585, Cartwright was imprisoned but then released. His last years were spent in Warwick, where he lived as a "rich and honored patriarch." Cartwright's views influenced the development of American **Congregationalism.**

CASTE. The hierarchical social grouping of Indian society reinforced by cultural tradition and Hindu religion. The caste system is based on occupation, race, class, economics, and other factors. Because one's place in the caste system is dictated by birth, some groups are able to dominate Indian society while other groups, such as the lower-caste "untouchables," are marginalized. Caste-based discrimination continues to be a problem in Indian society and in the Protestant churches. There have been some attempts to overcome the pressures of caste within urban Christian communities; in rural areas caste distinctions tend to dominate. Many Indian churches, including Reformed churches, have evolved along caste lines. In recent times, Protestant outreach among the untouchables (the Dalits) has shown great vitality. Dalit Christians have developed their own form of **liberation theology** and continue to struggle for social and economic justice. *See also* Dalit Theology

CATECHISMS (Greek *katæchein* "to instruct"). Instruction in the Christian **faith**, often in question-and-answer form, to set forth the basic beliefs of the **church.** In the early church, catechetical instruction was given to prepare catechumens for church membership. Reformed churches have made extensive use of catechisms as a means of educating members. **John Oecolampadius** and **Heinrich Bullinger** wrote catechisms; under **Martin Bucer** they became more widely used as preparation for the rite of **confirmation** (see *Inst.* 4.19.4, 13). Calvin's Geneva Catechism (1538, 1541) and the **Heidelberg Catechism** (1563) are important Reformed documents that convey both historic Christian doctrines and warm, devotional piety. The most influential Reformed catechism is the Westminster Shorter Catechism (1648). The catechism's 107 questions range through the whole of Christian doctrine and reflect the teachings of the **Westminster Confession.** Contemporary usage of Reformed catechisms has been minimal, although some denominations continue catechetical instruction.

CENTRAL AFRICA. More than half of the people of Central Africa practice Christianity. In the countries of the Central African Republic (50 percent) and the Congo (50 percent) religious practice is divided between Christianity and African traditional religions, along with a Muslim minority; there is a Christian majority in Rwanda (74 percent; 18 percent Protestant).

Central African Republic. During the 18th and 19th centuries, the people of the Central African Republic were involved in the slave trade as both slave traders and captives. By the beginning of the 20th century the region became a colony of France. With **colonialism** came Catholic and Protestant missionaries, some of whom provided medical services and established schools. The country became independent in 1960. The only Protestant church with Reformed roots is the Church of Christ the King. Organized as a French-speaking denomination, the church is composed of people of various nationalities and church backgrounds. Ministers are educated in Cameroon or France.

Congo. In 1997 the Congo reverted to its former name, Democratic Republic of the Congo (1960–1971; 1997–). The country has also been called the Congo Free State (1885–1908); the Belgian Congo (1908–1960); and Zaire (1971–1997). First the personal property of King Leopold II of **Belgium**, then a colony of Belgium, and following independence (1960) and civil war, under the autocratic rule of Mobutu Sese Seko (1965–1997), the people of the Congo have endured great hardships.

The first Protestants to arrive in the Congo were British Baptists, who in 1878 established the first of a series of **mission** stations on the Congo River. The first Reformed missionaries came from the Presbyterian Church in the United States, a denomination located in the southern part of the **United States.** In 1891 the Presbyterians founded a mission in the Kasai district, at Luebo. From this base the Presbyterian work spread throughout the Kasai. To serve this vast region, the mission educated evangelists, some of whom later became pastors. Early leaders include **Daniel Kalombo**, **Samuel Katshunga**, and **Pastor Musonguela**. Mission leaders **William H. Sheppard**, **William M. Morrison**, and others publicly denounced the abuses of the Leopold government; their criticism attracted international attention and forced social and political reforms during the early decades of the 20th century.

The period of Belgian colonial rule was followed by a difficult transition to independence. In a decree of 1970 the Mobutu government recognized only one Protestant church, the Church of Christ in Zaire (Eglise du Christ au Zaire), and forced the various missions and denominations to merge into this church. An ecumenical Congo Protestant Council, which had been in existence for many years, formed the basis of the new church. The various denominations in the Congo became "communities" of this united church. Each community retained its distinctive identity, making the new church more diverse that any other union church in Reformed Protestantism. Today more than 80 communities make up the Church of Christ in the Congo.

The Presbyterians are one of the largest groups in the united church, with approximately two million members in four communities. The Presbyterian Community in Congo (1891) grew out of the work of the American mission. Its first Congolese pastors were ordained in the second decade of the 20th century, and the church gradually became indigenous, achieving full autonomy in 1959. The Presbyterian Community of Kinshasa (1955) is an independent church organized to serve that city. The church has three presbyteries and established a synod in 1983. The Presbyterian Community of East Kasai and the Presbyterian Community of West Kasai were formed by a schism over the appointment of bishops in the Church of Christ in the Congo. Although the center of Presbyterian activity remains at Kananga in the Kasai, Presbyterian churches have spread throughout the country, and membership continues to increase. There is a growing interest in uniting these Presbyterian bodies in a single community.

Three other communities belonging to the Church of Christ in the Congo have Reformed roots. The Evangelical Community of the Congo evolved from the work of the Swedish Missionary Society. The church, which operates schools and hospitals, became independent in 1961. The Protestant Community in Shaba (Communauté protestante au Shaba) was organized in 1953 by a union of Belgian Protestant churches in the Congo. Later, some Baptist and Brethren congregations joined the church. **Henri Theophile de Worm** and **Edouard Dominique Antoine Pichal** were important representatives of the Belgian church who supported mission work in the Congo. The Reformed Presbyterian Community is a small church centered in the region of Mbuji-Mayi. The church emphasizes African liturgy and **music** in **worship.**

Rwanda. German Protestants arrived in Rwanda in 1907, crossing the border from Tanzania. These Lutheran missionaries from the Bethel Mission worked in Rwanda until World War I. After the war, Germans were not allowed to return to the country. Other mission organizations from Belgium, the **Netherlands**, and **Switzerland** carried on the work.

Beginning in 1921, the Belgian Society of Protestant Missions in the Congo (Société Belge des Missions Protestantes au Congo), the mission organization of the Reformed Church of Belgium, assumed a share of this responsibility. The work of the Belgian mission evolved into the Presbyterian Church of Rwanda (Eglise presbytérienne au Rwanda), which became independent in 1959. The church cooperates with other Protestant churches through the Protestant Council of Rwanda.

CENTRAL AFRICAN FEDERATION (1953–1963). A federation between the British colony of Southern Rhodesia **(Zimbabwe)** and the territories of Northern Rhodesia **(Zambia)** and Nyasaland **(Malawi).** Southern Rhodesia was a British settler colony developed by the British South Africa of Cecil Rhodes, whereas the territories were autonomous areas with an African majority who were governed by the British Colonial Office. First proposed in the 1920s, the federation was opposed by the black majority in the territories and by Church of Scotland missionaries who feared a complete domination of the population by a white minority. Supported by economic arguments, the federation was enacted by the British government. However, by 1959 pressure from the Church of Scotland forced the government to appoint the Devlin Commission, whose critical report helped to end the federation. In 1964 Malawi and Zambia became independent nations; after a tragic war, black majority rule was also achieved in Zimbabwe when it became an independent nation in 1980.

CENTRAL AFRICAN REPUBLIC. *See* CENTRAL AFRICA

CENTRAL AMERICA. *See* MESOAMERICA

CENTRAL AND EASTERN EUROPE. The countries of central and eastern Europe are affiliated with Christian churches. The Roman Catholic Church predominates in Hungary (67 percent), Austria (89 percent), Croatia, Slovenia, Czech Republic, Poland (95 percent), Latvia, and Lithuania (85 percent); and the Eastern Orthodox in Yugoslavia (65 percent), Ukraine (76 percent), Romania (87 percent), Slovakia, and Bulgaria (90 percent). The largest Reformed communities are found in Hungary (25 percent) and among Hungarian-speaking people in neighboring countries.

Hungary. The Reformed churches in Hungary were primarily influenced by the Reformation in Zurich. **Heinrich Bullinger** maintained contact with leaders of the Hungarian movement, and he sent the ***Consensus Tigurinus*** to Hungary for approval. The Hungarian **church** accepted Bullinger's Second Helvetic Confession at Debrecen (Constitutional Synod of Debrecen, 1567) and, like the Reformed church in Zurich, purged its churches of images, vestments, and musical instruments. Hungarian students studied at Heidelberg, Leiden, Basel, Cracow, and other centers of Reformed learning, but the Hungarian Reformation developed only gradually. **Reformed Theological Academy** was founded at Debrecen; a Hungarian translation of the Bible was published by **Gáspár Károlyi** (1590); the Hungarian educational system and the organizational life of the church were administered by Bishop **Péter Juhász** (Melius); and Hungarian theology was consolidated by **Stephen Kis** (Szegedi). One of the unique features of Hungarian church polity is the office of bishop, rarely used in Reformed **church government.**

During the first half of the 17th century, Hungarian Protestants gained full recognition by the government (1608), and the princes of Transylvania, István Bocskai and Bethlen Gábor, helped to establish the Hungarian church. **Albert Molnár** translated Calvin's *Institutes* and prepared a second edition of the Hungarian Bible. Hungarian students who studied abroad brought back the Puritan theology of **William Ames** and others. Several works by **William Perkins** were translated into Magyar, and Lewis Bayly's *Practice of Piety* was widely read in translation. The Puritan influence extended beyond theology and **spirituality** to the organizational life of the church. Puritan reformers pressed the Hungarian church to adopt a Presbyterian system of organization and advocated greater lay participation in church worship and service.

The Hungarian church was persecuted alternately by the armies of the Muslim Ottoman Turks and the Roman Catholic Habsburgs. The "dark decade" from 1671 to 1681 was a period of severe repression under the Habsburgs. Pastors were imprisoned, churches were occupied, and the Protestant population decreased sharply. The church did not resume normal activity until an Edict of Toleration (1781) was issued by Emperor Joseph II. More repression came during the mid-1800s, but by the last quarter of the century the organizational life of the church was renewed. After World War I, the defeat of the Austro-Hungarian Empire and the signing of the Treaty of Trianon (1919) caused the church to be divided into four separate bodies located in the successor states of Hungary (see Croatia, Slovenia, and Yugoslavia; Ukraine; Slovak Republic; and Romania below). The Hungarian church has approximately 1.5 million members in 1,100 parishes.

Austria. The Reformed Church in Austria (Evangelische Kirche HB [Reformiert] in Oesterreich) is a constituent part of the Helvetic Reformed and Augsburg Lutheran churches. The Reformed church began with Joseph II's Edict of Toleration that gave Reformed Christians in Austria a recognized status alongside Roman Catholics and Lutherans. The European revolution and counter-revolution of 1848–1859 led to the imperial edict of 1861 that extended civil rights and permitted the church to choose its own ministers. A national church was formed, gradually increasing its membership until 1898, when a national movement away from Catholicism brought many new converts into the church. The break-up of the Austro-Hungarian Empire (1918) and the period following World War II brought many refugees from Germany and eastern Europe into the Reformed churches. The constitution of 1949 granted full civil rights to Lutherans and Reformed who (since 1925) have met under one general synod as the Evangelical Church of the Augsburg and Helvetic Confession, but who are fully independent on issues of confessional identity and church administration.

Croatia, Slovenia, and Yugoslavia. The primary religions of the Balkan region are Islam (Bosnia), Roman Catholicism (Croatia), and Orthodoxy (Yugoslavia). The Protestant minority includes several Reformed churches with ethnic and historic ties to Hungary: the Reformed Christian Church in Croatia, the Reformed Christian Churches in Slovenia, and the Reformed Church in Yugoslavia. These churches trace their history to the Protestant Reformation, when numerous Protestant churches were established. Many of these Reformed churches were destroyed during the Counter-Reformation. The churches that survived retained the Reformed **confessions**, including the Second Helvetic Confession and the **Heidelberg Catechism.** Some churches continue to worship in the Hungarian language.

After World War I, the Trianon Treaty divided Hungary, and the southern parts were annexed to the newly created Kingdom of the Serbs, Croats, and Slovenians. In 1929 the country was named Yugoslavia. By 1946 Yugoslavia consisted of the republics of Slovenia, Croatia, Bosnia and Herzegovina, Serbia, Montenegro, Vojvodina, and Macedonia. After World War II communists came to power under Marshal (Josip Broz) Tito. Tito's regime unified the various ethnic groups in Yugoslavia. However, after Tito's death (1980) two decades of ethnic unrest followed. The collapse of communism in 1991 led to a breakup of Yugoslavia, to the independence of several republics, and to ethnic warfare in Bosnia-Herzegovina, Croatia, and Kosovo.

These conflicts have been devastating to the region with atrocities being committed by the Yugoslavian Serbs and other ethnic groups. In

Croatia, for example, autonomous areas were carved out by Croatian Serbs, causing loss of life and displacement among the civilian population. Church buildings were destroyed, local congregations were occupied, and two thirds of the Reformed church membership became refugees, most fleeing to neighboring Hungary. About 2,000 of these church members returned in 1992, living in and around Osijek and Vinkovci. In Slovenia there was a 10-day war with the Federal Army that resulted in independence with few casualties and little property damage.

During the 1980s the Croatian church reported 20 congregations and a membership of over 4,000. Because of the destruction and displacement caused by the Balkan war, there are now six Reformed congregations and six "preaching stations" in Croatia. The Croatian church cooperates with other Protestant churches and the Evangelical Theological Faculty in Osijek. The Reformed Christian Churches in Slovenia has six congregations in the northeast part of the country, near the Austrian and Hungarian borders. These congregations are ethnically Hungarian, and they are regularly visited by Reformed ministers from Hungary. The Reformed Christian Church in Yugoslavia has 15 congregations and over 17,000 members. Except for one Czech congregation located near the Romanian border, the church is primarily composed of ethnic Hungarians living in Vojvodina. In 1993 the Protestant Evangelical Alliance was formed to promote cooperation among the Protestant churches.

Ukraine. Carpatho-Ukraine was part of the Hungarian Empire and its Reformed churches, located in the western part of Ukraine, were part of the Reformed Church of Hungary until 1918. After World War I, the region became part of Czechoslovakia, and the Reformed churches were part of the Reformed Church of Slovakia until 1945. After World War II, national boundaries changed again and the Carpatho-Ukraine region became part of the Soviet Union. During this period, the Reformed churches became independent, but they also ceased to be a recognized denomination. The communist government closed many churches and sent ministers and church leaders to labor camps in Siberia. The collapse of the Soviet Union in 1989 enabled the church to reorganize its synod and adopt a new constitution. The Reformed Church in Carpatho-Ukraine has 95 congregations and over 120,000 members. Ministers of the church are educated in Hungary.

Romania. The Reformed Church in Romania was legalized by the Transylvanian parliament in 1564. Composed primarily of Hungarian-speaking people, the church maintained ties with Zurich, Geneva, and Heidelberg, adopting the Second Helvetic Confession and the **Heidel-**

berg Catechism as doctrinal standards. During the 18th century **Puritans** came to Romania from the Netherlands. These ministers met with opposition from feudal governments when they tried to promote **education**, Bible study, government by church "sessions," and spiritual renewal. The modern church is divided into two districts, each led by a bishop: the Transylvanian district consists of 16 dioceses and the Királyhágómelléki district consists of seven dioceses. A Presbyterian form of church government was adopted in the 19th century. The church has over 700,000 members in 777 parishes. Ministers are educated at the Protestant Theological Institute at Kolozsvár.

Slovak Republic. Part of the Reformed Church of Hungary until 1918, the Reformed Christian Church in Slovakia shares the heritage of the Hungarian church. More than three quarters of its approximately 327 congregations are Hungarian speaking; the rest are Slovak speaking. The church has about 120,000 members.

Czech Republic. The Reformed churches in the Czech Republic have a pre-Reformation heritage associated with the **Bohemian Brethren** movement. During the Reformation and post-Reformation period, Lutheran ideas were introduced into Bohemian lands, German-speaking Lutherans wrote a Bohemian Confession (1575), and educational reforms were carried out by **Jan Comenius.** The Brethren and Lutheran churches cooperated but remained separate churches until 1918. In that year the Brethren churches, which had grown to about 120,000 members, united with the 34,000-member Czech Lutheran church, creating the Evangelical Church of the Czech Brethren. The new body adopted the Presbyterian system of church government and reaffirmed its heritage by adopting both the Brethren Confession and Bohemian Confession. Its Reformation heritage was recognized by the acceptance of the Lutheran Augsburg Confession (1530) and the Reformed Second Helvetic Confession (1566). The church has over 260 congregations and carries out its work from offices in Prague.

The Czech church has produced several Bible scholars, theologians, and church leaders, including **Josef L. Hromádka, Viktor Hájek, Amedeo Molnár, Rudolf Říčan**, and **Josef B. Souček.**

The Church of the Brethren is a small Czech denomination of over 40 congregations and about 5,000 members. The church began in 1868, when a religious **revival** swept through eastern Bohemia and congregations were organized in Bystre. A similar revival began later in Prague under missionaries from the **American Board of Commissioners for**

Foreign Missions. This movement led to the organization of the Free Reformed Church in 1880. The two churches merged and became the Unity of Czech Brethren, a religious body governed by a congregational structure and guided by the Reformed confessions. An influx of Poles and Slovakians led the church to change its name in 1967 to the Church of the Brethren.

Poland. The Evangelical Church in Poland grew out of the Swiss Reformation, when Reformed preaching began to penetrate the country and the first congregations were organized in 1550. During the 16th century, the work of the Polish reformer **John Łaski** was especially important. Although Łaski failed in his attempt to create a Polish national Evangelical Church, he introduced Presbyterian church government and provided administrative and ecumenical leadership for the young church. The Sandomierz Consensus (1570), which pledged cooperation between the Polish Reformed, Lutheran, and Czech churches, and the Warsaw Confederacy (1573), which promoted religious toleration, were unable to prevent the Reformed churches from being virtually swept away by the Counter-Reformation, antitrinitarian divisions, and internal frictions.

The churches that survived the Counter-Reformation merged with Czech Brethren churches in 1634, and during the second half of the 18th century new congregations were organized. During World War II, Reformed congregations were dispersed and many ministers and **laity** were killed. After the war, Bishop Jan Niewieczerzaî (1953–1978) helped to rebuild the Reformed church. Today the Evangelical Church has 9 congregations, 10 preaching stations, and about 4,000 members. It is a member of the Polish Ecumenical Council (1946) and the **World Alliance of Reformed Churches** and cooperates with Reformed churches in **Switzerland**, **Germany**, and the **Netherlands.** The church subscribes to the Second Helvetic Confession and the Heidelberg Catechism. Its ministers are educated at the Christian Theological Academy in Warsaw.

The Polish Reformed community has been active in the theological, political, and cultural life of Poland. Polish Reformed scholars produced the Brzesc Bible (1563), and Daniel Mikolajewski prepared the Gdansk Bible (1632). Members of the Reformed church helped to develop the Polish parliamentary system during the 16th century. The church produced several composers, including Jakub Lubelczyk, Cyprian Bazylik, and **Waclaw z Szamotul.**

Bulgaria. The Congregational Church in Bulgaria was founded by missionaries from the American Board of Commissioners for Foreign

Missions in 1856 when Bulgaria was under Turkish rule. The church maintained a college in Sofia and began the first Bulgarian newspaper. When the country became independent after World War I the Congregational churches, located predominately in the southern part of the country, joined with other Protestant churches to form an Evangelical Union. The church endured persecution during the war years and under post-World War II Soviet rule. The church has over 30 congregations with a membership of about 5,000.

Latvia and Lithuania. The Reformed Church in Lithuania was founded in 1555. Reformed Protestantism spread throughout Lithuania, but its membership was considerably reduced during the Counter-Reformation. The country enjoyed a brief period of independence from 1918 to 1940, but for most of the last 200 years it has been dominated by the Russian Empire and the U.S.S.R. World War II and the post-war years were particularly devastating for the Reformed churches, with some of their membership and administrative functions relocated to Chicago. There were no synod meetings in Lithuania between 1957 and 1988, but the church has met annually since 1991. There are three regional centers of Reformed Protestant activity: Birzai, Kaunas, and Vilnius.

The church has similarities with the Dutch Reformed Church and the Church of Scotland, and it is organized according to a constitution produced at Thorn in 1637. The church subscribes to the Heidelberg Catechism and maintains a Presbyterian form of **church government**, with leading officers being superintendents rather than bishops. The synod is the highest governing body of the church. When the synod is not in session, a collegium, or executive board, meets to transact business. Laity have an active role in the church. The president of the collegium is always a lay person and lay people serve as members of the collegium. The church has 11 active parishes with approximately 2,000 members.

The Reformed Church in Latvia was organized in 1918 after the country became independent. After World War II, Latvia became a republic of the U.S.S.R. and the church was reduced to one congregation, which merged with a small Lutheran and Brethren community.

CHALMERS, JAMES (1841–1901). Scottish Congregationalist missionary in the **Cook Islands** and **New Guinea.** Chalmers was born in Ardrishaig, Argyleshire, in **Scotland.** In 1862 he entered the **London Missionary Society's** Cheshunt College, Cambridge, and was ordained in 1865. He went to the Cook Islands to continue the educational and evangelistic work of **John Williams** in Raratonga (1867–1877). He went to New Guinea in 1877 and established a base at Saguane and worked along the coasts and then into the interior. His explorations there resulted in the publication of *Work and Adventure in New Guinea* (1885) and *Pioneering in New Guinea* (1887). He was in favor of British rule of New Guinea but also saw the value of the indigenous cultures. He gave much of his time to educational work and tried to promote peaceful relations among hostile tribes. In 1901 Chalmers and several other teachers and missionaries were murdered on the island of Goaribari.

CHALMERS, THOMAS (1780–1847). Scottish minister and Free Church leader. Born in Anstruther and educated at St. Andrews University, Chalmers was minister at Kilmany in Fife (1803–1815), and at Tron Church (1815–1819) and St. John's (1819–1823) in Glasgow. After a **conversion** experience in 1810, Chalmers became an advocate of the **evangelical** wing of the Church of Scotland. He taught at St. Andrews (1823–1828), Edinburgh University (1828–1843), and the Free Church College, Edinburgh (1843–1847). Chalmers was a powerful orator and church organizer. His churches in Glasgow ministered to several thousand people, many from the poorest areas of the city. During the 1830s he organized over 200 congregations. After the Disruption of 1843, he became the leader of the Free Church of Scotland, serving as its first **moderator.** His *Institutes of Theology* (1849) and *Memoirs of Dr. Chalmers* (1849–1852) were published posthumously.

CHAMBERLAIN, JACOB (1835–1908). American Dutch Reformed missionary in **India.** A graduate of **New Brunswick Seminary** and the College of Physicians and Surgeons, New York, Chamberlain went as a medical missionary to Madras in 1859. In addition to practicing **medicine**, he worked on a translation of the Bible into Telugu, translated the Reformed liturgy and hymnody into Telugu, and taught biblical languages at the Theological Seminary in the Arcot Mission, Palmaner. He was the first **moderator** of the South India United Church Synod (1901) and published numerous devotional works in Tamil and Telugu. His publications include *A Telugu Bible Dictionary* (1906) and *The Kingdom in India* (1908).

CHILE. *See* SOUTHERN CONE OF SOUTH AMERICA

CHINA. *See* EAST ASIA

CHI-OANG (1872–1946). Taiwanese lay evangelist. Chi-Oang was a member of the Taroko Tribe, an ancient Polynesian-Malaysian people in **Tai-**

wan. She was converted to Christianity in 1924, when she was 52 years old. After attending the Tamsui Presbyterian Women's Bible School in 1929, Chi-Oang was sent as a missionary to her people by the Formosan Presbyterian Church. She was noted for her political skill when the Japanese occupied Taiwanese territory during World War II. Chi-Oang fearlessly continued her evangelistic work despite Japanese persecution of Christians. After the war, thousands of people were baptized as a result of her labors. By 1968 there were more than 400 churches with over 77,000 members in the mountains of Taiwan. In 1961 the Chi-Oang Church near Hualien was dedicated in her memory.

CHONGSHIN UNIVERSITY. An institution of the Presbyterian Church of Korea (Hap-tong). The school is one of two institutions that trace their roots to Pyongyang Theological Seminary. Pyongyang Seminary was organized by American missionary Samuel Moffet in 1901 and in 1905 became affiliated with the Presbyterian Church. In 1959 a doctrinal controversy split the school, and the theologically conservative Chongshin University became an institution of the Presbyterian Church of Korea. The institution, with 51 faculty members and 1,200 students, has graduate schools of liberal arts, divinity, and **education.** *See also* Presbyterian College and Theological Seminary

CHRISTIAN PEACE CONFERENCE (CPC). Organized in 1958 by **Josef L. Hromádka** and the **Comenius Theological Faculty** of the University of Prague, **Czechoslovakia**, the purpose of the CPC was to unite the churches of **Central and Eastern Europe** in the pursuit of world peace. With Hromádka serving as its president from 1958 to 1969, the CPC met every five years in a large assembly attended by several hundred delegates from Eastern Europe, the Third World, and the West. In between conferences, the president, general secretary, and the advisory committee carried out the business of the CPC. Since the 1980s, the Russian Orthodox Church assumed a major role in the affairs of CPC, with all major statements being published in the *Journal of the Moscow Patriarchate*. The CPC is known for its longtime support of Christian-Marxist dialogue and the demilitarization of both East and West, and its strong opposition to the nuclear arms race. The collapse of the Soviet Union in 1989 led to a reappraisal of the organization and its ties to the socialist social order. Although applauded for giving a public voice to Christians in Soviet-dominated countries during the years of the Cold War, the CPC has also been criticized for its close adherence to Soviet policy. *See also* Marxism and Christian Faith

CHRISTOLOGY. The study of the person of Jesus Christ. Christology attempts to explain the mysteries connected with the person and work of Christ. Reformed churches accept the early church creedal statements on the person of Christ as faithful reflections of scriptural teachings. These statements, which affirm Christ's full humanity and full divinity united in one person, include the Nicene Creed, Chalcedonian Formula, and the Athanasian Creed (Quicunque Vult). The Reformed **tradition** also ascribes to *enhypostasia*—that the full humanity of Christ was preserved but also included within the eternal person of the Word (Logos); and dyothelitism, that Christ had two wills, corresponding to his two natures, divine and human. Unlike the Lutheran tradition, the Reformed tradition rejects the ubiquity of the human nature of the exalted Christ (the presence of Christ's human nature in every place at every time; see **Heidelberg Catechism**, questions 47–48). The Reformed churches maintain that after the **incarnation**, Christ continues to be present and active beyond the flesh united to himself (the *extra-Calvinisticum*). The eternal Word exists "beyond the bounds of the humanity which it has assumed" (question 48). In eucharistic controversies, the Reformed tradition rejected the view that Christ was physically present in all places during the **Lord's Supper** (ubiquity), asserting that his ascended body was in heaven and that the whole Christ, but not everything that is Christ's, is genuinely present by the power of the Holy Spirit in the Lord's Supper. Calvin's Christology is developed by uniting the person with the work of Christ through use of the **threefold office** *(munus triplex)* of Christ as prophet, priest, and king (*Inst.* 2.15). **Friedrich Schleiermacher** sought to remove Christology from ontological to relational categories by portraying Jesus as the ideal of human God-consciousness. Jesus' perfect human consciousness of **God** was communicated to others and was of such intense power that it effected redemption from sin. **Karl Barth** maintained the traditional Reformed tendency to begin Christology "from above" (John 1:14), but in his later years more strongly emphasized "the humanity of God" as he oriented his whole theology to Christology, making a major shift in many doctrines, particularly **election** and **predestination.** Some contemporary Reformed theologians and confessions begin "from below," with the historical Jesus of Nazareth (cf. Jürgen Moltmann; the Confession of 1967). Moltmann's emphasis on "the crucified God" sees the cross as the foundation and criterion of Christian theology and focuses on the Father suffering the death of the Son in order to redeem humanity.

CHU, KI-CHOL (1897–1944). Korean Presbyterian minister and Christian martyr. Born in Kyongsangnamdo, in southeast **Korea**, Chu was the youngest son in a Christian family. He was educated at the Osan School, where both national consciousness and Christianity were encouraged by **Seung-Hoon Lee.** After graduation, Chu attended Yonsei College but withdrew because of poor health. In 1921 he attended a meeting held by Ik-Du Kim and made a profession of **faith.** Chu enrolled at the Pyongyang Theological Seminary in Pyongyang and was ordained in 1926. He spent the next nine years serving two churches in the southern part of Korea, in Pusan and Masan. In 1936 Chu became pastor of the San Chong Hyon Church in Pyongyang. During this time the Japanese government was attempting to unify its colonial subjects in Korea around the Shinto shrine. When the "Church Reform" group (Hyok-sin Kyodan) tried to persuade Christians to put "kamidana" (Shinto "god shelves") into Christian churches, Chu opposed it. Because of his opposition, he was arrested several times between 1938 and 1944. During his last arrest, Chu was tortured and killed in prison.

CHURCH. Those elected and called by **God** for **salvation** and service. In Reformed theology, the church is the people of God, the communion of saints, who are called by the **Holy Spirit** to receive the benefits of Christ's work and by **faith** to carry out God's will and purposes in the world. The church is grounded in God's action. The "invisible" church is the church known only to God and consists of all the elect, both living and dead. The "visible" church is the outward institution and those who publicly profess faith in Jesus Christ. The church, as the fellowship of believers, is an indispensable part of the Christian experience and exists as God's gracious provision to human weakness and the need for human relationships (*Inst.,* bk. 4). Theologically, the church is one, deriving its unity from Jesus Christ, the head of the church (Col. 1:18). **Karl Barth** called the church "the earthly-historical form of existence of Jesus Christ Himself" (*Church Dogmatics* 4.1: 661). Through mutual care and love, the church is a living community of those who are disciples of Jesus Christ and who embody his love and justice in the world.

CHURCH AND STATE. The Reformed understanding of the relationship between church and state grew out of the Swiss Reformation, and it was influenced by the experience of the **Huguenots** in **France**, Reformed Christians in **Hungary**, Presbyterians in **Scotland**, and the **Puritans** in **England** and the **United States.** In Reformation-era Geneva and Zurich church and state maintained different spheres of interest but were interdependent. This mutual dependence led to the growth in **Europe** and New England of established Protestant churches, which received state recognition and financial support. Although the **Peace of Westphalia** helped spread religious toleration and the disestablishment of religion throughout Europe, Protestant churches retained some privileges of establishment in **Germany, Switzerland, Great Britain,** and **Scandinavia.** In other Western countries such as the **United States, Canada, France,** and **Australia,** the separation of church and state was made complete. The spread of Reformed churches to non-Western countries beginning in the 18th century was influenced by the religious policies of colonial governments. With the end of **colonialism** and the emergence of independent indigenous churches, church–state relations have become more complex. Some Reformed churches serve minority communities that struggle for their existence in antagonistic political and religious settings (e.g., **Sudan**). During the 20th century religious toleration has increased, but communist ideology, religious fundamentalism, and various forms of religious intolerance have also influenced the spread of Reformed Protestantism.

CHURCH GOVERNMENT. There are three types of Protestant church polity: episcopal, led by bishops; congregational, in which the gathered members meet in democratic fashion; and presbyterian, led by representatives of the congregation (representative democracy). The Reformed churches have historically favored congregational or presbyterian government, although some churches, including the Hungarian Reformed Church, have made provision for bishops. In congregationalism, decisions are made by the vote of the congregation. Each congregation, though independent, is regarded as part of the universal church. Local congregations may belong to larger associations, which function as denominations. Congregational government is most associated with Congregational, Baptist, and independent churches. In presbyterianism, each congregation is governed by a "session" composed of ministers and elected **elders.** Congregations, church sessions, and ministers are governed by a higher body called a **presbytery**, which is composed of representatives from the congregations. The presbytery is responsible for the **ordination** of ministers within its jurisdiction. The highest presbyterian body is called a **General Assembly**, or synod, composed of representatives from the presbyteries. This body usually meets annually and directs the national and international work of the denomination. Presbyterian government is most associated with Presbyterian and Reformed denominations.

CHURCH GROWTH SCHOOL. Protestant school of thought that considers numerical growth to be an essential sign of a vibrant church. The "church growth school" emerged after World War II out of Donald McGavran's study of **people movements** to Christianity in **India.** McGavran transferred his insights to the Western church by developing principles that are more informed by sociology than the gospel (e.g., the creation of "homogenous congregations" in order to produce numerical growth). The concern for numerical growth has resulted in the development of a broad spectrum of methods and programs designed to produce "seeker-friendly" churches that are attractive to persons with a modern, unchurched outlook. Reformed theological response to this type of church growth is mixed, acknowledging that the growth of the church is of primary concern but unwilling to compromise the gospel by mixing it with Western market values of success, prosperity, and popularity, and reducing it to individual happiness.

CHURCH OF SCOTLAND ACT. Actions taken by the Parliament of the **United Kingdom**, including the Act of 1921, intended to heal the division between the Church of Scotland and the United Free Church of Scotland. Presbyterianism has been the dominant form of **church government** in **Scotland** since the Reformation. During the 19th century, a controversy arose over state patronage and the role of congregations in the election of ministers. This controversy resulted in the division of 1843, which led over one-third of the Presbyterian ministers to withdraw from the state church to form the United Free Church of Scotland. The Church of Scotland Act ensured the independence of the church from state control. This settlement, along with other reforms carried out during the 1920s, led to a reunion of the two churches in 1929.

COAN, TITUS (1801–1882). American Presbyterian minister, evangelist, and missionary in **Hawaii.** Born in Killingworth, Connecticut, Coan attended the academy at Madison, Connecticut, and became a schoolteacher. In 1826 he took charge of a school in Riga, New York, and in 1828 became a member of the Presbyterian church there under the **ministry** of his brother, George. Coan was influenced by evangelist **Charles G. Finney**, and entered Auburn Theological Seminary in 1831. After **ordination** by the **American Board of Commissioners for Foreign Missions** and a brief trip to Patagonia, Coan and his wife, Fidelia Church, went to Hawaii in 1835. Dispatched to Hilo, on the east coast of the island of Hawaii, Coan began a 30-day preaching tour in November 1836. Coan's emphasis on the love of **God** endeared him to his listeners. As a result of this and succeeding tours, the Hawaiian people began to flock to Coan's church in Hilo. Following a tidal wave that struck Hilo in November 1837, Coan's meetings became more crowded, and he soon began to preach twice a day. Nearly 10,000 people were encamped around Hilo during 1838. In 1838 and 1839, more than 5,200 new members were admitted to the church. On the first Sunday of July 1838, more than 1,700 converts were baptized. During the early 1840s Coan's church, with over 7,000 members, was one of the largest in the world. The Great Revival of 1838–1839 was followed by a period of relative calm until the great epidemics of 1848 and 1853–1854 decimated the Hawaiian population. In 1867 the Hilo church was divided into seven independent churches, six of them with Hawaiian pastors. In addition to the work in Hilo, Coan supported a **mission** to the **Marquesas Islands**, making voyages there in 1860 and 1867. He also published a book, *Life in Hawaii* (1882).

COLIGNY, GASPARD DE (1519–1572). French Protestant leader and admiral. Born into a powerful French family, Coligny served in the military and in public service during his early life. By 1560 he was converted and had joined the Reformed Church of France. He tried to plant Huguenot colonies in **Brazil** (1555) and Florida (1562), but failed. Throughout the first decade of French **Wars of Religion** (1562–1594), Coligny was the political leader of the Reformed Church. He arranged a peace between Calvinists and Catholics in **France** (1570) and was a feared rival of Catherine de Médicis. He was executed, along with several thousand **Huguenots**, in the **Saint Bartholomew's Day Massacres** (22 August 1572).

COLOMBIA. *See* ANDEAN REPUBLICS AND GREATER COLOMBIA

COLONIALISM. The expansion of one people's power and territory at the expense of another people's, resulting in structures of subjugation and economic exploitation. In its modern form, beginning with European colonial expansion in the 15th century, it has been reinforced by Western claims of cultural supremacy, linked to assumptions of the superiority of Christianity. Christian **mission** by the Roman Catholic Church in the 15th, 16th, and 17th centuries was an important part of Spanish and Portuguese colonial expansion. Protestant mission followed a similar pattern, moving overseas with Dutch, British, French, and German colonial conquests, especially during the 18th and 19th centuries. During the 19th century, American missionaries were seldom partners in U.S. expansion overseas (exceptions include **Hawaii** and the **Philippines**), but

U.S. cultural and economic imperialism often created problems as complex as those left by the colonial powers. Throughout history the relationship between Reformed mission and colonialism has been ambivalent: many missionaries opposed the exploitative policies of colonial administrations and advocated the rights of **indigenous** peoples; at other times mission workers were complicit in the colonial exploitation of peoples and resources. In the postcolonial period, there has been a global shift toward ecumenical partnerships and away from dependent relationships between Reformed churches in the West and those in **Africa**, **Asia**, **Latin America**, and the **Pacific** region.

COMBA, EMILIO (1839–1904). Waldensian minister and professor. Educated at the Protestant seminary, l'Oratoire, in Geneva, **Switzerland**, Comba was ordained in 1863 and served congregations in Tuscany, Lombardy, and Venice. In 1872 he was appointed professor of church history at the Waldensian Theological Seminary, where he became well-known for his studies of Waldensian origins and the history of Italian Protestantism. His many publications include the two-volume work, *I nostri Protestanti* (*Our Protestants*; 1895, 1898) and *Histoire des Vaudois* (1898, 1901), translated as the *History of the Waldenses of Italy: From Their Origin to the Reformation.*

COMENIUS, JAN AMOS (1592–1670). Czech Moravian minister and educational reformer. Born in Nivnice, Moravia (**Czech Republic**), Comenius studied theology at Herborn and Heidelberg. He fled Bohemia in 1818 at the beginning of the Thirty Years War, which was being waged in an effort to re-Catholicize the region. He served as a Moravian minister at Fulneck and in 1628 settled in Leszno, **Poland.** From 1641 to 1642 Comenius was in **England**, where he was invited to establish an experimental school. He traveled to Ebbing, **Sweden**, where he prepared educational textbooks. In 1648 the **Peace of Westphalia** ended Comenius's hopes of returning home, and he was consecrated bishop of the Moravians. After a brief period in **Hungary** (1650–1652), where he established a school at Sáros-Patak, Comenius settled in Amsterdam, remaining there for the rest of his life. His best-known works, *Janua Linguarum Reserata* and *Orbis Sensualium Pictus,* were Latin textbooks that taught the language by describing facts about the world rather than the rules of grammar. *Orbis* contained pictures accompanied by Latin sentences and vernacular translations. Comenius's works, based on his conviction that European culture and unity depended upon a common language, revolutionized Latin instruction.

COMENIUS THEOLOGICAL FACULTY. Czech Protestant theological seminary in Prague. Founded in 1950, the Comenius Faculty is the most widely known Protestant school in the **Czech Republic.** The school became noted for its distinguished theologians and biblical scholars, including **Josef Hromádka, Josef B. Souček, Rudolf Říčan**, and **Amedeo Molnár.**

COMMON ORDER, BOOK OF (1564). More popularly known as John Knox's Liturgy, the *Book of Common Order* was the official worship book of the Church of Scotland. In addition to standardizing the order and contents of Reformed **worship**, the book provides guidance on the administration of **baptism** and the **Lord's Supper** and instructions for marriages, funerals, and the election of church officers. The origin of the service book is found in the congregation of English exiles to whom **John Knox** ministered in Geneva. The first Geneva edition, *The Forme of Prayers and Ministration of the Sacraments, &c. used in the Englishe Congregation at Geneva,* was published in 1556. This was followed by the small editions of 1558 and 1561. The first Scottish edition was printed in 1562; it was followed by an enlarged edition of 1564, which included the metrical Psalter and for the first time was "Approved and Received by the Churche of Scotland." The *Book of Common Order* was also the first book to be printed in Gaelic in 1567. More than 60 Scottish editions were published before the book was replaced by the Westminster *Directory of Public Worship* in 1645.

COMMON PRAYER, THE BOOK OF. The official service book of the Church of England and the Anglican communion around the world. The book contains texts for morning and evening **prayer** and the administration of the **sacraments**, the Psalter, responsive readings, and other materials used in public and private **worship.** Primarily the work of **Thomas Cranmer**, the book was first issued in 1549. Because it was a product of compromise, it pleased neither the traditionalist nor the reformist elements in the Church of England. Under the influence of **Martin Bucer** and **Peter Martyr Vermigli**, substantive changes were made and the book, reissued in 1552, became a more Reformed work. The book has been revised several times since the Reformation. During the 1960s modern English was incorporated into the book and more recently Anglican churches in **Australia** (1978), **Canada** (1985), **South Africa** (1989), and other countries have carried out their own revisions.

COMMONWEALTH MISSIONARY SOCIETY (CMS). Organized by the Congregational Union of England and Wales in 1836, the CMS was complementary to, and smaller than, the **London Missionary Society.** Still, it was one of the main missionary societies of the Congregational churches in the **British Isles.** The CMS organized churches and provided a regular supply of pastors for several countries of the British Commonwealth, including **Canada**, **Australia**, and **New Zealand.** The society later extended its work to **South Africa, Guyana**, and **Jamaica.** In 1966 the CMS merged with the **London Missionary Society** to become the Congregational Council for World Mission. As a result of the 1972 merger of the Congregational Union of England and Wales with the Presbyterian Church of England, the council became the primary mission organization of the United Reformed Church.

COMMUNION. *See* LORD'S SUPPER

COMMUNITY. The service and gifts that individuals give one another, as well as the fellowship they enjoy, in the **church.** Community is the context in which the church cares for its members, shares its financial resources, ministers to those in physical and spiritual need, and prays and worships. Community is an activity and experience of the whole fellowship and a significant expression of the Christian life. For some churches in the West, Christian **faith** is expressed in individualistic terms (e.g., *personal* **salvation** and *personal* interpretation of **scripture**). However, for many churches in **Africa**, **Asia**, and the **Pacific Islands**, Christian life and Christian theology are communal enterprises. Salvation comes to a whole family or society, not just to individuals. This approach to faith is similar to the divine activity recorded in the Old Testament, when **God** saved a family, a tribe, or an entire people. African and Asian churches enjoy strong relational ties that are based on the concept of the extended family. In Japanese and Korean churches the idea of "belonging" is central to both personal and Christian identity.

CONFESSING CHURCH (Bekennende Kirche). The German churches opposed to the national and ecclesiastical policies of the Third Reich and the collaboration of the German Christians of the national church. The Confessing Church was organized at the Barmen Synod held in May 1934. It opposed the widespread political interference in the affairs of the German churches. This interference included Hitler's nomination of Ludwig Müller to preside over the German Evangelical Church in order to control its administrative affairs and organizational life; the integration of National Socialist ideology with Christian theology; the absorption of church youth into the Hitler youth movement; and the application of the Aryan Clause to the **church.** The Confessing Church and its leaders, including Martin Niemöller and Dietrich Bonhoeffer, tried to assert the freedom of the church based on God's Word. The objections of the Confessing Church movement are contained in its **Theological Declaration of Barmen**, largely drafted by **Karl Barth.** Many of the Confessing Church leaders were removed from their positions, imprisoned, or killed. Pastors were harassed by the Gestapo and pressured to sign an oath of allegiance to Hitler and to cooperate with the government-controlled church committees. The witness of the church, although often an embarrassment to the Reich government, was hindered by internal divisions and by the generally nationalistic and conservative outlook of its pastors.

CONFESSIONS. The expression of Christian beliefs in the form of theological affirmations. Reformed communities, from the early decades of their existence in the 16th century, produced many confessional documents. The profusion and variety of these documents have given the Reformed tradition a great range of expression. Several themes recur in these documents, including the **sovereignty of God**, God's **election** (choosing) for service and **salvation**, the convenantal nature of the **church**, stewardship, human sinfulness, engagement with the world, and obedience to the **Word of God.** The Reformed churches view all confessional documents, regardless of their content, as subordinate to **scripture.** Prominent among earlier Reformed confessional documents are **Huldrych Zwingli's** Sixty-Seven Articles (1523); the Theses of Berne (1528); the First Confession of Basel (1534); the First and Second Helvetic Confessions (1536; 1566); the Confession and Consensus of Geneva (1537; 1552); the Gallican Confession (1559); the Belgic Confession (1561); the Zurich **Consensus Tigurinus** (1549); Tetrapolitan Confession (1530); **Heidelberg Catechism** (1563); Scots Confession (1560); Irish Articles (1615); Canons of Dort (1619); **Westminster Confession** (1647); and the Helvetic Consensus Formula (1675). The 20th century has produced a number of new confessions that complement and clarify the earlier confessions but do not displace them. Many of these new confessions have been written by Reformed churches in **Africa** and **Asia.** The following are examples of new confessions: Statement of Faith (1958) of the Church of Jesus Christ in **Madagascar**; Constitution (1965) of the United Church of **Zambia**; Theological Declaration (1979) of the

Broederkring of the Dutch Reformed Church in **South Africa**; Confession of Faith (1954) of the United Church of Christ of **Japan**; New Confession (1972) of the Presbyterian Church in the Republic of **Korea**; and the Confession of Faith (1979) of the Presbyterian Church of **Taiwan**.

CONFIRMATION. A rite practiced in Reformed churches that allows young people to claim the promises made on their behalf by their parents when they were baptized as infants. Through the rite, recipients become full members of the **church**; their personal "confirmation" of baptismal vows constitutes a profession of **faith** in Jesus Christ as Lord and Savior. Traditionally, confirmation is initiated when children reach an "age of accountability" (often 12 years of age) and takes place at the end of a period of theological instruction—often catechetical in nature. Confirmation enables a person to be admitted to the **sacrament** of the **Lord's Supper.** This pattern in Reformed churches arose from the practice of **John Calvin** and **Martin Bucer** and was developed in the Church of Scotland.

Current practice in some Reformed churches in which baptized children are admitted to the Lord's Supper has led to a reexamination of confirmation in relation to both the sacraments of **baptism** and the Lord's Supper. Here elements of Christian identity, instruction, personal piety, and vocational discernment play a role, with some advocating that confirmation not be tied to a certain age but be linked to an individual's personal desire to profess faith in Jesus Christ.

CONGO. *See* CENTRAL AFRICA

CONGREGATIONALISM. *See* CHURCH GOVERNMENT

CONSENSUS TIGURINUS (1549). An agreement between **John Calvin** and **Heinrich Bullinger** on the **Lord's Supper.** The agreement was the result of an exchange of correspondence between Calvin and Bullinger, beginning in 1546. The two reformers met in Zurich in 1549 and prepared 26 articles on the **sacraments.** Published in 1551, the consensus was adopted by the Reformed churches in Zurich, Geneva, Basel, Neuchatel, and other European cities. The agreement is the basis for the Reformed understanding of the Lord's Supper as a spiritual partaking in which the soul of the believer is lifted up and united with Christ in a spiritual communion.

CONTEXTUALIZATION. The process by which the Christian **faith** is translated into a particular cultural context so that authentic Christian witness takes place in that culture. The term "contextualization" emerged in the 1970s under the aegis of the Theological Education Fund of the **World Council of Churches**, which placed emphasis on the preparation of church leadership in diverse cultural contexts. Western churches have long presented an absolute cultural form of Christianity, which was suprahistorical, objective, and preceded its missional translation. In the 20th century this ethnocentric view has gradually diminished with an increasing awareness by the Western churches that the very nature of faith is contextual: the gospel is known only in cultural forms and is communicated interculturally. Contemporary Reformed missiology seeks to integrate the contextual nature of the church's **mission** with the transcendent character of the gospel as God's self-disclosure, which is translatable into every culture but not reducible to any culture as normative.

CONVERSION. The transformation of human life by the personal experience of God's forgiving love and **grace.** Biblically understood, conversion means "turning" to a new direction on the basis of one's encounter with **God.** The act or process of conversion includes repentance for **sin,** the recognition and appropriation of God's grace in Jesus Christ, and the desire to live the "new life" of discipleship in Christ by the power of the **Holy Spirit.** Conversion is initiated by God's gracious action and is the outward expression of the inward regeneration or **justification** of the believer. The conversion experience has been a subject of controversy in the Reformed churches. The Calvinist/Arminian controversy turns in part on issues of **free will** and whether or not human beings are able to respond on their own to God's grace. In New England **Puritanism**, the **Half-Way Covenant** was enacted to address the question of whether the **church** should be composed only of those who have had a definite conversion experience or whether it should also include those who have not yet had this experience. Whether conversion was a single act or a gradual process (e.g., **Horace Bushnell**) was also debated. Reformed theology recognizes that conversion in some form ultimately occurs for every Christian; it also acknowledges both the variety and uniqueness of the conversion experience.

COOK ISLANDS. *See* PACIFIC OCEAN ISLANDS

COPTIC EVANGELICAL ORGANIZATION FOR SOCIAL SERVICES. Egyptian social service organization begun by the Coptic Evangelical Church. Begun as a literacy program based on the method of **Frank Laubach**, the organization grew into a rural and urban development agency with a staff of 400 people. The agency operates social programs intended to aid the poorest members of Egyptian society.

COSTA RICA. *See* MESOAMERICA

COTTON, JOHN (1585–1652). American Puritan minister and theologian. Born in Derby, Cotton graduated from Cambridge and was ordained in 1610. He served as vicar of Boston, Lincolnshire (1612–1633) before being ejected as a **Nonconformist** and emigrating to the Massachusetts Bay Colony, where he became a pastor in Boston (1633–1652). There he became a dominating theological figure known for his intense struggles with Roger Williams and **Anne Hutchinson**. Both Williams and Hutchinson were banished from the colony. Cotton was a convinced Calvinist who stressed the necessity for a **conversion** experience as evidence of God's **grace** in one's life. He advocated a congregational church polity in his *The Way of the Churches of Christ in New England* (1645) and *The Way of Congregational Churches Cleared* (1648). Cotton also helped construct the **Cambridge Platform.**

COUNTESS OF HUNTINGDON. *See* HUNTINGDON, SELINA HASTINGS

COVENANT. A binding relationship between **God** and humanity that brings God's gracious promise of blessing to the human **community** and evokes its response of faith. Covenant is a prominent theme in the Reformed theology developed by Johannes Cocceius and Hermann Witsius in the 17th century. It is also a prominent feature of the **Westminster Confession** (chaps. 7, 19) and other Reformed confessional documents. Some Reformed theologians taught that God first made a covenant of works that promised eternal life on the condition of Adam's obedience. This view is generally seen as lacking scriptural support. God's covenant of **grace** through Abraham is the means by which God interacts with a people through history, particularly the people of Israel. The culmination of God's covenantal purposes is to bring redemption and forgiveness in Jesus Christ. **John Calvin** and other Reformed theologians stress the essential unity of the Old and New Covenants of **scripture**, seeing the promise of a new covenant made to Jeremiah as fulfilled in Christ (Jer. 31:31–34). The Reformed tradition also understands infant **baptism** as an extension of God's covenant to believers and their children. The commitment of all life to God in Christ and participation in the **church** as the covenant community have also been marks of the Reformed tradition. *See also* Federal Theology

COVENANTERS. Scottish Presbyterians who signed public covenants during the 17th century. The most important covenants are the National

Covenant of 1638 and the Solemn League and Covenant of 1643. The purpose of these covenants was to pledge allegiance to the tenets of the Reformation and to the king as defender of Reformed principles. Many national leaders and citizens signed the covenants, including Charles II at his coronation in 1651. By 1660, though, the king broke his pledge and began to force an episcopal system on **Scotland.** Many Covenanters were imprisoned, killed, or forced to flee to the **Netherlands** or **America.** In 1690, William III restored **Presbyterianism** to Scotland, but a minority of Covenanters continued a separate existence as the Reformed Presbyterian Church. In addition to present-day descendants in Scotland and **Ireland**, the Covenanter tradition has established itself in America and **Australia.**

COWPER, WILLIAM (1731–1800). English poet. Born in Berkhampstead, Hertfordshire, **England**, Cowper attended Westminster School in London, studied law, and was admitted to the bar (1754). Cowper suffered throughout his life from mental illness and depression, and was hospitalized for 18 months. He went to live with the family of Morley Unwin, a Calvinist minister, and began writing religious poetry, publishing *Olney Hymns* (1779) with revivalist leader John Newton. His hymns, "God Moves in a Mysterious Way" and "Oh! For a Closer Walk with God," were widely used in Protestant churches. His most famous poems, "Hope," "The Progress of Error," and "The Task" (1785) contain elements of Calvinist theology and ethics. Cowper's works have been published in 15 volumes (1835–1837), and as *The Letters and Prose Writings* (2 vols., 1979–1980).

CRANMER, THOMAS (1489–1556). English reformer, theologian, and Archbishop of Canterbury. Born in Nottingham, Cranmer was educated at Cambridge, where he was exposed to humanist and Lutheran ideas. In 1529 Henry VIII sent Cranmer to Europe to inquire about his divorce from Catherine of Aragon, and in 1532 appointed Cranmer archbishop of Canterbury. Cranmer used this position to carry out gradual reforms in the Church of England, including the use of the English Bible. With the accession of Edward VI in 1547, sweeping changes took place in church **worship** and doctrine. A liturgical scholar, Cranmer produced the **Book of Common Prayer** (1549; 2d ed. 1552) and wrote *A Defence of the True and Catholic Doctrine of the Sacrament* (1550). He also had a hand in drafting the Forty-Two Articles of Religion, later reduced to **Thirty-Nine Articles** under Elizabeth I. The prayer book became the basis of Reformed worship in the Church of England, and the Thirty-Nine Articles incorporated Protestant doctrines of church **authority, scripture,**

justification, and the **sacraments.** When Mary ascended to the throne and temporarily reinstated Catholicism, Cranmer was arrested, imprisoned, and burned at the stake in Oxford.

CREATION. God's bringing into being of all that exists. The ultimate purpose of creation is to bring glory to **God.** The creation is a result of God's free act carried out through the eternal Word. Reformed theology links the identity of God the Creator with God the Redeemer, viewing creation as an action of the triune God and emphasizing God's ongoing involvement with the created order through **providence**—God's sustaining guidance of the creation. The Reformed tradition also affirms the goodness of creation and emphasizes human responsibility to use the gift of creation in ways that honor God. The exploitation and destruction of the creation is a powerful expression of the pervasiveness and perversity of human **sin.** The Reformed tradition encourages the exploration of the created order with the purpose of understanding its workings through scientific inquiry. Since God is the Lord of all creation, all aspects of human life and endeavor are proper arenas for Christian study and involvement.

CREEDS. *See* CONFESSIONS

CRESPIN, JEAN (ca. 1520–1572). French Protestant author and printer. Born in Arras, **France**, Crespin worked as a lawyer in Paris. After returning home to Arras, he was banished under suspicion of having Reformed tendencies. He moved to Strasbourg (1545) and later to Geneva (1548), where he became a citizen (1555). In Geneva he established a printing office where he issued his *Histoire des Martyrs (Book of Martyrs),* which provided narratives of Protestant martyrs beginning with John Huss. The first edition was published in 1554. As the years passed, Crespin added accounts of English martyrs from John Foxe's *Acts and Monuments* as well as other stories. The last edition published in his lifetime (1570) included seven volumes. After Crespin's death from plague in 1572, his son-in-law Jean Vignon continued the printing office while a minister, Simon Goulard, completed the *Book of Martyrs* in eight volumes. The work provided inspiration for many **Huguenot** martyrs, ranking behind only the Bible and the Psalter as the most widely read and influential publication.

CROATIA. *See* CENTRAL AND EASTERN EUROPE

CROMWELL, OLIVER (1599–1658). English soldier and political leader, the Lord Protector. Cromwell was born in Huntingdon and entered Sidney Sussex College, Cambridge, in 1616. He was an avid Bible reader who embraced a Calvinistic **faith.** In 1628 he was elected to Parliament by his hometown and in 1640 he represented Cambridge. During the Long Parliament, Cromwell was a vigorous advocate for the Puritan Party. He viewed the Civil War (1642) as a religious struggle and led the parliamentary forces in battle, winning victories at Marston Morr (1644) and Naseby (1645). After defeating the Scots at Preston (1648), Cromwell helped to overthrow the monarchy, signing the execution order of Charles I. In December 1653 Cromwell became Lord Protector, and he ruled the Commonwealth of England, Scotland, and Ireland until 1658. In a series of constitutional experiments he attempted to reform the government by developing a constitutional model. His Puritan **Calvinism** led him to oppose both the episcopacy of the established church and **Presbyterianism**, but he was also a strong advocate of religious toleration. After his death the English monarchy was restored.

CUBA. *See* CARIBBEAN

CULTURE AND THEOLOGY. The interaction between the Christian gospel and the learned behaviors of a society transmitted through its language, history, art, religion, morals, customs, and social and legal structures. Cultural identity is not synonymous with ethnic identity but may include elements of **ethnicity.** In the broadest sense, culture has to do with the way humans structure their existence in the world, shaping and developing the natural **environment**, creating structures of corporate life, relationships, communication, and continuity. In Reformed thought, this human activity takes place under the **providence of God**, who preserves **creation** and, through the **Holy Spirit**, makes known the divine purpose. Cultural diversity is a witness to the manifold nature of God and God's wondrous providence. The structures of society, human **labor** and **vocation**, and creative and artistic expression are all avenues of divine **grace** and power. While the diversity and dynamism of cultural pluralism challenges any theology which claims to be normative for all cultures, Reformed theology emphasizes the translatability of the gospel into all cultures; for the Christian gospel, no culture is normative but all cultures are potential bearers of the witness to God's love. *See also* Revelation; Contextualization; Inculturation

CZECH REPUBLIC. *See* CENTRAL AND EASTERN EUROPE

CZECHOSLOVAKIA. *See* CENTRAL AND EASTERN EUROPE

- D -

DABNEY, ROBERT LEWIS (1820–1898). American Presbyterian theologian and educator. Born in Louisa County, Virginia, Dabney was educated at Hampden-Sydney College (1836–1837), the University of Virginia (1842), and **Union Theological Seminary** in Virginia (1846). He was pastor of Tinkling Spring Church (1847–1853) and was a schoolteacher before serving as professor of church history and polity at Union Seminary (1859–1883). Failing health forced him to move to Texas, where he was professor of philosophy at the University of Texas (1883–1894), and one of the founders and a faculty member of Austin Presbyterian Theological Seminary (1884–1895). During the U.S. Civil War, Dabney was a strong supporter of the South and served as a chaplain (1861) in the Confederate army and as one of Stonewall Jackson's officers (1862). His views appeared in *A Defense of Virginia, and through Her of the South* (1867). Dabney's theology has affinities with Old School **Calvinism** and was influenced by Scottish Common Sense philosophy. His major works include *Systematic and Polemic Theology* (1871) and *Discussions* (4 vols., 1890–1897).

DA CONCEIÇÃO, JOSÉ MANOEL (1822–1873). Brazilian Presbyterian minister and evangelist. Born in São Pãulo, da Conceição was raised by his great uncle, a Catholic priest, after the death of his mother. He graduated from a Catholic seminary in São Pãulo in 1842, was ordained in 1845, and served as a priest in various parishes for 18 years. One of his first parish assignments put him into contact with English, German, and Danish Protestant immigrants. Later a journalist in São Pãulo gave him Protestant literature in German. As a result of these contacts and the guidance of Presbyterian missionary Alexander Blackford, Protestant ideas began to appear in his pastoral messages. In 1864 he professed **evangelical faith**, was ordained as the first Brazilian pastor by the Presbytery of Rio de Janeiro (1865), and went on to found churches in Brotas, Lorena, Sorocaba, and Borda da Mata. His defection from the Roman Catholic Church caused a great controversy. The events surrounding his departure, including his excommunication by the bishop of São Pãulo in 1867, were widely publicized and raised issues of religious freedom in worship, civil marriage, and the status of Protestant immigrants. The controversy that followed was sometimes violent. Da Conceição was known as the "Protestant St. Francis," traveling on foot, living simply, giving away his money to the poor, dispensing simple medicines, and evangelizing. In his sensitivity to the spiritual dimension of religious faith, he anticipated the later emergence of Brazilian charismatic Pentecostalism.

DA COSTA, ISAÄC (1798–1860). Dutch writer, poet, and leader of the Calvinist **Réveil**, a movement engaged in literary, political, and religious **revival.** Da Costa was born in Amsterdam and raised in a wealthy Portuguese-Jewish family. Through the witness of influential Dutch poet Willem Bilderdijk he converted to Christianity. Da Costa was editor of the *Nederlandsche Stemmen* from 1834 to 1840. He wrote poetry in both Latin and Dutch and developed a conservative religious and political outlook. Da Costa's works include *Objections to the Spirit of the Age* (1823), *Israel and the Gentiles* (1850), and *The Four Witnesses* (1851). He also prepared a biography of Bilderdijk and published an edition of his poems in 15 volumes. Da Costa's works were collected and published between 1861 and 1863.

DAGHER, IBRAHIM MILHAM (1901–1983). Lebanese pastor and executive secretary of the National Evangelical Synod of Syria and Lebanon. Born in Lebanon, Dagher attended Gerard Institute in Sidon, the Near East School of Theology, and Beirut University. He served churches in south Lebanon for 30 years (1927–1957), most notably in Hasbaya and in the Marjayoun Cooperative Parish. He was elected executive secretary of the synod (1958) and president of the Supreme Council (1965), a body that acts on behalf of the entire Lebanese Protestant community. Dagher managed the transition when American and European mission agencies withdrew from the region during the 1950s and 1960s, transferring their property and work to the Evangelical Synod. These transfers almost doubled the size of the synod. Dagher was head of the synod for 25 years, during which he presided over the church with a steady hand, especially during the years of warfare in Lebanon (1975–1991).

DAILLÉ (DALLAEUS), JEAN (1594–1670). French Protestant minister and theologian. Born at Châtellerault (in Poitou) to Protestant parents, Daillé was educated at Poitiers and at the Protestant university at Saumur (from 1612), where he studied philosophy and theology. At the same time he became tutor to the two grandsons of **Huguenot** leader **Philippe de Mornay.** Daillé was ordained in 1623 and became private chaplain to Mornay in lower Poitou. He was pastor at Saumur (1625) and Charenton (1626–1670), both centers of Reformed worship in Paris. Known as a gifted orator, apologist, and theologian, Daillé was the greatest Huguenot scholar after **John Calvin.** He was **moderator** of the last Huguenot national synod (1659) before the **Edict of Nantes** was revoked. He is famous for rejecting the **authority** of the early church fathers, arguing that Christian theology derives from **scripture** alone. His works include *Of the Use of the Fathers* (1631), *An Apology for the Reformed Churches* (1663), and 20 volumes of sermons, including sermons on Philippians and Colossians.

D'ALBRET, JEANNE (1528–1572). Queen of Navarre and leader of the French Reformed churches. The daughter of Henri d'Albret and the niece of Francis I, she married Antoine de Bourbon in 1548 and left her titles to her son, Henry IV of Navarre, later king of **France** and promulgator of the **Edict of Nantes.** At the death of her father in 1555, d'Albret succeeded to the throne of Navarre and Béarn, where she reigned with her husband until his death in 1562. Between 1560 and 1572, d'Albret exercised leadership in both the **Huguenot** party and the Calvinist movement, two overlapping but not identical movements. She helped develop the Calvinist religious establishment in Béarn and modeled church reorganization after **Calvin's** Geneva. Under her influence, the Reformed churches supported **education** and relief for the poor.

DALE, ROBERT WILLIAM (1829–1895). English Congregationalist minister and theologian. Born in London and educated at Spring Hill College, Birmingham, Dale came from a background of Nonconformity. He served as copastor (1853–1859) and pastor of Carr's Lane Chapel in Birmingham. There he exerted a powerful influence on the civic, social, religious and educational life of the city. In 1886 Dale helped establish Mansfield College, Oxford, to train Congregational ministers. He was the first president of the International Congregational Council (1891) and supported the revival meetings of D. L. Moody. Between 1871 and 1886 he published *The Congregationalist,* a monthly journal. In his major theological work, *The Atonement* (1875), Dale proposed an ethical rather than a legal defense of the penal substitutionary view and was critical of the views of Benjamin Jowett and **Horace Bushnell.** Among his other books are *A Manual of Congregational Principles* (1884), lectures on *Preaching* (1877), *Ephesians* (1882) and a *History of English Congregationalism* (1907), completed by his son.

DALIT THEOLOGY. A form of **liberation theology** unique to **India.** "Dalit" is the word for contemporary Indian "untouchables," people in the lowest castes in Indian society. The movement grew out of protest against the oppressive **caste** structure in India. The various Dalit groups hold Hinduism responsible for imposing a rigid, oppressive social system. As part of the rejection of Hinduism and the caste system, many Dalits have converted to Christianity, which provides an identity outside the caste system. However, many of these Christian Dalits have not been accepted in the mainline churches, where caste discrimination is also present. Dalit theology has emerged because of this "double alienation" (Christian Dalits do not receive government benefits extended to Hindu Dalits, nor are they fully welcomed in the Christian community). A Christian Dalit liberation movement was founded in 1985. Dalit theology emphasizes the sufferings, aspirations, and hopes of the people, and the desire for justice and freedom for Dalit Christians. In recent years many Christian Dalits have moved from mainline churches into Pentecostal groups.

DANCE AND DRAMA. Christian **tradition** has developed and preserved elements of movement and gesture, rhythm, and dramatic action, as ways to enact the story of **faith** and worship **God.** The liturgical action of Eastern Orthodox, Roman Catholic, and Anglican worship contain elements of dance and drama. Reformed worship, by contrast, has concentrated on the speaking and hearing of the Word, and has tended to be physically passive. Ecumenical interaction has led to a reexamination of Reformed worship and a new openness to many aspects of liturgical action, including the use of liturgical dance and drama. The worldwide expansion of the Reformed churches has also led to the introduction of non-Western forms of dance and drama that are enriching the worship life of the churches.

DAVIES, SAMUEL (1723–1761). American Presbyterian minister who led the southern phase of the **Great Awakening** and was the founder of southern **Presbyterianism.** Davies was educated in Samuel Blair's Foggs School and was ordained a Presbyterian evangelist in 1747. He was sent to preach to Presbyterian converts of the Great Awakening in Hanover County, Virginia, where he organized the first southern **presbytery** in 1755. In 1753 he accompanied Gilbert Tennent to the **British Isles**, where he raised £3,000, primarily from **Scotland**, for the College of New Jersey, now Princeton University. He also persuaded the king to grant legal status to **Dissenters** in Virginia. In 1759 Davies became president of the College of New Jersey, where he established high academic standards.

DAY, LAL BEHARI (1824–1894). Presbyterian minister in **India.** Raised a Hindu, Day enrolled in a mission school in Calcutta established by **Alexander Duff.** He converted to Christianity at the age of 19 under the influence of Duff and Thomas Smith. In 1846 he was appointed catechist; following theological study he was licensed to preach by the Free Church Presbytery (1851) and was ordained (1855). Day was a strong advocate of indigenous church leadership, challenging the European missionary control of the Indian church. He headed the mission in Culna and became pastor of the Free Church Native Congregation in Calcutta, before entering the Government Educational Service. He wrote many popular articles, especially about Bengali life and culture.

DE MORNAY, PHILIPPE. *See* MORNAY, PHILIPPE DE

DEACONS. Ordained officers in Reformed churches charged with ministering to those in need. The Reformed churches have recognized four ordained offices: pastor, teacher, **elder**, and deacon. The office of deacon is a permanent office. The forms of the office have varied widely. In some Reformed denominations deacons are responsible for the care of church property as well as the care of the congregation. Those who occupy the office are called to service *(diakonia)* and love of neighbor *(Inst.* 4.4.1ff.). The office of deacon provides a corporate structure for the church's benevolent activities. Diaconal ministries include service to both church members and to those outside the institutional church. Deacons attend to the needs of the sick, suffering, and poor, and they concern themselves with issues of social justice, peace, and other dimensions of social welfare. Reformed deacons have worked in cooperation with governmental structures to carry out specific ministries, but the spiritual character and benevolent work of the office is independent of these structures.

DEATH. The cessation of physical life. The Reformed tradition teaches that the appearance of death in the created order is the result of **sin** (Rom. 3:23) and that spiritual death, which is sin's consequence, leads to physical death (**Westminster Confession**, chap. 6). Deliverance is accomplished by Jesus Christ, who brings life eternal and defeats the power of sin and death through his own death and **resurrection** (1 Cor. 15). Reformed theology emphasizes the victory of Christ as God's final word and triumph so that the finality of physical death does not mean the ultimate end of existence. As **John Calvin** wrote, death "has been destroyed in such a way as to be no longer fatal for believers, but not in such a way as to cause them no trouble" *(Comm. on 1 Cor. 15:26).* The Christian hope and assurance of eternal life is expressed in the conviction that "in life and in death we belong to God" (**Brief Statement of Faith**, line 1).

DECLARATORY ACTS. Scottish legislative acts passed by the United Presbyterian Church in 1879 and the Free Church of Scotland in 1892 that relaxed the church's subscription to the **Westminster Confession.** The purpose of these acts was to allow liberty of conscience for those who disagreed with the Confession on particular matters of doctrine. While the Act of 1879 was passed unanimously in the United Presbyterian Church, the Act of 1892 evoked protest and controversy in the Free Church of Scotland. Passage of the act over strong opposition led to the secession of the Free Presbyterian Church, which continued strict adherence to the Confession. The Church of Scotland passed a similar act in 1910. The acts became part of the constitution of the reunited Church of Scotland in 1929.

DENMARK. *See* NORTHERN EUROPE

DENNEY, JAMES (1856–1917). Scottish theologian and New Testament scholar. Denney was born into a Reformed Presbyterian family in Paisley and was educated at the University of Glasgow and the Free Church College, Glasgow. He was ordained in 1886 and served the East Free Church in Broughty Ferry, near Dundee, from 1886 to 1897. In 1897 he became professor of systematic theology at the Free Church College, Glasgow, and later served as professor of New Testament (1900) and principal (1915). Denney's theology centered on Christ. "Christ is the whole of Christianity—Christ crucified and risen," he wrote. His emphasis was on Christ being known through what he had done rather than on speculative **Christology.** Denney also wrote: "I haven't the faintest interest in any theology which doesn't help us to evangelize." Denney's works include commentaries on *Thessalonians* (1892), *II Corinthians* (1894), and *Romans* (1900). He also wrote several theological works, including *Studies in Theology* (1894), *The Death of Christ* (1902), *Jesus and the Gospel* (1908), *The Way Everlasting* (1911), and a posthumously published work, *The Christian Doctrine of Reconciliation* (1917).

DE VALOIS, JOHN JAMES (1892–1988). American missionary in **India** with the Reformed Church in America. Following his education at Iowa State College and Moody Bible Institute, De Valois went to India as an agricultural missionary. An active layperson in the Church of South India, he pioneered in agricultural **education** and the improvement of poultry, livestock, and field crops. In 1920 he founded the Agricultural Institute at Katpadi, South India, to address the economic needs of rural people. He directed the institute for 40 years, leading it through initial public resistance to success and national recognition. The institute, when fully developed, included a 330-acre demonstration farm, elementary and continuing education programs, poultry extension activities, the World Neighbors Program recruiting workers for rural mission, a camp and conference **ministry**, and rural church development.

DE WORM, HENRI THEOPHILE (1893–1964). Belgian Reformed minister and missionary in the Belgian **Congo.** Born in Nukerke in eastern Flanders, De Worm served at the Belgian Front during World War I. Following the war he entered the Institute of Missions at Oegstgeest in the **Netherlands.** He received his license in theology from the Faculté de Montpellier (1924) and pursued studies at the School of Theology in Edinburgh (1925). Upon returning to Belgium De Worm organized evangelistic and religious meetings. In 1928 he revolutionized his church by giving **women** and communicants aged 21 and older the right to vote in church assemblies. He conducted tent **evangelism** campaigns and began a periodical, *Esprit et Vie.* In 1958 he became a missionary in Katanga, Belgian Congo, and at age 65 secretary-general of the Protestant Church of Katanga, affiliated with the Belgian synod. He returned to **Belgium** in 1964 and died at Oostduinkerke.

DIALECTICAL THEOLOGY. Theological perspective developed in the early 1920s by **Karl Barth, Emil Brunner**, and others, who criticized the prevailing liberal theology. These dialectical theologians were part of a movement called **neoorthodoxy.** They emphasized a "theology of the Word," considered **God** to be "wholly other" than humanity, and stressed the rupture of the human/divine relationship due to **sin.** A gulf exists between creature and Creator caused by human sin; this distance can only be overcome through divine self-revelation. In Jesus Christ, God has been fully self-disclosed. God stands in a dialectical relationship with humanity as judge yet redeemer, as crucified yet risen, as transcendent yet immanent, as one hidden yet revealed, as speaking no and yes. According to these theologians, all theologizing must be dialectical; it must correlate every position and its negation. Dialectical theology sought to recover the "Godness of God" at a time when many theologians emphasized human continuity with the divine. Eventually dialectical theologians took separate theological paths, paving the way for future developments in theology.

DIÉTRICH, SUZANNE DE (1891–1981). French Protestant lay leader in the ecumenical Student Christian Movement. Born in Niederbronn, **France**, Diétrich graduated from the University of Lausanne (1913) and embarked on a career with the World Student Christian Federation

(WSCF) and the World Young Woman's Christian Association (YWCA). She participated in many ecumenical conferences and taught the Bible to student groups. From 1946 to 1954 Diétrich was associate director of the Ecumenical Institute in Bossey, **Switzerland.** As a result of her ecumenical work in France and Switzerland, and extensive travels throughout the world, she gained a wide following. Her books include *God's Unfolding Purpose: A Guide to the Study of the Bible* (1960).

DISCIPLINE, BOOKS OF. The two foundational documents that organized the Reformed churches in **Scotland.** The First Book of Discipline, influenced by **John Knox** and modeled after **John Calvin's** Genevan polity, was published in 1560. The book recognized six offices within the congregation: minister, teacher, **elder**, **deacon**, superintendent, and reader. The book also organized the Reformed churches into congregational governing bodies called "sessions," regional bodies called "synods," and a churchwide body called an "assembly." The Second Book of Discipline, influenced by **Andrew Melville**, was published in 1578. Known for its discussion of the relations between **church and state**, the book strengthened the role of the church's governing bodies and offices including, on the congregational level, the office of ruling elder. Although Presbyterian organizational life was not fully developed in these two works alone, the Books of Discipline laid the foundation for Presbyterian **church government.**

DISCIPLINE, CHURCH. The spiritual oversight of churches and their members. Church discipline may include elements of both belief and practice. Three important models of **church discipline** are found in the Reformed tradition. **Huldrych Zwingli** and **Heinrich Bullinger** implemented a theory of church discipline in Zurich that placed discipline and excommunication in the hands of the civil government. The civil magistrate ruled over both church and society. **John Oecolampadius, Martin Bucer**, and **John Calvin** developed the view that church discipline and excommunication should be carried out by courts of church **elders** (presbyters) and thus be separate from the civil structures. Jean Morély proposed a third approach for the French Reformed Church in 1562. He believed that church discipline should be imposed by the local congregation. Reformed churches generally adopted either the presbyterial or congregational form, which are compatible with the modern separation of **church and state** and with pluralistic societies. Church discipline within Reformed churches is carried out in widely varying degrees, from strict oversight to permissiveness.

DISPENSATIONALISM. An interpretation of the Bible that understands history in terms of successive dispensational epochs ordained by **God.** John Nelson Darby (1800–1882) of the English Plymouth Brethren Church was largely responsible for this interpretative scheme. Dispensationalism, which includes complex and literal interpretations of apocalyptic and prophetic biblical texts, teaches that God has ordained different methods of **salvation** in each of seven distinct dispensational periods. Dispensationalism, or "Darbyism," was popularized in 19th-century America through annual biblical and prophetic conferences. Early dispensational leaders were drawn from Presbyterian and Baptist denominations. The *Scofield Reference Bible* (1909) also spread the method widely. In 1944 the General Assembly of the Presbyterian Church in the United States declared dispensationalism to be "out of accord" with Reformed confessional standards. The major scholarly voice of dispensationalism since 1933 has been the journal *Bibliotheca Sacra.*

DISSENTER. *See* NONCONFORMIST

DIVORCE. *See* MARRIAGE, THEOLOGY OF

DOCTRINE. *See* THEOLOGICAL METHOD

DODD, CHARLES H. (1884–1973). British Congregationalist minister and New Testament scholar. Dodd was born in Wrexham, North **Wales**, and graduated from the University of Oxford in 1906. He was ordained in the Congregational church in 1912 and served in the pastorate for three years. Dodd was then appointed lecturer (1915–1918) and professor (1919–1930) of New Testament at Mansfield College, Oxford. He served as professor of **biblical criticism** and exegesis at Manchester University (1930–1935) and in 1935 went to Cambridge, where he remained until 1949. He became general director of the translation of the New English Bible in 1970. Dodd was the dominant figure in British New Testament scholarship during the middle decades of the 20th century. He is known for his view of the teachings of Jesus described as "realized **eschatology**" (*Parables of the Kingdom,* 1935). According to this view, Jesus taught that the future had become the present in himself and that the kingdom was already present. Dodd also identified an outline of early Christian preaching *(kerygma)* common to all apostolic writings (*Apostolic Preaching and Its Development,* 1936). His other works include *The Authority of the Bible* (1928), *The Bible and the Greeks* (1935), *History and the Gospel* (1938), *According to the Scriptures* (1952), *The Interpretation* *of the Fourth Gospel* (1953), as well as commentaries on Romans (1932) and the Johannine epistles (1946).

DODDRIDGE, PHILIP (1702–1751). English **Nonconformist** minister, author, and hymn writer. Doddridge was born in London and educated at Kibworth Academy. He was minister of Kibworth from 1723 to 1729 when he began his Independent/Congregational chapel in Northampton (1729–1751). He also organized an academy for training ministerial students. Friends with John Wesley and Countess Selina Hastings of **Huntingdon,** Doddridge embraced a modified Puritan theology similar to that of **Richard Baxter.** He encouraged freedom of inquiry and sought unity among the various Nonconformists. Doddridge's work, *The Rise and Progress of Religion in the Human Soul* (1745), is considered a spiritual classic. He wrote more than 400 hymns, all published after his death. Among these are "Great God, We Sing That Mighty Hand," "Hark, the Glad Sound!" "O God of Bethel, by Whose Hand," and "O Happy Day, That Fixed My Choice."

DOGMA AND DOCTRINE. The First Indian Theological Conference (1942) distinguished between the two terms. Dogma is the central core of **faith**, the **Word of God**; doctrine is the relative element, the expression, interpretation, and application necessary to present the gospel in any given situation.

DON, ALEXANDER (1857–1934). New Zealand Presbyterian missionary. Don began his service in 1879 as a missionary to Chinese immigrants who had come to New Zealand during the gold rush of the early 1860s. He was sent to Canton, **China**, and there learned a rudimentary Chinese. He married in 1883 and spent the next 30 years traveling in the rugged mountainous region of central Otago, New Zealand. Often traveling by foot from one isolated Chinese encampment to the next, Don described his travels in *Memories of the Golden Road* (1936). Although he made few converts, the Chinese people trusted Don and often gave him messages and money to give to relatives in China. These communications led to Don's founding of the Canton Villages Mission (1898), north of Guangzhou City. He also organized Chinese congregations in Dunedin and Auckland, although the congregations remained small. In 1907 he became **moderator** of the General Assembly of the Presbyterian Church of New Zealand, and from 1914 to 1923 he served as foreign mission secretary. During the time of Don's ministry the Chinese were treated with contempt, regarded by many as diseased, as pagans, and as a blot on a white New Zealand. Initially Don shared many of these racist views, but as he grew older his attitude changed. His work enabled the Presbyterian Church to play an important role in changing the attitude of the nation.

DOOYEWEERD, HERMAN (1894–1977). Dutch law professor and Christian philosopher. Dooyeweerd was born in Amsterdam and graduated from the **Free University.** From 1922 to 1926 he was assistant director of the Abraham Kuyper Institute, The Hague. He was then appointed professor of the philosophy of law at the Free University, where he served from 1926 to 1965. In 1935 he founded an international Christian philosophical movement with D. H. T. Vollenhoven, his brother-in-law. Dooyeweerd also edited the movement's journal, *Philosophia Reformata* (1936–1976), and was active in the Association for Christian Philosophy. Dooyeweerd's philosophy was summarized in *De Wijsbegeerte der Wetsidee* (*The Philosophy of the Law-Idea,* 1935–1936), published in a four-volume English edition as *A New Critique of Theoretical Thought* (1953–1958; rpt. 1983). In this work Dooyeweerd rejected the absolutizing of human **reason** and criticized the notion of autonomous theoretical thought. He sought to develop a Christian philosophy that could maintain a unified worldview. Dooyeweerd's work contains a basic ontology and epistemology from which he addresses many of the basic problems in philosophy from a Christian and Reformed perspective. His other works include *Transcendental Problems of Philosophic Thought* (1948) and *In the Twilight of Western Thought* (1960).

DOUBLE STRUGGLE. An Indonesian term used to suggest a twofold struggle with the will of **God** and with the world. The term was adopted in 1970 by the Indonesian National Council of Churches to express the desire of the churches to be faithful to God's will and to adapt to the changes of the modern world. In order to remain relevant, the churches must engage in a double struggle.

DRUMMOND, HENRY (1851–1897). Scottish evangelist, theologian, and scientist. Born at Stirling and educated at the University of Edinburgh, Drummond joined D. L. Moody and Ira Sankey in a British evangelistic campaign from 1873 to 1875. Beginning in 1877, Drummond taught natural science at the Free Church College, Glasgow, and in 1883 he published a bestseller, *Natural Law in the Spiritual World*, in which he interpreted spiritual order in terms of natural order. Later, in *Natural Law and the Ascent of Man* (1894), he sought a reconciliation of Darwinism and Christian thought, an attempt for which he was criticized. Ordained in 1884, Drummond conducted successful evangelistic meetings at several British universities and was also a recognized geologist and explorer in **Africa** (*Tropical Africa,* 1888). He traveled widely and is known for his small devotional study on 1 Corinthians 13 entitled *The Greatest Thing in the World.*

DUBOSE, HAMPDEN C. (1845–1910). American Presbyterian missionary in **China.** Born in Darlington district, South Carolina, DuBose was educated at the University of South Carolina and Columbia Theological Seminary. He became a missionary with the Presbyterian Church in the United States and worked in Hangchow and Soochow, China. DuBose conducted evangelistic work and organized the Yang Yoh Hang Church in Soochow. His *Preaching in Sinim* (1893) served as a model for the Chinese **mission.** DuBose is well-known for his anti-opium campaign, and he served as president of the Anti-Opium League in Soochow. His concern about drug trafficking prompted the U.S. State Department to send a delegation to China to investigate the opium trade. His publications include *Preaching in Sinim* (1893) and *The Dragon, Image, and Demon: or, the Three Religions of China* (1899).

DUFF, ALEXANDER (1806–1878). Scottish Presbyterian missionary in **India** and the first cross-cultural missionary of the Church of Scotland. Born near Pitlochry and educated at St. Andrews University, Duff was sent to Calcutta in 1829 by the Presbytery of St. Andrews. With encouragement from the aged **William Carey**, he founded an English school (1830) with the Bible as the basic curriculum. **Lal Behari Day** was a notable graduate. Duff's educational leadership had lasting influence on the development of Western educational institutions in India. In addition to his work in **education**, Duff was editor of the *Calcutta Review* (1845–1849) and supported the formation of the Scottish Free Church (1843), serving as its **moderator** in 1851 and 1873. After three terms of service in India, he returned to **Scotland** to become the first professor of evangelistic theology at **New College**, **Edinburgh** (1867), and to guide the cross-cultural **mission** of the Free Church. Duff's university appointment is regarded by some as the first recognition of the study of mission as an academic discipline.

DUNSTER, HENRY (1609–1659). American Congregational minister and first president of Harvard College. Dunster was born in Bury, **England**, and graduated from Cambridge. He sought to escape high church practices by fleeing to Massachusetts in 1640, where he was immediately appointed president of the new Harvard College. He not only established Harvard's curriculum after the English model but also formulated administrative policies and gave the college 100 acres of land. Dunster's reputation enhanced Harvard's standing throughout the colonial period. However, in 1654 he was dismissed from the presidency for preaching against infant **baptism** and refusing to have his own child baptized. He became a pastor in Scituate, Massachusetts, where he served until his death. Dunster's revision of **John Eliot's** *Bay Psalm Book* (1640) was widely used in New England.

DWIGHT, TIMOTHY (1752–1817). American Congregationalist minister and educator. Dwight was born in Northampton, Massachusetts, attended Yale College, and served as a chaplain during the American Revolution. He was pastor of the Congregational church in Greenfield Hill, Connecticut, from 1783 to 1795 and founded several schools. In 1795 he became president and professor of divinity at Yale and remained there for the rest of his life. He advanced the college's standards, reorganized the administration, and tripled enrollment. His preaching caused a student **revival** at the college in 1802. Dwight encouraged religious revivals and taught a moderate **Calvinism.** He revised the theology of his grandfather, **Jonathan Edwards**, rejecting such doctrines as the imputation of Adam's **sin**, natural inability, and limited **atonement.** Dwight's chapel sermons were posthumously published as *Theology, Explained and Defended* (5 vols., 1818–1819).

- E -

EAST AFRICA. The people of East Africa practice Christianity and Islam. Kenya is primarily Christian (76 percent; 40 percent Protestant), and Sudan is primarily Muslim (70 percent). There are Reformed churches in both countries, with the largest bodies located in Kenya. Small churches have been organized in Uganda since the 1980s, but there are no Reformed churches in Tanzania.

Kenya. In 1891 a group of missionaries led by James Steward of **Scotland** arrived in British East Africa and established a Christian **mission** at Kibwezi among the Kamba and Masai people. During this early period the educational and social work of Thomas and **Minnie Watson, Arthur Ruffle Barlow**, and **Marion Scott Stevenson** made an impact on the emerging church. The East Africa Scottish Mission came under the authority of the Church of Scotland in 1901 and was later transferred to Kikuyu, near Nairobi (1908). The mission began work among the Kikuyu people at Tumutumu (1908) and the Mwimbi, Chuka, and Meru people at Chogoria (1915)—all in central Kenya. In 1908 regular services were begun for white members of the Church of Scotland living in Nairobi. These services led to the organization of a congregation under H. E. Scott and the dedication of St. Andrews Church (1910).

The church in Kenya organized its governance structure in 1920. In that year the first **elders** were ordained; church sessions were formed for the congregations of Kikuyu, Tumutumu, and St. Andrews, Nairobi; and the Presbytery of British East Africa was established. In 1930 Kenyan teacher and evangelist **Wanyoike-Wa-Kamawe** was ordained to the pastoral ministry. In 1933 the **presbytery** revised its constitution, allowing it to establish additional presbyteries and to organize the presbyteries under a synod.

The Presbyterian work in Kenya was divided in 1936. In that year the Scottish missionaries and the congregation of St. Andrews became part of the Church of Scotland as the "Overseas Presbytery of Kenya." This act separated the European and African wings of the church.

The Presbyterian Church of East Africa was organized in 1943. Two church unions subsequently occurred. In 1945 congregations organized by the Gospel Missionary Society united with the church as the Presbytery of Chania. In 1956 agreement was reached on a basis of union between the Presbyterian Church of East Africa and the Overseas Presbytery of Kenya. This union resulted in the creation of the modern church. Eight moderators have served the church since 1956, including **Charles Muhoro Kareri** (1961–1967). During the 1970s, the church adopted the slogan **Jitegemea** to indicate its commitment to self-reliance in all areas of its ecclesiastical life. The church, a joint sponsor of **St. Paul's United Theological College** at Limuru, manages a Pastoral Institute for Lay Training and Education by Extension and operates hospitals at Kikuyu, Tumutumu, and Chogoria.

The Reformed Church of East Africa dates from the years 1904 to 1909, when Dutch settlers began arriving from **South Africa.** More settlers arrived after World War I, when the British offered South African Boers land as a reward for their support during the war. Most of these settlers came to the "White Highlands" on the fertile plateau in Uasin Gishu and Trans-Nzoia Districts. They occupied vast tracts of land, displacing the indigenous population.

Dutch missionary Tini Loubser founded the Bwana Loubser Mission and ministered to these farming communities between 1909 and 1935, holding services for the white settlers. The Boers built churches at Eldoret and Kitale. In 1944 additional mission personnel arrived, pastors and evangelists were educated, and the Presbytery of Eldoret, Trans-Nzoia, and Plateau was organized.

In 1961 the Reformed Mission League of the Reformed Church of the Netherlands took control of the mission and began to send its own missionaries. In 1963 the mission and the presbytery merged and a church synod was formed. The new synod was part of the Dutch Reformed Church until 1979, when it became independent. In 1992 the church issued a revised constitution, which now regulates its organizational life. The church sponsors the Plateau Bible School for pastors, and a conference and lay training center in Eldoret. Ministers are educated at the Scott Theological College in Kapsabet.

Sudan. Sudan includes two distinct and divided cultures: Arab Muslims in the north, and black Africans, including many Christians, in the south. Parts of the country have been devastated by strife and civil war that began about the time of independence in the mid-1950s. The recent strife dates from the mid-1980s. Attempts by the government since 1992 to impose Islamic law has led to persecution of the Christian minority, and social and political unrest.

The Evangelical Church in Sudan was founded by missionaries of the United Presbyterian Church in the U.S.A. The first missionary, Gabra Hanna of **Egypt**, came to work among the Coptic and **evangelical** Christians from Egypt and **Syria** who were employed by the government in Sudan. Hanna's work spread from Omdurman to neighboring cities. Congregations were organized and churches constructed at Khartoum (1902), Atbara (1912), Wed-Madani (1939), Omdurman (1948), Portsudan (1948), Gerief (1958; 1961), Khartoum North (1960), Kosti (1970), and El Obeid. The church, with headquarters in Khartoum, operates a Bible school at Gerief West and Nile Theological College in Khartoum North. The church is primarily composed of Northern Sudanese people of Egyptian origin.

The Presbyterian Church in the Sudan was founded by J. Kelly Giffen and H. T. McLaughlin, missionaries of the United Presbyterian Church of North America. Work was begun in the southern part of the country at Dolleib Hill (1902). Schools were organized and a hospital was built at Nasir (1923). By 1945 schools and mission work were established at Abwong, Pibor, Malakal, Wauglel, Obel, and elsewhere. In 1946 the Reformed Church in America also began work in the southern part of Sudan.

The Reformed churches founded by these groups were organized into the Church of Christ in the Upper Nile. The church, which became autonomous in 1956, is involved in development projects, the resettlement of refugees, and the repair and rebuilding of churches.

EAST ASIA. East Asia includes the People's Republic of China (China) and the Republic of China (Taiwan). China is officially atheist, but traditional religions and Christianity are practiced by a minority of the population. Estimates regarding the number of Christians in China vary between 6 and 20 million. In Taiwan, Buddhism, Taoism, and Christianity are major religions.

China. The first Christian communities in China were Nestorian, flourishing from the seventh to the ninth centuries before they disappeared. Four centuries later, the Mongol dynasty allowed Franciscan **mission** work, but the Franciscan presence ended when the Khan patronage ceased. Modern Roman Catholic mission began with Portuguese and Italian Jesuits in 1552.

The first Reformed mission began in China in the early 19th century, when Bible translator **Robert Morrison** was sent by the **London Missionary Society** (1807). Medical mission was pioneered by the **American Board of Commissioners for Foreign Missions**, which sent physician **Peter Parker** in 1832. The expansion of Protestantism in China was linked with the political and commercial vicissitudes of European and North American **colonialism.** Initially, foreigners and foreign mission work were permitted only in Shanghai and the other coastal and port areas in which international commerce was allowed. The Opium War (1842) and Western political influence gradually opened more of China to mission, although burdening it with the linkage to colonialism. The "unequal treaties" of Nanking (1842) and Tientsin (1858) were, in part, negotiated with the help of missionaries. From 1858 these treaties allowed Protestant mission to move with official protection into the provinces and expand its outreach. Organizations such as Hudson Taylor's China Inland Mission soon made their way into remote areas of China.

Reformed mission was carried out primarily by British and North American agencies who sent **Elijah C. Bridgman, Hampden C. DuBose, Mary Hannah Fulton, Andrew P. Happer, James Legge**, and **Robert B. McClure.** The emerging shape of Chinese Protestantism would be broadly influenced by the Reformed theology and polity of these bodies and their missionaries. Characteristic of Reformed mission was its combination of **evangelism** and **education**, as well as medical and agricultural ministries. Especially significant was the organization of Reformed colleges and universities, which introduced Western science and technology, Christian thought, and Western political ideas to future Chinese leaders. Although numerically small (in 1949, 2 percent of the Chinese population was Christian), Protestantism had a disproportional influence through its educational institutions, hospitals, churches, and other organizations.

The number of **mission** societies grew rapidly in the second half of the 19th century. By 1864, 20 Protestant missionary societies were counted in China. In 1877 the first all-China Missionary Conference was held, at which it was reported that there were 6,000 Chinese Christians. By 1890 missionaries from 36 societies counted 40,000 Chinese Christians. By then the Bible had been published in Mandarin; Protestants had sent the first woman medical missionary and had initiated the first Chinese anti-footbinding society; and missions were active in disaster relief, occasioned by the famine of 1878–1879. At the Centenary Mission Conference of 1907, baptized Protestants were reported to number 190,000, among whom 4,000 foreign missionaries labored. The first indigenous church, the Chinese Independent Protestant Church, had been formed by **Yu Kuo-Chen.** Five Chinese delegates joined the large group from China that attended the World Missionary Conference in Edinburgh (1910).

Christian churches developed rapidly in the first 30 years of the 20th century, and a National Christian Conference met in 1922. The meeting led to the formation of the National Christian Council, with a Chinese majority. Around 1925 foreign missionary activity reached its peak, with over 8,500 persons in service and 400,000 Chinese Christians reported. Chinese Christianity followed theological and ecclesial movements typical of Western Christianity: mainline churches, conservative to fundamentalist factions and splits, and a variety of indigenous churches, some with Pentecostal characteristics. There was also a movement to consolidate the mission churches and to contextualize the gospel; this movement agreed with the Chinese cultural concern for unity and harmony. In 1927 the Reformed churches (Presbyterian, Reformed Church of America, English Baptist, Congregationalists, and others) merged into the Church of Christ in China (CCC), which became the largest denomination in China and since 1929 a member of the **World Alliance of Reformed Churches.**

The **fundamentalist-modernist controversy** had an impact in Reformed Chinese circles but was complicated by cultural issues in China, especially the growing resistance to Western influence. The credibility of Christian witness in the Chinese context continued to be complicated by its association with Western imperialism. The social implications of the Christian presence, articulated in various ways by the **social gospel** (and propagated by the YMCA and YWCA in their Chinese ministries), gained greater acceptance, whereas the doctrinal and confessional claims were often rejected as Western and un-Chinese. On the other hand, the turmoil and suffering of the war period, beginning with the Sino-Japanese conflict (1937), strengthened Christian witness as missionaries and Chinese church leaders were imprisoned or otherwise persecuted. The Church of Christ in China expanded its outreach during this period with the initiation of the Border Tribes Mission.

The postwar development of Reformed Chinese Christianity has been profoundly shaped by the communist takeover in 1949, which led to the expulsion of all non-Chinese missionaries. Before 1951, Protestantism consisted of about 270 distinctive denominations with about 1.3 million adherents, of which the Church of Christ in China was the largest. Beginning in 1958, the government Bureau of Religious Affairs sponsored the Three-Self Patriotic Movement, under which Protestant churches and organizations were consolidated and many churches were closed. All churches were closed during the 10-year Cultural Revolution (1966–1976). *See also* Three-Self Formula

After the revolution, a single Protestant church was organized, the China Christian Council, which incorporates most of the institutions and traditions formed by the missionary movement. **Peter Tsai** and **Teng Ek Kheng** were leaders in the new church. Dissenting forms of Christian community have persisted, mostly in the **house churches**, which have emerged as a major spiritual force in China. Estimates of the Christian population in the 1990s range from 6 to 20 million adherents; contemporary Chinese Christianity is a vital and growing movement with strong ecumenical commitments and connections to the worldwide church. The Reformed legacy is completely integrated into the contextualized Christianity of China.

Hong Kong. The Hong Kong Council of the Church of Christ in China (HKCCCC) has functioned as an independent unit since the establishment of the People's Republic of China. It was originally a **presbytery** in the Kwangtung Synod of the Church of Christ in China. The Hong Kong Council has ministries of education, social work, and **medicine**, operating 53 schools, Chung Chi College, and several hospitals. With Great Britain's return of Hong Kong to the People's Republic in 1997, the Hong Kong churches face an uncertain future as they seek to reintegrate with the China Christian Council. **Peter Wong** was an important leader in the church.

Taiwan. The development of Reformed Christianity in Taiwan parallels mainland China until the post–World War II period. Beginning in 1865, the first churches were organized as a result of the work of English and Canadian Presbyterian missionaries, including physician James L. Maxwell and **George L. Mackay.** In 1876 the Tainan Theological College was established by Thomas Barclay, followed by the Mackay Hospital in Tamsui (1880; moved to Taipei in 1912), and the Boys and Girls Middle Schools in Tainan (1885, 1887). Throughout the World War II period, the Taiwanese Presbyterian Church engaged in the evangelization of the Taiwanese mountain tribal people. **Chi-Oang**, a Taiwanese convert, was central to this mission.

The restrictive religious policies of the Japanese occupation of Taiwan (1895–1845) brought about a single Protestant church, presbyterian in doctrine and polity and, until 1950, the only Protestant denomination in Taiwan. Church ministry grew under the Japanese, both during the tranquil period from 1895 to 1931, and later under the persecution of Japan's militarist regime. After World War II, the arrival of mainland Chinese was joined by an influx of missionaries from many other traditions, resulting in rapid church growth and today's denominational pluralism. Although the Presbyterian Church in Taiwan is the largest Protestant denomination, other Reformed bodies have been established in Taiwan, including the Christian Reformed Church, the Orthodox Presbyterian Church, and the Mandarin-speaking Independent Presbyterian Churches.

ECONOMIC THEORY. Economics involves the production of goods and services, the structures and management of finance, ownership and distribution of wealth, and consumption. Economics and economic theory are central concerns of the Reformed **tradition.** The Reformed churches place economic realities, like every area of human endeavor, under the **sovereignty** of **God**; they are subject to the biblical standards of **salvation** and justice. The Calvinist **Protestant ethic** encourages hard work and frugality, virtues that have led to the accumulation of wealth. Individuals and groups with economic power have a capacity to influence political processes and comprehensively shape human life. In Reformed thought, such power is to be tempered with social responsibility or it will result in personal greed and socially destructive practices. The Reformed tradition affirms the practice of market economics as long as individuals and economic structures are engaged in responsible **stewardship.**

When wealth is misused and social responsibility is ignored, the Reformed churches call individuals and social structures to the standards of justice and righteousness found in the **Word of God.**

ECUADOR. *See* ANDEAN REPUBLICS AND GREATER COLOMBIA

ECUMENICAL MOVEMENT. The movement by which the divided Christian churches have united in common purposes, action, and, in many places, organic church union. The Reformed churches have long been committed to the visible unity and the cooperative fellowship of the ecumenical church. Although most Reformed churches support the modern movement that began at the World Missionary Conference in Edinburgh (1910), some remain skeptical about its agenda. The Presbyterian churches were the second body, after the Anglicans, to organize themselves as a "world confessional family" in 1875. The Congregationalists formed the **International Congregational Council** (ICC) in 1891. These two international bodies merged in 1970 to create the **World Alliance of Reformed Churches** (Presbyterian and Congregational). Many leaders of the ecumenical movement have been connected with the Reformed churches: **John Baillie, Donald Baillie, Karl Barth, Eugene Carson Blake, Suzanne de Diétrich, Josef Hromádka, John A. Mackay, Lesslie Newbigin, J. H. Oldham,** and **W. A. Visser 't Hooft.** Reformed theologians and church leaders have participated in various aspects of the ecumenical movement, including the Faith and Order and Life and Work movements, as well as in the **World Council of Churches,** bilateral dialogues among churches, the International Missionary Council, conferences on world religion and **evangelism,** and the World Evangelical Fellowship.

EDIKPO, UDO UDO (1901–1988). Nigerian Presbyterian evangelist and church leader. Edikpo was influenced by **Mary Slessor** as a youth and decided to pursue **mission education** as a **vocation.** He first served as an interpreter for missionaries and then was educated at the Goldie Lay Training Center in Arochukwu. At his mission station, Ukwok, he worked against certain cultural practices that threatened effective **evangelism.** He tried to reform indigenous culture by curtailing the practice of secret cults, sacrifices, immolation, and divination. At the same time, he introduced African rhythm, dance, and clapping into Nigerian Reformed worship. He was a pioneer in what is now called the **contextualization** of Christianity, showing others how to approach cultural issues with integrity and cultural sensitivity. Edikpo is regarded as the champion of cultural reformation in the Presbyterian Church of Nigeria.

EDINBURGH MEDICAL MISSIONARY SOCIETY. A society organized to support medical work as part of the worldwide missionary movement of the 19th century. Inspired by **Peter Parker**, an American doctor working in **China**, a group of physicians led by John Abercrombie
organized the Edinburgh Association for Sending Medical Aid to Foreign Countries in 1841. Renamed the Edinburgh Medical Missionary
Society in 1843, the organization supported medical students training for
mission service, supplied medical personnel for hospitals operated by
Scottish churches and missionary societies, and shipped medicines and
medical equipment to mission hospitals around the world, including those
in **Israel**, **Syria**, **India**, and China. The society also began medical work
in **Ireland** and **Scotland.**

EDUCATION. The Reformed churches have placed a high value on education, drawing on their historical roots in Renaissance **humanism** and
their theological roots in the doctrine of the **priesthood of all believers**. The twofold purpose of education was to produce pastors for a
"learned ministry" and to empower **laity** by extending the benefits of
education to the **community.** This pattern emerged in Geneva, where
John Calvin founded the Genevan Academy for training pastors, wrote
catechisms for adults and children, delivered expository sermons for the
whole community, and supported a public school system as vehicles of
instruction for laity. The emphasis on education continued with the
founding of Protestant universities throughout Europe and with the reforms of educators such as **Jan A. Comenius.**

Reformed churches organized schools wherever they spread throughout the world. Mission educational institutions were powerful and sometimes controversial centers from which **evangelism**, social development
(e.g., schools for girls, untouchables, and racial minorities), and nationalism (both political and ecclesiastical) grew. The influence of Reformed
educational institutions today in any given region is often greater than
the size of the local Christian community (e.g., **Japan** and **India**). The
Reformed commitment to education over the centuries has wedded Reformed thought to Western intellectual history, giving Reformed theology great influence but also subjecting it to the reductionist and secularizing tendencies of modern Western thought.

EDWARDS, JONATHAN (1703–1758). American Congregationalist minister and Puritan theologian. Born in East Windsor, Connecticut, Edwards
was educated at Yale (1716–1720) and pursued graduate studies there
(1721–1722). He was ordained to the Congregational ministry in 1727

and called to the Northampton, Massachusetts, church. There Edwards assisted his grandfather, Solomon Stoddard; he became pastor of the church following Stoddard's death in 1729. A strong Calvinist, Edwards denounced Arminian theological tendencies. The **Great Awakening** of 1734–1735 and of 1740–1741 occurred under his preaching. Edwards defended the revivals and probed the depths of God's **grace** and human response in works such as *The Distinguishing Marks of a Work of the Spirit of God* (1741), *Some Thoughts Concerning the Present Revival* (1742), and *A Treatise Concerning Religious Affections* (1746). In these works he argues that true religion consists of discernable "holy affections" that do not violate the reasonableness of **God** or Christianity. As the revivals declined, Edwards faced controversies with his congregation over pastoral issues and the question of admitting the unconverted to the **Lord's Supper.** As a result of these controversies, he was dismissed in June 1750. Edwards then became pastor to the Mohican Indians in Stockbridge, Massachusetts, where he wrote a number of significant theological works including *A Careful and Strict Enquiry into Modern Prevailing Notions of . . . Freedom of the Will* (1754) and *The Great Christian Doctrine of Original Sin Defended* (1758). In the latter work he argued that all humanity was present in Adam at the fall into **sin** and consequently all human beings share the propensity for sin that Adam initiated. In 1758 Edwards became president of the College of New Jersey in Princeton, where he died the same year after receiving an inoculation for smallpox. Edwards is often regarded as America's greatest theologian and his thought laid the groundwork for the **New England Theology.**

EGYPT. *See* MIDDLE EAST

ELDERS. Ordained officers in Reformed churches charged with the spiritual oversight of the congregation. The Reformed churches have recognized four ordained offices: pastor, teacher, elder, and **deacon.** The office of elder is a permanent office. Elders are ordained for preaching, teaching, and sacramental purposes and for the function of **church government.** Some distinguish between pastors as "teaching elders" and lay elders as "ruling elders." Pastors and lay elders together constitute the "session," or consistory, the principal corporate body that assumes responsibility for the various programs and ministries of the congregation. Representative lay elders also serve with pastors and teachers at **presbytery,** a higher governing body that is the focal point of Presbyterian polity. Most Reformed bodies now recognize the rightful place of **women** to serve as elders.

ELECTION. God's choosing of human beings to receive the gift of **salvation** and carry out divine purposes in the world. The doctrine is associated with predestination and has been particularly important in the Reformed theological tradition. Many theologians use the terms "election" and "**predestination**" synonymously. **John Calvin** saw God's "eternal election" as the way "by which **God** has predestined some to salvation, others to destruction" (*Inst.* 3.21). Election, then, pertains to salvation as the work of God, who initiates a salvation by **grace** through **faith** to those who are "elect." Calvin understood election as the outworking of God's "eternal and unchangeable plan" (*Inst.* 3.21.7). Election is not associated with God's **foreknowledge** of human merit; it took place "before the creation of the world" (Eph. 1:4; *Inst.* 3.22.2). Faith is the "work of election, but election does not depend upon faith" (*Inst.* 3.24.3). Election is solely the work of God's free grace. For Calvin, election is focused in Jesus Christ (cf. Eph. 1:4), who is the "mirror" of election (*Inst.* 3.24.5). Believers thus should humbly attribute their salvation to the work of God's saving grace in Jesus Christ. Some 17th-century Reformed theologians treated election (salvation) as parallel to reprobation (damnation)—considering both decrees of God. **Karl Barth** modified these earlier views in relation to **Christology**, seeing Jesus Christ as "the elect and rejected man." For Barth, all humanity is elect in Christ. This universal election does not divide humanity into "elect" and "non-elect." Instead, it opens the reality of salvation to all.

ELIOT, JOHN (1604–1690). American Puritan missionary among the Massachusetts Bay Colony Algonquian Indians. Eliot was born in **England**, educated at Cambridge (graduating in 1622), and ordained in the Church of England. He taught at **Thomas Hooker's** Essex School and became **Nonconformist** in his views. In 1631 he emigrated to Massachusetts and became pastor of the Roxbury church from 1632 until his death. Eliot began work among the Indians in 1646, and by 1674 some 3,600 Indians had been gathered into 14 self-governing communities. He helped to provide jobs, housing, and clothes for the people. Eliot collaborated with Richard Mather and Thomas Welch to produce the *Bay Psalm Book* (1640), the first book published in New England. He also wrote *The Christian Commonwealth* (1659), a work suppressed for its republican sympathies. Eliot translated many works, including the Bible (1661–1663), into the Algonquian language. His Algonquian Bible was the first publication of the scriptures in North America. He also produced an Algonquian grammar (1666).

ELIZABETHAN SETTLEMENT (1559). The establishment of a Reformed Protestantism in **England** during the reign of Elizabeth I (1558–1603). After the reign of Mary I (1553–1558), who was Roman Catholic, the Act of Uniformity (1559) reestablished the Church of England as it had been under King Edward VI (1547–1553). This included use of the second **Book of Common Prayer** (1552) and the reintroduction of the Articles of Religion (reduced to 39 from 42). Ecclesial appointments of archbishops and bishops were given to those who supported Reformation views. Although the settlement was opposed by both Catholics and **Puritans** (who wanted to establish **presbyterianism**), its middle course resulted in the formation of a national Protestant character. The Puritans who resisted the national settlement formed independent congregations and church structures.

ELLIS, WILLIAM (1794–1872). English minister and missionary in the **Pacific** Islands and **Madagascar.** Born at Wisbech, Cambridgeshire, **England**, Ellis was educated in the London Missionary Society Training School at Gosport and at Homerton Academy, South Hampstead, England. Following his **ordination** in 1815, Ellis worked in the **Society Islands** from 1816 to 1822, where he became fluent in the Tahitian language. He lived in Oahu, **Hawaii**, between 1822 and 1824, where he assisted Protestant missionaries from the **American Board of Commissioners for Foreign Missions.** Ellis brought the first printing press to the South Pacific and laid the foundations of literacy in **Tahiti** and Hawaii. He returned to England in 1825 and published *A Tour through Hawaii* (1925) and the well-known *Polynesian Researches* (2 vols., 1829), which contained ethnographic and other material on **New Zealand**, Tahiti, and other Pacific islands. In 1830 Ellis was appointed assistant foreign secretary and then chief foreign secretary (1832) of the **London Missionary Society** (LMS). In 1847 he became pastor of the Congregational church at Hoddesdon, Hertfordshire. At the direction of the LMS Ellis made four visits to Madagascar on behalf of persecuted Christians. His longest visit was from 1861 to 1865. Ellis's experience in Madagascar led to the publication of four literary works, including a two-volume *History of Madagascar* (1838) and *The Martyr Church of Madagascar* (1870).

ELLUL, JACQUES (1912–1994). French sociologist, historian, and Christian ethicist. Born in Bordeaux, **France**, Ellul was educated at the University of Bordeaux, where he received a doctor of law degree in 1936. He was appointed professor at Strasbourg University but lost his teaching position when he opposed Marshal Pétain and the Vichy government. During World War II Ellul was a leader in the French resistance. In 1944 he was appointed professor of the history and sociology of institutions at the University of Bordeaux, remaining until 1980. He was an active member of the Reformed Church of France, serving on its National Council from 1951 to 1970, as well as on the **World Council of Churches.** Ellul published more than 30 books, including a sociological trilogy: *The Technological Society* (1967), *Propaganda* (1973), and *The Political Illusion* (1972). He sought to engage sociology with biblical and theological perspectives and did so in *The Meaning of the City* (1970), *The New Demons* (1975), and *God and the Politics of Man* (1972). Influenced by Søren Kierkegaard, he proposed a radical, Bible-centered Christian ethic that stressed holiness, freedom, and love against the principalities and powers of the world's structures.

EL SALVADOR. *See* MESOAMERICA

EMPEROR SYSTEM (JAPAN). After imperial power was restored (1868), official Japanese opposition to the fledgling Christian missionary movement began to grow. The nationalistic religious tradition of Shinto and its reverence of the emperor as divine were reestablished in **Japan.** The new constitution (1889) and the Imperial Rescript on Education (1890) applied Confucian ethics to the national structure and placed rites of emperor worship at the center of national identity, requiring these rites to be practiced in all schools. Some Christian institutions resisted the demands of the Shinto public observances, arguing that such practices were religious as well as patriotic and political; most eventually gave in, seeing in Shinto practice a way to indigenize Christianity. In 1940 the Japanese government intensified control over religious life by requiring the Protestant churches to unite in a single body, the United Church of Christ (Nihon Kirisuto Kyodan). Member churches of this union generally cooperated in the Shinto-based reverence of the emperor, seeing it as essential to the Japanese war effort. Very few organizations resisted, and most of them were legally dissolved. The Kyodan continued after the war, but many groups broke away, notably the Reformed Church of Japan, partly in reaction to the failure of the Kyodan to resist the ideological influence of Shinto and emperor worship. Even though government-mandated emperor worship ended after World War II, the relation of Christian confession to Japanese culture continues to be a controversial subject in the Japanese churches.

ENGLAND. *See* UNITED KINGDOM

ENVIRONMENT. *See* NATURE AND THE ENVIRONMENT

EQUATORIAL GUINEA. *See* WEST AFRICA

ERWIN, ADAM H. (ca. 1824–1897). Irish Presbyterian lay missionary in **Colombia.** Erwin went to Barranquilla in 1871 to teach the children of **Henry Pratt.** On his own, he started an educational ministry, primarily among the children of the city. When the Presbyterian **mission** left Barranquilla, Erwin stayed on as an independent missionary. He taught poor children in his own home, organized Sunday school and church services, and was a beloved member of the community. His educational and evangelistic work increased literacy and laid the foundation for the Presbyterian church in the region of Barranquilla.

ESCHATOLOGY. The theological study of "last things" (Greek *eschaton*) and the end of history. Traditionally, eschatology includes such elements as the end of the world, the return of Christ, the "millennial" reign of Christ, the last judgment, and eternal destiny in heaven or hell. Reformed theology generally seeks a middle course between a literalistic reading of the biblical texts about the future and a radical demythologizing of the texts that would dissolve the future. Although **John Calvin** tried to dissuade millennial speculation, all three millennial views—pre-millennialism, postmillennialism, and amillennialism—are represented in the Reformed tradition. Of these views, the amillennial position has generally predominated. This position teaches that at the second coming of Christ the dead will rise and judgment will follow; there is no inter-mediate rule of Christ on earth before the last judgment. Eschatological thought from the Reformation period through the 19th century empha-sized the destiny of the individual. During the 20th century, Reformed theologians such as **Karl Barth** and Jürgen Moltmann brought a corpo-rate eschatology into prominence. Moltmann's "theology of hope" em-phasizes the tension of future with present and the power of the future—which is grounded in the effects of the **resurrection** of Jesus Christ—to transform the present, particularly political structures. The quest for hu-man justice is motivated by commitment to Jesus Christ, as crucified and raised from the dead, and as the one who conveys God's righteousness and justice in the present.

ETHICS, CHRISTIAN. The system of moral principles that guide indi-viduals and churches in decision making and in the activities of the Chris-tian life. Reformed ethics is rooted in the idea of God's active presence in the world and in the lives of believers, in the **law** of **God** contained in **scripture**, and in the idea of **covenant.** Reformed theology teaches that God's **Holy Spirit** is present and active in the lives of Christians and that those who are justified by **faith** express their gratitude to God by living in obedience to the will of God. The law of God, as interpreted by Jesus, is recognized as the foundation of moral living and the basis of the Christian life. The development of "covenant theology" in the Reformed churches has had far-reaching social and ethical implications. The idea of covenants (that bind parties together) has been applied to interpersonal relationships (e.g., **marriage** and friendship) as well as to political and economic life. The Reformed impulse for individuals and corporate structures to be faithful to the will of God leads to active involvement in social issues and to a corresponding stress on the Christian life as a life of holiness. Puritan theologians in particular stressed the need for theology to have an ethical expression and for ethical actions to be grounded in right theological understandings.

ETHNICITY AND RACE. The distinctive identity of groups of people sharing a common culture is expressed in a culture's ethnicity, that is, its particular form of language or dialect, art and **music**, tools and technology, social and familial relationships, religion, and racial identity. Ethnology, the study of ethnicity, has been strongly influenced by missionary research. Ethnology seeks to make cultures mutually understandable and accessible. The fragmentation of colonial empires worldwide has led to the reassertion of ethnic interests, and has generated many conflicts. Ethnicity raises difficult issues for churches that affirm the gospel's intent that the **community** of **faith** be unified and multicultural. *See also* Culture and Theology

Race generally refers to the differentiation of populations within the human species by social groupings with common physical characteristics (e.g., body type or blood type). Such distinctions are frequently made on social rather than physical grounds. Racism, or discrimination on the basis of race, is a worldwide problem. In the West racism grew with the practice of **slavery** and the transatlantic slave trade, the spread of colonial empires, and the acceptance of social Darwinism as a scientific justification for subjecting groups of non-European peoples. Although some Protestant churches worked to eradicate the slave trade, little was done to address the issue of racism.

In 1924 two books appeared that brought the issue to the attention of many in the Presbyterian and Reformed churches: **Robert E. Speer's** *Of One Blood: A Short Study of the Race Problem* and John H. Oldham's *Christianity and the Race Problem.* Racism began to be addressed by international bodies in which the Reformed churches participated. Such bodies included the International Missionary Council (Jerusalem, 1928) and the **World Council of Churches** (Amsterdam, 1948). In 1969 the WCC established a Program to Combat Racism. **Apartheid** in **South Africa** became a central concern for many years. In 1982 the **World Alliance of Reformed Churches** declared apartheid a sin and its theological defense a heresy. Although the Dutch Reformed Church in South Africa supported the system, many Reformed ministers participated in the struggle to end it. The problem of racism is deeply rooted and widespread in Western countries, in parts of east and west **Asia**, and in some African and Latin American countries. The Reformed churches reject all claims of racial, ethnic, or national superiority.

EUCHARIST. *See* LORD'S SUPPER

EUROPE. *See* CENTRAL AND EASTERN EUROPE; NORTHERN EUROPE; SOUTHERN EUROPE; UNITED KINGDOM

EVANGELICAL. In many languages "evangelical" is the preferred self-description of churches derived from the Reformation. The term emphasizes the distinctiveness of the Reformed churches from Roman Catholicism in their emphasis on the centrality of the gospel of **grace**, **scripture**, and **faith.** In **Latin America** the term "evangélico" describes non-Roman Catholic Christianity in the same way. In **Germany** the term *evangelikal* has been recently introduced to refer to fundamentalists. In **Great Britain** and **North America** since the 19th century, the term has become associated with an emphasis on the **authority** of scripture, Christocentricity, **salvation** by faith, experiential faith, and **mission** and **evangelism**—while critical of modernism and **liberalism** in theology and ecclesial practice. Although there are denominations and organizations that are evangelical by definition (e.g., Evangelical Alliance, National Association of Evangelicals), evangelical convictions characterize large segments of traditional denominations; thus the doctrinal stances of evangelicals are diverse, rendering a precise use of the term impossible in English. Evangelicalism is generally more centrist than fundamentalism, skeptical of the categories and assumptions of enlightened modernity, and concerned to be faithful to the apostolic and catholic faith while open to the cultural diversity of worldwide Christianity.

EVANGELICAL MISSION SOCIETY IN BASEL. Founded in 1815 by a group from the German Christian Fellowship, the Evangelische Missionsgesellschaft in Basel began as a school for missionaries. The curriculum of the school was rooted in the pietistic movement that emphasized the Bible, spiritual life, and ecumenical cooperation, especially among Reformed and Lutheran churches. The society received most of its support from south **Germany**, German-speaking **Switzerland**, **Austria**, and the Alsace region of **France**. Its graduates initially worked for other mission societies, but the school soon became its own sending society, placing missionaries in **Ghana** (1825), **India** (1834), **China** (1846), **Cameroon** (1886), Borneo (1921), **Nigeria** (1959), and other countries. The society also began auxiliary mission committees that grew into separate mission societies (e.g., the **Paris Evangelical Missionary Society**).

EVANGELICAL THEOLOGICAL SEMINARY IN CAIRO. The theological seminary of the Coptic Evangelical Church in **Egypt**. Founded in Asyūt by Presbyterian missionaries from the United Presbyterian Church in **North America** in 1863, the school moved several times until 1926, when it was permanently located in Cairo. The school has three buildings: an administrative building (1927), a building containing a library of 30,000 volumes (1970s), and a conference center and student dormitory (1995). The seminary has produced pastors, missionaries, and church leaders for Egypt, **Syria**, **Lebanon**, **Sudan**, and other countries in the region. In 1987 the seminary opened a branch campus in Alexandria. The school publishes *al-Awraq*, a periodical begun in 1997.

EVANGELISM. The witness of the **church** to the gospel of Jesus Christ and his lordship over the world. Reformed understandings of evangelism are grounded in the activity of **God**, whose initiating love in **creation** and redemption through Jesus Christ is proclaimed and enacted. The Reformed churches seek to communicate the gospel message in a holistic manner involving both proclamation and lives of Christian service. The power of the gospel message is born of the **Holy Spirit**, who brings about **conversion** and the transformation of societies. Contemporary Reformed evangelism emphasizes the reign of God as a summary of the evangelistic message of Jesus. In carrying out its witness, the Reformed community recognizes the cultural forms in which the gospel is proclaimed and enacted and understands the strong relationship that exists between evangelism and concerns of peace and justice.

- F -

FAIRBAIRN, ANDREW MARTIN (1838–1912). Scottish Congregationalist minister and educator. Born at Inverkeithing, Fife, Fairbairn studied at Edinburgh University but left without taking a degree. He attended the Evangelical Union theological college in Glasgow (1857) and ministered at Bathgate (1860–1872) and St. Paul's Street, Aberdeen (1872–1877). After studying in **Germany**, he wrote *Studies in the Philosophy of Religion and History* (1876), a work that led to his appointment as principal of the Airedale Theological College, a Congregational school in Bradford (1877–1886). Other works followed, including *Studies in the Life of Christ* (1881). He was then called to serve as principal of the newly organized Mansfield College, Oxford, where he remained until 1909. At Oxford, Fairbairn shaped the life of the college; wrote *The Place of Christ in Modern Theology* (1893) and *The Philosophy of the Christian Religion* (1902); debated the Roman Catholic intellectual, John Henry Newman; lectured widely, making trips to **India** and the **United States**; and served on two Royal Commissions that studied education in **Wales**. He is best known for his eloquence and learning, as well as for his attempt to bring the fruits of contemporary theology into the Congregational churches.

FAIRWEATHER, MARION (1846–1923). Canadian Presbyterian missionary in **India.** Fairweather initiated Canadian **mission** work in Indore, Central India. In 1872 the Foreign Mission Committee of the Presbyterian Church in **Canada** endorsed her work and additional missionaries were later sent from the Canadian church. Fairweather developed a full range of mission ministries at Indore, including orphanages, schools, village **evangelism**, literature distribution, and medical services. Recalled after six years of service because of disagreements among Canadian mission personnel, she fought for reinstatement, was educated as a physician, and returned to India to become superintendent of the Native Women's Medical College and the General Hospital for Women at Agra (1886). Her convictions about gender equality in ministry irritated many of her Canadian colleagues and jeopardized her place in Canadian mission. Although breaking ground for many who followed, her career represents the ambiguity faced by women missionaries who were encouraged to pursue vocations but faced resistance when they moved beyond prescribed roles.

FAITH. Belief and trust in the **God** who is revealed in **scripture** and personified in Jesus Christ. **John Calvin** defined faith as "a firm and certain knowledge of God's benevolence toward us, founded upon the truth of the freely given promise in Christ, both revealed to our minds and sealed upon our hearts through the Holy Spirit" (*Inst.* 3.2.7). Christian faith is "not an opinion or human conviction, but a most firm trust and a clear and steadfast assent of the mind, and then a most certain apprehension of the truth of God presented in the Scriptures . . . and especially of God's promise and of Christ who is the fulfillment of all promises" (Second Helvetic Confession, chap. 16). The Reformed churches teach that the idols of race, government, class, or religious experience cannot be the object of faith. Rather, faith is a relationship with God, involving an act of the mind, heart, and will that affects the whole person. Faith is also a gift of God that empowers believers to live new lives of discipleship and service. The faith that comes from hearing the gospel inevitably expresses itself in works of love and justice. Such expressions of faith shape and transform individual lives, societies, and cultures.

FAITH AND HISTORY. *See* HISTORY AND FAITH

FAITH AND REASON. The relationship that exists between **faith** and reason in the Christian life. Faith is understood as a personal belief and trust that enables the whole person to enjoy a relationship with **God** in Jesus Christ. Reason is the means by which one knows oneself, the world, and God. However, Reformed theology stresses that true and saving **knowledge of God** is not attainable by the power of human reason alone. The knowledge of God that is necessary for **salvation** comes only through the inner witness of God's Spirit, who testifies to the divine **revelation** in Jesus Christ. Reformed theology considers reason to be supplemental rather than antithetical to faith. Some Reformed theologians have taken a "reason leads to faith" stance, arguing that human finitude and **sin** restrict but do not cripple the ability to know God through human reason alone. Most Reformed theologians, however, follow **John Calvin** in the belief that since the fall into sin, human reason lacks the spiritual insight to discover God's will. Instead, reason serves the sinful self in rejecting God. Faith, as God's gift, produces an assurance and certitude of God's loving **grace** that reason cannot attain. After the gift of faith is received, the power of reason may be used to advance spiritual understanding. Thus faith leads to understanding. This is the classic view held by Augustine and Anselm, Calvin, and modern Reformed theologians such as **Karl Barth** and **G. C. Berkouwer**.

FAITH AND SCIENCE. *See* SCIENCE AND FAITH

FĀNŪS, AKHNŪKH (1856–1918). Egyptian educator and outspoken leader of the Coptic Evangelical Church. Born in Abnub, Fānūs attended mission schools in Asyūt and Cairo before going to Beirut at age 14 to enroll in the Syrian Protestant College (now American University in

Beirut). An excellent speaker, Fānūs used his talent to raise funds for relief of the 1878 famine in Asyūt. He is best known for his contribution to Egyptian **education**, having been one of 11 persons appointed to organize Cairo University in 1906. He also organized and supported both a girls' school and a boys' school in Abnub, and he worked as a lawyer in the national courts from 1884. Fānūs spread his views through the *Misr* and *al-Watan* newspapers, and he organized the Coptic Reform Society, which promoted human and religious rights for the Protestant Christian minority in **Egypt.** From this society grew the independent Egyptian Party, which championed a similar cause. Both groups were formed in response to the rise of Islamic-leaning political parties. Fānūs served as head of the Evangelical church in Egypt and **Sudan** from 1902 to 1911, and he was honored by American University in Beirut with an honorary doctor of law degree in 1910.

FAREL, WILLIAM (GUILLAUME; 1489–1565). Protestant Reformer in Neuchatel and French **Switzerland.** Born near Gap, in Dauphiné, Switzerland, Farel studied at the University of Paris under humanist Jacques Lefèvre d'Étaples (J. Faber Stapulensis). By 1520 he espoused the cause of the Reformation and began to assist in parish reforms in Meaux under Bishop Briçonnet. In 1523 his reading of Cornelius Hoen's treatise on the Eucharist led him to more radical ideas and, as a result of growing intolerance in **France**, he was expelled from that country. Farel returned to Switzerland and became involved in a Basel disputation with **John Oecolampadius.** His attacks on the theological faculty there led to a second expulsion. Farel spent the next decade, from 1626 to 1636, evangelizing areas of French-speaking Switzerland, and he took part in the Berne Disputation of 1528. From 1532, he devoted his energies to Geneva, which accepted the Reformation in 1535. In 1536 Farel persuaded **John Calvin**, who was passing through Geneva, to join the reform movement there. As a result of their work, both men were banished from the city in 1538. Calvin returned to Geneva in 1541, but Farel went to Neuchâtel, the place where he had begun the Reformation in 1530. Although he was gradually eclipsed by Calvin, Farel remained one of the most influential French-speaking Protestant theologians.

FASTI ECCLESIAE SCOTICANAE. A 10-volume reference work containing biographies of the ministers of the Church of Scotland since the Reformation. The first three volumes were written by Hew Scott between 1866 and 1871. In 1914 the work was completely revised by W. S. Crockett, bringing it up to date and expanding it to seven volumes.

Additional material was added in 1950, 1961, and 1981 under the editorships of Francis J. Grant, John A. Lamb and Donald F. M. Macdonald, respectively. The *Fasti* is now complete through 1975.

FEDERAL THEOLOGY. Associated with the name of 17th-century theologian Johannes Cocceius, federal theology stressed the covenantal dimensions of the divine-human relationship and the "federal headship" of Adam as representative of the human race. The theology has its roots in the New Testament (e.g., Rom. 5 and 1 Cor. 15:22) but was developed more fully during the Reformation and post-Reformation periods by **Huldrych Zwingli**, **John Calvin**, **Heinrich Bullinger**, **Zacharias Ursinus**, Kaspar Olevianus, Herman Witsius, and especially Cocceius. According to these theologians, **God** uses covenants to carry out the divine will, especially in regard to **predestination.** Heidelberg theologians Ursinus, Olevianus, and Junius teach an initial covenant of works made by God with Adam, the "federal" head of all humanity. This covenant requires obedience to God's moral **law** (made explicit in the Ten Commandments) and the law of **nature.** Since the fall into **sin** it is no longer possible for human beings to obey these laws. Instead the divine-human relationship now depends on a covenant of **grace**, in which Christ fulfills the law and offers **atonement**, thus acting as the "federal head" for those who profess Christian faith. This idea of a double covenant appears in the **Westminster Confession** and is a foundational theme in the works of Witsius and Cocceius. In addition to using the covenant theme as an organizing principle of theology, Puritan writers also used it to encourage piety. "Covenanting" is an important feature of congregational and political life in both English **Congregationalism** and Scottish **Presbyterianism.** The idea of the contractual nature of covenant relationships contributed to the development of democratic government. *See also* Covenant

FELLOWSHIP FOR A CHRISTIAN SOCIAL ORDER (FCSO; 1934–1945). Canadian fellowship and movement that considered the capitalist economic system to be at variance with Christian teachings and called for a new economic and social order based on Christian socialism. The movement was a social and religious reaction to the poverty, unemployment, **labor** conditions, and economic disenchantment that resulted from the great depression of the 1930s. Organized in Kingston, Ontario, the fellowship expanded across **Canada**, receiving such organizations as the League for Christian Social Action in British Columbia and the Alberta School of Religion as affiliate members. The FCSO organized units within the presbyteries of the United Church of Canada; it held conferences, issued reports, and produced Bible study materials and worship resources that articulated its social vision. Internal division between moderate reformers and radicals hurt the movement and it did not survive the transition to a second generation of leaders. Its message of Christian social transformation was carried on by the social justice movement of the 1980s. *See also* Capitalism

FEMINIST THEOLOGIES. The variety of theological approaches that seek to know and understand **God** through the experience of **women.** Although feminist theologies vary in emphasis and direction, they share a common concern for the liberation of those who are oppressed, particularly women. **Knowledge** of God emerges through the experience of the oppressed, marginalized, and voiceless members of society. Feminist theologies advocate the empowerment and equality of women in all areas of life. Feminist theological reflection tends to be communal in nature and critical, that is, examining and challenging **authority** and **tradition.** Reformed feminist theologies emphasize the radical nature of **sin** and its pervasive effect on the structures of society. The patriarchalism that shaped **scripture**, tradition, **church**, and theology is questioned. Feminist theologies also affirm God's love as a reality stronger than the forces of evil and **death**, and share Christian hope for the "mending of **creation**," for the end of injustice, and for the coming of God's peace. Black women have used the term "Womanist" and Hispanic women the term "Mujerista" to describe feminist theologies that consider class and race in addition to gender. Non-Western theologians will inevitably develop different feminist approaches based on their historical, cultural, and religious contexts.

FINLAND. *See* NORTHERN EUROPE

FINNEY, CHARLES GRANDISON (1792–1875). American Presbyterian evangelist and revivalist. Finney was born in Warren, Connecticut, and raised in Oneida County, New York. He became a lawyer in Adams, New York, and was converted in 1821 after intense Bible study. He was ordained by the Presbytery of St. Lawrence in 1824 and spent the next eight years conducting **revival** meetings in the eastern **United States.** Finney became pastor of the Second Presbyterian Church in New York City (1832–1836) and began lawyerlike theological lectures, which he published as *Lectures on Revival* (1835). The work describes the use of the "anxious bench," "protracted meetings," and other revivalistic methods. In 1836 he became professor of theology at Oberlin College, Ohio, where he developed his views on "Christian perfection," exhorting Christians to "cast out **sin**" and replace it with holiness. Finney became a Congregational minister and conducted many revivals in America and Great Britain. He served as the second president of Oberlin (1851–1866). Finney's revivalist methods and theological views departed from historic **Calvinism**; by emphasizing **salvation**, he broke with traditional **predestinarian** views and helped shape later revivalist preaching. His views became known as the Oberlin theology.

FLYNN, JOHN (1880–1951). Australian Presbyterian minister, superintendent of the Australian Inland Mission (AIM), and **moderator** of the Presbyterian church. Flynn was ordained in 1911 and appointed superintendent of the AIM in 1912. With the support of the **general assembly** of the Presbyterian Church, Flynn pioneered the use of technology to minister to people in the remote areas of the Australian interior. He used radio to transmit messages and organized the first air medical service in 1928. This service inspired the nationwide Royal Flying Doctor Service of Australia. Flynn also established several hospitals and homes for the poor. From 1939 to 1942, he served as moderator of the Presbyterian Church.

FOREKNOWLEDGE. God's eternal knowledge of past, present, and future experienced in an eternal present. Foreknowledge is one aspect of the **sovereignty of God** revealed in the **scriptures.** The doctrine is an important element in **John Calvin's** writings (*Inst.* 1.17.1) and is explored further by **Francis Turretin** and other Reformed theologians. Foreknowledge must be understood in the context of God's eternal existence, omniscience, will, and power. The doctrine should not be confused with determinism or fatalism. Contrary to determinism, foreknowledge does not preclude human freedom and responsibility. In this context, it is important to note that God does not know all things in the same way. God's necessary self-knowledge is distinct from God's free knowledge of human beings. Although most Reformed theologians recognize God's foreknowledge, a small group of Protestant "process theologians," influenced by philosopher Charles Hartshorne, deny God's full omniscience. According to these theologians, in God's free act of creating a temporal universe, God freely chose a correspondingly temporal and self-limiting relationship with it, so even God does not know its complete future.

FOREORDINATION. *See* PREDESTINATION

FORSYTH, PETER TAYLOR (1848–1921). Scottish Congregationalist minister and theologian. Born in Aberdeen, Forsyth graduated from the University of Aberdeen and studied theology at Göttingen and Hackney College, later New College, London. He became a member of Baldwin Brown's church at Brixton, South London. Brown later helped Forsyth secure his first pastorate at the Congregational church in Shipley, Yorkshire, in 1876. This began Forsyth's 25 year career in the ministry serving four urban churches and the university-based Emmanuel Church, Cambridge, 1894–1901. In 1901 he was appointed principal of Hackney College, where he taught, counseled students, and spoke widely on behalf of the school. In 1907 he was invited to present the Lyman Beecher Lecture on Preaching at Yale University, published as *Positive Preaching and the Modern Mind*. He also became a reluctant disputant with R. J. Campbell concerning the "New Theology," which he considered a grave danger to the church. Because the outbreak of World War I disrupted the academic life of the college, Forsyth began to devote more time to writing, producing six books during a period of four years. Forsyth broke with theological **liberalism** in 1894 and gradually developed a Christ-centered, cross-centered theology. He wrote 25 books and more than 260 articles. His books include *The Person and Place of Jesus Christ* (1909), *The Work of Christ* (1910), *The Principle of Authority* (1912), *The Justification of God* (1916), and *The Church and the Sacraments* (1917).

FRANCE. *See* SOUTHERN EUROPE

FREE CHURCHES. *See* NONCONFORMIST

FREE UNIVERSITY, AMSTERDAM. A Christian university founded in 1880 by **Abraham Kuyper.** The university has its origin in the Dutch Reformed theological heritage but now maintains a broad curriculum and embraces an ecumenical outlook. The university maintains 14 faculties, including theology, law, medicine, arts, economics, psychology, and philosophy, as well as seven additional faculties in the sciences. Several Dutch Reformed professors have ably served the university and its faculties, including **Herman Bavinck**, **G. C. Berkouwer**, **Herman Dooyeweerd**, and **Hendrik R. Rookmaaker.**

FREE WILL. The power to act and decide, as opposed to determinism. Free will can refer to free agency, according to which all humans are free to make choices and are responsible for the choices they make. Reformed theology, following Augustine, stresses that these free choices can never be good or virtuous in the eyes of **God** because they proceed from a sinful human nature. Reformed theologians, borrowing Martin Luther's phrase, refer to a "bondage of the will": the will always acts in accord with the nature of the one who acts—so the will is bound in sinfulness. In this sinful condition, human beings are unable to respond to **God** in love and service. Reformed theology teaches that human beings have "wholly lost all ability of will to any spiritual good accompanying salvation" (**Westminster Confession**, "Of Free Will," chap. 9). Only through God's **grace**, by the work of the **Holy Spirit** in **salvation**, is belief possible and the believer able "freely to will and to do that which is spiritually good" (Westminster Confession). *See also* Original Sin

FRELINGHUYSEN, THEODORE JACOBUS (1691–1747). American Dutch Calvinist minister. Frelinghuysen was born in East Friesland, where he was influenced by a pietistic Dutch **Calvinism.** He became a pastor in the **Netherlands**; but upon hearing of the need for clergy in America, he emigrated to New Jersey and was ordained in 1719 to the Dutch Reformed ministry. He preached in the Raritan Valley, stressing the need for **conversion** and spiritual **revival.** Frelinghuysen had a strong influence on other revivalist leaders, including Gilbert Tennent and Jonathan Dickinson. Frelinghuysen also organized a separate assembly *(coetus)* for American Dutch Calvinist churches.

FRENCH POLYNESIA. *See* PACIFIC OCEAN ISLANDS

FULTON, MARY HANNAH (1854–1927). American Presbyterian medical missionary in **China.** A missionary of the Presbyterian Women's Foreign Missionary Society, Fulton was a physician and teacher of **medicine.** She founded the Hacket Medical College for Women (1901) in Canton, the first women's medical school in China, and the Turner Training School for Nurses. She was an outspoken advocate of women's **health** issues in China and recognized the need for **women** physicians to treat Chinese women. She translated into Chinese several English medical books, which were widely distributed. Fulton also shared the religious dimension of her work with the Chinese people, helping to organize the Cantonese Union Church and the Shanghai (Cantonese) Union Church. Many of the students who attended her schools became Christian converts.

FUNDAMENTALIST-MODERNIST CONTROVERSY (1920s). American conflict between conservative Christianity and liberal theology (modernism). By the 1920s, new discoveries in the natural and social sciences, biblical studies, and history had changed the modern understanding of the **creation** of the world, the human person, the nature of life, and historical interpretation. Whereas Protestant conservatives (fundamentalists) responded to these developments by reaffirming traditional Christian doctrine, modernists tried to adapt traditional theology to the results of modern scientific, literary, and historical study. The danger in conservatism was the development of litmus tests for orthodoxy in conjunction with various polarizing campaigns to save denominations from modernist influences. Many conservatives urged subscription to basic, "fundamental" Christian doctrines, but not everyone could agree on which doctrines to consider fundamental. The danger in **liberalism** was a secularized Christianity that resulted from an embrace of classic German liberalism, evolutionary theory, higher criticism, and a social interpretation of Christian faith. Could Christian liberalism still claim a salvific message? The Scopes Monkey Trial (1925) in Dayton, Tennessee, focused wide attention on the issues when a public school teacher was convicted of teaching biological evolution. During the trial, the fundamentalist position, which favored a literal reading of the Genesis creation story, was discredited. The controversy subsided in the late 1920s, but tensions between conservatives and liberals led to several church divisions and an adversarial relationship within many denominations.

- G -

GEDDIE, JOHN (1815–1872). Canadian Presbyterian minister and missionary in New Hebrides **(Vanuatu).** Geddie was born in Banff, **Scotland**, and moved with his family to Pictou, Nova Scotia, when he was a year old. Geddie studied theology with Thomas McCulloch in Nova Scotia, and he was ordained in the Presbyterian Church in 1838. He served the congregation of Cavendish and New London on Prince Edward Island until 1845. Successful in organizing missionary societies in the churches of the Presbytery of Prince Edward Island, Geddie volunteered for service in New Hebrides, a group of about 30 islands in the South Pacific. He arrived at Aneityum, the southernmost of the inhabited islands, in 1848. Though troubled by malaria and opposition from white traders, Geddie began to translate the Bible and print **scripture** portions on his mission press. By 1859 the New Hebrides **mission** had organized 11 churches and 56 elementary schools. Geddie also built a 1,200-seat stone church to accommodate many of the 3,500 Aneityumese (virtually the entire island population) who professed Christian faith. In 1861 a measles epidemic swept through Aneityum, killing about one-third of the population. Despite this tragedy, Geddie continued the work on Aneityum and tried to reach other islands to the north. He died in Geelong, **Australia.**

GENERAL ASSEMBLY. In Presbyterian **church government**, the general assembly is the highest governing body, representing the unity of the synods, **presbyteries**, and sessions of the church. In some Reformed denominations the highest governing body is called a synod or national synod, and lower bodies colloquies or classes, and consistories. Reformed church governance is characterized by such ascending governing bodies.

The general assembly consists of equal numbers of ministers and elders, called commissioners. The commissioners are either elected or appointed by presbyteries, not by congregations. The general assembly usually conducts its business in an annual meeting. Commissioners elect a **moderator**, adopt a budget, hear reports from various committees and church boards charged with carrying out the mission of the church, review decisions of lower governing bodies, address controversial issues, and maintain ecumenical relationships. Some decisions of the general assembly have the force of law, while others must be approved by a vote of the presbyteries or congregations of the church. Not every Presbyterian denomination has held a general assembly.

GERMANY. *See* NORTHERN EUROPE

GHANA. *See* WEST AFRICA

GILLESPIE, THOMAS (1708–1774). Scottish Presbyterian minister and cofounder of the Relief Church. Born in Duddingston, near Edinburgh, Gillespie was educated at the University of Edinburgh. He pursued further studies at the Dissenting Academy in Northampton, England, under **Philip Doddridge.** Following **ordination** in 1741, Gillespie returned to **Scotland** and became pastor of Carnock in Fife, where he proclaimed an **evangelical** message. When he objected to the law of patronage, he was deposed by the **general assembly.** He then served a large church in Dunfermline for the remainder of his life. In 1761 Gillespie, Thomas Boston (the younger), and Thomas Colier organized themselves into the Presbytery of Relief "to act for relief of oppressed Christian congregations." In 1847 the Relief Church merged with the United Session Church to form the United Presbyterian Church of Scotland.

GLADDEN, WASHINGTON (1836–1918). American Congregationalist minister and leader of the early **Social Gospel movement.** Gladden was born in Pottsgrove, Pennsylvania, and graduated from Williams College in 1859. He served pastorates in Brooklyn and Morrisania, New York, as well as North Adams and Springfield, Massachusetts, before beginning a 32-year ministry at the First Congregational Church in Columbus, Ohio (1882–1914), where he became a tireless social reformer. As one of the best-known advocates of the social gospel, Gladden wrote more than 30 books and 100 articles and was in demand as a conference speaker. He taught a pragmatic social theology forged from the daily experience of his community. His theology addressed some of the most important social issues that confronted American society, including **labor**-management relations, taxation, political corruption, and racial and religious bigotry. He had an abiding **faith** that the **kingdom of God**, understood socially, would be brought to fruition by an America desirous of doing God's will. Gladden wrote the popular hymn "O Master, Let Me Walk with Thee."

GLASGOW MISSIONARY SOCIETY (GMS). The first Scottish missionary organization. Founded in 1796, this independent society was supported by members of the Church of Scotland, which did not have an official missionary agency until 1924. The GMS established its first **mission** in **Sierra Leone** in 1797. This West African mission failed; however, in 1821 the GMS sent William Thompson and John Bennie to **South Africa**, where they remained for many years. By 1836, the society operated mission stations in Chumie, **Lovedale**, Balfour, Burnshill, Pirie, and Iggibiha. In 1844 the GMS transferred its mission work and personnel to the Free Church, which continued the work through its Executive Committee of Foreign Missions.

GLOBALIZATION. The worldwide **mission** of the **church**, which includes **evangelism**, ecumenical cooperation, interreligious dialogue, and work for **social justice**, carried out in the context of the world community. Advocates of globalization believe that theological **education** and the individual ministries of the church should be carried out in a world context. Advances in technology, including modern communication systems, air transport, satellite TV, and computer networks, are making globalization possible. Positively, these globalizing forces reduce isolation, speed the interchange of ideas, open up new avenues of learning, and increase the possibilities for Christian **community.** Negatively, globalization brings a threat to traditional cultural values by an overwhelming world media and mega-culture and by the global marketing of consumer products that shape human life and self-identity.

GOD. The supreme being revealed in **scripture** as triune, who with Jesus Christ and the **Holy Spirit** is the source of all **creation** and redemption. The Reformed tradition accepts the doctrine of the **Trinity** as it was interpreted by the early church, in which Father, Son, and Holy Spirit are three persons and one God. God is the creator who freely sustains the cosmos. The Reformed **confessions** describe God as an eternal, invisible, omniscient, personal, holy, and living spirit. Such descriptions of God, called attributes, not only describe God but also contribute to our understanding of other Christian doctrines on which the nature of God depends. Although Reformed theology in the 17th century concentrated on the transcendent "being" of God, 18th- and 19th-century theology emphasized God's personal and immanent nature. Twentieth-century theologians continue to debate the relationship between God's transcendent/immanent and personal/impersonal nature. Reformed theologians emphasize God's **providence** in sustaining, guiding, and acting in creation, history, the **church**, and individual lives.

GOLD COAST. *See* WEST AFRICA

GOMAR, FRANCIS (1563–1641). Dutch Calvinist minister and theologian. Gomar was born at Bruges and studied at Strasbourg, Neustadt, Oxford, and Cambridge before receiving his doctorate at Heidelberg in 1594. He became pastor for the Dutch community of Frankfurt am Main in 1587 and was appointed professor of theology at Leiden in 1594. At Leiden he championed strict **Calvinism** and engaged in a protracted dispute with his colleague **Jacob Arminius.** The controversy, which resonated through the Dutch Reformed Church, concerned the supralapsarian theory of **predestination**, which Gomar supported and Arminius rejected. Gomar left the university in protest when, after the death of Arminius in 1610, Conrad Vorstius, an Arminian, was appointed his successor. Gomar then became pastor of the Reformed congregation in Middleburg (1611) and taught at the French Protestant seminary at Saumur (1614–1618), and at Groningen (1618–1641). Gomar and his party published a *Counter-Remonstrance* (1611) in response to the *Remonstrance* (1610) of the Arminians. The dispute was "settled" by the Synod of Dort, which formulated the "five points of Calvinism." Gomar was a prominent figure at Dort yet could not persuade the synod to adopt his supralapsarianism. His *Opera theologica omnia* was published posthumously in 1645.

GORDON, CHARLES WILLIAM (1860–1937). Canadian Presbyterian minister and novelist who wrote under the pen name of Ralph Connor. Born in Glengarry County, Ontario, Gordon was educated at the University of Toronto and the University of Edinburgh. He was ordained in 1890 and worked as a Presbyterian missionary in Banff, Alberta, for three years. He then became a pastor in Winnipeg, and in 1897, as a fund-raising effort, he published some short stories about **mission** work in the Canadian west. The success of these stories led to the publication of several widely read novels about the west, including *The Sky Pilot* (1899) and *The Prospector* (1904). A wide audience identified with Gordon's early works, which dramatized the conflict of good and evil. His later works, which incorporate more theology, were less popular. Gordon served as a chaplain in France during World War I and was elected **moderator** of the Presbyterian Church in Canada in 1921. He also wrote an autobiography, *Postscript to Adventure*, which was published posthumously in 1938.

GOSPEL AND CULTURE MOVEMENT. The missiological discussion initiated by **Lesslie Newbigin** in the early 1980s that builds on a theology of **mission** called the **Missio Dei** and is informed by the theology of **Karl Barth** and by Newbigin's encounter with non-Christian religions. The movement links academic theologians, church leaders, missionaries, and **laity** across all denominational lines in missiological research and exploration. The North American movement is broadly ecumenical, with Reformed participation being particularly strong. The movement represents a disciplined attempt at the **contextualization** of mission in cultures in which Christianity was once established and is now secularized.

GOUDIMEL, CLAUDE (ca. 1510–1572). French composer. Little is known of Goudimel's early life. Prior to 1565 he converted to Protestantism. He became interested in the metrical psalms and their tunes being compiled under **John Calvin's** influence in Geneva. After 1551 Goudimel published eight books, each containing eight of these Genevan psalms in extended motet settings. In 1564 he published the 150 Genevan psalms in simple four-part settings, and a more elaborate version in 1568. These enjoyed wide popularity throughout Europe. He died in the **Saint Bartholomew's Day Massacres** in Lyons.

GRACE. Unconditional blessing extended to humanity by **God** for the maintenance of life (common grace) and for the purpose of **salvation** and perseverance in the Christian **faith** (special grace). Common grace is the *sustaining* and *restraining* power of God that enables humanity to enjoy the blessings of life. Common grace is sustaining because God "makes the sun rise" and "sends the rain" (Matt. 5:45); it sustains the whole of **creation.** Common grace is restraining because God provides the "restraining hand" of civil government that orders society and prevents humanity from descending into chaos. God is also the provider of special grace, God's sovereign, forgiving love and mercy that, through the work of the **Holy Spirit**, both begins and completes the process of salvation. According to **John Calvin**, God's freely promised mercy is centered in Jesus Christ (*Inst.* 3.2.28–29). It is Christ's atoning **death** that makes **justification** and **sanctification** possible. During the 17th century, Calvinists and Arminians carried on lengthy debates about the relationship between God's grace and human effort in salvation. Reformed ministers and theologians who met at the Synod of Dort declared that human beings are "incapable of any saving good" and receive salvation only through the work of God who "graciously softens the hearts of the elect . . . and inclines them to believe." The whole of salvation rests on God's grace and not on human merit. Perseverance in the Christian life is made possible by God's continuing grace, which forms Christian character and leads to Christian service.

GRASSROOTS THEOLOGY. Theology that emerges from the experience of the Christian **community** as it interacts with the political, social, and economic structures of society. Primarily an oral theology, it takes the form of sermons, prayers, Bible studies, and discussions. Grassroots theology comes from "below," whereas "academic theology," in the form of written, analytical reflections addressed to a guild of scholars, comes from "above." In this view, grassroots theology precedes academic theology. According to African scholar Kwame Bediako, academic theology "should be delivered from the false burden of having to construct a theology"; rather, it "has the role of understanding, clarifying, and demonstrating the universal and academic significance of grassroots theology" ("Cry Jesus!: Christian Theology in Modern Africa," *Vox Evangelica* 23 [1993]: 23) and providing enrichment and correction. In the case of **Africa**, grassroots theology is on the cutting edge of Christian reflection.

GRAYBILL, ANTHONY THOMAS (1841–1905). American Presbyterian minister and missionary in **Mexico** and **Cuba.** Born in Botetourt County, Virginia, Graybill served in the Confederate army during the

Civil War. After the war he graduated from Roanoke College (1869) and **Union Theological Seminary** in Virginia (1872). He went to Mexico where he served in Matamoras (1874–1887) and Linares. During Graybill's 31 years in Mexico, the Presbyterian mission established 10 churches with more than 1,700 members. Graybill was also the founder of the Presbyterian church in Cuba. In 1890 he went to Cuba at the invitation of Evaristo Collazo, a layperson who pleaded for help with the small church he had started in his home. During his visit, Graybill baptized over 40 adults, helped the congregation elect two elders, and ordained Collazo as pastor. Graybill made other visits to Cuba, working principally in Santa Clara and Cárdenas.

GREAT AWAKENING. A religious revival in the British American colonies between the mid-1720s and the 1740s. The Great Awakening was part of a larger movement that swept through Europe toward the end of the 17th and early part of the 18th centuries. On the Continent pietism and the **Réveil** movement gained a large following while in **England** and **Wales** the Methodist movement grew under John and Charles Wesley. These movements were a reaction to deistic rationalism and religious formalism in Western life.

The Great Awakening in the American colonies reached its height with the arrival of **George Whitefield** in 1839–1840. Whitefield's outdoor preaching inspired thousands of conversions. By some estimates, the awakening movement in the colonies generated about 350 new churches. Critics such as Charles Chauncy of Boston objected to the emotionalism of the movement. The Great Awakening was defended by Jonathan Edwards, whose *Religious Affections* (1746) tried to explain the theology and psychology of religious experience. The awakening had a pivotal effect on American religious life. Not only did it hold back the tide of religious rationalism, but it inspired the founding of educational institutions and mission organizations, and introduced an **evangelical** spirit into American **Calvinism.** This spirit came to define a large segment of American religious life.

GREAT BRITAIN. *See* UNITED KINGDOM

GREECE. *See* SOUTHERN EUROPE

GREENWOOD, JOHN (d. 1593). English minister and separatist leader. Greenwood was educated at Corpus Christi College. He became chaplain to Lord Robert Rich, a Puritan, and conducted services in his home. In 1586 he was imprisoned in London for holding illegal services and remained jailed for seven years, enduring frequent examinations before the High Commission and other courts. Greenwood remained true to his convictions and, along with fellow prisoner **Henry Barrow**, wrote numerous pamphlets defending separatism. Greenwood and Barrow were hanged at Tyburn in April 1593 for publishing seditious material.

GRENADA. *See* CARIBBEAN

GRONINGEN SCHOOL. A prominent theological movement within the Dutch Reformed Church in the **Netherlands** from the 1830s to the 1860s. The movement was organized around the faculty at the University of Groningen. The senior theologian and spokesperson of the movement was Petrus Hofstede de Groot (1802–1886). The Groningen theology, which was influenced by Johann Gottfried Von Herder and Gotthold Ephraim Lessing, might be described as a blending of Christian **humanism** and Christian Platonism. To de Groot, the **Trinity** is symbol rather than fact (Arianism); Jesus was not a real man but only appeared to be so (docetism); Christ gave us the moral **law** in order for each person to reach maturity, eventually growing into the full image of **God.** The views of de Groot and the Groningen School were disseminated through the movement's periodicals, *Truth in Love: A Theological Journal for Cultured Christians* (1837–1867) and *Faith in Love* (1867ff). The movement rejected formalistic, pietistic, and liberal interpretations of Christian **faith** but was severely criticized by "modernist" and Kuyperian theologians by the end of the 19th century. *See also* Kuyper, Abraham

GRUCHY, LYDIA (1894–1992). Canadian Presbyterian educator and the first woman ordained in the United Church of Canada. Born in **France** and educated there and in **England**, Gruchy arrived in **Canada** with her father and three sisters in 1913. Gruchy graduated from the University of Saskatchewan in 1920 and taught immigrant children in Lilyvale, near Verigin, Saskatchewan. She entered the Presbyterian Theological College (later St. Andrew's College) to train in Christian **education** but took the normal theological course and graduated in 1923. The Home Mission Board appointed Gruchy to the village of Verigin and there she was asked to provide church services in addition to teaching. In 1926 Kamsack Presbytery asked for her **ordination**, but it wasn't until 1936, after the formation of the United Church of Canada, that Gruchy was ordained. For the next five years Gruchy worked as general secretary of the Committee on the Deaconess Order and Women Church Workers, recruiting young **women** for mission work and Christian education. Afterward she returned to rural ministry in Saskatchewan.

GUATEMALA. *See* MESOAMERICA

GUEIROS, JERÔNIMO (b. ca. 1880). Brazilian Presbyterian minister and educator. In 1899 Gueiros was one of the first students to attend the Presbyterian Seminary of the North, which was located first in Garanhuns, and after 1920 in Recife. In the 1920s he served as a professor at the school when it was a joint venture of the Presbyterian Church in the United States, the Presbyterian Church in the U.S.A., and Congregationalist churches. He taught systematic theology at the seminary and was also a teacher at the Normal School in Recife. He helped to organize several primary and secondary schools, including the secondary school in Natal, which became a model of pedagogy. An articulate conservative voice, Gueiros was critical of the teachings of both Roman Catholicism and Pentecostalism. He also spoke against the exploitation of the poor by industrialists and land owners.

GULF STATES. *See* MIDDLE EAST

GUTHRIE, JAMES (ca. 1612–1661). Scottish Presbyterian minister and Covenanter. Educated at the University of St. Andrews, Guthrie became a Presbyterian minister in 1642 through his friendship with Samuel Rutherford. He was a pastor at Lauder (1642–1649) and in 1646 was one of several commissioners who met with Charles I to press the claims of **Presbyterianism** and the **Solemn League and Covenant.** From 1644 to 1651 Guthrie was a member of the Presbyterian **general assembly.** He also served as minister at Stirling (1649–1661), where he became a vigorous Covenanter and a "protester" against the king's ecclesiastical jurisdiction. Guthrie rejected any compromises with the Crown and suggested that Scotland's problems stemmed from "an arbitrary government and an illimited power." His book, *Causes of the Lord's Wrath against Scotland* (1653), was condemned and burned along with Samuel Rutherford's *Lex Rex.* Guthrie withdrew his allegiance to the king in favor of **Oliver Cromwell.** After the Restoration in 1660 he called for Charles to abide by his covenant obligation. However, Charles ordered his arrest and he was tried, convicted of treason, and hanged in Edinburgh.

GUYANA. *See* CARIBBEAN

- H -

HABIB, SAMUEL (1928–1998). Egyptian church leader and president of the Protestant Council of Egypt. Born in Wasta (Bani Swaif), Habib graduated from American University in Cairo (1952), the University of Syracuse, New York (M.A., 1955), and San Francisco Theological Seminary (D.Min.). He founded the **Coptic Evangelical Organization for Social Services** (1950) and served as its general director. He served as president of the Protestant Council of Egypt from 1980 to 1997. In this capacity, Habib led the Protestant church of Egypt. He also served as vice president of the **World Alliance of Reformed Churches** (1977–1982) and president of the Middle East Evangelical Churches (1991–1997). Habib wrote more than 70 books.

HAHN, SANG-DONG (1901–1976). Korean Presbyterian minister and founder of the General Assembly of the Presbyterian Church of Korea (Koshin). Born in Kyongsangnam Province in southeastern **Korea**, Hahn enrolled at Dadaepo Silyoung School in 1910, the year of the Japanese annexation of Korea. When he converted to Christianity and was baptized in 1925, his family rejected him. From 1933 to 1936 Hahn attended the Pyongyang Theological Seminary. Following graduation he served several churches, including Choryang of Pusan, Munchang of Masan, and Sanjunghyoun of Pyongyang. In 1939 Hahn organized the Nonshrine Movement against the Japanese colonial government, which forced Koreans to worship at Shinto shrines. His activities led to arrest and imprisonment until the liberation of Korea in 1945. The following year he began Koshin Theological Seminary in Pusan under the banner of the Presbyterian Church of Korea (Koshin), a new denomination representing those who had not supported Japanese colonial rule. In 1972 Hahn became president of the school and worked to establish relations with the Reformed Church in the Netherlands.

HAHN, YOUNG-SHIN (1887–1969). Korean Presbyterian lay and political leader. Born in Pyounganbuk Province in northeast **Korea**, Hahn studied at Yangshil Girl's High School and later taught there. She organized the Korean Patriotic Women's Association, which launched an anti-Japan movement. She was imprisoned for her political activities from 1919 to 1923. Hahn was a founder and then student at Pyongyang Bible School, where she graduated in 1927. She later taught at the school and was three times elected president of the National Assembly of Presbyterian Women.

HÁJEK, VIKTOR. (1900–1968). Czech pastor and church **moderator.** Hájek was a pastor in Ruždka (1925–1929) and Brno (1929–1950). From 1950 to 1968 he served as moderator of the Evangelical Church of the Czech Brethren in Prague. He was active in ecumenical activities and was an effective spokesperson for the church during the post-World War II period.

HALDANE, JAMES (1768–1851). The first Scottish Congregationalist minister and evangelist. Brother of **Robert Haldane,** James was born in Dundee and studied at Edinburgh University before joining the navy and serving in the East India Company (1785). After settling in Edinburgh in 1795, he was converted by David Bogue, an Independent minister. In 1797 Haldane began an unauthorized program of **evangelism** throughout **Scotland.** He helped found the Society for Propagating the Gospel at Home as a permanent **evangelical** agency (1798). In 1799 he became the first Congregational minister in Scotland, serving an Independent congregation in Edinburgh, the "Tabernacle," where he ministered for 50 years. Haldane advocated weekly communion, encouraged public **discipline** and exhortation of church members, and held Baptist views on **baptism.** He and his brother helped lay groundwork for a broad acceptance of evangelical **Calvinism** in early 19th-century Scotland.

HALDANE, ROBERT (1754–1842). Scottish evangelist, writer, and philanthropist. The older brother of **James Haldane,** Robert was born in London and educated at Dundee and the University of Edinburgh. He joined the navy in 1780 but soon returned to his Stirlingshire estate and became a farmer. He was converted to Christian **faith** in 1795, committing all of his resources to Christian work. He sold his estate in 1796 and, when the Church of Scotland decided not to engage in foreign **mission** work, he used the proceeds to establish the Society for Propagating the Gospel at Home, several independent preaching "tabernacles," and theological seminaries. He also supported early Scottish **Congregationalism,** until he and his brother became Baptists in 1808. Haldane stimulated **evangelical Calvinism** in Geneva and Montauban, **France** (1816–1819), and was influential in the **conversion** of important Reformed Protestants such as Frederic Monod, Cesar Malan, and Merle d'Aubigné. He engaged in a prolonged controversy with the British and Foreign Bible Society over its decision to include the Apocrypha in Bibles it circulated in Roman Catholic countries. His writings include *The Evidence and Authority of Divine Revelation* (1816), *The Authenticity and Inspiration of the Holy Scriptures Considered* (1827), and *Exposition of the Epistle to the Romans*, 3 vols. (1836–1839).

HALF-WAY COVENANT (1657; 1662). A compromise that permitted children of baptized but not fully confirmed parents to be baptized if they acknowledged the **discipline** of the Congregational Church. A feature of 17th-century New England **Puritanism**, the Half-Way Covenant addressed a problem that arose because Massachusetts Puritans allowed only those who could testify to their **conversion** experience to become full members of the **church.** When the children of these members could not provide such a narration from their own experience and when these persons had children themselves, the issue was whether they could be baptized, since their parents were not full church members.

HALL, GORDON (1784–1826). American Congregationalist missionary in **India.** A graduate of Williams College and **Andover** Seminary, Hall studied **medicine** for the purpose of **mission** in India. He was sent to India by the **American Board of Commissioners for Foreign Missions** in 1812 and eventually worked in Bombay, where he was the pioneer of American Protestant missions on the western coast of India. He spent 13 years engaged in medical and evangelistic work, especially among the Brahmans. He translated the New Testament into Marathi and, with others, founded schools that taught in the vernacular. During a cholera epidemic in Nasick, he contracted the disease and died at the age of 42. Because of Hall's work and his publications, which were widely read in North America, the western Indian mission was firmly established at the time of his death.

HAMPTON COURT CONFERENCE (1604). A conference between Anglican bishops and English Puritan ministers convened by King James I to discuss Puritan demands for reform of the Church of England. The Calvinistic reforms sought by the **Puritans** included changes in the **Book of Common Prayer** and in the form of **church government**; they also wanted a new translation of the Bible. The king rejected most of the Puritan demands and some agreements were later blocked by the bishops so that the Puritan party suffered setbacks. The king did order a new Bible translation, resulting in publication of the Authorized or King James Version (1611).

HANSHIN UNIVERSITY. An institution of the Presbyterian Church in the Republic of **Korea** (Kichang). The school was founded in 1939 by Dae Hyun Kim. With 95 faculty and more than 2,800 students, the school has five colleges: theology, social work, liberal arts, economics and management, and natural sciences. The school's divinity school comes out of the liberal theological tradition.

HAPPER, ANDREW P. (1818–1894). American Presbyterian missionary, physician, and educator in **China**. Born near Monongahela, Pennsylvania, Happer was educated at Jefferson College, Western Theological Seminary in Pittsburgh (1840–1843), and the University of Pennsylvania (1843–1844). In 1844 he went to Guangzhou (Canton), China, where his medical and educational work flourished. Happer established two dispensaries which, under John G. Kerr, developed into a medical center. From 1850 Happer devoted himself to **education**, founding several schools, including Lingnan University (1886). He served on the committee to revise the Chinese Bible, chaired the editorial committee of the Presbyterian Press in Shanghai, and served as editor of the *Chinese Recorder* (1880–1884).

HAROUTUNIAN, JOSEPH (1904–1968). American Presbyterian minister and theologian. Born in Marash, Turkey, the son of a minister of the Armenian Evangelical Church, Haroutunian attended American University in Beirut, **Lebanon** (1919–1923), and Columbia College in New York City (1924–1926). He earned advanced degrees from **Union Theological Seminary** in New York and Columbia University. Haroutunian began his career at Wellesley College (1932–1940) in Wellesley, Massachusetts, and went on to teach at McCormick Seminary (1940–1962) and the University of Chicago (1962–1968). His dissertation, "Piety Versus Moralism: The Passing of the New England Theology" (1932), was a positive evaluation of Jonathan Edwards. He was also co-editor and translator of a selection of **John Calvin's** exegetical work, published as *Calvin: Commentaries* (1958). Haroutunian criticized theological **liberalism** in his *Wisdom and Folly in Religion* (1940). Also critical of aspects of **neoorthodoxy**, Haroutunian was an independent thinker who called for a renewal of the church under the banner of "theocentric Protestantism." His theology of Communion was articulated in his book *God with Us: A Theology of Transpersonal Life* (1965).

HARRIS, HOWEL (1714–1773). Welsh preacher and revivalist. Born at Talgarth, Breconshire, Harris worked as a schoolmaster before his **conversion** experience of 1735. Hoping to enter the ministry of the Church of England, he went to Oxford but remained there for only a week. A gifted revivalist rather than a scholar, Harris returned to **Wales**, where he embarked on preaching and revival campaigns. In 1737 he met Anglican minister Daniel Rowlands, and the two men started a religious revival through their preaching and the founding of Methodist associations. Unlike English Methodism, which was Arminian in its theology,

Welsh Methodism became Calvinistic. These associations eventually withdrew from the Church of England, becoming part of a Welsh Calvinist church. Although Harris was an inspiring preacher and leader, his theological and personal differences with Rowlands and George Whitefield led him to establish a separate religious community at Trefeca, Brecknockshire (1752). This community, supported by Countess Selina Hastings of **Huntingdon** who sent students there, became a center of Harris's revival activity in his later years. In addition to his letters and journals, Harris wrote several Welsh hymns.

HASTINGS, SELINA. *See* HUNTINGDON, SELINA HASTINGS OF, COUNTESS

HAWAII. *See* UNITED STATES OF AMERICA

HEALTH AND MEDICINE. The Christian **church** understands the practice of medicine, care for the sick, and restoration of health as a witness to God's salvific purpose and a sign of God's providential care. Christian medical work is inspired by the healing ministry of Jesus, the commandment of neighborly love, and the gospel of **salvation** (healing). Protestant medical work expanded around the world in the 19th century parallel to the expansion of the ministry of **deacons**, nursing orders in Continental churches, and church-related hospitals in North America. The medical infrastructure of many emerging nations was developed by generations of missionary doctors before governments assumed responsibility for health care. The International Missionary Council affirmed the essential "place of medical mission in the work of the church" (Jerusalem, 1928). Medical **mission** has been a driving force in the development of modern medical science, especially in tropical medicine. Advances in medical technology such as genetic engineering create ethical dilemmas, which constitute a new frontier of theological exploration and Christian witness.

HEIDELBERG CATECHISM. The most widely accepted statement of Reformed Protestantism, published in 1563. Commissioned by the Reformed ruler Frederick III of the Palatinate, the catechism was written primarily by the Reformed theologian **Zacharias Ursinus** and the court preacher Caspar Olevianus. Its purpose was to unite divergent Protestant views, especially in regard to the **Lord's Supper.** The catechism is divided into three parts following the New Testament book of Romans: on humanity's **sin** and guilt, on redemption and freedom, and on gratitude and obedience. Although the doctrine of **election** is briefly mentioned, there is no reference to limited **atonement, predestination**, and repro-bation. On the doctrine of the **Lord's Supper**, the catechism states clearly that the bread does not become the actual "body of Christ" and does not overly speculate regarding the nature of Christ's presence in the sacra-ment. The catechism is known for its beauty of expression and the per-sonal language it uses to explain Reformed beliefs.

HEPPE, HEINRICH JULIUS LUDWIG (1820–1879). German Re-formed church historian and theologian. Born in Kassel, **Germany**, Heppe was educated at the University of Marburg (1839–1843). He served as a minister in Kassel (1845–1848) and then returned to the uni-versity, where he taught from 1849 to 1879. He wrote a history of the church in Hessen (1876–1878) in which he argued that the Hessen church was originally a "German Reformed" rather than a Lutheran body. He believed that the Hessen church, which drew on the theology of Philip Melanchthon, **Martin Bucer**, and **John Calvin**, charted a middle course between Lutheranism and **Calvinism.** He also wrote a four-volume *History of German Protestantism during the Years 1555–1581* (1853–1859), a *History of Pietism and Mysticism in the Reformed Churches of the Netherlands* (1879), and compiled a *Reformed Dogmatics* (1861; English translation, 1950), which consists of excerpts from the writings of Re-formed theologians. Heppe was a liberal advocate of German philosophi-cal-theological unionism. His views helped prepare the way for the later **liberalism** of Wilhelm Herrmann and Rudolf Bultmann at Marburg.

HERMENEUTICS. The rules used to determine the meaning of **scripture. John Calvin**, like Martin Luther, emphasized the literal or historical meaning of scripture over the allegorical, tropological, and anagogical—the traditional medieval interpretations of scripture. He interpreted scrip-ture in relation to both its historical and its theological meanings, reflect-ing his conviction that scripture has both a "human" and a "divine" side. The study of the scriptural texts in their original languages and the work of the **Holy Spirit** are crucial components in scriptural interpretation. The **Westminster Confession** distinguishes between those things in scripture that are necessary to be believed for **salvation**—"clearly pro-pounded"—and those things that are not as plain and must be derived by a "due use of the ordinary means" (chap. 1., sec. 7). An important hermeneutical key is that scripture is to be compared with scripture, so that obscure texts are illuminated by clear ones.

Contemporary Reformed biblical scholars employ the tools of **bibli-cal criticism** and adopt differing hermeneutical approaches while honoring the **authority** of scripture. A resource document for the United Presbyterian Church in the U.S.A. (1982) presented theological guidelines for biblical interpretation drawn from Reformed **confessions.** These included a recognition of Christ as the center of scripture; a focus on scripture's plain text; dependence on the Holy Spirit's guidance as well as the doctrinal consensus of the "rule of faith"; interpretation in light of the "rule of love"; the earnest study of the biblical text in its historical and cultural context; and the interpretation of particular biblical passages in light of the whole Bible.

HESSE, JOHANN JAKOB (1741–1828). Swiss minister and theologian. The son of a watchmaker, Hesse was born in Zurich and raised by an uncle who was a pastor in Affoltern, near Zurich. He studied in Zurich from 1755 to 1760 and briefly served as assistant pastor at Neftenbach. In 1761 an inheritance from his father allowed Hesse to retire in order to pursue intensive biblical and theological study. In 1777 he was called to the main church of Zurich, where his preaching attracted large audiences. Manuscript copies of his sermons circulated widely among the people. Hesse was made superintendent of churches for the canton of Zurich in 1795 and he founded the Zurich Bible Society. Hesse's most important work is his studies of the life of Christ, *Geschichte der drei letzten Lebensjahre Jesu* (1768–1773; 8th ed., 3 vols., 1822–1823).

HISTORICAL CONSCIOUSNESS. A term used to describe the movement away from the "Germanic captivity" of Japanese theology toward an indigenous theology formulated within the Japanese context. Since the 1970s, the need has become apparent for a Japanese Christianity interpreted within its own historical and cultural context, rather than out of the European or American experience. Historical consciousness is a form of **inculturation** that is taking place among many Reformed churches in non-Western countries.

HISTORY AND FAITH. The relationship between historical events and the meaning and truth of Christian faith. The problem of history and **faith** arose in the 18th and 19th centuries, when the modern discipline of history began and when biblical and historical criticism were first used to test the dogmatic claims of Christianity. Historians and biblical scholars began to examine Christianity not as a supernatural **revelation** but as a product of a specific time, place, and culture. This procedure stirred up doubt about the content and uniqueness of Christian faith; the whole Christian enterprise became the subject of research and judgment. To safeguard the doctrinal core of Christianity, 20th-century neoorthodox theologians interpreted Christianity as a truth about existence rather than as claims about the world. An important distinction was made between the events of history (German *Historie*) and "salvation history" (German *Heilsgeschichte*) through which **God** is redemptively at work in the faith communities of Israel and the **church.** However, this disconnection of history and faith also posed problems, especially considering the historical nature of many Christian doctrines. Some contemporary theologians (e.g., Wolfhart Pannenberg) see history and faith as interdependent processes, both being necessary to Christianity. Reformed theologians emphasize the **sovereignty** of God in history, understand Christ as the primary hermeneutical event of history, and view history in relation to Christian **eschatology.**

HODGE, ARCHIBALD ALEXANDER (1823–1886). American Presbyterian minister and theologian. The son of **Charles Hodge**, A. A. Hodge graduated from Princeton University in 1841 and **Princeton Theological Seminary** in 1846. He was ordained by the Presbyterian Church for missionary work in Allahabad, **India**, where he served for three years. Hodge then held pastorates in Maryland, Virginia, and Pennsylvania until 1864, when he was appointed professor of didactic theology at Western Theological Seminary (now **Pittsburgh Theological Seminary**). While teaching there he also pastored the North Presbyterian Church and published *Atonement* (1867) and *Exposition of the Confession of Faith* (1869). In 1877 Hodge was called to assist his ailing father at Princeton Seminary and, following his death in 1878, succeeded him as professor of didactic and polemical theology. In 1880 Hodge published *The Life of Charles Hodge*. With **B. B. Warfield**, Hodge wrote a famous article on **inspiration** (*Presbyterian Review* [April 1881]) supporting the plenary verbal inspiration of the original autographs of **scripture.** This article helped define the theory of scriptural inerrancy that played an important role in subsequent theological controversies both within and outside American **Presbyterianism.** Hodge's major book, *Outlines of Theology* (1860; rev. 1879), originated from Sunday evening sermons and was gradually expanded to include the characteristic themes of the Old **Princeton theology** that Hodge had learned from his father and from **Archibald Alexander**, for whom he was named. His *Popular Lectures on Theological Themes* (1887) was published posthumously.

HODGE, CHARLES (1797–1878). American Presbyterian minister and theologian. Hodge was born in Philadelphia and graduated from

Princeton College in 1815, and **Princeton Theological Seminary** in 1819, where he studied under **Archibald Alexander.** He became an instructor at Princeton Seminary where, except for two years of study in Europe, he remained for the rest of his life. He served as professor of oriental and biblical literature (1820–1840) and professor of exegetical and didactic theology (1840–1878). During this time he taught more than 3,000 seminarians, contributed some 140 articles to Princeton's scholarly journal, and wrote several important books, including biblical commentaries on Romans (1835, 1864), Ephesians (1856), and 1 and 2 Corinthians (1857). His magnum opus is a three-volume *Systematic Theology* (1872–1873). Hodge commented on nearly every significant issue in Protestantism from the perspectives of the old **Princeton theology.** He was a major voice in the denominational struggles of American **Presbyterianism**, contributing works on church polity (*Constitutional History of the Presbyterian Church in the United States of America,* 1840; *Discussions in Church Polity,* 1878) and serving as **moderator** of the Old School General Assembly in 1846. He also wrote on the U.S. Civil War and on Darwinism (*What Is Darwinism?* 1874). His personal **faith** and piety are expressed in *The Way of Life* (1841) and *Conference Papers* (1879). Hodge's influence at Princeton Seminary, in the conservative wing of American Presbyterianism, and in the American **evangelical** movement, continued for many years.

HOLLAND. *See* NORTHERN EUROPE

HOLY SPIRIT. The Spirit of **God** revealed in **scripture** as the third person of the **Trinity.** Reformed theology affirms the views of the Spirit found in the early ecumenical creeds. As the Nicene Creed affirms (Niceno-Constantinopolitan; A.D. 381), the Spirit is "the Lord and Giver of Life, who proceeds from the Father and the Son, who with the Father and Son together is worshiped and glorified, who spoke by the prophets." The Reformed tradition emphasizes the mystery, power, and activity of the Holy Spirit in the world, the scriptures, the individual, and the **church.** The Spirit is not only the giver of life, but is the Spirit of life itself, who sustains the universe. The Spirit inspired the biblical writers and illuminates readers by an "internal witness" so that they are convinced that scripture is the **Word of God.** The Spirit is the bringer of individual **faith, sanctification**, and "spiritual gifts" that are used in Christian service. The Spirit also calls, guides, and sustains the church, ministering to its congregations through both word **(preaching)** and **sacraments (baptism** and the **Lord's Supper).**

HONDURAS. *See* MESOAMERICA

HONG KONG. *See* EAST ASIA

HOOKER, THOMAS (1586–1647). American Puritan minister and theologian. Hooker was born in Markfield, Leicestershire, **England**, and educated at Queen's College and Emmanuel College, Cambridge (1611). While serving parishes in Esher (1620–1626), and as theological lecturer at St. Mary's Church, Chelmsford (1626–1630), Hooker gradually embraced Puritan views. In 1630 he fled to **Holland** rather than appear before the Court of High Commission. Lacking opportunities in Holland, Hooker emigrated to **America** in 1636. He became a noted preacher in Newtown (now Cambridge), Massachusetts. He was also one of the founders of Hartford, Connecticut (1636), and helped draft its Fundamental Orders (1638), which relied upon the consent of the people in both church and civil government. He defended New World **Congregationalism**, argued against the views of Roger Williams on religious freedom (1635), and was co-**moderator** in the 1637 trial of **Anne Hutchinson.** Hooker's theological views were strongly Calvinistic and he emphasized **preaching.**

HOPKINS, HENRY (1787–1870). Australian merchant, philanthropist, and Congregationalist lay leader. Born in Deptford, **England**, Hopkins worked in the English wool trade for 16 years and in 1822 went to Hobart, Tasmania, **Australia.** He prospered in the wool trade, real estate, banking, and in other enterprises, and served for many years as chair of the Hobart Town General Sessions. Hopkins used his wealth to support the work of the **London Missionary Society** and to build Congregational churches. So extensive were his gifts that some have credited him with the founding of **Congregationalism** in Australia.

HOPKINS, SAMUEL (1721–1803). American Congregationalist minister, theologian, and social reformer. Hopkins was born in Waterbury, Connecticut, attended Yale College (1741), and studied theology with **Jonathan Edwards**, whose library he inherited. He was ordained as pastor of the Congregational church of Great Barrington, Massachusetts (1743–1769), and later served in Newport, Rhode Island (1770–1803). Hopkins's writings sought to systematize the thought of Edwards. His "consistent **Calvinism**" also became known as "Hopkinsianism" as he modified the Calvinistic system to include a governmental theory of the **atonement** and a definition of **sin** as self-love, yet without the legal imputation of Adam's sin to subsequent humanity. He believed that human beings could, with regenerate wills, participate in their own **conversion.** Such participation consists of a deliberate turning from sin to embrace gospel truths by a "disinterested benevolence." Hopkins wrote *System of Doctrines Contained in Divine Revelation, Explained and Defended* (2 vols., 1793). Hopkins was one of the first Congregationalists to denounce **slavery.**

HORTON, DOUGLAS (1891–1968). American Congregationalist minister, theologian, and ecumenical leader. Born in Brooklyn, New York, Horton attended Princeton University (1908–1912) and Hartford Theological Seminary, where he was ordained to the Congregationalist ministry in 1915. He studied at Edinburgh, Oxford, and Tübingen, before serving in the pastorate for 12 years. He then taught at Newton Theological Institute and **Union Theological Seminary** in New York, and served as dean of the Harvard Divinity School (1955–1959). Horton was one of the pioneers of the modern **ecumenical movement.** Serving the **World Council of Churches** as a member of its Central Committee (1948–1954) and as chair of its Committee on Faith and Order (1957–1963). He served as moderator of the **International Congregational Council** (1949–1953) and was a delegate observer from the ICC at the Second Vatican Council (1962–1965). He presided over discussions that led to the 1957 merger of the General Council of Congregational Christian Churches and the Evangelical and Reformed Church, forming the United Church of Christ. He translated Karl Barth's *The Word of God and the Word of Man* (1957), was editor of *Basic Formula for Church Unity* (1937), and wrote *Vatican Diary* (4 vols., 1962–1965) and *Toward an Undivided Future* (1967).

HOUSE CHURCH. A group of Christians who meet privately for mutual pastoral care and support, to celebrate their common **faith**, and to encourage common witness. Such gatherings for **prayer**, Bible study, and **worship** have roots in the New Testament **church** and have consistently been a part of the church's life and often its renewal, especially during times of persecution. House churches played a significant role in the emergence of German and Dutch Pietism, the Moravian church, the Methodist church, and the first generations of modern missionary groups in **Great Britain** and **North America.** During the 20th century, the house church has been of primary importance in the Protestant communities of **Latin America**, in "underground" Christian communities in totalitarian states, in Bible study and discipleship movements (often denominationally or congregationally organized), and in support group movements.

In **China** during the Cultural Revolution (1966–1976), house churches constituted a major movement, not only preserving but expanding Christian witness in that country in a time of severe persecution.

HOYOIS, EMILE-PHILIPPE (1888–1972). Belgian Reformed minister, professor, and president of the Federation of Protestant Churches of Belgium. Born at Saint-Josse-ten-Noode, Hoyois studied at the Royal Athenaeum in Ixelles, and at Geneva, Montauban, and Edinburgh. After serving churches at Hornu and Charleroi, he became an army chaplain during World War I (1915–1919). After the war he returned to pastoral work, serving at Namur and environs from 1920 to 1923. He served as president and vice president of the Federation of Protestant Churches and secretary-general of the independent Belgian Christian Missionary Church (1927–1935). He continued pastoral work at the Church of French Expression from 1936 to 1959. Hoyois and Geneva classmates **Matthieu Schyns** and W. Thomas organized a theological school, Faculté de Bruxelles, during the Nazi occupation. He later taught church history at the school (1950–1965) and served as dean of the French-speaking section (1955–1958) and as president of the council of administration (1959–1962). Hoyois was also the editor of *Le Chrétien Belge* (1920–1932) and contributed to its successor publication, *Revue Protestante Belge*. He died at Etterbeek.

HROMÁDKA, JOSEF LUKI (1889–1969). Czech Brethren theologian and ecumenical leader in central Europe. Hromádka was born in Northern Moravia and studied theology at Vienna, Basel, Heidelberg, and Aberdeen. He served as assistant pastor in Vsetín and in Prague. In 1920, Hromádka was appointed professor of theology at the **Comenius Theological Faculty** in Prague and taught there for almost half a century. During World War II, he accepted a guest professorship at **Princeton Theological Seminary**, where he became active in the **ecumenical movement** that led to the formation of the **World Council of Churches.** At the first assembly of the WCC in 1948, Hromádka's debates with U.S. Secretary of State John Foster Dulles drew wide attention. When he returned to Prague in 1947, Hromádka was the major voice of central European Protestantism. He became a controversial figure in the West by taking unpopular positions on the Korean War, the Hungarian uprising, and the Cuban Missile Crisis. In 1958 he organized the **Christian Peace Conference** and was awarded the Lenin Prize. The importance of Hromádka's work lies in his critique of Western civilization and his writings on Christian-Marxist dialogue. *See also* Marxism and Christian Faith

HUGUENOTS. A name given to Protestants of the Reformed Church of **France**, and their descendants who emigrated to other lands. The origin of the French Reformed Church can be traced to the 16th-century reform movement in Geneva and to the biblical and theological works of Jacques Lefèvre d'Étaples and **John Calvin.** The church was officially organized by a national synod, which met in Paris in 1559. Although the majority of French people were Catholic, at least half of the French aristocracy converted to Protestantism. The Crown viewed this growing minority as a threat, and tensions led to a civil war, which lasted from 1562 to 1598. The Huguenots were persecuted during this period, and many died in the infamous **Saint Bartholomew's Day Massacres** of 1572. The **Edict of Nantes** (1598) gave the Huguenots civil rights and freedom of worship for nearly a hundred years; the edict was revoked in 1685 and persecution resumed until the French Revolution of 1789. It is estimated that under the reign of Louis XIV (1643–1715) more than 250,000 Huguenots fled to **Holland, England, Germany, Switzerland,** and **North America.** These exiled groups helped spread the Reformed movement throughout Europe and abroad.

HUMAN RIGHTS. Modern legal and political theory that posits universal principles or values claimed on behalf of all human beings: liberty, equality, inviolability of life, and freedom of religion, expression, and assembly. Some of the earliest arguments for human rights by Thomas Aquinas and Hugo Grotius were based on natural law. The English philosopher John Locke and the French *philosophes* Denis Diderot and Jean-Jacques Rousseau were important modern theorists of human rights. The Magna Carta (1215), the English Bill of Rights (1689), and the U.S. Bill of Rights (1791) codified human rights theory into law. Most governments today support such rights as reflected in the United Nations Universal Declaration of Human Rights (1948). Debate continues regarding the nature and extent of these rights. Reformed Protestants have often introduced human rights issues into the context of ministry. In some countries (e.g., **Argentina**), the Reformed community has participated in human rights organizations. In contemporary Reformed theology human rights are seen to originate in the human relationship with **God** and the resulting dignity and worth of human existence. The human rights discussion is a dynamic process, focusing recently on issues such as the **environment** and the rights to existence of future generations. *See also* Caste; Slavery; Social Justice

HUMANISM. A term that grew out of the literary, artistic, and scientific movement of the Italian Renaissance. It emphasized the free and independent development of the human person, with special concern to free humanity from the dogmatic and authoritarian structures of late medieval Christianity. Early use of the term dates from 14th-century Italy and the writings of the Italian poet Petrarch. Characteristic of the movement was a return to the sources of Western civilization: Greek and Hebrew sources (along with textual criticism), and a revived interest in Aristotle, the Bible, and the arts. Humanistic ideas were spread throughout Europe by the scholarly use of Latin and the invention of the printing press. Renaissance humanism laid the intellectual foundations of the European Reformation.

Humanism also refers to a modern approach to life that rejects Christian definitions of human existence, opting for naturalistic, scientific, economic, or psychological systems. The biblical view of human beings as the center or pinnacle of **creation** is being challenged by the modern disciplines of science, philosophy, and religion. These disciplines have expressed a concern for the survival of all species as a result of human exploitation of **nature** (environmental ethics), debated the possibility of extraterrestrial life (astronomy), challenged the autonomous human capacity to determine one's fate (philosophy), and considered the impact of non-Christian religions and cultures **(interfaith dialogue).** Reformed theologians have developed various theological anthropologies to address the concerns of humanism, from traditional approaches, which define the human being in relation to God's purposes and judgment **(John Calvin, Karl Barth)**, to more anthropocentric approaches focusing upon religious self-consciousness **(Friedrich Schleiermacher)** or "religious affections" **(Jonathan Edwards).**

HUNDESHAGEN, KARL BERNARD (1810–1872). German Reformed theologian. Hundeshagen was born at Fridewald and attended the University of Giessen, where he studied philology, theology, and church history. After a year in Halle (1829) he returned to Giessen, where he joined the philosophy faculty and lectured in church history. He was called as professor to the newly established University of Berne in 1834, was received into the clergy in 1836, and became rector of the university in 1841. Hundeshagen became professor of New Testament exegesis and church history in Heidelberg (1847–1867), and from 1867 to 1872 he served as professor at Bonn. His work *Der deutsche Protestantismus, im Zusammenhang mit der gesammten nationalen Entwickelung, beleuchtet von einem deutschen Theologen* (Frankfurt, 1846) made him a well-known scholar. Hundeshagen argued that the depressed conditions of religious and national life in **Germany** were closely related. Each could be healed only in relation to the other. Hundeshagen called for a return to Christian **ethics** and a concern for conscience, which lay at the heart of the Protestant Reformation but was lost in the German preoccupation with intellectual life.

HUNGARY. *See* CENTRAL AND EASTERN EUROPE

HUNTINGDON, SELINA HASTINGS OF, COUNTESS (1707–1791). English lay leader of the 18th-century British **evangelical revival.** In 1728 she married Theophilus Hastings, ninth Earl of Huntingdon, whose sister Margaret inspired her **conversion.** In 1739 the Countess of Huntingdon became a member of Wesley's London society, and her residence became a center of evangelical activities and a gathering place for revival leaders. She appointed chaplains for her estates, one of whom was **George Whitefield** (1748). The Countess worked with **Howel Harris**, founding a college at Trevecca in Talgarth, Breconshire (1768), the first nondenominational evangelical academy. She also organized a sect of Calvinistic Methodists, sometimes referred to as the "Countess of Huntingdon's Connexion," siding with Whitefield and the Calvinistic wing during the evangelical revivals (1779). She licensed her chapels as Dissenting meeting houses under provisions of the Toleration Act. The countess's evangelical fervor, her wealth, and her network of alliances made her a formidable influence over the evangelical revival.

HUTCHINSON, ANNE MARBURY (1591–1643). New England Puritan colonist. Born in Alford, **England**, Hutchinson was influenced by **John Cotton** in Boston and emigrated to the American colonies in 1634. In Massachusetts, Hutchinson gathered a group in her home after church services to discuss religion. She came to believe that the reception of God's **grace** implied an actual indwelling by the **Holy Spirit**, which provided entire **sanctification.** This made the externals of conventional morality unnecessary. She criticized the colony's religious leaders for placing more emphasis on good behavior than on spiritual purity. Her critics, especially **John Winthrop**, considered her views close to Antinomianism and charged that they would lead to anarchy. The conflict led to a trial in which she was accused of threatening the religious stability of the community. Both the civil and religious courts found her guilty of heretical doctrines. She was banished and settled in Rhode Island, where she remained until 1642. She then moved to Long Island, where she and all but one of her children were killed by Indians. Hutchinson was later revered as an early advocate of religious liberty and women's rights.

- I -

IBIAM, FRANCIS AKANU (1906–1995). Nigerian medical missionary, educator, and political leader. Following medical **education** at St. Andrews University, **Scotland**, Ibiam chose to serve as a rural medical missionary under the Church of Scotland Nigerian **mission** rather than pursue a promising government career. He and his wife built a rural hospital in **Nigeria**, despite a constant struggle against the racism of colonial mission structures. His leadership in **medicine** and **education** was recognized with his knighting by Queen Elizabeth II of **Great Britain** (1951); he later renounced his knighthood during the Nigerian Civil War. Ibiam served as the first African principal of the Hope Waddell Institute (1956), as chair of the governing council of the University College in Ibadan (1957), and as the first African president of the Christian Council of Nigeria. He significantly shaped the All-Africa Church Conference, of which he was the first chair. In 1960 he was appointed governor of the Eastern Region of Nigeria. Ibiam was a founder of the Bible Society of Nigeria, and he served as president of the **World Council of Churches.** An advocate of African culture and an opponent of racism, he nevertheless worked for reconciliation and ecumenical cooperation.

IM, JONG-HO (1890–1972). Korean Presbyterian teacher, evangelist, and lay minister. Im was born in Vladivostok, Russia, of Korean parents. She went to **Korea** to study the Korean language and to learn about Christianity. In 1910 she graduated from Martha Wilson Seminary in Wonsan in northwestern Korea. She then studied at Aoyama Academy of Theology in **Japan.** Im organized several Korean churches. From 1931 to 1941 she taught at Pyongyang Women's Seminary. In 1947 she was imprisoned for her antishrine activities. She wrote several books, including *The Outline and Spiritual Interpretation of Genesis.*

INCARNATION. The act whereby the eternal **Word of God** assumed a human nature in the person of Jesus Christ. Christian theology strongly links the incarnation to the doctrine of the **Trinity.** The Reformed **confessions** assert that the second person of the Trinity took upon himself human nature, "with all the essential properties and common infirmities thereof, yet without sin" (**Westminster Confession,** chap. 8); they also affirm the two natures of Christ, who was both fully human and fully **God** (cf. Scots Confession, chap. 6; Second Helvetic Confession, chap. 11). **John Calvin** emphasized the unity of the person of Christ, while stressing the distinction between the two natures, and saw the union of the person to be a dynamic union as Jesus Christ carried out his **three-fold office** of prophet, priest, and king. The *extra Calvinisticum* associated with Reformed theology over against Lutheranism is the view that Christ as the eternal Word of God *(logos)* is also operative outside the work of the historical Jesus. This is based on Calvin's argument that nothing finite can contain the infinite *(finitum non capax infiniti).* If so, the eternal Word is present and active beyond the flesh *(etiam extra carnem)* of the incarnate Jesus.

INCARNATIONAL LANGUAGE. Language used in **worship** to express an intimate connection between **God** and the reality of human life. Incarnational language is modeled on the **incarnation** of Jesus and the words of Colossians 3:16, "Let the word of Christ dwell in you richly in all wisdom." Reacting against the propensity for abstraction in Reformed worship and life, incarnational language considers the concrete realities of the body, physical life, and religious experience as central to the Christian life. Incarnational language provides a vocabulary for incarnational living whereby the gospel is not merely truth to be understood, but a personal God who is experienced and whose gospel is embodied in activities of daily life.

INCLUSIVE LANGUAGE. *See* LANGUAGE, THEOLOGICAL

INCULTURATION. The process by which new content is incorporated into the worldview of a society. The term can describe the process by which the Christian gospel becomes part of a local culture. Jesus' **incarnation** is the example that guides the process of inculturation: in Jesus, and in the life and actions of the local **faith community**, God's **grace** "becomes flesh." The gospel is received into local cultures and reformulated in that context. In the 20th century, anthropological and ethnological insights have contributed to an understanding of the process of inculturation. The process is consistent with the Reformed emphasis on the need to constantly reformulate theology "according to the **Word of God**," relating all local theologies to the events of God's self-disclosure in Jesus Christ.

INDIA. *See* SOUTHERN ASIA

INDIAN OCEAN ISLANDS. There are three Reformed churches in the Indian Ocean region, on the islands of Réunion, Mauritius, and Madagascar.

    Réunion. Lying off the southeast coast of **Africa**, Réunion is about 420 miles (680 km) east of Madagascar. The island is about 30 miles (50 km) wide and 40 miles (65 km) long. It has three mountain peaks of volcanic origin, the largest of which is over 10,000 feet. The island was uninhabited until the mid-1600s, when the French East India Company began to use it as a stopping point for ships traveling around the Cape of Good Hope on their way to India. The French established coffee and sugar plantations on the island and imported slave labor from Africa until **slavery** was abolished in 1848. Subsequently, laborers were recruited from **India, Malaysia,** and **China.** Most of the population are descendants of these workers, with the majority being African. The island remained a French colony until 1946, when it became a French department. Since 1973 the island has served as the headquarters of French military forces in the Indian Ocean.

Although 95 percent of the island's population is Roman Catholic, there is a small Protestant church located in the capital city of Saint-Denis. The Reformed Church of Réunion has two congregations with about 600 adult members. The church ministers mostly to French civil and military personnel stationed on the island.

Mauritius. Lying about 130 miles (212 km) northeast of Réunion, Mauritius is about 25 miles (42 km) wide and 32 miles (53 km) long. Uninhabited when it was discovered by the Portuguese, the island was settled by the Dutch in 1598 and later abandoned. In 1715 it became a French possession and so it remained until 1910, when it was annexed by the British. The island served as an important stopping point for ships until the Suez Canal was completed in 1861. A sugar industry was established on Mauritius, and Indians were recruited to work on the plantations. The majority of the island's one million inhabitants are of Indian descent, with the balance being African, Chinese, and European. The official language is English, but the majority of the population have adopted the French language and culture. Mauritius remained a British colony until 1968, when it became an independent country and a member of the British Commonwealth. Although sugar and textiles are a major source of income, Mauritius has recently developed into a tourist destination.

In 1814 the **London Missionary Society** (LMS) sent Jean le Brun, who established a French-speaking "Independent Church," worked in the capital city of Port-Louis, and organized several schools. In 1851 the Church of Scotland sent Presbyterian minister Patrick Beaton, who established St. Andrew's Church in Port-Louis. The Scottish churches on Mauritius ministered primarily to the Scottish and English Presbyterians who served in the colonial government. Samuel Anderson, who was born in Mauritius, later extended the ministry of the church. Between 1870 and 1883 he served several congregations, organized an Indian congregation, and translated most of the New Testament into the Krio language of Mauritius. His brother James recorded the history of the Protestant church on Mauritius. In 1876 the LMS and Scottish churches merged.

In 1979 the church became independent, calling itself the Presbyterian Church of Mauritius. In 1980 it became a member of the **World Alliance of Reformed Churches.** With a membership of more than 600 people in six parishes, the church conducts evangelistic and youth programs, and sponsors a program that provides theological **education** by extension.

Madagascar. Lying 250 miles (400 km) off the southeast coast of Africa, Madagascar is about 355 miles (571 km) wide and 976 miles (1,570 km) long. Settled by Malay and Indonesian people, Madagascar was first reached by Europeans in 1500, when the Portuguese arrived. An 1868 treaty with the Merina kingdom gave France control of the northwest coast of the island and by 1896 Madagascar had become a French protectorate. In 1960 it became an independent nation and by the 1970s it had severed ties with France and nationalized much of the economy. National life since independence has been characterized by political and economic instability. Poverty, unemployment, corruption, infectious disease, and the threat of deforestation are major problems. A market economy was instituted in 1986 and the evolution of the political process continues. The official languages are Malagasy and French. Agriculture products, including coffee, vanilla, and cloves, provide most of Madagascar's income.

The **London Missionary Society** sent missionaries to Madagascar in 1818. The missionaries organized churches, translated the Bible into Malagasy, and began schools. The work progressed until 1835, when Queen Ranavalona began a period of religious persecution that lasted until 1861. During this time, the missionaries were forced to leave and hundreds of Malagasy Christians suffered, including about 50 who were put to death. Between 1861 and 1865 **William Ellis** visited the island and wrote his famous history of the church. By the 1870s Protestant Christianity was widespread. *See also* Rafaravavy Rasalama

The establishment of the French protectorate in 1896 brought important changes to the religious life of Madagascar, including a government policy that favored Catholics and restricted the activities of Protestants. However, the presence of the French presented an opportunity for the

Protestant **Paris Evangelical Missionary Society** (Société des Missions Evangéliques de Paris), which also sent missionaries. In 1968 the British and French Protestant churches, along with the Friends Foreign Mission Association (Quakers) who had sent missionaries in 1864, united to form the Church of Jesus Christ in Madagascar (Eglise de Jesus-Christ à Madagascar). The church has 4,500 parishes, about 900 ministers (100 of whom are **women**), 1.2 million members, 200 schools, and three theological colleges. A general synod is held every four years. Church leaders include **Joseph Andrianaivoravelona, "Masina" Rabary**, and Reverend **Ravelojaona.**

The church has been deeply involved in the political and social life of Madagascar. Recent church political involvement dates from student and worker demonstrations of 1972. The church requested taxation and other reforms, urged a revision of the Franco-Malagasy cooperation agreements, and tried to bring peace to the country. During the national demonstration of 1991, the church again served as the primary mediator between the government and the strikers. The church has tried to maintain a position of neutrality but has also urged democratic elections and policies that promote justice and freedom. In the social sphere, the church launched a Mission Through Development program in 1974 that seeks to improve rural life conditions by providing food security, a reliable and safe water supply, **health** programs and services, a program of women's issues, and protection of the **environment** through reforestation, improvement of the land, and the management of nature reserves.

INDIGENIZATION. *See* INCULTURATION

INDIGENOUS PEOPLES. Descendants of the original inhabitants of a region, conquered or otherwise displaced by persons of a different culture or ethnic origin. The term "indigenous" loosely applies to groups who have historical ties to the land, inhabiting the region long before the arrival of colonial conquerors They may even be counted as the majority population of a region (as in **South Africa** and **Guatemala**) yet often constitute a cultural and economic minority.

The traditional approach of the Reformed churches has been to assimilate indigenous populations into the **church** and its often dominant culture. In the latter half of the 20th century, this earlier, colonial approach has been widely rejected. Reformed Christianity now acknowledges the distinct worldview of indigenous societies and the unique cultural and religious traditions into which the gospel is received. The gospel comes to each society within its own cultural and religious traditions rather than out of the experience set by another culture.

INDIGENOUS RELIGIONS. Throughout most of its history, Christianity has understood itself as the superior and only true religion, which conquered and replaced other religions (e.g., Greek gods, Slavic and Germanic tribal religion, Celtic deities). This assumption has been challenged by the encounter with indigenous religions; they are now recognized to be as essential as language, history, art, and social structures for the cultural identity of a people. Indigenous religions are studied on their own terms, compared, engaged as conversational partners with biblical religion, and sometimes approached as various expressions of a universal religion underlying all cultural expressions. Rather than judgment and conquest, the challenge today is to formulate Christian **faith** as witness to the adherents of indigenous religions, to be open to the lordship of Christ and work of God's Spirit in other religions while retaining the uniqueness of God's self-disclosure in Israel and Jesus, and to facilitate a dialogue characterized by mutual respect.

INDONESIA. *See* SOUTHEAST ASIA

INSPIRATION OF SCRIPTURE. A phrase describing the divine origin of **scripture.** Its biblical origins are rooted in 2 Timothy 3:16 and the Greek term *theopneustos,* and 2 Peter 1:21. According to **John Calvin**, the scriptures proceed from "the mouth of the Lord" (*Comm. on 2 Tim. 3:16).* However, consistent with his view of God's **accommodation** to the limits of human capacity, Calvin also believed that **God** used human beings to communicate the divine **revelation.** The biblical writings reflect the personalities, styles, worldviews, and limitations of the human authors. Others in the Reformed tradition support the "verbal inspiration" of scripture, which leads to a view of scripture as "a pure word of God free from all human admixtures" **(B. B. Warfield).** Those who support verbal inspiration have often believed that other conceptions of inspiration do not adequately safeguard scripture's origination with God. By contrast, **Karl Barth** and other Reformed theologians have viewed the biblical writers as "witnesses" to God's act of **incarnation** in Jesus Christ. By the power of the **Holy Spirit**, the words of the biblical writers elicit **faith** in Christ and **salvation.** According to this view, God uses the biblical writings primarily for salvific purposes.

INTERCULTURALISM. The mutuality in relationship among all ethnic groups within the Reformed churches. Interculturalism affirms the plurality of cultures in which Christian **faith** is expressed. The Reformed churches reject the domination of one culture over another, and acknowledge the transforming power of the gospel to relativize all cultural norms. The Seoul statement on gospel and culture, prepared at the 1989 meeting of the **World Alliance of Reformed Churches**, says in part, "To every culture and to its expressions the church must listen reverently and with patience. When it is time to speak the church may then 'speak the truth in love.' "

INTERFAITH DIALOGUE. The form of encounter with non-Christian religions that has emerged in the late 20th century to replace the confrontational and judgmental approach of earlier centuries. As Christian "witness among people of living faiths" (WCC, 1982), dialogue represents the gospel both by the exchange of content and the form of interaction. It is characterized by intense seriousness, profound respect for the partner, courtesy, willingness to learn as well as teach, openness to changing one's mind in response to persuasive argumentation, vulnerability for criticism, and a desire to persuade while abjuring manipulation or pressure (Stephen Neill). Interfaith dialogue has been practiced in exemplary fashion by mission leaders (e.g., E. Stanley Jones, Kenneth Cragg, D. T. Niles, and **Lesslie Newbigin**) and has become a dominant Protestant witness to other religions. In practice, it serves to deepen mutual understanding, to replace arrogant confrontation with interpersonal encounter, and to deepen the **faith** of those who participate.

INTERNATIONAL CONGREGATIONAL COUNCIL (ICC). Group organized in London in 1891 with the purpose of expanding worldwide cooperation among Congregational churches. The council was composed of 450 representatives, two-thirds from **Great Britain** and the **United States** and one-third from other nations. In 1970 the ICC merged with the Presbyterian World Alliance. The new body, called the **World Alliance of Reformed Churches** (Presbyterian and Congregational), carries on the tradition of the ICC by promoting ecumenical ties in programs of world **mission**, service, **education**, and research.

INYANG, EDET OKON UDOFIA (1914–1978). Nigerian Presbyterian minister and educator. Inyang was an important contributor to the improvement of ministerial **education** in the Presbyterian Church of Nigeria (PCN). While chair of the Education Committee of the PCN, he obtained scholarships from ecumenical sources to improve the standards and education of the Nigerian clergy. He supported **women** in the pastoral ministry and helped to educate the first women ordained in the PCN. Sought out as a counselor by pastors, he guided and encouraged many colleagues, mediated church disputes, and recruited talented leaders for the church. He was a theological centrist who contributed to the strength and unity of his church while serving as a model for younger pastors of strong and committed ministerial leadership.

IONA COMMUNITY. An ecumenical fellowship founded in 1938 by George F. MacLeod (1895–1991) and based on the island of Iona. Although Iona is the community's spiritual center, the largest part of its work is carried out in urban centers throughout **Scotland.** The community also maintains several "Columban Houses," which practice the community ideals of Iona. Members adhere to a fivefold rule of **prayer**, economic sharing, planning of time, meeting together, and working for justice and peace. Community staff are engaged in various ministries, including urban **mission**, the promotion of peace and justice, and the reform and renewal of contemporary **worship.** The Iona Community consists of approximately 3,500 clerical and lay supporters. Since 1951 the community has operated under the auspices of the Church of Scotland.

IRAN. *See* MIDDLE EAST

IRAQ. *See* MIDDLE EAST

IRELAND, NORTHERN. *See* UNITED KINGDOM

ISRAEL. *See* MIDDLE EAST

ITALY. *See* SOUTHERN EUROPE

- J -

JACKSON, SHELDON (1834–1909). American Presbyterian minister and pioneer missionary in the western **United States** and Alaska. Jackson graduated from Union College in Schenectady, New York (1855), and **Princeton Theological Seminary** (1858). Ordained by Albany Presbytery, Jackson became a missionary in Indian Territory, Oklahoma, where he taught at Spencer Academy. He was then reassigned to churches in La Crescent (1858–1864) and Rochester, Minnesota (1864–1869). Appointed superintendent for the Presbyterian Board of Home Missions, Jackson organized churches in the western territories between 1869 and 1882. These churches were subsequently organized into seven presbyteries and three synods. In 1884 Jackson became superintendent of Alaska **missions.** The following year he was also appointed U.S. superintendent of public instruction. Jackson traveled widely in Alaska to advance both his mission and educational work. In 1891, in order to help native Eskimos and prevent their relocation to reservations, Jackson arranged the importation of herds of reindeer from Siberia. In 1887 he served as **moderator** of the General Assembly of the Presbyterian Church in the U.S.A.

JAMAICA. *See* CARIBBEAN

JAPAN. *See* NORTHEAST ASIA

JESSUP, HENRY HARRIS (1823–1910). American Presbyterian missionary in the **Middle East.** Born in Montrose, Pennsylvania, Jessup was educated at Yale and at **Union Theological Seminary** (N.Y.). He was ordained in 1855 and went to **Syria** as a missionary of the **American Board of Commissioners for Foreign Missions** (1856). He worked as an evangelist and teacher in Tripoli and Abeih, and with the Presbyterian Church's Foreign Mission Board in Beirut. In addition to being a church pastor in Beirut, Jessup was involved in the work of the American University located there. Jessup, a prominent figure in the Middle East, chronicled his life's work and the history of the Syria **mission** in *Fifty-Three Years in Syria* (1910).

JESUS CHRIST. *See* CHRISTOLOGY

JITEGEMEA. A Swahili word that means "a movement toward self-reliance." The word was adopted by the Presbyterian Church of East Africa in the 1970s to symbolize the church's commitment to self-reliance in all areas of its ecclesiastical life. By use of the word "Jitegemea," the Presbyterian Church of East Africa declared its intention to determine its own form of **church government, discipline,** and service. The concept is a reflection of the church's desire to create an institutional and organizational life harmonious with the values and traditions of **East Africa.**

JOHN KNOX INTERNATIONAL REFORMED CENTRE. Founded in 1953 as a student hostel, the John Knox House Association located in Geneva, **Switzerland,** was created by the Presbyterian Church in the U.S.A. and operated by an international committee. In 1974 the **World Alliance of Reformed Churches** (WARC) took over the property, closed the student hostel, and added a Europe-Third World Center. Renamed the John Knox Center, the facility operates independently from the WARC and functions primarily as an ecumenical guesthouse and conference center that sponsors seminars and carries out research programs. Seminars and conferences hosted by the Alliance and the center have included Confessions of Faith (1981), Reformed Pastors (1982), Peace and Justice (1985), and Human Rights (1989).

JONES, JOSEPH T. (1902–1983). American Presbyterian minister and hymn writer. Jones was the son of former slaves whose father was a minister in South Carolina. He studied at Johnson C. Smith University, where he became interested in **music.** After graduating in 1927, he became a Presbyterian Sunday school missionary based in Knoxville, Tennessee. Later, Jones graduated from Johnson C. Smith Theological Seminary and was ordained in the Presbyterian Church in the U.S.A. He traveled throughout the South, collecting the spirituals he popularized in the **church.** His collection was published under the title, *Great Day: Negro Spirituals as Sung and Directed by J. T. Jones* (1961).

JUDSON, ADONIRAM (1788–1850). American Baptist missionary in **Burma**, lexicographer, and Bible translator. A graduate of Brown University (1807) and **Andover** Theological Seminary, he was involved as a Congregationalist in the formation of the **American Board of Commissioners for Foreign Missions.** In 1812 Judson left for **Burma**; en route to Rangoon he changed his views about **baptism** and transferred to Baptist sponsorship. Once in Rangoon, Judson learned Burmese and began Bible translation. During his ministry, Judson suffered the deaths of two wives and spent 17 months in prison during the Anglo-Burmese War (1824). His written legacy includes the still used Burmese Bible, a grammar, a Burmese-English dictionary (1849), liturgies, and many letters and essays interpreting his **mission.** Judson was opposed to the missionary imposition of Western civilization and educational structures, and sought instead to evangelize through dialogue and gospel proclamation. By the time of his death, he had been instrumental in the organization of 63 churches with some 7,000 Burmese Christians.

JUHÁSZ, PÉTER SOMOGYI (MELIUS) (1536–1572). Hungarian Reformed pastor, theologian, and bishop in Debrecen. Born in **Hungary** in territory occupied by the Ottoman Turks, Juhász studied at Wittenberg (1556–1558). In 1558 he went to Debrecen, Hungary, where he was appointed bishop in 1561 and stopped the spread of **Unitarianism.** Debrecen was the spiritual center of the Hungarian Reformation and an economically prosperous city, but it was under constant threat by the armies of the Habsburgs and by the Ottoman Turks. There Melius organized the Reformed church and published *Book on the Order of Service* (1563) and *Book of Canon Law* (1567). Under his leadership the church adopted the Second Helvetic Confession as its doctrinal standard (1567) and introduced a Debrecen hymnal and the **Heidelberg Catechism** (1577). Melius was the author of the first Hungarian confession, the Debrecen Confession (1561), *Sermons on Christ's Intervention* (1561), a *Catechism* (1562), and many other works. He founded the Reformed College of Debrecen, which later became the University of Debrecen.

JUNOD, HENRI A. (1863–1934). Swiss Reformed missionary in **southern Africa.** Junod was educated at Neuchatel, Basel, and Berlin. After a brief pastorate and missionary training in **Scotland**, he went to **Mozambique** (1889). Junod joined **Paul Berthoud** in the Swiss Romande Mission, working first at Ricatla near Lourenço Marques; later he served as principal of the Bible School at Shiluwane, Transvaal, in **South Africa.** He studied Bantu languages, published a Ronga grammar (1896), and co-authored a Shangane dictionary and grammar (1909). Junod interpreted his African experience by publishing fictional and historical works; his ethnographical publications about southern Africa (especially *The Life of a South African Tribe* [1912]) received particular attention and acclaim. Upon his return to Europe, Junod served as president of the International Bureau for the Defense of Native Interests, helped African pastors to pursue advanced study in **Switzerland**, and consulted on African affairs with the Mandates Commission of the League of Nations. He was awarded an honorary doctorate by the University of Lausanne.

JUSTIFICATION. A legal term used to indicate humanity's righteous status before **God.** Justification is a declaration through Christ that humanity's deserved condemnation is suspended by God's forgiveness. With Lutheranism, the Reformed tradition teaches that humanity's righteousness comes by the merit and righteousness of Christ and not by any human work. **Faith** as the gift of God is the means by which justification is effected. The result is **salvation**, a new status for the believer as a forgiven sinner who is adopted into the family of God. **John Calvin** spoke of a twofold **grace** *(duplex gratia)* in justification that makes a person both righteous in Christ and sanctified by the **Holy Spirit** *(Inst.* 3.11.1). Thus in Reformed theology there is the closest possible relation between justification and **sanctification.**

- K -

KA'AHUMANU (1772–1832). Hawaiian queen. The favorite wife of Kamehameha I of **Hawaii**, Ka'ahumanu was the most powerful royal supporter of Protestant missionaries from the **American Board of Commissioners for Foreign Missions** (ABCFM). Ka'ahumanu was instrumental in the overthrow of the ancient Hawaiian religion and taboo system in 1819, which prepared the way for arrival of the first company of ABCFM missionaries in 1820. By 1825 she was a member of the church and thereafter exercised considerable influence on behalf of the Hawaiian **mission.**

KAGAWA, TOYOHIKO (1888–1960). Japanese Presbyterian minister, social worker, and evangelist. Born in Kobe, Kagawa was the illegitimate child of a wealthy government minister. He was disinherited at age 15, when he became a Christian under the influence of American Presbyterian missionaries Harold W. Myers and C. A. Logan. He was baptized in 1904 and studied in the theological department of **Meiji Gakuin** and then at Presbyterian-related Kobe Theological Seminary, where he graduated in 1911. After working in the slums of Kobe, Kagawa pursued further studies at **Princeton Theological Seminary** from 1914 to 1916. He then returned to **Japan** and was ordained in 1919 in the Church of Christ in Japan. Kagawa became widely known for his work with the poor, including his efforts to improve **labor** conditions. He was also a pacifist who endorsed Christian socialism and supported various cooperatives. In addition to his work for social and economic reform, Kagawa traveled throughout Japan in an evangelistic ministry that established many churches and schools. He became an internationally known figure who proclaimed his message to large audiences on four continents. He was the author of 169 books, including *Christ and Japan* (1934), *Song from the Slums* (1935), *Brotherhood Economics* (1937), and *Behold the Man* (1941).

KAIROS DOCUMENT. A South African confessional statement written by Congregationalist, Presbyterian, Reformed, and other church leaders. Issued in 1985, the statement opposed South African **apartheid** and called on the churches to resist the government. Some churches responded with silence while others, including the United Congregational Church of South Africa, were guided by the document.

KALLEY, ROBERT REID (1809–1888). Scottish medical missionary in Madeira and **Brazil.** After medical study, Kalley and his wife, **Sarah P.**

Wilson Kalley, went to the Portuguese island of Madeira (1838), where their preaching, medical practice, and educational work led to a large number of conversions. The Portuguese government and Roman Catholic Church opposed the work and expelled the Kalleys and their converts (1846) from the island. In 1852 Kalley continued Portuguese-language **mission** work in Brazil as the first Protestant missionary there. His work included Bible distribution, hymn composition and distribution, door-to-door **evangelism**, and church planting. He founded the first indigenous Protestant church in Brazil, the Fluminense Evangelical Church (1858), on Congregational principles. Kalley practiced **medicine**, evangelized among rich and poor, and lobbied the Brazilian government to allow freedom of worship for Protestant religious communities.

KALLEY, SARAH POULTON WILSON (1825–1907). Scottish missionary in **Brazil.** In 1852 Kalley went to Rio de Janeiro with her husband, **Robert Reid Kalley.** She helped to found the oldest continuing Protestant church in Brazil, the Fluminense Evangelical Church (1858). A linguist, musician, and hymn writer, Kalley compiled *Salmos e Hinos*, a Portuguese hymnal, which she published in Brazil. She influenced the strategy of door-to-door **evangelism**, which is still widely used in Brazil, and helped in the translation and writing of devotional books in Portuguese.

KALOMBO, DANIEL (1885?–1953). Presbyterian minister in the **Congo** and pastor of the Luebo congregation. Born in the village of Bena Muembia, Kalombo was hired in 1901 as a day laborer by the American Presbyterian Congo Mission in Luebo. He was ordained an elder in 1914 and assumed responsibility for the congregation of South Luebo, across the river. The capital of the Kasai district was also located there, along with the state prison. In addition to his church work, Kalombo developed a prison ministry of visitation, **preaching**, and caring for the sick and dying. He attended the first **presbytery** meeting held in the Congo in 1919, and was ordained to the **ministry** in 1922. He became pastor of the 10,000-member Luebo church and served it for many years.

KÂMA (LALROKÂM), PASTOR (d. 1972). Indian Presbyterian minister and evangelist. Born at Suongsang village in Manipur, **India**, Kâma was from a Hindu priestly family and became a priest. He held important administrative and religious positions in the village of Sartuinek. Influenced by his cousin, Kâma became a Christian in 1918. He was commissioned by the Sartuinek Church and settled in the village of Vongzawl in 1920. A great **revival** broke out in 1924 and many in the Hamar community responded to Kâma's **preaching.** Although he was without formal theological training, the success of his evangelistic and pastoral work led to his **ordination** as an evangelist (1934) and minister (1939). Kâma ministered among the Hamars and other tribal peoples of North Cachar Hills for more than 50 years.

KANGSEN, JEREMIAH CHI (1917–1988). Cameroonian Presbyterian minister, public servant, and **moderator** of the Presbyterian Church in **Cameroon.** Born in Aghem-Wum in the Northwest Province, Kangsen studied at the Catechist Training Institute in Nyasoso from 1936 to 1937, and received further theological training in Kumasi, **Ghana**, from 1945 to 1947. He served as a teacher and youth pastor before entering political life. He then served as a member of the Southern Cameroon House of Assembly, as minister of education, and as minister of health and social welfare. He was an active member of the Board of Southern Cameroon Development Agency and of the Inland Revenue Board of the Federation of Nigeria. After the retirement of **Abraham Ngole** in 1969, Kangsen became the second moderator of the Presbyterian Church in Cameroon, serving for 16 years.

KAP, THAN (1901–1974). Pastor and a founder of the Presbyterian Church of **Myanmar** (formerly Burma). Kap became a Christian during his adolescent years and in 1931 enrolled at the Baptist Bible School in Haka town. He was appointed a Baptist evangelist in 1932 and ordained as a pastor in 1936. In 1956 Kap was one of the Christian pastors who organized the Presbyterian Church of Myanmar. He served the church as a pastor and teacher for the rest of his life.

KARERI, CHARLES MUHORO (1898–1978). Kenyan Presbyterian minister and **moderator** of the Presbyterian Church of East Africa. The son of a medicine man, Kareri was trained in his father's art and developed a deep respect for the spiritual dimension of life. Impressed by missionary teachings, he attended school and entered government service as a clerk before returning to the Tumutumu Mission. He became headmaster of the Mission's Infant School, helped to translate the Psalms, and in 1930 began to study for the ministry under R. G. M. Calderwood. In 1933 he became a senior preacher and married Esther Gacoki. With fellow student Stevenson Githii, Kareri sailed from Mombasa to **South Africa**, where he studied theology at Fort Hare University College (1935–1936). He served as chaplain (1942–1945) of the army in the **Middle East** during World War II. During the crisis of the revival movement in East Africa, he chaired a Committee of Enquiry to bring about reconciliation between the movement and the church at Tumutumu. In 1961 he became the first African moderator of the Presbyterian Church of East Africa, serving until 1967. He guided the postindependence church in **Kenya** and was a counselor to Kenyan President Jomo Kenyatta.

KÁROLYI, GÁSPÁR (ca. 1520–1591). Hungarian reformer and Bible translator. Born in Nagykároly, Károlyi studied at Cracow, at Wittenberg with Philip Melanchthon, at Strasbourg, and at universities in **Switzerland.** After he returned to **Hungary**, Károlyi was forced to take refuge from the Ottoman Turks in the besieged city of Szatmár, and in 1562 he escaped to Göncz in northeast Hungary. There he became a pastor and church leader, convening the Council of Tarcal, which approved Reformed doctrine as the theology of the Hungarian church. Because of pressure from the Ottoman Turks, Göncz, like Geneva, became a city of Protestant refugees. Károlyi became an important political leader in Göncz and the surrounding region, helping to establish the city's school system and overseeing district churches. He is best known for his Hungarian translation of the Bible, for which he used the Hebrew, Greek, and Latin texts. Károlyi translated the New Testament and prepared most of the Old Testament in collaboration with Reformed pastors in his district. The complete Bible was published in 1590.

KATSHUNGA, SAMUEL (1880–1963). Presbyterian minister in the **Congo.** Born in the village of Bakua Kolela, Katshunga was captured during intertribal fighting and sold into **slavery** in Luebo. Put on the slave market a second time, Katshunga was redeemed by H. P. Hawkins of the American Presbyterian Congo Mission. In 1903 he began training as an evangelist. He became the language assistant of American Presbyterian missionary **William M. Morrison**, who published the first Tshiluba-language **Bible translations.** In 1905 Morrison and Katshunga traveled to London, New York, and to Morrison's home in Lexington, Virginia, where they completed a Tshiluba dictionary and grammar published in 1906. Katshunga worked at Luebo and at the Bible school at Mutoto. In 1916 he was one of the first Congolese to be ordained a pastor. Following **ordination**, Katshunga worked at Bibanga (1917), Lulenga and Bena Kalambai (1928), and later in the Bena Kanyoka area. In 1934 he was elected **moderator** of the **presbytery.**

KAWAI, MICHI (1877–1953). Japanese educator and general secretary of the YWCA in **Japan.** Kawai was the daughter of a Shinto priest. She was educated in Hokkaido and Sapporo at the North Star Girl's School (now

Hokusei Gakuen) begun by Presbyterian missionary Sarah C. Smith. Kawai was baptized at age 13 and continued her studies at Bryn Mawr College in the **United States**, graduating in 1904. After returning to Japan, she became a teacher at Tsuda Women's College and helped to organize the YWCA, becoming general secretary in 1912. In 1921 she organized Keisen Girl's High School, near Tokyo, which later added a college. This school produced many teachers, ministers, and social workers. The school's Christian emphasis was continued during World War II despite government disapproval. After the war, Kawai was appointed to the government's **education** council. She played an important role in the democratization of Japanese education and was instrumental in the founding of International Christian University in 1949. Her writings include *My Lantern* (1939) and *Sliding Doors* (1950).

KEASBERRY, BENJAMIN PEACH (1811–1875). British Presbyterian missionary in **Malaysia.** Keasberry went to **Singapore** in 1839 under the sponsorship of the **London Missionary Society** (LMS). He built the Malay chapel in Singapore (1843). This church was the forerunner of the Presbyterian Church of Singapore and was later renamed the Prinsep Street Presbyterian Church. Keasberry's ministry expanded to the local Chinese minority, who also spoke Malay; these people proved most receptive to **evangelism.** He translated portions of the Bible into Malay, wrote hymns, and published Christian literature. When the LMS abandoned the Malay mission (1847), Keasberry stayed on, supporting himself by running a printing press. He started a boarding school for Malay boys and founded the first Chinese-speaking church at Bukit Timah.

KEET, BAREND BARTHOLOMEUS (1885–1974). South African minister and theologian. Educated at Stellenbosch University (1901–1909), where he received degrees in philosophy and theology, Keet received his doctorate under **Herman Bavinck** at the **Free University of Amsterdam** (1913). He served churches in Northern Paarl (1914) and Graaff-Reinet (1916) and taught dogmatics and ethics. In addition to several publications, including *Ons Rededlike Godsdiens* (1945), *Sedelike Vraagstukke* (1945), and *Orde in Die Kerk* (1963), Keet was involved in the translation of the Bible into Afrikaans. He was one of the first South African ministers to oppose the scriptural justification of **apartheid.**

KEKELA, JAMES HUNNEWELL (1824–1904). Hawaiian Congregationalist minister and missionary in the **Marquesas Islands.** Born in Waialua, Oahu, Kekela attended a **mission** school and then the high school at Lahainaluna, Maui (1838–1843), under the patronage of James Hunnewell, whose name he took at **baptism.** Kekela studied theology under Sheldon Dibble and W. P. Alexander, and graduated in 1847. He then married and was sent to serve a church in Kahuku, Oahu. In 1850 Kekela became the first Hawaiian ordained to the pastoral ministry. In 1853 he was sent by the newly organized Hawaiian Missionary Society to the Marquesas Islands, where he worked at Fatuhiva until 1857; he later worked at Hivaoa, where he remained for 41 years. He returned to **Hawaii** in 1899 and is buried in the cemetery of Kawaiaha'o Church in Honolulu.

KELLER, ADOLF (1872–1963). Swiss Reformed minister and ecumenical leader. Keller was born in Rüdlingen, **Switzerland**, and studied theology at the universities of Basel, Berlin, and Geneva. He served churches in Cairo, **Egypt**, Stein am Rhein, and Geneva and Zurich, Switzerland. He held several ecumenical positions, including general secretary of the International Christian Social Institute, secretary of the Swiss Church Federation, and director of the European Central Office for Inter-Church Aid (1922). He was appointed assistant professor of ecumenism and descriptive ecclesiology at the universities of Zurich and Geneva (1929). He was also the founder and director of the Ecumenical Seminar, Geneva. His many books include *A Philosophy of Life* (1914), *Karl Barth and Christian Unity* (1933), *Church and State on the European Continent* (1936), and *Christian Europe Today* (1942).

KENYA. *See* EAST AFRICA

KERR, GUILHERME (1888–1956). Brazilian Presbyterian minister, professor, and president of the Presbyterian Church of **Brazil.** The son of an American Civil War refugee of Scottish descent, Kerr was converted through the **preaching** of Brazilian pastor **Álvaro Reis** in Rio de Janeiro. He studied at Gammon Institute in Lavras and graduated from the Presbyterian seminary in Campinas. Kerr served as pastor of the church in Sorocaba (1917–1927). While engaged in pastoral work in the area of Campinas and São Paulo, Kerr also served as professor of Hebrew and Old Testament literature at the Campinas seminary (1926–1956). He served as dean (1926–1930) and president (1931–1948) of the seminary, and was elected president (i.e., **moderator**) of the Supreme Council of the Presbyterian Church of Brazil. Under his leadership, the denomination organized a national mission board called the "mixed board." The board included representatives of the Brazilian church and the mission boards of American Presbyterian Churches that were active in Brazil. His publications include a Hebrew grammar, a history of the seminary in Campinas, and many articles on the Old Testament.

KIEK, WINIFRED (1884?–1975). Australian Congregationalist minister and ecumenical leader. Born in Manchester, **England**, Kiek moved to **Australia** in 1920, where she graduated from Melbourne College of Divinity and the University of Adelaide. She was the first woman to be ordained to the Congregational ministry in Australia. Kiek served the Colonel Light Gardens Congregational Church (1926–1933) and the Knoxville Congregational Church (1939–1946). She participated in the church struggle for gender equality, and after World War II became the **World Council of Churches** Australian liaison for work among **women.** Kiek was involved in ecumenical organizations and twice served as vice chair of the Congregational Union of South Australia.

KIL, SUN-JOO (1869–1935). Korean Presbyterian minister and evangelist. Kil was born in Anju, Pyongannam Province, in northwest **Korea.** He studied Taoism and Buddhism, entering the Anguk-Sa Buddhist monastery in 1892. He left the monastery after three years, having permanently damaged his eyesight. Kil then studied Oriental **medicine** *(han-yak),* hoping to cure his failing sight, and opened a drugstore in Pyongyang. He converted to Christianity under the missionary Graham Lee and was baptized in 1895. Kil entered the Presbyterian-founded Pyongyang Theological Seminary in Pyongyang (North Korea) and graduated with the first class in 1907. He then became pastor of Central Presbyterian Church of Pyongyang, where the Great Revival of 1907 originated. His practice of early morning **prayer** became a model for the "day-break prayer meetings" that have become a tradition in the Korean churches. Kil was elected president of the Mission Board of the Korean Presbyterian Church and, in 1919, signed the Korean Declaration of Independence (protesting Japanese colonial rule). In 1927 Kil resigned his pastorate to become an evangelist. Although nearly blind, and often harassed and imprisoned for his evangelistic work, Kil traveled throughout Korea and into Manchuria to lead evangelistic meetings.

KIM, JAE-JUN (1901–1987). Korean Presbyterian minister and theologian. Born in Hamkyoungbuk Province in northwest **Korea**, Kim studied in **Japan** and the **United States**, where he received a Th.M. degree in 1929 from **Princeton Theological Seminary.** He helped to establish Chosun Theological Academy in 1939 and served until 1961 as professor and president of the institution that became Hankuk Presbyterian Seminary, the seminary of the Presbyterian Church of the Republic of Korea (Kijang). In 1972 Kim was elected chairperson of Amnesty International in Korea and became deeply involved in the **human rights** and democratic movements in Korea. He wrote and translated many books on systematic theology and Christian ethics. *See also* Ethics, Christian

KINGDOM OF GOD. The reign of **God** in both its present and future dimensions. A central theme in the teachings of Jesus, the kingdom of God refers to God's sovereign reign over **creation** and history and the justice and truth that God's reign brings. **John Calvin** adapted the "two cities" theme found in Augustine's *The City of God* to express the idea of two kingdoms: a spiritual and a political kingdom (*Inst.* 3.19.15). These are distinct yet not separable kingdoms that exist throughout history. God in Jesus Christ is sovereign over both, over all life. Although God's reign is taking place in the present day, the church anticipates an ultimate, coming reign, which "represents the triumph of God over all that resists [God's] will and disrupts [God's] creation" ("Confession of 1967," pt. 3). This perspective energizes **mission** and **ministry.** The **church** "does not identify limited progress with the kingdom of God on earth, nor does it despair in the face of disappointment and defeat. In steadfast hope the church looks beyond all partial achievement to the final triumph of God" ("Confession of 1967," pt. 3).

KIRIBATI. *See* PACIFIC OCEAN ISLANDS

KIS, STEPHEN (SZEGEDI) (1505–1572). Hungarian reformer and theologian. Born in Szeged, Kis studied at Vienna and then at Cracow (1537), a center of Protestant activity. In 1543 he went to Wittenberg to study with Martin Luther and Philip Melanchthon. When he returned to **Hungary**, Kis began educational work but was soon imprisoned and tortured by the Hapsburg Catholic Inquisition, which confiscated his property, including an extensive library. After moving to Ottoman territory, he was suspected of being a spy and imprisoned. Freed in 1562, Kis was appointed a bishop in the Hungarian Protestant church. In addition to his work as a church organizer and pastor, Kis was the most important scholar of the Hungarian Reformation. His works include *Theological Common Topics* (1585), a textbook of Protestant teachings on theology, church organization, and **Christian ethics.** The book was an encyclopedic work that contained the opinions of Reformed authors, including

Wolfgang Musculus, **Heinrich Bullinger**, **Théodore Beza**, **Peter Martyr Vermigli**, as well as the irenic Melanchthon. Kis maintained close relations with Bullinger and Beza and formulated a position on the **Lord's Supper** that came close to the teachings of **John Calvin**.

KNOWLEDGE OF GOD. The apprehension of God's self-revelation in **nature**, in **scripture**, and in Jesus Christ. The extent and effect of God's self-revelation in nature has been a subject of debate among Reformed theologians. **Karl Barth** and **Emil Brunner** clashed over this point; whereas Brunner accepted a limited natural **revelation**, Barth rejected any **natural theology**. In the theology of **John Calvin** one finds that God's natural revelation and God's special revelation in Christ are intimately related. Books 1 and 2 of Calvin's *Institutes* concern "the Knowledge of God the Creator" and "The Knowledge of God the Redeemer." According to Calvin, knowledge of **God** is "not only sowed in men's minds" but "in the whole workmanship of the universe" (1.5.1). However, the effects of **sin** on human nature are such that people are not able by themselves to discern who God is or how to enjoy a relationship with God. A personal and saving knowledge of God is only possible through God's Word revealed in scripture. Reformed theology teaches that the **Holy Spirit** acts through God's self-revelation in scripture to bring a personal and saving knowledge of God in Jesus Christ. This personal and saving knowledge is a divine gift that involves mind, heart, and will.

KNOX COLLEGE (Canada). Presbyterian theological school in **Canada.** Founded in 1844, Knox College is the oldest Presbyterian theological school in Canada. Located near the center of the University of Toronto, the present college building was dedicated in 1915. Its Gothic architecture is modeled after the colleges at Cambridge and Oxford. When the United Church of Canada was organized in 1925, all of the faculty and most of the students left Knox College and joined the United Church. The college building remained with the Presbyterian Church in Canada and its membership, representing the 30 percent of Canadian Presbyterians who did not join the union. In 1969 the college became a member of the Toronto School of Theology, a federation of seven theological colleges. In 1991 the school merged with Ewart College, the school of Christian **education** for the Presbyterian Church in Canada. Faculty have included **John T. McNeill**, Thomas Eakin, and **Walter W. Bryden.**

KNOX COLLEGE (New Zealand). The major Presbyterian seminary in Dunedin, **New Zealand**. Organized in 1886, the Theological Hall held its first session in 1887 with lecturer William Salmond and two students. By the turn of the century the school served both the northern and southern Presbyterian churches in New Zealand. Following the 1901 merger of these churches, the school was reorganized and renamed Knox College (1909). Modeled after Ormond and St. Andrew's Colleges in Australia, Knox College housed the Theological Hall and general student accommodations. In 1965 a separate Theological Hall building was constructed for theological instruction. A 1984 addition to the Theological Hall now provides a student commons, where social and community activities are held. The school maintains close relations with the University of Otago, with full time teachers being members of the Faculty of Theology.

KNOX, JOHN (1514–1572). Scottish Protestant reformer. Knox was born at Haddington and educated at St. Andrews University. He was ordained by the bishop of Dunblane in 1536 and served as a notary (by 1540) and private tutor (by 1543). Knox was converted by Thomas Gillyem (Gwilliam) and was influenced by John Rough and George Wishart. He became a preacher in St. Andrews Castle in 1547 amid great social and theological ferment in **Scotland.** When the castle was captured by anti-Reformation forces, he was sent to **France**, where he was a galley slave for 19 months. He studied Martin Luther's writings and embraced the Protestant doctrine of **justification.** After his release in 1549 Knox went to **England**, where he spoke against the Catholic Mass in his **preaching.** In January 1554 he went into exile in Europe when Mary Tudor, a Catholic, became queen. In exile Knox met other Reformers, including **John Calvin** and **Heinrich Bullinger.** He also pastored English congregations at Frankfurt and Geneva. While in Geneva he wrote *The First Blast of the Trumpet against the Monstrous Regiment of Women* (1558), in which he argued that a female sovereign contradicts natural and divine **law.** A more important work was his Geneva Service Book, which became a model of Reformed **worship.** In May 1559 Knox returned to Scotland as leader of the Reformed Party. He helped to prepare the Scots Confession and the Book of **Discipline** (1560). When Mary Stuart returned to Scotland, Knox became one of her most vocal critics. After her abdication, Knox preached at the coronation of her son, James VI. Knox believed that it was the duty of Christians to revolt against idolatrous leaders and envisioned a "Christian Commonwealth" in which both civil and ecclesiastical powers would join in promoting "true religion." He tried to reform worship in accord with **scripture** and contributed to both the theology and polity of the Church of Scotland. His major work is the *History of the Reformation of Religion within the Realm of Scotland* (1644).

KOREA. *See* NORTHEAST ASIA

KORINGO A POO (1906–1971). Tahitian minister in the Evangelical Church of French Polynesia. Born in Papeete, **Tahiti**, Koringo studied at the Hermon Theological School. He was ordained in 1941 and became pastor of the Siloama Parish, one of the largest parishes in **French Polynesia**, located in Papeete. In 1952 he was elected vice president of the Protestant Tahitian churches. When the Polynesian churches became independent in 1963, Koringo and **Samuel Raapoto** guided the churches through the transition and gave important leadership during the early post-independence period.

KOSHIN UNIVERSITY. An institution of the Presbyterian Church of **Korea** (Koshin). The school was founded in 1949 in Pusan by **Sang-dong Hahn** and Nam Sun Chu. With 179 faculty and 5,000 students, the school has five colleges: theology, liberal arts, social sciences, natural sciences, and medicine.

KRAEMER, HENDRIK (1888–1965). Dutch ecumenical theologian and lay missionary in **Indonesia**. Following his **education** in oriental languages and cultures in **Holland**, Kraemer served for 16 years in Indonesia as a lay missionary of the Netherlands Bible Society. While there he devoted his energy to Bible translation and linguistics, and developed a theology of **mission** that considered the church's encounter with other religions. He returned to the **Netherlands** and became professor of the history and phenomenology of religions at the University of Leiden (1937). His study guide for the 1938 World Missionary Conference (Tambaram, **India**), *The Christian Message in a Non-Christian World*, documented his affinity for **dialectical theology** and the primacy of biblical **revelation** for Christian **faith** and **mission** ("biblical realism"); it evoked a theological controversy that continues today. Kraemer's postwar work in the Dutch Reformed Church called attention to mission as integral to the church's **vocation.** He became the first director of the **World Council of Churches** Ecumenical Institute at Bossey, **Switzerland.** Kraemer's later books examined the relationship between Christianity and other religions; these works are marked by his rejection of religious relativism and his commitment to the distinctiveness of the Christian faith.

KRUMMACHER, FRIEDRICH WILHELM (1796–1868). German minister and preacher to the Prussian court. Krummacher was born in Mörs, near Düsseldorf, and studied at the universities of Halle and Jena. He served churches in Frankfurt (1819), Ruhrort (1823), Gemarke in Wuppertal (1825), and Elberfeld (1834). In 1847 he was called to Trinity Church, Berlin, and in 1853 became preacher to the Prussian court at Potsdam. A strong critic of the prevailing rationalism, Krummacher led a revival among the Reformed churches in the Rhineland. He was a teacher of **Philip Schaff**, through whom he also exerted considerable influence in **America**. He is best known for his sermon series *Elijah the Tishbite* (1838).

KUMANO, YOSHITAKA (1899–1981). Japanese Presbyterian minister and professor of systematic theology at **Tokyo Union Theological Seminary**. Born in Tokyo, **Japan**, Kumano attended Waseda University, where he became a Christian. Following his **baptism** in 1917, he withdrew from the university to attend Tokyo Theological Seminary and came under the influence of **Masahisa Uemura**. Kumano was ordained in 1926 and briefly served churches in Tokyo and Hakodate. He also served as copastor of the Musashino Church in Tokyo. In 1934 Kumano was appointed to the faculty of Tokyo Seminary. In addition to teaching theology, Kumano published *An Outline of Christianity* (1947), *Essence of Christianity* (1949), and a three-volume *Dogmatics* (1954–1965). In these works Kumano tried to relate the whole of theology to **eschatology**. He was one of the first Presbyterian theologians to contextualize Christian theology within Japanese life and culture.

KUROSAKI, KOKICHI (1886–1970). Japanese Bible teacher and author. Kurosaki became a Christian while attending First Higher School in Tokyo, **Japan.** He graduated from Tokyo University and worked for the Sumitomo Company. After the death of his wife, he became an independent Bible teacher and evangelist. He studied in Berlin; Tübingen, where he was influenced by Karl Heim; and Geneva, where he studied **John Calvin** with E. Choisy. He published a monthly magazine, *The Eternal Life* (1929–1966), in which appeared his Bible studies. He held Bible study meetings in Kansai, Osaka, Kyoto, and Kobe. He published a series of New Testament commentaries (1929–1950); a *New Testament Concordance* (Greek-Japanese/Japanese-Greek); with others, a three-volume *Old Testament Short Commentaries*; and a book on Calvin.

KUWADA, HIDENOBU (1895–1975). Japanese theologian and president of **Tokyo Union Theological Seminary.** After graduating from **Meiji**

Gakuin University, Kuwada studied at Auburn Theological Seminary in New York under Scottish theologian **John Baillie**, and at Harvard Divinity School. He became professor at Meiji Gakuin (1923) and in 1930, following the merger of the Meiji Gakuin Divinity School and Tokyo Theological Seminary, he was appointed professor of systematic theology and served as president of Tokyo Union Theological Seminary from 1945 to 1967. Kuwada was the principal founder of the Japan Association for Theological Education (1966) and helped to shape Protestant **education** in **Japan** during the post-World War II period. He was also a member of the Central Committee of the **World Council of Churches** (1955). At first a liberal Ritschlian, he was converted by the **dialectical theology** of **Karl Barth** and became an advocate of **neoorthodoxy**. His books include *The Essence of Christianity* (1932), *Dialectical Theology* (1933), *Christian Theology in Outline* (1941), and *Understanding Theology* (1939). His collected works were published in seven volumes, *The Complete Works of Hidenobu Kuwada* (1974).

KUWAIT. *See* MIDDLE EAST

KUYPER, ABRAHAM (1837–1920). Dutch Reformed theologian, journalist, and political leader. Kuyper was born in Maassluis, near Rotterdam, and studied at Leiden (1858–1863). He served churches in Beest (1863–1868), Utrecht (1868–1870), and Amsterdam (1870–1874). Moved by the deep piety of the villagers in his first parish, Kuyper embraced Calvinistic orthodoxy. He was attracted to politics and became leader of the Calvinistic Anti-Revolutionary Party. Editor of a daily newspaper, *De Standaard*, published from 1872 to 1919, Kuyper developed a political following that enabled him to enter the Dutch Parliament in 1873. There Kuyper devoted himself to the party organization and to a national Christian day school association (1878). He also founded the **Free University of Amsterdam** in 1879, a Calvinistic university "free" from both church and state control, and taught theology there for 20 years. In 1886 Kuyper led a movement of secession from the state church that resulted in the formation of the independent Geereformeerde Kerk (Reformed Church). Kuyper served as prime minister of the **Netherlands** from 1901 to 1905. Throughout his career, Kuyper tried to develop a Reformed perspective on public and cultural issues, drawing Christians into the public arena on the basis of their distinctive Christian worldview. He was interested in giving lower-middle-class Calvinists a voice in religious and political affairs. His theological works establish him, along with **Herman Bavinck**, as a leading voice in the Dutch neo-Calvinist movement. His theological writings include *Principles of Sacred Theology* (English translation 1898), *The Work of the Holy Spirit* (1900), and his Stone Lectures at **Princeton Theological Seminary** published as *Lectures on Calvinism* (1899).

- L -

LABADIE, JEAN DE (1610–1674). French Reformed theologian and Pietist leader. Labadie was born near Bordeaux, the son of the governor of Guienne. He became a Roman Catholic priest with a strong interest in mysticism. Dissatisfied with the Jesuits, Labadie left the order in 1639 and by 1644 had organized several small pietist communities dedicated to holy living. These communities influenced Philip Jakob Spener (1635–1705), the founder of German Pietism. By 1650 Labadie had read Calvin's *Institutes* and embraced the Reformed **faith.** He became a pastor in Geneva (1659–1666) and in Middelburg, **Holland**, until 1670, when unorthodox theological views led to his excommunication by the Reformed Church. His Middelburg congregation became a religious **community** of simple living in which goods and meals were held in common. Among those drawn to the group was Anna Maria von Schürmann (d. 1678), who set forth the group's principles in *Eucleria*. These views included the continuance of prophecy and the continuous Sabbath. Dutch authorities considered the Labadists too independent, so the group of about 55 adherents moved to Herford in Westphalia in 1670, to Bremen in 1672, and to Altona. The Labadists dispersed when their leader died, and the group was dissolved in the **Netherlands** and in the Western Hemisphere by 1732. Labadie's works include *La Réforme de l'église par le pastorat* (1667; *The Reform of the Church*).

LABOR AND LAND REFORM. The Reformed tradition's emphasis upon the **sovereignty of God** has ethical implications for the continual reform of the structures of society, including the reform of labor practices and land ownership in both industrialized and developing societies. In **central Europe**, groups of **deacons** confronted problems of industrialization such as child labor and urban poverty. In North America the **social gospel movement**, with some involvement by Reformed churches, addressed similar urban problems. With the growing complexity of modern societies in the 20th century, the call for labor and land reform has become widespread. Protestant missionaries, for example, have fought for land rights with African peoples against the encroachment of colonial settlement; developed agricultural mission projects that made attempts at land redistribution; and worked to end child labor practices. These and other social reforms remain a concern of the indigenous churches in many countries. Latin American **liberation theology**, with participation by Reformed churches, has worked for labor and land reform and helped to empower the poor to work for change in oppressive and unjust structures.

LAITY. The word means "people." The term is often used to refer to those who are not ordained by the **church** for specific ministerial functions. The distinction it implies between ministers and nonministers is not found in the New Testament. In the Reformed tradition, care is taken to recognize **ordination** for specific ministerial tasks such as the ministry of Word and Sacrament, and the offices of teacher, **elder**, and **deacon**. In **church government**, however, Reformed churches stress the parity of clergy and laity in the composition of church governing bodies beyond local church consistories or sessions. For governing purposes, clergy and laity have equal voice and vote. Reformed theology, like Protestant theology in general, recognizes the necessity for a vital ministry of the laity in carrying out the church's **mission.** The Protestant doctrine of **vocation** indicates that all Christians are called to God's service and that persons may exercise their vocation as disciples of Christ through different forms of work and witness.

LAL BEHARI DAY. *See* DAY, LAL BEHARI

LAL BIHARI (1850–1915). East Indian Presbyterian minister in **Trinidad.** Born in **India,** Lal Bihari had not found peace in Hinduism. While he was bathing in the Ganges River, an unscrupulous Brahmin stole his possessions. Destitute, he boarded a ship bound for Trinidad, where he met Canadian missionary K. J. Grant. Four years after his arrival he converted to Christianity. He was ordained in 1882 and served with Grant at the San Fernando Presbyterian mission. Lal Bihari was the first East Indian catechist in Trinidad and served as pastor of the Susamachar congregation.

LAMPE, FRIEDRICH ADOLF (1683–1729). German Reformed theologian. Lampe was born in Detmold and studied at Bremen (1698–1702) and the University of Franeker (1702–1703). He became pastor at Weeze, near Cleves, in 1703, and served churches in Duisburg (1706) and Bremen (1709). He was professor of dogmatics and church history at Utrecht (1720–1727) and served as pastor of St. Ansgar's Church. Lampe was a biblical theologian who tried to revive the **federal theology** of

Johannes Cocceius. He was influenced by pietism and stressed the importance of the inner life. He viewed the **church** as a divine institution and was against all separatist movements. Many of Lampe's students became influential ministers in the Reformed churches. His most important theological work is *Geheimnis des Gnadenbundes, dem grossen Bundesgott zu Ehren und allen heilbegierigen Seelen zur Erbauung geöffnet* (6 vols.; 1712–). He also published **catechisms**, including *Milch der Wahrheit, nach Anleitung des Heidelberger Katechismus* (1718) and *Einleitung zu dem Geheimnis des Gnadenbundes*; and *Delineatio theologiæ activæ* (1727), the first system of **ethics** derived from federal theology. In addition to his scholarly work, Lampe wrote many hymns for the Reformed church.

LAND REFORM. *See* LABOR AND LAND REFORM

LANE, EDWARD (1837–1892). American Presbyterian missionary in **Brazil**. Born in Dublin, **Ireland**, Lane emigrated to the **United States** as an orphan and graduated from Oglethorpe College and **Union Theological Seminary** in Virginia (1868). He went to Brazil in 1869 as part of a growing colony of Confederate emigrants who settled near Campinas after the U.S. Civil War. With George Morton, he established a church and soon afterward helped organize the Presbytery of São Paolo, which was the first **presbytery** founded by southern Presbyterians in Brazil. In 1870 this group established a school, which failed, but was soon followed by the Colégio Internacional (1873). Lane founded and edited the *Pulpito Evangelico*, the first Protestant journal in Brazil, and wrote many religious pamphlets in Portuguese. He was active in the formation of the Presbyterian seminary in Campinas.

LANG, JOHN DUNMORE (1799–1878). Scottish Presbyterian minister, newspaper editor, and promoter of Scottish emigration to **Australia**. Born in Greenock, Lang was educated at Glasgow University (1820–1825). He was ordained in the Church of Scotland (1822) and went to Sydney, Australia (1826), to become a pastor to Scottish settlers. He was the founder of a weekly newspaper, the *Colonist*, and wrote *An Historical and Statistical Account of New South Wales* (1834), *Transportation and Colonization* (1837), and *Freedom and Independence for the Golden Lands of Australia* (1852). On trips to **Scotland** he recruited ministers and Scottish emigrants, and in 1837 he brought about 4,000 people to Australia. He campaigned for improvements in **education**, was active in the Legislative Assembly, and was **moderator** of the General Assembly of the Presbyterian Church in New South Wales (1872).

LANG, JOHN MARSHALL (1834–1909). Scottish Presbyterian minister, social reformer, and educator. Educated at the University of Glasgow, Lang was pastor at Aberdeen (1856–1858), Fyvie (1858–1865), Anderson in Glasgow (1865–1868), Morningside in Edinburgh (1868–1873), and Barony in Glasgow (1873–1900). He became principal of the University of Aberdeen (1900–1909) and published *The Expansion of the Christian Life* (1897) and *The Church and Its Social Mission* (1902). A member of the Scottish Christian Social Union, Lang supported a minimum wage law, an end to sweatshop labor, and the rights of the workers in the Scottish Railway strike (1890–1891). He also advocated government-supported housing for the poor.

LANGO, EZEQUIEL (b. 1883). Mexican Presbyterian pastor, evangelist, and **moderator** of the **general assembly.** Lango's family converted to Protestantism when he was a boy. As an adult he became a lay preacher, Sunday school teacher, and elder; then he experienced a call to **ministry.** After completing his training at United Seminary, he was ordained, served several parishes, and then moved to the Yucatan Peninsula. There he encouraged the development of Presbyterian congregations among the Mayans, initiating the tradition of Mayan hymns and preparing Bible studies in Mayan. Lango went on to do several years of evangelistic **mission** in Chiapas before serving the church in national offices: moderator and permanent secretary-treasurer of the Presbytery of the Gulf of Mexico; itinerant secretary and administrator of the Progressive movement; and moderator and stated clerk of the general assembly.

LANGUAGE. *See* INCARNATIONAL LANGUAGE; LANGUAGE, THEOLOGICAL

LANGUAGE, THEOLOGICAL. Intelligent speech about **God** that makes use of **analogy** but avoids excessive anthropomorphism. Theological language is possible because the God of the Bible created humans with the faculties of intelligence and language as vehicles for receiving divine **revelation.** God is not only the object of thought and speech but is known through personal **faith** and commitment.

For centuries, Western Christians assumed that the "biblical languages" of Hebrew, Greek, and Latin were the only fit languages for theological discourse. Authoritative status was ascribed to these languages, ignoring their cultural assumptions and limitations. However, the formation of a global **church** and **Bible translations** have revealed the fundamental translatability of theological content and have disclosed the often subtle cultural captivity of the classical theological languages. The heightened sensitivity to the need for continuing translation, supported by modern textual research, is reforming theological language. This reform is reflected, for example, in the concern for inclusive language, which acknowledges sexist assumptions in cultures and their languages, and seeks better ways to translate the biblical message so that it can be heard by all as good news while remaining faithful to the original texts. Theological language always struggles with the tension between accurate translation and effective communication in constantly changing cultural settings.

ŁASKI, JOHN (1499–1560). Polish Protestant reformer. Łaski studied at Wittenberg and Bologna (1514–1517) and was ordained a priest in 1521. He spent a year pursuing humanistic studies, staying in the house of Erasmus (1524–1525). He was influenced by contact with **Huldrych Zwingli**, **John Oecolampadius**, and other Protestant reformers. He became Bishop of Vesprim in 1529 and Archdeacon of Warsaw in 1538. Łaski became a skilled administrator and carried out diplomatic missions for his uncle, Jan Łaski, the archbishop of Gniezno. In 1538 he joined the Protestant cause and moved to Emden in **Holland** (1542), where he became a pastor and married. In 1543 he became superintendent of churches in Frisia, under Countess Anna of Oldenburg. He visited **England** in 1548 at the invitation of **Thomas Cranmer** and in 1550 returned to pastor a church for European Protestants in London. He fled England upon the accession of Mary. Łaski contributed to the **Book of Common Prayer** (1552 ed.) and published an Emden Catechism (1554) that was later used by the authors of the **Heidelberg Catechism.** He eventually returned to **Poland**, where he became superintendent of the Reformed Churches of South Poland. Łaski failed in his attempt to unify the Protestants there.

LATIN AMERICA. *See* ANDEAN REPUBLICS AND GREATER COLOMBIA; BRAZIL; MESOAMERICA; SOUTHERN CONE OF SOUTH AMERICA

LATVIA. *See* CENTRAL AND EASTERN EUROPE

LAUBACH, FRANK (1884–1970). American Congregationalist missionary in the **Philippines** and pioneer in the work of adult literacy. Educated at **Union Theological Seminary** (N.Y.) and Columbia University, Laubach went to the Philippines (1915). He labored 15 years on the island of Luzon before working among the Moros people on Mindanao. He began literacy work with the Moros and developed the "each one teach one" concept. Laubach's methods developed gradually into a worldwide program of adult literacy **education** known as Laubach Literacy, Inc. (1955). Literacy programs have been prepared in over 300 languages, and it is estimated that over 100 million people have been taught to read by the Laubach method. Although nonsectarian, the literacy work is carried on by "an organization of volunteers motivated to Christian compassionate service to the helpless half of the world."

LAUGHTON, JOHN GEORGE (1891–1965). New Zealand home missionary with the Presbyterian Church of Aotearoa New Zealand and advocate of the Maori people. Laughton entered **mission** work in 1914 and in 1918 labored among the Tuhoe people in the remote bush outpost of Maungapohatu in the Urewera mountains. There he began a lifelong ministry among the Maori, at the time a profoundly alienated people whose land had been confiscated and whose prophet, Rua Kenana, had been harassed by the police. Ordained in 1921, Laughton gradually internalized the Maori culture, learning to think and live in the Maori way. He learned the Maori language and translated hymns and liturgies into Maori, producing a *Maori Service Book* (1933). From 1933 to 1955 Laughton was superintendent of the Maori mission. He used his position to fight assimilationist policies in both church and society. He played an important role in the establishment of Turakina Girls College and Maori Theological College at Whakatane. In 1943 he was elected **moderator** of the Presbyterian **general assembly**, and from 1956 to 1962 he served as moderator of the new Maori Synod. His publications include *From Forest Trail to City Street* (1961).

LAW. Divine rules that govern human behavior toward **God** and in society. Broadly, the term refers to the legal, ritual, and moral rules of the Old Testament. Narrowly, the term can refer to the law of Moses embodied in the Ten Commandments. Reformed understandings of the law of God are marked by the threefold usage outlined by **Calvin.** The first purpose of the law is to make people aware of their own **sin** and their need of **grace** (*Inst.* 2.7.7ff.). The second purpose, according to Calvin, is to restrain human sinfulness by showing the punishments that may come to those who break the law. The third and "principal use" is to guide believers into an understanding of the will of God. Thus, in Reformed thought, the law has primarily a positive role for the Christian. **Scripture** emphasizes that humanity has been unable to keep the law; it has only been fulfilled by Jesus Christ. Through God's grace in Christ, Christians do the works of the law, not in order to gain salvation but as a joyful response to the **salvation** given to them. This point is emphasized in the **Heidelberg Catechism**, in which the Law of God (Decalogue) is treated in part 3 under "Thankfulness."

LAWES, WILLIAM GEORGE (1839–1907). English Protestant missionary in **Niue** and **New Guinea**. Born in Berkshire, **England**, Lawes was sent by the **London Missionary Society** to Niue in 1860, where he educated evangelists and translated the New Testament (1870). In 1871 he went to Port Moresby, New Guinea, where he educated ministers, prepared a grammar of the Motu Language (1885), and translated the New Testament into Motu (1891). Lawes served in New Guinea until 1906. He died in Sydney, **Australia.**

LAWS, ROBERT (1851–1934). Scottish Presbyterian medical missionary in **Malawi.** Following his **education** as a doctor and minister in Glasgow, Laws went to Malawi under the United Presbyterian Church (1875). Building on the foundation established by **David Livingstone**, he developed a large **mission** among the Abangoni people, providing vocational training programs, a hospital, and a printing press. Under his leadership, mission stations spread across Livingstonia; schools were founded, teachers were educated, and eight languages were put into writing. Laws's missionary leadership was recognized when he was elected **moderator** of the General Assembly of the United Free Church of Scotland (1908). By 1925 Livingstonia had 19,000 communicants and 43,000 children in mission schools, many taught by African teachers. Laws was elected first moderator of the Presbyterian Church of Central Africa (1924). He retired in 1927 after 52 years of mission service.

LEBANON. *See* MIDDLE EAST

LEE (YI), SANG-CHAI (1850–1927). Korean public servant and Presbyterian lay leader. Born into a family of scholars, Lee passed the official Confucian examinations in 1867 and accepted a government post in Seoul. In 1884 Lee helped to establish the first middle and primary school system patterned on a Western model. Two years later, he became minister of state. Lee was one of the founding members of the Independence Club, a group that worked for national reform. Lee's opposition to the pro-Russian party led to his imprisonment. While in prison Lee found a copy of the Gospel of Matthew and became a Christian. After his release from prison, the 56–year-old Lee began work with Korean youth through the YMCA. In 1921 Lee was appointed the first chair of the Korean Educational Association and was a delegate to the World Student Christian Movement conference held in Peking. Lee was the most widely known and influential lay Christian leader in **Korea.**

LEE (YI), SEUNG-HOON (1864–1930). Korean Presbyterian elder, educator, and supporter of the Korean independence movement who wrote under the pen name "Nam-Kang." Lee was born in Chongju, North Pyonganbuk Province, **Korea.** His parents died by the time he was 10 years old, and Lee lived in the home of a brass manufacturer for whom he worked. Following the Sino-Japanese War of 1894–1895 and the Russo-Japanese War of 1904–1905, Lee studied Confucian classics and then traveled to Pyongyang in 1907 to hear Chang-Ho An, a Korean patriot who sought to transform Korean customs into new learning. Lee became a follower and began working at the Osan School, where he developed democratic ideals and offered **education** regardless of social class. During the Japanese Annexation, Lee was imprisoned in Taegu along with other church leaders. After his release in 1915 he attended the Presbyterian-related Pyongyang Theological Seminary in Pyongyang. In 1916 Lee returned to Osan, became an elder, and constructed a church at the Osan School. In 1919, he signed the Korean Declaration of Independence. Lee viewed Christianity as a religion of the oppressed and the poor and as the source of deliverance for the Korean people.

LEGGE, JAMES (1815–1897). Scottish Congregationalist missionary in **China.** After a liberal arts education at Aberdeen, Legge was sent to China as an ordained educator by the **London Missionary Society** (1839). He began as principal of the Anglo-Chinese College in Malacca; three years later he moved the institution to **Hong Kong**, where it functioned as a theological college and boys' school. Legge was the first minister of the Union Church of Hong Kong (1843–1873), active in New Testament scholarship, and a gifted student of classical Chinese literature. He began publishing translations of Chinese classics (1861), completing five volumes by 1886. In 1873 he retired and went to Oxford as the university's first professor of Chinese (1876). His scholarly translations of Confucian and Taoist texts, the first in English, opened up a new field of study. Legge's work represented a more cosmopolitan and less Western approach to world religions, advocating "orientalism," the belief that an oriental renaissance must be based on Asian ideas.

LEHMANN, PAUL L. (1906–1994). American Presbyterian minister, moral theologian, and civil libertarian. Born in Baltimore, Maryland, Lehmann was educated at **Union Theological Seminary** in New York (1936) and at the University of Bonn, where he studied with **Karl Barth.**

He became a friend of Dietrich Bonhoeffer when the young theologian came to study at Union Seminary in the 1930s. Lehmann served as professor of systematic theology at Union Seminary until 1974. During his long career he spoke out against McCarthyism, participated in Christian-Marxist dialogue, wrote on issues of war and peace and human sexuality, and was one of the first white theologians to engage black theology. His most widely read book is *Ethics in a Christian Context* (1963). *See also* Marxism and Christian Faith

LESOTHO. *See* SOUTHERN AFRICA

LIBERALISM. Theological movement within Protestantism that began during the mid-17th century. The movement emphasized human reason, the immanence of **God**, and the improvement of human nature. It was not a static theology, but one that went through several stages, embracing the rationalism associated with René Descartes and the Enlightenment, emphasizing the religious experience associated with **Friedrich Schleiermacher** and Romanticism, and accepting the modernist impulse associated with Albrecht Ritschl, Wilhelm Herrmann, and Adolf von Harnack, who taught moral progressivism. The movement was criticized by **neoorthodoxy** during the early part of the 20th century, and by the end of the century it had fractured into various theological schools emphasizing political theology and **liberation theology**, and the psychology and sociology of religion.

LIBERATION THEOLOGY. A theological approach and method developed in Latin America since the 1960s in reaction to the failure of modern development programs to solve the problems of poverty and economic injustice. The biblical liberation theme is modeled after the Exodus, prophetic admonitions regarding the poor, and Jesus' proclamation of the reign of **God**; it shapes a theology that interprets the gospel out of the immediate reality of human suffering. Examining the structures of economic dependency in Latin America (often using Marxist categories), Catholic and Protestant theologians began to call for radical change; Catholic clergy further developed liberation theology after Vatican II and the 1968 Medellin Conference of Bishops. For its major proponents (Rubem Alves, Leonardo Boff, Jose Míguez Bonino, and Gustavo Gutiérrez), an authentic theology of liberation emerges from the Christian commitment to the struggle against injustice, as the Bible reveals God's consideration for the poor and empowers the **church** to practice liberation. This understanding of liberation expands the traditional understanding of redemption, by stressing that the gospel not only liberates the individual from **sin**, but confronts systemic and corporate bondage through Christian witness and action.

LIBERIA. *See* WEST AFRICA

LINDLEY, DANIEL (1801–1880). American Presbyterian missionary in **South Africa.** Educated at Ohio University and **Union Theological Seminary** at Hampden-Sydney, Virginia, Lindley was sent to South Africa by the **American Board of Commissioners for Foreign Missions** (1835). With his large family, he traveled across the Transvaal, working among the Zulu people and seeking to alleviate tensions with the Dutch settlers (the Voortrekkers). He transferred to Natal and served as a pastor to the settler community. Following a stay in the **United States**, Lindley went to Inanda to resume work among the Zulus. As an advocate of Zulu rights, he supported Zulu land rights, the **ordination** of African pastors, and the incorporation of Zulu customs in the **church** (an openness uncharacteristic of his contemporaries). He also remained close to the Voortrekkers, who opposed the work of the mission and viewed the Zulu people as enemies. Lindley was an effective interpreter of the African situation to audiences in **Europe** and **North America.**

LITHUANIA. *See* CENTRAL AND EASTERN EUROPE

LIVINGSTONE, DAVID (1813–1873). Scottish physician, missionary, and explorer in **Africa.** Born in Blantyre, Livingstone quit school at age 10, worked in a mill while attending night school, and studied **medicine** at the Andersonian Medical School in Glasgow. After completing medical school in London, he was sent by the **London Missionary Society** to **South Africa** (1841), where he worked with **Robert Moffat.** He became famous for his explorations of the African interior and his extensive written reports of Lake Ngami (1849), Victoria Falls, and other regions. His Zambezi River expedition in 1858 was an embarrassment; Livingstone failed to discover whether the river was navigable. Nevertheless, Livingstone saw Portuguese and Arab slavetrading during his travels in the interior, and in 1866 he became determined to end the practice. During Livingstone's last journeys, rumors reached the Western press that he had died. An American newspaper, the *New York Herald,* sent Henry M. Stanley to find him, and the two explorers met at Ujiji in November 1871. Livingstone published *Missionary Travels and Researches in South Africa* (1856). He is buried in Westminster Abbey.

LOETSCHER, LEFFERTS A. (1904–1981). American Presbyterian church historian. Loetscher was born in Dubuque, Iowa, and graduated from Princeton University and **Princeton Theological Seminary.** After earning a doctorate at the University of Pennsylvania (1943), he was appointed instructor of church history (1941), and later became professor of American church history (1954–1974) at Princeton Theological Seminary. Loetscher was a longtime member of the board of directors of the Presbyterian Historical Society (1947–1972) and served as president of the American Society of Church History in 1962. One of the premier historians of American **Presbyterianism,** Loetscher's works include *American Christianity: An Historical Interpretation with Representative Documents* (2 vols.; 1960, 1963), prepared with H. Sheldon Smith and Robert T. Handy, *The Broadening Church* (1954), *Twentieth Century Encyclopedia of Religious Knowledge* (1955), *A Brief History of the Presbyterians* (4th ed., 1983), *The Presbyterian Enterprise—Sources of American Presbyterian History* (1956), compiled with M. W. Armstrong and C. A. Anderson, and *Facing the Enlightenment and Pietism: Archibald Alexander and the Founding of Princeton Theological Seminary* (1983).

LONDON MISSIONARY SOCIETY (LMS). An independent English missionary organization with a global outreach and ecumenical outlook. Organized in 1795, the society was primarily a Congregationalist enterprise, but English and Scottish Presbyterians also played an important role, with almost half of the original committee being Scots. The LMS conducted **mission** work in **Tahiti** (1797), Sierra Leone (1797–1798), **India** (1798), **South Africa** (1799), the **West Indies** (1807), **China** (1807), and **Madagascar** (1818). Its most famous missionaries include **William Ellis** and **John Williams** of the Pacific, **Robert Moffat** and **David Livingstone** of **Africa, Robert Morrison of China**, and **William George Lawes** and **James Chalmers** of **New Guinea.** In addition to its evangelistic work, the LMS succeeded in establishing mission-related educational systems, transliterating indigenous languages into the Roman alphabet, and publishing religious and educational books in local languages. In 1966 the LMS became the Congregational Council for World Mission and in 1977, the Council for World Mission. The council, which maintains its headquarters in London, now carries out the work of its predecessor bodies, the LMS and the **Commonwealth Missionary Society**, in partnership with churches of LMS and English Presbyterian heritage.

LORD'S SUPPER. The central act of Christian **worship** and, together with **baptism**, one of the two **sacraments** of the **church.** Also referred to as the Eucharist or Communion, the Lord's Supper was instituted by Jesus Christ. The Reformed churches understand the Lord's Supper as a **covenant** sign of God's promises, and a means of **grace** that sustains the **faith** of the Christian **community.** The actions of the Lord's Supper include the reading of the words of institution, the breaking of the bread, and the distribution of the bread and cup. The Lord's Supper reminds the community of faith to be thankful for the promises of **God**; to remember the life, **death,** and **resurrection** of Jesus and the benefits received from his obedience to God; to participate in the fellowship of believers who eat, drink, and gather around the Lord; and to anticipate the future eternal life that awaits the church. The Supper is a divine **accommodation** to human weakness in which God's promises of **salvation** in Jesus Christ are sealed in the lives of those who believe (see *Inst.* 4.17). Reformed theology teaches that Christ is genuinely present in the Lord's Supper, though not physically or locally present. Through the power of the **Holy Spirit** worshipers "lift up their hearts" *(sursum corda)* to the heavenly realm where Christ dwells (*Inst.* 4.17.36). This spiritual communion brings Christ's benefits to believers so that "whenever they see symbols appointed by the Lord," they are "persuaded that the truth of the thing signified is surely present there" (*Inst.* 4.17.10). The Supper is a "visible word" that spiritually unites believers with Christ.

LORRAIN, REGINALD ARTHUR (1880–1944). British Congregationalist missionary in **Myanmar** (formerly Burma). Born in London, Lorrain was ordained in 1906 and went to Burma in 1907. He founded the Mara Grammar and Mission School (1909) and translated the New Testament into the Mara dialect (1927). Lorrain sent Mara evangelists, including **T. Mathao**, to various parts of the country. These evangelists founded over 20 congregations. Lorrain is known as the founder of the Mara Evangelical Church in **Myanmar.**

LOVEDALE. A Church of Scotland **mission** center and school founded in Alice, **South Africa** in 1824, named after John Love (1757–1825), the first secretary of the **Glasgow Missionary Society**. The stone buildings of Lovedale were destroyed in the frontier war (1834–1835) between colonists and Africans. In 1836 the missionary board of Lovedale decided to abandon the old site and to rebuild four miles to the west, within the boundary of the Cape Colony. In 1838 a church school was established at the new site and in 1841 the institution was officially opened under the principalship of William Govan. The Lovedale Institute educated South Africans and Rhodesians to preach, to teach in mission schools, and to work in various trades, including blacksmithing, bookbinding and printing, and agricultural work. The nondenominational institute became well-known for its program of industrial **education**. The educational work of Lovedale was assumed by the government and led to the formation of the University of Fort Hare; the Reformed Presbyterian Church in South Africa now operates the printing department of Lovedale.

LUTHULI, ALBERT JOHN (1898–1967). Congregationalist political leader in **South Africa**. After completing his education in **mission** schools and teaching at Adam's College until 1936, Luthuli was elected chief of the Abase-Makolweni people in the Groutville Mission Reserve. In this role, he addressed the expanding realities of structural racism as **apartheid** began to take legislated form. He joined the African National Congress (ANC) in 1945 and became its provincial president in 1951. Because of his political activism, the government deposed him from his chieftainship (1952). He led the nonviolent activities of the ANC with conviction, gaining an international reputation. Although banished from politics for the last 15 years of his life, tried for treason and found not guilty, and then detained under "state of emergency" regulations, Luthuli never wavered. His speeches articulated the black African struggle for freedom and justice and documented the struggle against apartheid. He was awarded the Nobel Peace Prize in 1961.

LUXEMBOURG. *See* NORTHERN EUROPE

LUZZI, GIOVANNI (1856–1948). Waldensian Bible translator in **Italy**. Born in Engadine, **Switzerland**, Luzzi graduated from the Theological College of the **Waldensians** in Florence and **New College, Edinburgh**. He was ordained in 1886 and served a Waldensian congregation in Florence from 1887 to 1902. He was then appointed professor at the Theological College, becoming an expert in biblical translation. In 1906 he was appointed chair of the interdenominational committee for the revision of the Diodati Bible. The Diodati translation (1607) had been prepared by Giovanni Diodati, a professor of Hebrew at the Academy of Geneva, and had since been used by the Protestant churches in Italy. Luzzi's revision of the New Testament was completed in 1915 and the complete Bible (*La Riveduta*) was published in 1924. Luzzi also prepared a personal translation, which he published between 1921 and 1930. Although the format of the work made it difficult to use, its ecumenical spirit and contemporary expression contributed to a better understanding of the Bible in the Waldensian churches.

- M -

MACHEN, J[OHN] GRESHAM (1881–1937). American Presbyterian New Testament scholar. Machen was born in Baltimore and graduated from Johns Hopkins University in 1901. He then studied at **Princeton Theological Seminary** (1902–1905) and the universities of Marburg and Göttingen (1905–1906). Machen became an instructor at Princeton Seminary in 1906, and then assistant professor of New Testament in 1915. His two major New Testament studies are *The Origin of Paul's Religion* (1921) and *The Virgin Birth of Christ* (1930). He also wrote a widely used textbook, *New Testament Greek for Beginners* (1923). An important voice of conservative Christianity, Machen played an important role in the **fundamentalist-modernist controversy** in the Presbyterian Church during the 1920s. He opposed modernism in his book *Christianity and Liberalism* (1923), arguing that **liberalism** and biblical Christianity were two different religions. When Princeton Seminary was reorganized in 1929 to allow a wider latitude of theological opinion, Machen and others left to found Westminster Theological Seminary near Philadelphia. At Westminster Machen served as professor of New Testament and was the primary financial backer of the school. In 1933 Machen founded an Independent Board for Presbyterian foreign **mission**. This action led to his suspension from the Presbyterian Church in 1936. Machen and others went on to form the Presbyterian Church of America, renamed the Orthodox Presbyterian Church. This denomination continues the tradition of the old **Princeton theology** championed by Machen.

MACKAY, ALEXANDER (1849–1890). Scottish missionary in Uganda. Born in Rhymie, Aberdeenshire, Mackay studied at the Free Church teacher's college and was educated in Berlin as an engineer. In 1875 he volunteered in response to a general appeal from Henry M. Stanley to go to Uganda with the Anglican Church Missionary Society. After arriving in Kampala in 1875, Mackay spent two years building a road to Lake Victoria and placing a large boat on the lake. His teaching and evangelistic work yielded the first converts in 1882. When additional **mission** personnel arrived at his station in 1887, Mackay moved south of Lake Victoria to Usambiro, where he undertook a translation of the Gospel of John in the Luganda language, and saw his translation of the Gospel of Matthew through the press. Although he survived much violence, including civil war, he succumbed to malaria.

MACKAY, GEORGE LESLIE (1844–1901). Canadian Presbyterian missionary in **Taiwan.** Born in Zorra, Ontario, Mackay was educated at

Princeton and Edinburgh Universities, and in 1871 was the first Canadian Presbyterian missionary sent to China. During his career in Taiwan he established more than 60 churches and founded the Tainan Theological College (1876), the Mackay Hospital (1880) in Tamsui, and the Boys and Girls Middle Schools in Tainan (1885, 1887). In 1894 he served as **moderator** of the Presbyterian Church in Canada. He told the story of the founding of the Taiwanese Presbyterian church in his book, *From Far Formosa* (4th ed. 1896).

MACKAY, JOHN A. (1889–1983). Scottish Presbyterian missionary in **Peru**, theological educator, and ecumenical leader. Born in Inverness, **Scotland**, Mackay studied at the University of Aberdeen, **Princeton Theological Seminary** in the **United States**, and with existentialist scholar Miguel de Unamuno in Madrid, **Spain.** He served as an educational missionary in Lima, Peru, where he was appointed to a professorship in philosophy at Peru's National University of San Marcos (1915) and was the founding principal of the Protestant Colegio San Andrés (1917). Mackay worked as a writer and evangelist with the South American Federation of YMCAs (1925–1932) and went to the United States, where he served as mission board secretary of Latin America and Africa for the Presbyterian Church in the U.S.A. (1932–1936) and president of Princeton Theological Seminary (1936–1959). At Princeton he was the founding editor of the journal *Theology Today* (1944) and taught ecumenics. Mackay was committed to the task of **mission** and was a world leader in the **ecumenical movement.** He served on committees of the **World Council of Churches** (1948–1954) and was chair of the International Missionary Council (1947–1958). He was elected **moderator** of the Presbyterian Church in the U.S.A. (1953) and president of the Presbyterian Alliance of Reformed Churches (1954–1959). During the era of McCarthyism in the United States, Mackay courageously opposed the Senate's inquisitional political tactics and committee hearings, which he viewed as state idolatry. His publications include *The Other Spanish Christ* (1933), *Spain and Latin America: Christianity on the Frontier* (1950), *The Presbyterian Way of Life* (1960), and *Ecumenics: The Science of the Church Universal* (1964).

MACKENZIE, JEAN KENYON (1874–1936). American Presbyterian missionary in **Cameroon.** Educated at Van Ness Seminary in San Francisco, at the Sorbonne, and at the University of California, Mackenzie went to the German Cameroon and engaged in evangelistic work in remote villages (1903–1913). She returned to New York (1914) and published reports on her African experience; her literary work contributed to the American understanding of **Africa** and Christian **mission** in general. Mackenzie returned to Cameroon (1916) to assist in the difficult transition from German to French colonial rule. After 1918 she remained in the United States, publishing short stories, articles, and poetry, all dealing with mission work. Her writings conveyed much of African life and culture.

MACKINTOSH, HUGH ROSS (1870–1936). Scottish Presbyterian minister and theologian. Mackintosh was born in Paisley and educated at the universities of Edinburgh, Freiburg, Halle, Hesse-Nassau, and Marburg. He was ordained in 1897 in the Free Church of Scotland. He served parishes in Tayport (1897–1901) and Aberdeen (1901–1904), and was then appointed professor of divinity at **New College**, **Edinburgh**, where he served from 1904 to 1936. He was also **moderator** of the General Assembly of the Church of Scotland in 1932. Mackintosh translated works by Albrecht Ritschl and **Friedrich Schleiermacher** and through his posthumously published book, *Types of Modern Theology* (1937), helped interpret German theology to the English-speaking world. In his later years Mackintosh moved away from **liberalism** and became absorbed in the works of **John Calvin**, **John Knox**, and **Karl Barth**. His major focus was on the forgiveness of sin as the center of the gospel (*The Christian Experience of Forgiveness* [1927]). His kenotic **Christology** is expressed in *The Doctrine of the Person of Jesus Christ* (1912). Other works include *Immortality and the Future* (1915); *The Divine Initiative* (1921); and *Some Aspects of Christian Belief* (1923).

MADAGASCAR. *See* INDIAN OCEAN ISLANDS

MAKEMIE, FRANCIS (1658?–1708). Founder of American **Presbyterianism.** Makemie was born of Scots-Irish parents in Donegal, **Ireland**, and was educated at the University of Glasgow (1676–1680). After **ordination** in 1682, Makemie went to **America** and worked as a traveling evangelist in North Carolina, Maryland, Virginia, and Barbados. In 1706, Makemie organized the first American **presbytery**, the Presbytery of Philadelphia, and became its first **moderator.** The following year he was arrested and imprisoned by Governor Cornbury of New York for preaching without a license. Makemie vigorously defended his right of free speech and religious liberty, and he was acquitted. Makemie's widely publicized case gained members for the Presbyterian Church and furthered the cause of religious freedom in America.

MALAWI. *See* SOUTHERN AFRICA

MALAYSIA. *See* SOUTHEAST ASIA

MALO, DAVID (1793–1853). Hawaiian Congregationalist minister, scholar, and superintendent of schools. Malo was born in Keauhou, North Kona, on the island of **Hawaii.** About 1823 he moved to Lahaina, Maui, where he met the missionary **William Richards** and became a Christian convert. Malo and Richards, who later served as Hawaiian minister of education, became lifelong friends. Malo wrote some of the early Hawaiian laws of 1827 and became a counselor to Hawaiian royalty, speaking out against the riotous conduct of foreign sailors and the exploitation of Hawaiian workers in the sandalwood and other industries. In 1828 Malo joined the church at Lahaina, taking the name David in **baptism.** In 1831 he was the first student to enter the newly organized **mission** school at Lahainaluna. There he learned to read and write Hawaiian and gradually accumulated a library of Hawaiian literature. In 1841 Malo was appointed general school agent for Maui, and he served as superintendent of schools until 1845. He also served as a member of the Hawaiian House of Representatives for the term of 1846 and played an active role in the Great *Mahele*, or division of the land of 1848–1849. He was ordained in 1852 and became pastor of Ke'oke'a Church, Maui, where he served until his death. Malo wrote a life of Kamehameha I (lost); a cultural history of ancient Hawaii titled *Ka mo'oolelo Hawaii* (1838), later expanded and translated as *Hawaiian Antiquities* (1898); and was the chief collaborator on Sheldon Dibble's *The History of the Sandwich Islands* (1843).

MANSON, T[HOMAS] W[ALTER] (1893–1958). British Presbyterian New Testament scholar. Manson was born in Tynemouth, Northumberland, and graduated from the University of Glasgow in 1913. He attended Westminster College, Cambridge, and following graduation became pastor at Falstone (1926–1932). Manson was then appointed professor of New Testament Greek and exegesis at Mansfield College, Oxford (1932–1936), and professor of **biblical criticism** and exegesis at the University of Manchester (1936–1958). His major work, *The Teaching of Jesus* (1931), written while he was still a pastor, argued that Jesus used the title "Son of Man" in a corporate sense until the end of his ministry; when his disciples showed they were not ready to endure suffering, Jesus endured it alone. His other works include *The Sayings of Jesus* (1949), *The Servant-Messiah* (1953), *Ministry and Priesthood: Christ's and Ours* (1958), and *On Paul and John* (1963).

MARBURG COLLOQUY (1529). A meeting of Protestant Reformers held at Marburg, **Germany.** The meeting was called as a result of Landgrave Philip of Hesse's desire for the Protestants to resolve their theological differences. Two groups of theologians attended the meeting: Martin Luther and his followers, Philip Melanchthon, Justus Jonas, Johann Brenz, Kaspar Cruciger, and Andreas Osiander; and the Swiss and Strasbourg theologians, **Huldrych Zwingli, John Oecolampadius, Martin Bucer,** Wolfgang Capito, Jakob Sturm, and others. The colloquy produced 15 articles of agreement on major theological doctrines including the **Trinity,** Christ's person, **justification** by **faith, baptism,** and the role of secular authority. The meeting was sharply divided over the issue of the **Lord's Supper.** Luther adhered to the actual words of Christ regarding the Supper and insisted on a literal presence, whereas Zwingli understood Christ's words in symbolic terms and advocated a symbolic presence only. Although the Colloquy established a substantial unity of belief, the disagreement over the Lord's Supper ultimately divided the Lutherans from the Swiss and German Reformed Protestants.

MARGARET OF ANGOULÊME (1492–1549). Sister of Francis I, king of **France,** Duchess of Alençon, Queen of Navarre, and supporter of the Reform movement in France. After the death in 1525 of her first husband, the Duke of Alençon, Margaret married Henry II of Navarre (1527). As Duchess of Alençon, Margaret supported church reform and gathered around her a group of French artists and humanist scholars, including Jacques Lefèvre d'Étaples, **William Farel,** Gérard Roussel, Michel d'Arande, Clement Marot, and Guillaume Briçonnet. She appointed Briçonnet bishop in Meaux, the capital of her duchy. Several of these scholars from Margaret's "group of Meaux" later became Protestant. Although she never left the Catholic Church, Margaret ordered the **preaching** of **justification** by **faith,** accepted the Protestant **sacraments,** supported religious services in the vernacular, urged the reform of monastic abuses, and rejected confession, indulgences, and the intercession of the saints. Margaret eventually lost influence with Francis I, who gave up the cause of reform, but she continued her policies in Navarre. Margaret composed prose works such as *l'Heptaméron* and poetry issued under the titles *Miroir de l'âme pécheresse* and *Les Dernières Poésies.*

MARIAN EXILES. Edwardian Protestants in the **British Isles** who fled the reign of Mary I from 1553 to 1558 and settled in Geneva, **Switzerland.** The exiles fled for religious, academic, and political reasons. They were a heterogeneous group, having differing opinions on several matters, including resistance to the "ungodly ruler." With regard to political resistance, the views of **John Knox** and Christopher Goodman were among the more radical. Much has been said about the influence of these exiles on their return to Britain, but it is clear that they did not intend to form a "Puritan Party." They did influence the reign of Elizabeth by serving as members of the Privy Council, as court preachers, and as members of the ecclesiastical commissions (1559). Seventeen exiles also became bishops. The exiles played an important part in the success of the **Elizabethan Settlement.**

MARQUESAS ISLANDS. *See* PACIFIC OCEAN ISLANDS

MARRIAGE, THEOLOGY OF. Marriage is the public union of a man and a woman in a relationship characterized by love, service, and faithfulness. Marriage regularizes sexual behavior and provides a legal basis for having children. Although marriage is not a specifically Christian institution, it fulfills God's plan for **creation** (Gen. 1:27). Reformed churches view marriage as a covenantal relationship analogous to God's **covenant** with humanity and to Christ's relationship with the **church.** The marriage relationship is acknowledged to be good in itself and to be a blessing from **God**, who is at the center of the marriage covenant. Marriage is further understood as a Christian **vocation** enabled by God's **grace** and as a means by which both partners may live out their lives in Christian discipleship. The faithfulness of God to biblical covenantal relationships and of Jesus Christ to doing the will of God are norms to which married persons may aspire with each other.

The Reformed churches recognize that factors may arise that prevent the marriage relationship from being a true life partnership and that divorce may occur. **John Calvin** was opposed to divorce and believed that divorced persons should not remarry. **Huldrych Zwingli**, who appealed to the divorce provisions of the Old Testament, was more liberal in his approach, as were **Martin Bucer**, **Heinrich Bullinger**, and **John Milton.** The **Puritans** generally held the position of Calvin. Gradually the more permissive approach has gained acceptance in many, but not all, Reformed churches. In matters relating to marriage and divorce, the Reformed churches emphasize the forgiveness and grace of God and the healing fellowship of the Christian **community.**

MARROW CONTROVERSY (1718–1723). A doctrinal controversy in the Church of Scotland that involved the relationship between the **sovereignty** of **God** and human responsibility in **salvation.** The controversy was triggered when Thomas Boston recommended Edward Fisher's book,

The Marrow of Modern Divinity (1645), to a fellow minister. The book was reprinted in 1718, with a preface by James Hog. Although *The Marrow* was an orthodox exposition of the Calvinist **federal theology** of its day, by the early 18th century Scottish theology had incorporated more legalizing tendencies. Principal James Hadow of St. Mary's College, St. Andrews, charged that the book's emphasis on **grace** implied a universal salvation. In 1720 the General Assembly of the Church of Scotland declared the book to be heretical and prohibited ministers from recommending it. Twelve "Marrow Brethren," including Boston and Ralph and Ebenezer Erskine, signed a document supporting the book because they regarded its suppression as an attack on **evangelical** truth. The protesters were admonished by the general assembly of 1722 and were subsequently persecuted by other ministers. Their own **preaching** attracted followers, and their theology eventually became that of the Secession churches, which formed the Associate Presbytery.

MARSHALL ISLANDS. *See* PACIFIC OCEAN ISLANDS

MARTYR, PETER. *See* VERMIGLI, PETER MARTYR

MARXISM AND CHRISTIAN FAITH. In Marxism, Christianity is rejected and its ultimate demise anticipated. In the Soviet version of Marxism, atheism was advanced as a political program to replace religion. Most churches have regarded Marxism with hostility; the official papal position denounced it. However, many Christian and Marxist thinkers have been able to separate Marxist philosophy, with its atheistic implications, from Marxist social and economic analysis, thus moving from mutual renunciation to dialogue. Marxist concepts such as "alienation," "exploitation," and "class struggle" have found their way into Christian social-ethical discussions (e.g., in the works of **Josef Hromádka**, **Karl Barth**, Helmut Gollwitzer, and Jürgen Moltmann). Liberation theologians have made use of Marxist economic analysis to interpret the Latin American context. Churches in former socialist countries have developed various strategies for interaction with governments, sometimes accompanied by controversy. Whether a "Christian socialism" is possible may be debated, but Christian-Marxist dialogue has not harmed Christianity and has refocused the theological discussion of themes like **eschatology**, hope (Jürgen Moltmann), freedom, solidarity, and social progress. Marxist influence has declined since the breakup of the Soviet Union. *See also* Liberation Theology

MASS MOVEMENTS. *See* PEOPLE MOVEMENTS

MATERIALISM AND WEALTH. The preoccupation of modern industrialized market societies with material possessions, property, and financial security has profound implications for the **church**. In the Bible, wealth and property are the result of God's blessing and require **stewardship** and accountability. The dangers of wealth and the oppression of the poor by the rich are major themes of prophetic and wisdom literature. The literature of the patristic period and the monastic movement encouraged self-denial and the renunciation of worldly goods for spiritual growth. The pressure of the free market system with its emphasis on success and measurable growth can influence churches to likewise define themselves. The disparities between the rich and poor and the struggle for material advancement create ethical challenges for all churches, and complicate ecumenical relationships. Particularly problematic is the "prosperity gospel," with its claim that **God** intends to bless Christian followers with wealth. *See also* Capitalism; Church Growth School

MATHAO, T. (1911–1990). Evangelist, pastor, and leader in the Mara Evangelical Church of Myanmar (formerly Burma). Born at Sabyh village, Mathao converted to the Christian **faith** in 1939. He was appointed evangelist in 1945, being one of a group of evangelists sent out by Congregationalist missionary **Reginald A. Lorrain** to organize churches. He organized the first Mara church in **Myanmar** and was ordained a pastor in 1950. He spent the next 39 years working there and saw the Mara Evangelical Church grow to over 15,000 members. Mathao retired in 1989 and died at Tisi village.

MATHER, COTTON (1663–1728). American Congregationalist minister in New England. Mather was the grandson of Richard Mather and **John Cotton** and the son of Increase Mather, all prominent Puritan clergy. He entered Harvard at age 12 and graduated in 1678 at age 15. With his father, he pastored Boston's Second (Congregational) Church, remaining there for his entire life. Mather tried to maintain the ideals of the original **Puritans** and was involved in virtually every religious controversy of his time. He desired the edification of the faithful and was consumed with a passion for religious devotion. He supported the court decisions in the Salem witchcraft trials (1692), a position that damaged his reputation. Mather was a colonial member of London's Royal Society and boldly defended a plan for inoculation against smallpox. He was firmly committed to the theology of the **Westminster Confession** and **catechisms**, and he emphasized the need for **conversion** and **election by**

God. He was mystically inclined, seeing divine **providence** at work in all events. His dream of universal piety, rooted in the Puritan vision, also led him to interpret moral standards in ways that fit the nation's growing spirit of individual liberty. Mather was a prolific author, producing some 450 books on numerous subjects. His major works include *The Wonderful Works of God Commemorated* (1690); *Magnalia Christi Americana: The Ecclesiastical History of New England from Its First Planting* (1702); and *Bonifacius: An Essay Upon the Good* (1710).

MAURITIUS. *See* INDIAN OCEAN ISLANDS

MAURY, PIERRE (1890–1956). French Reformed pastor, theologian, and ecumenical leader. Maury studied humanities, philosophy, and theology at the Sorbonne, the University of Berlin, and Harvard University. He was a pastor in Ferney and Passy-Paris, led the Federation of Christian Students, chaired the National Council of the French Reformed Church, and taught at the Faculty of Protestant Theology in Paris. He was a member of the Central Committee of the **World Council of Churches** for the Amsterdam (1948) and Evanston (1954) assemblies. As a friend and colleague of **Karl Barth**, he initiated the French encounter with **dialectical theology** and was credited for bringing renewal to French Reformed theology. Maury was especially noted for his efforts to rebuild connections to the German Protestant church following World War II; he was one of a group of ecumenical leaders who met with German church leaders in Stuttgart, resulting in the celebrated Stuttgart Confession (1945). In his sermons, lectures, articles, and books, Maury proclaimed Jesus Christ and challenged the secularizing European culture of the mid-20th century.

MAYFLOWER COMPACT (1620). The foundational document of civil and religious life in New England. The compact was made by the Pilgrims as their ship *Mayflower* lay at anchor off Cape Cod, Massachusetts. Although not all Pilgrims were **Puritans**, the document was a Puritan **covenant** that bound its 41 signers to a single colony and to the government and laws that would later be established. Thus it became the charter that established self-government in Plymouth colony. The compact remained in effect until 1691, when the colony became part of Massachusetts.

McBETH, SUE L. (1830–1893). American missionary among the Nez Percé. McBeth was born in **Scotland** and raised in America. She served as a teacher at Fairfield University, Iowa, before becoming a missionary among the Choctaw people of Indian Territory in the Southwest. She worked at Good Water Station from 1859 to 1861. The Civil War interrupted her work, and she went to St. Louis, where she served in several war hospitals. McBeth remained in St. Louis until 1873, when she resumed **mission** work, this time among the Nez Percé. She served as a missionary with the **American Board of Commissioners for Foreign Missions** at Lapwai (1873) and Kamiah, Idaho, where she was a teacher on the reservation. From 1885 to 1893 she worked in the nearby town of Mount Idaho. She organized educational and evangelistic work in an effort to produce Nez Percé leaders for self-sufficient Indian churches. McBeth also translated hymns and prepared a dictionary and grammar in the Nez Percé language.

McCLURE, ROBERT BAIRD (1900–1991). Canadian Presbyterian medical missionary. Born in Portland, Oregon, McClure was the son of medical missionaries in **China.** He worked as a surgeon and public **health** educator in Henan (Honan), China, from 1923 to 1937. During the war with Japan, McClure served as field director of the International Red Cross in central China. From 1941 to 1946 he led the Friends of the Ambulance Unit, providing mobile surgical, medical, and public health services. When China was closed to missionaries in 1949, McClure traveled to Gaza, where he served Palestinian refugees from 1950 to 1954. He then became superintendent of the Ratlam Hospital in **India** (1954–1967). He returned to **Canada** in 1968 and served as the first nonordained **moderator** of the United Church of Canada, serving from 1968 to 1971. He spent his retirement years working in Borneo, rural Peru, the Caribbean, and the **Congo.** McClure was an outspoken humanitarian who worked on behalf of the world's poor.

McCULLOCH, THOMAS (1776–1843). Canadian Presbyterian minister, educator, and author. Born in Ferenze, **Scotland**, McCulloch was educated at the University of Glasgow and Divinity Hall, Whitburn. He became a minister in the General Associate Synod, immigrated to **Canada**, and organized a Presbyterian congregation at Pictou, Nova Scotia, in 1803. McCulloch founded the Pictou Academy in 1808; a theological college at West River, Pictou County; and a newspaper, the *Colonial Patriot* (1827), which championed public support of **education.** From 1838 to 1843 he served as teacher and the first president of Dalhousie College (now University) in Halifax. McCulloch was the author of *The Nature and Uses of a Liberal Education* (1819), *Calvinism: The Doctrine of the Scriptures* (1849), and fictional works, including *Letters of*

Mephibosheth Stepsure (1821–1823), reprinted as *The Stepsure Letters* (1960).

McNEILL, JOHN T. (1885–1975). Canadian Presbyterian minister, historian, and **Calvin** scholar. McNeill was born in Elmsdale, Prince Edward Island, and graduated from McGill University; Westminster Hall (now United Theological College of British Columbia), Vancouver; and the University of Chicago. He was a pastor and professor at **Knox College** in **Canada** before becoming professor of the history of European Christianity at the University of Chicago (1927–1944), and then professor of church history at **Union Theological Seminary** in New York (1944–1953). He made a significant contribution to the history of the Reformed tradition with the publication of his book *The History and Character of Calvinism* (1954). He served as general editor of the Library of Christian Classics series (Westminster Press) and was the editor of Calvin's *Institutes of the Christian Religion*, translated by Ford Lewis Battles (2 vols.; 1960), which appeared in the series. His other works include *Calvin on God and Political Duty* (1950), *A History of the Cure of Souls* (1951), and *Unitive Protestantism: The Ecumenical Spirit and Its Persistent Expression* (1964).

MEDICINE. *See* HEALTH AND MEDICINE

MEIJI GAKUIN. The oldest and largest educational institution in **Japan** with a Reformed background. Founded in 1877, the school has elementary, junior, and senior high schools, and university and graduate schools. The school enrolls more than 13,000 students on four separate campuses. It has produced many pastors, theologians, and Christian leaders.

MELANESIA. *See* PACIFIC OCEAN ISLANDS

MELVILLE, ANDREW (1545–1622). Scottish Presbyterian Reformer. Melville was born near Montrose, attended the University of St. Andrews, and at 19 left **Scotland** to study in Paris. He studied and taught at Poitiers before going to Geneva in 1569, where **Théodore Beza** offered him the chair of humanities in the city college. In 1574 Melville returned to Scotland and became an educational reformer and worked to establish Presbyterian church polity. He modernized the university curriculum while serving as principal of Glasgow (1574–1580) and St. Andrews (1580–1606) universities and was credited with raising the standards and reputation of the Scottish schools. Melville also contributed to the church's second **Book of Discipline** (1578), which organized the Reformed Church in Scotland in light of the **Elizabethan Settlement.** For the next

30 years he defended Presbyterian church government against the encroachments of the episcopal system sought by the Crown. He is known as the founder of the Scottish **presbytery** and is considered to be **John Knox's** successor in the reform of the Scottish church. Melville was imprisoned for four years (1607–1611) for the "treasonous" satirizing of the king's worship. Afterward he was exiled to **France**, where he taught at the University of Sedan.

MELVILLE, HERMAN (1819–1891). American novelist and poet. Melville was born in New York City. His father died in 1832, leaving the family in poverty. The young Melville was employed as a bank clerk and worked on his uncle's farm before attending Albany Classical School (1835). In 1839 he found work as a cabin boy on the merchant ship *St. Lawrence,* bound for Liverpool. In 1841 he went to the south seas on the whaler *Acushnet.* His voyage and experience in the **Marquesas Islands** inspired his first novel, *Typee* (1846). His second novel, *Omoo* (1847), was based on his experiences in **Tahiti.** He worked on the whaler *Charles and Henry* and spent several months in Lahaina, Maui, in the Hawaiian Islands. Melville drew on these experiences in the Pacific to write his masterpiece, *Moby Dick* (1851), an exploration of good and evil, human nature, and the **providence of God**, in the context of New England **Calvinism.** Melville's novels and poetry brought him neither riches nor literary acclaim. In 1866 he became a customs inspector on the docks of New York, where he worked for 19 years. His literary works, neglected for many years, were only later recognized as masterpieces.

MERCERSBURG THEOLOGY. American theological movement at the German Reformed seminary in Mercersburg, Pennsylvania, during the 1840s and 1850s. Associated with the work of theologian John Williamson Nevin and church historian **Philip Schaff**, the Mercersburg theology was Christocentric, emphasized a corporate rather than individualistic view of **salvation**, stressed the importance of the **Lord's Supper** and **sacraments** (as opposed to the Protestant emphasis on the read and preached word in **worship**), and held an ecumenical view of the **church** (in contrast to the denominationalism of the 19th century). The stellar works of the movement were Nevin's *The Anxious Bench* (1843), which criticized revivalism, and *The Mystical Presence* (1846), which taught a real "spiritual presence" of Christ in the Lord's Supper. The movement embraced the **Heidelberg Catechism** and opposed the rationalistic theology found within both American **Puritanism** and Princeton **Calvinism.**

MESOAMERICA. The people of Mesoamerica are predominantly Roman Catholic. Protestants are a majority in Belize (55 percent) and a minority in Costa Rica (5 percent), El Salvador (9 percent), Guatemala (25 percent), Honduras (10 percent), Mexico (3 percent), and Nicaragua (5 percent). Several small Reformed churches minister to segments of the Protestant population in the Mesoamerican region. There are no Reformed churches in Panama; Reformed involvement in Nicaragua is limited to relief work and a small presence by the Christian Reformed Church of North America.

The initial Christianization of the Mesoamerican cultures from the 16th century on occurred under the aegis of Spanish **colonialism**, linking military conquest with evangelization. The operative pattern was the establishment of Roman Catholic Spanish Christendom, resulting in the imposition of hierarchical **church** structures and Roman Catholic religious practices. Resistance to heterodox forms of Christianity, such as Protestantism, was both a political and religious priority of the emerging states (the Inquisition was established in Latin America in 1568). Although freedom of religion was generally espoused with the formation of independent states in the 19th century, persecution of Protestants was widespread and has continued actively in various countries ever since. Nevertheless, from the 19th century on, Protestant **mission** efforts have established a great diversity of Protestant churches throughout Mesoamerica, of which the Reformed churches constitute a numerical minority.

Protestantism began in Central America through British colonialism accompanied by **slavery**; for this reason, the Christianity that evolved on the eastern coast continues to have an African influence, and the Anglican presence is strong. As Spanish colonialism ended and the **United States** asserted hegemony over Latin American (Monroe Doctrine, 1823), North American denominational and faith missions rapidly replaced those of **Great Britain** and became the dominant non-Catholic religious force. The acceptance and growth of Protestant mission, which was largely anti-Catholic, was based on the spiritual nature of the **faith**, personal experience of the gospel, and the formation of communities of convinced believers willing to practice their faith as minority groups. Most North American missions made both evangelization and **education** their priorities. The emerging churches were conservative theologically and politically, so that Mesoamerican Protestantism has until recently been apathetic to social processes and the political convulsions of the 20th century. That is beginning to change, particularly under the expanding influence of Pentecostalism. The North American influence has resulted in frequent splits of Mesoamerican Protestantism, over issues ranging from the contested dominance of North American missionaries to doctrinal disagreements. Nevertheless, many of these churches have continued to grow. In the latter part of the 20th century, the growth of the older Protestant movements has been eclipsed by the rapid expansion of contemporary Pentecostal Christianity, often emerging in indigenous faith movements.

Belize (Formerly British Honduras). The only English-speaking nation in Mesoamerica, Belize is the one exception to North American hegemony in Mesoamerican Protestant mission. The British colony on the east coast grew out of British settlements in the **Caribbean**, the earliest Protestant presence in Central America. The Church of England became the established church of the colony in the 1860s after a century of mission activity. Dissenters arrived early, including Scottish Presbyterians in the 1820s, who founded the Presbyterian Church of Belize. Protestants make up the majority of the population today (55 percent; 43 percent Roman Catholic); the Anglican church remains the dominant Protestant denomination.

Costa Rica. North American faith mission societies dominated Protestant expansion in Costa Rica, which began in the 19th century. The two major nondenominational mission societies, the Central American Mission (CAM) and the Latin American Mission (LAM), both based in Costa Rica, have been influenced by Reformed involvement. The North American Congregationalist pastor Cyrus I. Scofield founded the CAM, and its first missionaries were Presbyterian, the William McConnell family (1891). Among the founding evangelists of the LAM (1921) were Presbyterians such as Angel Archilla Cabrera from Puerto Rico. Reformed scholars and missionaries have also been involved in its various agencies, particularly at the Latin American Biblical University in San José. The only Costa Rican member of the **World Alliance of Reformed Churches**, the Fraternity of Evangelical Churches of Costa Rica, grew out of the LAM. The various institutions formed by the LAM joined together as the Association of Biblical Churches of Costa Rica in 1945. In 1985, five congregations left to form the Fraternity, reacting to the older group's sympathy to Pentecostal influences and insensitivity to social problems. Costa Rica's stability, democratic traditions, and educational progress have made it home to many mission organizations and agencies with which Reformed churches from around the world cooperate. Significant among these is the Spanish Language Institute in San

José, an agency of the former United Presbyterian Church (U.S.A.), which moved to Costa Rica from Colombia in 1950. The institute trains missionaries from many denominations for ministry in Latin America. **El Salvador.** The first Reformed Protestant missionary effort in El Salvador was the work of Francisco Penzotti, an Italian Waldensian pastor, who expanded his Bible distribution ministry from Guatemala in 1893. The Central American Mission (CAM) began to organize churches in 1896, soon to be followed by Baptists, Pentecostals (the Assemblies of God are the largest group), and Adventists. The total Protestant presence in El Salvador is under 10 percent of the population, of which the Pentecostals claim over 60 percent. The small Reformed Church of El Salvador (Iglesia Reformada de El Salvador) is a member of the World Alliance of Reformed Churches. The intense political turmoil of the 1980s, with its violent suppression of civil and human rights, led to increased ecumenical cooperation between Reformed and Lutheran organizations.

Guatemala. In 1873 North American Presbyterians began mission work in Guatemala, responding to an invitation from that country's president, who was seeking to moderate the control of the Roman Catholic Church. The National Evangelical Presbyterian Church of Guatemala resulted from the gradual expansion of the mission church, with the founding of schools and hospitals and outreach to the Quiché and Mam people. This outreach included the translation of the Bible into Mayan languages, the formation of Mayan Bible Institutes, and especially the development of Theological Education by Extension (TEE), a model since accepted around the world. The Guatemalan Presbyterian Church was the first in Central America to achieve autonomy, when the North American mission and the national presbyteries were integrated and became independent in 1961. Since 1967, Protestantism has experienced rapid growth in Guatemala, especially in the Pentecostal churches. The National Presbyterian Church has also grown, especially among the Mayans, but several splinter denominations have broken away since 1960. Protestants now number more than 25 percent of the total population; more than 50 percent are Pentecostal.

Honduras. Anglican mission work spread to Honduras from Belize in the first half of the 19th century. Several North American agencies followed over the next decades, among them the North American Evangelical and Reformed Board of International Missions in 1921. This mission initiative soon produced the Evangelical and Reformed Church of Honduras, which incorporated both Reformed and Lutheran traditions and expanded from its base in San Pedro Sula. The mission church founded schools, clinics, and congregations, and established the Evangelical Theological Seminary in 1934. From 1961 on, its North American mission partner was the United Church Board for World Mission. The Protestant churches of Honduras compose about 10 percent of the population; the evangelical non-Pentecostal groups outnumber the Pentecostals.

Mexico. The first Protestant mission initiative in Mexico was Bible distribution under the auspices of the British Foreign and Bible Society (1827). After a new constitution assured freedom of worship, North American Presbyterians entered Mexico. Following work in the border town of Brownsville, Texas (1854–1857), **Melinda Rankin** moved to Matamoros and later Monterrey, Mexico, where she taught school and distributed Bibles. Julius Mallet Prevost (1872; "Northern" Presbyterian) and **Anthony Graybill** (1874; "Southern" Presbyterian) were other pioneers. **Henry B. Pratt** sent evangelists into Mexico from his school (founded 1896) in Laredo, Texas. Indigenous leadership gradually emerged from Mexican pastors such as **Arcadio Morales, Leandor Garza Mora,** and **Ezequiel Lango.**

By 1901 the Presbyterian churches in Mexico were organized into a general synod with 11 presbyteries. In 1925 the Presbyterian Church in the U.S.A. transferred its evangelistic work among the Chiapas people to the Reformed Church in America. The congregations resulting from this mission are also part of the National Presbyterian Church (NPC) of Mexico, a member of the World Alliance of Reformed Churches since 1904. The church maintains two schools, several clinics and hospitals, an orphanage, five theological seminaries, two Bible institutes, and a publishing house.

Other Reformed denominations have organized churches in Mexico. The Associate Reformed Presbyterian Church in the U.S.A. sent its first missionaries to Mexico in 1878; the Associate Reformed Presbyterian Church of Mexico became self-governing in 1964, when it joined the World Alliance. The Independent Presbyterian Church of Mexico was formed in 1962 as the result of mission initiated by the Christian Reformed Church. The small Congregational Church of Mexico was founded in 1872 from North American Congregationalist mission work. Most of the Presbyterian and Reformed churches engage ecumenically with the Evangelical Council of Mexico, founded in 1927. Similarly, Presbyterian and Reformed **women** work together in the Interdenominational Union of Women's Christian Societies, founded in 1922; they support mission among several ethnic groups in Mexico.

Nicaragua. Except for eight congregations of the Christian Reformed Church, there is no appreciable organized Reformed presence in Nicaragua. Early mission among the Miskitos began with the British and continued from the early 19th century on with the Moravians, first from Europe and later from North America. The Moravian Church's diverse ministries have included Bible translation into Miskito and Sumo and have extended to other ethnic groups. From the mid-19th century, Baptist missions have proliferated, often dividing and generating indigenous movements. The Central American Mission (CAM) began work in 1900, and its churches have also split into parallel movements. Pentecostalism entered Nicaragua with the Assemblies of God in the 1930s. Today Pentecostal churches make up almost 50 percent of the Protestant population of Nicaragua. In 1973, about 40 Protestant churches and agencies formed the Evangelical Committee for Relief and Development (CEPAD) in response to an earthquake that devastated Managua. North American Reformed agencies and individuals have been actively involved in various aspects of CEPAD's ministry.

METHOD IN THEOLOGY. *See* THEOLOGICAL METHOD

MEXICO. *See* MESOAMERICA

MICRONESIA, FEDERATED STATES OF. *See* PACIFIC OCEAN ISLANDS

MIDDLE EAST. The region is primarily Muslim, with Christians a minority population in Egypt (16 percent), Iran (1 percent), and Syria (8 percent). The only exception is Lebanon (49 percent), which has a large Christian population. Reformed churches, particularly from Scotland, established a presence in many Middle Eastern countries during the 19th century. Today, these four countries have significant Reformed churches, with membership in the **World Alliance of Reformed Churches.**

Egypt. During the 18th and 19th centuries, Protestant **mission** organizations from **Europe** and the **British Isles** arrived in Egypt. These missionary groups included the Moravians, who conducted mission work between 1752 and 1782, and the Church Missionary Society, whose personnel served between 1825 and 1862, and then resumed work in 1882. The Moravians introduced a Protestant **spirituality** into the Coptic Orthodox Church (the largest Christian group in the country, established in the first century), while the CMS began a seminary to train Coptic ministers (1842) and distributed Bibles. Although both groups failed in their attempt to reach Muslims, they prepared the way for an Egyptian Protestantism that would later grow out of the Coptic Church.

The United Presbyterian Church of North America began its work in 1854, with the purpose of "revitalizing" the Coptic Church. Although the Coptic community resisted proselytization, the Presbyterians converted two important families of Asyūt (in Upper Egypt) to the **evangelical** faith: the Wīsā and the Khayyāt families. The evangelical community grew and soon began to organize churches. In Lower Egypt the first evangelical congregation was organized in Cairo (1863). By the turn of the century, the Evangelical church had 21 ordained Arab ministers, 39 churches, and more than 5,000 communicants. The American mission founded hospitals in Asyūt, Tanta, and Cairo; more than 170 primary schools; colleges, including American College in Asyūt and American University in Cairo; and the Evangelical Theological Seminary in Cairo. The Evangelical churches have cooperated with other Protestant churches and organizations, including the work of Reformed missionary **Samuel Zwemer.**

In 1926 the Evangelical Church–Synod of the Nile became an independent body still related to the United Presbyterian Church in the United States. In 1948 the creation of the state of **Israel** and other political events in the **Middle East** caused the church to sever its American ties, a process that was completed in 1958. Today, the Evangelical Church-Synod of the Nile, with its eight presbyteries, 300 congregations, and approximately 300,000 communicants, is the largest Reformed body in the Middle East. The Evangelical church continues to operate schools and conducts social work through the **Coptic Evangelical Organization for Social Services**, an independent church-related agency that also manages Dar al-Thiqafa in Cairo, the largest Christian publishing house in the Arab world. Church-sponsored mission work has been conducted in East African and Middle Eastern countries. Prominent Egyptian ministers, educators, and church leaders include **Alexander Abiskhairun**, **Akhnūkh Fānūs, Samuel Habib, Ibrahim Sa'id**, and **Tadrus Yusuf.**

Syria and Lebanon. In 1819 the **American Board of Commissioners for Foreign Missions** (ABCFM) sent Congregationalist missionaries Pliny Fisk and Levi Parsons to the Middle East. After the death of Parsons (1822), Fisk lived in Beirut and founded the American mission (1823–1825). Even before Fisk's premature death in 1825, Jonas King arrived from France (1822), and Isaac Bird and William Goodell were sent by the ABCFM (1823). The Free Church of Scotland also sent missionaries.

The gradual expansion of mission work led to the organization of Protestant churches. The Ottoman government recognized the first evangelical congregation in Beirut (1848); another in Hasbayya at Mt. Hermon was ready to be organized. During the next two decades mission work was begun in Syria (1848), additional congregations were organized in Lebanon, and the Syrian Protestant College (now American University) was founded in Beirut (1866). By the end of the 19th century, the ABCFM (1870s) and the Scottish Free Church mission (1899) had transferred their work in Syria and Lebanon to the Presbyterian Church in the U.S.A.

One exception was the Beirut congregation, which had been connected to the ABCFM, but became independent in 1890, taking the name National Evangelical Church of Beirut. In the 1960s the original parish and several smaller congregations located in the suburbs of Beirut became known as the National Evangelical Union.

The beginnings of the National Evangelical Synod of Syria and Lebanon date from 1920, when an independent synod was organized for both countries. The synod adopted a presbyterian polity and in 1959 assumed the educational and social service work that had been independently carried on by the American Presbyterians and other mission organizations from **Denmark, France, Holland,** and **Switzerland.** Synod secretary **Ibrahim Milham Dagher** managed the transition and became a prominent leader in the church. A 16-year civil war in Lebanon (1975–1991) caused destruction to churches and schools and dispersed some congregations. However, the synod continued to sponsor primary and secondary schools and a hospital in Lebanon and to cosponsor Beirut University and the Near East School of Theology.

The Union of Armenian Evangelical Churches in the Near East is the second largest Reformed denomination in Syria and Lebanon. Begun as a mid-19th century reform movement within the Armenian Orthodox Church, the denomination declared its independence in 1846. In that same year it was the first Protestant community to be recognized by the Ottoman government in Istanbul. Although the church spread throughout the Ottoman Empire and remains a regional presence in the Middle East, its membership is concentrated in the northern parts of Syria and Lebanon, where Armenians fled during the 20th-century massacres that decimated their population in Turkey. The Union is composed of autonomous congregations with a congregational form of government. In addition to its primary and secondary schools, and Haigazian College, the Union operates conference centers and is a sponsor of the Near East School of Theology in Beirut.

Iran. In 1834 Presbyterian missionary Justin Perkins arrived in Tabriz, where he founded the Persian mission. Other American missionaries joined the work and it was relocated to Rezaieh in northwestern Iran (1835). There, a mission to Nestorians (a Christian community dating from the fifth century) was organized. The purpose of the mission was to "revitalize" the Nestorian church. However, those who embraced evangelical views were forced to leave and a new evangelical church was organized in 1855. Converts from other ethnic and religious groups also joined new churches. By 1862 the first **presbytery** was organized, and in 1872 Presbyterian work was begun in Teheran and later expanded to Tabriz, Resht, Hamadan, and Meshed.

In 1934 the evangelical churches of Iran joined to create a single Protestant church, the Synod of the Evangelical Church of Iran. Presbyterian in polity, the church adopted a constitution in 1963. With a membership of 3,000 in 10 congregations, it is the largest Protestant church in Iran. Persecution and emigration since the Iranian Revolution (1979) have adversely impacted church life.

Other Churches. The Gulf States, Iraq, and Israel have small Reformed churches. These churches are the Evangelical Church of Abu Dhabi (United Arab Emirates), the National Evangelical Church of Bahrain, the Evangelical Church in Kuwait, the Evangelical Church of Iraq, and the Church of Scotland in Israel.

MIEGGE, GIOVANNI (1900–1960). Waldensian minister and professor. Born in Savona, Miegge received his **education** at the Waldensian Theological Seminary in Florence. He was ordained in 1927 and served churches in Massello, Aosta, and Como. In 1937 he was called to teach church history at the Waldensian Seminary (recently moved to Rome). He left after one year due to poor health but returned to teach at the seminary extension in Torre Pellice from 1942 to 1946 and at Rome from 1952 to 1960. Miegge is known for his many contributions to the journal *Gioventu Cristiana*. He also wrote several books including a biography of Martin Luther, a commentary on the Sermon on the Mount, and a translation of **Karl Barth's** commentary on Romans. Influenced by Barth, Miegge played an important role in the theological revitalization of the Waldensian Church following World War II.

MILLENNIALISM. A belief in the thousand-year reign of Jesus Christ, as derived from the New Testament book of Revelation (Rev. 20:2–7). As a form of Christian **eschatology**, three positions have emerged that try to interpret the return and millennial reign of Christ. Premillennialism asserts that Jesus Christ will return to earth before his millennial reign begins. Postmillennialism teaches that Christ's return will follow a millennial period on earth. Amillennialism rejects the notion of a literal thousand-year period and emphasizes the coexistence of God's **kingdom** with the kingdom of evil until the end of history. Reformed theologians have adopted all of these three views. Many favor amillennialism as the view held by Augustine, **John Calvin**, and a number of Reformed **confessions.**

MILNE, WILLIAM (1785–1822). Scottish Presbyterian missionary in **Malaysia.** Milne was sent to Asia by the **London Missionary Society** (1812). He went first to **China** and later settled in Malacca (1815) to work with a large Chinese community. He started a school for Chinese boys, developing his **mission** around **education**, literature, and **evangelism.** He supported the work by publishing Christian literature. With **Robert Morrison**, he founded the Ultra-Ganges Mission, with the goal of evangelizing China through the efforts of Chinese people living overseas. As part of their evangelistic goal, Milne and Morrison translated the Bible into Mandarin. Milne founded the Anglo-Chinese College (1819) to acquaint the Chinese people with Christianity and Western civilization, and to train Westerners in Chinese language and culture. An early convert, Liang A-Fah, became the first ordained Chinese Protestant evangelist in Malaysia.

MILTON, JOHN (1608–1674). English poet, historian, and pamphleteer. Milton was born in London and educated at St. Paul's School and Christ's College, Cambridge (1625–1632). From 1632 to 1638, he devoted himself to scholarly pursuits while living on his father's estate. Milton traveled in **Italy** and returned to London, where he joined the Presbyterians in 1641 and was involved in several controversies relating to **church government.** After his wife left him, Milton wrote *The Doctrine and Discipline of Divorce* (1643), arguing that marriage may be dissolved on the basis of incompatibility of character. Although he and his spouse reconciled in 1645, this work led him to break with the Presbyterians. He eventually favored Independency. Politically, Milton became a supporter of **Oliver Cromwell.** In *Tenure of Kings and Magistrates* (1649) he defended the execution of the king. He became secretary for foreign languages in Cromwell's government and wrote pamphlets advocating civil and religious liberty. He worked to prevent reestablishment of the monarchy after Cromwell's death, and he was imprisoned briefly for his support of the Puritan Commonwealth following the Restoration of Charles II in 1660.

Despite his church and political activity, Milton, who became blind, is best remembered as a poet. His earliest significant poem, *On the Morning of Christ's Nativity* (1629), concerns the **incarnation** and its results. Milton published his first collection of poems in 1645. His greatest work, the epic poem *Paradise Lost,* was published in 1667. Milton wrote two sequels, *Paradise Regained* and *Samson Agonistes,* published in 1671. These works are dramatic poems that convey many of the insights of the Reformation: the power of **sin**, redemption by God's **grace**, the **sovereignty of God**, and other doctrines. In *De Doctrina Christiana,* published posthumously, Milton turned away from Christian orthodoxy.

MINISTRY. The service of **God** in the **church** and in the world. Ministry is the calling of the whole people of God, by the power of the **Holy Spirit**, to many forms of service. The Reformed **tradition** teaches that Christian ministry extends to every activity of human life because all life is lived under the lordship of Jesus Christ, whose service to humanity "commits the church to work for every form of human well-being" ("Confession of 1967," 2.A.1). Ministry is carried out by individual Christians who, in their **vocations**, receive God's call to live a life of Christian discipleship. Ministers receive both an inward and an outward call; the inward call of the Spirit is confirmed by the "consent and approval of the people" (*Inst.* 4.3.15). In **ordination**, the church recognizes and sanctions ministries for specific functions. The Reformed tradition ordains church members in four offices: **elders**, **deacons**, pastors, and teachers. Through these offices, and through the vocations of its members, the church ministers in **worship**, **preaching**, and teaching, through corporate expressions of care and love, and in its work for peace and justice.

MINJUNG THEOLOGY. Korean theological movement rooted in the events and experience of oppressed people, or *minjung* ("from below"). The movement emerged during the socially and politically turbulent 1970s, when a group of Korean theologians and lay leaders began to interpret the gospel and the Korean experience in sociopolitical terms. As the movement intensified, many of its leaders were forced to leave teaching positions at seminaries and universities.

At the heart of Minjung theology is a concern for those who suffer exploitation, poverty, and sociopolitical and cultural repression. The minjung are plagued by *han* (a concept articulated by minjung poet Chi-Ha Kim), the anger and resentment resulting from continuous injustice. Liberation from han happens as the minjung recognize in the events of their lives the same **God** they encounter in the biblical stories of suffering peoples. In Jesus they encounter the Christ who identifies with minjung. God's work is to relieve the suffering of han and create a new and just society through the actions of the minjung. Korean critics of Minjung theology see it as a social and political program for human liberation rather than a theology of the gospel as God's action in Jesus Christ for the **salvation** of humanity.

MISSIO DEI. The theological assumption, which emerged in the 1930s (Karl Hartenstein, **Karl Barth**), that **God** is a missionary God whose saving purposes for the **creation** are accomplished in the calling and formation of God's missionary people: Israel and the engrafted Christian **church**. **Mission** is thus derived from the nature of God, and the church is an instrument of God's mission, not an end in itself. The theology of mission is rooted in trinitarian doctrine (the nature and mission of God), rather than soteriology (the question of **salvation**). Every dimension of the church's theology and ministry is to be defined and assessed in terms of its implications for faithfulness to mission. *Missio Dei* theology was explicated and endorsed by the International Missions Conference at Willingen (1953) and has been adopted in many Christian traditions.

MISSION AND MISSIONS. If mission defines the nature of the **church**, then the term "missions" becomes problematic. Historically the term "missions" *(missiones ecclesiae)* has been used to describe the outreach activities of the church that crossed cultural boundaries ("overseas missions"). This use of "missions" has become questionable as Reformed churches in **Africa**, **Asia**, and **Latin America** have come to maturity and as Western Reformed churches have recognized the need for mission work within Western societies. When the church itself *is* mission, then all of its activities are in a profound sense "missions." Some resist this merging of mission and missions as a denial of the worldwide scope of the missionary mandate (cf. Stephen Neill: "If everything is mission then nothing is mission"). It is more accurate to use the term "cross-cultural mission" when referring to the crossing of cultural boundaries. Today, the term "missions" is often used to refer to specific points or efforts in mission. *See also* Missio Dei; Mission, Theology of

MISSION SOCIETIES. The primary organizational form of Protestant global **mission** since the 18th century. Whereas the Roman Catholic orders tried to meet the challenge of Christian mission by becoming missionary orders, Protestantism required a new organizational form to carry out its mission work. The revivalist enthusiasm for cross-cultural mission (late 18th century) quickly led to the formation of voluntarist societies (e.g., Baptist Missionary Society, 1793), to both recruit and support missionaries. Free of the institutional constraints of traditional ecclesial structures, the societies made opportunities for mission available to many who were not educationally qualified for ecclesiastical office. Missionary societies proliferated in **Great Britain** and on the Continent, specializing in various regions of the world and developing forms of mutual cooperation that anticipated the later **ecumenical movement.** Notable Reformed missionary societies included the **London Missionary Society** (1795), **Glasgow Missionary Society** and **Scottish Missionary Society** (1796), **Netherlands Missionary Society** (1797), **American Board of Commissioners for Foreign Missions** (1810), **Evangelical Mission Society in Basel** (1815), and the **Paris Evangelical Missionary Society** (1822).

MISSION, THEOLOGY OF. The study of the biblical and doctrinal foundations of the Christian world **mission,** leading to the definition of the message, methods, and activities of mission. The missionary movement today no longer assumes that the Great Commission (Matt. 28:19) adequately defines and justifies mission. A modern comprehensive approach is based on the missionary character and purposefulness of the triune **God.** God's mission **(Missio Dei)** is the healing and restoration of all **creation,** and God is working toward the completion of that mission through the formation and "sending" *(missio)* of God's people as instruments of mission. Jesus, sent by God to complete the work of **salvation,** sends his apostolic **community** to continue that mission as witnesses to the gospel. Theologies of mission read **scripture** with a missional hermeneutic and seek to integrate Christian doctrine around the central assertion of the "sentness" of the **church** as God's apostolic people. The multicultural nature of the global church produces diverse "local" theologies of mission, all **contextualizing** the gospel.

MODERATOR. One of the church officers of a Reformed governing body, such as a church session, **presbytery,** synod, or **general assembly.** Moderators convene and adjourn meetings and preserve order for the conducting of business at each administrative level of the church. The pastor of a congregation is the moderator of its session. The moderators of a presbytery, synod, and general assembly are elected to that office. The term of service is generally one year, but in some Reformed denominations moderators are elected for longer terms. The moderator of the highest office in a Reformed denomination, usually a synod or general assembly, does not serve as a spokesperson for the church at large. The authority of the moderator relates solely to the governing body that he or she convenes.

MOFFAT, ROBERT (1795–1883). Scottish Congregationalist missionary in **southern Africa.** Born in Ormiston, East Lothian, Moffat was sent to southern Africa by the **London Missionary Society** (1816) and remained in southern Africa for 50 years. He began Christian **mission** work with the Tswana peoples north of the Orange River; his station at Kuruman (1825) became the base for northward expansion toward the Zambezi River. Moffat learned Setswana and printed the first books in that language, including his translation of the New Testament (1840), and, with colleague William Ashton, the complete Bible (1857). Under his leadership, the Christian Church of Botswana was organized. Moffat also worked in agricultural management, pioneered in the use of irrigation and natural fertilizers, introduced new crops, and began a program of forest preservation. He encouraged the exploration of Africa and influenced his son-in-law, **David Livingstone**, in that direction. Moffat resisted the Boer expansion onto native lands, advocated a continuing British presence, and described his life's work in the book *Missionary Labours and Scenes in Southern Africa* (1842).

MOFFATT, JAMES (1870–1944). Scottish Bible translator and New Testament scholar. Born in Glasgow, Moffatt was educated at Glasgow University and the Free Church College. He served churches in Dundonald (1896–1907) and Broughty (1907–1911) before his appointment as professor of Greek and New Testament exegesis at Mansfield College, Oxford. He became professor of church history at the United Free Church College in Glasgow in 1915, and then professor of church history at **Union Theological Seminary** in New York from 1927 to 1939. He is best known for his translation of the Bible (New Testament, 1913; Old Testament, 1924), the first unofficial translation to gain wide acceptance. Among his scholarly works are *An Introduction to the Literature of the New Testament* (1911; 1918), *Love in the New Testament* (1929), *Grace in the New Testament* (1931), *Hebrews* (International Critical Commentary; 1924), and *Corinthians* (1938) and *General Epistles* (1928) in the Moffatt New Testament Commentary series, which he edited.

Moffatt was a member of the translation committee of the Revised Standard Version of the Bible and served as its executive secretary.

MOLNÁR, ALBERT SZENCI (1574–1634). Hungarian Reformed scholar. Born in Szenc in the western part of **Hungary**, Molnár began his education at age 12 by traveling from city to city with a group of young Protestants. He was in Göncz when the **Károlyi** Bible was being published and studied at the Reformed College in Debrecen, Hungary. In 1590 he began a period of wandering throughout Europe, studying at Wittenberg, Heidelberg, and Strasbourg. After briefly returning to Hungary, he settled in Altdorf, Germany, and began to work as an author. He compiled a two-volume Latin-Hungarian dictionary, prepared a Hungarian psalter (1607), revised the Hungarian Bible (1608; 2d ed., 1612), wrote a Hungarian grammar, and translated **John Calvin's** *Institutes* into Hungarian (1624). Although Calvin had little direct influence on the early Reformed churches in Hungary, the publication of the *Institutes* made an impact on succeeding generations of the **church**.

MOLNÁR, AMEDEO (1923–1990). Czech historian and theologian. Born in Prague, Molnár studied there and in Strasbourg. In 1950 he was appointed professor of church history at the **Comenius Theological Faculty** in Prague. He was co-editor of the ecumenical journal *Communio Viatorum.* Molnár wrote extensively on the history of the **Waldensians** and Hussites, and he served as editor of the *Opera Omnia* of Bohemian Reformer John Hus.

MOON, IK-WHAN (1918–1994). Korean Presbyterian minister and political activist. Moon was born in Manchuria, **China.** His family returned to **Korea**, where Moon enrolled in Sungsil Middle School. In 1932 Moon quit the school because he objected to the Shinto shrine policies of the Japanese colonial government. He traveled to **Japan** and studied theology at Japan Theological School in Tokyo, and subsequently became a lay leader in the Manbosan Korean Church in Manchuria (1943). He graduated from Korea Theological Seminary (1947) and **Princeton Theological Seminary** (Th.M., 1954) before teaching Old Testament at Korea Theological Seminary and Yonsei University. Moon wrote the Democracy and National Salvation Manifesto (1976) and was a leader in the democratic and Korean unification movements. He served as chair of the Fourth Pan National Congress (1993) and was imprisoned for traveling to North Korea. In 1992, Moon was a candidate for the Nobel Peace Prize. He also published three volumes of poetry.

MOORE, WALTER W. (1857–1926). American Presbyterian minister and educator. Born in Charlotte, North Carolina, Moore was educated at Davidson College (1874–1878), **Union Theological Seminary** in Virginia (1878–1881), and Central University, Richmond, Kentucky (1885). He began teaching at Union Theological Seminary in Virginia in 1883 and became professor of Hebrew and Old Testament (1895–1915). He served as president of Union Seminary (1904–1926) and was responsible for its reorganization and move from Hampden-Sydney to Richmond, Virginia. Moore founded the seminary's periodical, *Union Seminary Magazine* (1889) (after 1913 the *Union Seminary Review*), to which he contributed many articles. His publications include *The Indispensable Book* (1910) and *The Teaching Values of the Old Testament* (1918). He was elected **moderator** of the General Assembly of the Presbyterian Church, U.S. (1908).

MORA, LEANDRO GARZA (1854–1938). Mexican Presbyterian minister and evangelist. Mora's parents lived in southern Texas, where his mother was a member of the Presbyterian church of Brownsville. The missionary **Anthony T. Graybill** engaged Mora as his Spanish teacher; this relationship resulted in Mora's **conversion** and preparation for the ministry. He was ordained in 1879 and devoted the remainder of his life to Presbyterian **evangelism** in northern **Mexico.** Mora was one of the first Mexican candidates to be ordained to the Presbyterian ministry, and he served as the first **moderator** of the Presbytery of Tamaulipas, organized in Matamoras (1884). He represented the General Synod of Mexico at the meeting of the **World Alliance of Reformed Churches** in Edinburgh (1904). His ministry facilitated the spread of **Presbyterianism** into Mexico from the **United States.**

MORALES, ARCADIO (1850–1922). Mexican Presbyterian minister and evangelist. As a young man, Morales studied the scriptures and became involved with a Protestant group that nurtured his **faith.** While working as a colporteur, he began to look for a church that was, in his view, consistent with **scripture.** Under the influence of M. N. Hutchison he was drawn to the Presbyterian Church and, with several friends, formed the nucleus of the first Presbyterian church in Mexico City. He was ordained to the Presbyterian ministry (1878) and pastored the church in Mexico City until his death.

MORNAY, PHILIPPE DE (1549–1623). Huguenot political leader during the French **Wars of Religion** (1562–1598). Born in Normandy, Mornay became Protestant after the death of his father. Mornay was educated at the University of Heidelberg and at Paris where he was taught by Peter Ramus. He escaped the **Saint Bartholomew's Day Massacres** of 1572 and fled to England; for the next decade, he was a Huguenot military leader and diplomat for **William III of Orange** and Henry of Navarre. He wrote many religious and political tracts, including *Traité de l'Église* (1578) and *Traité de la vérité de la religion chrétienne* (1579). He also published a work on the **Eucharist**, *De l'institution, usage et doctrine du saint sacrement de l'eucharistie en l'Église ancienne.* Mornay worked for the general synods of the French Reformed Church and sought a union of all Protestant churches. In 1589 he became governor of the Protestant stronghold of Saumur, where he built a Protestant church and university. He conducted negotiations with the Catholic Holy League until 1593, when Henry IV embraced Catholicism. Mornay was present when the **Edict of Nantes** was promulgated in 1598.

MOROCCO. *See* NORTH AFRICA

MORRISON, ROBERT (1782–1834). Scottish Congregationalist missionary in **China**. Born in Northumberland, England, of Scottish parents, Morrison went to China under the sponsorship of the **London Missionary Society** (1807). His evangelistic work in Canton, including Bible translation and distribution, was hindered by government regulations that allowed him to live and work in only one small section of the city. He learned Chinese, gained residence privileges as a translator for the East India Company, and completed his Chinese Bible (1818), assisted by **W. C. Milne.** The translation, though imperfect, was a remarkable achievement. Morrison then prepared a Chinese-English dictionary (1821) that opened up the serious study of Chinese for succeeding generations of Westerners. He provided many linguistic aids for missionaries and advocated the study of Chinese language and literature in the West. Although he saw only modest success in his evangelistic ministry, he laid the foundations for Chinese **mission** work that would follow.

MORRISON, WILLIAM McCUTCHAN (1867–1918). American Presbyterian minister, missionary, linguist, and social reformer in the **Congo**. Born in Lexington, Virginia, Morrison graduated from Washington and Lee University in 1887, and was employed for six years as a school teacher. He entered the Presbyterian Theological Seminary at Louisville and graduated in 1895. While at seminary Morrison volunteered for the African **mission** field and was sent to the American Presbyterian Congo Mission at Luebo. Morrison became leader of the mission and worked to reduce the Tshiluba language to writing. He published an important

Grammar and Dictionary of the Buluba-Lulua Language (1906) and translated into Tshiluba *Lessons from the Bible* (*Malesona* [1913]) and the *Gospels and Acts of the Apostles* (*Lumu Luimpe* [1919]). With British reformer E. D. Morel, Morrison publicly denounced the human and economic exploitation perpetrated by King Leopold in the Congo. In 1909 Morrison and missionary colleague **William H. Sheppard** were sued for libel by the government-controlled Kasai Rubber Company. The trial received international publicity. The acquittal of the missionaries, along with public pressure from **Great Britain** and the **United States**, resulted in the Belgian government's annexation of the Congo. Although important reforms were undertaken by the new government, **human rights** abuses continued in the Congo for many years.

MORTON, JOHN (1839–1912). Canadian Presbyterian minister and missionary in **Trinidad**. Born in Nova Scotia to Scottish immigrants, Morton attended the Free Church College at Halifax from 1855 to 1861. Following **ordination**, Morton became a country minister in Canada. A bout of diphtheria caused him to take passage to the warmer climate of the **West Indies** in 1864. While visiting in Trinidad, Morton became concerned for the 20,000 East Indians who worked the sugar plantations. Representing nearly a quarter of the population of the island, these laborers were recruited from India between 1850 and 1917. Workers spent five to 10 years in service to the plantations, after which they could return to India or remain in Trinidad. Conditions were harsh; the system was sometimes compared to **slavery.** Following his return to Canada, Morton lobbied his church for a Trinidad **mission** among the Indian people and offered himself as a missionary. He arrived in 1868 and settled in Iere village, taking over the closed American Presbyterian mission station. From there he moved first to San Fernando, then back to Iere in 1875, and then to Princestown. He finally settled in Tunapuna, where he spent the rest of his life. Morton's most important contribution was his pioneering educational work for East Indians. He organized several primary schools and supported the establishment of St. Andrews Theological College (1892) in San Fernando. He also promoted mission work in British **Guyana** (1880), St. Lucia (1883), and Grenada (1885). Morton was a friend of the sugar planters and conservative in his politics and theology. His failure to ordain Indian ministers slowed the development of an indigenous church, but he was a strong supporter of the effort to move Indians away from plantation work into small farming. His evangelistic and educational work laid the foundation of the Presbyterian Church in Trinidad and Tobago.

MOZAMBIQUE. *See* SOUTHERN AFRICA

MULTICULTURALISM. *See* INTERCULTURALISM

MURRAY, ANDREW, JR. (1828–1917). South African minister, **moderator** of the Dutch Reformed Church of South Africa, and writer of devotional books. Born at Graaff-Reinet, Murray was educated in Aberdeen, **Scotland**, and Utrecht. He served churches in Bloemfontein, Worcester, Cape Town, and Wellington (1871). He is one of the founders of the Faculty of Theology at Stellenbosch University (1857) and was elected moderator of the Dutch Reformed Church (1862), a position he held six times. Murray dominated the life of the South African church for five decades, leading evangelistic tours in **South Africa** and promoting **mission** work in the Transvaal and **Malawi**. Theologically conservative, he wrote nearly 250 devotional books and pamphlets. Among his best-known works are *Abide in Christ* (1887) and *Waiting on God* (1896).

MUSIC AND HYMNODY. The expression of Reformed **worship** and spiritual experience through instrumental sound and singing. As the Reformed churches have been ambivalent about the visual **arts**, so they have also been cautious about music. The reformers considered some music and instruments to be inappropriate, rejecting, for example, the use of organs in their churches. Early Reformed communities relied almost exclusively on psalmody for church worship. The Scottish songbook *The Guid and Godlie Ballatis* (ca. 1542–1546) featured verse translations of the Psalms but also included several hymns by Martin Luther and devotional verse. By 1562 Sternhold and Hopkins had completed the first metrical psalter. Published in Geneva under **John Calvin**, the book had wide influence. In the **United States John Eliot's** *Bay Psalm Book* replaced the Geneva psalter in 1640. English Congregationalist **Isaac Watts** revolutionized Reformed worship by introducing modern hymn compositions alongside the psalms of David. Congregationalists **Albert F. Bayly** and **Erik Routley** also made important contributions to Reformed hymnody. Routley was particularly concerned to develop a theological foundation for church music; he also encouraged the composition of contemporary music for use in worship. The churches of **Scotland** were influenced by the work of **Horatius Bonar**. In Germany, **Friedrich Adolf Lampe**, Johann Neander (1789–1850), and Adolf Brunner were important pioneers of church music. Brunner took up theological concerns in his book, *Musik in Gottesdienst* (1968). Protestant composer **Waclaw z Szamotul** made an important contribution to Polish a cappella music. English-speaking churches have benefited from the editorial work of

Louis Benson; hymns composed by such Calvinists as Philip Doddridge, **William Cowper**, and John Newton; and the organization of the Westminster Choir College (1926) by John Finley Williamson. Pietism, Methodism, revivalism, and the social gospel movements contributed to Reformed music and hymnody, as has the African-American gospel tradition. The Reformed tradition has also recognized the cultural basis of music and worship. Many churches in **Africa**, **Asia**, and the Americas incorporate indigenous music and singing in church services and use instruments such as guitars, pianos, and drums. More varied instrumentation is now being used in both Western and non-Western Reformed churches. New hymns have been written by pastors such as **Tiyo Soga** of **South Africa**, **Joseph Andrianaivoravelona** of **Madagascar**, and Trevor Rodborne of **India**.

MUSONGUELA, PASTOR (1870?–1929). Presbyterian minister and evangelist in the **Congo**. Born in the village of Bakwanga, Musonguela lost his father during a famine in 1886. After his mother was sold into **slavery**, Musonguela went to Malandi (Luluabourg), where he joined the military and served until 1893. He was employed by a white trader at Luebo and there came into contact with the American Presbyterian Congo Mission; he was converted and was baptized in 1897. Musonguela became an evangelist and worked at Kamuanga Kalamba. In 1906 he became a medical assistant to Llewellyn Coppedge. Musonguela was ordained an elder in the Luebo congregation in 1907 and in 1911 worked as an evangelist in a region 300 miles east of Luebo. He then worked at Mutoto (1912) and Lusambo (1913), where he continued as an itinerant evangelist. In 1916, he was one of the first Congolese to be ordained as pastor. He was chosen as the first pastor of the Lusambo church and remained there for 10 years. In 1919 Musonguela attended the first **presbytery** meeting held in the Congo. He died in church service at Mutoto.

MUTCHMOR, JAMES RALPH (1892–1980). Canadian minister in the United Church of Canada, and secretary of the Board of Evangelism and Social Service. Born in Providence Bay, Manitoulin Island, Ontario, Mutchmor studied at the University of Toronto, Columbia University, and **Union Theological Seminary** in New York. He served in the Royal Canadian Artillery during World War I (1916–1919) and was ordained upon his return to **Canada** in 1920. Mutchmor served the Robertson Memorial Church, Winnipeg, from 1919 to 1932, and John Black Memorial Church, Kildonan, Manitoba, until 1937, when he was appointed associate secretary of the United Church Board of Evangelism and Social Service. Two years later he was appointed secretary and remained in this position for 24 years. In 1962 he was elected **moderator** of the United Church. Mutchmor was a champion of the poor and the elderly. He supported **labor** unions and was an outspoken critic of gambling, the alcohol and tobacco industries, and greed in business. He believed that the **church** should speak out on public issues and was the most provocative United Church leader of his time.

MYANMAR. *See* SOUTHERN ASIA

MZIMBA, JAMES PHAMBANI. South African Presbyterian minister and founder of the Presbyterian Church of Africa. Mzimba worked with the Church of Scotland in **South Africa** until 1898, when he resigned from the denomination after being ill-treated by white colleagues. He organized independent churches at Dikeni (Alice) and was arrested on the charge of attempting to overthrow the government. After being found innocent, he organized the Presbyterian Church of Africa in Cape Colony. Within a few months most black church members joined Mzimba. He evangelized in the streets of Transvaal, especially at Germiston. Mzimba was joined by other black ministers and evangelists, including John Thomas Sibiya. Within three years the church had a membership of over 15,000 and continued to grow.

- N -

NAMIBIA. *See* SOUTHERN AFRICA

NANTES, EDICT OF (1598). A decree of Henry IV that ended the **Wars of Religion** in **France.** The edict was the result of negotiations between Henry IV and the **Huguenots** and was the last of several agreements intended to bring religious peace to France. It confirmed Catholicism as the dominant religion of the country but granted to the still powerful Huguenots free exercise of religion and the control of about 150 towns, including La Rochelle, Montaubon, and Montpellier. The edict was an act of religious toleration that temporarily relieved pressure on the Protestant minority. The government supported it only reluctantly, and in 1685 it was revoked by Louis XIV.

NARRATIVE THEOLOGY. The use of the literary genre of narrative or story to construct Christian doctrine and theological **ethics** and to understand human life and **community.** Neither a school of theology nor a movement, narrative theology is employed by modern theologians who use biblical narratives to construct various theologies. Narrative theologians use the biblical accounts of Israel's history, the gospel stories of Jesus, and the parables as the primary means of formulating Christian doctrine and ethics. The Christian story is the basis of the Christian community, directing its life and activity. **Karl Barth** viewed the narratives of **scripture** as telling the story of the **God** of Jesus Christ. To **H. Richard Niebuhr**, the scriptural narratives tell our own story rather than God's. Narrative theologians include such thinkers as Hans Frei, Eberhard Jüngel, Stanley Hauerwas, and James W. McClendon.

NATURAL THEOLOGY. The view that a knowledge of God's existence can be derived from the natural world through reason and experience, and apart from God's **revelation** in **scripture** and in Jesus Christ. Christian arguments for the existence of **God**, sometimes called "theistic proofs," have been criticized since the 18th century. Many theologians hold that the natural world offers compelling evidence rather than proof of God's existence. The subject of natural theology has been vigorously debated within the Reformed **tradition**, the most notable example being the controversy between **Emil Brunner** and **Karl Barth** in the 1930s. Brunner taught that God's general revelation could be recognized in the "orders" of **creation** such as **marriage**, the state, and God's image in humanity. Barth argued that true **knowledge of God** is found only in Jesus Christ. Both theologians appealed to **John Calvin**, who acknowledged a revelation of God in **nature** but also the debilitating effects of human **sin**; Calvin concludes that natural revelation cannot produce a saving knowledge of God's goodness and beneficence (*Inst.* 1.1–8; 2.1–4).

NATURE AND THE ENVIRONMENT. Reformed theology emphasizes the dependence of all **creation** upon **God**, the goodness and orderliness of all creation in God's design, and human responsibility for the care of the natural world. In the Reformed **tradition** the natural world is under God's rule and Christ's **authority**, but it is not a source of **revelation** about God's saving purposes. Although scientific modernity has tended to regard nature as an object for human manipulation and exploitation, the contemporary ecological crisis and the gospel's encounter with non-Western cultures is generating new understandings of Christian responsibility with regard to nature. Reformed approaches to a theology of the environment are informed by the concepts of the world as the theater of

God's glory, of **stewardship**, and of the integrity of creation. God's healing purposes include the natural world and human relationships with nature, which the Genesis image of humanity as creation's gardener implies. *See also* Natural Theology

NEESHIMA, JOSEPH HARDY (1843–1890). Japanese Congregationalist minister, missionary, and founder of Doshisha University in **Japan.** Born in Tokyo, Neeshima boarded an American schooner, befriended merchant Alpheus Hardy, and arrived in the **United States** in 1864. The merchant, a member of the **American Board of Commissioners for Foreign Missions**, paid for Neeshima's education at Amherst College (1866–1870) and **Andover** Theological Seminary (1870–1874). Returning to Japan in 1874 as a missionary of the American Board, Neeshima was determined to organize a Christian university. He obtained a site in Kyoto, across from the imperial palace, and named his school Doshisha ("One Purpose") College. The college, which began with eight students in 1875, grew into the largest Christian college in Japan. The school educated ministers for the Congregational Church of Japan and received university status in 1890.

NEOORTHODOXY. Twentieth-century theological movement that rejected the prevailing liberal theology and tried to recover the basic theological insights of the 16th-century Protestant reformers. Associated with prominent theologians including Rudolf Bultmann in **Germany, Karl Barth** and **Emil Brunner** in **Switzerland,** H. R. Mackintosh in **Great Britain,** and **Reinhold Niebuhr** in the **United States,** neoorthodox theology was also called crisis theology, **dialectical theology,** and Barthianism. Neoorthodox theologians stressed God's transcendence, humanity's creaturely responsibility, **sin,** and the uniqueness of Jesus Christ as God's mediator of **revelation** and **grace. God** is personally encountered in Jesus Christ, who restores the human-divine relationship lost through human sin. Neoorthodoxy was the dominant European-American theological view from the post-World War II era to the 1960s and continues to influence theologians.

NEPAL. *See* SOUTHERN ASIA

NETHERLANDS. *See* NORTHERN EUROPE

NETHERLANDS ANTILLES. *See* CARIBBEAN

NETHERLANDS MISSIONARY SOCIETY. An ecumenical Protestant missionary organization founded in 1797 at Rotterdam. The society carried out work begun by missionaries of the Dutch East India Company in eastern **Indonesia** (1609), sending its personnel to the Moluccas, the Timor Islands (1815), North Celebes (1822), and East Java (1848). Theological tensions over modernism during the mid-19th century caused the body to fracture into six separate groups. The parent body reorganized itself and began work in northeast Sumatra (1890), central Celebes (1891), north Celebes (1904), and Bali (1931). Beginning in 1900 the Dutch **mission** societies began to resolve their differences and mergers took place. The independent societies that remained were integrated into the structures of the Reformed church responsible for mission work. The formation of the Netherlands Reformed Church Board of Foreign Missions (1951) meant the continuation of Reformed mission work in Indonesia and the development of new work in **Cameroon**, **Nigeria**, **Ghana**, and **Senegal**.

NEWBIGIN, JAMES EDWARD LESSLIE (1909–1998). Scottish missionary in **India**, ecumenical leader, and missiologist. Born in Newcastle upon Tyne, Newbigin was influenced by the Student Christian Movement. He studied for the ministry at Cambridge and was ordained in 1936. That same year he entered missionary service, working in India under the Church of Scotland. He served as an evangelist and pastor in both rural and urban areas, became a respected student of Hinduism, began to develop his theology of **mission** based on the **Trinity**, and was a formative leader in the emergence of the church in South India (1947). Appointed bishop in Madurai and Ramnad, Newbigin's service was interrupted by many ecumenical assignments. He served as secretary of the International Missionary Council and guided its integration into the **World Council of Churches** (1959–1961), continuing his service as the first secretary of the Commission on World Mission and Evangelism of the WCC (1962–1965). On his return to India in 1966 he was appointed bishop of Madras, serving until his retirement. He returned to **England** in 1974, where he joined the staff of Selly Oaks College in Birmingham and became pastor of a United Reformed Church. He lectured widely and his books made an important contribution to ecumenical missiological discussion, generating the **Gospel and Culture Movement**, which challenged Western Christianity to see its context as a mission field. His works also present a Reformed understanding of mission that relates the gospel to the late 20th century.

NEW BRUNSWICK THEOLOGICAL SEMINARY. Founded in 1784 in New York City, the seminary is the oldest educational institution of the Reformed Church in America. The school moved to Brooklyn in 1796 and to New Brunswick, New Jersey, in 1810. The present New Brunswick campus dates from 1856 and now includes 12 buildings on an eight-acre site near Rutgers University. In 1986 the school established a second location on the campus of St. John's University in Queens, New York. The school is both Reformed and ecumenical, with almost 60 percent of its student body made up of African Americans, Hispanic Americans, and Asian Americans.

NEW CALEDONIA. *See* PACIFIC OCEAN ISLANDS

NEW COLLEGE, EDINBURGH. A theological college of the University of Edinburgh and the Church of Scotland, and one of the primary centers of Reformed scholarship and study. Planned during the early 1840s, the college began in 1846 and moved into its building on the Mound in 1850. The complex included the Free High Church, which became New College Library in 1936. In 1929 the school merged with the divinity faculty of the University of Edinburgh, and in 1961 the Church of Scotland ceded the college property to the university. Once a leading center of British **neoorthodoxy**, the college now supports the Centre for the Study of Christianity in the Non-Western World. The college maintains a relationship with the *Scottish Journal of Theology*. In addition to its founding principal, **Thomas Chalmers**, notable faculty include William Cunningham, James Buchanan, James Bannerman, A. B. Davidson, Robert Rainy, **Alexander Duff, H. R. Mackintosh**, A. C. Welch, Marcus Dods, **John Baillie**, William Manson, **James S. Stewart, J. H. S. Burleigh**, T. F. Torrance, and John McIntyre.

NEWELL, SAMUEL (1785–1821). American Congregationalist missionary in **India**. Following his education at Harvard University and **Andover** Theological Seminary, Newell went to India (1812), having been one of four students whose fervent call to **mission** had inspired the formation of the **American Board of Commissioners for Foreign Missions.** He was ordained at Salem with **Adoniram Judson**, Samuel Nott, and **Gordon Hall.** The East India Trading Company refused him landing in India, so he went to **Mauritius** and then to Ceylon (**Sri Lanka**), where he began the first American mission (1813). He went to India in 1814 and worked in Bombay with Nott and Hall until an early death from cholera in 1821. His book *The Conversion of the World, or the Claims of Six Hundred Millions* (1818) aroused much interest in cross-cultural mission.

NEW ENGLAND THEOLOGY. American Congregationalist movement that sought to explain the spiritual experiences of the **Great Awaken-**

ing and defend Congregational churches against **Unitarianism** and **Arminianism.** The theology was first associated with **Jonathan Edwards,** who wrestled with questions of free will and **original sin.** His followers, Joseph Bellamy, Jonathan Edwards Jr., and **Samuel Hopkins,** continued the movement but also introduced subtle changes that had important consequences for American **Calvinism.** Edwards's followers adopted a "governmental" view of the **atonement,** asserting that Christ's **death** was demanded by God's sense of "right and wrong," rather than by God's anger at **sin.** The New England theologians argued that unconverted persons have "natural ability" to choose virtue through the inclination of the will by the **Holy Spirit.** These subtle changes, which were more optimistic about human reason and ability than orthodox Calvinism, prepared the way for the **New Haven theology** of **Nathaniel W. Taylor** and 19th-century **evangelical liberalism.**

NEW GUINEA. *See* PACIFIC OCEAN ISLANDS

NEW HAVEN THEOLOGY. A modified American **Calvinism** associated with Congregationalist **Nathaniel W. Taylor** and his students at Yale Divinity School during the 1820s to 1840s. Sometimes called "Taylorism," the theological movement drew its inspiration from **Timothy Dwight** and served the needs of the Second **Great Awakening.** The movement rejected the doctrine of **original sin,** arguing that **sin** arises from sinful acts rather than a sinful nature inherited from Adam. Taylor argued that sin is simply a voluntary action; although it is inevitable and certain, there is always the "power of contrary choice" ("Man, a Free Agent without the Aids of Divine Grace" [1818]). This moral empowerment laid the theological groundwork for an **Arminianism** that dominated 19th-century American theology. Taylorism influenced Christian activism in social reform, **evangelism** and **missions,** and educational and political life. Although he rejected original sin, Taylor upheld the **Trinity** and experiential religion against a Unitarian movement that was spreading throughout the Congregational churches of New England. Hartford Seminary was founded in opposition to Taylorism (1834).

NEW LIFE MOVEMENT. Established in 1949 by the General Assembly of the Presbyterian Church of New Zealand, the movement sought to address an urgent need for new church extension and development following World War II. The movement sought to renew the inner life of the **church** through congregational **evangelism** and through an emphasis on individual **stewardship** of time and money. Led by two lay secretaries, T. I. Steele and D. N. Perry, the movement produced 66 new parishes, funding for theological scholarships, the construction of new buildings for Maori, and various cross-cultural **mission** projects. Although New Zealand's population increased by 24 percent between 1948 and 1958, as a result of the New Life Movement church attendance rose by 32 percent and those under pastoral care increased by 64 percent.

NEW ZEALAND. New Zealand is predominantly Christian (Roman Catholic, 12 percent; Anglican, 36 percent; Protestant, 34 percent). Located in the Pacific Ocean about 1,000 miles southeast of **Australia**, it consists of two main islands, the North Island, of about 44,000 square miles, and the South Island, of about 58,000 square miles. The main cities in the north are Auckland and Wellington, and Christchurch and Dunedin are located in the south. A third island to the south, Stewart Island, is just 670 square miles. New Zealand possesses an island group called the Chatham Islands that is scattered some 400 miles east of the main land masses. About three quarters of New Zealand is covered by snowcapped mountains or steep hills.

Congregational and Reformed Churches. In 1842 the **Commonwealth Missionary Society** established the first Congregational church in New Zealand. The Congregational Union of New Zealand was formally established in 1884; it had fewer than 30 congregations. A joint union with Australian churches lasted from 1892 to 1960. The post-World War II period saw an influx of Pacific Islanders to the churches. These immigrants came to compose two-thirds of the membership. In 1969, 19 congregations with nearly 3,000 members were received into the Presbyterian Church of New Zealand. The Congregational Union of New Zealand is a member of the **World Alliance of Reformed Churches.** Founded in 1952, the Reformed Churches of New Zealand consists of Dutch Reformed immigrants who organized themselves into 18 congregations under three presbyteries: Auckland, Wellington, and Christchurch. The church claims about 3,000 members.

Presbyterian Churches. The Presbyterian Church of Aotearoa New Zealand is by far the largest Reformed church in New Zealand. The church dates from 1840, when the Reverend John Macfarlane and 122 Scottish immigrants sailed into what is now known as Wellington. The Presbyterian church founded by this group is known as a "settler church," in contrast to the missionary churches of the Anglicans, Wesleyans, and Roman Catholics, which were already well established.

Although Presbyterians also met in Auckland, the major activity took place in the south with the formation of the Lay Association of the Free Church of Scotland (1844). In 1848 the Lay Association, together with

Wakefield's New Zealand Company, launched the Otago settlement on the east coast of the South Island. The settlement was intended for Scottish settlers of the Free Church tradition; it was to be a "Geneva of the Antipodes." The English and non-Free Church settlers who went to Otago, however, soon dashed the hopes of those who had dreamed of a covenantal community. Nevertheless, **Presbyterianism** took a strong hold on the settlement and Southland. The first **presbytery** was organized in 1854 in Otago, and thereafter D. M. Stuart (1819–1894), minister of Knox Church, Dunedin, exerted a strong influence on the community.

With growing prosperity the church spread into the countryside, and rural communities became the backbone of New Zealand Presbyterianism. Newly organized presbyteries and synods allocated resources and maintained educational standards for ministers who came mostly from **Scotland, Ireland,** and Australia. By 1876 a Theological Hall had been established in Dunedin. Traditionalists in Otago and Southland Synod (founded 1866) resisted the idea of union with the Presbyterian Church of New Zealand (founded 1862). David Bruce (1824–1911), who served as minister of St. Andrew's, Auckland, from 1853 to 1876, was the most important leader of the North Island church. Despite resistance, the two bodies merged in 1901. By 1909 the church had reorganized its Theological Hall and had founded, with the help of **Andrew Cameron, Knox College.**

The majority of New Zealand Presbyterians were **evangelical,** with a strong commitment to cross-cultural **mission** and church extension work (see **Alexander Don**). Conservatives and moderates sometimes clashed on such issues as evolution, **universalism, biblical criticism,** and adherence to the **Westminster Confession,** which were argued out in the presbyteries. Ministers were generally well-educated and well-read, and a good tradition of church journalism flourished. Church conflicts led to a succession of heresy trials, including a trial of the first professor at the Theological Hall, William Salmond, who had criticized hard-line Calvinist orthodoxy from a broad evangelical perspective. Although theological issues tended to polarize the church, crusades against violation of the Sabbath, gambling, drinking, and Roman Catholicism, as well as crusades in support of **education,** including the founding of the first university in Otago (1869), were cohesive forces. In this Victorian period the church was essentially a transplant from Scotland.

By the turn of the century the old evangelical tradition had split into liberal and revivalist wings. Middle-class and rural Presbyterians tended to be socially conservative and concerned about individual morality until the 1970s and 1980s, whereas the liberal wing of the church devoted its energies to social work, including the organization of **Presbyterian Support Services**, now the largest independent social service organization in the country. In the post-World War II period, a critical social analysis was introduced, following the lead of pioneering figures such as Rutherford Waddell and James Gibb. Many in the church came to support a wide range of social activities, including counseling and various community services.

Toward the end of the 19th century, New Zealand churches suffered a loss of support and membership, sometimes attributed to the establishment in 1877 of the public school system. The majority of New Zealand's population came from the British working classes, already alienated from the churches. A strong tradition of Sunday school and Bible classes, founded by George Troup, worked to counteract this trend. From the beginning of the century, a large number of church schools, for both girls and boys, had been established. The importance of these schools as centers of church influence continued to grow, though for a long time centrist Presbyterians were more committed to the public schools. As boarding schools, church schools had a particular attraction in rural areas. After World War II, the Bible Class movement flourished, and a renewed emphasis on Christian education, led by J. D. Salmond, was evident in the churches.

The turn of the century saw the emergence of women's movements in the church. The Women's Christian Temperance Union (1885) and the Women's Missionary Union were influential in the struggle for women's rights. New Zealand **women** were allowed to vote in 1893, years ahead of the rest of the world. The first Presbyterian deaconess, Sister **Christabel Waddell**, was appointed in 1901, and the deaconess order pioneered in many areas of social work and Maori mission work. In addition to service as missionaries, women began to serve as **elders** after World War II. In 1965 Margaret Reid became the first woman minister, and in 1979 Joan Anderson became the first woman to be **moderator** of the church.

Church work among the Maori people came late, despite some earlier forays into the field. **John G. Laughton** began work among the Tuhoe people in 1918. The Presbyterians were the first to move from a missionary engagement to an autonomous Maori Synod (1955). After the Congregational church merger of 1969, a substantial number of Pacific Islanders, from **Samoa**, the **Cook Islands**, **Niue**, and other islands, joined the church. Since then church leaders have considered forming a Pacific

Islands Synod. The Pacific Island churches are vibrant congregations, providing ministers to European as well as Pacific Island congregations. The contemporary church is consciously multicultural and recognizes the Maori as the "people of the land." In 1991 the church changed its name to the Presbyterian Church of Aotearoa New Zealand.

The church of the post-World War II era was characterized by the enthusiasm of the **New Life Movement** (1949), which had strong lay support and involvement under Norman Perry and **Thomas C. Brash**. The movement initiated new church extension and **stewardship** work and new Christian education programs, and it increased ecumenical and liturgical awareness, and lay activism. During the 1960s, as New Zealand slipped out of its old colonial deferences, and amid a furious controversy over liberal theology, church membership began a decline that continues today.

By the 1980s the church was deeply involved in the social and political life of New Zealand. This was evident in 1981, when a tour by the South African rugby team caused rioting and polarized the nation. The church had opposed the tour because of its theological opposition to **apartheid**, and church members were prominent in nonviolent protest. The church supported the legitimate obligations of the Treaty of Waitangi (1840), which had guaranteed the Maori lands and fishing rights in return for the recognition of British sovereignty. The church supported a nuclear-free and independent Pacific, and it joined with other churches in calling for a more just social order. This prophetic stance, which tended to be led by ministers, alienated many in the pews. One reaction has been some tendency toward a self-sufficient congregationalism. The church remains engaged in hymn writing, **evangelism**, new methods of theological education, and the ministry of Presbyterian Support Services. In 1993 the church reported 25 presbyteries and 41,000 members, with about 10 times this number under pastoral care.

NGOLE, ABRAHAM EBONG (1895–1980). Presbyterian minister and the first moderator of the Presbyterian Church in **Cameroon**. Ngole was born in the village of Jockte-Enyandong Bakossi. In his youth he was put into the care of German missionaries by his father, who feared that he would be conscripted into the German army to fight in World War I. In 1923 Ngole became a schoolteacher with the Cameroonian mission of the **Evangelical Mission Society in Basel**. In 1937, after 13 years of service, Ngole moved to Tombel Bakossi, where he became an evangelist and served as tutor in the Catechist Training Institution at Nyasoso. He was appointed pastor in 1946 and served in Itoki, where he was ordained in 1947. When the Cameroonian church became independent from the Basel Mission in 1957, Ngole was elected **moderator**. During 12 years in office he worked to ensure that congregations were staffed by Cameroonians, organized youth work, helped to found the Christian Women's Fellowship in 1961, and began **mission** work in Akwaya in 1963. Ngole retired in 1969 and died in Kumba.

NICARAGUA. *See* MESOAMERICA

NIEBUHR, H[ELMUT] RICHARD (1894–1962). American theologian, ethicist, and minister in the German Evangelical Synod of North America. The son of Gustav Niebuhr and brother of **Reinhold Niebuhr**, H. Richard Niebuhr was born in Wright City, Missouri. He received degrees from Elmhurst College (1912), Eden Theological Seminary (1915), and Washington University, St. Louis. He pursued further studies at Yale Divinity School and Yale University. Niebuhr served as a pastor in St. Louis (1916–1918) and taught theology and **ethics** at Eden Seminary (1919–1922). He served as president of Elmhurst College (1924–1927) and then as professor at Eden Seminary (1927–1931) before accepting the position of associate professor of Christian ethics at Yale Divinity School in 1931.

Niebuhr approached theology from an ethical and historical viewpoint, standing between **Friedrich Schleiermacher** and **Karl Barth**. He was influenced by the works of Ernst Troeltsch, on whom he wrote his doctoral dissertation, and argued that the meaning of church teachings could and should be rediscovered in contexts that were relevant to contemporary culture. His book *The Social Sources of Denominationalism* (1929) explores the relationship of Christian institutions to culture. *The Kingdom of God in America* (1937) traces the concept of the **kingdom of God** through American history. *Christ and Culture* (1951), with its typologies of the relationships between Christians and culture, is a classic. Niebuhr's theological and ethical works include *The Meaning of Revelation* (1941), *Radical Monotheism and Western Culture* (1960), and *The Responsible Self* (1963).

NIEBUHR, [KARL PAUL] REINHOLD (1892–1971). American theologian, ethicist, and Evangelical and Reformed church minister. The brother of **H. Richard Niebuhr**, Reinhold was born in Wright City, Missouri. He graduated from Elmhurst College and received degrees from Eden Theological Seminary (1913), Yale Divinity School (1914), and Yale University (1915). He was a minister in Detroit for 13 years (1915–1928) before being appointed to the faculty of **Union Theologi-**

cal Seminary in New York. There he served as associate professor of **philosophy of religion** (1928–1930) and professor of applied Christianity (1930–1960). Niebuhr was a committed social activist who served on numerous committees and allied himself with many political groups. He helped form Americans for Democratic Action and the Liberal Party of New York State. From 1941 to 1966 he was editor of the influential journal *Christianity and Crisis*. He was awarded the Presidential Medal of Freedom in 1964.

Niebuhr was a proponent of "Christian Realism," a view similar to **neoorthodoxy** but emphasizing **ethics** rather than theology. His writings examine the doctrine of humanity and concentrate on the problems of the nation and society. Niebuhr advocated a radical **social gospel** for a world affected by human **sin**. Niebuhr understood humanity's greatest problem to be its own self-understanding. He proposed a dialectical response: humanity as "free and bound, both limited and limitless." He advocated justice as the goal for society, and believed that sin makes political action necessary. Politics is the means by which justice is attained. Power is necessary to enforce compromises that approximate justice. Niebuhr recognized that societies cannot attain ideal justice, and that humanity's hope ultimately lies in the reign of **God**. Niebuhr's *The Nature and Destiny of Man* (2 vols.; 1941, 1943) is one of the most important theological works of the 20th century. He also wrote *Moral Man and Immoral Society* (1932), *The Children of Light and the Children of Darkness* (1944), and *The Irony of American History* (1952).

NIGERIA. *See* WEST AFRICA

NIUE. *See* PACIFIC OCEAN ISLANDS

NONCONFORMIST. Any Protestant in 17th-century **England** and **Wales** who did not conform to the Church of England as prescribed by the Act of Uniformity (1662). Nonconformists included Baptists, Congregationalists, Presbyterians, and other Protestants who left the Church of England. These dissenting groups were later called "Free Churches." The status of the nonconforming groups was changed by the Toleration Act (1689), which accorded limited rights to orthodox Protestant dissenters. In **Scotland**, where the Church of Scotland is the established church, Episcopal and other Protestant churches were considered Nonconformist.

NORTH AFRICA. The great majority of the people of North Africa practice Islam. In the countries of Algeria, Morocco, and Tunisia, where 99 percent of the population is Muslim, there are small communities of Reformed Christians.

Algeria. Among the first Protestants to arrive in Algeria were missionaries from the **Evangelical Mission Society in Basel**, but their work did not survive. The Reformed Church of France also sent missionaries who worked among the French Protestant community living in Algeria. In 1962 the Reformed Church in Algeria became independent. In 1971 the church united with the Methodist Church to become the Protestant Church of Algeria. The church ministers to French residents and African students from countries south of the Sahara.

Morocco. Reformed influence in Morocco has come from Reformed churches in **Scotland** and **France**. The work of the Scottish South Morocco Mission primarily emphasized **health** care. In 1959 this **mission** united with the North Africa Mission, which continued the same emphasis. The Reformed Church of France began mission work in 1922. This work was carried out among French citizens and other Protestant Europeans working in the country. In 1958 the church became the independent Evangelical Church in Morocco (Eglise evangélique du Maroc). The church, which is recognized by the government, has agreed not to proselytize.

Tunisia. The Reformed Church of France established a church in Tunisia that serves French citizens and other Protestant Europeans working in the country. With its four congregations, the Reformed Church in Tunisia remains small, having a limited influence in the country.

NORTH AMERICA. *See* CANADA, CARIBBEAN, UNITED STATES OF AMERICA

NORTHEAST ASIA. The region is primarily Buddhist (South Korea, 49 percent; Japan, 43 percent [and 51 percent Shinto]), with Christians being a large, growing minority in South Korea (42 percent) and a small minority in Japan (less than 1 percent). In North Korea religious activities are severely restricted.

Korea. Presbyterians are by far the largest Protestant group in South Korea. The history of the Presbyterian Church in Korea dates from the 1870s, when Korea denied entry to foreigners. To evangelize the Korean people, a Scottish **mission** was founded in Manchuria. Here the Bible was translated into Korean. Korean nationals became converts, and several of these converts returned to Korea with the gospel. One of the first nationals to return home was So Sang-Yoon, who organized a Christian group in his village. Although such activity brought Reformed Christianity to Korea, it was the Korean treaty with the **United States** (1882) allowing Western missionaries to enter the country that generated the growth of the Korean churches.

During the 1880s, mission work in Korea was carried out by Presbyterian churches of **Australia**, **Canada**, and the **United States**. Among the first American arrivals were Presbyterian missionaries **Horace Underwood** (1885) and Samuel A. Moffett (1890); both remained influential figures during their long careers. The Presbyterian missions and their leaders participated in a great revival that took place between 1903 and 1907 and spread from Korea to Manchuria and **China**. In 1907 the four Western missions united to form the Presbyterian Church of Korea. From 1905 through the end of World War II, a period of trials took place for Korean Christians. Korea was annexed by Japan in 1910 and thereafter the church endured periodic clashes with the Japanese colonial government, including the Independence Movement in 1919. The church suffered severe repression during World War II. Part of the suffering was a result of the colonial government's attempt to enforce Shinto shrine worship on the Korean people. A few Korean Christians resisted and were killed; some resisted passively; most reluctantly obeyed government orders. A small group of church leaders, called the "rationalizing group," willingly collaborated with the government. *See also* Emperor System

After World War II the church endured further turmoil. The country was divided into the North and the South, with North Korea under the control of a communist government. North Korea had been the historic center of Presbyterian activity, and many Reformed Christians fled to South Korea during the 1940s and 1950s. Presbyterians who remained were persecuted during the government's antireligion campaigns. Many Christians still live in North Korea, but religious expression is restricted. If the Reformed faith flourished in the South, the post-World War II years also saw divisions open up within its churches between those who had cooperated with Shinto shrine worship and those who had not, between theological liberals and conservatives, and between South Koreans and refugees from the North. Today there are four major Presbyterian denominations and more than 40 smaller ones. In spite of the divisions, the Presbyterian community doubled in size about every 10 years between 1940 and 1990. There are now approximately 6.5 million Presbyterians in South Korea.

The Korean churches have been active in the educational, social, and political life of the nation. After a military coup in South Korea in 1972,

President Park Chung Hee consolidated power and reorganized the government as a dictatorship. In theological and political protest, a group of Korean ministers formulated the **Theological Declaration of Korean Christians** (1973). The Presbyterian Church of Korea (1907; T'ong-hap), the largest of the Presbyterian bodies in Korea, is broadly evangelical and has participated in ecumenical activities. The Presbyterian Church in the Republic of Korea (Kijang), formed in 1953 as a result of a liberal-conservative theological division, was for some years the only Presbyterian Church in Korea that ordained **women**. **Minjung theology** arose from this church body, which supports Han-Kuk Theological Seminary. Among the many conservative groups is the Koryo Presbyterian Church (1946).

Important leaders of the Korean churches include theologian **Byung-mu Ahn**; **Ki-chol Chu**, who was killed for his opposition to Shinto shrine worship; lay and political leader **Young-shin Hahn**; educator and denominational leader **Sang-dong Hahn**; teacher and lay minister **Jong-ho Im**; evangelist **Sun-joo Kil**; theologian **Jae-jun Kim**; public servant and lay leader **Sang-chai Lee**; educator **Seung-hoon Lee**; professor and political activist **Ik-whan Moon**; educator **L. George Paik**; theologian and educator **Hyung-nong Park**; educator and mission leader **Dong-hyuck Shin**; and social activist **Jae-kee Yoo**.

Japan. Christianity was illegal in Japan prior to the Townsend Harris Treaty of 1858 with the United States. In 1859 two American Reformed denominations, the Presbyterian Church in the U.S.A. and the Reformed Church in America, established missions in Japan. James C. Hepburn, who was responsible for the transliteration of Japanese into Roman letters, and Guido F. Verbeck were early missionaries from these churches. During this period Western missions were confined to Yokohama and Nagasaki. In 1872 a revival began in Yokohama that eventually resulted in the formation of the first Japanese Presbyterian church and **Meiji Gakuin** (1874), the first Japanese educational institution with Reformed roots.

In 1876 missionaries from the American Presbyterian, Dutch Reformed, and Scottish United Presbyterian churches organized the Council of Three Missions to form a single Presbyterian-Reformed denomination. The following year the Church of Christ in Japan (Nihon Kirisuto Kokai; later called Nihon Kirisuto Kyokai) was established, incorporating the groups represented by the council, as well as other Protestant denominations and new churches that were founded as a result of an 1883 revival that broke out in Yokohama and spread throughout Japan. In 1890 the church adopted a statement of faith based on the historic Christian creeds and regulated **church government.**

A period of Japanese nationalism took place under the Meiji regime (1890–1912), when the government mandated the worship of traditional Shinto gods. After the end of the Meiji regime in 1912, Protestant churches saw a new period of growth. At the same time, a movement of **Social Christianity** was introduced into the churches. Japanese nationalism and Shinto practice gradually increased, however, and in 1939 the government passed the Law of Religious Bodies, which regulated the Protestant churches and ordered them to merge into a single denomination, the United Church of Christ in Japan (Nihon Kirisuto Kyodan; founded 1941). Protestant groups that refused to join were no longer recognized (e.g., the Salvation Army). The first **moderator** of the new denomination was Mitsuru Tomita, a Presbyterian minister.

The United Church of Christ continues as the largest Protestant denomination in Japan, with a sizable Reformed membership. However, the government-imposed Protestant unity came partially undone after World War II, when many Reformed Congregations left the kyodan. Also, after the war years more than 2,500 Protestant missionaries came to Japan, and many of the smaller Reformed churches organized by these missionaries did not join the Kyodan.

The Korean Church in Japan withdrew from the Kyodan and continues to serve the Korean minority in Japan. In 1946 the Reformed Church in Japan was organized, adopting the **Westminster Confession,** founding Shikoku Christian College at Zentsuji, and organizing six presbyteries. It drafted a Statement of Faith Concerning Church and State, emphasizing the prophetic role of the church toward the state, and a Statement of Faith of the Reformed Church in Japan, emphasizing the doctrine of the **Holy Spirit.** The Scottish Reformed Presbyterian Christian Church of Japan and the American Cumberland Presbyterian Church of Japan were organized in 1950. In 1951 a group of about 40 churches withdrew from the Kyodan and organized a new denomination under the former name, Church of Christ in Japan (Shin-Nikki). The Presbyterian Church in Japan was established in 1956. This church founded Japan Christian Theological Seminary and Tokyo Christian College, which became Tokyo Christian University (1990).

Japanese theologians and church leaders include **Toyohiko Kagawa,** internationally known Christian social reformer; **Michi Kawai,** ecumenical leader and founder of Kelsen Jogakuen (Fountain of Grace School for Women); **Yoshitaka Kumano**, professor of systematic theology at **Tokyo Union Theological Seminary**; **Kokichi Kurosaki**, Bible teacher and author; **Hidenobu Kuwada**, theological educator; **Joseph Hardy Neeshima**, Congregationalist missionary and founder of Doshisha University; **Toson Shimazaki**, novelist and poet; **Hisano Takahashi**, Presbyterian evangelist; **Tokutaro Takakura**, president of Japan Theological Seminary; **Masaichi Takemori**, professor and president of Tokyo Union Theological Seminary; **Masahisa Uemura**, Presbyterian evangelist and president of Tokyo Theological Seminary; and **Tamaki Uemura**, pastor of Kashiwagi Church.

NORTHERN EUROPE. Although in some countries religious practice is minimal, the people of northern Europe are affiliated with Christian churches: Belgium (75 percent) and Luxembourg (96 percent) are predominantly Roman Catholic; Denmark (88 percent), Finland (90 percent), and Sweden (93 percent) are Evangelical Lutheran; and Germany (34 percent Roman Catholic; 34 percent Protestant; 31 percent unaffiliated or other) and the Netherlands (36 percent Roman Catholic; 27 percent Protestant; 37 percent unaffiliated or other) are almost evenly divided, with Roman Catholics and Lutheran Protestants dominating in Germany and Roman Catholics and Reformed Protestants being the majority in the Netherlands. In each of these countries there are communities of Reformed churches. There are no Reformed churches in Norway.

Belgium. The Reformed churches in Belgium trace their history to the Protestant Reformation and Dutch Reformer Guy de Brès, who came to Belgium in 1561. Although the Counter-Reformation swept away much of the Reformed movement, Reformed missionaries from **France**, the Netherlands, and **Switzerland** came later to make new converts. Modern Reformed churches were organized after Belgian political independence in 1830. In that year the Evangelical Protestant Church of Belgium was founded. In 1969 the church merged with the Belgian Conference of the United Methodist Church to form the Protestant Church of Belgium.

In 1937 another branch of the Reformed movement began with the founding of the Belgian Christian Missionary Church, later called the Reformed Church of Belgium. This denomination was centered in Wallonia, the French-speaking part of Belgium. The **church** was noted for its commitment to **evangelism** and its refusal of government support for its ministers. In 1979 this Belgian Reformed church merged with the Protestant Church of Belgium to create the United Protestant Church of Belgium (Eglise Protestante unie de Belgique). The United Protestant Church is a member of the **World Alliance of Reformed Churches** and the **World Council of Churches.**

Belgian Reformed church leaders include **Leonard J. F. H. Anet, Henri Theophile de Worm, Emile-Philippe Hoyois, Edouard D. A. Pichal,** and **Matthieu G. Schyns.**

Denmark. The Reformed Church Synod in Denmark began from the German Reformed Church in Copenhagen, founded by Queen Charlotte Amalie, wife of Christian V of Denmark and a princess of Hesse-Cassel. The church began in 1685, the year the **Edict of Nantes** was revoked by Louis XIV of France, forcing many French Reformed Christians to flee to northern Europe. Four church communities compose the synod, the primary one being the Reformed church in Copenhagen, which was modeled after the **Huguenot** temple at Charenton near Paris. The church is the center of Reformed activity in Copenhagen.

Finland. A congregationalist church movement came from Sweden in 1878. This movement produced two denominations in Finland: the Finnish-speaking Free Church of Finland and the Swedish-speaking Free Mission Covenant Church (discussed below). The Free Church is the larger denomination, having over 90 congregations. The Free Mission Covenant Church has about 20 congregations.

Germany. Reformed congregations began in Germany at the time of the Reformation. **John Łaski,** who became pastor in Emden (1543), introduced Reformed **worship** modeled after the practice in Strasbourg and the Ecclesiastical Ordinances of Geneva. After Elector Frederick III of the Palatinate converted to Reformed Protestantism (1563), the Palatinate church order was issued. Reformed churches expanded in Lower Saxony and congregations were later begun in the Rhineland. By the beginning of the Thirty Years War (1618–1648), there were many Reformed congregations in Germany. The German churches were influenced by **Zacharias Ursinus** and the **Heidelberg Catechism.**

Reformed and Lutheran "union churches" were established in the early 19th century in the Prussian territories, and a pietistic movement led to the organization of the **Evangelical Mission Society in Basel** (1815). In 1882 more than 100 congregations united to form the Evangelical Reformed Church in Northwest Germany. Two years later the **Reformed Alliance** was formed, uniting member churches for the purpose of cultivating "the heritage of the Reformed churches in life, worship, and order." From 1933 onward the Reformed Alliance was part of the **Confessing Church** movement that produced the **Theological Declaration of Barmen.**

Since 1925 the Evangelical Reformed Church in Northwest Germany has been governed along Presbyterian lines, with a synod as the highest judicatory. In 1955 the church established headquarters in Leer (Ostfriesland). The church shares eucharistic Communion with all member churches of the Evangelical Church in Germany (Evangelische Kirche in Deutschland; EKD).

Smaller Reformed bodies include the Evangelical Church of the Palatinate and the National Church of Lippe. The Palatinate church resulted from a 1918 union of Reformed and Lutheran churches; it maintains a presbyterian government. The Church of Lippe is also governed by a presbyterian constitution, and it emphasizes the missionary nature of the local congregation.

German Reformed theologians and church leaders include **Heinrich J. L. Heppe, Karl Hundeshagen, Friedrich W. Krummacher, Friedrich A. Lampe, Friedrich Schleiermacher,** and **Otto Weber.**

Luxembourg. The largest Protestant church in Luxembourg is the Evangelical Protestant Church of the Grand Duchy of Luxembourg. The church began when Prussian soldiers occupied Luxembourg after 1813. Beginning in 1918, Reformed Christians from the Netherlands joined the church, making the body of both Lutheran and Reformed heritage. There are also several Dutch Reformed churches in Luxembourg.

Netherlands. Calvinism was brought to the Netherlands by European refugees. The movement spread quickly, enabling the first Synod of the Dutch Reformed Church to be held in 1571. The church adopted the Belgic Confession (1561) and the **Heidelberg Catechism** (1562) as its doctrinal standards. A 17th-century controversy between the followers of **Jacob Arminius** and **Francis Gomar** over **predestination** was settled by the Synod of Dort (1618–1619), which condemned the anti-predestinarian teachings of Arminius in its Canons of Dort. These canons were added as the third doctrinal standard of the church.

During the 17th century, the Dutch established a vast colonial empire in the East Indies (1598), Formosa (1624), India (1633), Brazil (1640), and Cape Town (1652). Dutch wealth led to the development of a rich cultural life, with the growth of a book publishing industry and the arts. The flowering of Dutch art began with **Rembrandt** (1606–1669) and his immediate predecessors.

Intellectual life in the Dutch church was influenced by the growth of pietism and scholasticism. The Further Reformation *(Nadere Reformatie)* movement emphasized experiential faith while theological scholasticism was articulated by Gisbert Voetius (1589–1676), an important Reformed theologian.

The 18th-century Dutch church was shaped as much by its mission outreach as by its theology. Dutch mission followed the global trading and colonial empire of the nation. Mission societies were founded and mission schools were later organized at Baarn and Oostgeest. The movement produced important mission literature and shaped the life of emerging churches throughout the Dutch empire. *See also* Netherlands Missionary Society

In 1816 the Dutch Reformed state church was reorganized by William I and renamed the Netherlands Reformed Church (Nederduitse Hervormde Kerk; NHK). During the 19th century, theological **liberalism** became widespread within the church and a conservative reaction led to the withdrawal of some groups and the development of theological diversity within the church. The NHK remains the largest Reformed church in the Netherlands, with its ministers being trained by the theological faculties at Dutch universities, including the Rijksuniversiteiten, and at the seminary in Driebergen.

During the 19th century, a revival **(Réveil)** movement broke out in Europe. In 1834 a group of Dutch Reformed churches influenced by this Réveil withdrew from the NHK. Another secession (the *Doleantie*), led by **Abraham Kuyper** in reaction to liberalism, took place in 1886. A unification of the two seceder communities took place in 1892. The new denomination called itself the Reformed Churches in the Netherlands (Nederduitse Gereformeerde Kerk; NGK). This denomination began as a very conservative church, strictly adhering to the theology of the Dutch **confessions** and emphasizing church **discipline**, the local nature of the **church**, the active responsibility of all church members **(priesthood of all believers)**, and mission outreach. Ministers of the NGK are trained at the **Free University of Amsterdam** and at the Theologische Hoogschool at Kampen. In recent years the NGK has become more moderate in its theological views, and there is some interest in reuniting the two denominations. Other Dutch groups include the Remonstrant Brotherhood, a small church that maintains membership in the **World Alliance of Reformed Churches.**

Theological faculties of Kampen and the Free University of Amsterdam have produced prominent theologians, including **Herman Bavinck, A. A. van Ruler**, and **Gerrit C. Berkouwer**; biblical scholars such as H. N. Ridderbos; and philosophers Herman Dooyeweerd and D.

H. T. Vollenhoven. The schools of the NHK have among their graduates **Willem A. Visser 't Hooft**, the first general secretary of the World Council of Churches, and theologian **Hendrikus Berkhof**.

Sweden. The Swedish Mission Covenant Church (Svenska Missionsförbundet) began in the context of the 19th century pietistic revival movement that swept through several European countries. In Sweden, the **evangelical** revival generated covenantal fellowships, the earliest founded in 1855. These fellowships evolved into churches with congregational government. One of the leaders of these fellowship groups was **Peter Waldenström**, whose pietism and views on the **atonement** were opposed by the Swedish government and the established church. This opposition led to the formation of a new denomination organized under the name Swedish Missionary Society (1878). By the end of the 19th century the denomination had over 100,000 members. The church participated in meetings of the **International Congregational Council** (ICC) and is now a member of the World Alliance of Reformed Churches.

The Swedish Mission Covenant Church recognizes the scriptures as the only authoritative guide to **faith** and does not subscribe to creeds. Ministers are educated at its seminary at Lidingö (1908) or at the theological faculties at Uppsala and Lund. The **general assembly** is the church's highest decision-making body.

NORTHERN IRELAND. *See* UNITED KINGDOM

NOTT, HENRY (1774–1844). English missionary in **Tahiti**. Nott was sent to Tahiti by the **London Missionary Society**. Arriving in 1797, he was the first Protestant missionary to work in the **Pacific Ocean islands**. He translated **scripture** into Tahitian and served as an adviser to the Tahitian chief Pomare I. Following Pomare's **baptism** in 1815 the Tahitian people began to embrace Christianity. In his capacity as royal adviser, Nott helped to produce the Pomare Law Code (1819), a set of Christian laws for Tahiti. He is buried in Matavai, Tahiti.

- O -

OBERMÜLLER, RODOLFO (1904–1991). Argentine New Testament theologian. Born in Esslingen, **Germany**, Obermüller was educated at Tübingen (1922–1926) and spent one semester studying with **Karl Barth**. He served a congregation in Stuttgart until 1930 and then other churches in Germany until accepting a call in 1933 to Congregación Alemana, the German congregation of Buenos Aires. In addition to his pastoral duties, Obermüller served his denomination, the Church of the River Plata, as head of its publications office (1934–1950) and editor of the church magazine (1936–1950). In 1948 he was appointed associate professor at the Evangelical School of Theology in Buenos Aires; he also served on the faculty at the Lutheran School of Theology. His publications include *Lexico Griego-Español del Nuevo Testamento* (1941), a translation of the New Testament that appeared in *Nueva Version de la Biblia al Castellano* (1966) and *Teologia del Nuevo Testamento* (4 vols., 1976–1979).

OBOOKIAH (OPUKAHAIAH), HENRY (1792–1818). Hawaiian Protestant and advocate of Christian **mission** in **Hawaii.** Born on the island of Hawaii, Obookiah lost his parents in a tribal war when he was 12. At the age of 15, Obookiah signed on with an American merchant ship and went to New England. He arrived in New Haven, Connecticut, in 1809 and was befriended by **Timothy Dwight.** He learned to read and write, and in 1812 he became a member of the Congregational Church in Torringford, Connecticut. A devout Christian, Obookiah dedicated himself to bringing the gospel to Hawaii. He prepared a Hawaiian dictionary and grammar and translated the book of Genesis into Hawaiian. He also urged missionaries to go to Hawaii. In 1818, after enrolling at a new school for missionaries in Cornwall, Connecticut, Obookiah contracted typhoid fever and died. His memoir, published posthumously, *Memoirs of Henry Obookiah* (1818), became a best-seller in New England and inspired a Hawaiian mission, which was established in 1820 under the leadership of **Hiram Bingham.**

OCEANIA. *See* AUSTRALIA, NEW ZEALAND, PACIFIC OCEAN ISLANDS

OECOLAMPADIUS, JOHN (1482–1531). German humanist scholar, preacher, and church reformer in **Switzerland.** Oecolampadius was born in Weinsberg, in the Palatinate, and was educated at Heidelberg. After tutoring the sons of the Palatinate's elector and serving as court preacher at Weinsberg (1510–1513), he went to Tübingen. In **Germany** Oecolampadius mastered Hebrew, Greek, and Latin, and in 1515 he moved to Basel, Switzerland, where he assisted humanist scholar Desiderius Erasmus (c. 1466–1536). In Basel, Oecolampadius helped to prepare Erasmus's edition of the Greek New Testament, translated various Greek patristic texts, including works by Gregory of Nazianzus, and obtained a doctoral degree from the University of Basel (1518). He spent five years as a preacher and pastor in Basel and became a professor at the university. He also became preacher at Saint Martin's Church and the leader of the reform movement in the city. He entered into the theological debates of the time, supporting the reform movement against Roman Catholicism at Baden (1526) and at the disputation at Bern (1528), and the Zwinglian side against Luther at the **Marburg Colloquy** (1529). Although he supported the Zwinglian position on the **Lord's Supper**, Oecolampadius retained a mystical element in his understanding of the sacrament. His theology also helped to shape the Reformed movement in such areas as the interpretation of **scripture, covenant,** and **worship.**

OLDHAM, JOSEPH HOULDSWORTH (1874–1969). Ecumenical missionary and churchman. Oldham was born in **India** and educated at Edinburgh Academy and Trinity College, Oxford (1892–1896). He was converted under the ministry of Dwight L. Moody in 1897 and spent three years as secretary of the YMCA in Lahore, India. He then attended **New College, Edinburgh** (1901–1904), and was licensed by the United Free Church but never ordained. In 1906 Oldham was appointed mission study secretary of the United Free Church. He organized the World Missionary Conference in Edinburgh (1910) and became secretary of its Continuation Committee. In 1912 he became the first editor of the *International Review of Missions.* He played a major role in the formation of the Life and Work Movement and the International Missionary Council (1921), which he served as joint secretary (1921–1938). He worked closely with John R. Mott and edited the *Christian Newsletter* from 1939 to 1945.

Oldham was deeply interested in the affairs of Africa and tried, especially after 1930, to promote lay missionary activity. In 1937, sensing the threat of Nazi influence, he helped organize the Oxford Conference on Church, Community, and State. He was a founder of the **World Council of Churches** and served as one of its presidents. His later years were spent improving social and educational standards among indigenous African peoples. His writings include *Christianity and the Race Problem* (1924) and *Life Is Commitment* (1953).

ORAL TRADITION. The cumulative lore, history, stories, and wisdom of a particular culture as preserved, memorized, and passed on verbally from one generation to the next. In nonliterate societies, oral tradition is the primary vehicle of continuing cultural identity. Literate societies have sometimes viewed it as primitive and deficient, but ethnological and anthropological studies have revealed the wealth, variety, and great complexity of oral tradition. The fact that two-thirds of the world's population is nonliterate or minimally literate has led the Reformed churches to take oral tradition seriously, developing forms of **inculturation** that use oral communication for **evangelism** and Christian **education.** However, the Reformed churches continue to promote literacy because of the centrality of **scripture** to Christian **faith** (*see also* Bible Translations; Frank Laubach).

ORDINATION. An act of the **church** in which persons are set apart for specific types of ministries. In the Reformed tradition, ordination is seen as a commissioning to an office of **ministry** and is carried out as an act of a **presbytery** or classis. It is ordination to the ministry of Jesus Christ and is performed by Christ's **authority.** Ordination has typically been to the ministries of Word and Sacrament (pastor), teaching, government **(elder),** and service **(deacon).** Ordination to special ministries authorized by a governing body also occurs. The public act of ordination carried out in the context of **worship** is marked by the laying on of hands, which signifies that the person no longer acts independently but is now in service "to **God** and the church" (*Inst.* 4.3.16). The Spirit of God is invoked as the power that will make the ministry effective. Ordination is the outward recognition of the inner call to ministry in which the church acknowledges the call to positions of Christian leadership and service and affirms the Spirit's gifts for that ministry.

ORIGINAL SIN. The **sin** that entered into God's good **creation,** together with its subsequent consequences for humanity's relationship with **God.** The origin of sin is a mystery. Theologians have refused to hold God responsible for it and have resisted the idea that it is inherent in human nature, since God created everything good. The Bible explains it as an act of disobedience (free choice) by the parents of the human race (Gen. 3). In Reformed theology, Adam and Eve are viewed as representatives of the human race who broke the **covenant** relationship with God. By their act of disobedience sin entered the world and infected all of humanity, though not through the biological transmission suggested by Augustine. Original sin is imputed guilt that alienates human beings from a right relationship with God, with one another, and with the creation. It is only through the power of the "Second Adam," Jesus Christ, that humanity is delivered from the curse of sin and **death:** "as one man's trespass led to condemnation for all, so one man's act of righteousness leads to **justification** and life for all" (Rom. 5:18). Although Reformed theology stresses the "total depravity" of humanity, it recognizes that human beings were created good, that sinfulness is an alien condition, and that human destiny is to be conformed to the image of Christ.

ORR, JAMES (1844–1913). Scottish Presbyterian theologian and apologist. Orr was born in Glasgow and studied arts and theology at Glasgow University (1865–1872). He served as pastor of East Bank Church in Hawick (1874–1891) and was appointed professor of church history at the United Presbyterian College, Edinburgh (1891–1900). From 1900 to 1913, he taught systematic theology and apologetics at the United Free Church College in Glasgow. Orr began his academic career with publication of a lecture series, *The Christian View of God and the World* (1893). He became one of the leading theologians of the United Free Church.

In his book, *The Ritschlian Theology and the Evangelical Faith* (1897), Orr became an early critic of the liberal theology of Albrecht Ritschl, insisting that it was antithetical to genuine Christianity. He also countered Adolf von Harnack's views of the history of doctrinal development in *The Progress of Dogma* (1901). In *Revelation and Inspiration*, Orr affirmed **scripture's** full **inspiration** but rejected its inerrancy. He supported an **evangelical Calvinism**, which interacts with contemporary philosophy and theology, and favored a modified subscription to the **Westminster Confession.** His work was influential throughout **Great Britain** and also in the **United States**, where he lectured. Orr was a contributor to *The Fundamentals* (1910–1915) and served as general editor of the *International Standard Bible Encyclopedia* (1915). His other works include *God's Image in Man* (1905), *The Problem of the Old Testament* (1906), and *The Virgin Birth of Christ* (1907).

OWEN, JOHN (1616–1683). English Congregationalist minister and Puritan theologian. Born in Stadhampton, Oxfordshire, Owen was educated at Queen's College, Oxford, where he became sympathetic to the Puritan cause. He served as pastor of a church in Fordham, Essex (1643) and, after reading a work by Congregationalist **John Cotton**, rejected Presbyterian church polity in favor of the congregational system of church government. While minister of a church in Coggeshall, Essex, Owen accompanied **Oliver Cromwell's** military expeditions in **Scotland** and **Ireland** (1649–1651), serving as a chaplain. In 1651 Parliament appointed Owen dean of Christ Church, and in 1662 Cromwell made him vice-chancellor. He served in this capacity until 1657, becoming active in state affairs and in the training of "godly and learned" men.

Owen was the chief religious force behind the Cromwellian state, and a major influence on the **Savoy Declaration of Faith and Order** (1658). After the Restoration of the Monarchy in 1660, Owen was expelled from Christ Church and became a **Nonconformist.** He rejected episcopacy and written liturgies and became a leader of the Nonconformist movement. He then became pastor of a small London Congregational church, which he served for the next 20 years. A critic of deism and Socinianism, Owen was a prolific writer who combined Calvinistic theology with a devotional zeal and concern for the work of the **Holy Spirit.**

- P -

PACIFIC OCEAN ISLANDS. The people of the Pacific Islands are predominantly Christian. The island nations with Reformed churches are loosely grouped into three areas: Melanesia (New Caledonia, Papua New Guinea, and Vanuatu), Micronesia (Kiribati, Federated States of Micronesia, and Marshall Islands), and Polynesia (Cook Islands, French Polynesia, Niue, Samoa, and Tuvalu). Reformed Protestants are the majority in the Cook Islands, Federated States of Micronesia, Tuvalu, Marshall Islands, Niue, French Polynesia, Western Samoa, and Vanuatu. Roman Catholics predominate in Kiribati (53 percent) and New Caledonia (66 percent). Papua New Guinea is divided between Christian and indigenous religion; Protestants form the majority of the Christian population.

New Caledonia. The territory is a French overseas possession in the southwestern Pacific Ocean, including the islands of New Caledonia and Walpole, and several island groups. Samoan missionaries with the **London Missionary Society** (LMS) arrived in the 1840s. The LMS work was transferred to the **Paris Evangelical Missionary Society** in 1922. The Evangelical Church of New Caledonia emerged from this work.

Papua New Guinea. The country consists of the eastern half of the island of New Guinea and surrounding islands, including the Bismark Archipelago and Bougainville, located in the southwest Pacific Ocean. The country became independent in 1975. The capital is Port Moresby.

William G. Lawes of the London Missionary Society (LMS) arrived in 1871 with Protestants from New Caledonia, and in 1877 **James Chalmers** came from the Cook Islands. These two missionaries laid the foundation of the church. Lawes engaged in Bible translation while Chalmers located his evangelistic base in Saguane and later worked his way into the interior of the country. In 1962 three Reformed communities on Papua, including the LMS, the Presbyterian Church of New Zealand, and the Kwato Mission, united to form the Church of Papua. In 1968 this Reformed church joined with the Methodist Church and the Union Church in Port Moresby to form the United Church of Papua New Guinea and the Solomon Islands. The church plays an important role in **health** care and **education**.

Vanuatu. Formerly called New Hebrides, in 1980 the country became an independent nation, composed of more than 13 islands in the southwestern Pacific Ocean. Governed by the British and French since the early 19th century, the people of the islands are called Ni-Vanuatu.

The London Missionary Society sent English and Samoan teachers to the islands between 1839 and 1841 with disastrous results; **John Williams** was killed on the island of Erromango (1839) and two Samoan teachers, Samuela and Apela, were killed on the island of Futuna (1841). The **mission** did not establish a foothold until **John Geddie** arrived in Aneityum in 1848. Geddie was followed by Scottish missionary **John G. Paton.** Geddie and Paton laid the foundation of the Presbyterian Church of Vanuatu The church became independent in 1948.

Today the church operates Onesua High School, two vocational schools, an agricultural training school, and the Talua Ministry Training Center. The training center educates Ni-Vanuatu for both lay and ordained positions in the church.

Kiribati. The country is composed of three island groups that stretch across the central Pacific Ocean. From west to east, the islands are the former Gilbert Islands, the Phoenix Islands, and the Line Islands.

The first missionaries to arrive in Kiribati were **American Board of Commissioners for Foreign Missions** (ABCFM) Congregationalists from Hawaii, who began work on Abaiang in 1856. These missionaries were followed in 1861 by LMS missionaries from the Cook Islands who arrived in Tuvalu in 1861 and by Samoan LMS pastors and teachers who began work in the southern islands of Arorae and Tamana in 1870. The struggling Protestant work was consolidated with the arrival of W. E. Goward, a LMS missionary who founded a school on Beru Island, supervised the work of the Samoan pastors, and pushed for the transfer of the American mission to the LMS. In 1917 the transfer was completed. The Kiribati Protestant Church emerged from this work, becoming independent in 1968. In that year Polynesian Reformed Protestants on Tuvalu withdrew to establish an independent church (see following). Pastors are educated at Tangintebu Theological College.

Federated States of Micronesia. Located in the northwest Pacific Ocean, the country includes the island states of Kosrae, Pohnpei, Chuuk (Truk), and Yap—all in the Caroline Islands. The area was colonized by **Spain**, and after World War II it became the United Nations Trust Territory of the Pacific Islands, administered by the **United States.** The country was admitted to the United Nations in 1991.

Missionaries from the ABCFM were sent to the islands of Micronesia during the 1850s. Various churches of Congregational heritage emerged from this work, including the Protestant Church of East Truk (1885), the United Church of Christ in Pohnpei (1852), and the United Church of Christ in the Marshall Islands.

Marshall Islands. Located in the northwest Pacific Ocean, the country is composed of two coral islands and 29 coral atolls in two island chains: the Ratak (Sunrise) and the Ralik (Sunset). The islands were ruled first by **Germany** (1885) and then by Japan (1914). Following World War II they became a Trust Territory of the United Nations administered by the United States. The country became self-governing in 1979. In 1982 the Marshall Islands entered into a Compact of Free Association with the U.S. government, which provides for its defense. The compact became effective in 1986. In 1991 the republic was admitted to the United Nations.

The first missionaries in the Marshall Islands were Hawaiian Congregationalists from the ABCFM, who arrived in 1857. Carl Heine, an Australian trader, was converted during the 1890s, began working for the ABCFM in 1902, and was ordained in 1906. Heine played an important role in the church for 40 years. The Congregational church joined other Protestants in the United Church of Christ in the Marshall Islands (Jarin Rarik Drom), a united Protestant church. However, in 1986 many former Congregational churches withdrew to establish the Reformed Congregational Churches in the Marshall Islands.

Cook Islands. The islands were explored by British Captain James Cook between 1773 and 1777. From 1888 to 1901 the islands were a British protectorate; in 1901 they were annexed by **New Zealand.** The Cook Islands became independent in 1965.

John Williams and two Tahitian missionaries from the London Missionary Society arrived in the Cook Islands in 1821. The mission expanded and created a theocracy in the islands that lasted until the beginning of the 20th century. Under the British protectorate, the mission church legislated moral laws and controlled social and political life.

Between 1872 and 1896 the church sent out more than 70 missionaries to Papua New Guinea. Except in the isolated northern Cook Islands, schools begun by the mission were taken over by the government of New Zealand in 1915. Out of this mission grew the Cook Islands Christian Church, the largest denomination in the islands. The church became autonomous in 1963.

French Polynesia. The territory consists of several island groups in the south central Pacific Ocean: the Society Islands, including Tahiti; the Leeward Islands, west of Tahiti; the Tuamotu Archipelago, east of the Society Islands; the Gambier Islands, south of Tuamotu; the Marquesas group, northeast of Tahiti; and the Austral Islands, south of Tahiti. Administered as an overseas territory of **France**, the island groups came under French control during the 19th century.

Missionaries from the London Missionary Society, including **Henry Nott**, **George Pritchard**, and **William Ellis** arrived in Tahiti at the beginning of the 19th century. Supported by **Queen Pomare IV**, the LMS worked in the islands until 1843. During this period American novelist **Herman Melville** made his way through French Polynesia and wrote about island life in Tahiti. In 1863 the LMS work was assumed by the Paris Evangelical Missionary Society. Through a French decree of 1884, the Tahitian church became an established church, with the French government paying the salaries of its ministers and missionaries, approving the location of pastors, and having veto power on decisions made by church councils. In effect, French support enabled the government to have a measure of control over the Tahitian Protestant church. This practice continued until 1927.

The disestablishment of the Tahitian church created an opportunity for the Reformed churches throughout French Polynesia to unite into a single church. The Marquesas had become mostly Catholic, but a small Reformed church was begun by missionaries from Hawaii (1854). The Leeward Islands were entirely Reformed Protestant. These and other Reformed churches came together to create the Evangelical Church of French Polynesia (1927). Beginning with the boys' and girls' schools founded in Papeete by **Charles Viénot**, the Evangelical Church developed a large Protestant school system in Tahiti during the first half of the 20th century. The church also established the Mount Hermon Theological School, for many years operated by French Protestant missionary **Georges Preiss**. Out of this school came **Koringo A Poo, Samuel Raapoto**, and other Tahitian church leaders. The Tahitian church became autonomous in 1963.

Niue. Located in the south central Pacific Ocean, Niue is a self-governing island in association with New Zealand. Captain James Cook landed on Niue in 1774. The London Missionary Society sent missionaries in 1830, but they were not welcome; an LMS Niuean Christian had more success in 1846. During the next two decades the Bible was translated and a church was organized. The church became part of the Niuean social fabric. Today about 75 percent of the population are members of the Church of Niue. *See also* Lawes, William George

Samoa. The Samoan archipelago is located in the central Pacific Ocean. Samoa was a German protectorate during the early part of the 20th century and became a possession of New Zealand in 1914. Western Samoa was also a United Nations Trust Territory. Today the archipelago is politically divided between the independent nation of Western Samoa (1962) and the eastern area of American Samoa, belonging to the United States. Western Samoa is composed of nine islands, with the capital in Apia. American Samoa includes six Samoan islands and Swains Island, a coral atoll to the north. The capital is Pago Pago on Tutuila.

The church in Samoa evolved from the work of John Williams and the London Missionary Society beginning in 1830. During the 1850s the first Samoan pastors were ordained and Samoan teachers and missionaries were sent to other Pacific islands and to New Guinea. The operation of Samoan schools was a large part of mission activity.

During the early years of the 20th century, church life was disrupted by a civil war and by the worldwide influenza epidemic of 1918 that devastated Samoa and Tahiti. In Samoa almost half of the LMS pastors died, resulting in a shortage of experienced leadership. During the 1930s the rise of Samoan nationalism led to increased independence for the church. The Congregational Christian Church, which became autonomous in 1942, is the largest denomination in the Pacific Islands.

Tuvalu. The island nation is composed of nine islands in the west central Pacific Ocean and shares the same missionary history as Kiribati. In 1968 the island's Reformed church became independent. Almost all Tuvaluans belong to the Church of Tuvalu.

PAIK, L. GEORGE (1895–1985). Korean Presbyterian minister, educator, and historian. Born in Jungju, Pyong-Buk Province, Paik was educated in **Korea** and in the **United States** at **Princeton Theological Seminary**, Princeton University, and Yale University, where he studied under historian Kenneth Scott Latourette. Paik was ordained by the Presbytery of Kansas City (1927) and then returned to Korea, where he served as professor of Bible and history at Yonsei University in Seoul until 1957.

From 1957 to 1960 Paik served as president of the university. Paik's work at the university spans the period of the Japanese occupation of Korea. He was instrumental in introducing a broad program of Korean studies at the university, despite threats from the Japanese colonial regime. Paik made a considerable contribution to the university and supported Korean participation in ecumenical and international organizations such as UNESCO.

PAKISTAN. *See* SOUTHERN ASIA

PAPUA NEW GUINEA. *See* PACIFIC OCEAN ISLANDS

PARAGUAY. *See* SOUTHERN CONE OF SOUTH AMERICA

PARIS EVANGELICAL MISSIONARY SOCIETY (PEMS). An interdenominational and international missionary society organized and headquartered in Paris, **France.** Established in 1822 by leading Protestants in Paris, the board of the Société des Missions Evangéliques de Paris included Reformed, Lutherans, and Congregationalists. Although the society is based in France, a significant part of its support has come from the French-speaking areas of **Switzerland.** Two early leaders of the society were general secretaries Eugène Casalis (1856–1882) and Alfred Boegner (1882–1912). The original purpose of PEMS was to train missionaries who would serve other missionary societies, including the **Evangelical Mission Society in Basel** and the **London Missionary Society.** In response to urgent demands in the **mission** field, the society established its own mission work among the Tswana people in **southern Africa** (1829), **Lesotho** (1833), and **Zambia** (1885). The society also assumed responsibility for mission work in **Senegal** (1863), at the request of Krio Protestants; in Gabon (1892), at the request of the American Presbyterian Church; in the Loyalty Islands (1863) and **New Caledonia** (1922), at the request of the London Missionary Society; in **Madagascar** (1892), to aid the mission work of other societies; in **Cameroon** (1917), to assume the work of expelled German missionaries; and in **Togo** (1929). By the mid-1960s the work of the society had produced nine autonomous churches. The society's journal, *Journal des missions Evangéliques,* has been published since 1826.

PARK, HYUNG-NONG (1897–1978). Korean minister and theologian in the Presbyterian Church of Korea (Hap-Dong). Born in Pyukdong, Park studied in **China**, where he graduated from the University of Nanking. From 1923 to 1926, he studied in the **United States** at **Princeton Theological Seminary**, earning Th.B. and Th.M. degrees. At Princeton he was influenced by conservative New Testament professor **J. Gresham Machen**. Park then received a Ph.D. from Southern Baptist Theological Seminary in Louisville, Kentucky. After returning to **Korea** in 1930, Park held teaching positions at Pyongyang Theological Seminary, Manchuria Theological Seminary, Korea Theological Seminary in Pusan, and Presbyterian Theological Seminary in Seoul. From 1951 to 1972 he served as professor and president of the General Assembly Theological Seminary (Hap-Dong). Park was the gatekeeper of conservative theology in the Presbyterian Churches of Korea and was deeply involved in the theological controversies that led to divisions within the church. Park is widely known for his theological writings, which have been collected in 14 volumes.

PARKER, PETER (1804–1888). American Congregationalist medical missionary in **China**. Having studied theology and **medicine** at Yale, Parker was the first Protestant medical missionary in China; he was sent to Canton by the **American Board of Commissioners for Foreign Missions** (1834). He founded the Ophthalmic Hospital and, by establishing a reputation for effective medical treatment, overcame the local prejudice against missionaries. He assisted in the foundation of the Medical Missionary Society (1838), which funded medical **mission** and helped Western mission boards recognize the role of medical work. After the Opium Wars, Parker combined his medical mission work with diplomatic service for the Chinese. He assisted in the negotiation of the first treaty between the **United States** and China (1844) and left the mission to become U.S. minister to China (1845). Parker played an important role in opening China to Western contact in the 19th century.

PASTORAL THEOLOGY. The theological study of the relationship of the **Word of God** to the work of **ministry** and to human life and experience. Pastoral theology has theological, psychological, and pastoral dimensions. First, pastoral theology formulates the principles or theoretical framework utilized in ministry. It also examines the role and duties of the minister and the methods employed in pastoral work. Second, pastoral theology advances the Christian understanding of personhood by examining such issues as human **sexuality**, the family, illness, and **death**. Finally, pastoral theology addresses issues of pastoral care in the context of the **church**, including repentance, reconciliation, and **ethics** and moral conduct. Such spiritual care arises out of the human need to experience wholeness of life and **salvation**. In its various dimensions, pastoral theology is rooted in the life of the Christian **community** gathered around the Word of God manifest in Jesus Christ, proclaimed in **scripture**, and celebrated in the **sacraments**.

PATON, JOHN GIBSON (1824–1907). Scottish Presbyterian missionary in New Hebrides (**Vanuatu**). Paton was born at Kirkmahoe, Dumfries, in **Scotland**. While working as a city missionary (1847–1857), he attended the University of Glasgow and studied **medicine** and theology. In 1858 he was ordained in the Reformed Presbyterian Church of Scotland and volunteered for **mission** work in New Hebrides. Soon after arriving at Port Resolution, Tanna, in 1859, Paton lost his wife and infant son in childbirth. Paton suffered from bouts of fever and by 1862 was driven from the island by the warlike Tannese people. Paton spent the next four years promoting the New Hebrides mission in **Australia** and in Scotland, where, in 1864, he met and married Margaret Whitecross, who helped him gain support for the mission. Paton returned to Vanuatu and worked on the island of Aniwa from 1866 to 1881. He then relocated to Melbourne, Australia, and continued to work on behalf of the New Hebrides mission. Paton spoke out against the exploitation of Pacific Islanders in the Pacific **labor** trade, and against the growing French presence in New Hebrides. He penned an influential autobiography, *John G. Paton, D.D., Missionary to the New Hebrides: An Autobiography* (1889).

PEACE. *See* WAR AND PEACE

PEACE OF WESTPHALIA (1648). The settlement that brought an end to the **Wars of Religion** in Europe. In addition to its territorial clauses that stabilized the political map of Europe, the settlement confirmed the Peace of Augsburg (1555) that granted toleration to Catholic and Lutheran churches, and extended this toleration to Reformed churches. The agreement recognized liberty of conscience in religious matters, permitted private **worship**, and extended the right of emigration to religious minorities. On the issue of religious property, the delegates decided that the territories possessed by each religious body in the year 1624 would revert to that body. These decisions became effective for most of Europe with the exception of lands ruled by the Habsburgs.

PEOPLE MOVEMENTS. The large-scale **conversion** of families or groups of people to Christianity. Such group conversions enable the family and social structure of a tribal group, **caste**, or segment of society to remain intact. People movements have taken place in **Indonesia**, northeast **India**, and elsewhere.

PEREIRA, EDUARDO CARLOS (b. ca. 1860). Brazilian Presbyterian minister and founder of the Independent Presbyterian Church. Pereira was converted in 1881 through the ministry of G. W. Chamberlain. In 1884 he founded the Brazilian Society for Evangelical Tracts, which developed Brazilian church literature. A nationalistic church leader, he wrote "A Plan of National Missions for the Presbyterian Church of Brazil," proposing that the Brazilian Presbyterian Church support its own **mission** work and become independent of church aid from abroad. In 1888 he became pastor of the First Presbyterian Church in São Paulo, which he served for 34 years. He argued with Horace Lane, president of Mackenzie College, São Paulo, over the inclusiveness and theological direction of that school. In 1892 Pereira and several other church leaders founded the Nova Friburgo Seminary in São Paulo, which emphasized Brazilian leadership in theological **education.** The institution later merged with the Instituto Teológico, with Pereira, Cerqueira Leite, and John R. Smith serving as its first professors. Pereira became embroiled in a denominational controversy over the acceptance of Freemasonry in the church. In 1903 Pereira founded the Independent Presbyterian Church (Igreja Presbiteriana Independente do Brasil), taking about one-third of the Brazilian church membership with him. The new denomination was founded on the basis of Brazilian nationalism and anti-Masonic views. An expert on Portuguese grammar, Pereira published two schoolbooks, *Gramática Expositiva Elementar* and *Gramática Expositiva Superior*; founded the first Presbyterian journal, *O Estandarte*; and wrote on the religious situation in Latin America.

PERKINS, WILLIAM (1558–1602). English Puritan theologian and preacher. Perkins was born in Marston Jabbet, Warwickshire, and graduated from Christ's College, Cambridge, in 1581. He was appointed lecturer (preacher) at Great St. Andrew's Church, Cambridge (1584–1602), and elected a Fellow of Christ's College (1584–1595). Many of his students, including **William Ames**, became well-known Puritan leaders, and Perkins gained an international reputation.

Perkins was a nonseparatist leader of Elizabethan **Puritanism.** He was a patristics scholar who wrote significant theological works and commen tᵣ es on **scripture.** He was a polemicist against Roman Catholicism, ᵣ and witchcraft. He addressed issues of pastoral renewal and iety, and his writings, although learned, were used widely by iences. His Latin preaching manual, *The Arte of Prophesy-* ıglish translation, 1606), was a mainstay of New England pastors for generations. His theology was Calvinistic, arranged according to the logic and method of French logician Peter Ramus. Ramism enabled Perkins to maintain an essential unity between theology and **ethics.** His most important works include *A Golden Chaine* (1590), *Manner and Order of Predestination* (1606), *Whole Treatise of Cases of Conscience* (1606), and biblical commentaries on Galatians, Jude, and Hebrews 11. Some consider him to be the most significant Puritan writer.

PERSEVERANCE OF THE SAINTS. The doctrine that those who are justified before **God** will be preserved by God to eternal **salvation.** Emphasizing God's persevering work rather than human faithfulness, the doctrine is the fifth of the "five points" of **Calvinism** developed by the Synod of Dort (1619). Although it is recognized that there may be times when believers fall into **sin,** the doctrine teaches that God's love will safeguard the elect so that no other power or influence can deter the work of God's Spirit in their lives. For this reason, the doctrine is also referred to as one of eternal security. The doctrine cannot be used as an excuse for wanton sin; to do so would indicate that genuine **faith** is not present and that one has not truly experienced **justification** and **sanctification.**

PERU. *See* ANDEAN REPUBLICS AND GREATER COLOMBIA

PHILIP, JOHN (1775–1851). Scottish Congregationalist missionary in **South Africa.** Following 15 years of parish ministry in Aberdeen, Philip went to South Africa under sponsorship of the **London Missionary Society.** He reviewed the work of the society and remained as resident director for 30 years. Philip administered the affairs of more than 30 mission stations and became a knowledgeable expert in the culture and politics of the region. He actively opposed the colonialists' repressive policies, especially toward the Hottentots, and enlisted the support of the British government for legislation guaranteeing full equality of all racial groups (1828 Parliamentary Ordinance). He also worked for judicial reform, freedom of the press, and enlightened policies toward **indigenous peoples.** Philip recruited other **mission** societies (e.g., the **American Board of Commissioners for Foreign Missions** and the **Paris Evangelical Missionary Society**) for work in Africa. Because of his enlightened view of indigenous rights, Philip was able to foresee the 20th-century struggle with the racial legacy of white South African **colonialism.**

PHILIPPINES. *See* SOUTHEAST ASIA

PHILOSOPHY OF RELIGION. The critical, philosophical study of the claims, beliefs, and practices of religion. The discipline examines such

244 • PICHAL, EDOUARD DOMINIQUE ANTOINE

questions as the existence of **God**, the relationship between **faith and reason**, issues related to religious experience, and the nature of religious language. The so-called proofs of the existence of God, championed during the medieval period, were largely discredited in the post-Enlightenment era. Attention was directed to the social and anthropological dimensions of religious experience. During the 20th century, the existentialism of Søren Kierkegaard was influential in the early work of **Karl Barth** and in the writings of French socialist **Jacques Ellul**. By the late 20th century a renewed interest in the rationality of theistic belief was in evidence. Reformed philosophers such as Alvin Plantinga and Nicholas Wolterstorff addressed the issue of rational belief, both with and without "proofs." These philosophers have also given serious attention to the problem of evil. Plantinga argues that the need for "proofs" rests on the modern acceptance of a mistaken Cartesianism. His Reformed epistemology, which claims legitimacy for Christian belief, draws upon the work of **John Calvin**. The question of what philosophical underpinnings are appropriate for Reformed theology continues to be discussed.

PICHAL, EDOUARD DOMINIQUE ANTOINE (1898–1983). Belgian Reformed minister and president of the Protestant Church of **Belgium**. After World War I, Pichal traveled to **Switzerland**, where he studied theology at Lausanne, Geneva, and Strasbourg. He worked as a pastor at Fives-Lille under the evangelist Henri Nick. He served in Verviers, Bordeaux, and Quaregnon (1925–1928) before becoming minister at Gand from 1928 to 1949. He also worked as a teacher and served as inspector of Protestant religious **education** in Royaume from 1949 to 1954. As president of the Belgian Synod, Pichal helped to obtain government recognition for 21 new parishes and constructed new church sanctuaries at Alost, Chimay, Courtrai, Genk, Renaix, Tournai, Wavre, and Zaventhem. He supported the **ecumenical movement** and guided formation of the Union of Evangelical Protestant Churches of Belgium. Pichal was interested in African **missions** and made three trips to the **Congo**; he also maintained an interest in the religious life of **Rwanda**. Under his guidance the Protestant church spread its influence throughout **Belgium**.

PIDGEON, GEORGE CAMPBELL (1872–1971). Canadian Presbyterian and United Church minister. Born in Grand-Cascapédia, Quebec, Pidgeon was ordained in 1872 and received a D.D. degree from Presbyterian College, Montreal. He served churches in Montreal, Toronto, and Streetsville, Ontario. Following a period of teaching practical theology at Westminster Hall, Vancouver (1909–1915), Pidgeon returned to the pastorate, where he served Bloor Street United Church, Toronto (1915–1948). In retirement he wrote a column on religion for the Toronto *Telegram* (1949–1960). Pidgeon was the first **moderator** of the United Church of Canada. He was a supporter of ecumenical activities and organizations, and the temperance and home mission movements. For many years he was one of the chief spokespersons for the United Church of Canada.

PITTSBURGH THEOLOGICAL SEMINARY. One of 10 theological institutions of the Presbyterian Church (U.S.A.). The school's origins go back to Service Seminary, an institution founded in 1794 by John Anderson (1748–1830) near Aliquippa, Pennsylvania. Other predecessor institutions include Western Seminary of Allegheny (1827) and Pittsburgh (1912) of the Presbyterian Church U.S.A. Two predecessor institutions affiliated with the United Presbyterian Church of North America were Xenia Seminary of Xenia, Ohio (1855), and St. Louis (1920), and Pittsburgh Seminary (1825). In 1930 these two schools merged to form Pittsburgh-Xenia Theological Seminary, located in Pittsburgh. The merger of the Presbyterian Church U.S.A. and the United Presbyterian Church in North America in 1958 led to the merger of Western Theological Seminary and Pittsburgh-Xenia Theological Seminary. In 1960 the schools were united in one campus, becoming Pittsburgh Theological Seminary. The school is known for its archaeological research, led by Melvin G. Kyle, James L. Kelso (Xenia), and Paul W. Lapp (Pittsburgh). Distinguished professors include Markus Barth, **Ford Lewis Battles**, David G. Buttrick, Arthur C. Cochrane, David Noel Freedman, Donald G. Miller, and Robert S. Paul.

POISSY, COLLOQUY OF (1561). Conference in Poissy, **France**, between French Roman Catholics and Reformed Protestants. Catherine de Médicis convened the conference for the purpose of reaching a religious settlement that would bring peace and unity to France. Held in the wake of the Council of Trent (1545–1563), which had further separated Catholics and Protestants, the colloquy was intended to carry out a program of church reform that would bring the parties together. The Reformed churches were represented by **Théodore Beza** and **Peter Martyr Vermigli**. Failure of the parties to reach an agreement led to civil war, the **Saint Bartholomew's Day Massacres**, and further conflict and violence, continuing into the 17th century.

POLAND. *See* CENTRAL AND EASTERN EUROPE

POLITICAL AND SOCIAL PHILOSOPHY. The study of the corporate structures of human life: the state and society in all their relationships. Influenced by **John Calvin**, the Reformed **tradition** orders all human enterprises, including political and social structures, under the **sovereignty of God**, thus restricting their claims to absolute validity. The impact of **Calvinism** on political and social philosophy has been twofold. First, Calvinism emphasizes the fallen condition of humanity. Building upon this doctrine, Calvinist political philosophy argues that no one person should be given absolute power. Political checks and balances act as restraining forces, limiting the human tendency toward evil. Second, Calvinism emphasizes human capacity and responsibility to shape national life according to God's rule, thus contributing to the growing modern emphasis on human agency, individual rights and freedoms, and the preference for democratic orders as most just.

POLITY, CHURCH. *See* CHURCH GOVERNMENT

POLYNESIA (FRENCH). *See* PACIFIC OCEAN ISLANDS

POMARE IV, QUEEN (1813–1877). Daughter of King Pomare II and Queen of **Tahiti.** In 1927, following the death of the king's half brother, Pomare III, she was recognized as queen of Tahiti and the adjacent islands and reigned for the next 50 years. She supported the work of the English Protestant missionaries from the **London Missionary Society** (LMS). In 1842 **France** established a protectorate over the islands, and the queen went into internal exile on Moorea and then Raiatea. She was forced to accept French rule when the British government failed to come to her aid. The LMS temporarily withdrew from the islands. When William Howe of the London Missionary Society encouraged permanent withdrawal of the LMS in favor of French Protestants, the queen welcomed the arrival of Thomas Arbousset in 1863. Arbousset was the first of several French Protestant missionaries who were sent from the **Paris Evangelical Missionary Society.** These missionaries would continue to play an important role in shaping the Tahitian church and society.

PORTUGAL. *See* SOUTHERN EUROPE

PRATT, HENRY BARRINGTON (1832–1913). American Presbyterian missionary in **Colombia.** Educated at Oglethorpe University and **Princeton Theological Seminary** (1855), Pratt was the first Protestant missionary in Colombia (1856). He founded Presbyterian churches in Bogotá (1861), Bucaramanga, El Socorro, and elsewhere. The work was difficult, and the newly established churches remained small. Pratt mastered the Spanish language and was an influential evangelist, lecturer, and writer. His most lasting contribution was his translation of the Bible into Spanish (the Modern Version), which is noted for its elegance. Following his service in Colombia, Pratt worked among the Mexicans in Texas, founding the Bible Training School for Christian Workers in Laredo (1896). His graduates went into **Mexico** to do evangelistic work. He has been criticized for underpaying Mexican Presbyterian pastors and fostering a dependence on Anglo ministers. In his later years Pratt devoted his time to writing Bible commentaries in Spanish.

PRAYER. The act of communicating with the personal, transcendent **God** revealed in the Bible. Christian prayer is made in the power of the **Holy Spirit** who prompts, inspires, and assures those who pray. **John Calvin** called prayer "the chief exercise of **faith**" (*Inst.* 3.20). Christian prayer is both vocal and meditative. Vocal prayer includes prayers of petition, confession, thanksgiving, and adoration. **John Knox** wrote that prayer is "an earnest and familiar talking with God, to whom we declare our miseries, whose support and help we implore and desire in our adversities, and whom we laud and praise for our benefits received" (*Declaration of the True Nature and Object of Prayer* [1554]). Of the types of vocal prayer mentioned above, the Reformed **tradition** emphasizes prayers of petition as most central in the Christian life. Meditative prayer may include aspects of vocal prayer but stresses silence and listening. The object of meditative prayer is not contemplation of God's divine nature but reflection on God's redemptive love for humanity centered in Jesus Christ. The object of both types of prayer is discernment of God's will. The Westminster Shorter Catechism states that "prayer is an offering up of our desires unto God, for things agreeable to his will, in the name of Christ, with confession of our sins, and thankful acknowledgment of his mercies" (question 98). According to Calvin, prayer brings "extraordinary peace and repose to our consciences" grounded in the trust that "none of our ills is hid from him who, we are convinced, has both the will and the power to take the best care of us" (*Inst.* 3.20.2).

PREACHING. Although homiletics is the study of the art and theology of preaching, preaching itself is the proclaimed **Word of God**; a primary means of conveying the saving benefits of the Christian gospel. The Reformed **tradition** emphasizes the primacy of the Word of God in preaching. The Second Helvetic Confession asserts that "the preaching of the Word of God *is* the Word of God" (chap. 1); it is the Word itself, and not the minister, that is to be regarded. The **Holy Spirit** works in conjunction with the Word to make the preached Word effectual for **salvation**. When the response to preaching is **faith** (Rom. 10:17), the Spirit has testified to the Word. Thus the living Word, Jesus Christ, becomes present through the proclamation of the written Word in preaching.

PREDESTINATION. The doctrine that **God** chooses human beings to receive the gift of **salvation**. **John Calvin** defined predestination as "God's eternal decree, by which he compacted with himself what he willed to become of each man" (*Inst.* 3.21.5). It is sometimes used synonymously with **election.** Reformed theology follows the biblical pattern in which God chooses Israel to be a covenant people and also chooses the **church** (the "new Israel") for salvation in Jesus Christ. Predestinarian teachings are rooted in the theology of Paul (Rom. 8:29f.) and developed in the works of Augustine (cf. "On the Predestination of the Saints") and Calvin ("Concerning the Eternal Predestination of God"). These teachings ascribe salvation solely to God's **grace** extended to undeserving sinners. Since the power of **sin** is so strong, the human will is in bondage to it and thus is not "free" to choose God's will or salvation. For salvation to occur, God must initiate the process and through the **Holy Spirit** convey the gift of **faith**, which entails a regeneration of the whole person, including the will. Because human beings are captive to sin, they cannot will themselves to faith; only God can predestine or elect them to salvation.

Calvin considered predestination and election in the context of salvation (*Inst.*, bk. 3). Reformed theologians of the 17th century developed predestination as part of the "order of God's decrees" and divided it into two parts: election to salvation and reprobation to damnation. Predestination was considered an expression of God's eternal decrees whereby God ordains "whatsoever comes to pass" (**Westminster Confession**, chap. 3). These developments led to debates over the ordering of the decrees and whether the decrees for salvation and damnation occurred logically in the mind of God before the decree of the fall of humanity (supralapsarianism) or after (infralapsarianism). To Calvin, the doctrine was intended to be of comfort and assurance, not cause for anxiety or a point of theological speculation (*Inst.* 3.22.2-13).

PREISS, GEORGES (1899–1968). French Reformed minister and missionary in **Tahiti.** Born in Hunawihr (Haut-Rhin), **France**, Preiss studied at Mulhouse and at the theology department of the Université de Montpellier. Ordained in 1937, Preiss was sent to Tahiti by the **Paris**

Evangelical Missionary Society. He arrived in the Leeward Islands in 1938, where he worked as a pastor until 1945. From 1945 to 1956 he served as principal of the Mount Hermon Theological School in Papeete. Preiss is considered the founder of the Tahitian churches because of his work to prepare indigenous pastoral leadership for the Protestant churches of Tahiti. Returning to France in 1956, Preiss died in Strasbourg.

PRENTISS, ELIZABETH PAYSON (1818–1878). American Presbyterian hymn writer and poet. Elizabeth Payson was born into an old New England family in Portland, Maine. At the age of 16 she began publishing stories and verses in the *Youth's Companion* of Boston. She taught at Persico's Young Ladies Seminary in Richmond, Virginia (1840–1844). In 1845 Payson married George L. Prentiss, a Congregationalist pastor in New Bedford, Massachusetts, and in 1851 went to New York City. After two of her children died, Elizabeth Prentiss began a literary career. Over the next 26 years she produced many volumes of children's stories. These stories, presenting Christian themes, reflect a strong devotion and piety. The most popular story, *Stepping Heavenward* (1869), sold more than 200,000 copies and was widely translated. Her hymn "More Love to Thee, O Christ" (ca. 1856; pub. 1869) was written during a time of great personal sorrow. Prentiss's *Life and Letters* was published posthumously in 1882.

PRESBYTERIAN COLLEGE AND THEOLOGICAL SEMINARY. An institution of the Presbyterian Church of **Korea** (Tong-hap). The school is one of two institutions that trace their roots to Pyongyang Theological Seminary. Pyongyang Seminary was organized by American missionary Samuel Moffet in 1901 and in 1905 became affiliated with the Presbyterian Church. In 1959 a doctrinal controversy split the school and the theologically moderate Presbyterian College and Theological Seminary became an institution of the Presbyterian Church of Korea (Tong-hap). The institution, with 37 faculty members and 2,500 students, has graduate schools of ministry, **education**, and world **mission**. *See also* Chongshin University

PRESBYTERIAN SUPPORT SERVICES. The largest independent social service organization in **New Zealand.** Working in partnership with local churches, Presbyterian Support Services serves about 12,000 New Zealanders through its **health** and welfare programs. The organization provides residential care for older persons; home-based care, including the preparation and delivery of meals; and many family and community services, including counseling, foster home facilities, and programs for children and young adults.

Support employs over 2,500 people and has a volunteer staff of 1,500. Governed by a board and national council, the organization is composed of seven independent regions, each administered by a chief executive.

PRESBYTERIANISM. *See* CHURCH GOVERNMENT; PRESBYTERY

PRESBYTERY. The basic governing body of Presbyterianism; in some Reformed churches this body is called a colloquy or classis. The presbytery is composed of ordained ministers and of **elders** elected by congregations. The parity of **laity** and clergy is a fundamental element of presbyterian polity, which is based on **scripture** (see Rom. 12:8; 1 Cor. 12:28; 1 Tim. 5:17) and summarized by **John Calvin** (*Inst.* 4.3.4–9). Presbyteries have oversight of local church sessions and are linked with other presbyteries in a region to form a synod. Synods, together, constitute the **general assembly** of the **church.** Presbyteries are governed by a book of church order that prescribes procedures and establishes processes to be followed so that the work of Christian **ministry** might be done "decently and in order" (1 Cor. 14:40).

Presbyterianism is a form of representative **church government**, since churches elect presbytery delegates through local sessions. Ordained ministers are members of a particular presbytery when they work within its bounds and are accepted into presbytery membership. Presbyteries ordain persons to the gospel ministry, validate areas of service, determine their own membership, provide resources, and carry out Christian **mission**; they are responsible for the **discipline**, church government, and **worship** of local congregations, through the local church sessions. Presbyteries maintain relationships with higher governing bodies of the church and with ecumenical partners.

PRIESTHOOD OF ALL BELIEVERS. A teaching of Martin Luther (1483–1546) in which the people of **God**, as the **church**, are seen as a "royal priesthood" (1 Pet. 2:9–10; Rev. 1:6; 5:10). Because the church is a priesthood, it does not need an ecclesiastical priest to serve as an intermediary between itself and God. People are able to approach God directly through the mediator Jesus Christ (Heb. 3:1; 4:14). They are able to enter God's presence to pray, **worship**, and offer themselves in Christian service (cf. **John Calvin**, *Inst.* 3.15.6.). The implication of the teaching is that ministerial service is not limited to those who have a specific ecclesiastical status but is the responsibility of all believers.

PRINCETON THEOLOGICAL SEMINARY. The oldest continuing Presbyterian seminary in the **United States** and one of 10 educational institutions serving the Presbyterian Church (U.S.A.). Organized in 1812, the seminary's first professors were **Archibald Alexander**, Samuel Miller, and **Charles Hodge**. During the 19th century the seminary was an Old School institution, which emphasized its Scottish theological roots, including Scottish Common-Sense philosophy and the **Princeton theology**. The seminary was reorganized in 1929 to allow for greater theological diversity within the faculty. The seminary became a focal point of the **fundamentalist-modernist controversy** in the Presbyterian Church during the 1930s. Under the presidency of **John A. Mackay** (1936–1959), Princeton became a center of **neoorthodoxy** and gained an international reputation. Several distinguished visiting professors taught at the seminary during this period, including **Emil Brunner, Josef Hromádka**, and Otto Piper. In 1944 Mackay founded *Theology Today,* which remains a leading theological journal. Under the presidency of James I. McCord (1959–1983), the endowment of the seminary increased substantially, campus construction was carried out, and ecumenical ties were broadened. The seminary's influence on both the Presbyterian Church and national life has been considerable. Faculty have included **Archibald Alexander Hodge, Charles Hodge, Lefferts A. Loetscher, J. Gresham Machen, B. B. Warfield**, and **Samuel M. Zwemer**.

PRINCETON THEOLOGY. A Presbyterian and Reformed theological **tradition** developed at **Princeton Theological Seminary** in Princeton, New Jersey. Articulated by its first professor, **Archibald Alexander**, and subsequently expounded by successive Princeton theologians including **Charles Hodge, A. A. Hodge, B. B. Warfield**, and **J. Gresham Machen**, the Princeton theology was a contemporary expression of a scholastic form of **Calvinism**. The Princeton theology looked to 17th-century Reformed theology as a guide, adopting **Francis Turretin's** *Institutes* (1679–85) as its theological textbook until 1873, when Charles Hodge completed his own *Systematic Theology,* also rooted in Turretin. The Princeton theology taught Reformed confessionalism, strongly adhering to the **Westminster Confession.** It also defended the inerrancy of **scripture** in clashes with modern science and **biblical criticism.** The theological movement continued at the seminary from its founding in 1812 until its reorganization in 1929. Thereafter, it declined at Princeton Seminary but continued to flourish among American fundamentalists who, during the **fundamentalist-modernist controversy** of the 1920s and 1930s, sought an intellectual defense of the Bible and its doctrines. The theology continues to have influence among fundamentalists and conservative **evangelicals.**

PRITCHARD, GEORGE (1796–1883). English missionary and British consul in **Tahiti** and **Samoa.** In 1824 Pritchard was sent to Tahiti by the **London Missionary Society.** He won the confidence of **Queen Pomare IV** and eventually became an influential adviser. In this capacity, Pritchard became embroiled in a dispute with the French government when he arranged the expulsion of French Catholic missionaries who arrived in 1836. Pritchard's attempt to keep the islands under British Protestantism failed when the French government established a protectorate in Tahiti. Pritchard himself was expelled from the islands in 1844. Appointed British consul in Samoa, Pritchard came into conflict with the French and European communities there and was forced to resign in 1856. The following year he returned to England, where he continued to serve the **London Missionary Society.**

PROCHET, MATTEO (1836–1907). Waldensian minister and president of the Waldensian Board of Evangelism (1871–1905). Born in Luserna San Giovanni, Prochet was educated at the Waldensian Theological Seminary and Assembly College in Belfast, **Ireland.** He was ordained in 1862 and sent as a missionary to Tuscany. In 1867 he went to serve the **Waldensian church** in Genoa. In 1871 he was appointed president of the Board of Evangelism of the Waldensian Church. Prochet guided the expansion of the church in **Italy** during the last quarter of the 19th century and traveled extensively in Europe and the Americas.

PROTESTANT ETHIC. The view, first articulated by German economist, historian, and philosopher Max Weber (1864–1920), that there is a close connection between **Calvinism** and early modern **capitalism.** The term "Protestant work ethic" is an extension of Weber's view. It describes the attempt by individuals to establish their self-worth through hard work, self-denial, and the accumulation of wealth. In his book *The Protestant Ethic and the Spirit of Capitalism* (1904–1905; English translation, 1930) Weber noted the great economic success achieved by monastic orders that were dedicated to the spiritual life, especially "ascetic" Protestant sects. To explain this paradox, Weber held that Puritan religion, drawing upon its Calvinistic underpinnings, stressed involvement in the world through secular callings rather than separation and through frugality rather than consumption. It was the unintended consequence of living active, frugal lives that led to the accumulation of wealth as savings and capital for investment. Weber argued that this Calvinistic outlook spurred economic productivity and was a major factor in the development of modern capitalism. Weber's theory has been debated for many years. Although some scholars have questioned his historiography, others have stressed the economic and social complexity that contributed to the growth of modern capitalism.

PROTESTANT PRINCIPLE. The Protestant conviction that human **sin** is expressed in the **worship** of that which is relative—rendering it a rival god—rather than the true **God.** This principle originates in the prohibition of the first commandment (Exod. 20:3). The term is associated with Paul Tillich, who wrote that the Protestant principle "contains the divine and human protest against any absolute claim made for a relative reality. . . . It is the prophetic judgment against religious pride, ecclesiastical arrogance, and secular self-sufficiency and their destructive consequences" (*The Protestant Era* [1948], 163). Idols can be made of philosophies, social movements, political parties, nations, or churches. The Reformed tradition's polemic against idolatry is expressed in a contemporary statement of **faith** in which the **Holy Spirit** is said to give believers courage "to unmask idolatries in Church and culture" ("A Brief Statement of Faith," Presbyterian Church [USA], 1:66, 69).

PROVIDENCE OF GOD. The preservation of **creation** and the guidance of all things in accord with God's ultimate purposes. In Reformed theology, the doctrine of providence is related to but more general than the doctrine of **predestination.** Providence deals with the whole created order, whereas predestination concerns individuals. God's providence is the continuing involvement with creation in preserving it from chaos, in working with and through human means, and in directing the universe toward divine ends. Jesus Christ is central to the providence of **God,** since it is through Christ that God carries out the divine purpose. Belief in providence does not relieve humans of responsibility, from "due prudence," nor does it excuse human wickedness, according to **John Calvin.** It is, however, beneficial to personal **faith,** as solace to believers who know that the world is not subject to chance or fate and that "their plans, wills, efforts, and abilities are under God's hand" (*Inst.* 1.17.6).

PSYCHOLOGY AND THEOLOGY. The relationship between the nature, functions, and phenomena of the human mind and the meaning, truth, and practice of Christian **faith.** During the 17th and 18th centuries psychology referred to the study of the soul. Psychology was closely tied to religion and religious experience through the writings of the **Puritans,** Pietists, and revivalists. **Jonathan Edwards** wrote two classic works of Christian psychology, *Religious Affections* (1746) and *Freedom of the Will* (1754), in which he probed the human mind and emotions to answer theological questions. A more focused study of the human mind was *Psychology* (1840), a scientific study by Frederick Rauch, a German Reformed theologian.

By the late 19th century the discipline of psychology developed a separate area of investigation known as the psychology of religion, which studied the influence of religion on people's mental and emotional life, and the phenomenon of religious **conversion.** These studies led to William James's *Varieties of Religious Experience* (1902). While Norman Vincent Peale was popularizing *The Power of Positive Thinking* (1952), 20th-century clinical and pastoral theologians such as Paul Tournier (1898–1986) and Seward Hiltner (1909–1984) were trying to integrate psychological and theological insights into Christian **ministry.**

PURITANISM/PURITANS. The late 16th- and 17th-century movement for reform of the Church of England. Influenced by the Swiss Reformation, English Puritanism was primarily Calvinistic in its theology and presbyterian or congregational in its **church government.** Following England's separation from Rome in 1534, Protestant influence grew under the reign of Edward VI (1547–1553). However, under Queen Mary (1553–1558) England returned to Catholicism, and Protestants came under severe persecution. English exiles fled to Geneva and were inspired by **John Calvin's** reform effort there. The English Protestant experience of persecution and exile during Mary's reign led to the publication of two remarkable books, the *Geneva Bible* (1560) and John Foxe's *Acts and Monuments* (1570), popularly known as *Foxe's Book of Martyrs.*

The Puritan movement began during the reign of Queen Elizabeth I (1558–1603) when these exiles and other Protestants, who had looked to Elizabeth to carry out church reforms, were disappointed in her settlement. There was both theological and ecclesiastical diversity within the Puritan movement. Some Puritans hoped to impose a presbyterian form of government on the Church of England; others advocated separation. Although it was resisted by the established church, the Puritan movement was advanced by its colleges at Oxford and Cambridge, by the **preaching** of its ministers, and through its pamphlet literature. However, the hope of church reform gradually faded when James I (1603) came to the throne and rejected Puritan complaints at the **Hampton Court Conference** (1604) and when Charles I (1625–1649) and Archbishop William Laud increased the opposition. The protracted conflicts between university-educated ministers and bishops and monarchs over the pace and direction of church reform helped trigger the English Civil War of the 1640s. Following the restoration of the English monarchy in 1660, those Protestants who were **Nonconformist** formed Baptist, Congregationalist, and Presbyterian churches. Finally, an Act of Toleration (1689) permitted the existence of these groups but also firmly positioned the established church. Although the Puritans failed to extend their idea of the **church** and the Christian life to the English nation, they hoped to succeed in an American experiment: the founding of American colonies in which the goal of Puritanism might be achieved. But here too, in New England, the idea of creating a holy commonwealth under congregational church government would not be realized. However, these great Puritan experiments did produce a way of life that strongly influenced both English and American theology, culture, and institutions. Puritan theologians, including **William Perkins, William Ames, John Owen, Samuel Willard**, and **Jonathan Edwards**, articulated aspects of the Puritan vision for ministers who imbibed the theology and taught it to their congregations. This Puritan way of life emphasized simplicity in **worship** and church life, a plain style of preaching, and **conversion** and the active presence of the **Holy Spirit** in the Christian life. The Puritans believed that the Christian life was not one of abstinence, asceticism, and withdrawal from the world, but one of holy activism, in which the sphere of **sanctification** extended to all areas of life, including **vocation, marriage**, commerce, and civic affairs.

- R -

RAAPOTO, SAMUEL (1921–1976). Tahitian minister and first president of the Evangelical Church of French **Polynesia.** Born in the district of Tevaitoa (Raiatea) in the Leeward Islands, Raapoto studied at Hermon Theological School from 1948 to 1951. In 1953 he became pastor of the Protestant community in Makatea, in the Tuamotus. He served as president of the Evangelical churches from 1963 to 1973. During his tenure the Protestant churches provided new activities and services for youth, including the development of a center for young girls. Raapoto also developed relations between the Tahitian church and other churches of the Pacific region. He supported ecumenical activities and Tahitian membership in the **World Council of Churches.**

RABARY, "MASINA" (1864–1947). Protestant minister and educator in **Madagascar.** After studying **medicine** in 1880, Rabary became a teacher. He taught at the Girl's Central School, Ambohipotsy College, Biblical

School, and Paul Minault College. He was ordained in 1900 and served Avaratr'andohalo Church for 47 years. Rabary worked as a chaplain at Antanimora Prison. During World War II he conducted pastoral work with soldiers and served as Madagascar's minister of finance. In addition to his book, *Malagasy Martyrs* (1910), Rabary wrote stories, poems, and theatrical pieces.

RACE AND RACISM. *See* ETHNICITY AND RACE

RANKIN, MELINDA (1811–1888). American Presbyterian missionary in Northern **Mexico**. In 1852 Rankin organized a school for Mexican girls in Brownsville, Texas, which later became the Rio Grande Female Institute. Rankin moved to Matamoros, Mexico, where she started a second school and organized Bible distribution. When the American Bible Society began its work in Mexico, Rankin was their first agent in Monterey (1865). In that role she traveled widely, establishing 14 congregations, six of which had schools attached; all were eventually incorporated into the Presbyterian Church. She arranged funding for evangelistic work and for the building of churches. Her **mission** was ultimately taken over by the **American Board of Commissioners for Foreign Missions**, which later ordained the first indigenous Mexican pastors for the Presbyterian Church, among them **Arcadio Morales.**

RASALAMA, RAFARAVAVY (1812–1837). The first Protestant martyr in **Madagascar**. Taught by missionaries from the **London Missionary Society**, Rasalama was baptized in May 1831. In 1835 Queen Ranavalona, who ruled Madagascar from 1835 to 1841, gave a speech forbidding Christianity. She ordered the closure of churches, the expulsion of missionaries, and the killing of any who were caught practicing Christianity. In 1837 Rasalama was suspected by the authorities, imprisoned, and killed. Her strength and commitment became an inspiration to many Malagasy Christians.

RAVELOJAONA (1879–1960). Protestant minister and educator in **Madagascar**. Ravelojaona taught at several schools, including Ambatobevenja School (1898–1904) and Paul Minault School (1914–1915). He was ordained in 1908 and served the Ambohitantely Church for many years. He spent two years of national service in Paris as a Malagasy military chaplain. In 1939 Ravelojaona was elected Malagasy representative to the Council of Overseas French Colonies. He was also active in the Malagasy Democratic Party and in 1915 was briefly imprisoned for writing articles critical of the government.

READ, JAMES (1777–1852). Congregationalist missionary in **South Africa**. Sponsored by the **London Mission Society** missionary (LMS), Read went first to Cape Town (1800). He helped set up the **mission** station at Bethelsdorp, where his ministry with the Khoi (Hottentot) people evoked much contempt from the Afrikaners. He married a Khoi woman, Sarah. One son, James Read Jr., became a noted **evangelical** pastor; another, Joseph Read, became a distinguished officer of the Cape Corps. The interracial marriage infuriated white farmers, as did Read's continuing activity to find redress for the cruel treatment of black Africans. When **John Philip** became the LMS superintendent in South Africa, he became aware of the agitation against Read and temporarily suspended him. Later, Philip changed his mind and made Read his adviser. Read became pastor at Kat River (1829), where he endured much hardship because of racial tension.

REASON AND FAITH. See FAITH AND REASON

REES, WILLIAM (1802–1883). Welsh Congregationalist minister and social reformer. Rees was born in Llansannan, Denbighshire, and spent his youth as a farm laborer and shepherd, acquiring a great knowledge of the Welsh language and culture. He became a Congregational minister and served churches at Mostyn (1831–1837), Denbigh (1837–1843), Tabernacle, Liverpool (1843–1853), and Salem, Liverpool, until 1875. Rees was an eloquent preacher and wrote an influential Welsh-language catechism, *Y Cyfarwyddwr* (1833). He published a treatise on the **authority** of **scripture**, and he was editor of the newspaper *Yr Amserau* (*The Times*) from 1843 to 1852. Through this paper, using the pen name Gwilym Hiraethog, Rees introduced liberal social and political ideas to Welsh readers. He played an important role in linking **evangelical** churches in **Wales** with **liberalism** while also maintaining a strong Calvinistic theological base.

REFORMED ALLIANCE. A voluntary organization, assembled biennially, which represents the interests of the Reformed churches in **Germany**. Established in 1884, the Reformed Alliance publishes literature and supports German Reformed educational institutions. During World War II it supported the Confessing Church. The Alliance is a member of the **World Alliance of Reformed Churches.**

REFORMED ECUMENICAL COUNCIL. A Reformed ecumenical organization of Dutch heritage, first proposed by Dutch theologian H. H. Kuyper. The idea of an international Reformed council was first approved in the Reformed Church in South Africa in 1924. The first meeting of delegates from the Reformed Churches in the **Netherlands**, **South Africa**, and the Christian Reformed Church in North America was convened in Grand Rapids, Michigan, in 1949. Membership in the organization, then called the Reformed Ecumenical Synod, was based upon adherence to the Reformed **confessions**, including the Second Helvetic Confession, the Belgic Confession, the **Westminster Confession**, the Gallican Confession, the **Heidelberg Catechism**, the Canons of Dort, and the **Thirty-Nine Articles**. Subsequent meetings have been held every three to five years. Issues studied include race relations and social problems. The 1988 meeting, held in Harare, was attended by 33 churches from 20 countries. The Reformed Ecumenical Council publishes a newsletter, *The News Exchanger*, a mission bulletin, and a quarterly journal, *Theological Forum*.

REFORMED ORTHODOXY. A systematic presentation of Reformed theology that modified the essential theological insights of first- and second-generation Reformed theologians in an attempt to present a detailed and unified dogmatic theology. Reformed orthodoxy is a product of the post-Reformation period, when theological controversies strained relations between Protestants and Catholics, and when the rise of enlightenment science called for greater precision in theological argumentation. It is identified by its attention to the structure of theology and its concern for a cohesive method and arrangement of doctrine. Sometimes called Reformed scholasticism, the theology is also marked by a heavy reliance on Aristotelianism in its sustained argumentation. Reformed theologians such as **Théodore Beza**, **Ursinus**, Olevianus, Girolamo Zanchi, and later **Francis Turretin** and J. H. Heidegger were important contributors to Reformed orthodoxy. Scholars continue to debate the degree to which Reformed orthodoxy represents continuity with the theology of **John Calvin** and the other first-generation reformers, and the degree to which it represents a departure. Nineteenth- and twentieth-century Reformed theologians such as **Heinrich Heppe**, **Charles Hodge**, and Louis Berkhof have preserved some of the features of Reformed orthodoxy.

REFORMED THEOLOGICAL ACADEMY OF DEBRECEN. The principal seminary of the Reformed Church in **Hungary**. Founded in 1538, the academy has long been the center of Hungarian Reformed academic life. The school educates ministers, provides academic leadership for the Hungarian Reformed churches, and with its library of over

600,000 volumes, serves as an educational resource for those engaged in parish ministry. The academy has 12 professors and enrolls more than 240 students.

REIS, ÁLVARO (d. 1925). Brazilian Presbyterian minister and church leader. Reis was educated for the **ministry** through an apprenticeship, which he completed in 1888. In 1897 he was called to First Presbyterian Church in Rio de Janeiro. When Reis arrived, the congregation consisted of a central church with 400 members, a smaller church in the suburb of Riachuelo, and an unorganized congregation in Niteroi. Through Reis's charismatic personality, **preaching**, and writing, the Rio de Janeiro church grew to be the largest Protestant church in Latin America, with five congregations and more than 1,800 members in 1914. Fourteen members of Reis's congregation entered pastoral ministry. Reis also founded the church newspaper *O Puritano*, the voice of the Presbyterian Church of Brazil (Igreja Presbiteriana do Brasil). For many years he carried on a debate with Roman Catholic polemicist Júlio Maria. Reis supported the American missionary presence in **Brazil** but also worked to create an indigenous Brazilian Presbyterian Church.

RELIGIOUS BROADCASTING. The growth of religious programming and broadcast ministries for radio and television has been an important feature of 20th-century Protestantism. In many countries the commercial and private structure of the broadcast media has enabled the proliferation of religious programming. Some influential North American radio programs include *The Back to God Hour* (1939–), produced by the Christian Reformed Church, and *Radio Bible Class* (1938–), an independent ministry of M. R. and Richard DeHaan, that comes out of the Christian Reformed tradition. Noted programs by Presbyterian ministers are *The Bible Study Hour* (1949–), by Donald Grey Barnhouse and his successor, James Montgomery Boice of Philadelphia; and *Truths That Transform*, by D. James Kennedy of Fort Lauderdale, Florida. Reformed Church in America minister Robert Schuller, of Garden Grove, California, developed an extensive following through his *Hour of Power* (1970–) radio program. Kennedy and Schuller also broadcast television programs. The North American mainline churches sponsor *The Protestant Hour Radio Program* and have recently launched the Faith and Values Channel (1988–), which broadcasts both Protestant and interfaith television programming.

Outside North America radio and television broadcasting is an important form of **evangelism** and Christian **education.** In **Scotland** the

Bible study radio programs (1962–1970) of **William Barclay** were very popular. A large network of Christian stations, mostly theologically conservative, broadcast all over the world. Stations such as HCJB, the *Voice of the Andes* in **Ecuador**, and HLKX in South **Korea** have drawn large audiences. In many countries, Reformed churches have taken advantage of access to public broadcasting. An early pioneer was **Antonie C. Sonneveldt** in **Argentina**. In **Indonesia** YAKOMA, an organization established by the Indonesian National Council of Churches, produces religious programs for the national television station. International networks such as the World Association for Christian Communication foster cooperation, study, and research on religious broadcasting. Media ministry is now taught in many church-related institutions.

REMBRANDT HARMENSZOON VAN RIJN (1606–1669). Dutch painter. Rembrandt was educated at Leiden but left to study painting with Jacob van Swanenburch of Leiden, Pieter Lastman of Amsterdam, and Jan Lievens, also of Leiden. In 1631 he moved to Amsterdam and married Saskia van Uylenburgh (1634). Though he was a popular and prosperous artist during the 1630s, Rembrandt's promising career faded during the 1640s and by 1656 he was bankrupt. During the same period, three of his four children died, followed by his wife in 1642. His wife's will prevented his remarriage, and seven years later Hendrickje Stoffels became Rembrandt's companion until her death in 1663.

Rembrandt's works include paintings, drawings, and etchings. His subjects range from the biblical and historical to the mythological. He is perhaps most famous for his self-portraits. The various stages of Rembrandt's work demonstrate his attention to light (as the revealer of both form and truth), shadow, and texture. His portraiture and sketches communicate a level of intelligence, emotion, character, and compassion equaled by few artists. It was the tragedy in his life that brought increasing depth to his mature work and renewed his interest in biblical themes.

In Rembrandt's religious art one finds clear expressions of Reformed Christianity. Rembrandt presented a Protestant "street-level religion" by depicting biblical characters as ordinary people. Evident, for example, in the *Raising of Lazarus* (etching, 1642), the *Departure of Tobias* (drawing), and the *Return of the Prodigal Son* is a Reformed notion of **grace.** In *John the Baptist Preaching* (ca. 1634) and *Christ Preaching the Remission of Sins* (etching, ca. 1652), one finds an emphasis on the **Word of God** and **preaching.** And in *Jesus Healing the Sick* (etching, ca. 1643–1649), *Peter and John Healing the Cripple at the Gate of the Temple* (etching), and *The Reconciliation of David and Absalom,* one finds the gospel message of healing and reconciliation. Rembrandt portrayed the various scenes of Christ's life: preaching, healing, death, and burial. He identified himself with a vulnerable Paul in *Self-Portrait as the Apostle Paul* (1661), and illustrated the **conversion** experience in the *Conversion of Paul*. Shaped by his reading of the Bible, by his personal hardships, and by the artistic and intellectual currents of his time and country, Rembrandt's religious art is also a remarkable expression of Reformed Protestantism.

RENVILLE, JOHN B. (ca. 1840–ca. 1890). Native American (Dakota) hymn writer. Renville was the first Native American ordained to the Presbyterian **ministry** (1865). For 20 years he was pastor of the Ascension Church on the Lake Traverse Reservation in Sisseton, South Dakota (1870–1890). Renville edited the first hymnal in the Dakota language, *Dakota Odowan* (1879). This hymnal continues to be used by Native American congregations. His hymn "Wotanin Waste Nahon Po" ("Hear the Good News of Salvation"), which first appeared in Renville's hymnbook, is now found in English translation in *The Presbyterian Hymnal* (1990).

RESURRECTION. The completion of God's work of redemption, whereby the dead in Christ are "conformed to the body of his glory" (Phil. 3:21). The idea of a general resurrection is strongly linked to God's raising of Jesus from the dead. The resurrection of Christ vindicates his sinless life, breaks the power of **sin** and evil, and delivers believers from death to eternal life (**Brief Statement of Faith**, lines 23–26). Christ's resurrection has an eschatological dimension that anticipates the consummation of history, promises a resurrection that is "spiritual" in nature (1 Cor. 15:44), and secures an ultimate destiny of eternal life (some Reformed **confessions** also refer to eternal judgment and condemnation [Belgic Confession, chap. 37; **Westminster Confession**, chaps. 32–33]). **Scripture** teaches that the resurrected state is a spiritual existence in which individual consciousness, personality, memory, and relationships are preserved.

RÉUNION. *See* INDIAN OCEAN ISLANDS

REVELATION. God's self-disclosure to humanity; a revealing of that which is true about God but previously concealed or unknown. God is the source and content of revelation, since all knowledge of God must originate in the divine will. God is revealed in nature and in the moral consciousness of humanity. However, this rudimentary knowledge falls short in disclosing the fullness of God's character and God's purposes for humanity. According to **John Calvin**, the Christian **scriptures**, which record God's deeds in history, provide a more complete, redemptive knowledge of God. This knowledge is centered in Jesus Christ, in whom God's Word and will are revealed. The revelation of Christ, the incarnate **Word of God**, is received by **faith** through the work of the **Holy Spirit**. God's will and purposes are also made known through the proclamation of the Word in Christian **preaching**. In these respects, God's revelation is both a written word and an activity. The Holy Spirit illuminates the written Word (as it witnesses to the living Word) through the means of the preached Word.

RÉVEIL, LE. An 18th-century movement of religious revival among European Protestant students and churches. The movement was influenced by Moravians, who ministered in **France** during the postrevolution antireligious regime (1792–1814), and by the outreach of British missionary societies. Réveil was centered in **Switzerland** and France in the early 19th century. In Geneva the movement was inaugurated by **Robert Haldane**, whose exposition of Romans to a group of theological students called into question the pervasive reformulation of Protestant Christianity by the Enlightenment. Because the established church structures and theological institutions were dominated by deists, Réveil adherents began independent and voluntarist organizational activities. Primarily through students, the movement spread to the **Netherlands, Belgium, Hungary**, and northern **Italy**, fostering the growth of independent **evangelical** congregations, **mission** and Bible societies, and schools. Although the French and Swiss movements subsided in the later 19th century, they revived interest in classical **Calvinism** and, through a small number of independent Reformed congregations, continued their influence into the 20th century in Geneva, the Netherlands, and elsewhere.

REVIVAL, RELIGIOUS. Spontaneous spiritual awakening or renewal of commitment that involves large groups of people. Revivalism can involve large meetings in which evangelistic and psychological techniques are used to solicit **conversion** or inspire renewed commitment. More often, however, revivals take place without such techniques as people are moved by the **Holy Spirit** in response to the gospel message. Examples of large revivals that have taken place in **Europe** and **North America** are the European Reformation (1500s), formation of the Independent churches in the United Kingdom (1600s), the German pietistic movement in Europe (1700s), the **Great Awakening** in North America and the United

Kingdom (1700s), the Réveil movement in **Switzerland**, **France**, and the **Netherlands** (1800s), the missionary movement (1800s–1900s), and the charismatic movement (1960s–). During the 19th and 20th centuries revivals have taken place outside the West: in the Pacific region (**Hawaii** under **Titus Coan** and Aneityum under **John Geddie**); in Africa (**East Africa, Madagascar, South Africa**, and **Congo**); Asia (**Indonesia, Korea**, and **China**); and in parts of Latin America. Reformed churches have been involved in many of these revival movements.

ŘÍČAN, RUDOLF (1899–1975). Czech historian and theologian. Říčan served as professor of church history at the **Comenius Theological Faculty** in Prague. He is the author of several works on the Unity of Czech Brethren (**Bohemian Brethren**) and Jan Amos Comenius. His definitive history of the Brethren has been translated into English as *The History of the Unity of Brethren: A Protestant Hussite Church in Bohemia and Moravia* (1992).

RICE, JOHN HOLT (1777–1831). American Presbyterian minister and educator. Born in Bedford County, Virginia, Rice studied with **Archibald Alexander**, worked as a schoolteacher, and, following **ordination** (1804), served as pastor of the Cub Creek Presbyterian Church. He helped to found Union Theological Seminary at Hampden-Sydney College in Virginia, and he organized the First Presbyterian Church in Richmond (1812). He founded the Virginia Bible Society and with others the American Bible Society (1816). Rice published the monthly *Virginia Evangelical and Literary Magazine* (1818–1828), was elected **moderator** of the Presbyterian **general assembly** (1819), and became president of Union Theological Seminary (1824). He advocated a moderate **Calvinism**, emphasizing **education, mission**, and ecumenical cooperation. He published several books, including *Irenicum or the Peacemaker* (1820).

RICHARDS, WILLIAM (1793–1847). American Congregationalist minister and missionary in **Hawaii**; ambassador to **England** and minister of public instruction in the Hawaiian kingdom. Born in Plainfield, Massachusetts, Richards graduated from Williams College in 1819 and **Andover** Theological Seminary in 1822. Following **ordination**, he was sent by the **American Board of Commissioners for Foreign Missions** to Hawaii, where he arrived in 1823. Richards was stationed at Lahaina, Maui, where he organized the Lahainaluna School and became a respected teacher. In 1838 he left the mission to become chaplain, translator, and political adviser to King Kamehameha III. His political influence can be seen in the Hawaiian Bill of Rights (1839), the Constitution of 1840, and various laws. Appointed ambassador to England in 1842, he was responsible for securing, from Great Britain, **France**, and the **United States**, official recognition of Hawaii's independence. In 1846 he was appointed minister of public instruction and carried out the task of organizing an educational system for the Kingdom of Hawaii. Richards prepared a *Translation of the Constitution and Laws of the Hawaiian Islands* (1842). He was a skilled Bible translator and prepared about a third of the Hawaiian-language Bible published in 1839.

RINGELTAUBE, WILHELM TOBIAS (1770–1816?). German-born British Congregationalist missionary in **India**. Ringeltaube combined Lutheran training with Moravian piety and became a Congregationalist. He was sent by the **London Missionary Society** to South India (1803). He evangelized and ministered in Tinnevelley district, and later went to work in Travancore (1806). As the first missionary in this region, Ringeltaube developed the Protestant church, beginning in the village of Mayiladi. He worked tirelessly, lived simply, and gave away whatever money he had. Ringeltaube built chapels and opened several schools. By 1813 he had formed a community of some 600 Christians. A short time later he departed the region in poor health; he found his way to Malacca, where he disappeared in 1816. The Kanyakumari diocese of the Church of South India remembers Ringeltaube as its pioneer missionary.

ROBINSON, JOHN (ca. 1575–1625). English Puritan minister and pastor of the Pilgrims. Robinson was born in Nottinghamshire, **England**, and probably graduated from Cambridge (ca. 1598). He was ordained in the Church of England and in 1602 became a curate at St. Andrew's Church, Norwich. He refused to obey the anti-Puritan decrees of 1604 and joined the separatist congregation at Scrooby, Nottinghamshire (1606 or 1607). To avoid persecution, he fled with the congregation from Scrooby to Amsterdam in 1608. The following year, he and 100 church members moved to Leiden, where Robinson was ordained as their pastor. The congregation grew to about 300 members, and in 1620, 35 members of the congregation sailed to Plymouth, England, on their way to the New World. Robinson gave a farewell sermon in which he said, "I am very confident that the Lord hath more truth and light yet to break forth out of His holy Word." The Pilgrims departed Plymouth on the *Mayflower*, bound for New England. Although Robinson died before he could go to New England, he assisted the Pilgrims in their preparations and encouraged them through his letters. The members of Robinson's congregation who remained in Leiden were incorporated into the Dutch Reformed Church in 1658. Robinson wrote *Justification of Separation* *from the Church of England* (1610) and *Apologia* (1619), in which he defended the principles of congregationalism; *A Defence of the Doctrine Propounded by the Synod of Dort* (1624); and 62 essays on spiritual and moral themes published posthumously as *Observations Divine and Moral* (1625).

RODBORNE, TREVOR (1902–1986). Indian Presbyterian minister and executive secretary of the Khasi-Jaintia Presbyterian Synod. Born in the state of Meghalaya, in northeast **India**, Rodborne was educated at Serampore College in Calcutta, where he earned a bachelor of divinity degree in 1928. He was ordained an evangelist (1929) and minister (1934), serving in Meghalaya until 1953. When India became independent in 1947, the Welsh missionaries who had organized the Presbyterian churches in northeast India departed. During this critical period Rodborne was elected executive secretary of the church, remaining in the position for three consecutive terms (15 years). Rodborne was an enthusiastic preacher, wrote more than 30 books, and composed and translated many hymns, 11 of which are in the Khasi-Jaintia Presbyterian hymnbook.

ROMANIA. *See* CENTRAL AND EASTERN EUROPE

ROOKMAAKER, HENDRIK ROELOF ("HANS") (1922–1977). Dutch professor and art historian. Born in The Hague, Rookmaaker was educated at the Municipal University of Amsterdam, where he earned degrees in 1952 and 1959. He was appointed lecturer in art history at Leiden University (1958–1965) and then served as professor of the history of art at the **Free University of Amsterdam** (1965–1977). He was influenced by the work of **Herman Dooyeweerd** and attempted to apply his Reformed philosophical vision to art history. His publications include *Synthetist Art Theories* (on Gauguin) and *Modern Art and the Death of a Culture* (1973).

ROUTLEY, ERIK (1917–1982). English Congregationalist minister, theologian, and hymn writer. Routley was born in Brighton, **England**, and educated at the University of Oxford (Magdalen College [1940], Mansfield College [M.A., 1943; B.Div., 1946], and the University [D.Phil., 1952]). Routley became pastor of the Dartford Congregational Church (1945) and later served churches in Edinburgh (1959) and Newcastle upon Tyne (1967). In 1975 he became visiting professor and director of **music** at **Princeton Theological Seminary**, and professor of church music at Westminster Choir College, Princeton. In 1978 Routley was named director of the Princeton chapel. He lectured widely, publishing many books and hymnals, including *The Church and Music: An Enquiry into the History, the Nature and the Scope of Christian Judgment on Music* (1950; enlarged, 1967), *The English Carol* (1958); *A Panorama of Christian Hymnody* (1979), *The Music of Christian Hymns* (1981), and *Rejoice in the Lord* (1985). Routley was one of the most influential figures in English and American church music during the 20th century.

RWANDA. *See* CENTRAL AFRICA

- S -

SABBATARIANISM. The view, following the Old Testament Decalogue prescription, that the seventh day should be set aside for rest and **worship** (Exod. 20:8). Sabbatarianism was an important part of English and American **Puritanism**, which practiced a Christian Sabbath on Sunday. Nicholas Bound's *The Doctrine of the Sabbath* (1595) and *Sabbathum veteris* (1606) identified three essential elements of Sabbatarianism: that the Decalogue **law** is to be understood universally, morally, and perpetually; that the Christian Sabbath is rooted in the divine will and not merely in the **tradition** of the **church**; and that the whole Sabbath day is to be marked by public and private worship. Rest is to be had by refraining from recreation and "worldly employments" (**Westminster Confession**, chap. 21). In New England, civil laws punished Sabbath breakers. Secularization, industrialization, and urbanization have led to many cultural changes in Sabbath observance. Some Reformed and Presbyterian bodies still maintain vestiges of Sabbatarianism.

SACRAMENTS. Visible signs and seals of **God's covenant** promises given in **baptism** and the **Lord's Supper**, the two sacraments acknowledged by Reformed churches. Reformed theology emphasizes the connections between the Old Testament rite of circumcision and baptism (Gen. 17:11; Col. 2:11–12) and between Passover and the Lord's Supper (Exod. 12:7–8, 13; 23:14–17; 1 Cor. 5:7). These rites serve as means of **grace** by which the covenant **community** is given an outward, visible expression of its **faith** and of God's provisions for **salvation.** Reformed theology also stresses the link between the sacraments and the **Word of God** as it is proclaimed, written, and incarnate in Jesus Christ. God uses common, earthly elements to convey the blessings of the gospel; the **Holy Spirit** uses earthly elements in conjunction with the Word to nourish and sustain the faith of those who receive the sacraments. Reformed theology adopted Augustine's understanding of a sacrament as "a sign and the thing signified," existing together in a "spiritual relation, or sacramental union" (**Westminster Confession**, chap. 27). By the work of the **Holy Spirit**, which makes the sacraments efficacious, the rites both present and represent the benefits given by Christ in the gospel.

SA'ID, IBRAHIM (1895–1970). Egyptian Presbyterian minister, professor, and pastor of Qasr al-Dubara Church in Cairo. Born in Mallawi, **Egypt**, Sa'id graduated from the American College in Asyūt in 1913 and Cairo Evangelical Theological Seminary in 1916. After a nine-year pastorate at Beni Mazâr Evangelical Church he returned in 1925 to the seminary as professor of Hebrew and biblical studies. In the 1930s he began serving a community of Arab Protestants in downtown Cairo, which in 1944 became the Qasr al-Dubara Church. From 1957 to 1970, Sa'id served as president of the Protestant Council, which represented all Protestant denominations in Egypt. A supporter of the 1952 Egyptian revolution, Sa'id was an early advocate of the Palestinian cause, communicating his views in newspaper articles and radio addresses. He wrote 42 books while supervising the work of Christi Publishing of the Nile from 1932 to 1970.

SAINT BARTHOLOMEW'S DAY MASSACRES (1572). Massacres in **France** of Protestants by Roman Catholics. The violence began in Paris on August 23 and 24, spreading to the provinces of Bordeaux, Boruges, Lyons, Orléans, and Rouen. It is estimated that 3,000 **Huguenots** were killed in Paris, and thousands more in the provinces. The violence was sparked by an assassination attempt on a prominent Huguenot leader **Gaspard II de Coligny** secretly ordered by Catherine de Médicis, mother of the French king, Charles IX. De Médicis, who feared reprisals after the failed assassination, persuaded her son to order the death of Coligny and other Huguenot leaders, who were in Paris for the marriage of Henry of Navarre. Although the massacres shocked the entire Reformed world, they did not destroy the Huguenot movement but only incited further hostilities that were part of the Wars of Religion.

SALVATION. God's activity to deliver humanity from the power and effects of **sin** and to restore wholeness and peace in humanity's relationship with **God**, with other human beings, and with nature and the environment. Reformed theology recognizes the destructive powers of sin to cause alienation, enslavement, fear, despair, and unbelief. Sin is so pervasive that human beings are unable to experience reconciliation with God. Salvation comes as a result of the active presence of God in the life of the believer, enabling the reconciling work of Jesus Christ to become effective. Through **faith** in Christ, the believer experiences forgiveness of sin and freedom from the unreachable demands of the **law** of God. In the process of salvation the sinner is justified, united with Christ by faith, and given the gift of the **Holy Spirit**, who empowers the believer to live a Christian life of obedience and freedom. **Health** and wholeness, which are dimensions of the biblical term *soz* ("to save"), are found in Reformed emphasis on **sanctification**, in which believers grow in the life of faith and Christian discipleship. The ultimate end of salvation is glorification—the eternal blessedness of heaven and everlasting life in unbroken fellowship with God.

SAMOA. *See* PACIFIC OCEAN ISLANDS

SANCTIFICATION. The condition and process of being made holy. Sanctification is both a present condition and a goal or process toward which **faith** is directed. It is a present condition in virtue of Christ's sacrifice by which believers are sanctified. It is a goal or process in that faith leads to moral transformation. The process of sanctification involves the whole person: body, mind, and spirit. The goal of sanctification is to be made complete and whole; it is a process whereby the gift of faith is expressed through the practice of love. As both a present condition and a process, there is a strong connection between justification and sanctification. Both justification and sanctification are dependent on the indwelling work of the **Holy Spirit**, as unbelievers are prompted to faith and motivated to love and service. Sanctification is a result of justification, and **justification** finds its natural expression in sanctification. Ultimately, the process of sanctification is a paradox: it is completely dependent upon the Holy Spirit yet requires human effort and obedience to the will of **God.**

SAVOY DECLARATION (1658). An English Congregationalist statement of **faith** and **church government** produced by 120 church representatives who met at Savoy Palace, London. The purpose of the conference was to modify points of the **Westminster Confession** and to produce a statement of Congregational church polity. The declaration produced by the conference consisted of three parts: a preface, a confession of faith, and a platform of **discipline**. The document was prepared by John Owen, Philip Nye, Thomas Goodwin, and William Bridge; all but Owen had been members of the **Westminster Assembly** (1643–1648). Departing

˜om the Westminster Confession, the Savoy Declaration introduced the language of **federal theology** and revised Westminster's chapter on repentance. It added a chapter on the extent of the **grace** of the gospel and it reduced the power of the civil magistrate. The declaration also omitted, where Westminster included, children of believers from the Catholic Church, and advocated the autonomy of local churches.

SCANDINAVIA. *See* NORTHERN EUROPE

SCHAFF, PHILIP (1819–1893). American church historian, theologian, and ecumenist. Born in Chur, **Switzerland**, Schaff studied at Tübingen (1837–1839), Halle (1839–1840), and Berlin (1840–1841). After serving as a lecturer at Berlin (1842–1844), he went to America to serve as professor of church history and biblical literature at the German Reformed Church's seminary at Mercersburg, Pennsylvania (1844–1864), now Lancaster Theological Seminary. From 1864 to 1869 Schaff served as secretary to the New York Sabbath Committee, as president of the American Committee for the revision of the Bible, and as a visiting seminary lecturer (1868–1871). His last professorship was at **Union Theological Seminary** in New York.

At Mercersburg, Schaff and colleague John W. Nevin developed the **Mercersburg theology**, which stressed Christ and the **incarnation** and tried to revive liturgical elements of the Reformed **tradition**, including the centrality of the **Lord's Supper**. Schaff's scholarly contributions were monumental. His works include *The Principle of Protestantism* (1844), *What Is Church History? A Vindication of the Idea of Historical Development* (1846), *The Creeds of Christendom* (3 vols., 1877), *History of the Christian Church* (7 vols., 1882–1892), and *Theological Propaedeutic: A General Introduction to the Study of Theology* (1892). Schaff was editor of the *Schaff-Herzog Encyclopedia of Religious Knowledge* (3 vols., 1882–1884) and an American edition of John Peter Lange's biblical commentaries (25 vols., 1864–1880). He was involved in many ecumenical organizations, including the Evangelical Alliance and the Sunday school movement. In 1888, the American Society of Church History was founded in Schaff's home. He was its first president.

SCHLATTER, ADOLF (1852–1938). Swiss minister and New Testament scholar. Schlatter was born in St. Gallen, **Switzerland**, and studied at Basel and Tübingen. He was ordained in 1875 and served in the pastorate for five years. He began teaching at Bern (1880–1888) and then was appointed to professorships at Greifswald (1888), Berlin (1893), and Tübingen (1898–1922). With A. H. Cremer, Schlatter edited the journal

Beiträge zur Förderung christlicher Theologie (from 1897), to which he contributed many articles. His major works include *Der Glaube im Neuen Testament* (1885), a two-volume New Testament theology, *Die Geschichte des Christus* (1921), and *Die Theologie der Apostel* (1922). He also wrote histories of Israel (1901) and the early church (1926; English translation, 1955). Schlatter was a conservative New Testament scholar who sought to mediate between liberalism and pietism. His writings emphasize the centrality of Jesus, the facts of **faith** instead of speculative thought, and the recognition of the acts of **God** in history. Schlatter believed in the priority of Matthew among the Gospels and was concerned with the social implications of Christianity. His influence continues within German **evangelical** theology.

SCHLEIERMACHER, FRIEDRICH DANIEL ERNST (1768–1834). German minister, theologian, and preacher. Born in Breslau and educated among Moravian Pietists, Schleiermacher studied at Halle and in 1794 was ordained in the Reformed Church. In 1796 he became chaplain at the Charité Hospital in Berlin, where he met Prussian intellectuals and leaders of the Romantic movement. These acquaintances encouraged Schleiermacher to write his first book, *On Religion: Speeches to Its Cultured Despisers* (1799; English translation, 1894), in which he argued for the place of religious experience in defining the essence of religion. Schleiermacher then served as professor of theology at Halle (1804–1807) until Napoleon's troops occupied the city and he was forced to return to Berlin. There he became pastor of the Trinity Church (1809) and dean of the faculty and professor of theology at the new university (1810). Schleiermacher helped organize the Evangelical Church of the Prussian Union, which united Lutheran and Reformed churches. He was an active preacher who sought to make the Christian **faith** intelligible to modern hearers. He is considered to be the founder of both modern hermeneutics and modern theology.

In his classic work, *The Christian Faith* (1821–1822; 2d ed., 1830–1831; English translation, 1928), Schleiermacher tried to reformulate Christian theology for the post-Enlightenment world. Theology, for Schleiermacher, is a thematization of the Christian experience of redemption through Jesus Christ. Doctrines are attempts to describe the contents of Christian faith in a particular church of a particular time and place, and are therefore subject to constant criticism and revision. Schleiermacher wrote a critical work on the synoptic Gospels and pastoral epistles, *Einleitung ins Neue Testament* (*Introduction to the New*

Testament, 1845), and his lectures on the life of Jesus (*Das Leben Jesu*, 1864) were published posthumously.

SCHWEIZER, ALEXANDER (1808–1888). Swiss theologian. Born in Murten, Schweizer studied at Zurich, Berlin, and Jena. While a student at Berlin, he was deeply influenced by the lectures of **Friedrich Schleiermacher.** Schweizer was ordained in 1831 and in 1833 became assistant preacher at the Reformed church in Leipzig. In 1834 he was appointed instructor at the University of Zurich, teaching New Testament and practical theology. He also took charge of the cathedral and regularly preached there. In 1840 he became a full professor and produced important works on reformed theology (*Die Glaubenslehre der Evangelisch—Reformierten Kirche*, 1844–1847; *Die protestantishen Centraldogmen in ihrer Entwicklung innerhalb der reformierten Kirche*, 2 vols., 1854–1856). His sermons were published in five volumes (1834–1862).

SCHYNS, MATTHIEU GUILLAUME (1890–1979). Belgian Reformed minister and president of the Synod of the Protestant Evangelical Churches of Belgium. Schyns studied at the Protestant Institute of Glay and the Faculté de l'Oratoire in Geneva. He maintained a lifelong interest in the relationship between philosophy and theology. He was pastor of the Church of the Museum in Brussels from 1918 to 1968. He served successively as member, vice president (1938–42), and president of the Belgian Synod (1942–1954). During World War II he spoke out against anti-Semitism and aided refugees of Nazi persecution. In 1942, when Nazi authorities refused to allow Belgian students to study in **Switzerland**, he helped to organize a theological school in Brussels. Schyns taught philosophy and theology at the school, which became the Faculté de Bruxelles.

SCIENCE AND FAITH. The relationship between the scientific study of the natural world and the meaning and truth of Christian **faith.** Because science and faith do different things, they are complementary enterprises. Science is concerned with the natural world and tries to answer the question, How? while faith addresses the supernatural world and tries to answer the question, Why? Scientific discoveries and theories may call into question theological assumptions. The Copernican theory of the solar system, the Darwinian theory of evolution, and Freudian analysis of theological belief are examples. In relation to the Bible, the discussion has centered on the meaning of biblical statements (e.g., the **creation** stories in Genesis) in light of their apparent conflict with scientific evidence. Three positions have been taken by Reformed theologians in response to perceived conflicts between science and the Bible. Some Reformed theologians have defended the "scientific" accuracy of the Bible and have challenged the validity of modern scientific research. Others have tried to harmonize scientific and scriptural teachings. A third approach has been to affirm the theological nature of **scripture** and reject the idea that the Bible is a source of scientific information. Some points at which science and faith intersect include the origin of life, preservation of the biosphere, genetic engineering, reproductive technology, end-of-life decisions, and nuclear energy and weaponry.

SCOTLAND. *See* UNITED KINGDOM

SCOTTISH MISSIONARY SOCIETY (SMS). An independent missionary society founded in 1796. The SMS was one of several local **mission societies**, including the **London Missionary Society** (1795) and the **Glasgow Missionary Society** (1796), organized to carry out interdenominational **mission** work. The SMS promoted its work through the Scottish *Missionary Register*. In 1824 the General Assembly of the Church of Scotland approved foreign mission work and established a mission committee. This body appointed **Alexander Duff** as its first missionary and received other missionaries from the SMS. With the church willing to assume responsibility for international mission, the work of the SMS was gradually brought to an end. The mission strategy of the Church of Scotland has been characterized as "**evangelism** by **education**." This educational approach was criticized for not being "gospel centered." After the Disruption of 1843, the Church of Scotland had to rebuild its mission infrastructure when most of its missionaries joined the Free Church.

SCRIPTURE. The **Word of God** in written form. The Protestant scriptures include the 39 books of the Old Testament, sometimes called the Hebrew Bible, and the 27 books of the New Testament. The Old Testament consists of the **Law** (the Pentateuch), the Prophets, and the Writings. The New Testament consists of the four Gospels, the Acts of the Apostles, the letters of Paul and the other apostolic writers, and the Revelation of John. Scripture is the means by which God's plan of **salvation**, including the revelation in Jesus Christ, is made known. By the work of the **Holy Spirit** God's authoritative Word is actualized, conveying God's actions and will. Reformed theology conceives of scriptural **authority** in various ways but always maintains a commitment to scripture's primacy as revelation over other sources such as **tradition, reason,** or religious experience.

The content of scripture as God's revelation is centered in Jesus Christ, to whom the Old Testament points and the New Testament testifies. In scripture, the **church** has "the most complete exposition of all that pertains to a saving faith, and also to the framing of a life acceptable to God." Through the proclamation of the Word in **preaching,** the message of scripture is made effective by the "inward illumination of the Spirit" (Second Helvetic Confession, chap. 1).

The Reformed tradition has understood the nature of scripture in diverse ways. The **Princeton theology** considered scripture to be a book of "inerrant" facts regarding both the spiritual and the natural world. **Karl Barth** understood scripture as the "witness to Jesus Christ." **John Calvin** and Dutch theologians **Abraham Kuyper, Herman Bavinck,** and **G. C. Berkouwer** emphasize the function of scripture as God's divine revelation that does not deceive about its central purpose, which is to proclaim the message of God's salvation in Jesus Christ.

SCUDDER, IDA S. (1870–1959). American medical missionary in **India** under the Reformed Church of America. The granddaughter of **John Scudder,** she followed the family tradition of missionary service in India. She became a medical doctor and devoted her missionary labors primarily to the training of Indian women as nurses and doctors. Her efforts led to the formation of the Christian Medical School in Vellore (1918), which, in spite of great opposition, educated Indian women to be doctors. By 1942 Vellore had achieved university status and developed a reputation for a high educational standard. Later it began to admit men (1947). Scudder's commitment and vision resulted in the establishment of a major institution of **medicine** in India.

SCUDDER, JOHN (1793–1855). American Dutch Reformed medical missionary in **India** and Ceylon (now Sri Lanka). Born in Freehold, New Jersey, Scudder graduated from Princeton College (1811) and the Medical College of New York (1815) and then began to practice **medicine.** His reading of *The Conversion of the World* (1819) by Bombay missionaries **Gordon Hall** and **Samuel Newell** inspired him to work in India under the **American Board of Commissioners for Foreign Missions** (1820). Scudder's first appointment was in Jaffna, Ceylon, where he built a hospital and evangelized throughout the district. Later he was transferred to Madras, where he opened the first American **mission.** On long journeys, often by foot, he cared for the sick, preached, and distributed

Christian literature. He returned to America because of poor health (1842–1846) and traveled widely speaking on behalf of missions, especially to children. In 1846 he went to Madurai to continue medical work; from there he went again to Madras (1849). Scudder's writings on Christian mission inspired many to work in India, including several members of his own family.

SECULARIZATION. The social and political movement of religion from a position of public and protected domination to the realm of the private and individual. The term also refers to the church's adapting of itself to this modern shift by incorporating "worldly" methods and ideas to guarantee its preservation, and to the intellectual process whereby ideas and concepts originally rooted in Christianity are separated from their religious context and continue as allegedly neutral concepts (e.g., **human rights**). The themes that cluster around the term "secularization" all address the modern paradigm shift from the structures of European Christianity: desacralization, Enlightenment, disestablishment, postmodernity, and Dietrich Bonhoeffer's description of Western civilization as a "world come of age." Although secularization has marginalized the church in some regions of the world, in Southern Europe, Latin America, and other regions, the process has also helped to free social and political life from clerical control. Secularization has challenged Western churches to become **mission** churches, especially in their own societies, since Christianity is no longer socially and politically dominant.

SENEGAL. See WEST AFRICA

SEPOY MUTINY (1857–1858). A loosely organized rebellion against the British East India Company, which ruled **India**. Named after the sepoys, privates in the Indian army who initiated the mutiny, the rebellion grew out of anti-Western and anti-Christian sentiment in India. Several factors contributed to the uprisings: the introduction of Western **education**, the Christian missionary challenge to Hindu beliefs, the threat to the traditional Indian **caste** system, the Indian nobility's loss of authority, and the Western control of Indian churches. The rebellion spread from Delhi throughout north India. The mutiny resulted in the transfer of the administration of India from the British East India Company to the British government; the creation of a new legislative council (1861), with Indian representatives; and, in the context of the Reformed churches, the beginning of the movement toward **inculturation** and **contextualization** of Christianity in India.

SEWARD, SARA CORNELIA (1833–1891). American Presbyterian missionary and physician in **India.** Born in New York, Seward was educated at the Women's Medical College in Philadelphia, now the Medical College of Pennsylvania. She volunteered for mission service with the Woman's Union Missionary Society and was sent to Allahabad, India, in 1871. The following year she opened a medical dispensary and in 1873 transferred her connection to the Presbyterian Church in the U.S.A. Seward expanded her medical practice during the 1880s and helped raise funds for a hospital. Following a furlough to New York in 1889, she contracted cholera and died in Allahabad. Her work led to the construction of the Sarah Seward Hospital in 1893.

SEXUALITY, CHRISTIAN ETHICS OF. The understanding of human sexuality in light of the teachings of the Bible, Christian experience, and scientific studies. Contrary to ascetic teachings and practices that elevate the spirit over the body, the Protestant Reformers affirmed the goodness of the body and human sexuality. Active sexuality involves human intimacy expressed in acts of intercourse and procreation. Both physical and emotional intimacy are important for human **health** and well-being. The Reformed tradition teaches that such intimacy should take place within the **covenant** of **marriage.** The Reformers emphasized the goodness of married life, referring to it as a **vocation** or calling of **God.**

On issues relating to human sexuality, the Reformed churches continue to study scriptural teachings and the judgments of the scientific community. There is no consensus on such issues as abortion, homosexuality, and the use of genetic and reproductive technology. The emergence of these issues has raised not only important ethical concerns but also important methodological questions about the **authority** for Christian **ethics.** Pastoral ministry has obligations to those considering abortion, to persons of homosexual orientation, and to the unmarried: single adults, the aging, and those who have handicaps that prevent marriage.

SHEPPARD, WILLIAM H. (1865–1927). American Presbyterian minister and missionary in the Congo Free State, 1890–1910. Born in Waynesboro, Virginia, Sheppard attended the Hampton Institute in Virginia and then studied for the **ministry** at Stillman Institute in Alabama. While at Stillman, Sheppard volunteered for mission work in Africa, and in 1890 he departed for the Congo with Samuel N. Lapsley. Together they founded the American Presbyterian Congo Mission at Luebo, Congo Free State. Lapsley died of African fever in 1891, leaving Sheppard to manage alone until additional personnel were sent in 1893. For most of his

20 years in Africa, Sheppard worked among the Kuba people with his wife, Lucy, and other African-American missionaries, including Maria Fearing and Lillian Thomas DeYampert. In 1908 Sheppard's article in the mission's newspaper, the *Kasai Herald*, was used as a pretext for a libel suit by the government-controlled Kasai Rubber Company. He and the *Herald's* editor, **William M. Morrison**, were acquitted in 1909 after a widely publicized trial that led to important social and political reforms in the Congo. Sheppard left the mission in 1910, served as pastor of Grace Church in Louisville, Kentucky, and was widely sought as a church and conference speaker. He was made a Fellow of the Royal Geographic Society in London (1893) for his explorations and discoveries in the Congo.

SHIMAZAKI, TOSON (1872–1943). Japanese novelist and poet. Educated at **Meiji Gakuin**, Shimazaki became a Christian and was baptized (1888). He taught at Meiji School for Women, one of the oldest Christian schools in **Japan**. A widely published author, Shimazaki wrote *Before the Dawn* (1932; 1935), *Breaking the Commandment* (1906), *A New Life* (1918–1919), and *Spring* (1908). His literary works focus on human selfhood.

SHIN, DONG-HYUCK (1932–1994). Korean minister and educator in the Presbyterian Church of Korea (Tong-hap). Born in Pyonganbuk Province in the northern part of **Korea**, Shin was raised in a Christian family. In 1957 he graduated from Presbyterian Theological Seminary in Seoul. Following **ordination** in 1959 he served several churches in Pusan, including Nambu, Yangjung Jungang, and Dongrae Jungang. He married Kumjong Yoo and together they founded the Isabell Girls Mission School in 1964. In 1968, following theological study at Southwestern Theological Seminary in the **United States**, he served as principal of the Rural Evangelical School for the southern part of Kyoungsangnam Province. Shin was involved in rural and world **mission** and helped to organize the Agape Mission Board, which carried out the collective mission work of the churches of Pusan. A strong opponent of communism, Shin articulated his ideas in his book, *Jesus or Marx?* (1977).

SIMATUPANG, TAHI BONAR (1920–1990). Indonesian ecumenical lay leader. Educated at the Royal Army Academy in Bandung, Simatupang was actively involved in guerrilla warfare during the Indonesian independence struggle. He became chief of the armed forces (1949) and had an uneasy relationship with Indonesian President Sukarno until he retired in 1959. Simatupang was instrumental in starting the first business school (MBA program) in **Indonesia**, and his thinking guided the formation of Indonesian development policies. Simatupang became involved in the **ecumenical movement**, was elected to serve as one of the chairpersons of the National Council of Churches (1964), and later served as a member of the Central and Executive Committees of the **World Council of Churches**; he was also active in the Conference of Churches in Asia. He was influenced by **Karl Barth, H. Richard Niebuhr**, and **Reinhold Niebuhr**, and he helped to shape the relationship of **church and state** in Indonesia, describing it as "critical and realistic, positive and active."

SIN. The human condition of alienation and moral corruption. Sin is both an individual and a corporate condition that affects humanity's relationship with **God**, with other human beings, and with the world of **nature** and the environment. Sin also describes the actions and dispositions that spring from the corrupted human state, expressed by the Westminster Shorter Catechism as the "want of conformity unto, or transgression of, the law of God" (question 14). In the concept of sin there is both an ontological dimension that describes human nature and the world, and an ethical dimension that describes disobedience toward God. Some theologians have tried to locate the origin of sin (i.e., **original sin**) in the freedom given by the Creator. Reformed theology teaches that sin has ruptured the intended relationship between God and humanity. It has corrupted the image of God in humanity and enslaved the human will so that human beings are unable to choose to act in accord with God's will. It is only by the **Holy Spirit's** gift of **faith** that the bonds of sin are broken; in regeneration sin is forgiven and reconciliation is accomplished through the **atonement** of Jesus Christ on the cross. By his **resurrection**, Christ won ultimate victory over the forces of sin and power of evil. Thus "the victim of sin became victor, and won the victory over sin and **death**" for all people (Confession of 1967, pt. 1, A, 1). Although the Christian life is not without sin, Christ makes possible **sanctification** and forgiveness.

SINGAPORE. *See* SOUTHEAST ASIA

SISTER. *See* BROTHER-SISTER

SLAVERY. The holding of one person by another in involuntary servitude. Slavery has an ancient history rooted in both Western and non-Western societies. Its modern form began during the late 15th century and continued, with varying degrees of severity, into the 20th century. The Arabs were for many years the dominant slave-holding power, whereas the Spanish and Portuguese needed slaves for their empires in the Americas. It was not until the last quarter of the 18th century that opposition to slavery began in **Great Britain.** The British abolished the slave trade in 1807 and extended the ban throughout their empire in 1833. The total abolition of slavery came about gradually: **France** banned slavery in the **West Indies** in 1848, followed by a ban in the **United States** (1865), **Brazil** (1888), **Nigeria** (1900), **Tanzania** (1922), the Arabian Peninsula (1962), and Mauritania (1980). Even after the abolition of slavery, some colonial powers maintained slavelike conditions in countries like the **Congo** well into the 20th century. Some modern forms of indentured servitude, often based on class, **ethnicity**, and race, continue. The Reformed churches have a mixed history in regard to slavery. Although the **Puritans** and the British Free Churches were generally against slavery, Reformed churches in **South Africa**, in the United States, and in other countries cooperated with governments that perpetuated racism and oppression of their citizens.

SLEBOS, CORNELIS LODEWIJK (1913–1978). Argentine educator. A resident of Haarlem, **Netherlands,** Slebos was 26 years old when he was recruited in 1939 to begin a grammar school in the Dutch community of Tres Arroyos, a small city in the southern part of the province of Buenos Aires, **Argentina.** The grammar school enrolled over 100 children by 1950 and over 250 by the late 1970s. In addition to his work as an educator, Slebos was a lay preacher and choir director in the Reformed church, helped publish a small youth magazine with pastor J. Pott, and translated Dutch works into Spanish, including Hans Ridderbos's *The Return of the King.*

SLESSOR, MARY (1848–1915). Scottish Presbyterian missionary in **Nigeria.** Slessor was sponsored by the United Presbyterian Church as a teacher for the Calabar **mission** (1865). After 12 years of intensive work ranging from **preaching** to medical care, she went on to Okoyong, which was in the midst of rapid social change. She worked to settle disputes without bloodshed, introduce trade, and teach useful occupations; she helped guide the process of social change and tried to enhance the lives of the people. She worked against the abuse of alcohol, the demonization of twin children, witchcraft ordeals, and ritual killings at funerals. Slessor became widely respected, even serving as a government magistrate. Her life's work laid the foundations for the subsequent growth of the Presbyterian Church in Nigeria.

SLOVAK REPUBLIC. *See* CENTRAL AND EASTERN EUROPE

SLOVENIA. *See* CENTRAL AND EASTERN EUROPE

SMITH, GEORGE ADAM (1856–1942). Scottish Presbyterian minister and Old Testament scholar. Smith was born in **India**, where his father was editor of the *Calcutta Review*. In 1877, at the age of 18, he earned a divinity degree from **New College, Edinburgh**. He studied at Tübingen and Leipzig, and he served as an assistant Free Church minister until called to teach Hebrew and Old Testament in the Free Church College, Aberdeen. Smith served as minister of Queen's Cross Church, Aberdeen (1882–1892), and as professor of Old Testament language and literature in the Free Church (later United Free Church) College, Glasgow (1892–1909). He then returned to Aberdeen to become principal and vice-chancellor of the university until 1935. Smith was knighted by King George V, was a Fellow of the British Academy, **moderator** of his church's **general assembly**, and a royal chaplain in **Scotland**. He traveled extensively in the **Middle East** and was in great demand as a lecturer in **England** and the **United States**. He advocated the modern, critical approach to the Bible and sought to "interpret to the present age the messages of the ancient prophets." He was nearly tried for heresy over the views expressed in *Modern Criticism and the Preaching of the Old Testament* (1901). His major works include commentaries on Deuteronomy (1918), Isaiah (1927), Jeremiah (1929), the minor prophets (1928), and his historical-geographical works, *Historical Geography of the Holy Land* (1894; rev. 1931) and *Jerusalem . . . From the Earliest Times to 70 A.D.* (2 vols., 1907–1908).

SOCIAL CHRISTIANITY. Japanese Christian social movement of the early part of the 20th century. Influenced by the work of **Toyohiko Kagawa**, a Japanese **labor** leader and social reformer, the majority of socialists in **Japan** were Christian rather than Marxist. However, unlike Christian socialism, which directed its efforts to those outside the **church**, Social Christianity was a movement that took place within the church. Social Christianity tried to develop a "socialized Christianity" as opposed to individualistic Christianity. One of the leaders of the movement was Shigeru Nakajima (1888–1946), who helped organize the National Alliance of Social Christianity, published a magazine, *Social Christianity*, and wrote *The Essence of Social Christianity: The Religion of Redemptive Love* (1937).

SOCIAL GOSPEL MOVEMENT (1890s–1930s). North American social and theological movement that addressed the social problems of an industrial and urban population. The term originated in the 1870s as ministers became aware of the increasing social problems caused by American and Canadian industrialization, immigration, and urbanization. The focus of the movement was on **labor** conditions, **health** care, housing, and urban renewal. The leading social gospel figures in America were Walter Rauschenbusch and William Newton Clarke (Baptists) and **Washington Gladden** and Josiah Strong (Congregationalists). In **Canada**, Presbyterians **Charles W. Gordon**, Robert A. Falconer, and John G. Shearer helped to lead the movement. The movement was generally Ritschlian in its theology, viewing church creeds and **confessions** as hindrances to the healing of social ills. Its leaders embraced progressive theological, social, and scientific views, including higher criticism of the Bible, an optimistic view of humanity and a belief in social progress, and evolutionary Darwinism. These views were expressed in books intended for educated ministers and lay readers, and in hymns, prayers, and educational materials prepared for the larger church. Such materials reinterpreted traditional Christian doctrines such as **atonement**, **kingdom of God**, **sin**, and **salvation** in progressive social terms.

SOCIAL JUSTICE. The actions of societies and individuals guaranteeing that all are treated fairly and protected in their pursuit of that which is considered good. Justice is central to **scripture**, describing both the character and purposes of **God** and of God's will for **creation**, revealed in divine **law** and in God's saving purposes. Reformed theology has emphasized justice in its interpretation of the gospel, especially in personal and corporate **ethics**, churchly witness to the world, and the third use of the law. The process of **secularization** has removed Western understandings of justice from their rooting in divine law and will and has made both the concepts and structures of societies religiously neutral. Reformed ethical thought has resisted banishment from the public arena, though, insisting upon the systemic and structural implications of the gospel, or social justice. Although modern Protestantism tends to stress individual **evangelism** and **salvation**, social justice is considered by many to be the comprehensive definition of the church's **mission**. *See also* Law

SOCIETY ISLANDS. *See* PACIFIC OCEAN ISLANDS

SOEDARMO, R. (1914–1990). Indonesian Reformed theologian. After completing his doctoral studies at the **Free University of Amsterdam** (1957), Soedarmo served as professor at Duta Wacana Theological Seminary (1945–1954) and at the Jakarta Theological Seminary (1957–1978).

His theological work focused on the way in which the Christian minority could confess its faith in **Indonesia** with integrity and credibility. He translated many theological works into Indonesian and worked on an Indonesian translation of the Bible. He also pastored churches and wrote for both the lay reader and the scholar; his best-known book is *In Search of a Church with Many Faces.*

SOGA, TIYO (1829–1871). First black Presbyterian minister in **South Africa**, prolific hymn writer, and Christian teacher. Soga received theological training at **Lovedale**, South Africa, and in Glasgow, **Scotland**. He returned to South Africa after having been ordained a minister of the United Presbyterian Church (1856). He served as a missionary in Mgwali (1857–1868) and Tutura (1868–1871), working among the Xhosa people in the eastern Cape region. Soga opposed white missionaries in their complicity in the destruction of Xhosa tribal structures but was ambivalent about some tribal customs (e.g., adolescent circumcision). His ministry helped to preserve the territorial and cultural integrity of blacks in the Cape frontier. Although he was not a political figure, Soga was a convinced black nationalist and a pioneer in the development of "African consciousness." Soga translated the Bible and other works, including *Pilgrim's Progress* (1866), into the Xhosa language.

SOLEMN LEAGUE AND COVENANT (1643). A civil and religious agreement between the English and the Scots that pledged **Scotland** to assist the Parliamentary side in the English Civil War. The religious dimension of the covenant pledged uniformity for **England**, Scotland, and **Ireland**, with the Reformed religion being established in Scotland and the "reformation" of English and Irish churches pledged on issues of doctrine, liturgy, **church government**, and **discipline.** Scottish commissioners were sent to participate in the **Westminster Assembly**, which approved the document in September 1643. However, Charles I and **Oliver Cromwell** rejected the Solemn League. In order to fulfill a condition for his coronation, Charles II swore allegiance to the covenant in 1651, only to renounce it and persecute its adherents after the Restoration (1660). Later **Dissenters**, the **Covenanters** and Seceders, made adherence to the Solemn League and Covenant (along with the National Covenant of 1638) a condition for membership in their sects.

SONNEVELDT, ANTONIE CORNELIS (1880–1959). Dutch Reformed minister and missionary in **Argentina**. Born in Willemstad, **Netherlands**, Sonneveldt was educated in Amsterdam, where he studied to be a schoolteacher and principal. He became headmaster of the school in

Haarlemmermeer and in 1907 principal in Brouwershaven. In 1910 he traveled to Argentina to work as a teacher and preacher for the small Dutch community in Buenos Aires. He also worked in Chubut, in the Patagonia, where people of Dutch descent, including Boers from **South Africa**, had settled in remote farming communities. Sonneveldt was a gifted preacher; the founding editor of two newspapers, *Church Paper for South America (De Kerkblad Voor Zuid Amerika)*, published in Buenos Aires from 1927 to 1959, and *The Faithful Word (La Palabra Fiel)*, published from 1933 to 1960; an organizer of churches and Christian schools; and the first Protestant to broadcast over the radio in Argentina.

SOUČEK, JOSEF BOHUMIL (1902–1972). Czech biblical theologian and the first **moderator** of the Evangelical Church of the Czech Brethren. Souček served as professor at the **Comenius Theological Faculty** in Prague. During World War II he risked imprisonment when he organized theological courses that provided **education** for church leaders. He contributed to a two-volume Bible dictionary (1956) and helped to edit a three-volume Bible concordance for the Czech Kralice Bible. In 1961 Souček was appointed New Testament editor for a new Czech Bible translation, completed in 1979. He was influenced by the theology of discipline, and he edited and translated works by **Josef Hromádka**. He wrote *The Theology of the Commentaries in the Kralice Six-Volume Bible* (1933).

SOUTH AFRICA. The majority of the people of South Africa practice Christianity (over 80 percent); there are Hindu and Muslim minorities. Although South Africa is part of **southern Africa**, its size, cultural and historical development, regional influence, and the complexity of its church life make it a unique area of the world.

Reformed Christianity came to South Africa with the settlement of Cape Town by the Dutch East India Company in 1652. White settlers brought with them the Dutch Reformed Church (Nederduitse Gereformeerde Kerk; NGK). During the occupation of the Cape by **Great Britain** (1795–1803), the **London Missionary Society** sent missionary **Johannes T. Vanderkemp**, who began a Congregationalist **mission**; the work was continued and expanded by **John Philip**. Scottish missionary activity was also initiated in the early 19th century by the **Glasgow Missionary Society** and missionaries **Robert Moffat** and **David Livingstone**. Thus the Dutch Reformed, Congregational, and Presbyterian churches of South Africa have been influenced by Dutch and British colonial expansion and mission society initiatives; they have also been shaped by cultural-ethnic identity and racism. **Dutch Reformed Churches.** The NGK served exclusively the Dutch community in South Africa until 1836, when the church appointed its first missionary to work among the African population. The Great Trek of Afrikaners from the Cape (1836–1844) led to the establishment of Natal, the Orange Free State, and Transvaal. In 1862 the NGK churches in these areas, and later in southwest Africa (presently **Namibia**), became autonomous. These four independent churches reunited with the NGK in 1962. The oldest seminary in the country, now part of the university, was founded by **Andrew Murray** and other church leaders in Stellenbosch. Many theologians and church leaders, including **Barend B. Keet**, have been educated at Stellenbosch.

During the mid-19th century the NGK divided into three forms of the Dutch Reformed Church. The Nederduitse Hervormde Kerk (NHK) was founded in the Transvaal in 1853; it opposed both **mission** work with blacks and British influence and control. The Gereformeerde Kerk (GK) withdrew from the NGK in 1859 over doctrinal issues. Today the church has more than 77,000 members in 297 congregations and maintains its seminary at Potchefstroom. The NGK represented the continuing Dutch Reformed church tradition. All three churches maintained strong ties with Reformed churches in the **Netherlands** and preserved a commitment to Calvinist orthodoxy as defined by the Canons of Dort.

Evangelistic work among African (Bantu) and "colored" (mixed races) populations was carried out by the Dutch Reformed Church. This work resulted in the formation of new African congregations. In 1857 the Synod of the NGK decided to maintain **worship** services and an institutional life that was separate from the black mission congregations. This decision was rooted in the Boer conviction that there was no equality between whites and "natives." Eventually, the decision led to the formation of various "mission churches" among the African populations of South Africa.

During the 19th century, NGK mission initiatives led to the formation of separate churches among Bantu people in the Cape Province, another in the Transvaal, and a third in the Orange Free State. These three daughter churches united to form the Dutch Reformed Church in Africa (Nederduitse Gereformeerde Kerk in Afrika) in 1963, a church composed of Sotho and Nquni people, with minorities from other groups. In 1880 the NGK created a daughter church for black Cape Colony Christians. This resulted in the formation of the Dutch Reformed Mission Church in South Africa (Nederduitse Gereformeerde Sendingkerk in Suid Afrika). In its synod meetings of 1974, 1978, 1982, and 1986 the church rejected **apartheid** and took a strong stand against South Africa's racial laws. In 1994 the Dutch Reformed Church in Africa and the Dutch Reformed Mission Church in South Africa merged to form the Uniting Reformed Church, with a membership of over 500,000.

In 1968 the NGK organized a mission church for the Asian Indian population, which became the Reformed Church in Africa (RCA). A small church, the membership of the RCA is composed primarily of converts from Hinduism.

The political policy of apartheid, formally enacted and implemented by the Republic of South Africa after World War II, became the confessional crisis of the Reformed Churches in South Africa. The global ecumenical community, the Reformed family of churches, and the indigenous African churches all challenged the white churches regarding their theological support of apartheid. The **World Alliance of Reformed Churches** suspended the membership of the NGK and NHK in 1982; the **Kairos Document**, opposing apartheid, was drafted by some South African church leaders in 1985; in 1986 the NGK began the process of theological renunciation of apartheid, concluding in 1990 with its confession that the policy and its theological rationale were "an error in judgment." However, the NHK's constitution still stipulates that only whites can be members of that church.

Presbyterian Churches. Presbyterian missionary work was begun among Xhosa-speaking Bantu people of the eastern Cape and Scottish soldiers in the Cape Town area. The first European church was opened in 1829, and as British settlement grew, Presbyterian congregations were planted elsewhere. The first **general assembly** convened in 1897, with 23 European and 10 African congregations. This church continues today as the Presbyterian Church of Southern Africa, which is a largely white church with generally conservative views.

Scottish work among the Bantu led to the formation of the Bantu Presbyterian Church of South Africa in 1923, which later became the Reformed Presbyterian Church in Southern Africa. One of the most notable results of the Scottish mission among indigenous Africans was the founding of the Institution of **Lovedale**, a center of high-quality schooling that in turn gave birth to the University of Fort Hare (whose graduates include Nelson Mandela and Robert Mugabe). Based in Umtata, in the eastern Cape, is the Reformed Presbyterian Church Women's Christian Association (1893). With a membership of more than 20,000 **women,** the association sponsors conferences and provides resources for women's **ministry** and leadership in the church.

In 1898 **James Phambani Mzimba** left the Free Church of Scotland and formed an exclusively black church, the Presbyterian Church of Africa, with two presbyteries and four ministers. The church, which emphasized the theological **education** of its ministers, grew rapidly and today has over 900,000 members. It maintains its headquarters, and operates Lamb of God Bible College, in Durban. The church also has presbyteries in **Zimbabwe** and **Malawi**. In 1973 the church's general synod determined that there was no theological reason for the church to remain exclusively black.

Swiss Reformed missionaries, including **Paul Berthoud** and **Henri Junod**, came to the Northern Transvaal in 1875 to work among the Tsonga people. They established a network of mission stations in the northern and eastern parts of the state. The mission grew with the expansion of the mining industry, and congregations were later formed in the Orange Free State and Zululand. The church became autonomous in 1962 as the Evangelical Presbyterian Church in South Africa; the Swiss church still contributes to its support. The church has been contextualizing its ministry with emphasis upon African liturgy and **music**.

Congregational Churches. The United Congregational Church of Southern Africa (UCCSA) was formed in 1967 through the union of three bodies: the Congregational Union of South Africa (CUSA), the London Missionary Society (LMS), and the Bantu Congregational Church (BCC) of the **American Board of Commissioners for Foreign Missions.** In 1972 the South African Association of the Disciples of Christ joined the union.

The London Missionary Society was the first English-speaking mission in South Africa. In 1799 Theophilus van der Kemp landed at the Cape; he was followed by many others over a period of 150 years, including John Philip, Robert Moffat, **John Brownlee**, David Livingstone, and John Mackenzie. Many of these missionaries played important roles in the establishment of the Cape Colony and its frontiers.

From the eastern Cape, the LMS moved to the north Cape frontier, and over the next century established missions in what is today the northwestern area of South Africa, as well as the Republics of **Botswana** and Zimbabwe. Education was the focus of the mission work, including Robert Moffat's translation of the Bible into Setswana. A printing press was established at Kuruman; the Tiger Kloof Native Institute (which served South Africa and Botswana until it was closed by apartheid) was organized; and Hope Fountain and Inyati mission schools were founded in Zimbabwe.

In 1877 LMS congregations in the eastern Cape were released to join the Congregational churches established by English settlers to the Cape and Natal Colonies in the Congregational Union of South Africa. The CUSA became established in the lower Orange River region, and from this presence a mission was begun in **Namibia** under Saul Damon. American Congregational churches sent their first missionaries to South Africa in 1835. They established several missions in Zululand and **Mozambique** under John Adams and others. Educational and medical institutions such as Inanda Seminary, McCord Hospital, and Adams College were established, and the Bantu Congregational Church was organized. The then president of the African National Congress (ANC) and Nobel Peace Prize winner, **Albert Luthuli**, was a deacon in this church.

During the 1960s, these three denominations (LMS, CUSA, and BCC) began to work together in the black mine hostels of the goldfields around Johannesburg. The mines drew migrant laborers from the Tswana nations in the west (LMS) and from the Zulu nation in the southeast (BCC). These workers began to worship together and developed a common vision and witness. Ministers from the CUSA were involved in these developments, and out of this process the UCCSA was organized in 1967. The church is transnational, with communicants in Botswana, Mozambique, Namibia, South Africa, and Zimbabwe. *See also* Southern Africa

The first years of unity were extremely difficult in the racial and political cauldron of southern Africa. The policy of apartheid put severe pressure on the fledgling church, and the bonds of unity among various racial groups (as well as across national boundaries) were put to the test. The church suffered a small split in the late 1970s, when a group withdrew in protest against continued participation in the **World Council of Churches.** This group became the Evangelical Fellowship of Congregational Churches (EFCC).

In the late 1980s the UCCSA took a strong stand against the homeland policy of the Nationalist Party government and against other apartheid acts, such as the prohibition of mixed-race marriages, military conscription, and the suspension of rights during a state of emergency. Opposition to apartheid reforms caused still other splinter groups to leave and join the EFCC.

The UCCSA is one of the mainline churches in southern Africa. Composed of a mixed-race membership, and with congregations speaking 10 different languages, the church is truly multicultural and multinational. It has elected **women** and **laity** to its highest office. The Office of Secretariat for the denomination is located in Johannesburg, and there are synodical offices in Botswana, Zimbabwe, and Mozambique. Current discussions suggest that in the first decade of the new millennium the UCCSA will form autonomous churches in these countries. Unity talks with the Presbyterian Church of Southern Africa floundered during the early 1980s, but a growing number of congregations in South Africa are established as Uniting churches involving both denominations and on occasion the Methodist and Anglican churches.

SOUTH AMERICA. *See* ANDEAN REPUBLICS AND GREATER COLOMBIA; BRAZIL; SOUTHERN CONE OF SOUTH AMERICA

SOUTHEAST ASIA. The people of Southeast Asia practice many religions, with Christians composing a very small percentage of the population in Malaysia (less than 1 percent), Singapore (3 percent), and Thailand (less than 1 percent). Large Christian populations are found in Indonesia (9 percent) and the Philippines (Roman Catholic 84 percent; Protestant 10 percent).

Indonesia. The oldest Reformed churches in Asia are found in Indonesia. The first churches were organized during the 17th century by ministers of the Dutch East India Company, who served the Dutch population of the East Indies, Java, and Sumatra. In 1816 the country became a Dutch colony and an independent Protestant Church of the Indies was organized. This church, supported by state funds, served Reformed, Lutheran, and other Dutch Protestants.

During the 19th century, Swiss, German, and Dutch (Netherlands Reformed Church) missionaries began indigenous churches. These churches were organized along regional or tribal lines. Churches that descend from the Dutch work include the Christian Church of East Java (1921; Gereja Kristen Jawi Wetan), Christian Churches of Java (1949; Gereja-Gereja Kristen Jawa), Evangelical Christian Church in Halmahera (1949; Gareja Masehi Injili di Halmahera), Evangelical Christian Church in West Irian (1956), and the Indonesian Christian Church (1962).

The 20th century brought many changes to the Indonesian churches. British, American, and Asian missionaries came to Indonesia and established new churches. Many of the European mission churches and their leaders were persecuted during the Japanese occupation (1942–1945) of

Indonesia during World War II. The postwar years saw the breakup of the Dutch colonial administration in Indonesia and the independence of the Protestant churches. Today some 26 Indonesian denominations are members of **World Alliance of Reformed Churches.** These churches make up about 60 percent of the membership of the ecumenical Communion of Churches in Indonesia.

The Protestant Church in Indonesia, with over 2 million members, is the largest Protestant church family in the country. It is a continuation of the Dutch state church begun in the 17th century, and it is now composed of several major regional churches, including the Christian Evangelical Church in Minahasa (1934), the Protestant Church in Moluccas, the Christian Evangelical Church in Timor (1947), and the Protestant Church in Western Indonesia (1948). Each regional church holds separate membership in the World Alliance of Reformed Churches.

The Reformed churches have been an important influence on national life in Indonesia. In church life they have played an important role in the establishment of the National Council of Churches (now the Communion of Churches in Indonesia) in 1950. They have been instrumental in developing **education** and modern **health** care in Indonesia. In political life, they established the Indonesian Christian Party (1945), which has become part of the larger Democracy Party of Indonesia. Several important social, political, and ecumenical leaders have come from the Reformed churches, including **Martinus Abednego**, W. Z. Johannes, J. Leimena, B. Probowinoto, and **Tahi Bonar Simatupang. Yap Thiam Hien** (1913–1989) was an important leader in the area of **human rights.**

Theological education in Indonesia is carried out in an ecumenical context. What is now the Jakarta Theological Seminary originated with the Higher School for Theological Studies founded by **Hendrik Kraemer**; B. M. Schuurman organized Bale Wiyata in East Java; the Theological Seminary of the Indonesian Evangelical Church is located in Halmahera at Tobelo; a Christian University in Salatiga (Satya Wacana) was begun by Reformed churches in central Java; and the GMIM Foundation for Christian Education is operated by the Evangelical Christian Church in Minahasa. Significant Reformed theologians and educators include P. D. Latuihamallo, **T. B. Simatupang**, **R. Soedarmo**, **Clement Suleeman**, and Josef Widyaatmadja. **Interfaith dialogue** with Muslims is carried out by such Reformed leaders as P. D. Latuihamallo, Victor I. Tanya, Eka Darmaputera, and Th. Sumartana.

Malaysia and Singapore. The Presbyterian Church in Malaysia (Gereja Presbyterian Malaysia) is found on the Malay Peninsula, and the

Presbyterian Church of Singapore is located on the island nation of Singapore, at the tip of the Malay Peninsula. These churches originated with Dutch traders who built the famous Christ Church Melaka in 1753. Following the Dutch, the British **London Missionary Society** sent several Presbyterian missionaries to Malaysia, most notably **Robert Morrison, William Milne, James Legge**, and **Benjamin P. Keasberry.** Milne and Morrison established the Ultra-Ganges Mission in Malacca (1815) to train missionaries for China. They also established the Anglo-Chinese College (1819).

The present-day Presbyterian churches of Malaysia and Singapore were founded in 1881 through the efforts of J. A. B. Cook and Benjamin Keasberry. In 1901 a Presbyterian synod was organized in Singapore. When Cook departed Malaysia in 1924, he left behind 13 Presbyterian congregations.

The period of Japanese occupation during World War II caused great suffering for Protestants in Malaysia. The Chinese-speaking Presbyterian churches, which had grown to 33 congregations, pooled their resources and continued to meet for weekly worship throughout the war. In 1948 Trinity Theological College was established in Singapore, with the Presbyterian church as a founding member.

Singapore became an independent nation in 1965. In 1975 the Singapore-Malaysia Synod divided into separate churches, one in each country. The Presbyterian Church in Malaysia meets in a synod composed of three Chinese-speaking presbyteries and one English-speaking **presbytery.** The Presbyterian Church of Singapore also meets in a synod and is predominantly Chinese.

Philippines. Presbyterian and other American missionaries began arriving in the Philippines in 1899. In 1901 a conference of American Protestant mission boards was held in Manila. This conference created the Evangelical Union of the Philippines, a group that divided Philippines mission work among several denominations. As a result of this meeting, Congregationalists from the **American Board of Commissioners for Foreign Missions** worked on the island of Mindanao and Presbyterians on the islands of Luzon, Negros, Leyte, Panay, and Samar. These two Reformed bodies established the United Evangelical Church. Two educational institutions with Reformed roots are Silliman University, founded by Presbyterians in Dumaguete City (1901), and Union Theological Seminary in Manila (1907), organized by Presbyterians and Methodists.

Today, the United Church of Christ in the Philippines is the largest Protestant group in the country. The church was formed in 1948 by a union of the United Evangelical Church of the Philippines, the Philippine Methodist Church, and the Evangelical Church in the Philippines. Its form of government is primarily presbyterian. It has local overseers (bishops), who have spiritual and pastoral oversight of the church. Major departments of the church include **mission, evangelism,** Christian education, and service (public welfare). **Frank Laubach** was an important missionary-educator.

Thailand. Missionaries from the London Missionary Society arrived in Thailand in 1828. Beginning in 1840, American Presbyterians carried out much of the Protestant work in the country. They established mission centers in Petchaburi (1860) and Chiengmai (1867). After the establishment of religious toleration in 1878, the Presbyterian work expanded. The two centers of activity merged in 1922 to form a single Presbyterian mission.

In 1932 a national Protestant church, the Church of Christ in Thailand, was organized; two years later the church held its first **general assembly.** The majority of its congregations are Presbyterian, although its membership includes Baptist and Disciples churches. Founded by Presbyterians, McGilvary Faculty of Theology of Payap University is the church's seminary. Church ministries include hospitals, schools, and a cooperative farm. It has been heavily involved in aiding refugees in Thailand.

SOUTHERN AFRICA. The majority of the people of southern Africa practice Christianity and traditional religions. In some countries there are Muslim, Hindu, and Baha'i minorities. Christianity is the dominant religion in Angola (85 percent, including 38 percent Protestant), Botswana (50–60 percent), Lesotho (80 percent, including 26 percent Protestant), Malawi (75 percent), Namibia (95 percent), Swaziland (60 percent), and Zambia (50–75 percent). Christianity is a minority religion in Zimbabwe (25 percent) and Mozambique (30 percent). *See also* South Africa

The history of many of the Reformed churches in southern Africa has been strongly influenced by **colonialism** and by the distinctive political processes of the Republic of South Africa. Namibia, Botswana, Lesotho, and Swaziland account for 10 percent of southern Africa's population and are economically dependent on the Republic of South Africa. As a consequence of World War I, South Africa was entrusted by the League of Nations with Namibia, the former German Southwest Africa; it did not gain independence until 1990. Botswana, Lesotho, and Swaziland escaped incorporation into South Africa because of their protectorate status under **Great Britain**; all three became independent in the 1960s.

Great Britain and **Portugal** exerted powerful influence in the region. Malawi was a British protectorate beginning in 1889 and achieved independence in 1964. The countries of Zambia and Zimbabwe emerged from the colonial region called Rhodesia: Northern Rhodesia became Zambia in 1964, but Zimbabwe (Southern Rhodesia) struggled for 15 years after the Unilateral Declaration of Independence in 1965. Independence under black African government was finally achieved in 1980. Angola and Mozambique were Portuguese colonies that became independent in 1975. The Portuguese hoped to link the two colonies, creating a Portuguese-controlled zone across the whole of southern Africa, but the British control of Zambia and Zimbabwe frustrated these plans.

Namibia. Although the **London Missionary Society** arrived in 1805, Protestantism in Namibia was dominated by the influence of German colonialism, which established Lutheranism in the former German Southwest Africa. Today, the Lutheran United Evangelical Church of Namibia composes 40 percent of the population. Reformed churches were organized by South Africans who settled in Namibia. At least six Reformed churches were founded, the largest of which is the 17,000-member Dutch Reformed Church in Namibia.

Botswana. Formerly known as Bechuanaland, Botswana has a Christian majority as a result of the work of **Robert Moffat** (1817), **David Livingstone** (1842), and other missionaries of the London Missionary Society (LMS). The Tswana royalty favored LMS missionaries, making **Congregationalism** almost a state religion. Since independence (1966), the Botswana Congregationalists have become part of the regional United Congregational Church of Southern Africa.

The Dutch Reformed Church in Botswana can be traced to the work of South African missionaries who began work among the Kgatla people in 1869, and Pieter Brink, a minister of the Dutch Reformed Church (NGK) in South Africa, who began work in 1877 among the Kgatla people of Mochudi. In 1979 the Dutch Reformed Church in Botswana became autonomous and began to integrate both white and black Dutch Reformed congregations into a multiracial church.

Lesotho. Formerly known as Basutoland, Lesotho was the destination of French Reformed missionaries from the **Paris Evangelical Mission Society** who arrived in 1833. Their work led to the organization of the Lesotho Evangelical Church, which held its first national synod in 1872. The church became autonomous in 1964. The seminary at Morija is an important center of theological **education**, but a major problem for the church is recruiting and educating a sufficient number of pastors for its congregations. The church operates schools, hospitals, and a literature center, and it sponsors development projects. Lesotho also has a small white Dutch Reformed Church (1957) and a Bantu mission church. **Swaziland.** Methodist missionaries arrived in the small kingdom of Swaziland in 1825. The Christian majority of Swaziland is made up of independent charismatic and Zionist groups (African indigenous churches), which have synthesized elements of traditional religion and Christianity. Their religious rites reflect this syncretism as subservience to the absolutist king. A small Dutch Reformed Church is also present in Swaziland. The Swaziland Reformed Church is made up of Afrikaners from the Transvaal; they have four congregations.

Malawi. David Livingstone urged the Free Church of Scotland to send missionaries to Malawi (formerly Nyasaland); these missionaries established the Livingstonia Mission in 1875. The following year the Church of Scotland founded the Blantyre Mission, and in 1888 the Dutch Reformed Church began work in the center of the territory. Between 1924 and 1926, these three mission churches became presbyteries of the Church of Central Africa Presbyterian. In 1956 the presbyteries became synods, and the church has since founded synods in Zambia and Zimbabwe for Malawians in those countries. The highest church body is the general synod; decisions of the general synod must be approved by the regional synods. The church has developed a network of mission hospitals, primary and secondary schools, and the Zomba Theological College. The leadership of the church joined a movement for multiparty democracy initiated by Roman Catholic bishops, which resulted in general and free elections in 1994. *See also* Laws, Robert

Zambia and Zimbabwe. Many Reformed churches have begun mission work within the large territory of these countries, formerly Northern and Southern Rhodesia. The London Missionary Society began work in Zambia in 1859, failed, and started again in 1885, when Presbyterians from **Scotland** also came. The Paris Evangelical Mission Society worked from 1884 among the Lozi people. In 1958 the English-speaking Reformed missions united in the Church of Central Africa in Rhodesia. This union ultimately led to a merger with other Protestant churches in 1965, which formed the United Church of Zambia.

The Reformed Church in Zambia traces its history to 1899, when Dutch Reformed missionaries arrived from South Africa. The church became autonomous in 1943. Expanding its work through the provinces of Zambia, the church operates a theological college and two hospitals.

There are at least 10 Reformed denominations in Zimbabwe. Three churches come out of the Dutch Reformed tradition in southern Africa: the Church of Central Africa Presbyterian (Harare Synod) (1912; CCAP), the Dutch Reformed Church Synod of Central Africa (1895), and the Reformed Church in Zimbabwe (1891; RCZ). The CCAP primarily serves the Chewa-speaking community in Zimbabwe. The church is one of the constituent synods of the CCAP General Synod in Malawi. The Dutch Reformed Church is one of 11 constituent synods of the Nederduitse Gereformeerde Kerk in South Africa. The RCZ developed from Dutch Reformed mission work among the Shona-speaking people of Zimbabwe. Church headquarters are in Masvingo, the province in which the church is most active. These three churches are involved in union discussions among Dutch Reformed churches in southern Africa.

Three churches come out of the Congregational tradition: the United Church of Christ in Zimbabwe (UCCZ), the United Congregational Church of Southern Africa (UCCSA), and the Church of Christ in Zimbabwe (CCZ). The UCCZ and the UCCSA have a British heritage; the UCCSA grew out of the work of Robert Moffat and the London Missionary Society (1859). The UCCSA maintains ties with the Congregational Church in South Africa. The CCZ developed from mission work performed by the Church of Christ of New Zealand.

The Presbyterian Church in Zimbabwe (1896), composed of white settlers from South Africa, is the largest Presbyterian denomination. The church remains affiliated with the Presbyterian Church of South Africa.

Three small Reformed denominations that are not active ecumenically include the Reformed Church of Zimbabwe (RCZ), which is a local **presbytery** of the South African Nederduitsch Hervormde Kerk; the Reformed Churches in South Africa (Trans Limpopo), which is the local presbytery of the Gereformeerde Kerke of South Africa; and the African Reformed Church (ARC), which withdrew from the RCZ. The RCZ operates the Copoto School for the Blind.

In 1988 the first meeting of the Reformed Ecumenical Council was held in Harare. The council is the ecumenical body of the Reformed churches in Zimbabwe.

In both Zambia and Zimbabwe, the Reformed churches have emphasized evangelization and church formation, education, **health** and medical services, and agricultural development. The Presbyterian Church (U.S.A.) has become involved with the Christian churches in Zimbabwe, emphasizing **evangelism** and church growth throughout southern Africa from a base in Harare.

Angola. The **American Board of Commissioners for Foreign Missions** (ABCFM) established a mission among the Ovimbundu people in 1880, and missionaries from **Canada** arrived in 1886; by 1927 Reformed mission work in the Portuguese colony was divided between the ABCFM and the United Church of Canada. The work centered in the Benguela plateau area and in Silva Porto and Lobito on the coast. As a result of this work the Evangelical Congregational Church in Angola was organized. The Angolan civil war, which lasted from 1975 to 1991, severely disrupted the life of the church. The church operates the United Emanuel Seminary and Bible Institute, schools, and several hospitals, including Bailundo Hospital.

The Evangelical Reformed Church of Angola was begun in 1922 with the arrival of a Swiss minister and an Anglican priest who began work in the province of Uige at Kikaya. The work progressed until the outbreak of the Angolan revolution in 1961, when churches, schools, and other buildings were destroyed and many pastors and church members were killed. After independence (1975) the church began to rebuild itself only to face another 15 years of war. In 1978 the church established the Biblical Institute at Sanza Pombo.

Mozambique. There are six churches in Mozambique that come out of the Reformed tradition. The first Protestants to work in the country were native Mozambicans who brought the gospel from neighboring countries. From 1880 the ABCFM was active in the southern part of Mozambique at Cambine (1883) and Chicuque (1890). This work led to the formation of the United Congregational Church in Mozambique, which in 1967 became a member of the United Congregational Church in Southern Africa.

The Swiss mission in South Africa sent one of its converts, the evangelist Josefa Mhalamhala, who began work in Mozambique in 1882. The mission was formally established in 1887 at Ricatla by **Paul Berthoud** and **Henri Junod** (arrived 1889). This mission evolved into the Presbyterian Church of Mozambique, which became autonomous in 1962 and achieved complete independence in 1970.

Other Reformed churches include the United Church of Christ in Mozambique, which grew out of the work of ABCFM missionary F. R. Bunker, Swiss missionary Pierre Loze, and pastor Guilherme Tapera Nkomo beginning in the 1890s; the Evangelical Church of Christ, which grew out of the work of Scottish missionary James Reid in 1912; the Reformed Church of Mozambique, begun in 1909 by South African Dutch Reformed missionary A. G. Murray; and the Evangelical Church of the Good Shepherd, founded in 1965 by Dutch Reformed minister Fernando Moisés Magaia.

Reformed Christians suffered persecution under colonial rule and during the years of civil war from 1975 (independence) until 1992. Eduardo Mondlane, who founded the Front for the Liberation of Mozambique, was a member of the Presbyterian church and his pastor Zedequias Manganhela, president of the denomination, was arrested and died in prison. Since independence, Reformed churches have carried out evangelization programs, built schools and hospitals, and sponsored agricultural projects. The United Seminary at Ricatla serves the Reformed churches and other Protestant communities in Mozambique. The Reformed churches have also established several Bible schools and a Presbyterian lay training school at Khovo.

SOUTHERN ASIA. The people of southern Asia practice Islam, Buddhism, Hinduism, and Christianity. Islam is the primary religion of Pakistan (97 percent) and Bangladesh (88 percent); Buddhism predominates in Sri Lanka (69 percent) and Myanmar (89 percent); and Hinduism is the majority religion in India (83 percent) and Nepal (90 percent). Christianity is a minority religion with a presence in Sri Lanka (8 percent), Myanmar (5 percent), and India (2 percent); Pakistan and Nepal have Christian populations of less than 1 percent. In each of these countries there are communities of Reformed churches.

The establishment of Reformed churches in southern Asia followed the labors of missionaries such as **William Carey** and **Adoniram Judson** beginning in 1793. During the 19th century, India and Pakistan were being assimilated into the British Indian Empire; Sri Lanka (Ceylon) was subject to the colonial government of the **Netherlands** and **Great Britain**; and Myanmar (Burma) was also being explored and exploited by the British. In this region Christian missionaries faced opposition from other religions: Hinduism, Islam, and Buddhism. In the 20th century, there has been evidence of the coming to maturity of the Reformed churches, often planted at great sacrifice.

India. Reformed Protestantism was first carried to India during the 17th century by the Dutch. Preacher Abraham Rogerius arrived in 1630, but Dutch influence was never established. At the behest of the Danish king, German Lutheran missionaries Bartholomäus Ziegenbalg (1683–1719) and Heinrich Plütschau (1678–1747) arrived at Tranquebar in 1706. British missionaries under the Society for Promoting Christian Knowledge (SPCK) expanded the Danish work and by 1714 the New Testament had been translated into Tamil. European mission zeal in India then ebbed until the 18th century, when William Carey arrived in Bengal (1793) and Nathaniel Forsyth was sent by the **London Missionary Society** (1798).

From 1813, with the revision of the East India Company's charter, **mission** across the Indian subcontinent by European and North American agencies steadily expanded. In addition to the Scottish work (sponsored by the **Scottish Missionary Society**, the Church of Scotland, and the Free Church of Scotland), the **Evangelical Mission Society in Basel** established a presence on the west coast of India, American Congregationalists began work in Mathurai (1834), English Congregationalists in Bellary, and Irish Presbyterians in Gujarat (1841). Notable was the work of Presbyterian and Reformed missionaries **W. T. Ringeltaube** in Travancore, **Alexander Duff** in Calcutta, and **John Wilson** in Bombay. The Reformed emphasis on **education** was reflected in Duff's founding of the Scotch Mission School in Calcutta (1830), in Wilson's inauguration of Bombay College (1835), and in the founding of St. Andrew's School in Madras (1837). Many prominent Indian Christians, such as **Lal Behari Day** and K. M. Banerjea, were educated at these schools.

When the British government took over administrative responsibility for India from the East India Company in 1858, missionary outreach was extended even more vigorously. Several **women** missionaries, among them **Ida Scudder**, **Sara Seward**, and **Marion Fairweather**, began to play a major role in mission. Many hospitals and schools were established, including Christian Medical College Hospital in Vellore, United Theological College in Bangalore, and the Agricultural Institute at Katpadi in Vellore. Mission efforts began to focus on the aboriginal and animistic peoples as well as the Dalits, the people in the lowest **caste** of Indian society. The **Sepoy Mutiny** (1857–1858) and criticism by Indian converts such as Lal Behari Day began in the second half of the 19th century to raise questions about the indigenization of Indian Christianity and the Western control of the churches. *See also* Dalit Theology

The difficulty of Christian mission in India, especially with growing religious resistance and the gradual emergence of nationalist pressure, was compounded by the enormous diversity of Christian movements and churches. Reformed Christians were early advocates of Protestant church union: in 1901 three Presbyterian missions merged to become the South India United Church; in 1908 this union was expanded to include the Congregationalists. A movement of church union was also at work in north India. In 1924 Congregationalists and Presbyterians formed the United Church of North India. Later, other Protestant denominations joined these united churches to form the Church of South India (1947) and the Church of North India (1970). Discussions are under way to unite the two churches into a single Indian church. The evangelistic outreach of these churches continues, especially among the Dalits.

The Reformed church tradition in northeast India has a very different history from that of the rest of the country. The people of this region, which was annexed in 1826, are predominately Christian and have not historically identified themselves as Indian. In 1841 Welsh Calvinistic Methodists (later Presbyterians) began work in the Khasi and Jaintia hills areas of northeast India (now part of Meghalaya). Welsh Presbyterian missionary Thomas Jones introduced the Roman script. Schools were founded, the Bible was translated, and churches were organized. In 1867 Khasi **presbytery** was formed, and by 1896 five presbyteries were organized into the Khasi Jaintia Presbyterian Synod. After 1873 the Indian government's control of mission work in the northeast favored the already established Presbyterians. Reformed Christianity expanded further and new synods were organized, including the Mizo Synod, the Cachar Hill Tribes Synod, and the Manipur Synod. In 1972 the Presbyterian synods united to form the Presbyterian Church in Northeast India.

Pakistan and Bangladesh. Reformed Christianity in the predominantly Muslim areas that became Pakistan (1947) and Bangladesh (1970) has struggled with the religious dominance of Islam, church division, and repressive government policies. American Presbyterians began their work at Lahore (1849) and founded several schools, including Gujranwala Theological Seminary (1877). The Presbyterians concentrated their efforts among the "scheduled castes" (the untouchables). Two churches emerged from this work, the United Presbyterian Church of Pakistan and the United Church in Pakistan: Lahore Christian Council. Their successors united in 1992 to form the Presbyterian Church in Pakistan. The smaller Associate Reformed Presbyterian Church was founded in 1906. These four Presbyterian bodies remain outside the Protestant union that created the Church of Pakistan in 1970. The Church of Pakistan is the largest Protestant denomination in the country, incorporating the Scottish Presbyterian mission. The united church retains some aspects of Presbyterian polity. The Protestant churches in Pakistan were profoundly weakened when the Muslim government expropriated their schools and institutions in 1972; steps are now being taken to restore these institutions to the churches.

There are two churches in Bangladesh with Reformed roots. The Church of Bangladesh (1970) grew out of the century-long labors of the

Church Missionary Society, the Oxford Mission to Calcutta, and the English Presbyterian Society. The church sponsors youth homes, medical facilities, and primary schools. Welsh Presbyterian activity led to the founding of the small Church of Sylhet.

Sri Lanka. Dutch colonialists brought Reformed Christianity to Ceylon in 1642. Its initial growth was prodigious, but when the British replaced the Dutch (1796), their mission's influence gradually waned. The church continues today as the Dutch Reformed Church in Ceylon (Presbytery of Ceylon); it was weakened in 1953 by the withdrawal of the Presbytery of Lanka over doctrinal issues.

In 1816 American Congregationalists began work on the Jaffna Peninsula among the Tamils. They founded Jaffna College (1823) and organized the Congregational Church in Ceylon. In 1947 the church became the Jaffna diocese of the Church of South India.

Myanmar. The British annexed the ethnically diverse country of Burma in 1886; it gained its independence in 1948. The Christian presence in Myanmar goes back to the work of Adoniram Judson (1813), but Christianity has grown slowly in a land with a strong and articulate Buddhist tradition. In 1962 the government assumed control of all Protestant schools, and in 1966 Western missionaries were asked to leave the country. Even before this period, the churches of Myanmar were developing into indigenous bodies.

Small Protestant churches have emerged among the non-Burmese peoples, especially the Karens. The largest Reformed communities are the Independent Church of Burma (1938) and the Presbyterian Church of Burma (1954). The Presbyterian Church was begun by Lushais, an immigrant people from Assam, India, who went to Burma after World War II and settled in the mountainous Chin State and adjacent areas. The church has since expanded to other parts of the country and operates a printing press as well as Tahan Theological College at Tahan. Another small church, the Mara Evangelical Church, was founded in 1907 by Congregationalist missionary **Reginald A. Lorrain.** Church membership is concentrated in Chin State and Rakhine State. **T. Mathao** was an important leader in this church.

Nepal. Christian missionary work in Nepal has only been possible since the 1950s because the country, which is constitutionally a Hindu state, prohibits proselytization. As a result of contacts between Nepalis and Christian neighbors in northeastern India, at least two churches have been formed. The Evangelical Christian Fellowship and the Nepal Church Fellowship are indigenous churches supported by North American Presbyterians. The United Mission in Nepal (1954) is an ecumenical agency that combines the efforts of many organizations, including Reformed groups, in social, **health**, and educational projects, with official government endorsement.

SOUTHERN CONE OF SOUTH AMERICA. Argentina, Chile, Paraguay, and Uruguay form the southern cone of South America. The Roman Catholic Church has dominated the religious life of the region. Controlled by the Spanish government, the Catholic Church provided the **education, health** care, and social welfare that was available. In all four countries immigrants from Europe played an important role in shaping modern cultural, political, and religious life. The descendants of these Europeans today constitute the majority of the population.

After the wars for independence (1810–1818), the legislative assemblies of Argentina and Chile adopted constitutions that granted official standing to the Catholic Church. The Liberal Parties gained control of the legislatures in the 1820s and worked to break up the old regime of Spanish hegemony and open the countries to free trade and modernization. The ports of Buenos Aires, Montevideo, and Valparaiso welcomed ships and traders from **Great Britain, Holland, France**, the **United States**, and other nations. With these commercial openings came the beginnings of the Protestant presence.

Protestant growth in the 19th century came by way of a Bible salesman, foreign Protestant residents (whose worship in foreign languages was tolerated), and later by a slowly growing atmosphere of religious liberty. In the early postindependence years, as the governments of Argentina and Chile attempted to modernize their countries, they welcomed Baptist missionary James Thomson, an agent of the British and Foreign Bible Society. Thomson distributed Bibles and began schools and literacy programs. His work in Buenos Aires (1818–1821) and Chile (1821–1822) was so successful that both governments granted him honorary citizenship. In the following decades many more Protestants arrived among the thousands of European immigrants. By the second half of the century Protestant Spanish-speaking congregations were allowed.

In the 1970s and early 1980s under military dictatorships in the Southern Cone, the Protestant churches struggled to find an authentic witness. Today Pentecostal churches outnumber Reformed churches, but the Reformed movement is vigorous and growing.

Argentina and Paraguay. German immigrants from Prussia began the Evangelical Church of the River Plate (Iglesia Evangélica del Rio de la Plata). Before emigrating, they had been a part of a Lutheran-Reformed union in 1817, called the Protestant Church of Old Prussia. Their first congregations appeared in Buenos Aires in 1843, Montevideo in 1846, and Asunción (Paraguay) in 1899. The arrival of additional immigrants led to the organization in 1899 of the German Evangelical Synod of the River Plate. For many decades the congregations remained transplanted enclaves of the German language, culture, and loyalties; however, following World War II, they increasingly identified with the Latin American people and cultures, and by 1965 they used the Spanish language and had changed their name to the Evangelical Church of the River Plate. The church established ecumenical ties with other Spanish-speaking Protestant churches for theological **education**, publication, social services, and other activities. In the 1990s the church numbered 45,000 members. **Rodolfo Obermüller** was an important scholar and church leader.

Other immigrants to Argentina who came from Germany and from the Volga region in Russia established the Evangelical Congregational Church in 1870. The denomination was formally organized in 1924 with its center in Concordia, north of Buenos Aires. The seminary, in Urdinarrain, emphasizes a conservative, spiritually disciplined life. The church counts about 5,500 communicants and belongs to the **World Council of Churches** and other regional ecumenical bodies.

Immigrants came to Argentina from the **Netherlands** and **South Africa** between 1889 and 1908. The Dutch organized congregations in Buenos Aires, Rosario, and Tres Arroyos while the South Africans established themselves in the province of Chubut. These churches organized the Synod of the Reformed Churches in Argentina (1961). During its formative years the synod was supported by the Reformed Church in the Netherlands; after 1958, support came from the Christian Reformed Church in the United States. The church uses the Spanish language and cooperates with other Protestant churches in theological **education** and various dimensions of church life and **mission**. It is a founder of the Argentina Bible Society and the Argentina Federation of Evangelical Churches. The church also participates in the Ecumenical Movement for Human Rights (MEDH). In the 1990s the synod consisted of 13 congregations with about 500 members. **Antonie C. Sonneveldt** and **Cornelis L. Slebos** were important church leaders.

The Waldensian Evangelical Church of the River Plate also has a presence in Argentina, although about 75 percent of its membership is located in Uruguay (discussed later).

Protestant immigrants from countries such as **Hungary**, **Scotland**, **Switzerland**, France, and Armenia also organized clusters of Reformed congregations. These small churches (under 1,700 members each), in order to increase cooperation and effectiveness, organized themselves into the Association of Reformed Churches.

Chile. The founder of the Evangelical Presbyterian Church in Chile, **David Trumbull,** was one of the early English-speaking settlers. This Congregationalist from the United States, later supported by the Presbyterian Church, U.S.A., began his ministry in 1845 among English-speaking seamen on British, American, and other ships at the port of Valparaiso. He began with **worship** services onboard these vessels and in 1847 established a Union Church for seamen and foreign residents of Valparaiso. Later he published Protestant newspapers and organized a Bible Society. In 1864 Protestants gained official toleration for public worship in Chile. In 1868 the first Spanish-language Protestant congregation was organized in Santiago and became the foundation of the Presbyterian Church of Chile. The church maintains a hospital, several schools, and social service centers. In 1964 it gained full ecclesiastical autonomy and membership in the **World Alliance of Reformed Churches.** By the 1990s, it had a membership of 1,250.

Uruguay. Most of the population is descended from Spanish and Italian forebears. Though the majority are nominally Roman Catholic, the country has a long history of anticlericalism, and the Catholic Church is not strong. Religious toleration came with the constitution of 1830, and full separation of **church and state** was declared in 1918. Many people from the Waldensian Evangelical Church of Italy were among the immigrants to Uruguay. In 1858 they formed a transplanted "district" of their home church. Over the decades, the Latin American **Waldensians** organized themselves into an independent synod with the name Waldensian Evangelical Church of the River Plate. With about 25 congregations, the church uses only the Spanish language, takes a leadership role in ecumenical cooperation, trains ministers at the Protestant Higher Institute of Theological Studies in Buenos Aires, and counts a membership of about 3,000.

SOUTHERN EUROPE. Although in some countries religious practice is minimal, the people of southern Europe are affiliated with Christian churches. Four countries are predominantly Roman Catholic: France (81 percent), Italy (99 percent), Portugal (97 percent), and Spain (99 percent); Greece is Greek Orthodox (98 percent); and Switzerland is evenly divided between Roman Catholics (49 percent) and Reformed Protestants (48 percent). In addition to their historic roots in Switzerland, Reformed church communities are found in each of these southern European countries.

France. The Reformed Church in France (RCF; Eglise Réformée de France) originated in 1520 and held its first national synod in 1559. It was inspired by **John Calvin, Martin Bucer,** and other Protestant reformers; was united by its confession of **faith,** the Confession of La Rochelle (1559); and was protected by **Margaret of Angoulême** and **Jeanne d'Albret.** The **Colloquy of Poissy** (1561) failed to resolve Protestant-Catholic differences, and French Protestants, led by **Gaspard de Coligny** and **Philippe de Mornay,** faced severe persecution during the **Wars of Religion** of the next decades and afterward. The **Saint Bartholomew's Day Massacres** (1572) were among the more infamous persecutions, claiming the life of Coligny and French composer **Claude Goudimel.** Protestant resistance as a religious minority in France came to an end at the fall of La Rochelle (1628). When Louis XIV revoked the **Edict of Nantes** in 1685, more than 250,000 French Protestants or **Huguenots** fled to **England, Holland, Germany,** and the **United States.** The French Revolution (1789) finally brought religious toleration to France.

During the 19th century an **evangelical** revival **(Réveil)** increased church membership and strengthened its **mission** and social work. In 1848 the Reformed church convened its second national synod. However, government support of the church caused an evangelical group to withdraw. In 1905 the French government ceased to support the Reformed Church, and in 1938 the church reunited with the Evangelical Synod. Today the church maintains strong ecumenical ties with the Roman Catholic Church in France as well as with other Reformed churches in surrounding countries. It numbers approximately 180,000 members in 350 parishes and is a member of the **World Alliance of Reformed Churches** (WARC).

The Reformed Church of Alsace and Lorraine originated in the 16th century. Its churches are spread through the region of the Rhine and Moselle Rivers. When the region was annexed in 1648 by France, the Alsace-Lorraine Reformed Church, because of its separate history, remained distinct from the French Reformed Church. Its members constitute a minority among French Protestants. The church is composed of approximately 50 churches and 33,000 members and is a member of the WARC. In Alsace-Lorraine, Reformed ministers are paid by the government; this has created a long-standing theological controversy over **church** and state relations.

French Reformed theologians and church leaders include **Marc Boegner, Jacques Ellul, Jean Daillé, Suzanne de Diétrich,** and **Pierre Maury.**

Greece. The Greek Evangelical Church (Helleniki Evangeliki Ekklesia) traces its history to the work of D. Jonas King of the **American Board of Commissioners for Foreign Missions**, who went to Greece in 1828. King's work made an impression on Michael Kalopathakis, a physician, who went on to study at **Union Theological Seminary** (New York), returned to Greece as a Protestant missionary, and founded the church's first congregation (1858). Similar mission work in 1815 caused the growth of Protestantism among the Greek people in Turkey. After the Greek invasion of Turkey (1922), members of these congregations fled and sought refuge in Greece. These refugees helped form the Evangelical Church, the only Protestant church in Greece, which now has 34 congregations and 5,000 members. The church's **general assembly** meets every two years. Heavy emphasis is placed on Sunday schools and youth work.

Italy. The Italian Reformed tradition is represented by the Waldensian Evangelical Church of Italy. A small Reformed church centered primarily in the Piedmont or Italian side of the Alps, the denomination has congregations in Turin, Florence, and Rome. The Waldensian church traces its roots to 12th-century French reformer Peter Waldo, a lay preacher from Lyons, who rejected the theological excesses of medieval Catholicism, including prayers for the dead, purgatory, indulgences, veneration of images, and the sacramental doctrine of transubstantiation. Waldo and his followers were excommunicated by the Council of Verona (1184) and Waldensians were then persecuted; by the 13th century only a few groups remained in isolated areas of the Alps. *See also* Southern Cone of South America

In 1526 the Waldensians received **William Farel** and other reformed pastors and became part of the Reformed movement. Although many Waldensian churches did not survive the Counter-Reformation and the persecutions of 1655 and 1686–1689, those in the Italian Alps persisted. A revival took place in the 1820s, strengthening the churches, and in 1848 a declaration by King Carol Alberto established religious freedom in Italy. In 1855 a theological college was organized at Torre Pellice (near Turin) and the church later added a publishing house, Claudiana, and social agencies. In 1979 the church federated with the Italian Methodist Church; each group maintains its own international connections and denominational ties, as well as some administrative agencies. The Waldensian Church has produced several prominent scholars and church leaders, including **Matteo Prochet**, president of the Board of Evangelism; **Emilio Comba**, professor of church history and Waldensian scholar; **Giovanni**

Luzzi, Bible translator and commentator; **Giovanni Miegge**, professor and theologian; and **Augusto Armand Hugon**, lay leader, historian, and mayor of the city of Torre Pellice.

Portugal. The Reformed tradition was first established in Portugal by a Scottish physician, **Robert Kalley**, who founded a small hospital and school and began mission work on the Portuguese island of Madeira (1838). After some local residents burned Kalley's home, Portuguese Protestants dispersed to **Brazil** and other countries.

During the 1940s missionaries arrived in Portugal from Brazil and organized the Presbyterian Church of Lisbon. With aid and administrative help from Presbyterian churches in the United States, the church began to grow. The first Synod of the Evangelical Presbyterian Church of Portugal (Igreja Evangélica Presbiteriana do Portugal) met in Lisbon (1952). The church has approximately 1,300 members in 22 congregations, and it operates the Evangelical Theological Seminary and St. Luke's Presbyterian Hospital in Lisbon.

Spain. The 16th-century Reformed movement did not establish itself in Spain, which was under the Inquisition. Only Spanish Protestants living outside the country were able to use Spanish-language **Bible translations** (1478; Basel, 1569) and translations of the **Heidelberg Catechism** and John Calvin's *Institutes.*

Religious toleration in Spain came after the Spanish Revolution (1868). The following year the Spanish Christian Church was born. Its first general assembly met in Seville (1872), and in 1874 the church changed its name to the Spanish Evangelical Church (Iglesia Evangélica Española). A union church, the denomination is composed of Presbyterians, Methodists, Congregationalists, and Lutherans. In 1980 the church gained official governmental recognition for the first time. The church, which has more than 2,700 members, emphasizes Christian **education**, **evangelism**, and ecumenical cooperation with other Protestant bodies.

Switzerland. Swiss Protestant churches grew from the 16th-century Reformation led by **John Calvin**, **William Farel**, and **Théodore Beza** in Geneva and **Huldrych Zwingli** and **Heinrich Bullinger** in Zurich. The Reformation spread through Reformed preaching, the academy founded in Geneva by Calvin in 1559, and the publications of printers such as **Jean Crespin.** Calvinist churches were formed in French-speaking areas, and Zwinglian churches in German-speaking areas. A major source of unity among the Swiss churches was the Second Helvetic Confession (1566), written by Heinrich Bullinger.

Because Protestant churches are based in the Swiss cantons, there is no national Reformed church in Switzerland. The Protestant churches vary in legal status: some are independent, some are state churches, and some have concordat relationships with the state. The churches are diverse in their church constitutions, liturgies, and teaching materials. Most cantonal churches are governed by the synod as a legislative body.

In 1920, a Federation of Swiss Protestant Churches (Schweizerischer Evangelischer Kirchenbund; Fédération des Eglises protestantes de Suisse) was organized. It was initially composed of national churches, the Methodist Church, and the Protestant Association (Evangelische Gemeinschaft). Its constitution was revised in 1950. The federation is divided into various departments and is characterized by a strong concern for **human rights** and religious liberty, social justice, and peace.

The Swiss churches have produced Bible scholars and theologians, including **Karl Barth, Emil Brunner, Johann Jakob Hesse, Adolf Schlatter, Alexander Schweizer**, and **Francis Turretin**; missionaries **Paul Berthoud** and **Henri A. Junod**; and church leader **Adolf Keller.**

SOVEREIGNTY OF GOD. A doctrine of **Calvinism** that emphasizes the power and purpose of **God.** The doctrine stresses God's ultimacy and primacy over all things and considers the being and will of God supreme realities. In biblical terms "sovereignty" refers to God's "lordship" (Eph. 1:11; Rev. 4:11). God's will is supreme in electing human beings to **salvation**, willing events and actions, directing the course of history, and sustaining and governing the universe **(providence).** Some recent Reformed theologians such as Jürgen Moltmann (b. 1928) have considered God's sovereignty in relation to **Christology.** God's supreme and ultimate purposes are known in and through Jesus Christ, who offered his life in self-giving service (Phil. 2:5–8). Thus sovereignty is not to be perceived in terms of power but rather in being able to effect the divine will by way of love and humility, as conveyed in the person of Jesus. Sovereignty is particularly related to the doctrines of providence, **election**, and **predestination.**

SPAIN. *See* SOUTHERN EUROPE

SPEER, ROBERT E. (1867–1947). American Presbyterian lay leader and a central figure in the American missionary movement. Speer was born in Huntingdon, Pennsylvania, and graduated from Princeton University in 1889. He studied at **Princeton Theological Seminary** for one year (1890–1891), and then became secretary of the Board of Foreign Missions of the Presbyterian Church in the U.S.A. and served from 1891 to 1937. Speer quickly became a leader of the Protestant **mission** movement. He was chair of the Committee on Cooperation in Latin America (1916–1937) and participated in international conferences in Edinburgh, Geneva, Jerusalem, and Madras. A talented speaker, he traveled widely in **Asia** and **Latin America.** Speer urged cooperative efforts in all phases of Protestant mission. Although his views were criticized by **J. Gresham Machen,** he remained resolute in carrying out his program. He believed that the missionary purpose was to "present Christ to the world" and expounded his views in *The Finality of Jesus Christ* (1933). Speer worked to increase missionary funding within the Presbyterian Church. He served as **moderator** of its **general assembly** in 1927 and wrote 67 books, including many works on mission.

SPIRITUALITY. The transforming power of God's Spirit in the Christian life. Related Protestant terms are piety, godliness, and spiritual formation. Reformed spirituality has been influenced by the writings of **John Calvin** and other Protestant reformers, and by **Puritanism,** pietism, movements of religious **revival,** and ecumenical dialogue. Spirituality concerns the doctrine of **sanctification** and the forms and practices followed to enhance communion with **God** and Christian discipleship. The Reformed **tradition** emphasizes the activity of the **Holy Spirit** and the spiritual union of the believer with Christ (*Inst.* 4.17.10). Of equal importance are the various means of **grace** through which growth in **faith** and service may occur. These means include participation in **worship,** the **sacraments, prayer,** and Bible study. The social dimension of spirituality is also stressed, including simplicity of life, submission to one another in love, and service to those in need. Christian activism is recognized as naturally inherent in Christian faith. Personal experiences of grace and **salvation** are ultimately inseparable from corporate connections with **church,** society, and culture. A complete Reformed spirituality is theologically grounded and personally and socially expressed.

SRI LANKA. *See* SOUTHERN ASIA

STEVENSON, MARION SCOTT (d. 1930). Scottish missionary and educator in **Kenya.** Arriving in Kenya in 1907, Stevenson worked at the Scottish Kikuyu Mission, where she operated a school for girls and worked in the **mission** hospital. In 1910 she went to the Scottish station at Tumutumu and remained there for 20 years. She taught school, educated Kenyan teachers who worked in the Nyeri area around Mt. Kenya, wrote Gikuyu language books for her students, and assisted with

Bible translation. She believed that **education** would bring an end to **colonialism.**

STEWARDSHIP. A biblical concept that refers to the responsibility and accountability of individuals for the management of another's property. Theologically, the term relates to both human responsibility for **creation** (the creation command, Gen. 1:28; 2:15) and to the entrusting of the gospel to the **church** as its **mission** (1 Cor. 4:1–2). With the disestablishment of Western churches and their loss of state support, stewardship re-emerged as a theological motif to guide patterns of church funding and involvement (tithing, pledging, voluntarism). The crises of modern civilization (economic injustice, war, ecological disaster) have stimulated a theological broadening of the understanding of stewardship toward a fuller understanding of the human calling to witness to God's rule in every arena of life. Reformed theologian Douglas John Hall proposes stewardship as a primary biblical metaphor for Christian **faith** and action. The **World Council of Churches** made it a central emphasis in its study of "Justice, Peace, and the Integrity of Creation" (since 1983).

STEWART, JAMES (1831–1905). Scottish missionary and educator in **South Africa.** Born in Edinburgh, Stewart was educated at the University of Edinburgh (1854–1861), where he studied theology and **medicine.** After a brief trip to Africa where he was part of **David Livingstone's** Zambezi expedition (1862–1864), he returned to Edinburgh to complete his medical degree (1866). He went to Cape Colony and joined the staff of **Lovedale** Institute, becoming principal in 1870. He was an advocate of racial equality, expressing his views in a newspaper he founded in 1870. In his book *Lovedale: Past and Present* (1884), he documented the careers of the African students who had attended the school. He was instrumental in the founding of the Livingstonia Mission in **Malawi** and the Kikuyu Mission in **Kenya.**

STEWART, JAMES STUART (1896–1990). Scottish preacher. Born in Dundee, Stewart was educated at the University of St. Andrews. He served in the military during World War I, before completing his education at **New College, Edinburgh** (1918–1921), and the University of Bonn (1921–1922). Stewart served three churches in **Scotland** (1924–1946) and was professor of New Testament at the University of Edinburgh (1947–1966). His publications include a translation of Friedrich Schleiermacher's *The Christian Faith* (1928), *A Man in Christ: The Vital Elements of St. Paul's Religion* (1935), and *A Faith to Proclaim* (1953). An eloquent preacher, Stewart published his sermons in several volumes, including *The Wind of the Spirit* (1968). He was elected **moderator** of the General Assembly of the Church of Scotland (1963–1964).

STOWE, HARRIET BEECHER (1811–1896). American Congregationalist writer. The daughter of **Lyman Beecher**, Harriet Beecher Stowe was born in Litchfield, Connecticut. She attended girls' schools in Litchfield and Hartford before becoming a teacher at the Western Female Institute. She moved to Cincinnati in 1832 when her father became president of Lane Seminary. In 1836 she married Calvin Ellis Stowe, a minister and professor at the school. She lived on the border of slave-holding territory for 18 years and sheltered fugitive slaves in her home.

After moving to Brunswick, Maine, in 1850, Stowe drew on her experiences to write *Uncle Tom's Cabin, or Life among the Lowly* (1852), one of the most popular and controversial works ever written in the **United States.** Abraham Lincoln said her book began the Civil War. Ten thousand copies were sold in a week. The work stirred antislavery sentiment and galvanized public opinion. During the next 30 years, Stowe wrote nearly one book per year. Many of her works convey spiritual themes and the conviction that America is "consecrated" to righteousness. She was especially influenced by **Cotton Mather's** *Magnalia.* Among Stowe's writings are *The Mayflower* (1843), *The Minister's Wooing* (1859), *Religious Poems* (1867), *Oldtown Folks* (1869), and *Poganuc People* (1878).

ST. PAUL'S UNITED THEOLOGICAL COLLEGE. A united theological college located in Limuru, **Kenya.** Founded in 1903 in Freretown, Mombasa, by the Church Missionary Society, the school was moved to Limuru in 1930. In 1949 the Presbyterians and Methodists joined the Anglicans in operating the college. During this period there were two principals, one Anglican and one Presbyterian. In 1954 a college council was formed to govern the school, and in 1955 the new school was formally established. In 1973 the Reformed Church of East Africa joined in sponsorship of the school. Students and staff are drawn from many nations, races, and denominations.

STUART, JOHN LEIGHTON (1876–1962). American Presbyterian missionary, educator, and ambassador to **China.** Born in Hangzhou, China, the son of American missionaries, Stuart was educated at Hampden-Sydney College and **Union Theological Seminary** in Virginia. He worked for the Executive Committee of Foreign Missions of the Presbyterian Church in the United States, and in 1904 he was sent to Hangchow. After 10 years of evangelistic work, Stuart became professor of New Testament at Nanking Theological Seminary and published the *Greek-Chinese-English Dictionary of the New Testament* (1918). In 1919 he was appointed president of Yenching University, Beijing, the most influential of the Protestant-supported universities. He kept the university open during the Sino-Japanese war and the Japanese occupation, and he served as a mediator between the Japanese and Chinese. He sought to influence the U.S. government to support Chinese interests while averting hostilities. President Truman appointed him ambassador to the Republic of China (1946); he attempted unsuccessfully to mediate between the Nationalist and Communist political parties in China. Stuart served as ambassador through the communist takeover (1949), when Mao Tse-Tung came to power and the Western missionaries were expelled from China.

SUDAN. *See* EAST AFRICA

SULEEMAN, CLEMENT (LEE SIAN HUI) (1919–1988). Indonesian Chinese theological educator. As a young man Suleeman studied **medicine**, and after World War II he went to Jakarta Theological Seminary and then studied Christian **education** at **Princeton Theological Seminary.** He returned to **Indonesia** to become **moderator** of the Indonesian Christian Church in West Java. Suleeman introduced the subject of Christian education throughout Indonesia, chairing the Christian Education Committee of the National Council of Churches. He promoted church union in East Java, and his work led to the union of several churches.

SUNG THEOLOGY. An indigenous Korean theology rooted in Confucian philosophy, especially as formulated by Korean philosopher Yul Gok (1536–1584). The term "Sung" combines the Chinese characters for "logos" (word) and "fulfillment" and means "fulfillment of the word," "sincerity," or "integrity." Contemporary Methodist theologian Sung Bum Yun, who developed Sung theology, proposed that the gospel be indigenized in Korean culture by interpreting it on the basis of Confucian thought rather than Old Testament biblical **revelation.** The logos assumed to be already present in Confucian philosophy is now linked and reinterpreted with the Christ-logos; Christ is said to have been present from the beginning in Confucian thought. Korean Reformed response has been mixed. Many theologians have rejected Sung theology as unorthodox; others have sought to indigenize Christian theology through the exposition of the gospel's social implications in Korean culture; some of these have received Sung theology favorably. *See also* Minjung Theology

SUTNGA, KHNONG (1850–1986). Indian Presbyterian minister and educator. Born at Shangpung village in Jaintia Hills, Meghalaya, in northeast **India**, Sutnga attended a school opened by Welsh missionary Thomas Jones and became one of the first Christians in the village. He continued his **education** at the Teacher's Training School in Sohra (Cherrapunji), graduating in 1878. He remained at the school and taught for 17 years. He attended theology classes in the evening and was ordained in 1899. While continuing to teach at the Training School, Sutnga served four churches in the Sohra area. In 1907 he was relieved of his teaching responsibilities and became the pastor of 16 congregations. Five years later he was transferred to another area to serve 12 congregations. The educational and pastoral work of Sutnga laid the foundation of the Presbyterian Church in northeast India.

SWAZILAND. *See* SOUTHERN AFRICA

SWEDEN. *See* NORTHERN EUROPE

SWITZERLAND. *See* SOUTHERN EUROPE

SYRIA. *See* MIDDLE EAST

SZAMOTUL, WACLAW Z (ca. 1524–1560). Polish composer. Born in Szamotuly near Poznań, Szamotul was educated at Lubranscian College in Pozna and at Kraków University. After serving as secretary to the governor of Troki, **Lithuania** (1545–1547), he was appointed composer to Sigismund II August. For three years Szamotul provided **music** for the chapel choir, and in 1550 he became involved in the Protestant movement. By 1555 he was working at the court of Mikolaj Radziwill, a Calvinist Lithuanian, where he remained until his death. He composed sacred polyphony and developed Polish a cappella music during the 1550s. Although much of his music is lost, seven pieces for Protestant **worship** survive.

- T -

TAHITI. *See* PACIFIC OCEAN ISLANDS

TAIWAN. *See* EAST ASIA

TAKAHASHI, HISANO (1871–1944). Japanese Presbyterian minister and evangelist. Born on Sado Island off Niigata, Takahashi studied in Tokyo. During her student years she was influenced by the sermons of **Masahisa Uemura** and received **baptism** upon her graduation in 1892. She then returned to Sado Island, where she became a schoolteacher and married. When her husband died, Takahashi moved to Tokyo to teach at Aoyama Girl's High School. She was active in evangelistic work throughout Japan and was instrumental in organizing several churches. At 40 years of age she enrolled at Tokyo Theological Seminary and graduated in 1913. She became an evangelist at Fujimicho Church and was ordained in 1932, at 62 years of age, and went to serve Sado Church. Takahashi was the first woman to be ordained in Japan.

TAKAKURA, TOKUTARO (1885–1934). Japanese Presbyterian minister, professor, and president of Japan Theological Seminary. Takakura was educated at Tokyo University and Tokyo Theological Seminary, graduating in 1910. He was ordained in 1912 and served churches in Kyoto and Sapporo. Takakura was appointed professor of theology at Tokyo Theological Seminary in 1918. From 1921 to 1924 he studied at **New College, Edinburgh**, and at Oxford and Cambridge, being particularly influenced by the work of **P. T. Forsyth.** After **Masahisa Uemura** died, he became president of Tokyo Theological Seminary (1925) and continued to teach systematic theology. In 1927, when another minister was elected over Takakura as pastor of Fujimicho Church, 100 church members withdrew and followed Takakura to the newly established Shinanomachi Church. In 1932 Takakura became president of Japan Theological Seminary, which later became **Tokyo Union Theological Seminary.** He is responsible for introducing the theology of **John Calvin** into **Japan**, and his thought continued to be influenced by Forsyth. His books include *Grace and Faithfulness* (1921); *Grace and Calling* (1925), a collection of sermons that present the Christian **faith**; and *Evangelical Christianity* (1927), a widely read book that reflects his mature theology.

TAKEMORI, MASAICHI (1907–1990). Japanese Presbyterian minister and professor and president of **Tokyo Union Theological Seminary.** Born in Manchuria, **China**, to Japanese parents, Takemori graduated from Manchuria Teacher's College (1931) and Nihon Theological Seminary (1936). He served as pastor of Shirakane Church (1936) and Kichijoji Church (1941). After serving as associate professor at Tokyo Union Seminary (1949) and earning a S.T.M. degree at **Union Theological Seminary** in New York (1950), Takemori was appointed professor at Tokyo Union Seminary (1950). Except for two years when he served as visiting professor at Western Theological Seminary in Michigan (1968) and the University of Heidelberg (1969), Takemori taught at the seminary. He served as its president from 1973 to 1979. His publications include the widely read *Introduction to the New Testament* (1958) and New Testament commentaries, including works on Acts (1965), 1 Peter (1983), 1 Corinthians (1985), 2 Corinthians (1988), Ephesians (1988), and Philippians (1990). Takemori translated into Japanese Hugh T. Kerr's abridgment of John Calvin's *Institutes*, titled *A Compendium of the Institution of the Christian Religion* (1958), and prepared a Japanese edition of the **Heidelberg Catechism** (1961). As an important member of the Calvin Translation Society (1960) Takemori encouraged the preparation of a new Japanese translation of Calvin's *Institutes*. The work was undertaken by Nobuo Watanabe and published in 1965.

TAYLOR, NATHANIEL WILLIAM (1786–1858). American Congregationalist minister and theologian. Taylor was born in New Milford, Connecticut, and graduated from Yale College in 1807. He studied theology under **Timothy Dwight** in New Haven from 1808 to 1812, became pastor of the First Congregational Church (1812–1822), and was appointed professor of didactic theology at Yale Divinity School (1822–1857). Taylor was the founder of the **New Haven theology**, which tried to modify traditional **Calvinism** to be more compatible with contemporary revivalism. He worked closely with **Lyman Beecher** in support of the Second **Great Awakening** and initiated a crusade against Sabbath breaking and drunkenness. Taylor spread his views through class lectures, articles in the *Quarterly Christian Spectator*, and published sermons.

Although he maintained the Christian concept of **sin,** Taylor also gave a place to the individual decision of **faith,** as fostered by the revivalist tradition. He believed that human sin, although inevitable, also carried with it the "power to the contrary." People may choose not to sin and possess the will to choose faith. His position held people morally responsible for their actions. Taylor's views originated in his concept of God's moral government of the universe rather than God's divine sovereignty (*Lectures on the Moral Government of God*, 2 vols. [1859]). Human nature is the locus for sin, but it does not preclude nonsinning. Sin is moral failure, that is, free human choice acting in wrong ways. Taylorism contributed to the Old School–New School schism that divided American **Presbyterianism. Charles Hodge** accused Taylor of Pelagianism and **Arminianism.** Taylor's theology was popularized by revivalists such as **Charles G. Finney** and was attractive to New School Presbyterians and Congregationalists who supported the revival movement.

TEMPERANCE MOVEMENT. Societies organized during the 19th century advocating abstinence and later legal restriction or prohibition of alcoholic beverages. The rise of the Temperance Movement coincided with widespread production of distilled liquors in Europe during the 18th century. Increased consumption heightened awareness of the adverse effects of drinking upon individual health and the strength of the social fabric. Significant temperance movements, often of religious origin, arose in **North America**, in the **British Isles**, and in **Denmark**. Scottish religious societies, for example, included the Personal Abstinence Society (1845), the Free Church Temperance Society (1849), and the Church of Scotland Temperance Society (1876). In 1913 the Scottish Temperance Act was passed in an attempt to restrict or prohibit liquor sales. When the act became effective in 1920, however, it was not welcomed by the voting public and failed in all but a few wards. American societies included the American Temperance Society (1826) and the Women's Christian Temperance Union (1874). The American experiment with prohibition lasted from the passage of the Eighteenth Amendment in 1920 to its repeal in 1933. Churches also struggled with issues of abstinence, to the point of controversy over the use of fermented or unfermented wine in Communion. Although the Temperance Movement waned during the late 20th century, Reformed churches have remained active in substance abuse counseling and rehabilitation programs for alcoholics.

TENG EK KHENG (1891–1981). Chinese Presbyterian minister in **China** and Singapore. Born in East Hweian, Fujian, China, Teng was educated at the theological academy in South Fujian, Gulangsu (Gulang-yu). Following graduation he returned to East Hweian and married in 1912. In 1913 Teng was invited to Amoy (Xiamen), where he served as a teacher for four years. He then became a preacher and teacher in Pho-lam. In 1927, when the Sino-Japanese War broke out, he returned to Hweian as pastor of the city church. Invited to the Lai-chhuo church at Gulangsu in 1950, Teng served as secretary and then clerk of Minnan Synod, to which he belonged for 40 years. In 1955 he went to Singapore and pastored several congregations. An authority on **church government** and constitutional questions, Teng was appointed chair of the Law and Constitution Committee of Singapore Synod, which drafted a church constitution after Singapore gained political independence from **Malaysia** in 1965.

THAILAND. *See* SOUTHEAST ASIA

THEOLOGICAL DECLARATION OF BARMEN (1934). A confession of **faith** unanimously adopted by 134 delegates at the Confessing Synod of the German Evangelical Church, held in Wuppertal-Barmen on May

29–31, 1934. The declaration, written largely by **Karl Barth**, opposed the German Christian Movement, the ideology of National Socialism, and Hitler's attempt to dominate the faith and life of the German church. The declaration was also the basis upon which the **Confessing Church** carried out the church struggle in Germany. The **Reformed Alliance** adopted the Theological Declaration of Barmen, and it is now considered one of the historic documents of the Reformed confessional tradition. The declaration continues to influence the writing of modern Reformed creeds and **confessions**. The declaration's six articles contain positive statements of scriptural teaching, affirming the **scriptures** as the unique **revelation** of **God** and declaring that Jesus Christ alone is Lord. The positive statements are followed by negative statements, repudiating any political intrusion that seeks to modify the church's gospel or usurp its **authority**.

THEOLOGICAL DECLARATION OF KOREAN CHRISTIANS (1973). A theological declaration formulated and circulated by a group of Korean ministers after South Korean president Park Chung Hee came to power (1972) and reorganized the government as a dictatorship. Reminiscent of the **Theological Declaration of Barmen**, the document confesses the authors' allegiance to **God**, their **vocation** as witness to the messianic rule of Christ, and their responsibility to speak out against injustice and oppression. The authors particularly emphasize their call to speak for and live among the oppressed and poor. They decry the regime as illegitimate, and they denounce its violation of **human rights** and its manipulation and exploitation of the public.

THEOLOGICAL METHOD. The ways of formulating Christian theology. The **authority** for Christian theology is derived from **scripture**, **tradition**, reason, and experience. Reformed theologians use these sources in the development of a theological method. During the Reformation period, theologians adopted the principle of scripture alone, and theological method took the form of *scriptural commentary,* both in **preaching** and theological exposition. John Calvin's *Institutes* (1559) is such an exposition, although it is based on the Apostles' Creed and draws heavily on the writings of Augustine and Chrysostom. During the 17th and 18th centuries, *Aristotelian syllogistic reasoning* was applied to theological exposition, resulting in the development of a Protestant scholasticism. The ensuing reaction of pietism and the work of **Friedrich Schleiermacher** produced a theological method that emphasized *religious experience.* The early part of the 20th century witnessed the emergence of **neoorthodoxy** as a reaction to theological **liberalism**. With its emphasis on the scriptures and *scriptural exegesis,* methodology had come full circle. The recent period has witnessed the emergence of a variety of new methods, including **liberation theology, feminist theologies,** and **narrative theology.**

THIRD WORLD. Term coined in 1961 by Franz Fanon to describe the colonized and underdeveloped countries of the world, drawn from the analogy of the Third Estate of the French Revolution. Peter Worsley (*The Third World,* 1967) defined the Third World as the attempt to find a third way to practice independence over against the capitalist First World (the United States and its allies) and the communist Second World (Soviet Empire). The churches that have emerged as a result of modern **mission** have come to be identified as Third World churches, although the term is frequently criticized as discriminatory. "Third World theologies" include black or African theologies, Asian theologies, and Latin American theologies, such as **liberation theology** and **Minjung theology.** The Ecumenical Association of Third World Theologians (EATWOT) emerged in 1976 and has continued as a major ecumenical force.

THIRTY-NINE ARTICLES (1563). A document containing short summaries of theological doctrines that defined the position of the Church of England in relation to the theological controversies of the English Reformation. The document was a result of earlier theological work that included the publishing of the Ten Articles (1536), the Bishops' Book (1537), the Six Articles (1539), the King's Book (1543), and the Forty-Two Articles (1553) of Archbishop **Thomas Cranmer.** The Thirty-Nine Articles, largely the work of Cranmer, are part of the doctrinal standards of the Church of England and the worldwide Anglican communion. Reformed emphasis is evident in the doctrines of **scripture, salvation, church** authority, and the **sacraments.** The articles insist on the sufficiency of scripture for salvation (art. 6); they affirm that **predestination** and **election** in Christ is "full of sweet, pleasant, and unspeakable comfort to godly persons" (art. 17); they assert that the general councils of the church are not infallible (art. 21); and they reject the doctrine of transubstantiation in relation to the **Lord's Supper** (art. 28). Subscription to the articles is not required in the Church of England, and they are freely interpreted throughout the Anglican communion.

THORNWELL, JAMES HENLEY (1812–1862). American Presbyterian minister and theologian. Thornwell was born in the Marlborough district of South Carolina and graduated from South Carolina College (1831) and Columbia Theological Seminary (1834). In 1834 he pursued further theological study at **Andover** Seminary and Harvard University. Thornwell served churches in Lancaster (1835–1838) and Columbia (1840–1841; 1855–1861), South Carolina. He was appointed professor of moral philosophy at South Carolina College (1841–1851) and served as president of the University of South Carolina from 1852 to 1855. In 1847 he was elected **moderator** of the General Assembly of the Old School Presbyterian Church and became the founding editor of the *Southern Presbyterian Review*. From 1855 to 1862 he served as professor of systematic theology at Columbia Theological Seminary.

Thornwell's theology was based upon the principles of Scottish Common Sense philosophy, emphasizing the "moral government" of **God** in juridical terms. He taught the immediate imputation of Adam's **sin** and Christ's righteousness through **federal, covenant** theology. He was described by **Charles Hodge** as a "hyper-hyper-hyper Calvinist." Thornwell was concerned about the nature of Presbyterian **church government**, arguing that church courts rather than independent "boards" were the true agencies for **mission**. He supported the institution of **slavery** because he believed it was sanctioned by **scripture.** Thornwell also taught the "spirituality of the church," a doctrine that interpreted the **church** as a purely spiritual institution concerned with personal **faith** and morals alone. Thornwell believed that the church should not be directly involved in politics. He was a principal organizer of the Presbyterian Church in the United States at the beginning of the U.S. Civil War in 1861.

THREEFOLD OFFICE *(Munus triplex).* The person and work of Christ according to his work as prophet, priest, and king. **John Calvin** used these three images *(Inst.* 2.15) as a way of uniting Christ's person and describing his work as mediator. Christ is the teacher of "perfect doctrine" (prophet) in which "all parts of perfect wisdom are contained" (2.15.2). Christ is the everlasting intercessor (priest) who died on the cross to wash away **sin,** sanctify us, and obtain for us "that grace from which the uncleanness of our transgressions and vices debars us." This provides "trust in prayer" and also "peace for godly consciences" (2.15.6). Christ is the king who exercises an eternal and spiritual reign over the **church** and over each individual. Believers find comfort in the reign of Christ, knowing that "our King will never leave us destitute, but will provide for our needs until, our warfare ended, we are called to triumph" (2.15.4). This formulation of the threefold office of Christ also appears in the **Heidelberg Catechism** (question 31) and the **Westminster Confession** (chap. 8).

THREE-SELF FORMULA. Protestant **mission** policy that tried to develop self-governing, self-supporting, and self-propagating churches. The policy was articulated by Henry Venn (1796–1873), secretary of the Anglican Church Missionary Society, and **Rufus Anderson** of the **American Board of Commissioners for Foreign Missions.** The purpose of the formula was to establish independent churches throughout the world. In a few regions of the world Protestantism reflected the policy, but in many countries Protestant work developed into a pattern of ecclesiastical and cultural paternalism. Roland Allen (1868–1947), a missionary in **China**, further developed the policy by emphasizing the indigenous nature of the entire missionary enterprise. Allen's thinking on indigenization in China helped inspire a movement by Three-Self Chinese Protestants who sought independence from the Western mission boards and from missionary control of the churches.

TOGO. *See* WEST AFRICA

TOKYO UNION THEOLOGICAL SEMINARY. The leading Protestant theological seminary in **Japan** and one of the major graduate schools in the Far East, enrolling students from **South Korea**, **Taiwan**, and other Asian countries. The seminary was founded in 1949 by the United Church of Christ in Japan (Nihon Kirisuto Kyodan). The origin of the school goes back to Tokyo Theological Seminary founded by **Masahisa Uemura** in 1904. In 1926 this school merged with the theological department of **Meiji Gakuin** University to form the Japan Theological Seminary. During World War II the Japanese government forced the Japan Theological Seminary to merge with other theological seminaries representing several denominations. These mergers led to the formation of the Tokyo Union Theological Seminary.

In 1951, with the support of the Interboard Committee, a body representing the overseas denominations that cooperated with the United Church of Christ in Japan, the school moved to a new campus in Kichijoji, western Tokyo. The government education agency (Monbusho) recognized the school's master of divinity program in 1952, and in 1954 it authorized the granting of a doctorate in theology. The seminary relocated again in 1966, this time in Osawa (further west in Tokyo), adjoining the International Christian University campus and the Lutheran Theological Seminary. The seminary library, expanded in 1986, houses more than 100,000 volumes and all major theological journals, including 80 publications in Japanese. One of these publications is the seminary's own journal, *Shingaku* (Theology), published annually since 1949.

Members of the seminary faculty come from diverse denominational backgrounds, but the dominant theological strain is Presbyterian and Reformed. The school's first president, Hidenobu Kuwada, its current president, Kikuo Matsunaga, and its major theologian of the modern period, Yoshitaka Kumano, come out of the Presbyterian and Reformed tradition.

TRADITION. That which is received (from Latin *tradere* "to hand over") as the cumulative beliefs and practices of the **church** through the centuries. On the basis of the scriptural witness, the Protestant Reformers rejected Roman Catholic teaching, codified at the Council of Trent (1545–1563), that placed tradition on an equal footing with **scripture** as an independent and parallel **authority** for the church. However, the Dogmatic Constitution on Divine Revelation issued by the Second Vatican Council (1962–1965) seems to have softened the earlier Roman Catholic view. Although the Reformed tradition stresses the primacy of scripture over tradition, it also recognizes the importance of tradition as a kind of commentary on the scriptures and the Christian life. Much can be learned from church tradition as expressed in creeds and **confessions**, the decrees of church councils, and the writings of Bible commentators and theologians. While maintaining their emphasis on scriptural primacy, the Reformed churches are also aware of the historical process of doctrinal development that enriches the church's understanding of God's **revelation** in scripture.

TRINIDAD AND TOBAGO. *See* CARIBBEAN

TRINITY. The one **God** in three persons, traditionally expressed as Father, Son, and **Holy Spirit.** Reformed churches inherited the trinitarian theology articulated by the fourth-century Western **church**, which maintained that the Godhead is three coequal persons who share the same "substance" or "essence" (Greek *ousia*; Latin *substantia*). Although this definition grew out of the church's need to define Christ's relationship to God, it is not a definition explicitly found in **scripture.** The New Testament contains trinitarian language, but this language generally refers to the order of **salvation** rather than the essence of the persons. There also continues to be debate on the place of the Spirit within the Trinity. The Reformers preferred to emphasize the activity of the three persons of the Trinity rather than their essence: God is the Creator who is revealed in Jesus Christ whose spirit dwells in the believer. Although the Trinity is a mystery, the church's trinitarian doctrine is central to its understanding of God and salvation and remains a major theological dividing line separating it from Islam and Judaism.

Reformed theologians have creatively used the doctrine of the Trinity to explain various aspects of Christian **faith**. In the 20th century, **Karl Barth** used the Trinity as a major organizing theme in his doctrines of **revelation** and theological anthropology, in which the three persons are seen as Revealer, Revelation, and Revealedness. According to Jürgen Moltmann, the Trinity is a divine community that can stand as a model for human communities (*The Trinity and the Kingdom* [1982]). Letty Russell writes that the doctrine of the Trinity conveys the idea of "partnership," an image of mutuality, reciprocity, and a totally shared life. The characteristics of partnership, or *koinonia,* may be "discovered in their perfection in the Trinity, where there is a focus of relationship in mutual love between the persons and toward **creation**" (*The Future of Partnership* [1979], p. 35).

TRUMBULL, DAVID (1819–1889). American Presbyterian missionary in **Chile.** After completing his **education** at Yale College and **Princeton Theological Seminary**, Trumbull went to Valparaiso, Chile, under the auspices of the Foreign Evangelical Society, to serve as seamen's chaplain (1845). His ministry expanded to the expatriate communities in that city, along the western coast of Latin America, and to the Chilean people as a whole. He preached, taught Reformed theology, opened the Union Church (1847), and founded an orphans' home, a public school, a YMCA, and a temperance society. He organized the Presbyterian Church among the Spanish-speaking people; Trumbull is known as the founder of Protestantism in Chile. He advocated religious toleration and fostered minority rights and progressive legislation; for this purpose, he published two newspapers. He became a Chilean citizen in 1886, when religious toleration was incorporated into the Chilean constitution.

TSAI, PETER (CAI WENHAO) (1913–1993). Chinese Protestant minister and vice president of the China Christian Council (1980–1993). After studying literature at Shanghai University and theology at the Yanjing School of Religion (Beijing) and Nanjing Theological Seminary, Tsai did graduate work under **John Mackay** at **Princeton Theological Seminary** (1946–1948). Upon his return to Hangzhou (Zhejiang Province) he served as pastor of the Sicheng Church and worked in a number of national and regional offices. He was involved in the Chinese Christian Three-Self Patriotic Movement (TSPM) from the early 1950s, serving as president of both the Zhejiang TSPM and Church Council until his death. During the Cultural Revolution he suffered severe persecution. Under Tsai's evangelistic leadership the Christian population in the province grew from 200,000 in 1950 to over 1,000,000 in 1993. Although denominational legacies have been merged in the contemporary Chinese church, Tsai was a noted Reformed voice in the formation of contemporary Chinese Christianity. He was co-author of a draft of a new constitution for the China Christian Council, a polity that shows Reformed influence. *See also* Three-Self Formula

TUNISIA. *See* NORTH AFRICA

TURRETIN, FRANCIS (1623–1687). Swiss Reformed minister and theologian. Turretin was the son of Benedict Turretin, a leading Swiss theologian. He was born in Geneva and educated at theological schools in Geneva, Leiden, Utrecht, Paris, Saumer, Montauban, and Nîmes. In 1647 he became pastor of the Italian Protestant congregation in Geneva. He was named professor of theology at the Geneva Academy in 1653. Turretin was a rigorous adherent of **Calvinism** and supported the Helvetic Consensus Formula (1675), which taught the verbal **inspiration** of **scripture** to the degree that even the Hebrew vowel points were said to be inspired. His four-volume *Institutio Theologicae Elencticae* (1679–1685) contains a full exposition of scholastic Calvinism on such topics as the divine decrees, **election**, and **predestination.**

Turretin's work emerged out of Calvin's theological framework but went beyond it to develop a precise scholastic system designed to refute his opponents. His son and successor, Jean-Alphonse (1671–1737), worked to reverse his father's scholastic emphasis. Turretin's *Institutes* exercised considerable influence in the **United States**, particularly at **Princeton Theological Seminary** in the 19th century, where it was used by **Archibald Alexander** and **Charles Hodge** as the standard text in theology from the founding of the seminary in 1812 until the publication of Hodge's *Systematic Theology* (1871–1873).

TUVALU. *See* PACIFIC OCEAN ISLANDS

- U -

UEMURA, MASAHISA (1858–1925). Japanese Presbyterian minister, evangelist, and president of the Tokyo Theological Seminary (Tokyo Shingakusha). Uemura was born into a samurai family in Edo. Following the Meiji Restoration, his family lost its wealth and standing. Uemura left home and traveled to Yokohama, where he became a Christian. He was baptized in 1873 and entered S. R. Brown's theological training school, which later became the theological department of **Meiji Gakuin.** He was ordained in 1880 and began a small church in Tokyo, now Fujimicho Church, which grew to 1,600 members during the 1920s. In 1890 he organized a monthly journal, *Nippon Hyoron* (Japan Review), which discussed the political and social questions of the time but, like his *Fukuin-Shinpo* (Gospel News, 1924), also stressed **evangelism,** Uemura's greatest concern. Uemura reorganized the evangelistic work of the Church of Christ in Japan (Nihon Kirisuto Kyokai), which became independent and self-supporting. In 1904 he organized Tokyo Theological Seminary, which later became **Tokyo Union Theological Seminary.** He was a critic of modern currents in theology that try to reduce Christian **faith** to a cultural or social expression.

UEMURA, TAMAKI (1890–1982). Japanese Presbyterian minister. Uemura was born in Tokyo, **Japan,** the third daughter of **Masahisa Uemura.** She graduated from Joshi Gakuin (1910), went to the **United States** to attend Wellesley University (1911–1915), and returned to **Japan.** After the death of her father in 1925, she went to **New College, Edinburgh,** to study theology. She returned to Japan in 1930 and taught at several Christian colleges. In 1931 she founded Kashiwagi Church (Nihon Kirisuto Church) in Tokyo and was ordained in 1934. She became a principal of Tainan Women's School (1937–1938), was chairperson of the YWCA in Japan (1937), and visited the United States in 1946 as a guest of the Women of the Presbyterian Church. During the 1950s she worked on behalf of world peace, principally as cofounder of the Committee of Seven Persons, a Christian group that opposed nuclear bomb testing, the presence of U.S. nuclear submarines in Japan, and the U.S. bombing of North Vietnam. In 1973 she became pastor emeritus of Kashiwagi Church.

UKRAINE. *See* CENTRAL AND EASTERN EUROPE

UNDERWOOD, HORACE GRANT (1859–1916). American Reformed Church missionary in **Korea.** Born in London, Underwood emigrated to the **United States** with his family in 1872. He graduated from New York University (1881) and **New Brunswick Theological Seminary** (1884) and pursued graduate studies in **France.** Underwood went to Korea in 1885. He organized the first Christian orphanage in Seoul, founded the Korean Tract Society (1888), and published a Korean dictionary, a grammar, and the first Korean hymnal (1889). In 1895 he founded the Jesus Hospital in order to treat cholera patients. He also organized Union Medical College and Pierson Bible Institute (1912–1913). Both schools eventually became part of Yonsei University in Seoul. A founder of the Sai Mun An Church, Underwood was a teacher, author, and tireless advocate of Korean **mission.**

UNION THEOLOGICAL SEMINARY (NEW YORK). American Protestant seminary in New York City. Founded by New School Presbyterians in 1836, the school was incorporated by 1839. First located at University Place, the seminary grew to occupy buildings on Park Avenue at 70th Street. In 1910 the seminary moved to Morningside Heights, a campus quadrangle of Gothic-style buildings. Ever conscious of its urban setting, the seminary initially recruited from the New York metropolitan area but eventually drew students from all over the world. The seminary was independent until 1870, when the Presbyterian Church in the U.S.A. began to confirm its faculty appointments. This system continued until 1893, when the denomination suspended **Charles A. Briggs** for heresy. The seminary refused to dismiss Briggs and severed its ties to the Presbyterian Church. Union Seminary is known for its extensive theological library and its distinguished faculty. The faculty have included **William Adams Brown, Paul L. Lehmann, John T. McNeill, James Moffatt, Reinhold Niebuhr,** and **Philip Schaff.**

UNION THEOLOGICAL SEMINARY AND PRESBYTERIAN SCHOOL OF CHRISTIAN EDUCATION (VIRGINIA). The oldest Presbyterian seminary in the American South and one of 10 theological institutions serving the Presbyterian Church (U.S.A.). The seminary dates from 1806, when the Presbytery of Hanover established a theological library and a fund to educate ministers at Hampden-Sydney College in Virginia. In 1807 Moses Hoge was appointed president of the college, and in 1812 he was elected professor of divinity. Hoge educated more than 30 ministers before his death in 1820. His successor, **John Holt Rice,** was appointed professor of theology in 1824. Under Rice's leadership Union Theological Seminary constructed buildings and established a faculty. The remainder of the 19th century was turbulent for the seminary, with the division of the Presbyterian Church and the Civil War (1861–1865). In the two decades following the war, Benjamin M. Smith gradually brought the war-ravaged institution back to life. In 1895 the seminary moved to Richmond, Virginia, where it began to flourish under the leadership of **Walter W. Moore.** Moore expanded the seminary faculty and arranged for the endowment of the Sprunt Lectureship (1911). Under five subsequent presidents, Union Seminary assembled a distinguished faculty, expanded programs and facilities, founded *Interpreta-*

tion: A Journal of Bible and Theology (1946), became a founding member of the Richmond Theological Consortium of schools (1968), and constructed a new library (1996–1997). In 1997 the seminary merged with the Presbyterian School of Christian Education in Richmond, Virginia. The institution now maintains a 60-acre campus with 43 buildings and 32 faculty members. Faculty have included John Holt Rice, Walter W. Moore, and **John Bright.**

UNIQUENESS OF CHRIST. The gospel is the historical event of Jesus the Christ, in which **God** accomplished the promised work of **salvation.** Since the era of the apostolic **church,** theology has sought to understand the person and work of Jesus Christ: his humanity and deity, relationship to the Godhead, historical particularity, and eternal rule. The encounter with world religions resulting from the expanding **mission** movement has made the assertion of the uniqueness of Christ an important issue of contemporary **Christology.** The discussion oscillates between emphasis upon the "Jesus of history" and the "Christ of faith," with various attempts to unlink them by rendering the "Christ" into a religious principle or idea found in many religions. Reformed theology generally rejects that uncoupling and insists that God's self-revelation in Jesus Christ is unique. But this uniqueness does not preclude the universal lordship of Christ, found in various elements of human religious experience. *See also* Interfaith Dialogue

UNITARIANISM. A theology that espouses belief in the oneness of **God** and a church movement that emerged from this theology. Unitarian movements began in 16th-century **England** and **Hungary.** Sometimes called Socinianism, after Socinus of Siena (1539–1604), Unitarianism rejects the **Trinity** and has an optimistic view of humanity in contrast to the Calvinistic view that accepts human sinfulness. Unitarian thinking, which also embraced an Arian **Christology** and **universalism**, was eventually wed to Enlightenment rationalism and deism to produce a new Unitarian church movement. The first British congregation was organized in London (1774), and the first American congregation appeared in Boston (1785). British adherents included Joseph Priestley (1733–1804) and James Martineau (1805–1900). In the **United States** William E. Channing (1780–1842), Ralph Waldo Emerson (1802–1882), and Theodore Parker (1810–1860) were leading figures. Unitarian churches have congregational polities and emphasize a rational approach to religion.

UNITED ARAB EMIRATES. *See* MIDDLE EAST

UNITED KINGDOM. The people of the United Kingdom are affiliated with Christian churches, although religious practice is minimal. The country is predominantly Protestant (Anglican, 45 percent; other Protestants, 10 percent), with Roman Catholics (9 percent) being a minority. Of the non-Anglican Protestant churches, the Presbyterians are the largest group, followed by Methodists and Baptists.

England. The Reformation in England was ignited when Pope Clement VII refused to grant Henry VIII's request for a divorce. In response, the English king renounced papal authority and in 1534 established the Church of England. This break with Rome began a process of church reform that lasted several decades. Following Henry's death in 1547, **Thomas Cranmer** produced the **Book of Common Prayer** (1549), which reformed **worship** in the **church**, and the Forty-Two Articles (1553), later reduced to **Thirty-Nine Articles**, which reformed its doctrine. The **Elizabethan Settlement** (1559) created an Anglican Church that retained aspects of both Catholicism and Protestantism.

The settlement was a compromise opposed by English **Puritans**, many of whom became Presbyterian or Congregationalist. The Presbyterian Puritans wanted greater reform but were unsuccessful in their attempt to establish a Presbyterian form of government within the Church of England. However, during the 1640s, when they controlled the English Parliament, the Presbyterians were able to convene the **Westminster Assembly** (1643–1649). Their strength led to the adoption by Parliament (1648) of the **Westminster Confession.** When **Oliver Cromwell** and his army came to power, Parliament was purged of its 140 Presbyterian members, and Cromwell gave favored treatment to the Congregationalists. Presbyterian reform was undone when, during the reign of Charles II (1660–1685), episcopal **church government** was reestablished. *See also* Cartwright, Thomas

In 1689 English Protestants were granted toleration. By this time the Presbyterian Church was in decline, and many of its ministers became Congregationalists. The church was revived during the 18th century, when an influx of Scots led to the organization of new congregations. In 1847 English and Scottish congregations merged to form the United Presbyterian Church. In 1876 the United Presbyterian Church merged with other English and Scottish churches to form the Presbyterian Church of England.

Presbyterians wanted to reform the Church of England; Congregationalists (also called Independents) separated from it. Early Congregationalists suffered for their separatist views. Some, like **Henry Barrow** and **John Greenwood**, were killed. Others, including **Robert Browne**, went to **Holland** or the **United States**. The movement was shaped by the writings of **Richard Baxter**, **William Ames**, and **John Owen**. During the 1640s some exiled Congregationalists returned to England. Congregationalists were present at the Westminster Assembly and expressed their views more fully in the **Savoy Declaration** (1658). The movement became influential in Oliver Cromwell's army and during the Commonwealth of the 1650s. However, persecution resumed with the reign of Charles II. Passage of the Act of Uniformity (1662) led to Black Bartholomew's Day, when 2,000 Protestant ministers, including many Congregationalists, were ejected from the Church of England. Even after the Act of Toleration, Congregationalists were persecuted under the reign of Queen Anne (1702–1714).

Congregationalism was profoundly influenced by the Methodist revival associated with John and Charles Wesley, **George Whitefield**, Countess Selina Hastings of **Huntingdon**, and **Philip Doddridge**. During this period churches were renewed and the **London Missionary Society** was founded. The society went on to make British Congregationalism a worldwide movement. In 1832 Congregational churches united to form a national denomination, the Congregational Union of England and Wales.

In addition to its theologians, the English Congregationalist tradition produced hymn writers and editors **Albert F. Bayly**, **Erik Routley**, and **Isaac Watts**; literary figures **John Bunyan** and **John Milton**; and church leader **Robert W. Dale**.

In 1972 English Congregationalists and the Presbyterian Church of England merged to form the United Reformed Church in the United Kingdom. The union marked the first time two transconfessional bodies had come together in England since the time of the Protestant Reformation. In 1981 the Reformed Association of Churches of Christ (Disciples of Christ) also joined the United Church. The church holds an annual **general assembly** and has 12 provinces with a presiding **moderator**, local district councils, and, in the local congregation, joint government by **elders** (from the Presbyterian tradition) and the meeting of all church members (from the Congregational tradition). It accepts the validity of both infant and believers' **baptism**. The World Missions Council succeeds the London Missionary Society.

Wales. The Presbyterian Church of Wales, also known as the Calvinist Methodist Church, has its origin in 18th-century **evangelical** revivals. These revivals were led by **Howel Harris** (1714–1773), Daniel

Rowlands (1713–1790), and others, who began religious societies patterned on the Methodist societies of England founded by John Wesley. Unlike the English **revival** movement, which was Arminian in its theology and developed a version of presbyterial church polity, the Welsh movement adopted Whitefield's **Calvinism** and became Presbyterian. The Calvinist Methodist movement took place within the Church of England. Lay "exhorters," as well as ministerial and lay superintendents, worked with the Welsh religious societies between 1735 and 1752. By the beginning of the 19th century, Thomas Charles of Bala, an Anglican minister who had become a leader in the movement, ordained nine exhorters (1811); this action, along with increasing persecution, led to a break with the Church of England.

The Calvinistic Methodists organized their church into two synods, one for North Wales and one for South Wales. The church drafted its own Confession of Faith (1823) based on the Westminster Confession, Rules of Discipline, and church polity. In 1864 it organized a general assembly to unite the two synods. An amended constitution was adopted in 1933. More than three quarters of the congregations are Welsh speaking.

The Union of Welsh Independents, or Congregationalists, share the same tradition as the English Congregationalists. The first Congregational church in Wales was founded in 1639 at Llanfaches, Monmouthshire. After a period of government persecution, the 18th-century evangelical revivals stimulated the formation of new congregations. These churches were united in 1872 by the formation of the Union of Welsh Independents. During the 20th century these Welsh churches declined to join the United Reformed Church. Most congregations continue to worship in the Welsh language; **William Rees** and other ministers have helped to preserve Welsh culture.

Scotland. The roots of the Church of Scotland lie in the missionary work of St. Ninian (A.D. 400) and St. Columba (ca. 563 at Iona), and in the influence of the early Celtic church. The Scottish Reformation of the 16th century was led by **John Knox**, who was the primary author of the Scots Confession and the **Book of Common Order.** Knox brought church reform in the pattern of 16th-century Geneva. The church adopted a Presbyterian polity with church courts that included a kirk (church) session, **presbytery**, synod, and a general assembly. This system was put in place by John Knox's **Book of Discipline** and developed further by **Andrew Melville** in the second Book of Discipline. The Act of 1592 ("the Magna Carta of the Kirk") was a recognition of the Scottish church system by king and Parliament. **Presbyterianism** in Scotland was permanently established in 1689.

A number of church schisms occurred in the Church of Scotland during the 18th and 19th centuries, the most important being the Disruption of 1843. This division was the result of a break between moderates, who controlled the church, and evangelicals, who supported **mission** work and the **Calvinism** of the Westminster Confession. Led by **Thomas Chalmers**, the evangelicals organized a Free Church of Scotland composed of about one-third of the ministers and laity of the Scottish church. The new denomination also attracted almost all of the church's missionaries and many of its best scholars.

After the 1843 Disruption two other Presbyterian bodies, the United Secession Church and the Relief Church, merged in 1847 to form the United Presbyterian Church of Scotland. In 1900 the Free Church of Scotland and the United Presbyterian Church united to form the United Free Church of Scotland. In 1929 the United Free Church and the Church of Scotland reunited as the Church of Scotland, in effect reconstituting the national church. Today the Church of Scotland is committed to ecumenical relations and **interfaith dialogue**, international mission work, and social and educational work. Saint Andrew Press is the church's publishing house.

Presbyterian congregations that declined to join the 1929 union continue as the United Free Church of Scotland. This denomination has emphasized the voluntary support of the church by its members, freedom from state control, and religious equality. Other Presbyterian church bodies include the Free Presbyterian Church of Scotland, Associated Presbyterian Churches, and Reformed Presbyterian churches.

The Congregational Union of Scotland emerged in 1812 from evangelical revivals of the late 18th century. Congregational churches were dissatisfied with the Church of Scotland's lack of support for mission. These churches stressed the independence of local congregations, toleration in doctrine, church mission, and personal Christian commitment. In 1896 the Congregational Union united with another free association of churches, the Evangelical Union, to form the Congregational Union of Scotland.

The Scottish churches have produced many theologians, Bible scholars, church leaders, and missionaries, including **Donald M. Baillie, John Baillie, William Barclay, John H. S. Burleigh, John McLeod Campbell, Andrew Martin Fairbairn, P. T. Forsyth, Thomas Gillespie, James Guthrie, David Livingstone, John Marshall Lang, Hugh Mackintosh, Robert Moffat, James Orr,** and **George Adam Smith.**

Northern Ireland. The Presbyterian Church in Ireland began with the arrival of English Puritans and Scottish settlers in Ulster during the 17th century. Ulster became dominated by an English landholding aristocracy and Scottish and English merchants. The original Irish population became landless and their condition as an underclass led to an insurrection in 1641 that was suppressed by **Oliver Cromwell** in the 1650s. By the next decade the "Ulster Plantation" was reestablished. The Protestant population was augmented during the late 17th and early 18th centuries with the arrival of **Huguenot** linen merchants from France.

Following a 1798 rebellion, the British Parliament passed the Act of Union (1800), which placed Irish Protestants under the protection of the British government. Social and economic difficulties continued and many Scotch-Irish Presbyterians emigrated to America, Australia, and other countries during the 18th and 19th centuries. At home, Protestant and Roman Catholic communities became segregated, and in 1922 the country was politically partitioned, creating the Protestant British-ruled entity of Northern Ireland. Since the 1960s the Protestant majority and Roman Catholic minority have renewed their violent social and political struggle over Northern Ireland.

The Presbyterian Church in Ireland was formed in 1840 by the merger of congregations linked to the secession in Scotland, with Presbyterian congregations organized in the Synod of Ulster. The political partition of 1922 did not divide the churches. The Presbyterian Church draws its membership from the whole of Ireland but has gradually become concentrated in Northern Ireland, where Presbyterians make up approximately one-fourth of the population, compared with the Republic of Ireland, where they total less than 1 percent. The church has carried out mission work in several countries in **Asia**, **Africa**, and **South America**, including **India**, Manchuria, **Kenya**, and **Brazil**. In 1951 the Free Presbyterian Church of Ulster was organized by a conservative branch of the Presbyterian Church of Ireland.

The Congregational Union of Ireland was formed in 1828 with eight churches. It was suspended in 1845 but reconstituted in 1860. The union is conservative in its theology, recently withdrawing from the Council for World Mission. Most of its ministerial candidates are educated at the Congregational College in Manchester, England.

UNITED STATES OF AMERICA. The country is primarily Christian, with Protestants making up 61 percent of the population; Roman Catholics (25 percent), Jews (2 percent), other religions (5 percent), and those who profess no religion (7 percent) are minorities.

The Reformed tradition in the United States developed out of the religious experience and traditions of several immigrant groups. During the 16th and 17th centuries English **Puritans** who adhered to a Congregationalist **Calvinism** settled in New England. The American Puritan tradition was an important theological and cultural force in the early history of the United States. **Francis Makemie, John Witherspoon, Samuel Davies**, and Scotch-Irish settlers established Presbyterian Calvinism in New Jersey, the middle colonies, and southward into the Shenandoah Valley and the Piedmont region of the South. Dutch Calvinism began in New Netherlands (New York) and spread to the American heartland. German and Hungarian Reformed immigrant groups also established Reformed churches in the United States.

Congregational Churches. Congregationalism was brought to America by the Pilgrims and their pastor, **John Robinson**, who arrived in Plymouth, Massachusetts (1620), and the Puritans who settled Massachusetts Bay Colony (1629). The **Cambridge Platform** (1648) and the Saybrook Platform (1708) organized early congregational life. Church membership increased through the **preaching** of **Jonathan Edwards** and **George Whitefield** during the **Great Awakening**, and the Congregational churches became the most influential Reformed bodies of the colonial era. Although the Great Awakening increased the size and strength of the churches, it also created conflict. Two factions emerged within the churches: a New Light group, which supported **revival**, and an Old Light group, which opposed it. Many New Light churches later became Baptist, whereas many Old Light churches moved toward **Unitarianism.** Congregationalists developed a New England theology and a **New Haven theology.**

In spite of internal difficulties, Congregationalism continued to expand westward through its **American Home Missionary Society** (1826) and internationally through the **American Board of Commissioners for Foreign Missions** (1810). One Congregational stronghold was in Hawaii. Protected by Queen **Ka'ahumanu** and assisted by **William Richards**, Americans **Hiram Bingham, William Richards**, and **Titus Coan** made a considerable impact on the Pacific region. Hawaiian converts **Henry Obookiah, James H. Kekela**, and **David Malo** made important contributions.

The Congregational churches extended their ministry by joining with the Presbyterian Church in the Plan of Union (1801–1837), which unified Reformed churches in the Midwest. Congregationalism was not organized on a denominational level until 1871, when it formed a National Council of Congregational Churches.

Church leaders emerged from Harvard and Yale Universities, **Andover** Theological Seminary, and other educational institutions founded by Congregationalists. The church produced many theologians, historians, educators, and social reformers, including **Roland Bainton, Horace Bushnell, Timothy Dwight, Washington Gladden, Samuel Hopkins, Cotton Mather, Harriet Beecher Stowe, Nathaniel W. Taylor**, and **Samuel Willard**.

United Churches. The Congregational expression of the Reformed tradition in the United States is now embodied in the United Church of Christ (UCC). The UCC was founded in 1957 as the result of a merger between the Congregational Christian Churches and the Evangelical and Reformed Church, a German Reformed church founded by John Philip Boehm and Michael Schlatter in the early 1700s. The German church had been organized in 1934 when immigrants in the East and Midwest united two separate denominations with a combined membership of 600,000. The German Reformed tradition was influenced by the **Mercersburg theology** of **Philip Schaff** and **John Williamson Nevin**, and later by the theology of **Reinhold Niebuhr** and **H. Richard Niebuhr**. Two Congregational churches that did not enter the 1957 union are the Conservative Congregational Christian Conference and the National Association of Congregational Christian Churches.

Presbyterian Churches. The American Presbyterian tradition was begun by New England Puritans who embraced Presbyterian government, by Scotch-Irish immigrants who were known for their rigorous theology and adherence to strict **church government**, and by English and Welsh settlers who held a pietistic faith. Although these Presbyterians adopted a common statement of faith (the **Westminster Confession**) in 1729, the different backgrounds and outlooks of the settlers led to tension within the church.

An early schism took place over the issue of religious revivals (1741–1758), with the Scotch-Irish (Old Side, against revival) and the New Englanders (New Side, favoring revival) pitted against each other. The Presbyterian Church reunited in 1758, but in 1837 the old tension resurfaced and caused another split. A group in the North (New School) and a predominantly Scotch-Irish group (Old School) differed on theological questions, the validity of the Plan of Union (1801) enacted with the Congregationalists for joint ministry and **mission** work, and the issue of **slavery.** However, these church divisions did not prevent an important merger in 1858 between the Associate Synod of North America (founded in 1753 by Covenanters) and the Associate Reformed Synod (founded in 1782), to form the United Presbyterian Church of North America (UPCNA).

Presbyterians joined with Congregationalists in supporting the American Board of Commissioners for Foreign Missions and eventually organized their own Board of Foreign Missions. Mission work was carried out in the west and Alaska by **Sheldon Jackson**, and in Oregon by Marcus and **Narcissa Whitman**. These missionaries helped the church expand westward during the 19th century.

The Civil War (1861–1865) led to further division of the church along regional lines, with Old School Presbyterians in the South withdrawing to form a separate denomination. A southern Presbyterian Calvinism was articulated by **Robert Lewis Dabney** and **James Henley Thornwell**. After the war, New School and Old School groups united with the northern and southern churches, but the Presbyterian Church in the U.S.A. (PCUSA, Philadelphia and New York) and the Presbyterian Church in the United States (PCUS, Atlanta) remained separate denominations for over a century, finally reuniting in 1983 to form the largest Presbyterian body in the United States, the Presbyterian Church (U.S.A.), centered in Louisville, Kentucky. In 1998 the church reported approximately 3.6 million members in over 12,600 congregations.

During the last quarter of the 19th century and the early part of the 20th century, Presbyterians struggled with theological, social, and scientific questions, including the acceptance of **biblical criticism** and evolutionary theory. In response to these challenges, the old **Princeton theology** of **Archibald Alexander, Charles Hodge, A. A. Hodge**, and **B. B. Warfield** became widespread. As a result of industrialization and urbanization the nation faced new moral issues. These issues led many Presbyterians to participate in the **social gospel movement** and in benevolent organizations and causes.

During the 20th century, the Presbyterian churches and their leaders also embraced a global vision of the church. Leaders such as **Henry Pitney Van Dusen** and **Eugene Carson Blake** promoted ecumenical cooperation and church union. **Robert E. Speer** and **John A. Mackay** did much to promote the international mission work of the church, and through that work they exerted a powerful influence on the worldwide spread of **Presbyterianism.**

Church conflict persisted during the 20th century, and smaller Presbyterian denominations were organized as a result of theological, social, and ethnic differences within the churches. The Orthodox Presbyterian Church (OPC, 1936), led by **J. Gresham Machan**, and the Bible Presbyterian Church (BPC, 1937) emerged as a result of the **fundamentalist-modernist controversy** that took place within the Presbyterian Church in the U.S.A. during the 1930s. The Presbyterian Church in America (PCA, 1973) and the Evangelical Presbyterian Church (EPC, 1981) recently emerged from the PCUS; they adhere to a conservative Calvinistic theology. The Korean Presbyterian Church in America (KPCA, 1976) was organized in the Korean-American community. The confessional standard of American Presbyterianism has been the **Westminster Confession.** In 1967 the UPCUSA adopted the Book of Confessions, which includes as doctrinal standards the Nicene and Apostles' Creeds, the Scots Confession, the **Heidelberg Catechism,** the Second Helvetic Confession, the Westminster Confession, the Larger and Shorter **Catechisms,** the **Theological Declaration of Barmen,** and the Confession of 1967. These documents represent the variety of Reformed thought. In 1990 the Presbyterian Church (USA) added a **Brief Statement of Faith** to this Book of Confessions. Other Presbyterian bodies have maintained the Westminster Confession as their sole standard.

Dutch Reformed Churches. The Dutch Calvinist tradition was begun in 1628, when Jonas Michaelius settled in New Amsterdam and founded what is today the Collegiate Church. The Reformed Church in America was formally organized in 1792, and until the mid-19th century its activity was concentrated in New York and New Jersey. The church founded Rutgers University (1766) and **New Brunswick Theological Seminary** (1784) in New Jersey. During the 19th century Dutch immigrants settled in Michigan and Iowa, increasing church membership. The pioneer founder of Holland, Michigan, A. C. van Raalte, was instrumental in founding Hope College and Western Theological Seminary, also institutions of the Reformed Church in America. Some of the more theologically conservative settlers organized the Christian Reformed Church (1857). The church founded Calvin College and Calvin Theological Seminary and located its headquarters in Grand Rapids, Michigan. The Christian Reformed tradition was perpetuated by Louis Berkhof (1873–1957), who drew aspects of his theology from Dutch theologians **Abraham Kuyper** and **Herman Bavinck.** Other Dutch denominations include the Netherlands Reformed Congregations and the Free Reformed Churches of North America. Most of the Dutch Reformed churches accept the Belgic Confession, the Heidelberg Catechism, and the Canons of Dort as doctrinal standards.

UNITING ABORIGINAL AND ISLANDER CHRISTIAN CONGRESS. Australian congress of aboriginal Christians within the Uniting Church that oversees all ministry with aboriginal people. Founded by Charles Enoch Edward Harris, the congress was sanctioned by the Uniting Church in 1985. The congress addresses spiritual, economic, and political issues that affect aboriginal Christians.

UNIVERSALISM. The belief that ultimately all people will be pardoned of **sin** and restored to **God.** With its emphasis on the love of God, universalism has been part of the Christian **tradition** since the early patristic era. Clement (ca. 155–ca. 220) and Origen of Alexandria (ca. 185–ca. 254) and Gregory of Nyssa (330–ca. 395) were leading proponents of the doctrine. Its teachings were rejected by Augustine and by an overwhelming majority of theologians in both the Eastern and Western church. During the Reformation, Anabaptist theologian Hans Denck taught universalism, but the Lutheran and Reformed churches held that divine judgment was part of the ultimate workings of God. Although the doctrine has never been embraced by the Reformed churches, the theology of **Karl Barth** is said to come to the "brink of universalism." In sections of his *Church Dogmatics* Barth writes of Christ as both the elected and rejected One. In this view, Christ is the **covenant** head of all humanity and as such includes all in the covenant of **grace.**

URSINUS, ZACHARIAS (1534–1583). German Reformer and theologian. Born in Breslau, Silesia, Ursinus was educated at Wittenberg and Zurich. He taught dogmatics at Heidelberg (1561–1568), served as rector of the seminary (1561–1576), called the Collegium Sapientiae, and was a lecturer at Neustadt (1577–1583). Ursinus was one of the authors of the **Heidelberg Catechism**, a document known for the beauty of its language and its presentation of a moderate **Calvinism.** This same moderate theological consensus is reflected in Ursinus's lectures on the Heidelberg Catechism, which were later collected and published. Ursinus did much to solidify the Reformed movement in the Palatinate, and as such is considered one of the principal founders of the German Reformed Church.

URUGUAY. *See* SOUTHERN CONE OF SOUTH AMERICA

- V -

VANDERKEMP, JOHANNES THEODOSIUS (1747–1811). Dutch Reformed medical missionary in **South Africa.** Following his **education** at Leiden, 16 years in the army, and study at Edinburgh, Vanderkemp became a physician in Rotterdam. After the death of his wife and child, he became a Christian and went as the first European medical missionary to Africa (1799), when he was over 50. With his entry into Xhosa culture, he opened up the first **mission** among indigenous African people in South Africa. At first his efforts met with little success, so he shifted his work to the Hottentot people and settled at Bethelsdorp (1803), which became the base for his mission. He resisted the racist policies of the Dutch and the British and chose to adopt the lifestyle of the people with whom he lived. His message was consistently evangelistic, emphasizing what he regarded as the universal principles of the gospel. He was a pioneer in the struggle for racial justice in South Africa and in the cross-cultural communication of the gospel.

VAN DUSEN, HENRY PITNEY (1897–1975). American Presbyterian minister, theologian, and ecumenical leader. Van Dusen was born in Philadelphia and graduated from Princeton University (1919), **Union Theological Seminary** in New York (1924), and the University of Edinburgh (1932). He was ordained in 1924 in the Presbyterian Church in the U.S.A. and was appointed professor at Union Seminary in New York (1926–1963), where he served as president (1945–1963). Van Dusen became concerned about cross-cultural **mission** work while he was a student worker with the YMCA and later vice president of the Board of Foreign Missions of the Presbyterian Church. He became a leading ecumenical spokesperson, participating in the meetings of the **World Council of Churches** (WCC) between 1948 and 1961. Many of Van Dusen's ideas were incorporated into the structure of the WCC.

Van Dusen was a strong adherent of liberal theology, maintaining his views throughout his presidency at Union Seminary, even when **neoorthodoxy** had became the dominant theological voice. Under Van Dusen's leadership, Union Seminary emerged as an international center for theological study, with scholars such as **Reinhold Niebuhr** and Paul Tillich joining its faculty. Van Dusen's books include *The Plain Man Seeks for God* (1933), *Life's Meaning* (1951), *One Great Ground of Hope* (1961), and *The Vindication of Liberal Theology* (1963).

VAN RULER, A. A. (1908–1970). Dutch minister and theologian. Born in Apeldoorn, the **Netherlands**, Van Ruler was ordained in the Dutch Reformed Church and received a doctorate from the University of Groningen. He became professor at the University of Utrecht (1947), where he remained for many years. A popular lecturer, Van Ruler became widely known for his radio addresses on the Bible and various Christian themes. He was a creative theologian who rejected the Christocentric theology of **neoorthodoxy** popular among his colleagues. His theology emphasized the **Holy Spirit** rather than Christ. He viewed the present age as one in which the Spirit extends the redemptive work of Christ to all that exists. His provocative ideas were developed in *Die christliche Kirche und das Alte Testament* (The Christian Church and the Old Testament, 1955; English translation, 1972). His emphasis on the relation between the Spirit and **creation** also appeared in other works. A collection of his essays was published as *Calvinist Trinitarianism and Theocentric Politics: Essays toward a Public Theology* (1989).

VANUATU. *See* PACIFIC OCEAN ISLANDS

VENEZUELA. *See* ANDEAN REPUBLICS AND GREATER COLOMBIA

VERMIGLI, PETER MARTYR (1500–1562). Italian Reformer. Vermigli was born in Florence, the son of a prosperous shoemaker. He became an Augustinian friar in 1514 and attended the University of Padua from 1518 to 1526. He was elected public preacher and served as vicar of Bologna, and then abbot of Spoleto and of St. Peter ad Aram in Naples. Influenced by Juan de Valdés and the works of the reformers, Vermigli fled the Inquisition to Zurich and Basel. He went to Strasbourg at the invitation of **Martin Bucer.** He was appointed professor of theology (1542–1547) and lectured on the Old Testament. In 1547, at the invitation of **Thomas Cranmer**, Vermigli became Regius Professor of Divinity at Oxford and Canon of Christ Church. He participated in a major disputation on the Eucharist in 1549. His eucharistic views were close to those of **John Calvin** and Bucer. With Queen Mary's accession, he was imprisoned for six months. Following his release, he returned to Strasbourg and was reappointed professor of theology (1553–1556). In 1556, when his views on the Eucharist again caused conflict, Vermigli moved to Zurich and became professor of Hebrew. In 1561 he participated with **Théodore Beza** in the Colloquy of Poissy. Vermigli is best known for his contributions to eucharistic theology. *See also* Poissy, Colloquy of

VIÉNOT, CHARLES (1839–1903). French Reformed minister, educator, and missionary in **Tahiti.** Born in Couthenans, **France**, Viénot was sent to Tahiti by the **Paris Evangelical Missionary Society** in 1865. Viénot organized the first Protestant school in Tahiti and ran the mission press. He also drafted the constitution of the Tahitian church and founded its governing council, the Conseil Supérieur. In controversies with the French Catholics, Viénot was an important advocate of the Protestant minority in Tahiti. He remained in the islands as an educator, and as a member and vice president of the Tahitian legislature in the early 20th century.

VISSER 'T HOOFT, WILLEM ADOLF (1900–1985). Dutch ecumenical leader. Visser 't Hooft was born in Haarlem, **Netherlands**, and educated at Leiden. He joined the staff of the YMCA (1924–1928) and worked as secretary (1928–1932) and general secretary (1932–1938) of the World Student Christian Federation (WSCF). In 1938 he began work with the Provisional Committee of the **World Council of Churches** (WCC) in Process of Formation (1938–1948) and went on to serve as general secretary of the WCC (1948–1965). He was honorary president from 1965 to 1985. A versatile linguist, Visser 't Hooft served as editor of *The Student World* (1928–1938) and *Ecumenical Review* (1948–1966). He was a theologian, administrator, analyst of world events, and author. His books include *The Kingship of Christ: An Interpretation of Recent European Theology* (1947), *The Ecumenical Movement and the Racial Problem* (1954), *No Other Name: The Choice between Syncretism and Christian Universalism* (1963), *Has the Ecumenical Movement a Future?* (1974), *The Fatherhood of God in an Age of Emancipation* (1982), and *The Genesis and Formation of the World Council of Churches* (1982).

VOCATION. One's calling as a Christian to work that glorifies **God**. The Reformed tradition emphasizes that all things are to be done for the glory of God (1 Cor. 10:31). **John Calvin** perceived that God "called" persons not only to **salvation** in Jesus Christ ("effectual calling," **Westminster Confession**, chap. 10) but also to the specific church and secular vocations through which they would serve God and live out their salvation experience in **sanctification.** The effect of this was to legitimate all manner of work and occupations by which one's Christian **faith** may be expressed. The idea of vocation gives the individual reassurance that even in a transitory world one's labor, as Calvin expressed it, "which is under God's direction, and in which He stretches out His hand to us, will not be in vain" (*Comm. 1 Tim. 6:12*). Calvin recognized that God may call a person first to one kind of work and later to another. He also asserted that a strong sense of vocation leads to contentment (*Comm. 1 Cor. 7:20*).

- W -

WADDELL, CHRISTABEL (1876–1932). The first deaconess in the Presbyterian Church of Aotearoa **New Zealand.** Waddell was educated in the Deaconess College, Melbourne, and in 1901 went to serve St. Andrew's Church in Dunedin. There she took an active role in young girls' groups,

Christian Endeavor, Bible classes, and attending to the poor and sick. Along with her husband, Rutherford Waddell, she began a **ministry** to **women.** Waddell served as the first traveling secretary of the Presbyterian Women's Missionary Union (1918–1920), a position that brought her national attention.

WALDENSIAN CHURCH. *See* SOUTHERN EUROPE

WALDENSTRÖM, PETER (1838–1917). Swedish Congregationalist theologian and preacher. Waldenström was born in Lulea and studied theology and classical languages at Uppsala. He was ordained in the Lutheran state church in 1863 but later demitted his ministerial status over differences with the Lutheran hierarchy. He became associated with the revivalism of C. O. Rosenius (d. 1868), whom he succeeded as editor of *Pietisten*, a widely read revivalist newspaper. In 1878 Waldenström founded the Swedish Mission Covenant Church, and in 1905 he became director of the Swedish Mission Society. Members of the Swedish Mission Covenant Church later emigrated to America and formed the Evangelical Covenant Church. Waldenström served as a member of the Swedish House of Representatives from 1884 to 1905.

Waldenström advocated the gathering of Christians into small groups for Bible study and **prayer**, and he believed that living **faith** was the central mark of the **church.** His participation in the **sacraments** outside existing church structures led him to reject Lutheran and creedal **authority.** Waldenström advanced a view of the **atonement** that conflicted with the teachings of the state church. He argued that the death of Christ proceeded from God's love, not God's wrath; the cross did not reconcile **God** to humanity but rather reconciled humanity to God. His view that on the cross Christ had won victory over **death**, evil, and Satan anticipated the work of fellow Scandinavian Gustav Aulén (*Christus Victor* [1930]). Waldenström understood the atonement as a continuing process as each new convert is reconciled to God through faith.

WALES. *See* UNITED KINGDOM

WANYOIKE-WA-KAMAWE (ca. 1888–1978). Kenyan Presbyterian minister and educator. While still a young boy, Wanyoike joined the Kambui Mission of the Gospel Missionary Society (GMS). The society was founded by W. P. Knapp in 1902. Wanyoike lived with the Knapp family and, after four years of Bible instruction, was one of the first Gikuyu converts to be baptized. At age 14 he began eight years of schooling at the Kambui Mission. He was tutored for three years and, in turn, helped to instruct Knapp in the Gikuyu language. Wanyoike taught at Kambui (1910–1913) and at Komothai, and he began schools at Mitahato and Gathugu. In addition to his work in **education**, Wanyoike was a member of the Local Native Council and helped arbitrate civil cases in the district magistrate's court. Between 1926 and 1929 he studied for the **ministry** at Kambui; he was ordained in 1930 and conducted mission work at Kambui and Ng'enda. In 1945, when the GMS and the Church of Scotland Mission merged, Wanyoike was among the negotiators and signers of the agreement. He retired in 1959 but continued to be active in community development work and in the Presbyterian Church of East Africa.

WAR AND PEACE. The gospel message proclaims peace and defines peacemaking as an essential expression of Christian witness. Yet the witness of the Protestant and Reformed churches has been mixed. The European churches endured the **Wars of Religion**, and subsequent hostilities between Catholics and Protestants have been played out in many countries. The 20th-century world wars had a catastrophic impact on the global **mission** and witness of the Protestant churches. In the view of non-Western countries, the "Christian" West was at war with itself. Protestant mission work ceased in many countries, missionaries were interned, and churches and ministries were left unsupported.

Protestants have also been seen as peacemakers, especially in regional and tribal conflicts. During the colonial era, Protestants often tried to reduce hostilities between colonizing forces and **indigenous peoples.** The rapid expansion of mission work after 1945 has been characterized by tangible commitments to peacemaking, with some indigenous churches serving as mediators in areas of political tension (e.g., Mizoram).

WARFIELD, B[ENJAMIN] B[RECKENRIDGE] (1851–1921). American Presbyterian minister and theologian. Warfield was born near Lexington, Kentucky, and graduated from Princeton University (1871) and **Princeton Theological Seminary** (1876), where he studied under **Charles Hodge.** He was assistant pastor at the First Presbyterian Church, Baltimore, Maryland (1877–1878), before becoming professor of New Testament exegesis and literature at Western Theological Seminary (now **Pittsburgh Theological Seminary**) from 1878 to 1887. During that time, he and **A. A. Hodge** of Princeton published a famous article on **inspiration** in the *Presbyterian Review* (April 1881) that supported the verbal inspiration and inerrancy of the original autographs of **scripture**. Warfield succeeded A. A. Hodge as professor of didactic and polemic theology at Princeton Seminary, where he served from 1887 to 1921.

Warfield's scholarly work was wide-ranging and influential. His *Introduction to the Textual Criticism of the New Testament* (1886) appeared in nine editions. He was editor of the *Presbyterian and Reformed Review* (1890–1902) and the *Princeton Theological Journal* (from 1903). He wrote many articles, which were later collected in several volumes. His theological position continued the old **Princeton theology** of **Archibald Alexander** and the Hodges. Warfield opposed attempts to modify the **Westminster Confession.** His writings include major studies of Augustine, **John Calvin,** and the **Westminster Assembly.** He also wrote on the inspiration of scripture, **predestination** and God's decrees, the person and work of Christ, and perfectionism. Warfield's conservative views have been embraced by many who do not share his **Calvinism,** and his influence extends beyond the Presbyterian and Reformed churches to American **fundamentalism.**

WARS OF RELIGION. Wars between Protestant and Catholic forces during the Counter-Reformation in the late 16th and early 17th centuries. The wars began over issues of religious freedom, but also involved the balance of power in **Europe.** The religious question in **Germany** was addressed by the Peace of Augsburg (1555), which mandated that the population of each state conform to the religion of its ruler. This granted a measure of tolerance to Catholics and Lutherans but not to the emerging Calvinists. In **France,** the conflict between Catholics and Protestant **Huguenots** led to the **Saint Bartholomew's Day Massacres** (1572). A stalemate between the two sides resulted in the **Edict of Nantes** (1598), a decree that granted toleration to the Huguenots and allowed them to retain Protestant-controlled lands. In the **Netherlands,** the south remained Catholic and Spanish, but the north was controlled by the Protestants, who formed an independent federation. The **Peace of Westphalia** (1648) finally brought religious peace in Europe, except for lands ruled by the Habsburgs.

WATERSTON, JANE ELIZABETH (1843–1933). Scottish Free Church missionary and physician in **South Africa.** Born and educated in Inverness, Waterston went to the **Lovedale** mission in South Africa (1866), where she was head of the Lovedale Girls School. She resigned to pursue medical studies (1873), but the British system did not allow **women** to be examined in **medicine.** Waterston persisted and was educated in London; she obtained her M.D. in **Belgium.** She returned to South Africa to work as a medical missionary but struggled there just to be recognized as a physician. Eventually she left the **mission** and established a private general practice in Cape Town (1883). Over the next 50 years Waterston practiced medicine and became known for her philanthropic and political activities. In 1925 she was elected a fellow of the Royal College of Physicians in **Ireland**.

WATSON, MINNIE CUMMING (ca. 1870s–1930s). Scottish missionary and educator in **Kenya**. In 1898 Minnie Cumming arrived in Mombasa, **East Africa**, and married missionary colleague Thomas Watson. When her husband died two years later, Minnie Watson stayed on to work at Thogoto, where she operated a day school for refugee children. In 1907 she and colleague Ruffel Barlow decided to open a boarding school for boys, and in 1909 she started a boarding school for girls in her own home. Watson taught English, hygiene, sewing, and the catechism that prepared students for baptism. She tried to improve the social conditions of Gikuyu **women** and girls and spoke out against the practice of female circumcision. Watson was placed in charge of **education** at all mission schools, and by 1919 enrollment had increased to 370 students. Watson served the Kikuyu mission for 32 years. *See also* Catechisms

WATTS, ISAAC (1674–1748). English **Nonconformist** minister and hymn writer. Watts was born in Southampton, Hampshire, **England**, and educated at Stoke Newington Academy. In 1696 he became tutor to the family of John Hartopp, and he preached in the family chapel. He became assistant pastor (1699) and then pastor (1702) of Mark Lane Independent Chapel in London. In 1712 he fell ill and was taken in by the Thomas Abney family. He remained with them for the rest of his life. His publications include works on grammar, pedagogy, **ethics**, psychology, theology, and several volumes of sermons. Watts is best known as a hymn writer, having composed 600 hymns, including a volume of children's hymns. His hymn writing helped establish the tradition of using hymns, instead of psalmody exclusively, in Reformed **worship**. Watts wrote hymns based on the psalms but with modern words and Christianized ideas. His publications include *Hymns and Spiritual Songs* (1707), *Divine Songs* (1715), and *The Psalms of David Imitated in the Language of the New Testament* (1719). Among his most popular hymns are "O God, Our Help in Ages Past," "Joy to the World," "When I Survey the Wondrous Cross," and "Jesus Shall Reign." Watts is regarded as the founder of English hymnody.

WEBER, OTTO (1902–1966). German Reformed theologian. Weber served as professor at the Theological Seminary at Elberfeld, **Germany** (1928–1934), and then as professor of Reformed Theology at Göttingen

(1934–1966). He was a member of the Nazi Party and the "German Christians" (1933). Following World War II he publicly renounced Nazism and a recommendation from **Karl Barth** permitted him to continue to teach. His scholarly work was in the area of Reformed dogmatics. He translated Calvin's *Institutes* into German and prepared an evaluation of Karl Barth's dogmatics (*Karl Barth's Church Dogmatics: An Introductory Report* [English translation, 1953]). Weber also wrote his own two-volume systematic theology, *Foundations of Dogmatics* (English translation, 1982–1983), a detailed work in the theological tradition of Barth. Weber understands dogmatics as the church's response (German *Antwort*) to the **Word of God.** Christian dogmatics is closely related to proclamation, since neither dogmatics nor **preaching** is complete without the other. Weber emphasizes God's faithfulness in history and the centrality of Jesus Christ, who is the foundation of Christian **faith.**

WEST AFRICA. The people of West Africa practice traditional religions, Islam, and Christianity. Traditional religions predominate in Burkina Faso (45 percent; Muslim 43 percent; Christian 12 percent), Cameroon (51 percent; Muslim 16 percent; Christian 33 percent), Liberia (70 percent; Muslim 20 percent; Christian 10 percent), and Togo (70 percent; Muslim 10 percent; Christian 20 percent); Islam in Nigeria (50 percent; Christian 40 percent; traditional religions 10 percent) and Senegal (92 percent; Christian 2 percent; traditional religion 6 percent); and Christianity in Ghana (75 percent; Muslim 18 percent; traditional religion 6 percent). Growing Christian populations are evident in Cameroon, Ghana, and Nigeria. In each of these countries there are communities of Reformed churches.

The first Christian missionaries, primarily Roman Catholic, accompanied the gradual expansion of European settlement along the western coast of Africa beginning in the 16th century. The establishment and growth of Reformed churches took place in the 19th and 20th centuries, with the arrival of British, North American, Swiss, French, and German missionaries. British, French, and German **missions** were usually linked with their respective colonial expansion. By the end of the 19th century much of Africa south of the Sahara was under European colonial rule. The European wars upset the patterns of **colonialism** during the first half of the 20th century. The end of colonialism and the emergence of independent West African states have often been preceded by the formation of autonomous churches out of a great diversity of missionary endeavors.

Protestant mission agencies carried out a broad agenda in West Africa. The abolition of the slave trade became the focus of most Reformed mission organizations. Missionaries developed educational systems in many areas. Churches were organized and African evangelists were educated, a smaller number being ordained. Bible translation, the reduction of African languages to writing, and the development of indigenous literatures both preserved and profoundly shaped West African cultures. The use of European languages is also a legacy. Although vernacular languages are spoken by a majority of the population of West Africa, sub-Saharan states have adopted French or English (Spanish in Equatorial Guinea), or both languages. *See also* Slavery

Cameroon. The expansion of Reformed Christianity in Cameroon began with Jamaicans of African descent, whose vision to evangelize their ancestral homeland led the London Baptist Mission Society to send them to what was to become Cameroon. By 1845 two mission stations were established on the Cameroon River, and the ministry was developed largely by Jamaicans in partnership with English missionaries. German colonization of the region from 1884 onward resulted in a transfer of the mission work to the **Evangelical Mission Society in Basel**, which was joined by American Presbyterians in 1892 (see **Jean Kenyon Mackenzie**) as the mission expanded inland. The French and British divided the German colony in 1918, and French mission work was carried out by the **Paris Evangelical Mission Society.** With independence in 1960, the anglophone and francophone societies (four-fifths of the country is officially French speaking) were reunited.

After independence was established in Cameroon, three major Reformed churches and several smaller bodies continued their already well-established ministries. In 1957 the Presbyterian Church in Cameroon, the Evangelical Church of Cameroon (Eglise évangélique du Cameroun), and the Presbyterian Church of Cameroun (Eglise presbytérienne Camerounaise) became autonomous. Language and tribal concentrations contribute to their distinctiveness, but they cooperate in many ministries, especially in their joint sponsorship of the Protestant Theological Faculty in Yaoundé. These churches face many challenges, including the encounter with Islam and traditional African religions, ecumenical interaction with the Roman Catholic Church, and relations with diverse Protestant denominations. **Abraham Ebong Ngole** and **Jeremiah Chi Kangsen** have been leaders of the Presbyterian Church in Cameroon.

Equatorial Guinea. Equatorial Guinea (formerly Spanish Guinea) is made up of several islands and the mainland enclave of Rio Muni. It is the only officially Spanish-speaking nation of sub-Saharan Africa.

American Presbyterian missionaries arrived in 1850, and the Presbytery of Rio Muni was founded in 1860, initially connected with Cameroon and later made a **presbytery** of the Synod of New Jersey of the United Presbyterian Church. After the territory became Spanish in 1900 (colonial fluctuations have made the territory Portuguese, Spanish, and French at various times), the establishment of the Roman Catholic Church severely restricted Protestant activity.

In 1960 the Evangelical Presbyterian Church of Guinea became independent. The church formed an alliance with the World Mission Crusade and the Methodist Church of England in 1973; in 1987 these churches united to form the Reformed Church of Equatorial Guinea (Iglesia Reformada de Guinea Ecuatorial). Since national independence in 1968, the church has endured a period of dictatorial rule, suffering the confiscation of its property and the banning of its churches, hospitals, and schools. Religious liberty was restored in 1979.

Ghana. A Christian presence on the coast of Ghana can be traced to the 15th century and to sporadic missionary activity during the 18th century. The establishment of Protestant churches in Ghana did not occur until the 19th century with the growth of German, Swiss, and British mission work.

The Presbyterian Church of Ghana traces its roots to the work of the **Evangelical Mission Society in Basel**, beginning in 1828 in Akropong. Work among the Twi and Ashanti people expanded throughout the 19th century, with strong emphasis on **education.** When the British colonial authorities required that the Basel missionaries leave in 1917, Scottish missionaries assumed the work, shaping the emerging autonomous church along Presbyterian lines. The church has recently established the Akrofi-Christaller Memorial Centre in Akropong-Akuapem, which promotes research in West African Christianity.

The parallel work of the Bremen Mission Society (1836) of northern Germany led to the formation of the Evangelical Presbyterian Church, Ghana, in 1847. The roots of this church are primarily among the Ewe people. Scottish missionaries replaced the Germans after World War I, and the church became autonomous. After World War II missionaries from the Evangelical and Reformed Church in America (now part of the United Church of Christ) expanded the work. A newly formed denomination, the Evangelical Presbyterian Church of Ghana, has emerged from the Evangelical Presbyterian Church, Ghana.

Presbyterianism in Ghana is characterized by vigorous mission outreach that combines church planting with medical, educational, agricultural, and social ministries. The churches' ecumenical commitments include sponsorship of Trinity Theological College (1943), a united school serving several Protestant traditions.

Liberia. Christianity arrived in the region with freed American slaves who founded Liberia in 1822; in 1847 the country became independent. From 1833 North American Presbyterians carried out mission work in Liberia. Initially, only African-American missionaries were sent, but that policy was later abandoned. Between 1843 and 1850 the **American Board of Commissioners for Foreign Missions** also sent missionaries to Liberia, including **J. Leighton Wilson.** Although the last American missionaries arrived in 1887, the emerging Liberian church continued to receive financial aid from its North American partners. The Presbytery of Liberia in West Africa became an independent church in 1928. The church is noted for the important role played by its ordained **women** evangelists. Of more than 150 denominations in the country, it is among the smallest.

Nigeria. British colonization of what would become Africa's most populous nation was carried out between 1851 and 1914. The **Scottish Missionary Society** sent the first Presbyterians in 1846, at the urging of Jamaican Christians of African descent. The first group came from the **West Indies** to Old Calabar, under the leadership of Hope Waddell. The work expanded until there was a Presbyterian presence in the entire territory. Indigenous leadership was encouraged with the founding of the Hope Waddell Training Institution (1895); and educational, **health,** and medical services accompanied evangelistic ministry. Through literacy programs and Bible translation, the Presbyterian church encouraged the development of vernacular literature.

In 1954 the autonomous Presbyterian Church of Nigeria (PCN) was established. With over 120,000 members in 14 presbyteries, the PCN is one of the smaller denominations in Nigeria. It is characterized by a strong commitment to evangelistic ministry, while struggling at various times with civil war (in Biafra), continuing political turmoil, and tensions with the Muslim population. In addition to the PCN, there are seven other denominations linked in the Reformed Ecumenical Council of Nigeria (RECON), which was organized in 1991 to strengthen Reformed witness in the country. In 1994 the Presbyterian Theological College was established at Akwa, Ibom state. Noted leaders include Hope Waddell, **Mary Slessor, E. N. Amaku, Udo Udo Edikpo, Francis Akanu Ibiam,** Lady Ibiam, and Samuel Efern Imoke.

Senegal. The Protestant Church of Senegal (Eglise protestante du Sénégal) resulted from French **evangelical** mission efforts begun in 1863.

The church became independent in 1972. Its membership of 250 is concentrated in two congregations in Dakar and three preaching stations. It is part of a relatively small Christian minority in a predominantly Muslim country.

Togo. The Evangelical Church of Togo (Eglise évangélique du Togo) resulted from missionary efforts of the North German Mission Society, which from 1893 to 1921 worked in the western region of Togo. English- and French-speaking Togos were united in one synod when the church became independent in 1922. The **Paris Evangelical Mission Society** and the United Church of Christ (U.S.A.) continued to support the church in Togo, especially in its educational and evangelistic endeavors, until 1959, when the church became fully responsible for all its ministries. The church works ecumenically with several other Protestant churches that together make up about one quarter of the total Christian population of the country.

Burkina Faso. About 2.4 percent of the population of Burkina Faso (formerly Upper Volta) is Protestant. The Protestant community is affiliated with approximately 20 different churches. One of these churches is the Reformed Evangelical Church of Burkina Faso. This Reformed church is a growing community of about 3,000 members.

WESTERN SAMOA. *See* PACIFIC OCEAN ISLANDS

WEST INDIES. *See* CARIBBEAN

WESTMINSTER ASSEMBLY (1643–1648). A meeting of 121 English clergy with lay assessors and Scottish commissioners in Westminster Abbey, which produced doctrinal and **church government** standards. The Assembly met during the English Civil War and was instructed by the Long Parliament to suggest ways of making the Church of England "more agreeable to the **Word of God**." The **Puritan** character of the Parliament ensured that the proposed documents would be Calvinistic in character. The Assembly produced a Confession of Faith, the Larger and Shorter **Catechisms**, the Directory for Public Worship, and a Form of Church Government. In Scotland the Westminster Standards were adopted by the national church; in **England**, the rise of Independency led to the adoption of other doctrinal statements. The Westminster documents played a significant role in America, where they were for over two centuries the primary doctrinal standards of American **Presbyterianism.**

WESTMINSTER CONFESSION (1648). English confession produced by the **Westminster Assembly.** Influenced by the Irish Articles of Religion (1615) and the European Reformed **confessions**, the Westminster

Confession was completed in 1646 and approved by Parliament in 1648. It was accorded official status in **England** only until the restoration of the monarchy in 1660. Thereafter it was replaced in England by Episcopalian **church government**. The confession was adopted by the Church of Scotland (1647), by many Presbyterian denominations worldwide, and by some Congregational and Baptist groups in Great Britain and **North America**. The confession is divided into 33 chapters, including chapters on **scripture, God**, the **covenant** of **grace**, free will, redemption, the **law**, the **church**, and the last things.

WHARTON, ROBERT LESLIE (1871–1960). American Presbyterian minister, missionary, and educator in **Cuba**. Born in McLeansville, North Carolina, Wharton graduated from Davidson College (1892) and **Union Theological Seminary** in Virginia (1898). He went to Cuba in 1899 and settled in Cárdeñas, where **Anthony Graybill** had worked. With John G. Hall, Wharton organized churches and schools in Caíbarién and Remédios. He was appointed superintendent of the Presbyterian mission when Hall died in 1904. He was the main force behind *La Progresiva*, a secondary school in Cárdenas that had grown to almost 2,000 students when it was taken over by the Castro government in 1961. Wharton was also the first **moderator** of Cuba's Central Presbytery, organized in 1914. In 1918 the two American Presbyterian denominations working in Cuba combined their work, forming the United Presbytery of Havana. Thereafter, Wharton concentrated on teaching and educational work, serving as superintendent of schools. He died in Cárdenas.

WHITEFIELD, GEORGE (1714–1770). Church of England evangelist. Whitefield was born in Gloucester and educated at Pembroke College, Oxford. After his **conversion** in 1735, he joined John and Charles Wesley in their Holy Club. The following year he became a **deacon** in the Church of England and in 1738 traveled to America, where he worked with orphans in Georgia. During a return trip to **England** to raise money for an orphanage, Whitefield began open-air **preaching** in Bristol. After returning to America in 1739, he preached throughout the colonies. In 1740 his preaching tour reached its zenith in New England, where he preached daily for over a month to crowds of up to 8,000 people. This exhibition was a pivotal event in New England's **Great Awakening.** Whitefield made seven trips to America and 14 tours to **Scotland.** He broke with the Wesleys' **Arminianism** and preached a **Calvinism** shaped primarily by English Puritan theologians. His success in preaching was attributed to his direct, plain speech to the common people, and his appeal to their hearts and emotions. He preached over 15,000 times during a 33-year ministry.

WHITMAN, NARCISSA PRENTISS (1808–1847). American Congregationalist missionary. Whitman was born in Prattsburg, New York. In 1834 she applied to the **American Board of Commissioners for Foreign Missions** to become a missionary in Oregon. In 1836 she married missionary-physician Marcus Whitman (1802–1847) and went to work among the Nez Percé, Flathead, and Cayuse Indians in Oregon. The Whitmans, and co-workers Henry and Eliza Spalding, traveled overland along the Oregon Trail to the Northwest. Narcissa Whitman conducted a school at the Waiilatpu Mission, near Walla Walla, Washington, and cared for homeless children. In 1839 the Whitmans' two-year-old daughter drowned. Narcissa's eyesight began to fail, and work became increasingly difficult. Tensions increased between the Cayuse Indians and the settlers, and in 1847 Narcissa and her husband, along with 12 others, were killed in an attack by the Cayuse. Narcissa Whitman's work enabled the mission to become the pioneering Protestant work in the Pacific Northwest. Her writings, including 126 letters and diaries, were published posthumously.

WIERENGA, CORNELIUS R. (1894–1971). American missionary in **India** with the Reformed Church in America. A native of the **Netherlands**, Wierenga emigrated with his family to the **United States** and graduated from Hope College (1917). After a short term of missionary service in India, he returned to the United States to complete his theological **education** at Western Theological Seminary (1923). Returning to India, Wierenga worked for three years in village evangelistic ministry and then took charge of the Arcot Theological Seminary at Vellore, which educated village pastors and catechists for evangelistic outreach. He was a leader in the South India United Church, serving as its last **moderator** and preparing the way for the formation of the Church of South India (1947). He was one of a small group of non-Anglican clergyman who consecrated Anglican bishops in the new Church of South India.

WILKES, HENRY (1805–1886). Canadian Congregationalist minister and agent of the Colonial Missionary Society in **Canada**. Born in **England**, Wilkes emigrated to Canada in 1819. In 1827 he was appointed secretary to the newly organized Canada Education and Home Missionary Society. Wilkes developed contacts with missionary societies in the British Isles and went to Glasgow to study for the Congregational **ministry**.

As a student, Wilkes recruited Congregational ministers to serve in Canada and received a large donation from the **London Missionary Society** to further his efforts. Following a three-year pastorate in Edinburgh, he returned to Canada and served as pastor of a new Congregational church in Montreal and agent of the Colonial Missionary Society in Canada, a subsidiary of the London Missionary Society. Wilkes is credited with organizing more than 25 Congregational churches and raising funds to support more than 30 Congregational ministers. His efforts helped to establish the Congregational churches in Canada.

WILLARD, SAMUEL (1640–1707). American Congregationalist minister and theologian. Willard was born in Concord, Massachusetts, and graduated from Harvard College in 1659. He was a pastor in Groton, Massachusetts (1663–1676), until the city was destroyed by Native Americans in King Philip's War. In 1678 Willard moved to Boston and became pastor of the Old South Church, remaining there for the rest of his life. He also served as vice president (1700–1707) and acting president (1701–1707) of Harvard.

Willard's fame rests on his *Compleat Body of Divinity*, sometimes called "New England's *Summa*," published posthumously in 1726. The book emerged from Willard's monthly lectures, delivered between 1678 and 1707, on the Westminster Shorter Catechism. It is the largest volume published during colonial times (914 folio pages). The work stands as a second-generation **Puritan** summary of the Christian **faith.** Because Willard's work reflects many of the views of the first generation, it was somewhat dated at its publication. Nevertheless, the work remains a valuable summary of Puritan teachings and was an important resource for later generations of New England divinity students. Willard's other works include *Covenant-Keeping, the Way to Blessedness* (1682), *A Brief Discourse on Justification* (1680), and *The Truly Blessed Man* (1700).

WILLIAM III, OF ORANGE (1650–1702). Stadholder of the **Netherlands** (1672–1702), king of **Great Britain** (1689–1702), and defender of Protestantism. Born in The Hague, William was the son of William II, prince of Orange, and Mary, the daughter of Charles I of **England.** As stadholder, he opposed the armies of Louis XIV of **France** and was able to keep **Holland** a prosperous and free nation. As the ruler of Great Britain, he was never accepted by the upper classes but was hailed by the public for his support of Protestantism. He carried out political reform in England, establishing an independent judiciary and securing the British parliamentary system.

WILLIAMS, JOHN (1796–1839). English missionary in the Pacific Islands. Born in London, Williams was apprenticed at the age of 14 to an ironmonger. He experienced a **conversion** at the age of 18 and joined the Calvinistic congregation at the Tabernacle, Moorfields. In 1816 he volunteered for missionary service with the **London Missionary Society** and was sent to the Pacific Islands. In 1817 Williams arrived in the **Society Islands** and visited Huahine and Ra'iatéa in 1818. Williams established a printing press in Huahine and printed **scripture** portions and elementary lessons in Tahitian. In order to reach scattered island populations, Williams purchased the schooner *Endeavour* and sailed to the **Cook Islands** in 1823. Unable to meet the expenses of operating the vessel, he was forced to sell the schooner and relocate to Rarotonga in 1827. There he translated the New Testament into the Rarotongan language and built a second vessel, *The Messenger of Peace,* on which he traveled to other distant islands. He returned to **England** for seven years (1832–1838) and wrote the autobiographical *Narrative of Missionary Enterprises in the South Sea Islands* (1837). He raised money for a third vessel, the *Camden,* on which he and 16 other missionaries sailed to **Samoa**, the Society Islands, and **Vanuatu.** He was killed by Erromango islanders in Vanuatu.

WILSON, JOHN (1804–1875). Scottish Presbyterian missionary in **India.** After studying linguistics, philosophy, and theology at Edinburgh University, Wilson went to Bombay as a missionary for the **Scottish Missionary Society** (1829). He learned Indian languages (Marathi, Gujarati, Hindustani, and Persian), evangelized, founded schools, ministered to the poor, and engaged in discussions with representatives of other religions. Wilson founded an English school in Bombay and was appointed vice-chancellor of the University of Bombay (1857). **Education** and **evangelism** were the two emphases of his work, always informed by intensive study of Indian literature and culture. He explored widely in India, strategizing and encouraging the expansion of **mission** work. Wilson was elected **moderator** of the Free Church (1870) and published works on Hinduism, Islam, and the Parsi religion.

WILSON, JOHN LEIGHTON (1809–1886). American Presbyterian missionary in **West Africa** and secretary of foreign **missions** for the Presbyterian church. Born in Sumter County, South Carolina, Wilson was educated at Union College, Schenectady, New York, and Columbia Theological Seminary. He developed an interest in Africa and was sent by the **American Board of Commissioners for Foreign Missions** to **Liberia**

and Gabon, where he served from 1834 to 1853. He then served as secretary of the Presbyterian Board of Foreign Missions (1853–1860). With the outbreak of the U.S. Civil War, the Presbyterian Church divided into two bodies. Wilson aligned himself with the southern body, the Presbyterian Church in the United States, serving as secretary of its Executive Committee of Foreign Missions (1861–1886). Wilson helped break up the slave trade in **Africa.** He compiled a dictionary and grammar of the Grebo and Mpongwe languages, translated parts of the Bible, and published the first literature in a western equatorial language. During his extensive travels in West Africa to treat the sick and to found schools and churches, Wilson collected vast amounts of information, which ultimately appeared in his encyclopedic work *Western Africa, Its History, Conditions, and Prospects* (1856). He was editor of the *Foreign Record* (New York, 1853–1861) and the *Missionary* (Baltimore, 1861–1885). He inspired the founding of the American Presbyterian Congo Mission, which had a wide influence under **William M. Morrison.**

WINTHROP, JOHN (1588–1649). Puritan governor of Massachusetts Bay Colony. Winthrop studied at Trinity College, Cambridge (1603–1605), became a justice of the peace of Lord of Groton Manor (after 1619), practiced law in London (ca. 1613–1629), and emigrated to Massachusetts Bay Colony in 1629. Winthrop was influenced by Puritan teachings in college and became a person of deep piety while practicing law in London. He decided to emigrate, hoping to live in a land in which the reform of religion could be more completely carried out. He became an executive in the Massachusetts Bay Company and was elected the first governor of the Massachusetts Bay Colony, serving several terms between 1629 and 1649.

Winthrop's *A Model of Christian Charity* (1630) set the life of the colony in the context of the **covenant** of **God,** patterned after Old Testament Israel. The people of Massachusetts Bay were to render corporate obedience to God's law of love. Their faithfulness or disobedience evoked God's blessings or judgments. The civil magistrate was to maintain both moral purity and theological integrity. Winthrop conceived of the holy commonwealth as a "city set on a hill." He banished **Anne Hutchinson** and Roger Williams from the colony because of their divergent theological views. He also served as the first president of the New England Confederation (1643).

WITHERSPOON, JOHN (1723–1794). American Presbyterian minister, president of the College of New Jersey, member of the Continental Congress, and signer of the Declaration of Independence. Witherspoon was born in Yester in Haddonshire and attended the University of Edinburgh (M.A., 1739). He studied theology at Edinburgh (1739–1743), was ordained in 1745, and served a congregation in Beith, **Scotland**. In 1757 Witherspoon was called to the Leigh church in Paisley and became a leader in the **evangelical** party, opposing patronage and arguing for the right of a local church to have **authority** in choosing its own clergy rather than accepting those sent by the national church.

In 1768 Witherspoon became the sixth president of the College of New Jersey (now Princeton University). He improved the finances of the college and the quality of instruction in the natural sciences and languages. He lectured in divinity, moral philosophy, and "eloquence." Witherspoon introduced the Scottish Common Sense philosophy to American intellectual life, opposing both idealism and skepticism. His students later distinguished themselves in government service as state governors, members of Congress, and Supreme Court justices. Their records bore out his conviction that **education** should lead to public service. Witherspoon was elected to the Continental Congress and was the only minister to sign the Declaration of Independence. He served in Congress (1776–1782) and helped to negotiate an alliance with France. He sought to stabilize American **Presbyterianism** by uniting various groups. In 1789 he became **moderator** of the Presbyterian Church's first **general assembly**. His theological writings include *Practical Treatise on Regeneration* (1764) and *Essay on Justification* (1756).

WOMEN. The status of women in Reformed churches has been characterized by the traditional discrimination that has existed in many societies; nevertheless, there has been a gradual movement toward gender equality. Modern ecumenical and missionary movements have provided women with remarkable opportunities for service and leadership in non-Western cultures (e.g., **Chi-Oang, Mary Hannah Fulton, Sarah P. W. Kalley, Michi Kawai, Winifred Keik, Jean K. Mackenzie**, and others). In Western countries, such leadership roles developed slowly, with many changes coming in the wake of secular emancipatory movements. The **ordination** of women to the diaconate, the eldership, and the pastorate have gained widespread approval only in the latter half of the 20th century. Reformed churches continue to deal with discriminatory cultural patterns and theological resistance, making the participation of women still incomplete. As of 1998, approximately one-third of the member churches of the **World Alliance of Reformed Churches** do not ordain women.

WONG, PETER (1914–1984). Educator and general secretary of the Hong Kong Council of the Church of Christ in China (HKCCCC). Wong was born in Guangzhou, **China.** He was educated at Ying Wa Boys College, **Hong Kong**, and studied theology at Union Theological College in Guangzhou. He traveled to the **United States** and studied at Oberlin College. Upon his return to Hong Kong, Wong was appointed executive secretary and then general secretary of the Synod of the Church of Christ in China. Over a 25-year career Wong established the HKCCCC as a separate entity and built a self-supporting, self-governing, and self-propagating Chinese church in Hong Kong. The HKCCCC became an important contributor to church programs in **Africa** and **India.** As an educator, Wong developed a network of over 60 primary, secondary, and vocational schools in Hong Kong. He developed innovative programming and educational activities. Upon his retirement in 1983, the HKCCCC collected and published his writings in a book titled *The Words of the General Secretary* (1984).

WORD OF GOD. God's self-revelation. The Bible contains many references to the word of God. In the Old Testament, prophets received instructions from the mouth of **God.** In the New Testament, Jesus speaks the word of God with the **authority** of God. In the Acts of the Apostles, the early **church** regarded the preached gospel as the word of God (cf. Acts 4:31). This oral gospel of the early church was later set down in **scripture** so that it became the written word of God. Finally, in the Gospel of John, Jesus is referred to as the living Word of God. It is out of this multiplicity of meanings that **Karl Barth** expounded a threefold Word of God characteristic of the **neoorthodox** movement: Jesus Christ is the *incarnate,* living, "revealed" Word of God; the scriptures are the *written* Word of God; and the **preaching** of the church is the *proclaimed* Word of God. Each dimension of the Word of God is related to the others and cannot exist in isolation. The living Word (Jesus Christ) is revealed in and through the written Word (scripture) and made present through the proclaimed Word (preaching). The **Holy Spirit** is active in conjunction with the written and preached Word to make effective the living Word who conveys the **knowledge** of God (Calvin, *Inst.* 1.9.3). This is why the **Theological Declaration of Barmen** (Art. 1) speaks of the one Word of God, Jesus Christ, who is known in these three forms.

WORLD ALLIANCE OF REFORMED CHURCHES (WARC). The most important international organization of Reformed churches representing about 70 percent of the world's Reformed Christians. Founded in 1875, the "Alliance of Reformed Churches Throughout the World Holding the Presbyterian System" was headquartered in Edinburgh until 1948. The Alliance offices were then relocated to Geneva, where they remain today. In 1970 the Alliance merged with the **International Congregational Council** (ICC) to form the World Alliance of Reformed Churches (Presbyterian and Congregational). The World Alliance is a federation of 211 (1998) Reformed churches (with 70 million communicants) organized into a General Council, which meets every five to seven years, an executive committee, which meets annually, and various regional bodies, which meet intermittently. The member churches of World Alliance of Reformed Churches, while sharing a common Calvinian heritage, are extremely diverse. These churches subscribe to more than 60 different Reformed **confessions** and differ in **worship** practices and church organization. The World Alliance of Reformed Churches serves primarily as a consultative and advisory body, engaging in theological study, **interfaith dialogue**, and benevolent work. The organization carries on conversations with other Christian world communions, including the Orthodox, Anglican, and Lutheran World Federation. In addition to theological studies and reports, the World Alliance publishes a journal, the *Reformed World.*

WORLD COUNCIL OF CHURCHES (WCC). Composed of more than 300 Eastern Orthodox and Protestant (including Anglican) denominations from more than 100 countries, the WCC is the largest Christian **ecumenical** body. Organized in 1948, the WCC incorporated other ecumenical organizations formed during the 20th century, including the Faith and Order movement and the Life and Work movement (1948), the International Missionary Council (1961), and the World Council of Christian Education (1971).

The WCC meets in an assembly attended by more than 800 delegates from around the world. Seven assemblies have been held: Amsterdam (1948), Evanston, Illinois (1954), New Delhi (1961), Uppsala (1968), Nairobi (1975), Vancouver (1983), Canberra (1991), and Harare (1998). Between assemblies, the work of the WCC is carried out by a Central Committee composed of 150 elected members. The WCC operates several program units, including Faith and Witness, Justice and Service, and Education and Renewal. It maintains an Ecumenical Institute at Bossey, Switzerland, and publishes the *Ecumenical Review* (established 1948) and the *International Review of Mission* (est. 1912).

Reformed churches have been involved in the WCC from its inception. Approximately 50 Reformed denominations and several union churches with Reformed heritage maintain membership in the world organization. The WCC has drawn on the Reformed heritage for aspects of its organizational life and theology. WCC leaders from the Reformed tradition include **John Baillie**, Roswell Barnes, Madeleine Barot, **Hendrikus Berkhof, Marc Boegner, Emil Brunner**, Samuel Cavert, **Douglas Horton, Josef Hromádka**, Alphonse Koechlin, **Hendrik Kraemer, John A. Mackay, Reinhold Niebuhr** and **H. Richard Niebuhr**, and **Henry P. Van Dusen**. In addition, **W. A. Visser 't Hooft** and **Eugene Carson Blake** have served as general secretary, the chief WCC executive.

WORSHIP, PUBLIC. The reverence, adoration, praise, supplication, and thanksgiving offered by a **community** of **faith** to **God**. Worship is given in response to the mystery of God's being and to the wonders of God's activity in **creation** and redemption. In public worship the gathered community uses liturgical language, **music** and singing, symbolic actions, and silence to communicate with God. God speaks to the worshiping community through **scripture, sacraments**, sermon, and silence and song. The Reformed tradition stresses the need for all worship to conform to God's word as found in the scriptures. The scriptures contain the "whole counsel of God" concerning all things necessary for God's glory, human **salvation**, and life (**Westminster Confession**, chap. 1).

The scriptural elements of Reformed worship include music, both instrumental and vocal, especially the singing of psalms; congregational confession of **sin** and declaration of pardon; **prayer**, especially prayers of intercession and supplication; reading of scripture; the sermon or proclamation of the **Word of God**; creeds or **confessions** recited in unison as expressions of faith and as a response to God's Word; an offering given in gratitude for God's goodness and for use in the church's **mission** and **ministry**; and sacraments administered as visible signs and seals of God's presence and as a means of nourishing the faith of the worshiping community. The renewal of worship has been an important emphasis of the Reformed churches during the 20th century. As a result, much attention has been given to the modernization of music and hymnals and to the use of liturgical forms that communicate to differing national, social, and cultural contexts.

Many churches in **Africa, Asia**, and **Latin America** still use a set liturgy brought from the missionary churches of **Europe** and **North America**. These services usually feature formal prayers, translated hymns, and limited participation by the congregation. Other churches, especially those influenced by the charismatic movement, desire more spontaneity in worship and have incorporated traditional music and singing, congregational participation, and traditional musical instruments. Regardless of the type of liturgy employed, Reformed churches try to maintain the unity of Word and sacrament. **Preaching** continues to be of primary importance in weekly worship, whereas the **Lord's Supper** may be celebrated weekly, monthly, or a few times a year.

- Y -

YAP THIAM HIEN (1913–1989). Indonesian Chinese lawyer and lay leader. Educated as a lawyer in **Indonesia** and the **Netherlands**, Yap was a founder of the Regional Council on Human Rights in **Asia** and the Legal Aid Institute in Jakarta. He was appointed one of the Asian representatives on the International Commission of Jurists and supported the judicial impartiality of Asian courts. As a member of the Indonesian Chinese minority, Yap supported the assimilationist movement and opposed discrimination against Chinese; he was a critic of communism and supported Asian liberation movements. Yap was active in various bodies of the **World Council of Churches** and was known for the integrity of his Christian witness. He was awarded an honorary doctor of law degree by the **Free University of Amsterdam** for his **human rights** work.

YOO, JAE-KEE (1907–1949). Korean Presbyterian minister and pioneer of the **labor** union, rural cooperative, and credit union movements in **Korea**. Born in Yongju, Kyong-Buk Province, Yoo received his early **education** in Korea, and in 1923 he traveled to **Japan**, where he was influenced by the Christian social movement. Yoo brought the tenets of the movement to Korea by launching the "Jesus village" movement in the southeastern part of Korea (the Youngnam region) in 1926. Yoo then attended Pyongyang Theological Seminary and graduated in 1932. After graduation, he directed the rural division of the General Assembly of the Korean Presbyterian Church. Yoo's articles on rural cooperatives were serialized in the Christian newspaper, *Keedokko Shinmoon,* in 1927 and in the *Chosen Daily* in 1933. In 1938 Yoo was imprisoned by the Japanese government because his activism was viewed as an independence movement. Following his release from prison, Yoo served Uisong Church in Uisong and First Presbyterian Church in Taegu. In 1945 Yoo organized the Christian Brethren for National Revival in Seoul and published the *National Revival Newspaper.*

YUGOSLAVIA. *See* CENTRAL AND EASTERN EUROPE

YU KUO-CHEN (1856–1932). Chinese Reformed church leader. Born in Chekiang (Zhejiang) Provence, Yu became pastor of Hongkou Presbyterian Church in Shanghai (1894). He was one of the leaders who worked to free the Chinese church from the control of Western **mission** boards. In 1903 he organized the Chinese Christian Union and changed the name of his church to the Independent Presbyterian Church (1906). By 1911 Yu had organized the Chinese Independent Protestant Church (CIPC), which grew to include hundreds of congregations. As head of the CIPC, Yu was its major voice for over 20 years.

YUSUF, TADRUS (1842–1903?). Egyptian Presbyterian minister; the first graduate of a seminary. Yusuf was educated at the Coptic Egyptian Christian school. In 1857 he became headmaster of the Coptic school at Haret al-Saqa'een in Cairo. Appointed supervisor of the American Boys School in Cairo in 1862, Yusuf remained there for four years. He was then appointed director of the American school at al-Fayoum, where he established an **evangelical** fellowship. This fellowship grew into the Evangelical Church in Sinnoris. After attending seminary, Yusuf was ordained and installed as pastor of al-Nakhayla Church in 1871, remaining there for 31 years. He served as executive secretary of the first Egyptian **presbytery.** In 1886, along with G. Khayyat and Khalil Ibrahim, Yusuf became an editor of *al-Nuzha,* the first weekly regional newspaper published in **Egypt.** Yusuf's eyesight began to fail, and by age 50 he was blind. He nevertheless ministered for another 10 years, until 1903.

- Z -

ZAMBIA. *See* SOUTHERN AFRICA

ZIMBABWE. *See* SOUTHERN AFRICA

ZWEMER, SAMUEL MARINUS (1867–1952). American Reformed Church missionary in the **Middle East**, Islamic specialist, and author. Born in Michigan, Zwemer attended Hope College and **New Brunswick Theological Seminary**, from which he graduated in 1890. He traveled to the Arabian Gulf area to join James Cantine in **mission** work in Basrah, **Bahrain**, and Muscat. In 1894 the Reformed Church in America assumed sponsorship of Zwemer's work, which became its Arabian mission. Between 1905 and 1910 Zwemer traveled throughout the **United States** on behalf of Islamic mission work and the Student Volunteer Movement. He organized Christian conferences on Islam in Cairo (1906) and Lucknow (1911). In 1911 he became the founding editor of *The Moslem World*, a scholarly periodical that he edited for 36 years. In 1912 he began a long residence in Cairo, where he worked with the Nile Mission Press and traveled to **India, China,** and other countries with Islamic populations. Returning to the United States in 1929, Zwemer became a professor of mission and the history of religion at **Princeton Theological Seminary.** Among his publications, which number about 50 volumes, including works in Arabic, are *Arabia, the Cradle of Islam* (1900), *Islam: A Challenge to Faith* (1907), and *Across the Moslem World* (1929).

ZWINGLI, HULDRYCH (1484–1531). Swiss Protestant Reformer. Zwingli was born in Wildhaus, part of the Swiss Confederacy. He studied at Berne and Vienna before attending the University of Basel (B.A., 1504; M.A., 1506), where he excelled in humanistic studies. Zwingli was ordained a Catholic priest and served in Glarus (1506–1516) and Einsiedeln (1516–1518) until he became the People's (Preaching) Priest at the Great Minster in Zurich. The Reformation in Zurich may be dated from 1519, when Zwingli began to preach the Gospel of Matthew. For the next decade, he led the reform movement in **Switzerland.** He wrote tracts and **confessions** of faith, and he promoted the cause of the Reformation through his friendship with **John Oecolampadius** and other reformers. He tried to thwart the Anabaptist movement and disagreed with Martin Luther over the **Lord's Supper** at the **Marbury Colloquy** (1529).

Zwingli studied the works of Erasmus and was influenced by the ideas of Origen, Augustine, and Martin Luther, which he incorporated into his own theology. He stressed the **sovereignty of God** in **election.** He emphasized simplicity in **worship,** achieved by removing statuary, pictures, stained glass windows, and organs from churches. To Zwingli, the Bible was the cradle of **faith,** and the focus of worship was **preaching.** He accepted two **sacraments: baptism** as a sign of membership in the visible **church** and the Lord's Supper as a memorial of the benefits of Christ's **death.** Zwingli believed that Christ's presence in the Supper is symbolic, not physical. He interpreted Christ's words "this is my body" to mean "this signifies my body." He proposed the unity, rather than the separation, of **church and state.** Zwingli's views spread from Switzerland and southern **Germany** to **England** and **Scotland.** His theology developed into a distinct Protestant ethos having both affinities with and differences from the views of Luther and **John Calvin.** Zwingli was killed on the battlefield in the Second Battle of Kappel.

ZWINGLIANISM. A Reformed movement separate from **Calvinism** that stressed the centrality of **faith**, primacy of **scripture**, and simplicity of **worship**. Zwinglianism grew out of the work of **Huldrych Zwingli**, who introduced church reform to the German-speaking areas of **Switzerland** from his base in Zurich. Zwingli attempted to reform Swiss congregational life by organizing worship around the **Word of God** in scripture rather than around visual images, whether in stained glass, statuary, or other depictions. Simplicity in worship also meant the rejection of church organs. The center of worship was to be **preaching**, and sermons were to be biblically grounded so that congregations would be able to hear the living Word of God. The movement was Christ centered in its theology and differed from both the Lutheran and Calvinist churches in its understanding of the **sacraments**. Zwinglianism taught that the **Lord's Supper** is a simple memorial in which Christ is neither physically present (Lutherans) nor spiritually present (Calvinists). **Baptism** is merely a sign of one's membership in the **church** and in civil society. Zwinglian influences are still present in many Reformed churches that trace their heritage to this movement.

Bibliography

INTRODUCTION

No bibliography of the Reformed tradition can be exhaustive. The tradition is too theologically diverse, ecclesiastically complex, multilingual, and ever changing. The Reformed churches in some countries are small and have little or no literature, whereas in other countries the churches are large, and the literature is vast. In many countries, like Korea, a wealth of material is in a language that is inaccessible to most Westerners. And the shifting boundaries of the Reformed faith, as churches advance and retreat around the world, means constant revisions in bibliographical coverage. For these and other reasons, an exhaustive bibliography is not possible.

What is offered here is a basic guide for English-language readers. The bibliography is divided into four parts. Part 1 is a general orientation to Protestant Christianity in a global context. Part 2 focuses on the Reformation and the literature produced by and about the Protestant Reformers, especially John Calvin. Part 3 is a general orientation to the history, theology, and life of the modern Reformed tradition. Part 4 is an orientation to the world Reformed churches organized by seven regions of the world. It contains materials on the history of the Reformed churches in specific countries. For a few European countries, the citations listed in parts 2 and 4 should be read together.

The focus of the bibliography is on English-language books. Literature in German, French, and other languages has been cited, whenever possible, in English translation. Where no translations exist, significant works are cited in the original European languages. Whenever the monographic literature is inadequate, dissertations and journal articles have been cited. In recent years there has been a flurry of activity to document the history and faith of the younger, non-Western churches and some progress can be seen in the bibliography. Nevertheless, regional balance, which has been a concern throughout, has not always been possible to achieve.

The individual works listed in the bibliography may vary in their helpfulness. A few works by Reformed theologians such as John Calvin or Karl Barth are enduring classics in their field. Some historical or theological works may be dated but still provide an important perspective on the history and life of the Reformed churches. Some biographies and missionary literature may be flawed in perspective but still provide the only available coverage on a topic. In every case, the reader is advised to use discernment in making use of the bibliography.

A few books can be mentioned by way of general orientation to each part of the bibliography. In part 1, David B. Barrett's *The World Christian En-*

cyclopedia, 3 vols. (Oxford: Oxford University Press, forthcoming) is a mine of historical and statistical information. Anglican in perspective, *The Oxford Dictionary of the Christian Church*, 3d ed. (Oxford: Oxford University Press, 1997) is a prized handbook on many aspects of the Christian tradition. *The Encyclopedia of Christianity* (Grand Rapids, Mich.: Eerdmans, 1999–) is a Protestant work with an ecumenical outlook and worldwide coverage. For global mission Gerald H. Anderson's *Biographical Dictionary of Christian Missions* (New York: Simon & Schuster, 1997) will be a standard for many years. The ecumenical movement is well covered in Nicholas Lossky's *Dictionary of the Ecumenical Movement* (Grand Rapids, Mich.: Eerdmans, 1991) and Ans Joachim van der Bent's *Historical Dictionary of Ecumenical Christianity* (Metuchen, N.J.: Scarecrow Press, 1994).

In part 2, Euan Cameron's *The European Reformation* (Oxford: Clarendon Press, 1991) and Hans J. Hillerbrand's *Historical Dictionary of the Reformation and Counter-Reformation* (Lanham, Md.: Scarecrow Press, 1999) are basic guides. The reform in France is examined in Mark Greengrass's *The French Reformation* (Oxford: Blackwell, 1987). The situation in Geneva is described in Robert M. Kingdon's *Geneva and the Consolidation of the French Protestant Movement, 1554–1572* (Madison, Wis.: University of Wisconsin Press, 1967) and in William G. Naphy's *Calvin and the Consolidation of the Genevan Reformation* (Manchester: Manchester University Press, 1994). Among the recent biographies of John Calvin are William J. Bouwsma's *John Calvin: A Sixteenth-Century Portrait* (New York: Oxford University Press, 1988) and a translation of A. Ganoczy's *The Young Calvin* (Philadelphia: Westminster Press, 1987). Calvin's best-known theological work, considered one of the classics of Reformed theology, is his *Institutes of the Christian Religion*, trans. Ford Lewis Battles, 2 vols. (Philadelphia: Westminster Press, 1960). Two classic works on the English Reformation are A. G. Dickens's *The English Reformation*, 2d ed. (New York: Peter Bedrick Books, 1990) and Patrick Collinson's *The Elizabethan Puritan Movement* (Berkeley: University of California Press, 1967). Diarmaid MacCulloch's *Thomas Cranmer: A Life* (New Haven, Conn.: Yale University Press, 1996) is sure to become a standard work. Several studies are available on the Scottish Reformation, including Ian B. Cowen, *The Scottish Reformation: Church and Society in Sixteenth Century Scotland* (New York: St. Martin's Press, 1982).

In part 3, aspects of the modern Reformed tradition are summarized in Donald K. McKim's *Encyclopedia of the Reformed Faith* (Louisville, Ky.: Westminster John Knox, 1992) and in Jean-Jacques Bauswein and Lukas

Vischer's *The Reformed Family Worldwide* (Grand Rapids, Mich.: Eerdmans, 1999). The former summarizes the historical and theological tradition, whereas the latter is a catalog of the world Reformed churches with statistical information. French readers will greatly benefit from Pierre Gisel's *Encyclopédie du Protestantisme* (Paris: Cerf, 1995). A classic history of the Reformed movement, now showing its age, is John T. McNeill's *The History and Character of Calvinism* (New York: Oxford University Press, 1967). Two works on the World Alliance of Reformed Churches are Marcel Pradervand's *A Century of Service: A History of the World Alliance of Reformed Churches, 1875–1975* (Grand Rapids, Mich.: Eerdmans, 1975) and Alan P. F. Sell's *A Reformed, Evangelical, Catholic Theology: The Contribution of the World Alliance of Reformed Churches, 1875–1982* (Grand Rapids, Mich.: Eerdmans, 1991). A helpful collection of Reformed confessions is Lukas Vischer's *Reformed Witness Today: A Collection of Confessions and Statements of Faith Issued by Reformed Churches* (Bern: Evangelische Arbeitsstelle Ökumene Schweiz, 1982).

In part 4, historical surveys of Africa, Asia, and Latin America include Adrian Hastings's *A History of African Christianity, 1950–1975* (New York: Cambridge University Press, 1979) and *The Church in Africa, 1450–1950* (New York: Oxford University Press, 1994), J. W. Hofmeyr and G. J. Pillay's *A History of Christianity in South Africa* (Pretoria: HAUM, 1994), Alan Hunter and Kim-Kwong Chan's *Protestantism in Contemporary China* (New York: Cambridge University Press, 1993), Stephen Neill's *A History of Christianity in India 1707–1858*, 2 vols. (New York: Cambridge University Press, 1984–1985), Wilton M. Nelson's *Protestantism in Central America* (Grand Rapids, Mich.: Eerdmans, 1984), and H. McKennie Goodpasture's *Cross and Sword: An Eyewitness History of Christianity in Latin America* (Maryknoll, N.Y.: Orbis Books, 1989).

For Europe, an older work still helpful for English readers is Émile G. Léonard, *A History of Protestantism*, 2 vols. (London: Nelson, 1965, 1967), which should be supplemented by Jacob Rosenberg's *Dutch Art and Architecture 1600–1800* (New Haven, Conn.: Yale University Press, 1987) and other studies. In the British Isles, the Congregational side of the Reformed family is surveyed in R. Tudur Jones's *Congregationalism in England, 1662–1962* (London: Independent Press, 1962) and Harry Escott's *A History of Scottish Congregationalism* (Glasgow: The Congregational Union of Scotland, 1960). For Presbyterian Scotland, an important reference work is Nigel M. de S. Cameron et al., *Dictionary of Scottish Church History & Theology* (Downers Grove, Ill.: InterVarsity Press, 1993). A multivolume history of the Scottish church is Andrew L. Drummond, and James

Bulloch's *The Scottish Church, 1688–1843: The Age of the Moderates* (Edinburgh: Saint Andrew Press, 1973), *The Church in Victorian Scotland, 1843–1879* (Edinburgh: Saint Andrew Press, 1975), and *The Church in Late Victorian Scotland 1874–1900* (Edinburgh: Saint Andrew Press, 1978). For North America, two complementary histories are Robert T. Handy's *A History of the Churches in the United States and Canada* (New York: Oxford University Press, 1977) and Mark A. Noll's *A History of Christianity in the United States and Canada* (Grand Rapids, Mich.: Eerdmans, 1992). Henry Warner Bowden's *Dictionary of Religious Biography* (2d ed.; Westport, Conn.: Greenwood Press, 1993), Randall Balmer and John R. Fitzmier's *The Presbyterians* (Westport, Conn.: Greenwood Press, 1993), and J. William Youngs's *The Congregationalists* (Westport, Conn.: Greenwood Press, 1990) are standard works.

For Australia and the Pacific region standard works include Roger C. Thompson's *Religion in Australia: A History* (New York: Oxford University Press, 1994), Charles W. Forman's *The Island Churches of the South Pacific: Emergence in the Twentieth Century* (Maryknoll, N.Y.: Orbis Books, 1982) and John Garrett's *To Live Among the Stars: Christian Origins in Oceania* (Geneva: World Council of Churches, 1982) and *Footsteps in the Sea: Christianity in Oceania to World War II* (Suva: Institute for Pacific Studies, 1992).

PROTESTANT CHRISTIANITY IN THE MODERN WORLD

Reference Works

1. Atlases

Hartmann, Karl. *Atlas-Tafel-Werk zu Bibel und Kirchengeschichte: Karten, Tabellen, Erläuterungen.* 5 vols. Stuttgart: Quelle Verlag, 1979–.

Jedin, Hubert, Kenneth Scott Latourette, and Jochen Martin, eds. *Atlas zur Kirchengeschichte: Die christlichen Kirchen in Geschichte und Gegenwart.* Freiburg im Breisgau: Herder, 1970.

Littel, Franklin H. *The Macmillan Atlas History of Christianity.* New York: Macmillan, 1976.

2. Bibliographies

Bibliographia Missionaria, 1933– . Vatican City: Pontifical Urban University. Published annually.

Fahey, Michael A. *Ecumenism: A Bibliographical Overview.* Westport, Conn.: Greenwood Press, 1992.

Fritze, Ronald H., Brian E. Coutts, and Louis A. Vyhnanek. *Reference Sources in History: An Introductory Guide.* Santa Barbara: ABC-Clio, 1990.

Gorman, G. E., and Lyn Gorman. *Theological and Religious Reference Materials*. 3 vols. Westport, Conn.: Greenwood Press, 1984–1986.

Hartley, Loyde H. *Cities and Churches: An International Bibliography*. 3 vols. Metuchen, N.J.: Scarecrow Press, 1992.

Latham, A. J. H. *Africa, Asia, and South America Since 1800: A Bibliographical Guide*. New York: St. Martin's Press, 1995.

Melton, J. Gordon, and Michael A. Köszegi. *Religious Information Sources: A Worldwide Guide*. New York: Garland Publishing, 1992.

Missionary Research Library. *Dictionary Catalog of the Missionary Research Library (New York)*. 17 vols. Boston: G. K. Hall, 1967. The collection is now housed at Union Theological Seminary in New York.

———. *Missionary Biography: An Initial Bibliography*. New York: Missionary Research Library, 1965.

3. Indexes to Christian Literature

American Theological Library Association. *ATLA Religion Database on CD-ROM*. Chicago: ATLA, 1993. Updated annually, this product indexes periodical articles, book reviews, and multiauthor works in religion from 1949.

American Theological Library Association. *International Christian Literature Documentation Project: A Subject, Author and Corporate Name Index to Nonwestern Christian Literature*. Vol. 1, *Subject Index*; vol. 2, *Author-Editor Index/Corporate Name Index*. Evanston, Ill.: ATLA, 1993.

Historical Abstracts: Bibliography of the World's Periodical Literature. Edited by E. H. Boehm. Santa Barbara: ABC Clio, 1955–.

Index to the World Council of Churches Official Statements and Reports, 1948–1978. Geneva: World Council of Churches, 1978.

Myklebust, O. G. *International Review of Missions: Index 1912–1966*. Geneva: International Review of Missions, 1968.

4a. Dictionaries and Encyclopedias, General Works

Barrett, David B., ed. *The World Christian Encyclopedia*. Rev. ed. 3 vols. Oxford: Oxford University Press, forthcoming.

Brauer, Jerald C., ed. *The Westminster Dictionary of Church History*. Philadelphia: Westminster Press, 1971.

Campenhausen, Hans von, et al., eds. *Die Religion in Geschichte und Gegenwart: Handwörterbuch für Theologie und Religionswissenschaft*. 7 vols. 3d. ed. Tübingen: Mohr, 1957–1965.

Cross, F. L., and E. A. Livingstone, eds. *The Oxford Dictionary of the Christian Church*. 3d ed. Oxford: Oxford University Press, 1997.

Douglas, J. D., ed. *The New International Dictionary of the Christian Church*. Grand Rapids, Mich.: Zondervan, 1978.

————. *New 20th-Century Encyclopedia of Religious Knowledge*. 2d ed. Grand Rapids, Mich.: Baker Book House, 1991.

Fahlbusch, Erwin, Jan Milic Lochman, John Mbiti, and Lukas Vischer, eds. *Evangelisches Kirchenlexikon: Internationale theologische Enzyklopädie*. 4 vols. Göttingen: Vandenhoeck & Ruprecht, 1986–.

Fahlbusch, Erwin, et al., eds. *The Encyclopedia of Christianity*. Translated by Geoffrey W. Bromily. 5 vols. Grand Rapids, Mich.: Eerdmans, 1999–.

Hauck, A., ed. *Realencyclopaedie für protestantische Theologie und Kirche*. 24 vols. 3d ed. Leipzig: J. C. Hinrich, 1896–1913.

Jackson, Samuel Macauley, et al., eds. *The New Schaff-Herzog Encyclopedia of Religious Knowledge*. 12 vols. New York: Funk & Wagnalls, 1908–1914.

Krause, Gerhard, and Gerhard Müller, eds. *Theologische Realenzyklopädie*. 30 vols. Berlin and New York: de Gruyter, 1976–.

Loetscher, L. A., ed. *Twentieth Century Encyclopedia of Religious Knowledge*. 2 vols. Grand Rapids, Mich.: Baker Book House, 1955. Continues Jackson above.

4b. Dictionaries and Encyclopedias, Biographies

Anderson, Gerald H., ed. *Biographical Dictionary of Christian Missions*. New York: Simon & Schuster, 1997.

Who's Who in Religion [1992–1993]. 4th ed. Wilmette, Ill.: Marquis Who's Who, 1992.

4c. Dictionaries and Encyclopedias, Mission and Ecumenism

Goddard, Burton L., ed. *The Encyclopedia of Modern Christian Missions: The Agencies*. New Jersey: Thomas Nelson & Sons, 1967.

Jongeneel, J. A. B. *Philosophy, Science, and Theology of Mission in the Nineteenth and Twentieth Centuries: A Missiological Encyclopedia*. 2 vols. Frankfurt, Germany: Peter Lang, 1995–1997.

Lossky, Nicholas, et al., eds. *Dictionary of the Ecumenical Movement*. Grand Rapids, Mich.: Eerdmans, 1991.

Müller, Karl, et al., eds. *Dictionary of Mission: Theology, History, Perspectives*. Maryknoll, N.Y.: Orbis Books, 1997.

Neill, Stephen, Gerald H. Anderson, and John Goodwin. *Concise Dictionary of the Christian World Mission*. Nashville, Tenn.: Abingdon Press, 1971.

Van der Bent, Ans Joachim. *Historical Dictionary of Ecumenical Christianity*. Metuchen, N.J.: Scarecrow Press, 1994.

4d. Dictionaries and Encyclopedias, Religion and Theology

Crim, Keith, ed. *Abingdon Dictionary of Living Religions*. Nashville, Tenn.: Abingdon Press, 1981.

Edwards, Paul, ed. *The Encyclopedia of Philosophy*. 8 vols. New York: Macmillan, 1972.

Eliade, Mircea, ed. *The Encyclopedia of Religion*. 16 vols. New York: Macmillan, 1987.

Hastings, James, ed. *Encyclopedia of Religion and Ethics*. 13 vols. Edinburgh: T. & T. Clark, 1908–1926.

McGrath, Alister E., ed. *The Blackwell Encyclopedia of Modern Christian Thought*. Oxford: Blackwell, 1993.

McKim, Donald K. *Westminster Dictionary of Theological Terms*. Louisville, Ky.: Westminster John Knox, 1996.

Richardson, Alan, and John Bowden, eds. *The Westminster Dictionary of Christian Theology*. Philadelphia: Westminster Press, 1983.

Russell, Letty M., and J. Shannon Clarkson, eds. *Dictionary of Feminist Theologies*. Louisville, Ky.: Westminster John Knox, 1996.

Wuthnow, Robert, ed. *The Encyclopedia of Politics and Religion*. 2 vols. Washington, D.C.: Congressional Quarterly Books, 1998.

The History and Theology of Protestantism

1. Handbooks

Barzun, Jacques, and Henry F. Graff. *The Modern Researcher*. 4th ed. San Diego, Calif.: Harcourt, Brace, Jovanovich, 1985.

Bradley, James E., and Richard A. Muller. *Church History: An Introduction to Research, Reference Works, and Methods*. Grand Rapids, Mich.: Eerdmans, 1995.

2. Theologies of History

Baillie, John. *The Belief in Progress*. London: Oxford University Press, 1950.

Bebbington, David. *Patterns in History: A Christian Perspective on Historical Thought*. Grand Rapids, Mich.: Baker Book House, 1990.

Berkhof, Hendrikus. *Christ and the Meaning of History*. Grand Rapids, Mich.: Baker Book House, 1966.

Butterfield, Herbert. *The Origins of History*. New York: Basic Books, 1981.

Cullmann, Oscar. *Christ and Time: The Primitive Christian Conception of Time and History*. Philadelphia: Westminster Press, 1950.

———. *Salvation in History*. London: SCM Press, 1967.

Gilkey, Langdon Brown. *Reaping the Whirlwind: A Christian Interpretation of History*. New York: Seabury Press, 1976.

Harvey, Van A. *The Historian and the Believer: The Morality of Historical Knowledge and Christian Belief*. Reprint, Philadelphia: Westminster Press, 1981.

Himmelfarb, Gertrude. *The New History and the Old.* Cambridge, Mass.: Harvard University Press, 1987.

McIntire, C. T., ed. *God, History, and Historians: An Anthology of Modern Christian Views of History.* New York: Oxford University Press, 1977.

————. *Herbert Butterfield: Writings on Christianity and History.* New York: Oxford University Press, 1979.

Niebuhr, Reinhold. *Faith and History: A Comparison of Christian and Modern Views of History.* Reprint, New York: Macmillan, 1987.

Richardson, Alan. *History Sacred and Profane.* London: SCM Press, 1964.

Rust, Eric C. *The Christian Understanding of History.* London: Lutterworth Press, 1947.

3. Histories of Protestantism

Chadwick, Henry, and Owen Chadwick, eds. *Oxford History of the Christian Church.* 20 vols. New York: Oxford University Press, 1977–. In progress.

Cragg, Gerald. *Church & Age of Reason, 1648–1789.* New York: Penguin Books, 1961.

González, Justo. *The Story of Christianity.* Vol. 2, *The Reformation to the Present Day.* New York: Harper & Row, 1985.

Latourette, Kenneth S. *Christianity in a Revolutionary Age: A History of Christianity in the Nineteenth and Twentieth Centuries.* 5 vols. Reprint, Westport, Conn.: Greenwood Press, 1973.

————. *History of Christianity.* Vol. 2, *Reformation to 1975.* New York: Harper & Row, 1975.

McNeill, John T., and James H. Nichols. *Ecumenical Testimony: The Concern for Christian Unity within the Reformed and Presbyterian Churches.* Philadelphia: Westminster Press, 1974.

Neill, Stephen. *A History of Christian Missions.* Rev. ed. New York: Penguin, 1986.

Rouse, Ruth, Stephen C. Neill, and Harold E. Fey, eds. *A History of the Ecumenical Movement.* Vol. 1, *1517–1948;* vol. 2: *1948–1968.* One vol. ed. Geneva: World Council of Churches, 1993.

Walker, Williston. *A History of the Christian Church.* 4th ed. Revised by Richard A. Norris, David W. Lotz, and Robert T. Handy. New York: Macmillan, 1985.

Yates, Timothy. *Christian Mission in the Twentieth Century.* New York: Cambridge University Press, 1994.

4. Histories of Protestant Theology

Dillenberger, John, and Claude Welch. *Protestant Christianity: Interpreted through its Development.* 2d ed. New York: Macmillan, 1988.

Küng, Hans. *Christianity: Essence, History, and Future.* New York: Continuum, 1995.

Pelikan, Jaroslav. *The Christian Tradition.* 5 vols. Chicago: University of Chicago, 1971–1989.

Welch, Claude. *Protestant Thought in the Nineteenth Century.* 2 vols. Reprint, New Haven, Conn.: Yale University Press, 1988.

THE EUROPEAN ORIGINS OF THE REFORMED TRADITION

The Reformation

1. Bibliographies

Adams, Herbert M., comp. *Catalogue of Books Printed on the Continent of Europe, 1501–1600, in Cambridge Libraries.* 2 vols. Cambridge: Cambridge University Press, 1967.

Archiv für Reformationsgeschichte, Beiheft: Literaturbericht/Archive for Reformation History. Supplement: Literature Review. St. Louis, Mo.: American Society for Reformation Research, 1972–. Published annually.

Bainton, Roland H., and Eric W. Gritsch. *Bibliography of the Continental Reformation: Materials Available in English.* 2d ed., rev. and enl. Hamden, Conn.: Archon Books, 1972.

Chrisman, Miriam Usher. *Bibliography of Strasbourg Imprints, 1489–1599.* New Haven, Conn.: Yale University Press, 1982.

Ozment, Steven E., ed. *Reformation Europe: A Guide to Research.* St. Louis, Mo.: Center for Reformation Research, 1982.

Pollard, Alfred W., and Gilbert R. Redgrave. *A Short Title Catalogue of Books Printed in England, Scotland, and Ireland and of English Books Printed Abroad, 1475–1640.* 2d ed., rev. and enl. by W. A. Jackson, F. S. Ferguson, and Katherine F. Pantzer. 2 vols. London: The Bibliographical Society, 1976, 1986. See also, Rider, Philip R. *A Chronological Index to the Revised Edition of the Pollard and Redgrave Short-Title Catalogue.* London: Bibliographical Survey, 1978.

Van den Brink, J. N. B., et al., eds. *Bibliographie de la Réforme 1450–1648.* 7 vols. Leiden: E. J. Brill, 1958–1970.

2. Dictionaries and Encyclopedias

Hillerbrand, Hans J., ed. *Historical Dictionary of the Reformation and Counter-Reformation.* Lanham, Md.: Scarecrow Press, 1999.

————. *The Oxford Encyclopedia of the Reformation.* 4 vols. New York: Oxford University Press, 1996.

3. Primary Sources

Bretschneider, Karl, et al., eds. *Corpus Reformatorum.* 101 vols. Halle, Berlin, Leipzig, and Zürich, 1834–1962. Includes the works of Calvin (vols. 29–87) and Zwingli (vols. 88–101).

Center for Reformation Research Microform Holdings. 8 vols. St. Louis, Mo.: The Center, 1977–1979.

Cochrane, Arthur C., ed. *Reformed Confessions of the 16th Century.* Philadelphia: Westminster Press, 1966.

Duke, Alastair, Gillian Lewis, and Andrew Pettegree, eds. *Calvinism in Europe, 1555–1610: A Collection of Documents.* Manchester: Manchester University Press, 1992.

Durr, Emil. *Aktensammlung zur Geschichte der Basler Reformation in den Jahren 1519 bis Anfang 1534. Im Auftrage der Historischen und antiquarischen Gesellschaft zu Basel.* 6 vols. Basel: Verlag der Historischen und antiquarischen Gesellschaft, 1921–1950.

Early English Books I, 1475–1640. Ann Arbor, Mich.: University Microfilms. Microfilm editions of almost all of the works from the short title catalog of Pollard and Redgrave.

Leith, John H., ed. *Creeds of the Churches.* 3d ed. Louisville, Ky.: Westminster John Knox, 1982.

Johnson, William Stacy, and John H. Leith, eds. *Reformed Reader: A Sourcebook in Christian Theology.* Vol. 1, *Classical Beginnings, 1519–1799.* Louisville, Ky.: Westminster John Knox, 1993.

Müller, E. F. Karl. *Die Bekenntnisschriften der reformierten Kirche.* Leipzig: A Deichert, 1903.

Niesel, Wilhelm, ed. *Bekenntnisschriften und Kirchenordnungen der nach Gottes Wort reformierten Kirche.* 2d ed. Zürich: Evangelischer Verlag A. G. Zollikon, 1938.

Reformed Protestantism: Sources of the 16th and 17th Centuries on Microfiche. 1.A. Heinrich Bullinger and the Zürich Reformation; I.B. Geneva; 2.A. Strasbourg; 2.B. France, 3. The Netherlands and Germany. Zug, Switzerland/New York: Inter Documentation Company/Norman Ross Publishing. Swiss microfiche contains 543 titles; Geneva, Strasbourg, and France contain 229 titles; Netherlands and Germany contain 262 titles.

Schaff, Philip. *The Creeds of Christendom, with a History and Critical Notes.* 3 vols. New York: Harper, 1919.

Strickler, Joannes. *Actensammlung zur schweizerischen Reformationsgeschichte in den Jahren 1521–1532: im Anschluss an die gleichzeitigen eidgenossischen Abschiede.* 5 vols. Zürich: Theologische Buchhandlung, 1989.

Torrance, Thomas F., ed. *The School of Faith: The Catechisms of the Reformed Churches.* New York: Harper, 1959.

4a. Histories and Studies, General Works

Brady, Thomas A., Heiko A. Oberman, and James D. Tracy, eds. *Handbook of European History, 1400–1600: Late Middle Ages, Renaissance, & Reformation.* 2 vols. Grand Rapids, Mich.: Eerdmans, 1996.

Cameron, Euan. *The European Reformation.* Oxford: Clarendon Press, 1991.

Eire, Carlos M. N. *War against the Idols: The Reformation of Worship from Erasmus to Calvin.* Cambridge: Cambridge University Press, 1986.

Oberman, Heiko A. *The Reformation: Roots and Ramifications.* Grand Rapids, Mich.: Eerdmans, 1994.

Ozment, Steven E. *The Age of Reform (1250–1550): An Intellectual and Religious History of Late Medieval and Reformation Europe.* New Haven, Conn.: Yale University Press, 1980.

4b. Histories and Studies of Switzerland, Bibliographies

Heyer, Henri, and Eugène Pallard, eds. *Bibliographie de l'Eglise Evangélique Réformée de la Suisse.* Berne: K. J. Wyss, 1918.

Martin, Paul Edmond. *Catalogue de la collection des manuscrits historiques* [Archives d'Etat de Genève]. Geneva: A. Jullien, 1936.

Ruchat, Abraham, and Louis Vulliemin. *Histoire de la réformation de la Suisse.* 7 vols. Lausanne: Ducloux, 1835–1838.

4c. Histories and Studies of Switzerland, Primary Sources

Fatio, Olivier. *Registres de la Compagnie des pasteurs de Genève.* Geneva: Droz, 1962–.

Hughes, Philip E. *The Register of the Company of Pastors of Geneva in the Time of Calvin.* Grand Rapids, Mich.: Eerdmans, 1966.

4d. Histories and Studies of Switzerland, General

Innes, William C. *Social Concern in Calvin's Geneva.* Allison Park, Pa.: Pickwick, 1983.

Kingdon, Robert M. *Adultery and Divorce in Calvin's Geneva.* Cambridge, Mass.: Harvard University Press, 1995.

———. *Geneva and the Coming of the Wars of Religion in France, 1555–1563.* Geneva: L. Droz, 1956.

———. *Geneva and the Consolidation of the French Protestant Movement, 1554–1572.* Madison, Wis.: University of Wisconsin Press, 1967.

Monter, E. William. *Calvin's Geneva.* New York: John Wiley, 1967.

Naphy, William G. *Calvin and the Consolidation of the Genevan Reformation.* Manchester: Manchester University Press, 1994.

See "Zwingli" and "Calvin" under Continental Reformers.

4e. Histories and Studies of Germany

Holborn, Hajo. *A History of Modern Germany: The Reformation.* 1959. Reprint, Princeton, N.J.: Princeton University Press, 1982.

Spitz, Lewis W. *The Protestant Reformation, 1517–1559: The Rise of Modern Europe.* New York: Harper & Row, 1985.

Visser, Derk, ed. *Controversy and Conciliation: The Reformation and the Palatinate, 1559–1583.* Allison Park, Pa.: Pickwick Press, 1986.

4f. Histories and Studies of Central and Eastern Europe

Evans, R. J. W. "Calvinism in East Central Europe: Hungary and Her Neighbours." In *International Calvinism*, edited by Menna Prestwich, 167–96. Oxford: Clarendon Press, 1985.

Fudge, Thomas A. *The Magnificent Ride: The First Reformation in Hussite Bohemia.* Brookfield, Vt.: Ashgate, 1998.

Kool, A. M. *God Moves in a Mysterious Way: The Hungarian Protestant Foreign Mission Movement, 1756–1951.* Zoetermeer: Uitgerverij Boekencentrum, 1993.

Lubieniecki, Stanislas. *History of the Polish Reformation and Nine Related Documents.* Translated and interpreted by George Huntston Williams. Minneapolis: Augsburg Press, 1994.

Maag, Karin, ed. *The Reformation in Eastern and Central Europe.* Brookfield, Vt.: Ashgate, 1997.

Tóth, K. "The Helvetic Reformation in Hungary." In *John Calvin: His Influence in the Western World.* Edited by W. S. Reid. Grand Rapids, Mich.: Zondervan Publishing House, 1982.

Unghváry, Alexander S. *The Hungarian Protestant Reformation in the Sixteenth Century under the Ottoman Impact.* Lewiston, N.Y.: Mellen Press, 1989.

4g. Histories and Studies of Italy

Cantimori, Delio. *Italian Heretics of the Sixteenth Century.* Cambridge, Mass.: Harvard University Press, 1979.

Church, Frederic C. *The Italian Reformers, 1534–1564.* New York: Octagon Books, 1974.

Martin, John. *Venice's Hidden Enemies: Italian Heretics in a Renaissance City.* Berkeley: University of California Press, 1993.

4h. Histories and Studies of France

Bainton, Roland H. *Women of the Reformation in France and England.* Minneapolis: Augsburg Publishing House, 1973.

Davis, Natalie Z. *Society and Culture in Early Modern France.* Stanford, Calif.: Stanford University Press, 1975.

Garrison, Janie. *Les protestants au XVIe siècle.* Paris: Fayard, 1988.

Greengrass, Mark. *The French Reformation*. Oxford: Blackwell, 1987.

Higman, Francis. *La diffusion de la réforme en France, 1520–1565*. Geneva: Labor et Fides, 1992.

———. *Piety and the People: Religious Printing in France, 1511–1551*. Aldershot: Scolar Press, 1996.

Salmon, J. H. M. *Society in Crisis: France in the Sixteenth Century*. New York: St. Martin's Press, 1975.

4i. Histories and Studies of the Netherlands

Bremmer, R. H. *Reformatie en rebellie*. Franeker: Wever, 1984.

Crew, Phyllis M. *Calvinistic Preaching and Iconoclasm in the Netherlands, 1544–1569*. New York: Cambridge University Press, 1978.

Duke, Alastair. "The Ambivalent Face of Calvinism in the Netherlands, 1561–1618." In *International Calvinism*, edited by Menna Prestwich, 109–34. Oxford: Clarendon Press, 1985.

Freedberg, D. "Art and Iconoclasm, 1525–1580: The Case of the Northern Netherlands." In *Kunst and Beeldenstorm*, Rijksmuseum Exhibition Catalogue, The Hague, 1986.

Geyl, Pieter. *The Revolt in the Netherlands, 1555–1609*. London: E. Benn, 1966.

Ijssewijn, J. "The Coming of Humanism in the Low Countries." In *Itinerarium Italicum: Essays in Honour of P. O. Kristeller*, edited by H. A. Oberman, 193–304. Leiden: E. J. Brill, 1975.

Parker, G. *The Dutch Revolt*. Ithaca, N.Y.: Cornell University Press, 1977.

Pettegree, Andrew. *Emden and the Dutch Revolt: Exile and the Development of Reformed Protestantism*. New York: Oxford University Press, 1992.

4j. Histories and Studies of Scotland

Cowen, Ian B. *The Scottish Reformation: Church and Society in Sixteenth Century Scotland*. New York: St. Martin's Press, 1982.

Donaldson, Gordon. *The Scottish Reformation*. Cambridge: Cambridge University Press, 1960.

Lynch, Michael. "Calvinism in Scotland, 1559–1638." In *International Calvinism*, edited by Menna Prestwich, 225–55. Oxford: Clarendon Press, 1985.

———. *Edinburgh and the Reformation*. Edinburgh: Donald, 1981.

Wormald, Jenny. *Court, Kirk, and Community: Scotland 1470–1625*. 1981. Reprint, Toronto: University of Toronto Press, 1990.

4k. Histories and Studies of England

Bainton, Roland H. *Women of the Reformation in France and England*. Minneapolis: Augsburg Publishing House, 1973.

Collinson, Patrick. *The Birthpangs of Protestant England.* New York: St. Martin's Press, 1988.

————. *The Elizabethan Puritan Movement.* Berkeley: University of California Press, 1967.

————. "England and International Calvinism, 1558–1640." In *International Calvinism,* edited by Menna Prestwich, 197–223. Oxford: Clarendon Press, 1985.

————. *English Puritanism.* London: Historical Association, 1983.

————. *The Religion of Protestants: The Church in English Society, 1559–1625.* Oxford: Clarendon Press, 1992.

Dickens, A. G. *The English Reformation.* 2d ed. New York: Peter Bedrick Books, 1990.

Elton, G. R. *Reform and Reformation: England, 1509–1558.* Cambridge, Mass.: Harvard University Press, 1977.

Pettegree, Andrew. *Marian Protestantism: Six Studies.* Aldershot: Scolar Press, 1996.

Scarisbrick, J. J. *The Reformation and the English People.* Oxford: Basil Blackwell, 1984.

Shiels, W. J. *The English Reformation, 1530–1570.* London: Longman, 1989.

5. The Theology of the Reformation

Bierma, Lyle D. *German Calvinism in the Confessional Age: The Covenant Theology of Caspar Olevianus.* Grand Rapids, Mich.: Baker Book House, 1997.

Dickens, A. G., and John M. Tonkin. *The Reformation in Historical Thought.* Cambridge, Mass.: Harvard University Press, 1985.

George, Timothy. *The Theology of the Reformers.* Nashville, Tenn.: Broadman, 1987.

McGrath, Alister E. *Reformation Thought: An Introduction.* Oxford: Blackwell, 1989.

Muller, Richard A. *Christ and the Decree: Christology and Predestination in Reformed Theology from Calvin to Perkins.* Durham, N.C.: Labyrinth Press, 1986.

Platt, J. *Reformed Thought and Scholasticism: The Arguments for the Existence of God in Dutch Theology, 1575–1650.* Leiden: E. J. Brill, 1982.

Schweizer, Alexander. *Die protestantishen Centraldogmen in ihrer Entwicklung innerhalb der reformirten Kirche.* 2 vols. Zürich: Orell, Fuessli, 1854–1856.

Weir, David A. *The Origins of Federal Theology in Sixteenth-Century Reformation Thought.* New York: Oxford University Press, 1990.

The Continental Tradition

1a. Huldrych Zwingli, Bibliographies

Gäbler, Ulrich. *Huldrych Zwingli im 20. Jahrhundert: Forschungsbericht und annotierte Bibliographie, 1897–1972*. Zürich: Theologischer Verlag, 1975.

Pipkin, H. Wayne. *A Zwingli Bibliography*. Pittsburgh: Clifford E. Barbour Library, 1972.

Thompson, Bard. "Zwingli Study Since 1918." *Church History* 19 (1950): 116–128.

1b. Huldrych Zwingli, Biographies

Gäbler, Ulrich. *Huldrych Zwingli: His Life and Work*. Translated by Ruth C. L. Gritsch. Philadelphia: Fortress Press, 1986.

Potter, G. R. *Zwingli*. Cambridge: Cambridge University Press, 1976.

1c. Huldrych Zwingli, Primary Sources

Bromiley, G. W., ed. *Zwingli and Bullinger*. Library of Christian Classics, vol. 24. Philadelphia: Westminster Press, 1953.

Furcha, E. J., ed. *The Defense of the Reformed Faith*. Vol. 1. Huldrych Zwingli Writings. Allison Park, Pa.: Pickwick Publications, 1984.

Jackson, Samuel Macauley, ed. *Early Writings: The Latin Works of Huldrych Zwingli*. Vol 1. 1912. Reprint, Durham, N.C.: Labyrinth Press, 1986.

Jackson, Samuel Macauley, and Clarence Nevin Heller, eds. *Commentary on True and False Religion: The Latin Works of Huldrych Zwingli*. Vol. 3. 1929. Reprint, Durham, N.C.: Labyrinth Press, 1983.

Jackson, Samuel Macauley, and William John Hinke, eds. *On Providence and Other Essays: The Latin Works of Huldrych Zwingli*. Vol. 2. 1922. Reprint, Durham, N.C.: Labyrinth Press, 1981.

Pipkin, H. Wayne, ed. *In Search of True Religion: Reformation, Pastoral and Eucharistic Writings*. Vol. 2, Huldrych Zwingli Writings. Allison Park, Pa.: Pickwick Publications, 1984.

1d. Huldrych Zwingli, Studies

Büsser, Fritz, ed. *1484–1984: Zwingli und die Züricher Reformation*. Zürich: Theologischer Verlag, 1984.

Courvoisier, Jacques. *Zwingli, A Reformed Theologian*. Richmond, Va.: John Knox Press, 1963.

Furcha, E. J. *Huldrych Zwingli, 1484–1531: A Legacy of Radical Reform*. Montreal: McGill University, 1985.

Furcha, E. J., and H. W. Pipkin, eds. *Prophet, Pastor, Protestant: The Work of Huldrych Zwingli after Five Hundred Years*. Allison Park, Pa.: Pickwick Publications, 1984.

Garside, Charles. *Zwingli and the Arts*. New Haven, Conn.: Yale University Press, 1966.

Locher, Gottfried W. *Zwingli's Thought: New Perspectives*. Studies in the History of Christian Thought, vol. 25. Leiden: Brill, 1981.

Oberman, Heiko A., et al., eds. *Reformiertes Erbe: Festschrift für Gottfried W. Locher zu seinem 80. Geburtstag*. Vol. 1. Zürich: Theologischer Verlag, 1992.

Pollet, J. V. *Huldrych Zwingli et le Zwinglianisme*. Paris: Vrin, 1988.

Rilliet, Jean. *Zwingli: Third Man of the Reformation*. Philadelphia: Westminster Press, 1964.

Stephens, W. P. *The Theology of Huldrych Zwingli*. New York: Oxford University Press, 1986.

———. *Zwingli: An Introduction to his Thought*. Oxford: Clarendon Press, 1992.

2a. John Calvin, Bibliographies

Bourilly, E., et al., eds. *Calvin et la Réforme en France*. 2d ed. Aix-en-Provence: Librairie Dragen, 1974. "Bibliographie Calvinienne abrégée," 137–64.

De Klerk, Peter. "Calvin Bibliographies, 1971–." *Calvin Theological Journal* 7 (1972): 221–50; 9 (1974): 38–73, 210–40; 10 (1975): 175–207; 11 (1976): 199–243; 12 (1977): 164–87; 13 (1978): 166–94; 14 (1979): 187–212; 15 (1980): 244–60; 16 (1981): 206–21; 17 (1982): 231–47; 18 (1983): 206–24; 19 (1984): 192–212; 20 (1985): 268–80; 21 (1986): 194–221; 22 (1987): 275–94; 23 (1988): 195–221; 24 (1989): 278–99; 25 (1990): 225–48; 26 (1991): 389–411; 27 (1992): 326–52; 28 (1993): 393–419; 29 (1994): 451–85; 30 (1995): 419–47; 31 (1996): 420–63; and Paul Fields 32 (1997): 368–94.

Dowey, Edward A., Jr. "Studies in Calvin and Calvinism since 1948." *Church History* 24 (1955): 360–367.

———. "Studies in Calvinism since 1955." *Church History* 29 (1960): 187–204.

Erichson, Alfred, ed. *Bibliographia Calviniana. Catalogus Chronologicus Operum Calvini*. Nieuwkoop, Netherlands: B. de Graaf, 1960.

Fraenkel, Pierre. "Petit supplement aux bibliographies calviniennes 1901–1963." *Bibliothèque d'Humanisme et Renaissance* 33 (1971): 385–413.

Kempff, Dionysius. *A Bibliography of Calviniana, 1959–1974*. Medieval and Reformation Thought, vol. 15. Leiden: E. J. Brill, 1975.

McNeill, John T. "Thirty Years of Calvin Study." *Church History* 17 (1948): 207–240.

Niesel, Wilhelm. *Calvin-Bibliographie, 1901–1959*. Munich: Chr. Kaiser, 1961. Continuation of Erichson.

Peter, Rodolphe, and Jean-François Gilmont. *Bibliotheca Calviniana: Les oeuvres de Jean Calvin publiées au xvi siècle*. Vol. 1, *Écrits théologiques, littéraires et juridiques, 1532–1554*. Geneva: Librairie Droz, 1991.

———. *Bibliotheca Calviniana*. Vol. 2. Geneva: Librairie Droz, 1994.

Tylenda, Joseph N. "Calvin Bibliography, 1960–1970." Edited by Peter De Klerk. *Calvin Theological Journal* 6 (1971): 156–193.

2b. John Calvin, Biographies

Bouwsma, William J. *John Calvin: A Sixteenth-Century Portrait*. New York: Oxford University Press, 1988.

Doumergue, Emile. *Jean Calvin, les hommes et les choses de son temps*. 7 vols. Lausanne: Georges Bridel, 1899–1927.

Ganoczy, A. *The Young Calvin*. Translated by David Foxgrover and Wade Provo. Philadelphia: Westminster Press, 1987.

McGrath, Alister E. *A Life of John Calvin*. Oxford: Basil Blackwell, 1990.

Parker, T. H. L. *John Calvin: A Biography*. Philadelphia: Westminster Press, 1975.

2c. John Calvin, Primary Sources

Battles, Ford Lewis, trans. *Institutes of the Christian Religion*. Edited by John T. McNeill. Library of Christian Classics, 20, 21. Philadelphia: Westminster Press, 1960.

———. *Institution of the Christian Religion: 1536 Edition*. Grand Rapids, Mich.: Eerdmans, 1986.

Battles, Ford Lewis, trans. and ed. *The Piety of John Calvin: An Anthology Illustrative of the Spirituality of the Reformer*. Grand Rapids, Mich.: Baker Book House, 1978.

Battles, Ford Lewis, and André Malan Hugo, trans. and ed. *Calvin's Commentary on Seneca's De Clementia*. Leiden: E. J. Brill, 1969.

Beaty, Mary, and Benjamin W. Farley, trans. *Calvin's Ecclesiastical Advice*. Louisville, Ky.: Westminster John Knox, 1991.

Beveridge, Henry, trans. and ed. *John Calvin's Tracts and Treatises*. 3 vols. Reprint, Grand Rapids, Mich.: Eerdmans, 1958.

Bonnet, Jules, ed. *Letters of John Calvin*. 4 vols. 1858. Reprint, New York: Burt Franklin, 1972–1973.

Dillenberger, John, ed. *John Calvin: Selections from His Writings*. Atlanta, Ga.: Scholars Press, 1975.

Farley, Benjamin W. *John Calvin's Sermons on the Ten Commandments*. Grand Rapids, Mich.: Baker Book House, 1980.

Farley, Benjamin W., trans. and ed. *Treatises against the Anabaptists and against the Libertines*. Grand Rapids, Mich.: Baker Book House, 1982.

Fraser, John W., trans. *Concerning Scandals*. Grand Rapids, Mich.: Eerdmans, 1978.

Haroutunian, Joseph, ed. *Calvin: Commentaries.* Library of Christian Classics, vol. 23. Philadelphia: Westminster Press, 1958.

Hesselink, I. John. *Calvin's First Catechism: A Commentary.* Louisville, Ky.: Westminster John Knox, 1997.

Miller, Graham, ed. *Calvin's Wisdom.* Edinburgh: Banner of Truth Trust, 1992.

Potter, G. R., and M. Greengrass. *John Calvin.* Documents of Modern History. New York: St. Martin's, 1983.

Reid, J. K. S., ed. *Calvin: Theological Treatises.* Library of Christian Classics, vol. 22. Philadelphia: Westminster Press, 1954.

————. *Concerning the Eternal Predestination of God.* London: James Clarke, 1961.

Torrance, David W., and Thomas F. Torrance. *Calvin's New Testament Commentaries.* 12 vols. Grand Rapids, Mich.: Eerdmans, 1963–1974.

Wright, David F., ed. *Calvin's Old Testament Commentaries.* Grand Rapids, Mich.: Eerdmans, 1994–.

2d. John Calvin, Studies

Balke, William. *Calvin and the Anabaptist Radicals.* Grand Rapids, Mich.: Eerdmans, 1981.

Barth, Karl. *The Theology of John Calvin.* Translated by Geoffrey W. Bromiley. Grand Rapids, Mich.: Eerdmans, 1995.

Battles, Ford Lewis. *Analysis of the "Institutes of the Christian Religion" of John Calvin.* Grand Rapids, Mich.: Baker Book House, 1980.

————. *Interpreting John Calvin.* Edited by Robert Benedetto. Grand Rapids, Mich.: Baker Book House, 1996.

Benoît, J. D. *Calvin directeur d'âmes: Contribution à l'histoire de la piété réformée.* Strasburg: Editions Oberlin, 1947.

Biéler, A. *La Pensée économique et sociale de Calvin.* Geneva: Librairie de l'Université, 1959.

————. *The Social Humanism of Calvin.* Translated by Paul T. Fuhrmann. Richmond, Va.: John Knox Press, 1964.

Breen, Quirinus. *John Calvin: A Study in French Humanism.* 2d ed. New York: Archon Books, 1968.

DeVries, Dawn. *Jesus Christ in the Preaching of Calvin and Schleiermacher.* Louisville, Ky.: Westminster John Knox, 1996.

Douglass, Jane Dempsey. *Women, Freedom and Calvin.* Philadelphia: Westminster Press, 1985.

Doumergue, Emile. *L'art et le sentiment dans l'oeuvre de Calvin.* Reprint, Geneva: Slatkine, 1970.

Dowey, Edward A. *The Knowledge of God in Calvin's Theology.* 3d ed. Grand Rapids, Mich.: Eerdmans, 1994.

Duffield, G. E., ed. *John Calvin*. Courtenay Studies in Reformation Theology, vol. 1. Appleford, England: Sutton Courtenay Press, 1966.

Gamble, Richard C., ed. *Articles on Calvin and Calvinism*. 14 vols. Hamden, Conn.: Garland Publishing, 1992.

George, Timothy, ed. *John Calvin and the Church: A Prism of Reform*. Louisville, Ky.: Westminster John Knox, 1990.

Gerrish, Brian A. *Grace & Gratitude: The Eucharistic Theology of John Calvin*. Minneapolis: Fortress Press, 1993.

———. *The Old Protestantism and the New: Essays on the Reformation Heritage*. Chicago: University of Chicago Press, 1982.

Graham, W. Fred. *The Constructive Revolutionary: John Calvin and His Socio-Economic Impact*. Richmond, Va.: John Knox Press, 1971.

Hancock, Ralph Cornel. *Calvin and the Foundations of Modern Politics*. Ithaca, N.Y.: Cornell University Press, 1987.

Harkness, Georgia E. *John Calvin: The Man and His Ethics*. New York: Henry Holt, 1931.

Hass, Guenther H. *The Concept of Equity in Calvin's Ethics*. Waterloo, Ont.: Wilfrid Laurier University Press, 1997.

Hesselink, I. John. *Calvin's Concept of the Law*. Allison Park, Pa.: Pickwick Publications, 1992.

Höpfl, Harro. *The Christian Polity of John Calvin*. New York: Cambridge University Press, 1982.

Jansen, J. F. *Calvin's Doctrine of the Work of Christ*. London: James Clarke, 1956.

Kelly, Douglas F. *The Emergence of Liberty in the Modern World: The Influence of Calvin on Five Governments from the 16th through 18th Centuries*. Phillipsburg, N.J.: Presbyterian & Reformed, 1992.

Kingdon, Robert M., and Robert D. Linder, eds. *Calvin and Calvinism: Sources of Democracy?* Lexington: D. C. Heath, 1970.

Leith, John H. *John Calvin's Doctrine of the Christian Life*. Louisville, Ky.: Westminster John Knox, 1989.

McDonnell, Kilian. *John Calvin, The Church and the Eucharist*. Princeton: Princeton University Press, 1967.

McKee, Elsie Anne. *John Calvin on the Diaconate and Liturgical Almsgiving*. Geneva: Librairie Droz, 1984.

McKee, Elsie Anne, and Brian G. Armstrong, eds. *Probing the Reformed Tradition: Historical Studies in Honor of Edward A. Dowey, Jr.* Louisville, Ky.: Westminster John Knox, 1989.

McKim, Donald K., ed. *Readings in Calvin's Theology*. Grand Rapids, Mich.: Baker Book House, 1984.

Milner, Benjamin C., Jr. *Calvin's Doctrine of the Church.* Leiden: E. J. Brill, 1970.

Neuser, Wilhelm H., ed. *Calvinus Sacrae Theologiae Professor: Calvin as Confessor of Holy Scripture.* Grand Rapids, Mich.: Eerdmans, 1994.

Niesel, Wilhelm. *The Theology of Calvin.* Translated by Harold Knight. Philadelphia: Westminster Press, 1956.

Parker, T. H. L. *Calvin's Doctrine of the Knowledge of God.* 2d ed. Edinburgh: Oliver & Boyd, 1969.

———. *Calvin's New Testament Commentaries.* 2d ed. Louisville, Ky.: Westminster John Knox, 1993.

———. *Calvin's Old Testament Commentaries.* 1986. Reprint, Louisville, Ky.: Westminster John Knox, 1993.

Partee, Charles. *Calvin and Classical Philosophy.* Leiden: E. J. Brill, 1977.

Puckett, D. L. *John Calvin's Exegesis of the Old Testament.* Louisville, Ky.: Westminster John Knox, 1995.

Richard, Lucien J. *The Spirituality of John Calvin.* Atlanta: John Knox Press, 1974.

Schnucker, Robert V., ed. *Calviniana: Ideas and Influence of Jean Calvin.* Kirksville, Mo.: Sixteenth Century Journal, 1988.

Schreiner, Susan E. *The Theater of His Glory: Nature and the Natural Order in the Thought of John Calvin.* Durham, N.C.: Labyrinth Press, 1991.

Schulze, Ludolf F. *Calvin and "Social Ethics": His Views on Property, Interest and Usury.* Pretoria: Kital, 1985.

Steinmetz, David. *Calvin in Context.* New York: Oxford University Press, 1995.

Tamburello, Dennis E. *Union with Christ: John Calvin and the Mysticism of St. Bernard.* Louisville, Ky.: Westminster John Knox, 1994.

Torrance, Thomas F. *Calvin's Doctrine of Man.* London: Lutterworth, 1949.

———. *The Hermeneutics of John Calvin.* Edinburgh: Scottish Academic Press, 1988.

Van Buren, Paul. *Christ in Our Place: The Substitutionary Character of Calvin's Doctrine of Reconciliation.* Edinburgh: Oliver & Boyd, 1957.

Wallace, Ronald S. *Calvin's Doctrine of the Christian Life.* Edinburgh: Oliver & Boyd, 1959.

———. *Calvin's Doctrine of Word and Sacraments.* Edinburgh: Oliver & Boyd, 1953.

Wencelius, Léon. *Calvin et Rembrandt.* Paris: Société d'Edition "Les Belles Lettres," 1937.

———. *L'esthétique de Calvin.* Paris: Société d'Edition "Les Belles Lettres," [1937].

Wendel, François. *Calvin et l'humanisme.* Paris: Presses universitaires de France, 1976.

———. *Calvin: The Origins and Development of His Religious Thought.* Translated by Philip Mairet. 1963. Reprint, Grand Rapids, Mich.: Baker Book House, 1997.

Wilterdink, Garret A. *Tyrant or Father? A Study of Calvin's Doctrine of God.* Bristol, Ind.: Wyndham Hall, 1985.

Wulfert de Greef. *The Writings of John Calvin: An Introductory Guide.* Translated by Lyle D. Bierma. Grand Rapids, Mich.: Baker Book House, 1993.

Zachman, Randall. *The Assurance of Faith: Conscience in the Theology of Martin Luther and John Calvin.* Minneapolis: Fortress Press, 1993.

3a. Other Continental Reformers, Bibliographies

Donnelly, John Patrick, with Robert M. Kingdon. *A Bibliography of the Works of Peter Martyr Vermigli.* Kirksville, Mo.: Sixteenth Century Journal, 1990.

Thompson, Bard. "Bucer Study Since 1918." *Church History* 25 (1956): 62–82.

3b. Other Continental Reformers, Primary Sources

Bèza, Théodore de. *Du Droit Magistrats.* Edited by Robert M. Kingdon. Geneva: Droz, 1970.

Bucer, Martin. *The Commonplaces of Martin Bucer.* Translated and edited by David F. Wright. Appleford, England: Sutton Courtenay Press, 1972.

———. "De Regno Christi." In *Melanchthon and Bucer.* Edited by Wilhelm Pauck. Library of Christian Classics, vol. 19. Philadelphia: Westminster Press, 1969.

Bullinger, Heinrich. "Of the Holy Catholic Church." In *Zwingli and Bullinger.* Translated and edited by G. W. Bromiley. Library of Christian Classics, vol. 24. Philadelphia: Westminster Press, 1953.

Ursinus, Zacharias. *The Commentary of Dr. Zacharius Ursinus on the Heidelberg Catechism.* 2d American ed. Translated by G. W. Williard. 1852. Reprint, Grand Rapids, Mich.: Eerdmans, 1954.

Vermigli, Peter Martyr. *The Life, Early Letters and Eucharistic Writings of Peter Martyr.* Edited by G. E. Duffield and J. C. McLelland. Appleford, England: Sutton Courtenay Press, 1989.

3c. Other Continental Reformers, Biographies

Bietenholz, Peter G., and Thomas B. Deutscher, eds. *Contemporaries of Erasmus: A Biographical Register of the Renaissance and Reformation.* 3 vols. Toronto: University of Toronto Press, 1985.

3d. Other Continental Reformers, Studies of Théodore de Bèza

Bray, John S. *Theodore Beza's Doctrine of Predestination.* Nieuwkoop, Netherlands: B. De Graaf, 1975.

Geisendorf, P. F. *Théodore de Bèze.* 1949. Reprint, Geneva: Labor et Fides, 1971.

Maruyama, T. *The Ecclesiology of Theodore Beza: The Reform of the True Church.* Geneva, 1978.

Raitt, Jill. *The Eucharistic Theology of Theodore Beza: Development of the Reformed Doctrine.* Chambersburg, Pa.: American Academy of Religion, 1972.

3e. Other Continental Reformers, Studies of Martin Bucer

Eells, H. *Martin Bucer.* New Haven, Conn.: Yale University Press, 1931.

Greschat, Martin. *Martin Bucer: Ein Reformator und seine Zeit.* Munich: Verlag C. H. Beck, 1990.

Krieger, Christian, and Marc Lienhard, eds. *Martin Bucer and Sixteenth Century Europe: actes du colloque de Strasbourg (28–31 aout 1991).* 2 vols. Leiden: E. J. Brill, 1993.

Stephens, W. P. *The Holy Spirit in the Theology of Martin Bucer.* Cambridge: Cambridge University Press, 1970.

3f. Other Continental Reformers, Studies of Heinrich Bullinger

Baker, J. Wayne. *Heinrich Bullinger and the Covenant: The Other Reformed Tradition.* Athens, Ohio: Ohio University Press, 1980.

3g. Other Continental Reformers, Studies of Jacques Lefèvre d'Étaples

Hughes, Philip. *Lefèvre: Pioneer of Ecclesiastical Renewal in France.* Grand Rapids, Mich.: Eerdmans, 1984.

3h. Other Continental Reformers, Studies of Marguerite de Navarre

Reynolds-Cornell, Régine, ed. *International Colloquium Celebrating the 500th Anniversary of the Birth of Marguerite de Navarre.* Birmingham, Ala.: Summa Publications, 1995.

3i. Other Continental Reformers, Studies of Zacharias Ursinus

Hinkle, G. H. "The Theology of the Ursinus Movement." Ph.D. diss., Yale University, 1964.

Klooster, Fred. "'Ursinus' Primacy in the Composition of the Heidelberg Catechism." In *Controversy and Conciliation: The Reformation and the Palatinate, 1559–1583.* Edited by Derk Visser. Allison Park, Pa.: Pickwick Publications, 1986.

Visser, Derk. *Zacharias Ursinus. The Reluctant Reformer: His Life and Times.* New York: United Church Press, 1983.

3j. Other Continental Reformers, Studies of Peter Martyr Vermigli

Di Gangi, Mariano. *Peter Martyr Vermigli 1499–1562: Renaissance Man, Reformation Master.* Lanham, Md.: University Press of America, 1993.

——. *Calvinism and Scholasticism in Vermigli's Doctrine of Man and Grace*. Leiden: Brill, 1976.

McLelland, J. C. *The Visible Words of God: An Exposition of the Sacramental Theology of Peter Martyr Vermigli, A.D. 1500–1562*. Edinburgh: Oliver and Boyd, 1957.

McNair, P. *Peter Martyr in Italy*. Oxford: Clarendon Press, 1967.

3k. Other Continental Reformers, Studies of Pierre Viret

Linder, Robert D. "Pierre Viret and the Sixteenth-Century French Protestant Revolutionary Tradition." *Journal of Modern History* 38 (June 1966): 125–37.

——. *The Political Ideas of Pierre Viret*. Geneva: Droz, 1964.

The British Tradition

1a. John Knox, Bibliographies

Hazlett, Ian. "A Working Bibliography of Writings of John Knox." In *Calviniana: Ideas and Influence of Jean Calvin*, edited by Robert V. Schnucker, 185–93. Kirksville, Mo.: Sixteenth Century Journal Publishers, 1988.

1b. John Knox, Biographies

Murray, Iain. *John Knox*. London: Evangelical Library, 1973.

Percy, Eustace. *John Knox*. London: Hodder & Stoughton, 1937.

Reid, W. S. *Trumpeter of God: A Biography of John Knox*. New York: Scribner's, 1974.

Ridley, Jasper. *John Knox*. New York: Oxford University Press, 1968.

1c. John Knox, Primary Sources

Bray, Gerald, ed. *Documents of the English Reformation*. Minneapolis: Fortress Press, 1994.

Knox, John. *John Knox's Genevan Service Book, 1556*. Edited by William D. Maxwell. Edinburgh: Oliver and Boyd, 1931.

——. *John Knox's History of the Reformation in Scotland*. Edited by W. C. Dickinson. New York: Philosophical Library, 1950.

1d. John Knox, Studies

Greaves, R. L. *Theology and Revolution in the Scottish Reformation*. Grand Rapids, Mich.: Eerdmans, 1980.

Kyle, R. G. *The Mind of John Knox*. Lawrence, Kans.: Coronado Press, 1984.

McEwen, James S. *The Faith of John Knox*. Richmond, Va.: John Knox Press, 1961.

Sefton, Henry R. *John Knox: An Account of the Development of His Spirituality*. Edinburgh: Saint Andrew Press, 1993.

2a. English Reformers, Bibliographies

Abbott, Wilbur Cortez. *A Bibliography of Oliver Cromwell: A List of Printed Materials Relating to Oliver Cromwell, Together with a List of Portraits and Caricatures*. Cambridge, Mass.: Harvard University Press, 1929.

2b. English Reformers, Biographies

Cocks, H. F. L. *The Religious Life of Oliver Cromwell*. London: Independent Press, 1960.

Daniell, David. *William Tyndale*: A Biography. New Haven, Conn.: Yale University Press, 1994.

Dickens, A. G. *Thomas Cromwell and the English Reformation*. London: English Universities Press, 1959, 1972.

MacCulloch, Diarmaid. *Thomas Cranmer: A Life*. New Haven, Conn.: Yale University Press, 1996.

Paul, Robert S. *The Lord Protector: Religion and Politics in the Life of Oliver Cromwell*. London: Lutterworth Press, 1955.

2c. English Reformers, Primary Sources

Barrow, Henry. *The Writings of Henry Barrow, 1587–1590*. Edited by Leland H. Carlson. London: Allen and Unwin, 1962.

———. *The Writings of Henry Barrow, 1590–1591*. Edited by Leland H. Carlson. London: Allen & Unwin, 1966.

The Book of Common Prayer. Oxford: Oxford University Press, 1552.

Cartwright, Thomas. *Cartwrightiana*. Vol. 1. Edited by A. Peel and Leland H. Carlson. London: Allen & Unwin, 1951.

Cranmer, Thomas. *Cranmer's Selected Writings*. Edited by Carl S. Meyer. London: SPCK, 1961.

———. *The Work of Thomas Cranmer*. Edited by G. E. Duffield. Appleford, England: Sutton Courtenay Press, 1964.

Greenwood, John. *The Writings of John Greenwood, 1587–1590. Together with the Writings of Henry Barrow and John Greenwood, 1587–1590*. Edited by Leland H. Carlson. London: G. Allen and Unwin, 1962.

Greenwood, John, and Henry Barrow. *The Writings of John Greenwood and Henry Barrow, 1591–1593*. London: Allen and Unwin, 1970.

Harrison, Robert, and Robert Browne. *The Writings of Robert Harrison and Robert Browne*. Edited by A. Peel and L. H. Carlson. London: Allen & Unwin, 1953.

Parker, T. H. L., ed. *The English Reformers*. Library of Christian Classics, vol. 26. Philadelphia: Westminster Press, 1966.

Perkins, William. *The Work of William Perkins*. Edited by Ian Breward. Appleford, England: Sutton Courtenay Press, 1970.

Pierce, William. *The Marprelate Tracts, 1588, 1589.* London: A. Constable, 1908.

2d. English Reformers, Studies

Brooks, Peter N. *Thomas Cranmer's Doctrine of the Eucharist.* 2d ed. Basingstoke, England: Macmillan Academic and Professional, 1992.

Dent, C. M. *Protestant Reformers in Elizabethan Oxford.* Oxford: Oxford University Press, 1983.

Hopf, C. *Martin Bucer and the English Reformation.* Oxford: Oxford University Press, 1946.

Hughes, Philip E. *The Theology of the English Reformers.* Grand Rapids, Mich.: Eerdmans, 1965.

McKim, Donald K. *Ramism in William Perkins' Theology.* New York: Lang, 1987.

Whitaker, E. C. *Martin Bucer and the Book of Common Prayer.* Great Wakering, England: Alcuin Club, 1974.

THE MODERN REFORMED TRADITION

History of Reformed Protestantism

1. Bibliographies and Indexes

Dexter, Henry Martyn. *The Congregationalism of the Last Three Hundred Years As Seen in Its Literature.* 1880. Reprint, 2 vols. New York: Bert Franklin, 1970.

Perret, Edmond. *World Alliance of Reformed Churches: General Index, 1875–1992.* Geneva: World Alliance of Reformed Churches, 1994.

2. Dictionaries and Encyclopedias

Gisel, Pierre, ed. *Encyclopédie du Protestantisme.* Paris: Cerf, 1995.

McKim, Donald K., ed. *Encyclopedia of the Reformed Faith.* Louisville, Ky.: Westminster John Knox, 1992.

3. Directories and Handbooks

Bauswein, Jean-Jacques, and Lukas Vischer. *The Reformed Family Worldwide.* Grand Rapids, Mich.: Eerdmans, 1999.

Price, Ernest J. *A Handbook of Congregationalism.* London: Independent Press, 1957.

World Alliance of Reformed Churches. *Directory of Theological Schools Related to WARC Member Churches.* Geneva: WARC, 1996.

4. Primary Sources

American Board of Commissioners for Foreign Missions. Primary Source

Media, 12 Lunar Dr., Woodbridge, CT 06525. ABCFM papers on microfilm.

Council for World Mission Archives, 1775–1940. Zug, Switzerland/New York: Inter Documentation Company/Norman Ross Publishing Co. The collection consists of 23,343 microfiche. Incorporates the archives of the London Missionary Society.

Proceedings of the Councils of the World Presbyterian Alliance, 1877–1964; the International Congregational Council, 1891–1966; and the WARC, 1970–. *See* theological sources.

5. Biographies

Peel, A. *The Congregational Two Hundred.* London: Independent Press, 1948.

Who's Who in Congregationalism: An Authoritative Reference Work and Guide to the Careers of Ministers and Lay Officials of the Congregational Churches. London: Shaw Publishing, 1933–.

6a. Histories, General

Graham, W. Fred, ed. *Later Calvinism: International Perspectives.* Kirksville, Mo.: Sixteenth Century Journal, 1994.

McNeill, John T. *The History and Character of Calvinism.* New York: Oxford University Press, 1967.

Pradervand, Marcel. *A Century of Service: A History of the World Alliance of Reformed Churches, 1875–1975.* Grand Rapids, Mich.: Eerdmans, 1975.

Prestwich, Menna, ed. *International Calvinism, 1541–1715.* Oxford: Clarendon Press, 1985.

Reid, W. Stanford, ed. *John Calvin: His Influence in the Western World.* Grand Rapids, Mich.: Zondervan, 1982.

Sell, Alan P. F. *A Reformed, Evangelical, Catholic Theology: The Contribution of the World Alliance of Reformed Churches, 1875–1982.* Grand Rapids, Mich.: Eerdmans, 1991.

6b. Histories, Congregational

Calder, Ralph F. G. *To Introduce the Family.* London: Independent Press, 1953.

Peel, Albert, and Douglas Horton. *International Congregationalism.* London: Independent Press, 1949.

Routley, Erik. *The Story of Congregationalism.* London: Independent Press, 1961.

United Church of Christ. *The Living Theological Heritage of the United Church of Christ.* 7 vols. Cleveland, Ohio: Pilgrim Press, 1995–.

6c. Histories, Presbyterian

Drury, Clifford M., ed. *Four Hundred Years of World Presbyterianism*. San Francisco: Privately published, 1961. Microfilm.

Moffatt, James. *The Presbyterian Churches*. London: Methuen, 1928.

Reed, R. C. *History of the Presbyterian Churches of the World*. Philadelphia: Westminster Press, 1927.

6d. Histories, Reformed

Bratt, John H., ed. *The Rise and Development of Calvinism: A Concise History*. Grand Rapids, Mich.: Eerdmans, 1959.

Reformed Theology

1. Bibliographies and Indexes

Benedetto, Robert. *Interpretation: Fifty Year Index, 1947–1995*. Richmond, Va.: Interpretation, 1996.

———. *P. T. Forsyth Bibliography and Index*. Westport, Conn.: Greenwood Press, 1993.

Kwiran, Manfred. *Index to Literature on Barth, Bonhoeffer, and Bultmann*. Basel: Friedreich Reinhardt Verlag, 1977.

McKim, Mark G. *Emil Brunner: A Bibliography*. Lanham, Md.: Scarecrow Press, 1996.

Princeton Theological Seminary. *Theology Today Fifty Year Index, 1944–1994*. Princeton: Theology Today, 1994.

Robertson, D. B. *Reinhold Niebuhr's Works: A Bibliography*. Rev. ed. Lanham, Md.: University Press of America, 1983.

Sittler, J. "A Selected Haroutunian Bibliography." *Journal of Religion* 50 (1970): 323–26.

Tice, Terrence. *Schleiermacher Bibliography*. Princeton, N.J.: Princeton Theological Seminary, 1985.

Wildi, Hans Markus. *Bibliographie Karl Barth*. Zürich: Theologischer Verlag, 1984.

2a. Theological Sources, Primary Sources

Christian Reformed Church in North America. *Ecumenical Creeds and Reformed Confessions*. Grand Rapids, Mich.: CRC Publications, 1988.

Presbyterian Church (U.S.A.). *Book of Confessions*. Louisville, Ky.: Office of the General Assembly, 1994.

Stroup, George, ed. *Reformed Reader: A Sourcebook in Christian Theology*. Vol. 2, *Contemporary Trajectories, 1799–Present*. Louisville, Ky.: Westminster John Knox, 1993.

Vischer, Lukas, ed. *Reformed Witness Today: A Collection of Confessions and Statements of Faith Issued by Reformed Churches.* Bern: Evangelische Arbeitsstelle Ökumene Schweiz, 1982.

Walker, Williston, ed. *The Creeds and Platforms of Congregationalism.* 1893. Reprint, Boston: Pilgrim Press, 1960.

2b. Theological Sources: Studies of Confessions, Catechisms, and Creeds

Dowey, Edward A., Jr. *A Commentary on the Confession of 1967 and an Introduction to the Book of Confessions.* Philadelphia: Westminster Press, 1968.

Guthrie, Shirley C. *Always Being Reformed: Faith for a Fragmented World.* Louisville, Ky.: Westminster John Knox, 1996.

Placher, William C., and David Willis-Watkins. *Belonging to God: A Commentary on A Brief Statement of Faith.* Louisville, Ky.: Westminster John Knox, 1992.

Plantinga, Cornelius, Jr. *A Place to Stand: A Reformed Study of Creeds and Confessions.* Grand Rapids, Mich.: Board of Publications of the Christian Reformed Church, 1979.

Rogers, Jack B. *Presbyterian Creeds: A Guide to the Book of Confessions.* Louisville, Ky.: Westminster John Knox, 1991.

Rohls, Jan. *Reformed Confessions: Theology from Zurich to Barmen.* Louisville, Ky.: Westminster John Knox, 1998.

Stotts, Jack L., and Jane Dempsey Douglass, eds. *To Confess the Faith Today.* Louisville, Ky.: Westminster John Knox, 1990.

World Alliance of Reformed Churches. *Confessions and Confessing in the Reformed Tradition Today.* Geneva: WARC, 1982.

3a. General Introductions, Congregational

Cadoux, C. J., and T. T. James. *The Congregational Way.* Oxford: Basil Blackwell, 1945.

Jenkins, Daniel Thomas. *Congregationalism: A Restatement.* New York: Harper, 1954.

Rouner, A. A., Jr. *The Congregational Way of Life.* Englewood Cliffs, N.J.: Prentice-Hall, 1960.

Whale, J. S. *The Protestant Tradition.* Cambridge: Cambridge University Press, 1955.

3b. General Introductions, Presbyterian

Leith, John H. *An Introduction to the Reformed Tradition: A Way of Being the Christian Community.* Rev. ed. Atlanta: John Knox Press, 1981.

Mackay, John A. *The Presbyterian Way of Life.* Englewood Cliffs, N.J.: Prentice-Hall, 1960.

McKim, Donald K., ed. *Major Themes in the Reformed Tradition.* Grand Rapids, Mich.: Eerdmans, 1992.

3c. General Introductions, Reformed

Hesselink, I. John. *On Being Reformed: Distinctive Characteristics and Common Misunderstandings.* New York: Reformed Church Press, 1988.

Kuyper, Abraham. *Calvinism: Six Stone Foundation Lectures.* 1899. Reprint, Grand Rapids, Mich.: Eerdmans, 1931.

Osterhaven, Eugene M. *The Spirit of the Reformed Tradition.* Grand Rapids, Mich.: Eerdmans, 1971.

4. International Reformed Dialogue

Baptists and Reformed in Dialogue. Geneva: WARC, 1984.

Bender, Ross T., and Alan P. F. Sell, eds. *Baptism, Peace, and the State in the Reformed and Mennonite Traditions.* Waterloo, Ont.: Wilfrid Laurier University Press, 1991.

Berg, Hans Georg vom, et al., eds. *Mennonites and Reformed in Dialogue.* Geneva: WARC, 1986.

Confessing Jesus Christ in Dialogue. Geneva: John Knox International Reformed Center, 1986.

God's Reign and Our Unity: The Report of the Anglican-Reformed International Commission, 1981–1984. Edinburgh: Saint Andrew Press, 1984.

Reformed and Methodists in Dialogue. Geneva: WARC, 1988.

Sell, Alan P. F., ed. *Reformed and Disciples of Christ in Dialogue.* Geneva: WARC, 1985.

———. *Reformed Theology and the Jewish People.* Geneva: WARC, 1986.

Torrance, T. F., ed. *Theological Dialogue between Orthodox and Reformed Churches.* Edinburgh: Scottish Academic Press, 1985.

Toward Church Fellowship [with the Roman Catholic Church]. Geneva: WARC, 1989.

Towards Closer Fellowship: Report of the Dialogue between Reformed and Disciples of Christ. Geneva: WARC, 1988.

5. Western Philosophy and Theology

Allen, Diogenes. *Christian Belief in a Postmodern World.* Louisville, Ky.: Westminster John Knox, 1989.

———. *Philosophy for Understanding Theology.* Louisville, Ky.: Westminster John Knox, 1992.

Conradie, A. L. *The Neo-Calvinistic Concept of Philosophy: A Study in the Problem of Philosophic Communication.* Natal: University Press, 1960.

Heslam, Peter S. *Creating A Christian Worldview: Abraham Kuyper's Lectures on Calvinism.* Grand Rapids, Mich.: Eerdmans, 1998.

Hoitenga, Dewey J. *Faith and Reason from Plato to Plantinga: An Introduction to Reformed Epistemology.* Albany, N.Y.: State University of New York Press, 1991.

Migliore, Daniel L. *Faith Seeking Understanding: An Introduction to Christian Theology*. Grand Rapids, Mich.: Eerdmans, 1991.

Plantinga, Alvin. *God, Freedom and Evil*. Grand Rapids, Mich.: Eerdmans, 1974.

———. *God and Other Minds: A Study of the Rational Justification of Belief in God*. Ithaca, N.Y.: Cornell University Press, 1990.

———. *The Nature of Necessity*. Oxford: Clarendon Press, 1974.

Plantinga, Alvin, and Nicholas Wolterstorff, eds. *Faith and Rationality: Reason and Belief in God*. South Bend, Ind.: University of Notre Dame Press, 1984.

Spykman, Gordon. *Reformational Theology: A New Paradigm for Doing Dogmatics*. Grand Rapids, Mich.: Eerdmans, 1992.

Young, William. *Toward a Reformed Philosophy: The Development of a Protestant Philosophy in Dutch Calvinistic Thought since the Time of Abraham Kuyper*. Grand Rapids, Mich.: Piet Hein, 1952.

6. Gender and Theology

Chopp, Rebecca S. *The Power to Speak: Feminism, Language, God*. New York: Crossroad, 1989.

Groothuis, Rebecca M. *Good News for Women: A Biblical Picture of Gender Equality*. Grand Rapids, Mich.: Baker Book House, 1997.

Japinga, Lynn. *Feminism and Christianity: An Essential Guide*. Nashville, Tenn.: Abingdon Press, 1999.

Ruether, Rosemary Radford. *Sexism and God-Talk: Toward a Feminist Theology: With a New Introduction*. Boston: Beacon Press, 1993.

Russell, Letty M. *Household of Freedom: Authority in Feminist Theology*. Philadelphia: Westminster Press, 1987.

7a. Representative Works of Systematic Theology, Seventeenth- and Eighteenth-Century European Works

Beardslee, John W., III, ed. *Reformed Dogmatics: Seventeenth-Century Reformed Theology through the Writings of Wollebius, Voetius, and Turretin*. New York: Oxford University Press, 1965.

Pictet, Benedict. *Christian Theology*. 1696. Translated by F. Reyroux. Philadelphia: Presbyterian Board of Publication, 1834.

Turretin, Francis. *Institutes of Elenctic Theology*. 3 vols. 1688. Edited by James T. Dennison. Phillipsburg, N.J.: Presbyterian & Reformed, 1992–1993.

Wollebius, Johannes. *Compendium theologiae Christianae*. 1626. 3d ed. London: T. Mabb, 1660. Reprint, Ann Arbor, Mich.: University Microfilms.

7b. Representative Works of Systematic Theology, Seventeenth- and Eighteenth-Century British and American Puritanism

Ames, William. *The Marrow of Theology.* 1623. Translated and edited by John D. Eusden. 1968. Reprint, Grand Rapids, Mich.: Baker Book House, 1996.

Edwards, Jonathan. *The Works of Jonathan Edwards.* Edited by Paul Ramsey and John E. Smith. Yale University Press, 1957–.

Forbes, John. *Instructiones Historico-Theologicae.* Amsterdam: Apud Henricum Wetstenium, 1702.

Perkins, William. *A Golden Chaine.* Cambridge: John Legat, 1600.

Willard, Samuel. *A Compleat Body of Divinity.* Boston: B. Green and S. Kneeland, 1726.

7c. Representative Works of Systematic Theology, Nineteenth-Century European Works

Bavinck, Herman. *Gereformeerde Dogmatiek.* Kampen: J. H. Bos, 1895–1901. Translated and abridged as *Our Reasonable Faith.* Grand Rapids, Mich.: Eerdmans, 1956.

Heppe, Heinrich, ed. *Reformed Dogmatics Set Out and Illustrated from the Sources.* London: George Allen & Unwin, 1950. Reprint, Grand Rapids, Mich.: Baker Book House, 1978.

Kuyper, Abraham. *Encyclopedia of Sacred Theology: Its Principles.* New York: Charles Scribner's Sons, 1898.

Schleiermacher, Friedrich D. E. *The Christian Faith.* 2d ed. 1830–1831. Reprint, Philadelphia: Fortress Press, 1976.

Schweizer, Alexander. *Die Glaubenslehre der Evangelisch–Reformierten Kirche.* Zürich: Orel, Füssli, 1844–1847.

7d. Representative Works of Systematic Theology, Nineteenth-Century North American Works

Dabney, Robert Lewis. *Systematic and Polemic Theology.* 1871. 2d ed. St. Louis, Mo.: Presbyterian Publishing Company, 1878.

Hodge, A. A. *Outlines of Theology.* 1860. Reprint, New York: R. Carter and Brothers, 1871.

Hodge, Charles. *Systematic Theology.* 3 vols. New York: Scribner's, 1871.

Shedd, William. *Dogmatic Theology.* 3 vols. New York: Scribner, 1888–94.

Smith, Henry B. *System of Christian Theology.* New York: A. C. Armstrong, 1884.

7e. Representative Works of Systematic Theology, Twentieth-Century European Works

Barth, Karl. *Church Dogmatics.* 13 vols. Edinburgh: T. & T. Clark, 1936–1977.

Berkhof, Hendrikus. *Christian Faith: An Introduction to the Study of the Faith.* Rev. ed. Grand Rapids, Mich.: Eerdmans, 1985.

Berkouwer, Gerrit Cornelius. *Studies in Dogmatics.* 14 vols. Grand Rapids, Mich.: Eerdmans, 1952–76.

Brunner, H. Emil. *Dogmatics.* 3 vols. Philadelphia: Westminster Press, 1949–62.

Gollwitzer, Helmut. *An Introduction to Protestant Theology.* Philadelphia: Westminster John Knox, 1982.

Lecerf, Auguste. *An Introduction to Reformed Dogmatics* (1931). London: Lutterworth, 1949.

Lochman, Jan M. *The Faith We Confess: An Ecumenical Dogmatics.* Translated by David Lewis. Philadelphia: Fortress Press, 1984.

Moltmann, Jürgen. *The Coming of God: Christian Eschatology.* Minneapolis: Fortress Press, 1996.

———. *The Crucified God: The Cross of Christ as the Foundation and Criticism of Christian Theology.* Minneapolis: Fortress Press, 1991.

———. *God in Creation: A New Theology of Creation and the Spirit of God.* Minneapolis: Fortress Press, 1991.

———. *The Spirit of Life: A Universal Affirmation.* Minneapolis: Fortress Press, 1992.

Weber, Otto. *Foundations of Dogmatics.* Translated by Darrell Guder. 2 vols. Grand Rapids, Mich.: Eerdmans, 1981–1983. Work originally published in 1955.

7f. Representative Works of Systematic Theology, Twentieth-Century North American Works

Berkhof, Louis. *Systematic Theology.* New ed. Grand Rapids, Mich.: Eerdmans, 1996.

Bloesch, Donald G. *A Theology of Word and Spirit.* 7 vols. Downers Grove, Ill.: InterVarsity Press, 1992–.

Brown, William Adams. *Christian Theology in Outline.* New York: C. Scribner's Son, 1906.

Fackre, Gabriel J. *The Christian Story.* 2 vols. Rev. ed. Grand Rapids, Mich. Eerdmans, 1984–1987.

———. *Ecumenical Faith in Evangelical Perspective.* Grand Rapids, Mich.: Eerdmans, 1993.

Guthrie, Shirley C. *Christian Doctrine.* Rev. ed. Louisville, Ky.: Westminster John Knox, 1994.

Strong, Augustus Hopkins. *Systematic Theology.* 3 vols. 1907. Reprint, Valley Forge, Pa.: Judson Press, 1967.

8a. Representative Theological Studies, Africa

Akrong, Abraham Ako. "An Akan Christian View of Salvation from the Perspective of John Calvin's Theology." Ph.D. diss., Lutheran School of Theology at Chicago, 1991.

Appiah-Kubi, Kof, and Sergio Torres, eds. *African Theology en Route: Papers from the Pan African Conference of Third World Theologians, December 17–23, 1977, Accra, Ghana.* Maryknoll, N.Y.: Orbis Books, 1995.

Bediako, Kwame. *Christianity in Africa: The Renewal of Non-Western Religion.* Maryknoll, N.Y.: Orbis Books, 1995.

De Gruchy, John W., and Charles Villa-Vicencio, eds. *Doing Theology in Context: South African Perspectives.* Cape Town: David Philip, 1994.

Maimela, Simon S., ed. *Culture, Religion and Liberation: Proceedings of the EATWOT Pan African Theological Conference, Harare, Zimbabwe, January 6–11, 1991.* Pretoria, South Africa: All Africa Conference of Churches, 1994.

Martey, Emmanuel. *African Theology: Inculturation and Liberation.* Maryknoll, N.Y.: Orbis Books, 1993.

Mugambi, J. N. K. *African Christian Theology: An Introduction.* Nairobi: East African Educational Publishers, 1989.

Parratt, John. *Reinventing Christianity: African Theology Today.* Grand Rapids, Mich.: Eerdmans, 1996.

Parratt, John, ed. *A Reader in African Christian Theology.* Rev. ed. London: SPCK, 1997.

Pauw, B. A. *Christianity and Xhosa Tradition: Belief and Ritual among Xhosa-Speaking Christians.* Cape Town: Oxford University Press, 1975.

Pobee, John. *Toward an African Theology.* Nashville, Tenn.: Abingdon Press, 1979.

Shorter, Aylward. *African Christian Theology—Adaptation or Incarnation?* Reprint, Maryknoll, N.Y.: Orbis Books, 1977.

Udoh, Enyi Ben. *Guest Christology: An Interpretative View of the Christological Problem in Africa.* Frankfurt am Main, Germany: Peter Lang, 1988.

8b. Representative Theological Studies, Asia

Anderson, Gerald H., ed. *Asian Voices in Christian Theology.* Maryknoll, N.Y.: Orbis Books, 1976.

Balasundaram, Franklyn. J. *EATWOT in Asia: Towards a Relevant Theology.* Bangalore, India: Asian Trading Corporation, 1994.

Barth, Christoph. *God with Us.* Grand Rapids, Mich.: Eerdmans, 1991.

Batumalai, S. *An Introduction to Asian Theology.* Delhi, India: Indian Society for Promoting Christian Knowledge, 1991.

Bo, Bong Rin. *The Bible and Theology in Asian Contexts*. Taichung, Taiwan: Asia Theological Association, 1984.

Boyd, R. H. S. *An Introduction to Indian Christian Theology*. Rev. ed. Madras, India: Christian Literature Society, 1975.

Carino, Feliciano V. *Like a Mustard Seed: Commentaries on the UCCP Statement of Faith*. Quezon City, Philippines: UCCP, 1987.

Devasahayam, V., ed. *Frontiers of Dalit Theology*. Madras: Gurukul, 1996.

Elwood, Douglas, J., ed. *Asian Christian Theology: Emerging Themes*. Philadelphia: Westminster Press, 1980.

England, John C., ed. *Living Theology in Asia*. Maryknoll, N.Y.: Orbis Books, 1981.

Fabella, Virginia, Keng-hsin Lee, and Kwang-sun Suh, eds. *Asian Christian Spirituality: Reclaiming Traditions*. Maryknoll, N.Y.: Orbis Books, 1992.

Fabella, Virginia, and Mercy Amba Oduyoye, eds. *With Passion and Compassion: Third World Women Doing Theology*. Maryknoll, N.Y.: Orbis Books, 1988.

Gutheinz, Luis, and Timothy Yongxiang Liau. *Theology of the Earth: Ecological Theology in Christian Perspective, Unity of Heaven and Man*. Taipei, Taiwan: Kuangchi Press, 1994.

Hedlund, Roger E. *God and the Nations: A Biblical Theology of Mission in the Asian Context*. Delhi: ISPCK [Indian Society for Promoting Christian Knowledge], 1997.

Kim, Yong Bock. *Minjung Theology: People as the Subjects of History*. Maryknoll, N.Y.: Orbis Books, 1983.

Lak, Yeow Choo, ed. *Doing Theology with the Festivals and Customs of Asia*. Singapore: ATESEA, 1994.

Moon, Cyris H. S. *A Korean Minjung Theology: An Old Testament Perspective*. Maryknoll, N.Y.: Orbis Books, 1985.

Song, C. S. *Tell Us Our Names: Story Theology from an Asian Perspective*. Maryknoll, N.Y.: Orbis Books, 1984.

Sugirtharajah, R. S., and Cecil Hargreaves, eds. *Readings in Indian Christian Theology*. London: SPCK, 1993.

Takenaka, Masao. *Cross and Circle*. Hong Kong: Christian Conference of Asia, 1990.

8c. Representative Theological Studies, Europe and British Isles: Europe

Barth, Karl. *Learning Jesus Christ through the Heidelberg Catechism*. Grand Rapids, Mich.: Eerdmans, 1981.

Gollwitzer, Helmut. *The Existence of God As Confessed by Faith*. Philadelphia: Westminster Press, 1965.

Hromádka, Josef L. *Doom and Resurrection.* Richmond, Va.: Madrus House, 1945.

———. *Impact of History on Theology: Thoughts of a Czech Pastor.* Notre Dame, Ind.: Fides, 1970.

———. *Sprung über die Mauer: Ein Hromádka-Lesebuch.* Edited by Milan Opocensky. Wuppertal: Hammer, 1991.

———. *Theology between Yesterday and Tomorrow.* Philadelphia: Westminster Press, 1957.

Jüngel, Eberhard. *God as the Mystery of the World.* Translated by Darrell Guder. Grand Rapids, Mich.: Eerdmans, 1983.

Kraemer, Hendrik. *The Christian Message in a Non-Christian World.* New York: Harper Brothers, 1938.

Kuyper, Abraham. *Abraham Kuyper: A Centennial Reader.* Edited by James D. Bratt. Grand Rapids, Mich.: Eerdmans, 1998.

———. *Calvinism.* New York: Revell, 1899.

Lochman, Jan M. *The Church in a Marxist Society: A Czechoslovak View.* New York: Harper & Row, 1970.

Moltmann, Jürgen. *The Crucified God: The Cross of Christ as the Foundation and Criticism of Christian Theology.* London: SCM Press, 1974.

———. *Theology of Hope: On the Ground and the Implications of a Christian Eschatology.* London: SCM Press, 1964.

8d. Representative Theological Studies, British Isles

Baillie, Donald. *God Was in Christ: An Essay on Incarnation and Atonement.* New York: Scribner's, 1948.

Baillie, John. *The Interpretation of Religion.* New York: Scribner, 1928.

Campbell, John McLeod. *The Nature of the Atonement.* 1856. Reprint, with a new introduction by James B. Torrance, Grand Rapids, Mich.: Eerdmans, 1996.

Cunningham, William. *Historical Theology.* 1862. Reprint, 2 vols. Edmonton, Canada: Still Waters Revival Books, 1991.

Denney, James. *The Christian Doctrine of Reconciliation.* 1917. Reprint, Minneapolis: Klock & Klock, 1985.

———. *The Death of Christ.* 1911. Reprint, New Canaan, Conn.: Keats Publishing, 1981.

Fairbairn, Andrew Martin. *The Philosophy of the Christian Religion.* London: Hodder & Stoughton, 1902.

Forsyth, P. T. *The Person and Place of Jesus Christ.* 1909. Reprint, Grand Rapids, Mich.: Eerdmans, 1965.

———. *Positive Preaching and the Modern Mind.* 1907. Reprint, Grand Rapids, Mich.: Eerdmans, 1966.

Fraser, James. *A Treatise on Justifying Faith.* Edinburgh: William Gray, 1749.

Hendry, George. *God the Creator.* London: Hodder & Stoughton, 1937.

Mackintosh, Hugh Ross. *The Christian Experience of Forgiveness.* New York, London: Harper & Brothers, 1927.

————. *The Person of Jesus Christ.* London: Student Christian Movement, 1912.

Oman, John. *Honest Religion.* Cambridge: The University Press, 1941.

Orr, James. *The Christian View of God and the World.* New York: Scribner's, 1897. Reprint, Grand Rapids, Mich.: Kregel, 1989.

Owen, John. *The Works of John Owen.* 16 vols. London: Johnstone & Hunter, 1850–1853.

Torrance, Thomas F. *Theology in Reconstruction.* Grand Rapids, Mich.: Eerdmans, 1965.

————. *The Trinitarian Faith.* Edinburgh: T. & T. Clark, 1988.

8e. Representative Theological Studies, North America

Bushnell, Horace. *God in Christ.* 1849. Reprint, New York: Scribner's, 1903.

————. *Horace Bushnell.* A Library of Protestant Thought. Edited by Shelton H. Smith. New York: Oxford University Press, 1965.

Calhoun, Robert L. *God and the Common Life.* New York: Scribner's, 1935.

Haroutunian, Joseph. *God with Us: A Theology of Transpersonal Life.* 2d ed., enl. Allison Park, Pa.: Pickwick Publications, 1991.

Lehmann, Paul. *Ethics in a Christian Context.* New York: Harper & Row, 1963.

Nevin, John W. *The Mystical Presence.* 1846. Reprint, Philadelphia: S. R. Fisher, 1867.

Niebuhr, H. Richard. *Christ and Culture.* New York: Harper, 1951.

————. *The Meaning of Revelation.* New York: The Macmillan Company, 1941.

————. *Radical Monotheism and Western Culture.* 1960. Reprint, Louisville, Ky.: Westminster John Knox, 1993.

Niebuhr, Reinhold. *The Essential Reinhold Niebuhr: Selected Essays and Addresses.* Edited by Robert McAfee Brown. Reprint, New Haven, Conn.: Yale University Press, 1987.

————. *An Interpretation of Christian Ethics.* New York: Harper & Brothers, 1935.

————. *The Nature and Destiny of Man.* 2 vols. New York: Scribner's, 1941, 1943. Reprint, Louisville, Ky.: Westminster John Knox, 1996.

Ramsey, Paul. *Basic Christian Ethics.* New York: Scribner's, 1950. Reprint, Louisville, Ky.: Westminster John Knox, 1993.

Rauschenbusch, Walter. *Christianity & the Social Crisis.* 1907. Reprint, Louisville, Ky.: Westminster John Knox, 1992.

———. *A Theology for the Social Gospel.* New York: Macmillan, 1917.

Taylor, Nathaniel. *Lectures on the Moral Government of God.* 1859. Reprint, Chicago: Library Resources, 1970. Microfiche.

Thornwell, James Henley. *The Collected Writings of James Henley Thornwell.* 4 vols. Edited by John B. Adger and John L. Girardeau. 1871–1881. Reprint, London: Banner of Truth Trust, 1975.

Van Dusen, Henry P. *The Plain Man Seeks for God.* New York: Scribner's, 1933.

Warfield, Benjamin B. *Calvin and Calvinism.* New York: Oxford University Press, 1931.

8f. Representative Theological Studies, Mesoamerica and South America

Alves, Rubem A. *What Is Religion?* Maryknoll, N.Y.: Orbis Books, 1984.

Ortega, Ofelia, ed. *Women's Visions: Theological Reflection, Celebration, Action.* Geneva: WCC Publications, 1995.

Palomino Lopez, Salatiel. "Toward Reformed-Liberating Hermeneutics: A New Reading of Reformed Theology in the Latin American Context." Ph.D. diss., Princeton Theological Seminary, 1993.

Tamez, Elsa. *Woman's Theology from Latin America.* Maryknoll, N.Y.: Orbis Books, 1989.

8g. Representative Theological Studies, Oceania

Hayes, Victor C. *Toward Theology in an Australian Context.* Bedford Park, S.A.: Australian Association for the Study of Religion, 1979.

Houston, Jim, ed. *The Cultured Pearl: Australian Readings in Cross-Cultural Theology and Mission.* Melbourne: Victorian Council of Churches, 1986.

Knight, James, ed. *Christ in Melanesia: Exploring Theological Issues.* Goroka, Papua New Guinea: Melanesian Institute, 1977.

May, John D'Arcy, ed. *Living Theology in Melanesia: A Reader.* Goroka, Papua New Guinea: Melanesian Institute, 1985.

Pattel-Gray, Anne, and John P. Brown, eds. *Indigenous Australia: A Dialogue about the Word Becoming Flesh in Aboriginal Churches.* Geneva: World Council of Churches, 1997.

Trompf, G. W., ed. *The Gospel Is Not Western: Black Theologies from the Southwest Pacific.* Maryknoll, N.Y.: Orbis Books, 1987.

9. Studies of Theologians

Barth, Karl. *Protestant Theology in the Nineteenth Century: Its Background and History.* Reprint, Valley Forge, Pa.: Judson Press, 1973.

———. *The Theology of Schleiermacher.* Grand Rapids, Mich.: Eerdmans, 1982.

Bauckham, Richard. *The Theology of Jürgen Moltmann*. Edinburgh: T. & T. Clark, 1995.

Beardslee, John W., III. "Theological Developments at Geneva under Francis and Jean-Alphonse Turretin (1648–1737)." Ph.D. diss., Yale University, 1956.

Berkhof, Hendrikus. *Two Hundred Years of Theology: Report of a Personal Journey*. Grand Rapids, Mich.: Eerdmans, 1989.

Gerrish, Brian A. "Friedrich Schleiermacher." In *Nineteenth Century Religious Thought in the West*. Edited by Ninian Smart et al. Vol. 2. New York: Cambridge University Press, 1985.

———. *Schleiermacher: A Prince of the Church*. Philadelphia: Fortress Press, 1984.

Hunsinger, George. *How to Read Karl Barth: The Shape of His Theology*. New York: Oxford University Press, 1990.

Jenson, Robert W. *America's Theologian: A Recommendation of Jonathan Edwards*. New York: Oxford University Press, 1988.

Johnson, William Stacy. *The Mystery of God: Karl Barth and the Postmodern Foundations of Theology*. Louisville, Ky.: Westminster John Knox, 1997.

McCormack, Bruce L. *Karl Barth's Critically Realistic Dialectical Theology: Its Genesis and Development, 1909–1936*. Oxford: Oxford University Press, 1995.

Muller, Richard A. *Post-Reformation Reformed Dogmatics*. Vol. 1, *Prolegomena to Theology*. Grand Rapids, Mich.: Baker Book House, 1987.

———. *Post-Reformation Reformed Dogmatics*. Vol. 2, *Holy Scripture: The Cognitive Foundations of Theology*. Grand Rapids, Mich.: Baker Book House, 1993.

Ottati, Douglas. *Meaning and Method in H. Richard Niebuhr's Theology*. Washington, D.C.: University Press of America, 1982.

Sell, Alan P. F. *Defending and Declaring the Faith: Some Scottish Examples, 1860–1920*. Colorado Springs, Colo.: Helmers & Howard, 1987.

Reformed Life

1a. Church and Ministry, Reference Words

Cully, Kendig Brubaker. *The Westminster Dictionary of Christian Education*. Philadelphia: Westminster Press, 1963.

Davies, J. G., ed. *The New Westminster Dictionary of Liturgy and Worship*. Philadelphia: Westminster Press, 1986.

Peterson, Eugene H. *Take and Read, Spiritual Reading: An Annotated List.* Grand Rapids, Mich.: Eerdmans, 1996.

Thompson, Bard. *A Bibliography of Christian Worship.* Metuchen, N.J.: Scarecrow Press, 1989.

1b. Church and Ministry, Christian Education

Aleshire, Daniel. *Faithcare.* Philadelphia: Westminster Press, 1988.

Bushnell, Horace. *Christian Nurture.* Hartford: E. Hunt, 1847. Reprint, Cleveland, Ohio: Pilgrim Press, 1994.

Carroll, Jackson. *As One with Authority: Reflective Leadership in Ministry.* Louisville, Ky.: Westminster John Knox, 1991.

Farley, Edward. *The Fragility of Knowledge: Theological Education in the Church and the University.* Philadelphia: Fortress Press, 1988.

Harris, Maria. *Fashion Me a People.* Louisville, Ky.: Westminster John Knox, 1989.

Little, Sara. *To Set One's Heart.* Atlanta: John Knox Press, 1983.

Nelson, C. Ellis. *Where Faith Begins.* Atlanta: John Knox Press, 1967.

Oppewal, Donald, ed. *Voices from the Past: Reformed Educators.* Lanham, Md.: University Press of America, 1997.

Osmer, Richard. *Teaching for Faith.* Louisville, Ky.: Westminster John Knox Press, 1992.

Stronks, Gloria Goris, and Doug Blomberg, eds. *A Vision with a Task: Christian Schooling for a Responsive Discipleship.* Grand Rapids, Mich.: Baker Book House, 1993.

Williamson, Clark M., and Ronald J. Allen. *The Teaching Minister.* Louisville, Ky.: Westminster John Knox, 1991.

1c. Church and Ministry, the Church

Alston, Wallace M., Jr. *The Church.* Atlanta: John Knox Press, 1984.

Avis, Paul D. L. *The Church in the Theology of the Reformers.* Atlanta: John Knox Press, 1981.

Leith, John H. *From Generation to Generation: The Renewal of the Church According to Its Own Theology and Practice.* Louisville, Ky.: Westminster John Knox, 1990.

———. *The Reformed Imperative: What the Church Has to Say That No One Else Can Say.* Philadelphia: Westminster Press, 1988.

Paul, Robert S. *The Church in Search of Its Self.* Grand Rapids, Mich.: Eerdmans, 1972.

1d. Church and Ministry, Church Government and Ministry

Goodykoontz, Harry G. *The Minister in the Reformed Tradition.* Richmond, Va.: John Knox Press, 1963.

Henderson, Robert W. *The Teaching Office in the Reformed Tradition: A History of the Doctoral Ministry*. Philadelphia: Westminster Press, 1963.

Horton, Douglas. *Congregationalism: A Study in Church Polity*. London: Independent Press, 1952.

McKee, Elsie Anne. *Diakonia in the Classical Reformed Tradition and Today*. Grand Rapids, Mich.: Eerdmans, 1989.

Paul, Robert S. *Ministry*. Grand Rapids, Mich.: Eerdmans, 1965.

Peterson, Eugene H. *The Contemplative Pastor: Returning to the Art of Spiritual Direction*. Grand Rapids, Mich.: Eerdmans, 1993.

———. *Working the Angles: The Shape of Pastoral Integrity*. Grand Rapids, Mich.: Eerdmans, 1987.

Sell, Alan P. F. *Saints: Visible, Orderly & Catholic: The Congregational Idea of the Church*. Allison Park, Pa.: Pickwick Publications, 1986.

Sprott, George W. *The Worship and Offices of the Church of Scotland*. Edinburgh: William Blackwood, 1882.

Torrance, Thomas F. *The Eldership in the Reformed Church*. Edinburgh: Handsel Press, 1984.

———. *Royal Priesthood: A Theology of Ordained Ministry*. New ed. Edinburgh: T. & T. Clark, 1993.

Vischer, Lukas, ed. *The Ministry of the Elders in the Reformed Church*. Geneva: World Alliance of Reformed Churches, 1992.

Witherspoon, Henry J., and J. M. Kirkpatrick. *A Manual of Church Doctrine According to the Church of Scotland*. 2d ed. London: Oxford University Press, 1965.

1e. Church and Ministry, Hymnody

Chenoweth, Vida. "Spare Them Western Music." *Evangelical Missions Quarterly* 20 (1984): 30–35.

Christian Conference of Asia. *Sound the Bamboo, CCA Hymnal*. Singapore: Asian Institute for Liturgy and Music and the Christian Conference of Asia, 1990.

McKim, LindaJo H. *The Presbyterian Hymnal Companion*. Louisville, Ky.: Westminster John Knox, 1993.

McKim, LindaJo H., ed. *The Presbyterian Hymnal: Hymns, Psalms, and Spiritual Songs*. Louisville, Ky.: Westminster John Knox Press, 1990.

Routley, Erik. *Christian Hymns Observed: When in Our Music God Is Glorified*. Princeton, N.J.: Prestige Publications, 1982.

———. *The Music of Christian Hymns*. Chicago: G.I.A. Publications, 1981.

Sydnor, James R. *Hymns: A Congregational Study*. Carol Stream, Ill.: Hope Publishing, 1983.

White, Linda, ed. *Lift Up Your Hearts: Songs for Creative Worship*. Louisville, Ky.: Westminster John Knox, forthcoming.

1f. Church and Ministry, Mission and Evangelism

Armstrong, Richard S. *The Pastor-Evangelist in the Parish*. Louisville, Ky.: Westminster John Knox, 1990.

Blauw, Johannes. *The Missionary Nature of the Church*. 1962. Reprint, Grand Rapids: Eerdmans, 1974.

Bosch, David J. *Transforming Mission: Paradigm Shifts in Theology of Mission*. Maryknoll, N.Y.: Orbis Books, 1991.

———. *Witness to the World: The Christian Mission in Theological Perspective*. Atlanta: John Knox Press, 1980.

Coalter, Milton J., and Virgil Cruz, eds. *How Shall We Witness? Faithful Evangelism in a Reformed Tradition*. Louisville, Ky.: Westminster John Knox, 1995.

Coalter, Milton J., John M. Mulder, and Louis B. Weeks, eds. *The Diversity of Discipleship: The Presbyterians and Twentieth-Century Christian Witness*. Louisville, Ky.: Westminster John Knox, 1991.

Costas, Orlando. *Liberating News: A Theology of Contextual Evangelization*. Grand Rapids, Mich.: Eerdmans, 1989.

Guder, Darrell L. *Be My Witnesses: The Church's Mission, Message, and Messengers*. Grand Rapids, Mich.: Eerdmans, 1985.

Guder, Darrell L., ed. Missional Church: *A Vision for the Sending of the Church in North America*. Grand Rapids, Mich.: Eerdmans, 1998.

Hunsberger, George R. *Bearing the Witness of the Spirit: Lesslie Newbigin's Theology of Cultural Plurality*. Grand Rapids, Mich.: Eerdmans, 1998.

Johnson, Ben Campbell. *An Evangelism Primer: Practical Principles for Congregations*. Atlanta: John Knox Press, 1983.

———. *Rethinking Evangelism: A Theological Approach*. Philadelphia: Westminster Press, 1987.

———. *Speaking of God: Evangelism as Initial Spiritual Guidance*. Louisville, Ky.: Westminster John Knox Press, 1991.

Lovell, Arnold B., ed. *Evangelism in the Reformed Tradition*. Decatur, Ga.: Columbia Theological Seminary Press, 1990.

Newbigin, Lesslie. "Can the West Be Converted?" *International Bulletin of Missionary Research* 11 (1987): 2–7.

———. *The Open Secret: An Introduction to the Theology of Mission*. Rev. ed. Grand Rapids, Mich.: Eerdmans, 1995.

Scherer, James A., and Stephen B. Bevans, eds. *New Directions in Mission and Evangelization*. Vol. 1, *Basic Statements, 1974–1991*. Maryknoll, N.Y.: Orbis Books, 1992.

Van Engen, Charles. *Mission on the Way: Issues in Mission Theology.* Grand Rapids, Mich.: Baker Book House, 1996.

Verkuyl, Johannes. *Contemporary Missiology: An Introduction.* Translated by Dale Cooper. Grand Rapids, Mich.: Eerdmans, 1978.

Visser 't Hooft, W. A. "Evangelism among Europe's Neo-Pagans." *International Review of Mission* 66 (1979): 349–57.

1g. Church and Ministry, Prayer and Spirituality

Baillie, John. *A Diary of Private Prayer.* New York: Scribner's, 1936.

Barth, Karl. *Church Dogmatics.* Vol. 4.4, *The Christian Life.* Grand Rapids, Mich.: Eerdmans, 1981. An unfinished exposition of the Lord's Prayer.

———. *Prayer.* Edited by Don E. Saliers. 2d ed. Philadelphia: Westminster Press, 1985.

Bloesch, Donald G. *The Struggle of Prayer.* San Francisco: Harper & Row, 1980.

Ellul, Jacques. *Prayer and Modern Man.* New York: Seabury Press, 1970.

Old, Hughes Oliphant. *Leading in Prayer.* Grand Rapids, Mich.: Eerdmans, 1995.

Ramsey, Robert H., Jr., and Ben Campbell. *Living the Christian Life: A Guide to Reformed Spirituality.* Louisville, Ky.: Westminster John Knox, 1992.

Rice, Howard L. *Reformed Spirituality: An Introduction for Believers.* Louisville, Ky.: Westminster John Knox, 1991.

Rice, Howard L., and Lamar Williamson, eds. *A Book of Reformed Prayers.* Louisville, Ky.: Westminster John Knox Press, 1998.

Scougal, Henry. *The Life of God in the Soul of Man.* Philadelphia: Westminster Press, 1948.

Speer, Wayne R. *The Theology of Prayer.* Grand Rapids, Mich.: Baker Book House, 1979.

Thompson, Marjorie. *Soul Feast: An Invitation to the Christian Spiritual Life.* Louisville, Ky.: Westminster John Knox, 1995.

Westerhoff, John. *Spiritual Life: The Foundation for Preaching and Teaching.* Louisville, Ky.: Westminster John Knox, 1994.

1h. Church and Ministry, Preaching

Achtemeier, Elizabeth R. *Creative Preaching: Finding the Words.* Nashville, Tenn.: Abingdon Press, 1980.

———. *Preaching as Theology and Art.* Nashville, Tenn.: Abingdon Press, 1984.

Barth, Karl. *Homiletics.* Louisville, Ky.: Westminster John Knox, 1991.

Brueggemann, Walter. *Finally Comes the Poet: Daring Speech for Proclamation.* Minneapolis: Fortress Press, 1989.

Buttrick, David. *Homiletic: Moves and Structures.* Philadelphia: Fortress Press, 1987.

Craddock, Fred B. *As One without Authority: Essays on Inductive Preaching.* Enid, Okla.: Phillips University Press, 1971.

———. *Preaching.* Nashville, Tenn.: Abingdon Press, 1985.

Forsyth, P. T. *Positive Preaching and the Modern Mind.* Grand Rapids, Mich.: Eerdmans, 1964.

Long, Thomas G. *Preaching and the Literary Forms of the Bible.* Philadelphia: Fortress Press, 1988.

———. *The Senses of Preaching.* Louisville, Ky.: Westminster John Knox, 1988.

———. *The Witness of Preaching.* Louisville, Ky.: Westminster John Knox, 1989.

Parker, T. H. L. *Calvin's Preaching.* Louisville, Ky.: Westminster John Knox, 1992.

1i. Church and Ministry, Psychology and Theology

Boisen, Anton T. *Religion in Crisis and Custom: A Sociological and Psychological Study.* 1955. Reprint, Westport, Conn.: Greenwood Press, 1973.

———. *Vision from a Little Known Country: A Boisen Reader.* Edited by Glenn H. Asquith, Jr. Decatur, Ga.: Journal of Pastoral Care Pub., 1991.

Cohen, Charles L. *God's Caress: The Psychology of Puritan Religious Experience.* New York: Oxford University Press, 1986.

Hiltner, Seward. *Theological Dynamics.* Nashville, Tenn.: Abingdon Press, 1972.

Menninger, Karl A. *Man against Himself.* 1938. Reprint, San Diego: Harcourt Brace Jovanovich, 1988.

———. *What Ever Became of Sin?* New York: Hawthorne Books, 1973.

Tournier, Paul. *Guilt and Grace: A Psychological Study.* New York: Harper, 1962.

———. *The Healing of Persons.* New York: Harper & Row, 1965.

———. *The Meaning of Persons.* New York: Harper, 1957.

1j. Church and Ministry, Sacraments and Rites

Baillie, Donald M. *The Theology of the Sacraments.* London: Faber, 1957.

Barclay, William. *The Lord's Supper.* London: SCM Press, 1967.

Barth, Markus. *Rediscovering the Lord's Supper: Communion with Israel, with Christ, and among the Guests.* Atlanta: John Knox Press, 1988.

Bromiley, G. W. *Children of Promise.* Grand Rapids: Eerdmans, 1979.

Cullmann, O. *Baptism in the New Testament.* London: SCM Press, 1950.

Fisher, J. D. C. *Christian Initiation: The Reformation Period.* London: SPCK, 1970.

————. *Confirmation Then and Now*. London: SPCK, 1978.

Molnar, Paul D. *Karl Barth and the Theology of the Lord's Supper*. New York: Peter Lang, 1996.

Monkres, Peter R., and R. Kenneth Ostermiller. *The Rite of Confirmation: Moments When Faith Is Strengthened*. Cleveland, Ohio: Pilgrim Press, 1995.

Myers, William R., ed. *Becoming and Belonging: A Practical Design for Confirmation*. Cleveland, Ohio: United Church Press, 1993.

Old, Hughes Oliphant. *The Shaping of the Reformed Baptismal Rite in the Sixteenth Century*. Grand Rapids, Mich.: Eerdmans, 1992.

Osmer, Richard Robert. *Confirmation: Presbyterian Practice in Ecumenical Perspective*. Louisville, Ky.: Geneva Press, 1995.

Paul, Robert S. *The Atonement and the Sacraments: The Relation of the Atonement to the Sacraments of Baptism and the Lord's Supper*. New York: Abingdon Press, 1960.

Sell, Alan P. F. *Responding to 'Baptism, Eucharist and Ministry': A Word to the Reformed Churches*. Geneva: World Alliance of Reformed Churches, 1984.

1k. Church and Ministry, Worship

Baird, Charles W. *The Presbyterian Liturgies: Historical Sketches*. Grand Rapids, Mich.: Baker Book House, 1957.

Barkley, John M. *The Worship of the Reformed Church*. Richmond, Va.: John Knox Press, 1967.

Esther, James R., and Donald J. Bruggink. *Worship the Lord*. Grand Rapids, Mich.: Eerdmans, 1987.

Forrester, Duncan. *Studies in the History of Worship in Scotland*. 2d ed. Edinburgh: T. & T. Clark, 1996.

Forrester, Duncan, Ian McDonald, and Gian Tellini. *Encounter with God*. 2d. ed. Edinburgh: T. & T. Clark, 1996.

Hageman, Howard G. *Pulpit and Table: Some Chapters in the History of Worship in the Reformed Churches*. Richmond, Va.: John Knox Press, 1962.

Jewett, Paul K. *The Lord's Day: A Theological Guide to the Christian Day of Worship*. Grand Rapids, Mich.: Eerdmans, 1971.

Maxwell, Jack Martin. *Worship and Reformed Theology: The Liturgical Lessons of Mercersburg*. Pittsburgh: Pickwick Press, 1976.

Maxwell, William D. *Concerning Worship*. London: Oxford University Press, 1949.

Nichols, James H. *Corporate Worship in the Reformed Tradition*. Philadelphia: Westminster Press, 1968.

Old, Hughes Oliphant. *The Patristic Roots of Reformed Worship*. Zürich: Theologischer Verlag Zürich, 1975.

———. *Worship That Is Reformed According to Scripture*. Atlanta: John Knox Press, 1984.

Schroeder, Frederick. *Worship in the Reformed Tradition*. Boston: United Church Press, 1966.

2a. Church and Culture, Culture

Dooyeweerd, Herman. *Roots of Western Culture: Pagan, Secular and Christian Options*. New York: Shiloh Books, 1979.

Hunsberger, George, and Craig van Gelder, eds. *The Church between Gospel and Culture: The Emerging Mission in North America*. Grand Rapids, Mich.: Eerdmans, 1996.

Kraft, Charles H. *Christianity in Culture*. Maryknoll, N.Y.: Orbis Books, 1979.

Newbigin, Lesslie. *The Gospel in a Pluralist Society*. Grand Rapids, Mich.: Eerdmans, 1989.

Niebuhr, H. Richard. *Christ and Culture*. New York: Harper, 1951.

Sanneh, Lamin. *Translating the Message: The Missionary Impact on Culture*. Maryknoll, N.Y.: Orbis Books, 1989.

Van Til, Henry R. *The Calvinistic Concept of Culture*. Grand Rapids, Mich.: Baker Book House, 1959.

Wolf, Miroslav. *Exclusion and Embrace: A Theological Exploration of Identity, Otherness, and Reconciliation*. Nashville: Abingdon, 1996.

Wilson, H. S., ed. *Gospel and Cultures: Reformed Perspectives*. Geneva: World Alliance of Reformed Churches, 1996.

2b. Church and Culture, Architecture

Bieler, Andre. *Architecture in Worship: The Christian Place of Worship*. Philadelphia: Westminster Press, 1965.

Bruggink, Donald J., and Carl H. Droppers. *Christ and Architecture: Building Presbyterian/Reformed Churches*. Grand Rapids, Mich.: Eerdmans, 1965.

Drummond, Andrew Landale. *The Church Architecture of Protestantism*. Edinburgh: T. & T. Clark, 1934.

Goetz, Ronald. "Protestant Houses of God: A Contradiction in Terms." *Christian Century* 102 (March 1985): 294–99.

Rosenberg, Jacob. *Dutch Art and Architecture 1600–1800*. New Haven, Conn.: Yale University Press, 1987.

Takenaka, Masao. *The Place Where God Dwells: An Introduction to Church Architecture in Asia*. Hong Kong: Pace Publishing, 1995.

White, James. *Protestant Worship and Church Architecture*. New York: Oxford University Press, 1964.

2c. Church and Culture, Arts (Visual)

Buechner, Frederick. *The Faces of Jesus.* Croton-on-Hudson, N.Y.: Riverwood Publishers, 1974.

Communion of Churches in Indonesia. *Many Faces of Christian Art in Indonesia.* Jakarta: Persekutuan Gereja-Gereja di Indonesia, 1993.

Dillenberger, John. *The Visual Arts and Christianity in America: From the Colonial Period to the Present.* Rev. and enl. ed. New York: Crossroad, 1988.

Elavathingal, Sebastian. *Inculturation and Christian Art: An Indian Perspective.* Rome: Urbaniana University Press, 1990.

Lüthy, Hans. *Swiss Painting: From the Middle Ages to the Dawn of the Twentieth Century.* Geneva: Skira, 1976.

Parshall, Linda B., and Peter W. Parshall. *Art and the Reformation: An Annotated Bibliography.* Boston: G. K. Hall, 1986.

Spelman, Leslie P. "Calvin and the Arts." *Journal of Aesthetics and Art Criticism* 6 (1947–48): 246–52.

Takács, Béla. *"The Habitation of Thy House, Lord, I have Loved Well . . .": Reformed Ecclesiastical Art in Hungary.* Budapest: Officina Nova, [1991?].

See the Netherlands (Dutch art).

2d. Church and Culture, Literature and Literary Criticism

Coats, Catharine Randall. *Subverting the System: D'Aubigné and Calvinism.* Kirksville, Mo.: Sixteenth Century Journal Publishers, 1990.

Fibiny, Tibor. *The Lion and the Lamb: Figuralism and Fulfilment in the Bible, Art, and Literature.* New York: St. Martin's Press, 1992.

Frye, Northrop. *The Great Code: The Bible and Literature.* New York: Harcourt Brace Jovanovich, 1982.

Jasper, David, and Colin Crowder, eds. *European Literature and Theology in the Twentieth Century: Ends of Time.* New York: St. Martin's Press, 1990.

Kazin, Alfred. *God and the American Writer.* New York: Knopf, 1997.

Wheeler, Michael. *Death and the Future Life in Victorian Literature and Theology.* New York: Cambridge University Press, 1990.

Wright, T. R. *Theology and Literature.* New York: Blackwell, 1988.

3a. Church and Society, Reference Works

Childress, James F., and John Macquarrie, eds. *The Westminster Dictionary of Christian Ethics.* Philadelphia: Westminster Press, 1986.

3b. Church and Society, Economics

Besnard, P. *Protestantisme et Capitalisme: la Controverse Post-weberienne.* Paris: A. Colin, 1970.

Bonk, Jonathan. *Missions and Money: Affluence as a Western Missionary Problem.* Maryknoll, N.Y.: Orbis Books, 1991.

Ellul, Jacques. *Money and Power.* Downers Grove, Ill.: InterVarsity Press, 1984.

Lüthy, Herbert. *From Calvin to Rousseau: Tradition and Modernity in Socio-Political Thought from the Reformation to the French Revolution.* New York: Basic Books, 1970.

―――. "Variations on a Theme by Max Weber." In *International Calvinism,* edited by Menna Prestwich, 369–90. Oxford: Clarendon Press, 1985.

Marshall, Gordon. *Presbyteries and Profits: Calvinism and the Development of Capitalism in Scotland, 1560–1707.* New York: Oxford University Press, 1980.

Poggi, Gianfranco. *Calvinism and the Capitalist Spirit: Max Weber's Protestant Ethic.* Amherst: University of Massachusetts Press, 1983.

Stackhouse, Max, ed. *On Moral Business: Classical and Contemporary Resources for Ethics in Economic Life.* Grand Rapids: Eerdmans, 1995.

Weber, Max. *The Protestant Ethic and the Spirit of Capitalism.* 1926. Reprint, New York: Scribner's, 1958.

3c. Church and Society, Ethics and Human Rights

Barclay, William. *Ethics in a Permissive Society.* London: Fontana, 1971.

Barth, Karl. *The Holy Spirit and the Christian Life: The Theological Basis of Ethics.* Reprint, Louisville, Ky.: Westminster John Knox, 1993.

Boulton, Wayne G., Thomas D. Kennedy, and Allen Verhey, eds. *From Christ to the World: Introductory Readings in Christian Ethics.* Grand Rapids, Mich.: Eerdmans, 1996.

Fairweather, Ian C. M., and James I. H. McDonald. *The Quest for Christian Ethics: An Inquiry into Ethics and Christian Ethics.* Edinburgh: Handsel Press, 1984.

Gustafson, James M. *Theology and Christian Ethics.* Philadelphia: United Church Press, 1974.

John Knox Center. *Forms of Solidarity: Human Rights.* Geneva: John Knox Center, 1988.

McDonald, J. Ian H. *Christian Values: Theory and Practice in Christian Ethics Today.* Edinburgh: T. & T. Clark, 1995.

Miller, Allen O., ed. *A Christian Declaration on Human Rights.* Grand Rapids, Mich.: Eerdmans, 1977.

Niebuhr, Reinhold. *The Nature and Destiny of Man.* 2 vols. New York: Scribner's, 1941–1943.

Ramsey, Paul. *Basic Christian Ethics.* Reprint, Louisville, Ky.: Westminster John Knox, 1993.

Schaeffer, Jill, and Adrienne Reber. *Against Torture*. Geneva: WARC, 1987.

Smylie, James H., ed. "Human Rights and the Bill of Rights." *Affirmation* 6, no. 1 (Spring 1993).

Stackhouse, Max. *Christian Social Ethics in a Global Era*. Nashville, Tenn.: Abingdon Press, 1995.

————. *Creeds, Society, and Human Rights: A Study in Three Cultures*. Grand Rapids, Mich.: Eerdmans, 1984.

————. *Ethics and the Urban Ethos: An Essay in Social Theory and Theological Reconstruction*. Boston: Beacon Press, 1972.

Verhey, Allen. *Living the Heidelberg: The Heidelberg Catechism and the Moral Life*. Grand Rapids, Mich.: CRC Publications, 1986.

World Alliance of Reformed Churches. *Theological Basis of Human Rights*. Geneva: WARC and Lutheran World Federation, 1976.

3d. Church and Society, Health and Medicine

Bouma, Hessel, III, et al., eds. *Christian Faith, Health, and Medical Practice*. Grand Rapids, Mich.: Eerdmans, 1989.

Lammers, Stephen E., and Allen Verhey, eds. *On Moral Medicine: Theological Perspectives in Medical Ethics*. Grand Rapids, Mich.: Eerdmans, 1987.

Smylie, James H. "The Reformed Tradition." In *Caring and Curing: Health and Medicine in the Western Religious Traditions*, edited by Ronald L. Numbers and Darrel W. Amundsen, 204–39. New York: Macmillan, 1986.

Vaux, Kenneth. *Health and Medicine in the Reformed Tradition: Promise, Providence, and Care*. New York: Crossroad, 1984.

Verhey, Allen, and, Stephen E. Lammers, eds. *Theological Voices in Medical Ethics*. Grand Rapids, Mich.: Eerdmans, 1993.

Wiest, Walter E. *Health Care and Its Costs: A Challenge for the Church*. Lanham, Md.: University Press of America, 1988.

3e. Church and Society, Politics and Law

Ellul, Jacques. *Anarchy and Christianity*. Grand Rapids, Mich.: Eerdmans, 1991.

————. *The Theological Foundation of Law*. Translated by Marguerite Wieser. New York: Doubleday, 1960.

Hunt, George L., ed. *Calvinism and the Political Order*. Philadelphia: Westminster Press, 1965.

Jenkins, Daniel T. *The Church Meeting and Democracy*. London: Independent Press, 1944.

Lehmann, Paul. *The Transfiguration of Politics*. New York: Harper & Row, 1975.

Moltmann, Jürgen. *Religion and Political Society*. New York: Harper & Row, 1974.

Niebuhr, Reinhold. *Faith and Politics*. New York: George Braziller, 1968.

Richardson, Alan. *The Political Christ*. Philadelphia: Westminster Press, 1973.

Stackhouse, Max L. *Public Theology and Political Economy: Christian Stewardship in Modern Society*. 1987. Reprint, Lanham, Md.: University Press of America, 1991.

Stringfellow, William. *The Politics of Spirituality*. Philadelphia: Westminster Press, 1984.

Van Ruler, A. A. *Calvinist Trinitarianism and Theocentric Politics: Essays toward a Public Theology*. Lewiston, N.Y.: Mellen Press, 1989.

Yardeni, Myriam. "French Calvinist Political Thought, 1534–1715." In *International Calvinism*, edited by Menna Prestwich, 315–37. Oxford: Clarendon Press, 1985.

3f. Church and Society, Science and Technology

Dillenberger, John. *Protestant Thought and Natural Science: A Historical Interpretation*. South Bend, Ind.: University of Notre Dame, 1988.

Ellul, Jacques. *The Technological Bluff*. Grand Rapids, Mich.: Eerdmans, 1990.

———. *The Technological Society*. New York: Knopf, 1964.

Hooykaas, Reijer. *Religion and the Rise of Modern Science*. Grand Rapids, Mich.: Eerdmans, 1972.

Kaiser, Christopher B. *Creation and the History of Science*. Grand Rapids, Mich.: Eerdmans, 1991.

Klaaren, Eugene M. *Religious Origins of Modern Science*. Grand Rapids, Mich.: Eerdmans, 1977.

Nebelsick, Harold P. *The Renaissance, the Reformation and the Rise of Science*. Edinburgh: T. & T. Clark, 1992.

Torrance, Thomas F. *Christian Frame of Mind: Reason, Order and Openness in Theology and Natural Science*. Colorado Springs, Colo.: Helmers Howard, 1989.

———. *Preaching Christ Today: The Gospel and Scientific Thinking*. Grand Rapids, Mich.: Eerdmans, 1994.

———. *Space, Time and Incarnation*. London: Oxford University Press, 1969.

———. *Theological Science*. 1969. Reprint, Edinburgh: T. & T. Clark, 1996.

3g. Church and Society, Sociology

Albrecht, Gloria H. *The Character of Our Communities: Toward an Ethic of Liberation for the Church*. Nashville: Abingdon Press, 1995.

Dekker, Gerard, ed. *Rethinking Secularization: Reformed Reactions to Modernity*. Lanham, Md.: University Press of America, 1977.

Ellul, Jacques. *The Humiliation of the Word.* Grand Rapids, Mich.: Eerdmans, 1985.

Lenski, Gerhard E. *The Religious Factor: A Sociological Study of Religion's Impact on Politics, Economics, and Family Life.* Reprint, Westport, Conn.: Greenwood Press, 1977.

Niebuhr, H. Richard. *The Social Sources of Denominationalism.* Reprint, Gloucester, Mass.: Peter Smith, 1987.

Stackhouse, Max L. *Covenant and Commitments: Faith, Family, and Economic Life.* Louisville, Ky.: Westminster John Knox, 1997.

Wuthnow, Robert. *Christianity in the 21st Century: Reflections on the Challenges Ahead.* Princeton: Princeton University Press, 1993.

THE WORLD REFORMED CHURCHES

Africa

1a. General Works, Bibliographies

Cochrane, J. R., I. W. Henderson, and G. O. West, eds. *Bibliography of Contextual Theology in Africa.* Pietermaritzburg: Cluster Publications, 1993–.

Facelina, Raymond. *African Theology: International Bibliography 1968– June 1977 Indexed by Computer.* RIC Supplement 30. Strasbourg, France: Cerdic-Publications, 1977.

Tropical Africa and the Old Testament: A Select and Annotated Bibliography. Oslo: University of Oslo Faculty of Theology, 1996.

Young, Josiah U., III. *African Theology: A Critical Analysis and Annotated Bibliography.* Westport, Conn.: Greenwood Press, 1993.

1b. General Works, Histories and Studies

Baur, John. *2000 Years of Christianity in Africa: An African History, 62– 1992.* Nairobi: Paulines Publications, 1994.

Fasholé-Luke, Edward, et al., eds. *Christianity in Independent Africa.* Bloomington: Indiana University Press, 1978.

Hastings, Adrian. *The Church in Africa, 1450–1950.* New York: Oxford University Press, 1994.

———. *A History of African Christianity, 1950–1975.* African Studies Series, no. 26. New York: Cambridge University Press, 1979.

Isichei, Elizabeth. *A History of Christianity in Africa.* Grand Rapids, Mich.: Eerdmans, 1995.

1c. General Works, African Religions

Idowu, Bolaji. *African Traditional Religion: A Definition.* London: SCM Press, 1973.

Mbiti, John S. *African Religions and Philosophy.* 2d ed. Portsmouth, N.H.: Heinemann, 1990.

Olupona, Jacob K., ed. *Religious Plurality in Africa: Essays in Honor of John S. Mbiti.* New York: M. de Gruyter, 1993.

p'Bitek, Okot. *African Religions in Western Scholarship.* Nairobi: East African Literature Bureau, 1970.

Taylor, John V. *The Primal Vision: Christian Presence Amid African Religion.* Reprint, London: SCM Press, 1982.

2a. Central Africa (Central African Republic, Congo, and Rwanda), Central African Republic

Barrett, David B., ed. "Central African Republic." In *World Christian Encyclopedia,* 220–22. New York: Oxford University Press, 1982.

Kalck, Pierre. *Historical Dictionary of the Central African Republic.* Metuchen, N.J.: Scarecrow Press, 1980.

2b. Central Africa (Central African Republic, Congo, and Rwanda), Congo: Primary Sources

Benedetto, Robert, ed. *Presbyterian Reformers in Central Africa: A Documentary Account of the American Presbyterian Congo Mission and the Human Rights Struggle in the Congo, 1890–1918.* Leiden: E. J. Brill, 1996.

2c. Central Africa (Central African Republic, Congo, and Rwanda), Congo: Histories and Studies

Braekman, E. M. *Histoire du Protestantisme au Congo.* Flavion, Belgium: Librairie des Eclaireurs Unionistes, 1961.

Diakubikwa, Komy-Nsilu. "L'Église de Christ au Zaïre à la recherche d'une unité, 1902–1977." Ph.D. diss., Faculté universitaire de théologie protestante, Bruxelles, 1984.

Hakira, Serufuri. "Les auxiliaires autochtones des missions protestantes au Congo, 1878–1960: étude de cinq sociétés missionnaires." Ph.D. diss., Université de Louvain-la-Neuve, 1984.

Kabombi, Dijinda. "Daily Life as Worship and Gospel Communication in the Presbyterian Community of Kinshasa." Ph.D. diss., Fuller Theological Seminary, 1991.

Kabongo-Mbaya, Philippe B. *L'Église du Christ au Zaïre: Formation et adaptation d'un protestantisme en situation de dictature.* Paris: Karthala, 1992.

Morel, E. D. *History of the Congo Reform Movement.* Edited by William Roger Louis and Jean Stengers. Oxford: Clarendon Press, 1968.

Mulundi, Mulumba. "Witchcraft among the Kasaian People of Zaire: Challenge and Response." Ph.D. diss., Fuller Theological Seminary, 1988.

Ranger, T. O., and John Weller, eds. *Themes in the Christian History of Central Africa.* Berkeley: University of California Press, 1975.

Shaloff, Stanley. *Reform in Leopold's Congo.* Richmond, Va.: John Knox Press, 1970.

Slade, Ruth. *English-Speaking Missions in the Congo Independent State, 1878–1908.* Brussels: Academie Royale des Sciences Coloniales, 1959.

———. *King Leopold's Congo.* 1962. Reprint, Westport, Conn.: Greenwood Press, 1974.

Wharton, E. T. *Led in Triumph.* Nashville, Tenn.: Board of World Missions, 1953.

2d. Central Africa (Central African Republic, Congo, and Rwanda), Congo: Biography

Vinson, Thomas C. *William McCutchan Morrison.* Richmond, Va.: Presbyterian Committee of Publication, 1921.

Williamson, Lamar. *Ishaku: An African Christian between Two Worlds.* Lima, Ohio: Fairway Press, 1992.

2e. Central Africa (Central African Republic, Congo, and Rwanda), Rwanda

Longman, Timothy Paul. "Christianity and Democratisation in Rwanda: Assessing Church Responses to Political Crisis in the 1990s." In *The Christian Churches and the Democratisation of Africa,* edited by Paul Gifford, 188–204. Leiden: E. J. Brill, 1995.

McCullum, Hugh. *The Angels Have Left Us: The Rwanda Tragedy and the Churches.* Geneva: World Council of Churches, 1995.

———. "Reconciling: Rebuilding Rwanda." *One World* 204 (1995): 6–8.

Twagirayesu, Michael, and Jan van Butselaar, eds. *Ce don que nous avons reçu. Histoire de l'Eglise Presbyterienne au Rwanda.* Kigali: Eglise Presbyterienne au Rwanda, 1982.

3a. East Africa (Kenya and Sudan), East African Region

Anderson, William B. *The Church in East Africa, 1840–1974.* Reprint, Nairobi, Kenya: Uzima, 1981.

Nthamburi, Zablon, ed. *From Mission to Church: A Handbook of Christianity in East Africa.* Nairobi, Kenya: Association of Theological Institutions in East Africa, 1991.

Oliver, Roland. *The Missionary Factor in East Africa.* 2d ed. London: Longman, 1965.

Temu, A. J. *British Protestant Missions*. London: Longman, 1972.

3b. East Africa (Kenya and Sudan), Kenya

Barrett, David B., et al., eds. *Kenya Churches Handbook: The Development of Kenyan Christianity, 1498–1973*. Kisumu, Kenya: Evangel Publishing House, 1973.

Macpherson, Robert. *The Presbyterian Church in Kenya: An Account of the Origins and Growth of the Presbyterian Church of East Africa*. Nairobi: Presbyterian Church of East Africa, 1970.

McIntosh, Brian G. "The Scottish Mission in Kenya, 1891–1923." Ph.D. diss., Edinburgh University, 1969.

Muriuki, Godfrey. *A History of the Kikuyu 1500–1900*. Nairobi: Oxford University Press, 1974.

3c. East Africa (Kenya and Sudan), Sudan

Boer, Jan Marm. *Missionary Messengers of Liberation in a Colonial Context: A Case Study of the Sudan United Mission*. Amsterdam: Rodopi, 1979.

International Institute for the Study of Islam and Christianity. "The Church in the Sudan." *Evangelical Review of Theology* 20 (1996): 141–51.

Vantini, Giovanni. *Christianity in the Sudan*. Bologna, Italy: EMI, 1981.

4. North Africa (Algeria, Libya, Morocco, and Tunisia)

Horner, Norman A. "Christianity in North Africa Today." *Occasional Bulletin of Missionary Research* 4 (1980): 83–88.

O'Donnell, Joseph Dean. *Lavigerie in Tunisia: The Interplay of Imperialist and Missionary*. Athens, Ga.: University of Georgia Press, 1979.

Schmidt, Elizabeth. *When God Calls a Woman: The Struggle of a Woman Pastor in France and Algeria*. New York: Pilgrim Press, 1981.

5a. South Africa (Republic of South Africa), Bibliographies

Borchardt, C. F. A., and Willem S. Vorster, eds. *South African Theological Bibliography/Suid-Afrikaanse Teologiese Bibliografie*. Pretoria: University of South Africa, 1983–.

Chidester, David, Judy Jobler, and Darrel Wratten, eds. *Christianity in South Africa: An Annotated Bibliography*. Westport, Conn.: Greenwood Press, 1997.

Hofmeyr, J. W., and K. E. Cross, eds. *History of the Church in South Africa: A Select Bibliography of Published Material*. Vol. 2, *1981–1985;* vol. 3, *1986–1989*. Pretoria: University of South Africa, 1988, 1993.

Hofmeyr, J. W., J. H. Rykheer, and J. M. Nel, eds. *A Select Bibliography of Periodical Articles on Southern African Church History, 1975–1989*. Vol. 1. Pretoria: University of South Africa, 1991.

Turnbull, C. E. P. *The Work of Missionaries of Die Nederduits*

Gereformeerde Kerk van Suid-Afrika: An Annotated Bibliography of Materials in the Johannesburg Public and University of Witwatersrand Libraries. Johannesburg: University of Witwatersrand, Dept. of Bibliography, Librarianship, and Typography, 1965.

Young, Josiah U., III. *African Theology: A Critical Analysis and Annotated Bibliography.* Westport, Conn.: Greenwood Press, 1993.

5b. South Africa (Republic of South Africa), Primary Sources

Hofmeyr, J. W., J. A. Millard, and C. J. J. Froneman, eds. *History of the Church in South Africa: A Document and Source Book.* Pretoria: University of South Africa, 1991.

5c. South Africa (Republic of South Africa), Histories and Studies

Bloomberg, Charles. *Christian-Nationalism and the Rise of the Afrikaner Broederbond in South Africa, 1918–48.* Bloomington: Indiana University Press, 1989.

Boesak, Allan A. *Black and Reformed: Apartheid, Liberation, and the Calvinist Tradition.* Maryknoll, N.Y.: Orbis Books, 1984.

Comaroff, J. *Of Revelation and Revolution: Christianity, Colonialism, and Consciousness in South Africa.* Chicago: University of Chicago Press, 1991.

De Gruchy, John W. *The Church Struggle in South Africa.* 2d ed. Grand Rapids, Mich.: Eerdmans, 1986.

Dinnerstein, Myra. "The American Board Mission to the Zulu, 1835–1900." Ph.D. diss., Columbia University, 1971.

Du Plessis, Johannes. *A History of Christian Missions in South Africa.* London: Longmans, Green, 1911.

Froise, Marjorie, ed. *World Christianity: South Africa: A Factual Portrait of the Christian Church in South Africa, Botswana, Lesotho, Namibia, and Swaziland.* Monrovia, Calif.: MARC, 1989.

Hexham, Irving. *The Irony of Apartheid: The Struggle for National Independence of Afrikaner Calvinism against British Imperialism.* New York: Mellen Press, 1981.

Hofmeyr, J. W., and G. J. Pillay, eds. *A History of Christianity in South Africa.* Pretoria: HAUM, 1994.

Logan, Willis H., ed. *The Kairos Covenant: Standing with South African Christians.* New York: Friendship, 1988.

Mostert, Noël. *Frontiers: The Epic of South Africa's Creation and the Tragedy of the Xhosa People.* New York: Knopf, 1992.

Réamonn, Páraic. *Farewell to Apartheid? Church Relations in South Africa.* Geneva: World Alliance of Reformed Churches, 1994.

Shepherd, Robert Henry W. *Lovedale, South Africa. The Story of a Century, 1841–1941.* Lovedale, C. P., South Africa: Lovedale Press, [1940].

Van der Merwe, W. J. *The Development of Missionary Attitudes in the Dutch Reformed Church in South Africa*. Cape Town: Nasionale Pers, 1936.

5d. South Africa (Republic of South Africa), Theological Studies

De Gruchy, John W. *Liberating Reformed Theology: A South African Contribution to an Ecumenical Debate*. Grand Rapids, Mich.: Eerdmans, 1991.

Gerstner, Jonathan Neil. *The Thousand Generation Covenant: Dutch Reformed Covenant Theology and Group Identity in Colonial South Africa, 1652–1814*. Leiden: E. J. Brill, 1991.

Landman, Christina. *The Piety of Afrikaans Women*. Pretoria: Unisa, 1994.

Moore, Basil, ed. *The Challenge of Black Theology in South Africa*. Atlanta: John Knox Press, 1974.

5e. South Africa (Republic of South Africa), Biographies

Gobledale, Ana K. *The Learning Spirit: Lessons from South Africa*. St. Louis, Mo.: Chalice Press, 1994.

Lindner, William, Jr. *Andrew Murray*. Minneapolis: Bethany House, 1996.

Ross, A. *John Philipp (1775–1851): Mission, Race, and Politics in South Africa*. Aberdeen, Scotland: Aberdeen University Press, 1986.

Ryan, Colleen. *Beyers Naudé: Pilgrimage of Faith*. Grand Rapids, Mich.: Eerdmans, 1990.

Van Der Vyver, G. C. P. *Professor Dirk Postma, 1818–1890*. Potchefstroom: Pro Rege, 1958.

6a. Southern Africa (Angola, Botswana, Lesotho, Malawi, Mozambique, Zambia, and Zimbabwe), The Region of Southern Africa

Froise, Marjorie, ed. *World Christianity: South Central Africa: A Factual Portrait of the Christian Church*. Monrovia, Calif.: MARC, 1991.

Livingstone, David. *Letters and Documents, 1841–1872: The Zambian Collection at the Livingstone Museum*. Edited by Timothy Holmes. Bloomington: Indiana University Press, 1990.

Seaver, George. *David Livingstone: His Life and Letters*. Reprint, New York: Harper, 1965.

Weller, John, and Jane Linden. *Mainstream Christianity to 1980 in Malawi, Zambia, and Zimbabwe*. Gweru, Zimbabwe: Mambo Press, 1984.

6b. Southern Africa (Angola, Botswana, Lesotho, Malawi, Mozambique, Zambia, and Zimbabwe), Angola

Henderson, Lawrence W. *The Church in Angola: A River of Many Currents*. Cleveland, Ohio: Pilgrim Press, 1992.

6c. Southern Africa (Angola, Botswana, Lesotho, Malawi, Mozambique, Zambia, and Zimbabwe), Botswana

Amanze, James, ed. *Botswana Handbook of Churches: Churches, Ecumeni-*

cal Organizations, Theological Institutions and Other World Religions. Gaborone: Pula Press, 1994.

Shepherd, P. M. *Molepolole, A Missionary Record.* [Glasgow?]: Youth and Overseas Committees of the United Free Church of Scotland, 1947.

6d. Southern Africa (Angola, Botswana, Lesotho, Malawi, Mozambique, Zambia, and Zimbabwe), Lesotho

Haliburton, Gordon M. *Historical Dictionary of Lesotho.* Metuchen, N.J.: Scarecrow Press, 1977.

Mohapeloa, J. M. *From Mission to Church: Fifty Years of the Work of the Paris Evangelical Missionary Society and the Lesotho Evangelical Church, 1933–1983.* Morija, Lesotho: Morija Sesuto Book Depot, 1985.

Revet, Roland. "Lesotho and France: 150 years of Friendship." *Reformed World* 39 (1986): 539–45.

6e. Southern Africa (Angola, Botswana, Lesotho, Malawi, Mozambique, Zambia, and Zimbabwe), Malawi: Histories and Studies

Forster, Peter G. "Missionaries and Anthropology: The Case of the Scots of Northern Malawi." *Journal of Religion in Africa* 16 (1986), 101–20.

McCracken, John. *Politics and Christianity in Malawi, 1875–1940. The Impact of the Livingstonia Mission in the Northern Province.* Cambridge: Cambridge University Press, 1977.

Mufuka, K. Nyamayaro. *Missions and Politics in Malawi.* Kingston, Ont.: Limestone Press, 1977.

Ross, Andrew C. *Blantyre Mission and the Making of Modern Malawi.* Blantyre, Malawi: Christian Literature Association in Malawi, 1996.

Sindima, Harvey J. *The Legacy of Scottish Missionaries in Malawi.* Lewiston, New York: Mellen Press, 1992.

Thompson, T. J. *Christianity in Northern Malawi: Donald Fraser's Missionary Methods.* Leiden: E. J. Brill, 1995.

6f. Southern Africa (Angola, Botswana, Lesotho, Malawi, Mozambique, Zambia, and Zimbabwe), Malawi: Biographies

Ballantyne, M. M. S., and Robert Henry W. Shepherd, eds. *Forerunners of Modern Malawi: The Early Missionary Adventures of Dr. James Henderson, 1895–1898.* Lovedale: n.p., 1968.

Ncozana, Silas S. *Sangaya: A Leader of the Church of Central Africa Presbyterian.* Blantyre, Malawi: Christian Literature Association in Malawi, 1996.

6g. Southern Africa (Angola, Botswana, Lesotho, Malawi, Mozambique, Zambia, and Zimbabwe), Mozambique

Helgesson, Alf. *Church, State, and People in Mozambique.* Uppsala, Sweden: University of Uppsala Press, 1994.

Koevering, Helen van. "Recent Developments in Mozambiquean Christianity." In *New Dimensions in African Christianity*, edited by Paul Gifford, 103–34. Nairobi: All African Conference of Churches, 1992.

Van Butselaar, Jan. *Africains missionnaires et colonialistes. Les origines de l'Église presbytérienne du Mozambique (Mission suisse), 1880–1896.* Leiden: E. J. Brill, 1984.

Vines, Alex, and Ken Wilson. "Churches and the Peace Process in Mozambique." In *The Christian Churches and the Democratization of Africa*, edited by Paul Gifford, 130–47. Leiden: E. J. Brill, 1995.

6h. Southern Africa (Angola, Botswana, Lesotho, Malawi, Mozambique, Zambia, and Zimbabwe), Zambia

Bolink, Peter. *Towards Church Union in Zambia: A Study of Missionary Cooperation and Church Union Efforts in Central Africa.* Franeker, Netherlands: T. Wever, 1967.

Hinfelaar, Hugo F. *Bemba-Speaking Women of Zambia in a Century of Religious Change (1892–1992).* Leiden: E. J. Brill, 1994.

Ipenburg, At. *"All Good Men": The Development of Lubwa Mission, Chinsali, Zambia, 1905–1967.* Frankfurt am Main, Germany: Peter Lang, 1992.

Taylor, John V., and Dorothea A. Lehmann. *Christians of the Copperbelt: The Growth of the Church in Northern Rhodesia.* London: SCM Press, 1961.

Verstraelen-Gilhuis, Gerdien. *From Dutch Mission Church to Reformed Church in Zambia.* Franeker, Netherlands: T. Wever, 1982.

6i. Southern Africa (Angola, Botswana, Lesotho, Malawi, Mozambique, Zambia, and Zimbabwe), Zimbabwe

Cuppen, G., B. Dijkstra, and P. Linhoud. *A New People, A New Church: Zimbabwe.* Hertogenbosch: Dutch Missionary Council, 1980.

Hallencreutz, Carl F., and Ambrose Moyo, eds. *Church and State in Zimbabwe.* Gweru, Zimbabwe: Mambo Press, 1988.

Maxwell, David J. "The Church and Democratisation in Africa: The Case of Zimbabwe." In *The Christian Churches and the Democratization of Africa,* edited by Paul Gifford, 108–29. Leiden: E. J. Brill, 1995.

Van der Merwe, W. J. *From Mission Field to Autonomous Church in Zimbabwe.* Pretoria: NG Kerkboekhandel, 1981.

Zvobgo, Chengetai J. M. *A History of Christian Missions in Zimbabwe, 1890–1939.* Gweru, Zimbabwe: Mambo Press, 1996.

7a. West Africa (Cameroon, Equatorial Guinea, Ghana, Liberia, Nigeria, Senegal, and Togo), The West African Region

Agbeti, J. Kofi. *West African Church History: Christian Missions and Church Foundations, 1482–1919.* Leiden: E. J. Brill, 1986.

Faure, Jean. *Histoire des missions et Églises protestantes en Afrique occidentale des origines à 1884.* Yaoundé: Editions Clé, 1978.

Kalu, O. U., ed. *The History of Christianity in West Africa.* New York: Longman, 1980.

Sanneh, Lamin O. *West African Christianity: The Religious Impact.* Maryknoll, N.Y.: Orbis Books, 1983.

7b. West Africa (Cameroon, Equatorial Guinea, Ghana, Liberia, Nigeria, Senegal, and Togo), Cameroon

Beanland, Lillian L. *African Logs.* New York: Board of Foreign Missions of the Presbyterian Church in the U.S.A., 1945.

Brown, Arthur Judson. *One Hundred Years: A History of Foreign Missionary Work of the Presbyterian Church in the U.S.A.*, 217–51. New York: Fleming H. Revell, 1936.

Efesao, Mokosso, Henry Teddy. "The United Presbyterian Mission in Cameroon, 1879–1957." Ph.D. diss, Howard University, 1987.

Slageren, J. V. *Les origines de l'Église Évangélique de Cameroun.* Leiden: E. J. Brill, 1972.

7c. West Africa (Cameroon, Equatorial Guinea, Ghana, Liberia, Nigeria, Senegal, and Togo), Equatorial Guinea

Barrett, David B., ed. "Equatorial Guinea." In *World Christian Encyclopedia*, 280–82. New York: Oxford University Press, 1982.

Vischer, Lukus. "Equatorial Guinea." *One World* 183 (1993): 6–7.

7d. West Africa (Cameroon, Equatorial Guinea, Ghana, Liberia, Nigeria, Senegal, and Togo), Ghana: Histories and Studies

Anguandah, James. *Together We Sow and Reap: The Christian Council of Ghana, 1929–1979.* Accra: Asempa, 1979.

Debrunner, Hans W. *A History of Christianity in Ghana.* Accra: Waterville Publishing House, 1967.

Parsons, Robert T. *The Churches and Ghana Society, 1918–1955: A Survey of Three Protestant Mission Societies.* Leiden: E. J. Brill, 1963.

Pobee, J. S. *Religion and Politics in Ghana.* Accra: Asempa, 1991.

Smith, Noel. *The Presbyterian Church of Ghana, 1835–1960: A Younger Church in a Changing Society.* Accra: Ghana Universities Press, 1966.

7e. West Africa (Cameroon, Equatorial Guinea, Ghana, Liberia, Nigeria, Senegal, and Togo), Ghana: Biography

Kpobi, David Nii Anum. *Mission in Chains: The Life, Theology, and Ministry of the Ex-Slave Jacobus E. J. Capitein (1717–1747); With a Translation of His Major Publications.* Zoetermeer: Vitgeverij Boekencentrum, 1993.

Odjidja, E. M. L. *Mustard Seed: The Growth of the Church in Kroboland.* Accra: Waterville Publications, 1973.

Prah, Kwesi Kwaa. *Jacobus Eliza Johannes Capitein, 1717–1749: A Critical Study of an Eighteenth Century African.* Braamfontein: Skotaville Publications, 1989.

7f. West Africa (Cameroon, Equatorial Guinea, Ghana, Liberia, Nigeria, Senegal, and Togo), Liberia

Cason, J. W. "The Growth of Christianity in the Liberian Environment." Ph.D. diss., Columbia University, 1962.

Gifford, Paul. *Christianity and Politics in Doe's Liberia.* New York: Cambridge University Press, 1993.

Moore, Moses N., Jr. "Edward Blyden and the Presbyterian Mission in Liberia." *Union Seminary Quarterly Review* 48 (1994): 59–114.

Murray, Andrew E. "Bright Delusion: Presbyterians and African Colonization." *Journal of Presbyterian History* 58 (1980): 224–37.

Wiley, Bell I., ed. *Slaves No More: Letters from Liberia, 1833–1869.* Lexington, Ky.: University Press of Kentucky, 1980.

7g. West Africa (Cameroon, Equatorial Guinea, Ghana, Liberia, Nigeria, Senegal, and Togo), Nigeria

Ajayi, J. F. Ade. *Christian Missions in Nigeria, 1841–1891: The Making of a New Elite.* Evanston, Ill.: Northwestern University Press, 1965.

Aye, E. U. *Hope Waddell Training Institution.* Calabar: Paico Press, 1986.

———. *Presbyterianism in Nigeria.* Calabar: Wusen Press, 1987.

Daniel, W. "Missionary Preaching in the Scottish Calabar Mission, 1846–1930." Ph.D. diss., Edinburgh University, 1993.

Johnston, Geoffrey. *Of God and Maxim Guns: Presbyterianism in Nigeria, 1846–1946.* Waterloo, Ont.: Wilfrid Laurier University Press, 1988.

Kalu, Ogbu. *Divided People of God. Church Union Involvement in Nigeria, 1867–1966.* New York: NOK Publishers, 1978.

McFarlan, Donald M. *Calabar: The Church of Scotland Mission, 1846–1946.* London: T. Nelson, 1957.

Tasie, G. O. M. *Christian Missionary Enterprise in the Niger Delta, 1864–1918.* Leiden: E. J. Brill, 1978.

Taylor, W. H. *Mission to Educate: A History of the Educational Work of the Scottish Presbyterian Mission in East Nigeria, 1846–1960.* Leiden: E. J. Brill, 1996.

7h. West Africa (Cameroon, Equatorial Guinea, Ghana, Liberia, Nigeria, Senegal, and Togo), Senegal

Barrett, David B., ed. "Senegal." In *World Christian Encyclopedia,* 606–08. New York: Oxford University Press, 1982.

7i. West Africa (Cameroon, Equatorial Guinea, Ghana, Liberia, Nigeria, Senegal, and Togo), Togo

Debrunner, Hans Werner. *A Church between Colonial Powers: A Study of the Church in Togo.* London: Lutterworth Press, 1965.

Prempeh, Samuel. "The Basel and Bremen Missions and Their Successors in the Gold Coast and Togoland, 1914–1926." Ph.D. diss., Aberdeen University, 1977.

Asia

1. The Asian Region

Anderson, Gerald H., ed. *Christ and Crisis in Southeast Asia.* New York: Friendship Press, 1968.

Hoke, Donald E., ed. *The Church in Asia.* Chicago: Moody Press, 1975.

Lak, Yeow Choo, comp. *Women in Theological Education.* Singapore: ATESEA, 1994.

Moffett, Samuel H. *History of Christianity in Asia.* 2 vols. San Francisco: Harper Collins, 1992–.

Weber, Hans-Ruedi. *Asia and the Ecumenical Movement: 1895–1961.* London: SCM Press, 1966.

2a. East Asia (China and Taiwan), China: Reference Works

Crouch, Archie R., et al., eds. *Christianity in China: A Scholar's Guide to Resources in the Libraries and Archives in the United States.* Armonk, N.Y.: M. E. Sharpe, 1989.

Lodwick, Kathleen. *Chinese Recorder Index.* 2 vols. Wilmington, Del.: Scholarly Resources, 1986.

Marchant, Leslie R. *A Guide to the Archives and Records of Protestant Christian Missions from the British Isles to China, 1796–1914.* Nedlands, Western Australia: University of Western Australia Press, 1966.

Yu, David C., ed. *Religion in Postwar China: A Critical Analysis and Annotated Bibliography.* Westport, Conn.: Greenwood Press, 1994.

Zurndorfer, H. T. *China Bibliography: A Research Guide to Reference Works about China Past and Present.* Leiden: E. J. Brill, 1995.

2b. East Asia (China and Taiwan), China: Primary Sources

Jones, Francis P., ed. *Documents of the Three-Self Movement: Source Materials for a Study of the Protestant Churches in Communist China.* New York: National Council of Churches, 1963.

2c. East Asia (China and Taiwan), China: Histories and Studies

Bays, Daniel H., ed. *Christianity in China: From the Eighteenth Century to the Present.* Stanford, Calif.: Stanford University Press, 1996.

Bear, James Edwin. "The Mission Work of the Presbyterian Church in the United States in China, 1867–1971." 5 vols. Manuscript, Union Theological Seminary in Virginia.

Brown, G. Thompson. *Christianity in the People's Republic of China*. Rev. ed. Atlanta: John Knox Press, 1986.

———. *Earthen Vessels and Transcendent Power: American Presbyterians in China, 1837–1952*. Maryknoll, N.Y.: Orbis Books, 1997.

Cohen, P. A. *China and Christianity: The Missionary Movement and the Growth of Chinese Anti-Foreignism, 1860–1870*. Cambridge, Mass.: Harvard University Press, 1963.

De Jong, Gerald F. *The Reformed Church in China, 1842–1951*. Grand Rapids, Mich.: Eerdmans, 1992.

Fairbank, John K. *The Missionary Enterprise in China and America*. Cambridge, Mass.: Harvard University Press, 1974.

Fulton, Austin. *Through Earthquake, Wind, and Fire: Church and Mission in Manchuria, 1867–1950*. Edinburgh: Saint Andrew Press, 1967.

Hood, George A. *Mission Accomplished? The English Presbyterian Mission in Lingtung, South China*. Frankfurt: Verlag Peter Land, 1986.

———. *Neither Bang nor Whimper: The End of a Missionary Era in China*. Singapore: The Presbyterian Church in Singapore, 1991.

Hunter, Alan, and Kim-Kwong Chan. *Protestantism in Contemporary China*. New York: Cambridge University Press, 1993.

Johnston, James. *China and Formosa: The Story of the Mission of the Presbyterian Church of England*. New York: F. H. Revell, 1897.

Korson, Thomas E. "Congregational Missionaries in Foochow during the 1911 Revolution." *Chinese Culture* 8 (1967): 44–103.

Latourette, Kenneth S. *The Chinese: Their History and Culture*. 2d ed., rev. New York: Macmillan, 1941.

———. *A History of Christian Missions in China*. 1929. Reprint, New York: Paragon Book Gallery, 1975.

Lian, Xi. *The Conversion of Missionaries: Liberalism in American Protestant Missions in China, 1907–1932*. University Park: Pennsylvania State University Press, 1997.

Lodwick, Kathleen L. *Crusaders against Opium: Protestant Missionaries in China, 1847–1917*. Lexington, Ky.: University Press of Kentucky, 1996.

Lutz, Jessie G. *China and the Christian Colleges 1851–1864*. Ithaca, N.Y.: Cornell University Press, 1971.

MacInnis, Donald E. *Religion in China Today: Policy and Practice*. Maryknoll, N.Y.: Orbis Books, 1989.

Rubinstein, Murray A. *The Origins of the Anglo-American Missionary Enterprise in China, 1807–1840*. Lanham, Md.: Scarecrow Press, 1996.

T'ien Ju-K'ang. *Peaks of Faith: Protestant Mission in Revolutionary China*. Leiden: E. J. Brill, 1993.

Towery, Britt E., Jr. *The Churches of China: Taking Root Downward, Bearing Fruit Upward.* Waco, Tex.: Baylor University Press, 1990.

Wickeri, Philip L. *Seeking the Common Ground: Protestant Christianity, the Three-Self Movement, and China's United Front.* Maryknoll, N.Y.: Orbis Books, 1988.

2d. East Asia (China and Taiwan), China: Biographies

Chao, Charles H. *Out of the Tiger's Mouth: The Autobiography of Dr. Charles H. Chao.* Fearn, England: Christian Focus Publications, 1991.

Chao, Samuel Hsiang-En. "John Livingston Nevius, 1829–1893: A Historical Study of his Life and Mission Methods." Ph.D. diss., Fuller Theological Seminary, 1991.

Chiow, Samuel. "Religious Education and Reform in Chinese Mission: The Life and Work of Francis Wilson Price." Ph.D. diss., St. Louis University, 1988.

Covell, Ralph R. "The Legacy of W. A. P. Martin." *International Bulletin of Missionary Research* 17 (1993): 28–31.

Fung, Raymond, ed. *Households of God on China's Soil.* Reprint, Maryknoll, N.Y.: Orbis Books, 1983.

Kang, Wi Jo. "The Legacy of Horace Newton Allen." *International Bulletin of Missionary Research* 20 (1996): 125–28.

Lodwick, Kathleen L. *Educating the Women of Hainan: The Career of Margaret Moninger in China.* Lexington: University Press of Kentucky, 1995.

Moffett, Eileen. "Betsey Stockton: Pioneer American Missionary." *International Bulletin of Missionary Research* 19 (1995): 71–76.

Price, Frank P. *Our China Investment.* Nashville, Tenn.: Executive Committee of Foreign Missions, 1927.

Shaw, Yu Ming. *An American Missionary in China: John Leighton Stuart and Chinese-American Relations.* Cambridge, Mass.: Harvard University Press, 1992.

Stuart, J. Leighton. *Fifty Years in China: The Memoirs of John Leighton Stuart, Missionary, and Ambassador.* New York: Random House, 1954.

Wong, Peter C. *The Blessed Journey.* Hong Kong: Streams Press, 1962.

2e. East Asia (China and Taiwan), Taiwan

Band, Edward. *Barclay of Formosa.* Tokyo: Christian Literature Society, 1936.

———. *He Brought Them Out: The Story of the Christian Movement among the Mountain Tribes of Formosa.* London: British & Foreign Bible Society, 1950.

Campbell, W. *An Account of the Missionary Success in the Island of Formosa.* 2 vols. London: Trübner, 1889.

Copeland, Margaret. *Chi-Oang: Mother of the Taiwan Tribes Church.* Taipei: The Presbyterian Church of Formosa, 1962.

Freytag, J. *A New Day in the Mountains.* Taiwan: Tainan Theological College, 1968.

Kuepers, J. J. A. M. *The Dutch Reformed Church in Formosa 1627–1662: Mission in a Colonial Context.* Immensee: Neue Zeitschrift für Missionwissenschaft, 1978.

MacKay, George L. *From Far Formosa.* New York: F. H. Revell, 1896.

Song, Choan-Seng. *Testimonies of Faith: Letters and Poems from Prison in Taiwan.* Geneva: World Alliance of Reformed Churches, 1984.

Swanson, A. J., ed. *I Will Build My Church: Ten Case Studies of Church Growth in Taiwan.* Tai Chung: Taiwan Church Growth Society, 1977.

Tong, H. *Christianity in Taiwan: A History.* Taipei: China Post, 1961.

3a. Indian Ocean Islands (Madagascar, Mauritius, and Reunion Island), Madagascar

Covell, Maureen. *Historical Dictionary of Madagascar.* Lanham, Md.: Scarecrow Press, 1995.

Ellis, William. *The Martyr Church of Madagascar.* London: John Snow, 1852.

Gow, Bonar A. *Madagascar and the Protestant Impact: The Work of British Missions, 1818–1895.* London: Longman & Dalhousie University Press, 1979.

3b. Indian Ocean Islands (Madagascar, Mauritius, and Reunion Island), Mauritius

Anderson, James Forrester. *Esquisse de l'histoire du Protestantisme à l'île Maurice et aux îles Mascaregnes, 1505 à 1902,* Paris: Societe Francaise d'imprimerie et de Librairie, 1903.

3c. Indian Ocean Islands (Madagascar, Mauritius, and Reunion Island), Reunion Island

Prudhomme, Claude. *Histoire religieuse de la Réunion.* Paris: Karthala, 1984.

4a. Northeast Asia (Korea and Japan), Northeast Asian Region

Ion, A. Hamish. *The Cross and the Rising Sun: The British Protestant Missionary Movement in Japan, Korea, and Taiwan, 1865–1945.* Waterloo, Ont.: Wilfrid Laurier University Press, 1993.

———. *The Cross and the Rising Sun: The Canadian Protestant Missionary Movement in the Japanese Empire, 1872–1931.* Waterloo, Ont.: Wilfrid Laurier University Press, 1993.

4b. Northeast Asia (Korea and Japan), Korea: Histories and Studies

Choi, Doug Sung. "The Roots of the Presbyterian Conflicts in Korea, 1910–

1954, and the Predominance of Orthodoxy." Thesis, Emory University, 1992.

Clark, Allen D. *A History of the Church in Korea*. Seoul: Christian Literature Society of Korea, 1971.

Clark, Donald N. *Christianity in Modern Korea*. Lanham, Md.: University Press of America, 1986.

Grayson, James H. *Korea: A Religious History*. Oxford: Clarendon Press, 1989.

Huntly, Martha. *Caring, Growing, Changing: A History of the Protestant Mission in Korea*. New York: Friendship Press, 1984.

Kim, Chai Choon. "Presbyterian Church in Korea." *Reformed and Presbyterian World* 28 (1964): 21–26.

Kim, Sung Tae. "Contextualization and the Presbyterian Church in Korea." Ph.D. diss., Fuller Theological Seminary, 1991.

Lee, Chang-sik. "A Historical Review of Theological Thought for the Last One Century in Korea." *East Asia Journal of Theology* 3 (1985): 321–326.

Min, Kyong-pai. *The History of the Korean Christian Church*. 2d ed. Seoul: Korean Christian Publishing, 1983. Standard Korean-language text.

Moffett, Samuel Hugh. *The Christians of Korea*. New York: Friendship Press, 1962.

Rhodes, Harry A., and Archibald Campbell. *History of the Korea Mission, Presbyterian Church in the USA*. New York: United Presbyterian Church, 1964.

Yang, Nak Heong. *Reformed Social Ethics and the Korean Church*. New York: Peter Lang, 1996.

4c. Northeast Asia (Korea and Japan), Korea: Missions

Brown, G. Thompson. *Mission to Korea*. Atlanta: Board of World Mission, 1962.

———. *Not by Might: A Century of Presbyterians in Korea*. Atlanta: General Assembly Mission Board, Presbyterian Church (U.S.A.), 1984.

Hunt, Everett Nichols, Jr. *Protestant Pioneers in Korea*. New York: Orbis Books, 1980.

Huntley, Martha. *Caring, Growing, Changing: A History of the Protestant Mission in Korea*. New York: Friendship, 1984.

———. *To Start a Work: The Foundations of Protestant Mission in Korea, 1884–1919*. Seoul: Presbyterian Church of Korea, 1987.

Paik, L. George. *The History of Protestant Missions in Korea, 1832–1910*. 3d ed. Seoul: Yonsei University Press, 1980.

Rhodes, Harry A., ed. *History of the Korea Mission: Presbyterian Church*

U.S.A., 1884–1934. Korean church centennial ed. Seoul: Presbyterian Church of Korea, 1984.

Rhodes, Harry A., and Archibald Campbell, eds. *History of the Korea Mission: Presbyterian Church U.S.A., 1935–59*. New York: United Presbyterian Church in the U.S.A., 1964.

Ro, Bong-Rin, and Marlin L. Nelson. *Korean Church Growth Explosion*. Seoul: Word of Life Press, 1983.

4d. Northeast Asia (Korea and Japan), Korea: Biography

Kim, In Soo. *Protestants and the Formation of Modern Korean Nationalism: A Study of the Contribution of Horace G. Underwood and Sun Chu Kil*. New York: Peter Lang, 1996.

Shim, Koon Kik. *"Till the End of the Age": The Life of Rev. Sang Dong Han, A Living Witness of the Korean Church*. Pusan, Korea: Kosin College, 1984.

Shin, Young Keol. *Yawoldo: A Story of Faith and Freedom*. DeBary, Fla.: Longwood Communications, 1995.

4e. Northeast Asia (Korea and Japan), Japan: Bibliography

Ikado, Fujio, and James R. McGovern, eds. *A Bibliography of Christianity in Japan: Protestantism in English Sources (1859–1959)*. Tokyo: International Christian University, 1966.

4f. Northeast Asia (Korea and Japan), Japan: General Histories and Studies

Drummond, Richard H. *A History of Christianity in Japan*. Grand Rapids, Mich.: Eerdmans, 1971.

Furuya, Yasuo. *A History of Japanese Theology*. Grand Rapids, Mich.: Eerdmans, 1997.

Germany, Charles H. *Protestant Theologies in Modern Japan*. Tokyo: IISR Press, 1965.

Iglehart, Charles W. *A Century of Protestant Christianity in Japan*. Rutland, Vt.: Charles E. Tuttle, 1959.

Irifune, Takasni, et al., eds. *Following after Calvin: A Selection of Six Essays by Japanese Calvin Scholars*. Tokyo: Komine Book Publishers, 1978.

Kagawa, Toyohiko. *Christ and Japan*. London: SCM Press, 1935.

Kumazawa, Yoshinobu, and David L. Swain. *Christianity in Japan, 1971–1990*. Tokyo: Kyo Bun Kwan, 1991.

Lande, Aasulv. *Meiji Protestantism in History and Historiography: A Comparative Study of Japanese and Western Interpretation of Early Protestantism in Japan*. Frankfurt am Main, Germany: Peter Lang, 1989.

Phillips, James M. *From the Rising of the Sun: Christians and Society in Contemporary Japan*. Maryknoll, N.Y.: Orbis Books, 1981.

Picken, Stuart D. B. *Christianity and Japan: Meeting, Conflict, Hope.* Tokyo: Kodansha International, 1983.

Ryder, Stephen Willis. *A Historical Sourcebook of the Japan Mission of the Reformed Church in America (1859–1930).* York, Pa.: York Printing Company, 1935.

Thomas, Wilburn T. *Protestant Beginnings in Japan.* Tokyo: Tuttle, 1959.

Yoshinobu, Kumazawa, and David L. Swain. *Christianity in Japan, 1971–90.* Tokyo: Kyo Bun Kwan/Friendship Press, 1991.

4g. Northeast Asia (Korea and Japan), Japan: Biographies

Kilson, Marion. *Mary Jane Forbes Greene (1845–1910), Mother of the Japan Mission: An Anthropological Portrait.* Lewiston, N.Y.: Mellen Press, 1991.

Sasa, Sho. *Mrs. A. E. Randolph: The Life of a Missionary, 1827–1902.* Nagoya, Japan: Kinjo Gakuin, 1994.

Schildgen, Robert. *Toyohiko Kagawa: Apostle of Love and Social Justice.* Berkeley: Centenary, 1988.

5a. Southeast Asia (Indonesia, Malaysia and Singapore, Philippines, and Thailand), Indonesia

Aritonang, J. S. *Mission Schools in Batakland (Indonesia), 1861–1940.* Leiden: E. J. Brill, 1994.

Cooley, Frank L. "Altar and Throne in Central Moluccan Societies." Ph.D. diss., Yale University, 1961.

———. *The Growing Seed: The Christian Church in Indonesia.* New York: Division of Overseas Ministries, NCCUSA, 1982.

———. *Indonesia: Church and Society.* New York: Friendship Press, 1968.

Kipp, Rita Smith. *The Early Years of a Dutch Colonial Mission: The Karo Field.* Ann Arbor: University of Michigan Press, 1990.

Pederson, Paul. *Batak Blood and Protestant Soul: The Development of National Batak Churches in North Sumatra.* Grand Rapids, Mich.: Eerdmans, 1970.

Sumartana, Th. *Mission at the Crossroads: Indigenous Churches, European Missionaries, Islamic Association, and Socio-religious Change in Java, 1812–1936.* Jakarta: BPK-GM, 1991.

Van Akkeren, Philip. *Sri and Christ: A Study of the Indigenous Church in East Java.* London: Lutterworth Press, 1970.

5b. Southeast Asia (Indonesia, Malaysia and Singapore, Philippines, and Thailand), Malaysia and Singapore

Band, Edward. *Working His Purpose Out. The History of the English Presbyterian Mission, 1847–1947.* London: Wellington Press, 1948.

Goh Keat Peng, ed. *Readings in Malaysian Church and Mission.* Selangor, Malaysia: Pustaka SUFES, 1992.

Greer, Robert M. *A History of the Presbyterian Church in Singapore.* Singapore: N.p., 1956.

Harcus, A. Drummond. *History of the Presbyterian Church in Malaya.* London: Albert Clark, 1955.

Hunt, Robert, Lee Kam Hing, and John Roxborogh, eds. *Christianity in Malaysia: A Denominational History.* Selangor Darul Ehsan, Malaysia: Pelanduk Publications, 1992.

Sng, Bobby E. K. *In His Good Time: The Story of the Church in Singapore, 1819–1992.* 2d ed. Singapore: Graduates' Christian Fellowship, 1993.

5c. Southeast Asia (Indonesia, Malaysia and Singapore, Philippines, and Thailand), Philippines

Anderson, Gerald H., ed. *Studies in Philippine Church History.* Ithaca, N.Y.: Cornell University Press, 1969.

Clymer, Kenton J. *Protestant Missionaries in the Philippines, 1898–1916.* Urbana, Ill.: University of Illinois, 1986.

Deats, Richard L. *Nationalism and Christianity in the Philippines.* Dallas: Southern Methodist University, 1967.

Guillermo, Merlyn L., and L. P. Verona. *Protestant Churches and Missions in the Philippines.* Manila: World Vision Philippines, 1982.

Kwantes, Ann C. *Presbyterian Missions in the Philippines: Conduits of Social Change (1899–1910).* Quezon City: New Day Publishers, 1984.

Rigos, Cirilo. "The Development of the United Church of Christ in the Philippines." S.T.M. thesis, Union Theological Seminary in New York, 1958.

Rogers, James. *Forty Years in the Philippines: A History of the Philippine Mission of the Presbyterian Church in the United States of America, 1899–1939.* New York: Board of Foreign Missions, 1940.

Spindler, Marc R. "Creeds and Credibility in the Philippines." *Exchange: Journal of Missiological and Ecumenical Research* 19 (1990): 152–171.

5d. Southeast Asia (Indonesia, Malaysia and Singapore, Philippines, and Thailand), Thailand

Hudson, Cornelia Kneedler. "Daniel McGilvary in Siam: Foreign Missions, the Civil War, and Presbyterian Unity." *American Presbyterians* 69 (1991): 283–93.

Wells, Kenneth E. *History of Protestant Work in Thailand, 1828–1958.* Bangkok: Church of Christ in Thailand, 1958.

6a. Southern Asia (India, Pakistan, Myanmar, and Sri Lanka), India and Pakistan: Bibliographies

Anderson, Bernard, comp. *Annual Bibliography of Christianity in India, 1988.* Bombay: Heras Institute of Indian History and Culture, St. Xavier's College, 1989.

Hambye, E. R. "A Bibliography of Christianity in India." New Delhi: Church History Association of India, 1976.

6c. Southern Asia (India, Pakistan, Myanmar, and Sri Lanka), India and Pakistan: Histories and Studies

Ali, Muhammad Moher. *The Bengal Reaction to Christian Missionary Activities, 1833–1857.* Chittagong: Mehrub Publications, 1965.

Anderson, Rufus. *History of the Missions of the American Board of Commissioners for Foreign Missions in India.* Boston: Congregational Publishing Society, 1874.

Arles, Siga. *Theological Education for the Mission of the Church in India, 1947–1987.* New York: Peter Lang, 1991.

Brouwer, Ruth Compton. *New Women for God: Canadian Presbyterian Women and India Missions, 1876–1914.* Toronto: University of Toronto Press, 1990.

Campbell, Ernest Y. *The Church in the Punjab: Some Aspects of its Life and Growth.* Nagpur: 1961. Also in Victor E. W. Hayward, ed., *The Church as Christian Community: Three Studies of North Indian Districts.* London: Lutterworth Press, 1966.

David, Immanuel. *Reformed Church in America Missionaries in South India, 1839–1938: An Analytical Study.* Bangalore: Asian Trading Corp., 1986.

Davis, Walter Bruce. "A Study of Missionary Policy and Methods in Bengal: 1793–1905." Ph.D. diss., Edinburgh University, 1942.

Day, Lal Behari. *Recollections of Alexander Duff, D.D., LL.D., and of the Mission College Which He Founded in Calcutta.* London: Nelson, 1879.

DiBona, Joseph, ed. *One Teacher, One School: The Adam Reports on Indigenous Education in Nineteenth Century India.* New Delhi: Biblia Impex, 1983.

Downs, Frederick S. *History of Christianity in India.* Vol. 5, pt. 5, *North East India in the Nineteenth and Twentieth Centuries.* Bangalore, India: Church History Association of India, 1992.

Firth, Cyril B. *An Introduction to Indian Church History.* Madras: Christian Literature Society, 1961.

Grafe, Hugald. *History of Christianity in India.* Vol. 4, no. 2, *Tamilnadu in the Nineteenth and Twentieth Centuries.* Bangalore: Church History Association of India, 1990.

Ingham, Kenneth. *Reformers in India, 1793–1833: An Account of the Work of Christian Missionaries on Behalf of Social Reform.* Cambridge: Cambridge University Press, 1956.

Kellock, James. *Breakthrough for Church Union in North India and Pakistan*. Madras: Christian Literature Society, 1965.

Kooiman, Dick. *Conversion and Social Equality in India: The London Missionary Society in South Travancore in the 19th Century*. New Delhi: Manohar, 1989.

Laird, Michael A. *Missionaries and Education in Bengal, 1793–1837*. Oxford: Clarendon Press, 1972.

Majumdar, R. C., ed. *The History and Culture of the Indian People*. 11 vols. Bombay: Bharatiya Vidya Bhavan, 1951–1977.

Moraes, G. M. *A History of Christianity in India*. Bombay: Manaktalas, 1964.

Mundadan, A. Mathias. *Indian Christians: Search for Identity and Struggle for Autonomy*. Placid Lectures Series, no. 4. Banagalore: Dharmaram, 1984.

Neill, Stephen. *A History of Christianity in India, 1707–1858*. 2 vols. New York: Cambridge University Press, 1984–1985.

Pickett, J. Waskom. *Christian Mass Movements in India*. Lucknow, India: Lucknow Publishing House, 1933.

Richter, J. *A History of Protestant Missions in India*. Edinburgh: Oliphant, 1908.

Sahu, Dhirendra Kumar. *The Church of North India*. New York: Peter Lang, 1994.

Sen Gupta, Kanti P. *The Christian Missionaries in Bengal, 1795–1871*. Calcutta: Firma K.L. Mukhopadhyay, 1966.

Singh, D. V., ed. *History of Christianity in India*. 6 vols. Bangalore: Church History Association of India, 1982–.

Stock, Frederick, and Margaret Stock. *People Movements in the Punjab, with Special Reference to the United Presbyterian Church*. South Pasadena, Calif.: William Carey Library, 1975.

Sundkler, Bengt. *Church of South India. The Movement towards Union, 1900–1947*. London: Lutterworth Press, 1954.

Thangaraj, C. P. *Whither Indian Christianity?* Madras, India: Christian Literature Society, 1990.

United Presbyterian Church of North America. *A Century for Christ in India and Pakistan, 1855–1955*. Lahore: United Presbyterian Church, 1955.

Urquhart, Anne M. *Near India's Heart: An Account of the Free Church of Scotland Mission Work in India during the 20th Century*. Edinburgh: Knox Press, 1990.

Varghese, V. Titus, and P. P. Philip. *Glimpses of the History of the Christian Churches in India*. Madras: Christian Literature Society, 1983.

Webster, John C. B. *The Christian Community and Change in Nineteenth Century North India.* Delhi: Macmillan, 1976.

———. *A History of Dalit Christians in India.* Lewiston, N.Y.: Mellen Press, 1992.

Wilfred, Felix. *Beyond Settled Foundations: The Journey of Indian Theology.* Madras: Dept. of Christian Studies, University of Madras, 1993.

World Alliance of Reformed Churches. *The Presbyterian Church of Mizoram.* Geneva: WARC, 1989.

Young, William G. *Days of Small Things? A Narrative Assessment of the Work of the Church of Scotland in the Punjab in "the Age of William Harper, 1873–1885."* Rawalpindi, Pakistan: Christian Study Centre, 1991.

6d. Southern Asia (India, Pakistan, Myanmar, and Sri Lanka), India and Pakistan: Biography

Hess, Gary R. *Sam Higginbottom of Allahabad: Pioneer of Point Four to India.* Charlottesville, Va.: University Press of Virginia, 1966.

Johnson, Rachel Kerr. *Affectionately, Rachel: Letters from India, 1860– 1884.* Kent, Ohio: Kent State University Press, 1992.

Macpherson, G. *Life of Lal Behari Day, Convert, Pastor, Professor, and Author.* Edinburgh: T. & T. Clark, 1900.

Morris, Henry. *The Life of John Murdoch, LL.D., the Literary Evangelist of India.* London: Christian Literature Society for India, 1906.

Phillip, T. V. *Krishna Mohan Banerjea, Christian Apologist.* Madras: Christian Literature Society, 1982.

6e. Southern Asia (India, Pakistan, Myanmar, and Sri Lanka), Myanmar

Anderson, Courtney. *To the Golden Shore: Life of Adoniram Judson.* Reprint, Valley Forge: Judson, 1987.

Becka, Jan. *Historical Dictionary of Myanmar.* Metuchen, N.J.: Scarecrow Press, 1995.

6f. Southern Asia (India, Pakistan, Myanmar, and Sri Lanka), Sri Lanka

Arasaratnam, Sinnappah. *Dutch Power in Ceylon, 1658–1687.* Amsterdam: Djambatan, 1958.

Franciscus, S. D., ed. *Faith of Our Fathers: History of the Dutch Reformed Church in Sri Lanka (Ceylon).* Colombo: Pragna, 1983.

Goonewardena, K. W. *The Foundation of Dutch Power in Ceylon, 1638– 1658.* Amsterdam: Djambatan, 1958.

Wilson, D. Kanagasabai. *The Christian Church in Sri Lanka: Her Problems and Her Influence.* Colombo: Study Centre for Religion and Society, 1975.

Europe

1a. United Kingdom (England, Wales, Scotland, Northern Ireland), England and Wales: Atlases

Currie, Robert, Alan Gilbert, and Lee Horsley. *Churches and Churchgoers: Patterns of Church Growth in the British Isles since 1700.* Oxford: Clarendon Press, 1977.

Gay, John D. *The Geography of Religion in England.* London: Gerald Duckworth, 1971.

1b. United Kingdom (England, Wales, Scotland, Northern Ireland), England and Wales: Bibliographies

Annual Bibliography of British and Irish History. Brighton: Royal Historical Society, 1975–.

Baker, Derek, ed. *The Bibliography of the Reform 1450–1648 Relating to the United Kingdom and Ireland for the Years 1955–70.* Oxford: Blackwell, 1975.

Bibliography of British History. Oxford: Clarendon Press, 1951–. Volumes include Brown, Lucy M., and Ian R. Christie. *1789–1851* (1977); Davies, Godfrey. *Stuart Period, 1603–1714.* 2d ed. edited by Mary Frear Keeler (1970); Hanham, H. J. *1851–1914* (1976); Pargellis, Stanley M., and D. J. Medley. *The Eighteenth Century, 1714–1789* (1951); Read, Conyers. *The Tudor Period, 1485–1603.* 2d ed. (1959).

Booty, John E. *The Godly Kingdom of Tudor England: Great Books of the English Reformation.* Wilton, Conn.: Morehouse-Barlow, 1981.

Conference on British Studies Bibliographical Handbooks. Cambridge: Cambridge University Press, 1968–. Volumes include Altholz, Josef L. *Victorian England, 1837–1901* (1970); Levine, Mortimer. *Tudor England, 1485–1603* (1968); Sachse, William L. *Restoration England, 1660–1689* (1971); Smith, Robert A. *Late Georgian and Regency England, 1760–1837* (1984).

Hadidian, Dikran, ed. *Bibliography of British Theological Literature, 1850–1940.* Pittsburgh, Pa.: Clifford E. Barbour Library, Pittsburgh Theological Seminary, 1985.

Johnson, Dale A. *Women and Religion in Britain and Ireland: An Annotated Bibliography from the Reformation to 1993.* Lanham: Md.: Scarecrow Press, 1995.

Milward, Peter. *Religious Controversies of the Elizabethan Age: A Survey of Printed Sources.* Lincoln: University of Nebraska Press, 1977.

Smeeton, Donald D. *English Religion, 1500–1540: A Bibliography.* Macon, Ga.: Mercer University Press, 1988.

1c. United Kingdom (England, Wales, Scotland, Northern Ireland), England and Wales: Catalogues and Guides

Altholz, Josef L. *The Religious Press in Britain, 1760–1900*. New York: Greenwood Press, 1989.

Foster, Janet, and Julia Sheppard. *British Archives: A Guide to Archive Resources in the United Kingdom*. 2d ed. New York: Stockton Press, 1989.

Gillett, Charles Ripley, ed. *Catalogue of the McAlpin Collection of British History and Theology*. 5 vols. New York: Union Theological Seminary, 1927–1930.

Nineteenth-Century Short Title Catalogue. Series 1, 1801–15, 6 vols.; Series 2, 1816–1870, 7 vols. Newcastle upon Tyne: Avero Publications, 1984–.

Wing, Donald. *Short-Title Catalogue of Books Printed in England, Scotland, Ireland, Wales, and British America and of English Books Printed in Other Countries, 1641–1700*. 2d ed. 3 vols. New York: Modern Language Association, 1972–1988.

1d. United Kingdom (England, Wales, Scotland, Northern Ireland), England and Wales: Primary Sources

Archives of the Huguenot Community in London. World Microfilms, Microworld House, 2–6 Foscote Mews, London, England W9 2HH.

Congregational Church in England and Wales. *A Declaration of Faith*. New rev. ed. London: Independent Press, 1967.

Matthews, A. G., ed. *The Savoy Declaration of Faith and Order 1658*. London: Independent Press, 1959.

Paul, Robert S., ed. *An Apologeticall Narration*. Boston: United Church Press, 1963.

Presbyterian Church of England, 1847–1950. Zug, Switzerland/New York: Inter Documentation Company/Norman Ross Publishing Co. Church archives on 2,850 microfiche.

Trinterud, Leonard J., ed. *Elizabethan Puritanism*. New York: Oxford University Press, 1971.

Wallace, D. D., Jr., ed. *The Spirituality of the Later English Puritans*. Macon, Ga.: Mercer University Press, 1987.

Williams, Pettit, Herget and Bush, eds. *Thomas Hooker: Writings in England and Holland, 1626–1633*. Cambridge, Mass.: Harvard University Press, 1975.

1e. United Kingdom (England, Wales, Scotland, Northern Ireland), England and Wales: Histories and Studies

Bolam, C. Gordon, Jeremy Goring, H. L. Short, and Roger Thomas. *The*

English Presbyterians, from Elizabethan Puritanism to Modern Unitarianism. Boston: Beacon Press, 1968.

Clarkson, George E. *George Whitefield and Welsh Calvinistic Methodism*. Lewiston, N.Y.: Mellen Press, 1996.

Cottret, Bernard. *The Huguenots in England: Immigration and Settlement, 1550–1700*. New York: Cambridge University Press, 1991.

Cragg, Gerald R. *Puritanism in the Period of the Great Persecution, 1660–1688*. Cambridge: Cambridge University Press, 1957.

Dale, R. W. *History of English Congregationalists*. New York: A. C. Armstrong, 1907.

Davies, Horton. *The English Free Churches*. London: Oxford University Press, 1952.

George, Timothy. *John Robinson and the English Separatist Tradition*. Macon, Ga.: Mercer University Press, 1981.

Haller, William. *The Rise of Puritanism*. New York: Columbia University Press, 1938.

Jones, R. Tudur. *Congregationalism in England, 1662–1962*. London: Independent Press, 1962.

Kendall, Robert T. *Calvin and English Calvinism to 1649*. Oxford: Oxford University Press, 1979.

Knappen, Marshall M. *Tudor Puritanism; A Chapter in the History of Idealism*. Chicago: University of Chicago Press, 1939.

Le Huray, Peter. *Music and the Reformation in England, 1549–1660*. Cambridge, N.Y.: Cambridge University Press, 1978.

Leith, John H. *Assembly at Westminster: Reformed Theology in the Making*. Richmond, Va.: John Knox, 1973.

Loades, D. M. *The Oxford Martyrs*. London: Batsford, 1970.

McConica, James K. *English Humanists and Reformation Politics under Henry VIII and Edward VI*. Oxford: Clarendon Press, 1968.

Neal, Daniel. *History of the Puritans*. 2 vols. New York: Harper & Brothers, 1844. Many editions.

Nuttall, Geoffrey, and Owen Chadwick. *From Uniformity to Unity, 1662–1962*. London: SPCK, 1962.

Paul, Robert S. *The Assembly of the Lord: Politics and Religion in the Westminster Assembly and the "Grand Debate."* Edinburgh: T. & T. Clark, 1985.

Peel, A. *A Brief History of English Congregationalism*. London: Independent Press, 1931.

Rupp, E. G. *Studies in the Making of the English Protestant Tradition*. Cambridge: Cambridge University Press, 1947.

Sell, Alan P. F. "Confessing the Faith in English Congregationalism." In *Dissenting Thought and the Life of the Churches: Studies in an English Tradition*. Lewiston, N.Y.: Mellen Press, 1990.

Waddington, John. *Congregational History*. 5 vols. London: Snow, I:1869; London: Longmans, Green, II-V: 1874–1880.

Williams, William. *Welsh Calvinistic Methodism: A Historical Sketch of the Presbyterian Church of Wales*. 2d ed. London: Presbyterian Church of England, 1884.

1f. United Kingdom (England, Wales, Scotland, Northern Ireland), England and Wales: Missions

Ellis, W. *History of the London Missionary Society*. Vol 1. London: J. Snow, 1844.

Goodall, Norman. *A History of the London Missionary Society, 1895–1945*. London: Oxford University Press, 1954.

Lovett, Richard. *The History of the London Missionary Society, 1795–1895*. 2 vols. London: London Missionary Society, 1899.

Thorogood, Bernard, ed. *Gales of Change, Responding to a Shifting Missionary Context: The Story of the London Missionary Society, 1945–1977*. Geneva: World Council of Churches, 1994.

1g. United Kingdom (England, Wales, Scotland, Northern Ireland), England and Wales: Theological Studies

Davies, Horton. *Like Angels from a Cloud: The English Metaphysical Preachers, 1588–1645*. San Marino: Huntington Library, 1986.

———. *The Worship of the English Puritans*. Glasgow: Dacre Press, 1948.

———. *Worship and Theology in England*. 3 vols. Princeton: Princeton University Press, 1970–. Reprint, Eerdmans, 1996.

Fisher, Edward. *The Marrow of Modern Divinity*. 3d ed. London: Giles Calvert, 1646.

Lake, Peter. *Anglicans and Puritans: Presbyterianism and English Conformist Thought from Whitgift to Hooker*. London: Allen & Unwin, 1988.

Manning, Bernard Lord. *Essays in Orthodox Dissent*. 1939. Reprint, London: Independent Press, 1953.

Nuttall, Geoffrey. *Visible Saints: The Congregational Way, 1640–1660*. Oxford: Oxford University Press, 1957.

Peel, Albert, ed. *Essays Congregational and Catholic Issued in Commemoration of the Centenary of the Congregational Union of England and Wales*. London: Congregational Union of England and Wales, 1931.

Riesen, Richard A. *Criticism and Faith in Late Victorian Scotland*. Lanham, Md.: University Press of America, 1985.

Rooy, S. H. *The Theology of Missions in the Puritan Tradition*. Grand Rapids, Mich.: Eerdmans, 1965.

Sell, Alan P. F. "Rhetoric and Reality: Theological Reflections upon Congregationalism and its Heirs." In *Commemorations: Studies in Christian Thought and History*. Calgary: University of Calgary Press, 1993.

Tomes, Roger, ed. *Christian Confidence: Essays on a Declaration of Faith of the Congregational Church in England and Wales*. London: SPCK, 1970.

Toon, Peter. *Puritans and Calvinism*. Swengel: Reiner, 1973.

Wallace, Dewey D. *Puritans and Predestination: Grace in English Theology, 1525–1695*. Durham: University of North Carolina, 1982.

White, B. R. *The English Separatist Tradition*. London: Oxford University Press, 1971.

1h. United Kingdom (England, Wales, Scotland, Northern Ireland), England and Wales: Biographies

Dale, A. W. W. *The Life of R. W. Dale of Birmingham*. London: Hodder & Stoughton, 1899.

Dallimore, A. A. *George Whitefield*. 2 vols. London: Banner of Truth Trust, 1970–1980.

Davis, Authur Paul. *Isaac Watts*. London: Independent Press, 1948.

Dictionary of National Biography. 63 vols. with supplements. London: Macmillan, 1885–.

Evans, Eifion. *Daniel Rowland and the Great Evangelical Awakening in Wales*. London: Banner of Truth Trust, 1985.

Evans, Joseph. *Biographical Dictionary of Ministers and Preachers of the Welsh Calvinist Methodist Body or Presbyterians of Wales*. Carnarvon: D. O'Brien Owen, 1907.

Kaye, Elaine. *C. J. Cadoux, Theologian, Scholar, Pacifist*. Edinburgh: Edinburgh University Press, 1988.

Lewis, Donald M. *Dictionary of Evangelical Biography, 1730–1860*. 2 vols. Oxford: Blackwell, 1995.

Micklem, Nathaniel. *The Box and the Puppets (1888–1953)*. London: Geoffrey Bles, 1957.

Nuttall, Geoffrey F. *Howel Harris, 1714–1773: The Last Enthusiast*. Cardiff: University of Wales Press, 1965.

———. *Richard Baxter*. London: Nelson, 1965.

Nuttall, Geoffrey F., ed. *Philip Doddridge 1702–51: His Contribution to English Religion*. London: Independent Press, 1951.

Owen, W. T. *Edward Williams, D.D., His Life, Thought and Influence*. Cardiff: University of Wales Press, 1963.

Parker, Joseph. *A Preacher's Life: An Autobiography and an Album*. London: Hodder & Stoughton, 1903.

Robinson, W. Gordon. *William Roby (1766–1830) and the Revival of Independency in the North*. London: Independent Press, 1954.

Selbie, W. B. *The Life of Andrew Martin Fairbairn*. London: Hodder & Stoughton, 1914.

Sell, Alan P. F. *Robert Mackintosh: Theologian of Integrity*. Bern: Peter Lang, 1977.

Shuffelton, Frank. *Thomas Hooker, 1588–1647*. Princeton: Princeton University Press, 1977.

Stout, Harry S. *Divine Dramatist: George Whitefield*. Grand Rapids, Mich.: Eerdmans, 1991.

Toon, Peter. *God's Statesman: The Life of Dr. John Owen*. Grand Rapids, Mich.: Zondervan, 1973.

Welch, Edwin. *Spiritual Pilgrim: A Reassessment of the Life of the Countess of Huntingdon*. Cardiff: University of Wales Press, 1995.

Williams, J. B. *The Lives of Philip and Matthew Henry*. Reprint, Edinburgh: Banner of Truth Trust, 1974.

1i. United Kingdom (England, Wales, Scotland, Northern Ireland), Scotland: Bibliographies

Kirk, James. "The Scottish Reformation and Reign of James VI: A Select Critical Bibliography." In *Records of the Scottish Church History Society*, vol. 23, pt. 1, 1987.

Macgregor, Malcolm Blair. *The Sources and Literature of Scottish Church History*. Glasgow: J. McCallum, 1934.

1j. United Kingdom (England, Wales, Scotland, Northern Ireland), Scotland: Dictionaries

Cameron, Nigel M. de S., David F. Wright, David C. Lachman, and Donald E. Meek, eds. *Dictionary of Scottish Church History and Theology*. Downers Grove, Ill.: InterVarsity Press, 1993.

1k. United Kingdom (England, Wales, Scotland, Northern Ireland), Scotland: Histories and Studies

Brown, Stewart J. *Thomas Chalmers and the Godly Commonwealth in Scotland*. New York: Oxford University Press, 1982.

Burleigh, J. H. S. *A Church History of Scotland*. London: Oxford University Press, 1960.

Burnet, George B. *The Holy Communion in the Reformed Church of Scotland, 1560–1960*. Edinburgh: Oliver & Boyd, 1960.

Douglass, J. D. *Light in the North: The Story of the Scottish Covenanters*. Grand Rapids, Mich.: Eerdmans, 1964.

Drummond, Andrew L., and James Bulloch. *The Church in Victorian Scotland, 1843–1879*. Edinburgh: Saint Andrew Press, 1975.

————. *The Church in Late Victorian Scotland, 1874–1900*. Edinburgh: Saint Andrew Press, 1978.

————. *The Scottish Church, 1688–1843: The Age of the Moderates*. Edinburgh: Saint Andrew Press, 1973.

Escott, Harry. *A History of Scottish Congregationalism*. Glasgow: Congregational Union of Scotland, 1960.

Free Presbyterian Church. *History of the Free Presbyterian Church of Scotland* (1893–1970). N.p.: Publications Committee, [c. 1970].

Hart, Trevor, ed. *Justice the Only True Mercy: Essays on the Life and Theology of Peter Taylor Forsyth*. Edinburgh: T. & T. Clark, 1995.

Herron, A. *Kirk by Divine Right: Church and State, Peaceful Coexistence*. Edinburgh: Saint Andrew Press, 1985.

Kirk, James. *Patterns of Reform*. Edinburgh: T. & T. Clark, 1989.

Louden, R. Stuart. *The True Face of the Kirk*. London: Oxford University Press, 1963.

Macleod, John. *Scottish Theology in Relation to Church History since the Reformation*. 1943. Reprint, Edinburgh: Knox Press and the Banner of Truth Trust, 1974.

Maxwell, William D. *A History of Worship in the Church of Scotland*. London: Oxford University Press, 1955.

McCoy, F. N. *Robert Baillie and the Second Scots Reformation*. Berkeley: University of California Press, 1974.

Morton, T. Ralph. *The Iona Community Story*. London: Lutterworth Press, 1957.

Scorgie, G. G. *A Call for Continuity: The Theological Contribution of James Orr*. Macon, Ga.: Mercer University Press, 1989.

Torrance, T. F. *Scottish Theology: From John Knox to John McLeod Campbell*. Edinburgh: T. & T. Clark, 1996.

Watt, Hugh, ed. *New College Edinburgh: A Centenary History*. Edinburgh: Oliver & Boyd, 1946.

————. *Thomas Chalmers and the Disruption*. New York: Thomas Nelson, 1943.

11. United Kingdom (England, Wales, Scotland, Northern Ireland), Scotland: Missions

Hewet, Elizabeth G. K. *Vision and Achievement, 1796–1956: A History of the Foreign Missions of the Churches United in the Church of Scotland*. London: Thomas Nelson, 1960.

Smith (Swan), Annie S. *Seed Time and Harvest. The Story of the Hundred Years Work of the Women's Foreign Mission of the Church of Scotland*. London: Thomas Nelson, 1937.

Weir, Robert W. *A History of the Foreign Missions of the Church of Scotland.* Edinburgh: T. & T. Clark, 1900.

1m. United Kingdom (England, Wales, Scotland, Northern Ireland), Scotland: Biographies

Barclay, William. *William Barclay: A Spiritual Autobiography.* Grand Rapids, Mich.: Eerdmans, 1975.

Bonar, Andrew A., ed. *Letters of Samuel Rutherford with a Sketch of His Life.* Edinburgh: Oliphant Anderson & Ferrier, 1894.

Bradley, William R. *P. T. Forsyth: The Man and His Work.* London: Independent Press, 1952.

Brown, David. *The Life of Rabbi Duncan.* Reprint, Glasgow: Free Presbyterian Publications, 1986.

Coffey, John. *Politics, Religion, and the British Revolutions: The Mind of Samuel Rutherford.* New York: Cambridge University Press, 1997.

Collins, G. N. M. *John Macleod.* Edinburgh: Publications Committee of the Free Church of Scotland, 1951.

Darlow, T. H. *William Robertson Nicoll: Life and Letters.* Hodder & Stoughton, 1925.

Ferguson, R. *George MacLeod.* London: Collins, 1990.

Leckie, J. H. *Fergus Ferguson, D.D., His Theology and Heresy Trial: A Chapter in Scottish Church History.* Edinburgh: T. & T. Clark, 1923.

MacKenzie, Robert. *John Brown of Haddington.* Reprint, London: Banner of Truth Trust, 1964.

Martin, James. *William Barclay: A Personal Memoir.* Edinburgh: Saint Andrew Press, 1984.

MacEwen, A. R. *The Erskines.* Edinburgh: Oliphant, Anderson, & Ferrier, 1900.

———. *Life and Letters of John Cairns.* London: Hodder & Stoughton, 1898.

MacMillan, Donald. *The Life of Robert Flint.* London: Hodder & Stoughton, 1914.

McNaughton, William D. *The Scottish Congregational Ministry, 1794–1993.* Glasgow: Congregational Union of Scotland, 1993.

Newbigin, Lesslie. *Unfinished Agenda: An Autobiography.* Grand Rapids, Mich.: Eerdmans, 1985.

Scott, Hew. *Fasti Ecclesiae Scoticanae: The Succession of Ministers in the Church of Scotland from the Reformation.* 8 vols. Edinburgh: Oliver & Boyd, 1915–1981.

Simpson, P. C. *The Life of Principal Rainy.* London: Hodder & Stoughton, 1907.

Triggs, Kathy. *Alexander Whyte, the Peacemaker*. Basingstoke, Hants., England: Pickering & Inglis, 1984.

Worthies of the Evangelical Union. Glasgow: Thomas D. Morison, 1883.

Wright, Ronald Selby, ed. *Fathers of the Kirk: Some Leaders of the Church of Scotland from the Reformation to the Reunion*. London: Oxford University Press, 1960.

1n. United Kingdom (England, Wales, Scotland, Northern Ireland), Northern Ireland: Bibliographies

Annual Bibliography of British and Irish History. Brighton: Royal Historical Society, 1975–.

Baker, Derek, ed. *The Bibliography of the Reform 1450–1648 Relating to the United Kingdom and Ireland for the Years 1955–70*. Oxford: Blackwell, 1975.

1o. United Kingdom (England, Wales, Scotland, Northern Ireland), Northern Ireland: Histories and Studies

Anderson, A. C. *The Story of the Presbyterian Church in Ireland*. N.p.: General Assembly Committees, 1965.

Ball, J. T. *The Reformed Church of Ireland, 1537–1889*. London: Longmans, 1890.

Brooke, Peter. *Ulster Presbyterianism: The Historical Perspective, 1610–1970*. 2d ed. Belfast: Athol Books, 1994.

Dunlop, John. *Presbyterians and the Conflict in Ireland*. Belfast: Blackstaff Press, 1995.

Falconer, Alan D. "Churches in the European Community, 1: The Irish Churches." *Expository Times* 104 (1993): 101–05.

Finlay, Holmes. *Our Irish Presbyterian Heritage*. Belfast: Presbyterian Church in Ireland, 1985.

Leyburn, James G. *The Scotch-Irish: A Social History*. Chapel Hill: University of North Carolina Press, 1962.

Loughridge, Adam. "The Reformed Presbyterian Church of Ireland." Thesis, University of Dublin, 1963.

Mawhinney, Brian, and Ronald Wells. *Conflict and Christianity in Northern Ireland*. Grand Rapids, Mich.: Eerdmans, 1975.

McDowell, R. B. *The Church of Ireland, 1869–1969*. London: Routledge & Kegan Paul, 1975.

Seymore, St. John Drelincourt. *The Puritans in Ireland, 1647–1661*. Oxford: Clarendon Press, 1969.

1p. United Kingdom (England, Wales, Scotland, Northern Ireland), Northern Ireland: Biographies

Loughridge, Adam, ed. *Fasti of the Reformed Presbyterian Church of Ireland*. Belfast: Presbyterian Historical Society, 1970.

McConnell, James. *Fasti of the Irish Presbyterian Church, 1613–1840*. Revised by Samuel G. McConnell. Belfast: Presbyterian Historical Society. Reprint, University Microfilms, 1979.

2a. Central and Eastern Europe (Bulgaria; Croatia, Slovenia, Yugoslavia; Czech Republic and Slovak Republic; Hungary; Latvia and Lithuania; Romania; Poland; and Ukraine), General Region

Bailey, J. Martin. *The Spring of Nations: Churches in the Rebirth of Central and Eastern Europe*. New York: Friendship Press, 1991.

Broun, Janice. *Conscience and Captivity: Religion in Eastern Europe*. Washington, D.C.: Ethics and Public Policy Center, 1988.

Evans, Robert J. W., and T. I. V. Thomas, eds. *Crown, Church, and Estates: Central European Politics in the Sixteenth and Seventeenth Centuries*. New York: St. Martin's Press, 1991.

Greinacher, Norbert, and Virgil Elizondo, eds. *Churches in Socialist Societies of Eastern Europe*. Concilium, no. 154. New York: Seabury, 1982.

Nielsen, Niels, C. *Revolutions in Eastern Europe: The Religous Roots*. Maryknoll, N.Y.: Orbis Books, 1991.

Swatos, William H., Jr., ed. *Politics and Religion in Central and Eastern Europe: Traditions and Transitions*. Westport, Conn.: Greenwood Press, 1994.

Walters, Philip, ed. "Repentance and Reconciliation in Eastern Europe after Communism." *Religion, State, and Society* 21 (1993): 243–53.

2b. Central and Eastern Europe (Bulgaria; Croatia, Slovenia, Yugoslavia; Czech Republic and Slovak Republic; Hungary; Latvia and Lithuania; Romania; Poland; and Ukraine), Bulgaria

Matheeff, Mitko. *Document of Darkness: A Document of 35 years of Atheist-Communist Terror against the Christians in the People's Republic of Bulgaria*. St. Catherines, Ont.: Mission Bulgaria, 1980.

2c. Central and Eastern Europe (Bulgaria; Croatia, Slovenia, Yugoslavia; Czech Republic and Slovak Republic; Hungary; Latvia and Lithuania; Romania; Poland; and Ukraine), Croatia, Slovenia, Yugoslavia

Alexander, Stella. *Church and State in Yugoslavia since 1945*. New York: Cambridge University Press, 1979.

2d. Central and Eastern Europe (Bulgaria; Croatia, Slovenia, Yugoslavia; Czech Republic and Slovak Republic; Hungary; Latvia and Lithuania; Romania; Poland; and Ukraine), Czech Republic and Slovak Republic

Daniel, David P. *Historiography of the Reformation in Slovakia*. Sixteenth Century Bibliography no. 10. St. Louis, Mo.: Center for Reformation Research, 1977.

Ecumenical Council of Churches in the Czech Socialist Republic. *Czech Ecumenical Fellowship*. Praha: Ecumenical Council, 1981.

Evangelical Church in Prague. *The Evangelical Church of Czech Brethren (Presbyterian)*. Edinburgh: Saint Andrew Press, 1970.

Lochman, Jan Mili. *Church in a Marxist Society: A Czechoslovak View*. New York: Harper & Row, 1970.

Otter, Jirí. *The First Unified Church in the Heart of Europe*. Prague: Kalich, 1992.

———. *The Witness of Czech Protestantism*. Prague: Kalich, 1970.

Spinka, Matthew. *John Hus and the Czech Reform*. Chicago: University of Chicago Press, 1941.

———. "The Religious Situation." In *Czechoslovakia*. Edited by Robert J. Kerner. Berkeley: University of California Press, 1949.

2e. Central and Eastern Europe (Bulgaria; Croatia, Slovenia, Yugoslavia; Czech Republic and Slovak Republic; Hungary; Latvia and Lithuania; Romania; Poland; and Ukraine), Hungary

Churches, Denominations, and Congregations in Hungary, 1991. Budapest: Ministry of Foreign Affairs, 1991.

Dercsény, Balázs, Gábor Hegyi, Ernö Marosi, and Béla Takács. *Calvinist Churches in Hungary*. Budapest: Hegyi, 1992.

Evans, R. J. "Calvinism in East Central Europe: Hungary and Her Neighbours." In *International Calvinism, 1541–1715*. Edited by M. Prestwich. Oxford: Clarendon Press, 1985.

Gombos, Gyula. *The Lean Years: A Study of Hungarian Calvinism in Crisis*. New York: Kossuth Foundation, 1960.

Have No Fear, Little Flock. Budapest: Reformed Church in Hungary, 1987.

Kádár, Imre. *The Church in the Storm of Time: The History of the Hungarian Reformed Church During the Two World Wars, Revolutions, and Counter-Revolutions*. Budapest: Bibliotheca, 1958.

Kool, Anna Maria. *God Moves in a Mysterious Way: The Hungarian Protestant Foreign Missions Movement, 1756–1951*. Zoetermeer, Netherlands: Uitgeverij Boekencentrum, 1993.

Révész, E. *History of the Hungarian Reformed Church*. Translated by George A. F. Knight. Washington, D.C.: Hungarian Reformed Federation of America, 1956.

2f. Central and Eastern Europe (Bulgaria; Croatia, Slovenia, Yugoslavia; Czech Republic and Slovak Republic; Hungary; Latvia and Lithuania; Romania; Poland; and Ukraine), Latvia and Lithuania

Kahle, Wilhelm. "Baltic Protestantism." *Religion in Communist Lands* 7 (1979): 220–25.

2g. Central and Eastern Europe (Bulgaria; Croatia, Slovenia, Yugoslavia; Czech Republic and Slovak Republic; Hungary; Latvia and Lithuania; Romania; Poland; and Ukraine), Poland

Fox, Paul. *The Reformation in Poland: Some Social and Economic Aspects.* Reprint, Westport, Conn.: Greenwood Press, 1971.

Lasco, John à. *Works.* Edited by A. Kuyper. 2 vols. Amsterdam: Muller, 1866.

Mazierski, Roman K. *A Concise History of the Polish Reformed Church.* London: Polish Reformed Church in Great Britain, 1966.

Müller, Michael G. "Protestant Confessionalisation in the Towns of Royal Prussia and the Practice of Religious Toleration in Poland-Lithuania." In *Tolerance and Intolerance in the European Reformation,* edited by O. Grell, 262–81. New York: Cambridge University Press, 1996.

Tazbir, Janusz. *A State without Stakes: Polish Religious Toleration in the Sixteenth and Seventeenth Centuries.* New York: Kosciuszko Foundation, 1973.

Williams, George Huntston. *The Polish Brethren.* 2 vols. Missoula, Mont.: Scholars Press, 1980.

2h. Central and Eastern Europe (Bulgaria; Croatia, Slovenia, Yugoslavia; Czech Republic and Slovak Republic; Hungary; Latvia and Lithuania; Romania; Poland; and Ukraine), Romania

The Churches in Romania. Geneva: World Council of Churches, 1982.

Corley, Felix, and John Eibner. *In the Eyes of the Romanian Storm: The Heroic Story of Pastor Laszlo Tokes.* Old Tappan, N.J.: Revell, 1990.

Reformed Church in the Socialist Republic of Romania. [Bucharest?]: The Church, 1976.

Tokes, Laszlo. *The Fall of Tyrants.* Wheaton, Ill.: Crossway Books, 1990.

2i. Central and Eastern Europe (Bulgaria; Croatia, Slovenia, Yugoslavia; Czech Republic and Slovak Republic; Hungary; Latvia and Lithuania; Romania; Poland; and Ukraine), Ukraine

Bushkovitch, Paul. *Religion and Society in Russia: The Sixteenth and Seventeenth Centuries.* New York: Oxford University Press, 1992.

Spinka, Matthew. *The Church in Soviet Russia.* New York: Oxford University Press, 1956.

3a. Northern Europe (Austria, Belgium, Denmark, Finland, Germany, Netherlands, and Sweden), Austria

Barton, Peter Friedrich. *Die Geschichte der Evangelischen in Österreich und Südostmitteleurope.* Vienna: H. Böhlaus Nachf, 1985.

Bierbraver, Peter. *Die unterdrückte Reformation: Der Kampf der Tiroler um eine neue Kirche, 1521–1527.* Zurich: Chronos, 1993.

Jahrbuch für die Geschichte des Protestantismus in Österreich. Vienna: Evangelischer Pressevervand in Österreich, 1980–. Annual.

Reingrabner, Gustav, and Karl Schwarz, eds. *Quellentexte zur österreichischen evangelischen Kirchengeschichte zwischen 1918 und 1945.* Vienna: Vorstand der Gesellschaft für die Geschichte des Protestantismus in Österreich, 1988–1989.

3b. Northern Europe (Austria, Belgium, Denmark, Finland, Germany, Netherlands, and Sweden), Belgium

Boudin, Hugh Robert. "Churches in the European Community, 2: The Churches in Belgium." *Expository Times* 104 (1993): 132–36.

Braekman, E. M. *Histoire de l'église protestante de Dour.* Brussels: R. Leys, 1977.

CRISP, *Le Protestantisme en Belgique Courrier Hebdomadaire N, 1430–1431.* Brussels: Centre de Recherche et d'Information Socio-politique, n.d.

Pichal, E. *De geschiedenis van het protestantisme in Vlaanderen.* Antwerp: Standaard Wetenschappleijke Uitgeverij, 1975.

Slory, Michaël. *Een andere weg.* Amstelveen: Luyten, 1986.

3c. Northern Europe (Austria, Belgium, Denmark, Finland, Germany, Netherlands, and Sweden), Denmark

Chetwynd, I. "Churches in the European Community, 6: Nestling in the Life of the People: Denmark." *Expository Times* 104 (1993): 258–63.

3d. Northern Europe (Austria, Belgium, Denmark, Finland, Germany, Netherlands, and Sweden), Finland

Barrett, David B., ed. "Finland." In *World Christian Encyclopedia*, 292–94. New York: Oxford University Press, 1982.

3e. Northern Europe (Austria, Belgium, Denmark, Finland, Germany, Netherlands, and Sweden), Germany: Libraries and Archives

German Historical Institute. *Guide to Inventories and Finding Aids of German Archives at the German Historical Institute.* Washington, D.C.: The Institute, 1989.

Welsch, Erwin K. *Libraries and Archives in Germany.* Pittsburgh: Council for European Studies, 1975.

3f. Northern Europe (Austria, Belgium, Denmark, Finland, Germany, Netherlands, and Sweden), Germany: Histories and Studies

Barth, Karl. *The German Church Conflict.* Translated by P. T. A. Parker. Richmond, Va.: John Knox Press, 1965.

Beckmann, Joachim. *Das Wort Gottes bleibt in Ewigkeit: Erlebte Kirchengeschichte.* Neukirchen: Neukirchener Verlag, 1986.

Bredt, Johann Victor. *Die Verfassung der Reformierten Kirche in Cleve-Jülich-Berg-Mark.* Neukirchen: K. Moers, 1938.

Cochrane, Arthur. *The Church's Confession under Hitler.* Philadelphia: Westminster Press, 1962.

Cohn, Henry J. "The Territorial Princes in Germany's Second Reformation, 1559–1622." In *International Calvinism*, edited by Menna Prestwich, 135–65. Oxford: Clarendon Press, 1985.

Good, James I. *The Origin of the Reformed Church in Germany*. Reading, Pa.: Daniel Miller, 1887.

Holloway, James Y., ed. *Barth, Barmen, and the Confessing Church Today*. Lewiston, N.Y.: Mellen Press, 1995.

Nischan, Bodo. *Prince, People, and Confession: The Second Reformation in Brandenburg*. Philadelphia: University of Pennsylvania Press, 1994.

Podmore, Colin J. "Churches in the European Community, 3: Churches in Germany." *Expository Times* 104 (1993): 164–69.

Schilling, Heinz. *Civic Calvinism in Northwestern Germany and the Netherlands: Sixteenth to Nineteenth Centuries*. Kirksville, Mo.: Sixteenth Century Journal, 1991.

Vorländer, Herwart. *Aufbruch und Krise: Ein Beitrag zur Geschichte der deutschen Reformierten vor dem Kirchenkampf*. Neukirchen-Vluyn: Neukirchener Verlag, 1974.

3g. Northern Europe (Austria, Belgium, Denmark, Finland, Germany, Netherlands, and Sweden), Germany: Biographies

Easton, M. G., trans. *Friedrich Wilhelm Krummacher: An Autobiography*. New York: Robert Carter, 1869.

Robertson, E. H. *Paul Schneider: The Pastor of Buchenwald*. London: SCM, 1956.

Wentorf, Rudolf. *Paul Schneider. The Witness of Buchenwald*. Tucson, Ariz.: American Eagle, 1993.

3h. Northern Europe (Austria, Belgium, Denmark, Finland, Germany, Netherlands, and Sweden), Netherlands: Archives

Okkema, J. C. *Inventaris van de synodale archieven van de Gereformeerde Kerken in Nederland*. Kampen: Kok, 1975.

3i. Northern Europe (Austria, Belgium, Denmark, Finland, Germany, Netherlands, and Sweden), Netherlands: Primary Sources

Kossmann, E. H., and A. F. Mellink, eds. *Texts Concerning the Revolt of the Netherlands*. New York: Cambridge University Press, 1974.

Netherlands Reformed Church Archives, c. 1560–1810. Zug, Switzerland/ New York: Inter Documentation Company/Norman Ross Publishing Co. Collection consists of 3,143 microfiche.

3j. Northern Europe (Austria, Belgium, Denmark, Finland, Germany, Netherlands, and Sweden), Netherlands: Histories and Studies

Bolt, John, ed. "The Dutch Connection: Dutch Reformed Church History and Theology." *Calvin Theological Journal* 28 (1993): 266–442.

Carter, A. C. *The English Reformed Church in Amsterdam in the Seventeenth Century.* Amsterdam: Scheltema & Holkema, 1964.

Cerny, Gerald. *Theology, Politics, and Letters at the Crossroads of European Civilization: Jacques Basnage and the Baylean Huguenot Refugees in the Dutch Republic.* Dordrecht: M. Nijhoff, 1987.

Cracknell, Kenneth R. "Churches in the European Community, 5: The Churches in the Netherlands." *Expository Times* 104 (1993): 228–32.

Israel, Jonathan I. *The Dutch Republic: Its Rise, Greatness, and Fall, 1477–1806.* New York: Oxford University Press, 1995.

Sprunger, K. L. *Dutch Puritanism: A History of the English and Scottish Churches in the Netherlands.* Leiden: E. J. Brill, 1982.

3k. Northern Europe (Austria, Belgium, Denmark, Finland, Germany, Netherlands, and Sweden), Netherlands: Dutch Art

Haak, Bob. *The Golden Age: Dutch Painters of the Seventeenth Century.* New York: Abrams, 1984.

Kahr, Madlyn M. *Dutch Painting in the Seventeenth Century.* 2d ed. New York: HarperCollins, 1993.

Rosenberg, Jacob, and Seymour Slive. *Dutch Painting 1600–1800.* New Haven, Conn.: Yale University Press, 1995.

Westermann, Mariët. *A Worldly Art: The Dutch Republic, 1585–1718.* New York: Abrams, 1996.

3l. Northern Europe (Austria, Belgium, Denmark, Finland, Germany, Netherlands, and Sweden), Netherlands: Biographies

Bangs, Carl D. *Arminius: A Study in the Dutch Reformation.* Rev. ed. Nashville, Tenn.: Abingdon Press, 1971.

Boerkoel, J. D. *Sola Gratia. Shets van de Geschiedenis en de Werkzaamneid van de Theologische Hogeschool der Gereformeerde Kerken in Nederland, 1854–1954.* Kampen: Kok, 1954.

Braekman, E. M. *Guy de Brès.* Brussels: Éditions de la Librairie des éclaireurs unionistes, 1960.

Martin, Linette. *Hans Rookmaaker: A Biography.* Downers Grove, Ill.: InterVarsity Press, 1979.

Nauta, Doede, ed. *Biographisch Lexicon voor de Geschiedenis van het Nederlandse Protestantisme.* 2 vols. Kampen: Kok, 1983.

Schwartz, Gary. *Rembrandt: His Life, His Paintings.* New York: Penguin Books, 1985.

Van Halsema, Thea B. *Glorious Heretic: The Story of Guy de Brès.* Grand Rapids, Mich.: Eerdmans, 1961.

3m. Northern Europe (Austria, Belgium, Denmark, Finland, Germany, Netherlands, and Sweden), Sweden

Barrett, David B., ed. "Sweden." In *World Christian Encyclopedia*, 646–50. New York: Oxford University Press, 1982.

Gustavsson, Anders. "Free-Church Membership and Folk Beliefs." *Temenos: Studies in Comparative Religion* 20 (1984): 40–51.

4a. Southern Europe (France, Greece, Italy, Luxembourg, Portugal, Spain, and Switzerland), France: Bibliography

Bourgeois, Émile, and Louis André. *Les Sources de l'histoire de France: XVII siècle (1610–1715)*. 4 vols. Paris: Picard, 1913–24.

Geisendorf, Paul-F. *Bibliographic Raisonné de l'Histoire de Genève des Origines a 1798*. *Memoires et documents de la Société d'histoire et d'archéologie de Genève XLIII*. Geneva: Alex. Jullien, 1966.

Hauser, Henri. *Les Sources de l'histoire de France XVI siècle (1494–1610)*. 4 vols. Paris: Picard, 1906–1915.

4b. Southern Europe (France, Greece, Italy, Luxembourg, Portugal, Spain, and Switzerland), France: Histories and Studies

Armstrong, Brian G. *Calvinism and the Amyraut Heresy: Protestant Scholasticism and Humanism in Seventeenth Century France*. Madison: University of Wisconsin Press, 1969.

Chrisman, Miriam Usner. *Strasbourg and the Reform*. New Haven, Conn.: Yale University Press, 1967.

Delumeau, J. *Naissance et affirmation de la Réforme*. Paris: Presses universitaires de France, 1973.

Dodge, G. H. *The Political Theory of the Huguenots of the Dispersion: With Special Reference to the Thought and Influence of Pierre Jurieu*. New York: Octagon, 1922.

Garrisson-Estèbe, J. *Protestants du Midi, 1559–1598*. Toulouse: Privat, 1980.

Gray, Janet Glenn. *The French Huguenots*. Grand Rapids, Mich.: Baker Book House, 1981.

Gwynn, Robin D. *Huguenot Heritage*. London: Routledge and Kegan, 1985.

Hanlon, Gregory. *Confession and Community in Seventeenth Century France: Catholic and Protestant Coexistence in Aquitaine*. Philadelphia: University of Pennsylvania Press, 1993.

Heller, Henry. *The Conquest of Poverty: The Calvinistic Revolt in Sixteenth-Century France*. Leiden: E. J. Brill, 1986.

Kingdon, Robert M. *Myths about the St. Bartholomew's Day Massacres, 1572–1576*. Cambridge, Mass.: Harvard University Press, 1988.

Labrousse, Élisabeth. "Calvinism in France, 1598–1685." In *International Calvinism*, edited by Menna Prestwich, 285–314. Oxford: Clarendon Press, 1985.

Lavender, Abraham. *French Huguenots: From Mediterranean Catholics to White Anglo-Saxon Protestants.* New York: Peter Lang, 1990.

Léonard, Émile G. *A History of Protestantism.* 2 vols. London: Nelson, 1965, 1967.

Ligou, Daniel. *Le Protestantisme en France de 1598 à 1715.* Paris: Société d'édition d'enseignement Supérieur, 1968.

Magdelaine, M., and Thadden, R. von, eds. *Le Refuge Huguenot, 1685–1985.* Paris: A. Colin, 1985.

Milligan, W. J. "Churches in the European Community, 7: The Churches in France." *Expository Times* 104 (1993): 292–95.

Mours, Samuel. *Les églises réformées en France.* Paris: Librairie Protestante, 1958.

————. *Les galériens protestants (1683–1775).* Paris: Librairie Protestante, 1971.

————. *Le protestantisme en France au XVIᵉ siècle.* Paris: Librairie Protestante, 1959.

————. *Le protestantisme en France au XVIIᵉ siècle.* Paris: Librairie Protestante, 1967.

Prestwich, Menna. "Calvinism in France, 1555–1629." In *International Calvinism,* edited by Menna Prestwich, 71–107. Oxford: Clarendon Press, 1985.

Rothrock, G. A. *The Huguenots.* Chicago: Nelson-Hall, 1979.

Salmon, J. H. M. *Society in Crisis: France in the Sixteenth Century.* London: E. Benn, 1975.

Soman, Alfred, ed. *The Massacre of St. Bartholomew: Reappraisals and Documents.* The Hague: Martinus Nijoff, 1974.

Sutherland, N. M. *The Huguenot Struggle for Recognition.* New Haven, Conn.: Yale University Press, 1980.

————. *The Massacre of St. Bartholomew and the European Conflict, 1559–1572.* New York: Barnes & Noble, 1973.

Wendel, F. *L'Eglise de Strasbourg: sa constitution et son organization.* Paris: Presses Universitaires de France, 1942.

4c. Southern Europe (France, Greece, Italy, Luxembourg, Portugal, Spain, and Switzerland), France: Biography

Engel, Claire-Eliane. *L'Admiral de Coligny.* Geneva: Labor et Fides, 1967.

Haag, M. M., ed. *La France Protestante.* 10 vols. Geneva: Slatkine Reprints, 1966.

Jacques, Andre. *Madeleine Barot.* Geneva: World Council of Churches, 1991.

Osen, James L. *Prophet and Peacemaker: The Life of Adolphe Monod.* Lanham, Md.: University Press of America, 1984.

Spink, Kathryn. *A Universal Heart: The Life of Brother Roger of Taizé.* San Francisco: Harper & Row, 1986.

Weber, Hans-Reudi. *Suzanne de Dietrich (1891–1981): La Passion de Vivre.* Paris/Strasbourg: Les Bergers et les Mages et Oberlin, 1995.

4d. Southern Europe (France, Greece, Italy, Luxembourg, Portugal, Spain, and Switzerland), Greece

Barrett, David B., ed. "Greece." In *World Christian Encyclopedia,* 328–33. New York: Oxford University Press, 1982.

Walker, Mary A. "American Board and the Oriental Churches: A Brief Survey of Policy Based on Official Documents." *International Review of Mission* 56 (1967): 214–23.

4e. Southern Europe (France, Greece, Italy, Luxembourg, Portugal, Spain, and Switzerland), Italy: Bibliography

Armand-Hugon, Augusto, and Giovanni Gonnet. *Bibliografia Valdese.* Torre Pellice: Tipografia Subalpina, 1953.

Tedeschi, John A. *The Literature of the Italian Reformation: An Exhibition Catalogue.* Chicago: The Newberry Library, 1971.

4f. Southern Europe (France, Greece, Italy, Luxembourg, Portugal, Spain, and Switzerland), Italy: Primary Sources

Evers, Meindert, ed. *Gabriel de Convenant, Avoué de la "Glorieuse Rentrée" des Vaudois: Correspondance avec les Etats-Généraux des Provinces-Unies 1688–1690.* Geneva: Librairie Droz, 1995.

4g. Southern Europe (France, Greece, Italy, Luxembourg, Portugal, Spain, and Switzerland), Italy: Histories and Studies

Armand-Hugon, Augusto. *Storia dei Valdesi, II, dall'adesione alla Riforma all'Emancipazione (1532–1848).* Turin: Claudiana, 1989.

Cameron, Euan. *The Reformation of the Heretics: The Waldenses of the Alps, 1480–1580.* Oxford: Clarendon Press, 1984.

Comba, Emilio. *History of the Waldensians of Italy: From Their Origin to the Reformation.* 1889. Reprint, New York: AMS Press, 1978.

———. *I nostri Protestanti.* Turin: Claudiana, 1895.

Ducker, R. F. "Churches in the European Community, 4: The Churches in Italy." *Expository Times* 104 (1993): 196–201.

Gonnet, Giovanni. *Le confessioni di fede valdesi prima della Riforma.* Turin: Claudiana, 1967.

Molnár, Amedeo. *Storia dei Valdesi, I, dalle orinini all'adesione alla Riforma (1176–1532).* 2d ed. Turin: Claudiana, 1989.

Tourn, Giorgio. *The Waldensians: The First 800 years (1174–1974).* Turin: Claudiana, 1980.

Vinay, Valdo. *Storia dei Valdesi, III, dal movimento evangelico italiano al movimento ecumenico (1848–1978).* Turin: Claudiana, 1980.

World Council of Churches. *The Churches in Italy.* Geneva: WCC Commission on Inter-Church Aid, 1984.

4h. Southern Europe (France, Greece, Italy, Luxembourg, Portugal, Spain, and Switzerland), Luxembourg

Barrett, David B., ed. "Luxembourg." In *World Christian Encyclopedia*, 462–64. New York: Oxford University Press, 1982.

4i. Southern Europe (France, Greece, Italy, Luxembourg, Portugal, Spain, and Switzerland), Portugal

Cardoso, Manuel Pedro. "The Churches in Portugal." *Expository Times* 104 (1993): 323–28.

The Churches in Portugal: The Pathway to the Future. Geneva: World Council of Churches, 1984.

4j. Southern Europe (France, Greece, Italy, Luxembourg, Portugal, Spain, and Switzerland), Spain

Commission on Inter-Church Aid. *The Churches in Spain.* Geneva: World Council of Churches, 1984.

Estuch, J. *Los Protestantes Españoles.* Barcelona: Nova Terra, 1968.

Mackay, John A. *The Other Spanish Christ.* New York: Macmillan, 1933.

Vought, Jule G. *Protestants in Modern Spain: A Struggle for Religious Pluralism.* South Pasadena, Calif.: William Carey Library, 1973.

4k. Southern Europe (France, Greece, Italy, Luxembourg, Portugal, Spain, and Switzerland), Switzerland: Histories and Studies

Beardslee, John W. "Theological Development at Geneva under Francis and Jean-Alphonse Turretin (1648–1737)." Ph.D. diss., Yale University Press, 1956.

Bonjour, E., H. S. Offler, and G. R. Potter. *A Short History of Switzerland.* Reprint, Westport, Conn.: Greenwood Press, 1985.

Good, James I. *History of the Swiss Reformed Church Since the Reformation.* Philadelphia: Reformed Church in the United States, 1913.

Hadorn, Wilhelm. *Geschichte des Pietismus in den schweizerischen reformierten Kirchen.* Constance: Carl Kirsch, 1901.

Schenkel, Karl. *Ratgeber für evangelische Gemeindeglieder: eine Orientierung über das Leben unserer Kirche.* Basel: F. Reinhardt, 1961.

4l. Southern Europe (France, Greece, Italy, Luxembourg, Portugal, Spain, and Switzerland), Switzerland: Biographies

Burnett, Stephen G. *From Christian Hebraism to Jewish Studies: Johannes Buxtorf (1564–1629) and Hebrew Learning in the Seventeenth Century.* Leiden: E. J. Brill, 1996.

Busch, Eberhard. *Karl Barth: His Life from Letters and Autobiographical Texts.* Philadelphia: Fortress Press, 1976.

Selth, Jefferson P. *Firm Heart and Capacious Mind: The Life and Friends of Etienne Dumont.* Lanham, Md.: University Press of America, 1997.

Mesoamerica and South America

1a. Mesoamerica and South America, General Region: Bibliography
Bibliografía Teológica Comentada. Buenos Aires: Instituto Superior Evangélico de Estudios Teológicos, 1973–. Published annually.

Musto, Ronald G. *Liberation Theologies: A Research Guide.* New York: Garland Publishing, 1991.

Sinclair, John H. *Protestantism in Latin America: A Bibliographical Guide.* South Pasadena, Calif.: William Carey Library, 1976.

Wilson, Stanton. "Bibliography of Dr. John A. Mackay." *Studies in Reformed History and Theology.* Princeton, N.J.: Princeton Theological Seminary, 1994.

1b. Mesoamerica and South America, General Region: Primary Sources
Goodpasture, H. McKennie, ed. *Cross and Sword: An Eyewitness History of Christianity in Latin America.* Maryknoll, N.Y.: Orbis Books, 1989.

1c. Mesoamerica and South America, General Region: Histories and Studies
Beeson, Trevor, and Jenny Pearce. *A Vision of Hope: The Churches and Change in Latin America.* Philadelphia: Fortress Press, 1984.

Berryman, Phillip. *The Religious Roots of Rebellion: Christians in Central American Revolutions.* Maryknoll, N.Y.: Orbis Books, 1984.

Cleary, Edward L. *Crisis and Change: The Church in Latin America Today.* Maryknoll, N.Y.: Orbis Books, 1985.

Cook, Guillermo, ed. *New Face of the Church in Latin America.* Maryknoll, N.Y.: Orbis Books, 1994.

Costas, Orlando E. *Mission to Latin America.* Grand Rapids, Mich.: Eerdmans, 1989.

Curlee, Robert R., and Mary Ruth Isaac-Curlee. "Bridging the Gap: John A. Mackay, Presbyterians and the Charismatic Movement." *American Presbyterians* 72 (1994): 141–56.

Gibellinni, Rosino, ed. *Frontiers of Theology in Latin America.* New York: Orbis Books, 1979.

Tomás, Gutiérrez S., ed. *Protestantismo y Política en America Latina y el Caribe: Entre la Sociedad Civil y el Estado.* Lima, Peru: Comisión de Estudios de Historia de la Iglesia en América Latina, 1996.

Langer, Erick, and Robert H. Jackson, eds. *The New Latin American Mission History.* Lincoln: University of Nebraska Press, 1995.

Levine, Daniel H., ed. *Religion and Political Conflict in Latin America.* Chapel Hill: University of North Carolina Press, 1986.

Mackay, John A. "An Introduction to Christian Work among South American Students." *International Review of Missions* 17 (1928): 278–90.

Nelson, Wilton M. *Protestantism in Central America*. Grand Rapids, Mich.: Eerdmans, 1984.

Pattnayak, Satya, ed. *Organized Religion in the Political Transformation of Latin America*. Lanham, Md.: University Press of America, 1997.

Prien, Hans Jurgen. *Historia del Cristianismo en América Latina*. Salamanca: Sigame, 1985.

Sinclair, John H. "W. Stanley Rycroft, Latin America Missiologist." *American Presbyterians* 65 (1987): 117–33.

Stoll, David. *Is Latin America Turning Protestant?* Berkeley, Calif.: University of California Press, 1990.

Walsh, Thomas G., and Frank Kaufmann, eds. *Christianity in the Americas: Ecumenical Essays*. New York: Berkley, 1997.

Willems, Emílio. *Followers of the New Faith: Culture Change and the Rise of Protestantism in Brazil and Chile*. Nashville, Tenn.: Vanderbilt University Press, 1967.

2a. Mesoamerica and South America, Argentina and Uruguay

Dalmas, Marcelo. *Historia de los Valdenses en el Río de la Plata*. Buenos Aires: La Aurora, 1987.

Davis, John Merle. *The Evangelical Church in the River Plate Republics: A Study of the Economic and Social Basis of the Evangelical Church in Argentina and Uruguay*. New York: International Missionary Council, 1943.

Drysdale, J. Monteith. *A Hundred Years in Buenos Aires*. Buenos Aires: Presbyterian Church, 1929.

Enns, Arno W. *Man, Milieu, and Mission in Argentina: A Close Look at Church Growth*. Grand Rapids, Mich.: Eerdmans, 1971.

Monti, Daniel P. *Presencia del Protestantismo en el Río de la Plata durante el Siglo XIX*. Buenos Aires: La Aurora, 1969.

Rooy, Sidney. "Argentina." In *Lengthened Cords*. Edited by Roger S. Greenway. Grand Rapids, Mich.: Baker Book House, 1975.

Rullmann, J. A. C. *Een Geslaagde Mislukking*. Netherlands: Zendingcentrum, Baarn, n.d.

Schmidt, Hermann. *Deutsche Evangelische La Plata Synode, 1899–1949*. Buenos Aires: Delps, 1949.

Villalpando, Waldo Luis, ed. *Las Iglesias del Trasplante*. Buenos Aires: Centro de Estudios Cristianos, 1970.

2b. Mesoamerica and South America, Bolivia, Peru, and Ecuador

Escobar, Samuel. "The Legacy of John Alexander Mackay." *International Bulletin of Missionary Research* 16 (1992): 116–22.

Goffin, Alvin Matthew. *The Rise of Protestant Evangelicalism in Ecuador, 1895–1990*. Gainesville: University Press of Florida, 1994.

Goodpasture, H. McKennie. "Latin American Soul of John A. Mackay." *Journal of Presbyterian History* 48 (1970): 265–92.

Kuhl, Paul E. "Protestant Missionary Activity and Freedom of Religion in Ecuador, Peru, and Bolivia." Ph.D. diss., Southern Illinois University at Carbondale, 1982.

MacPherson, John M. *At the Roots of a Nation: The Story of Colegio San Andrés, a Christian School in Lima, Peru*. Edinburgh: Knox Press, 1993.

Money, Herbert. *The Money Memoirs: New Zealand and Peru*. Tayport, England: MAC Research, 1989.

Wagner, C. Peter. *The Protestant Movement in Bolivia*. South Pasadena, Calif.: William Carey Library, 1970.

3a. Mesoamerica and South America, Brazil: Bibliography

Asher, Georg Michael. *A Bibliographical and Historical Essay on the Dutch Books and Pamphlets Relating to New Netherland and to the Dutch West-India Company and to Its Possessions in Brazil*. Amsterdam: N. Israel, 1960.

3b. Mesoamerica and South America, Brazil: Primary Sources

Ferreira, Julio Andrade. *Historia de Igreja Presbiteriana do Brasil, 1859–1959*. 2 vols. São Paulo: Casa Presbiteriana, 1959–1960.

3c. Mesoamerica and South America, Brazil: Histories and Studies

Alves, Rubem A. *Protestantism and Repression: A Brazilian Case Study*. Maryknoll, N.Y.: Orbis Books, 1985.

Arnold, Frank L. "American Presbyterians in Brazil: A Brazilian Perspective." *American Presbyterians* 73 (1995): 66–68.

Bear, James. *Mission to Brazil*. Nashville, Tenn.: PCUS Board of World Missions, 1961.

Boxer, C. R. *The Dutch in Brazil, 1624–54*. New ed. Hamden: Conn.: Archon Books, 1973.

Braga, Erasmo. *Panamericanismo: Aspecto Religioso*. New York: Sociedade de Preparo Missionario, 1916.

———. *The Republic of Brazil: A Survey of the Religious Situation*. New York: World Dominion Press, 1932.

Comissão Presbiterians Unida do Centenario. *Presbyterianismo no Brazil. Presbyterianism in Brazil, 1859–1959*. São Paulo: Casa Editora Presbiteriana, 1959.

McIntire, Robert L. *Portrait of Half a Century: Fifty Years of Presbyterianism in Brazil (1859–1910)*. Th.D. thesis, Princeton Theological Seminary, 1959.

ANTES

Pierson, Paul. *A Younger Church in Search of Maturity: Presbyterianism in Brazil from 1910 to 1959*. San Antonio: Trinity University Press, 1973.

Read, William R. *New Patterns of Church Growth in Brazil*. Grand Rapids, Mich.: Eerdmans, 1965.

Wedemann, Walter. "A History of Protestant Missions to Brazil, 1850–1914." Ph.D. diss., Southern Baptist Theological Seminary, 1977.

4a. Mesoamerica and South America, Chile

Goodpasture, H. McKennie. "David Trumbull: Missionary Journalist and Liberty in Chile, 1845–1889." *Journal of Presbyterian History* 56 (1978): 149–65.

Kessler, Jean Baptiste August, Jr. *A Study of the Older Protestant Missions and Churches in Peru and Chile*. Goes: Costerbaan & Le Cointre, 1967.

4b. Mesoamerica and South America, Colombia

Goff, James E. *The Persecution of Protestant Christians in Colombia, 1948–1958, with an Investigation of Its Background and Causes*. Cuernavaca: Centre Intercultural de Documentatión, 1968.

4c. Mesoamerica and South America, Costa Rica

Gomez, Jorge I. "Protestant Growth and Desertion in Costa Rica . . . as Affected by Evangelicalism . . . and Discipleship Practices." Ph.D. diss., Columbia International University, 1996.

Millett, Richard. "Protestant-Catholic Relations in Costa Rica." *Journal of Church and State* 12 (1970): 41–57.

4d. Mesoamerica and South America, El Salvador

Coleman, Kenneth M., et al., eds. "Protestantism in El Salvador: Conventional Wisdom Versus the Survey Evidence." In *Rethinking Protestantism in Latin America*, edited by Virginia Garrard-Burnett and David Stoll, 111–42. Philadelphia: Temple University Press, 1993.

4e. Mesoamerica and South America, Guatemala

Bodas de Diamante Comité. *Historia de la obra evangélica presbiteriana en Guatemala, 1892–1957*. Quezaltenango, Guatemala: Noticiero Evangélico, 1957.

Schäfer, Heinrich. *Church Identity between Repression and Liberation: The Presbyterian Church in Guatemala*. Geneva: World Alliance of Reformed Churches, 1991.

5a. Mesoamerica and South America, Mexico: Histories and Studies

Baldwin, Deborah J. *Protestants and the Mexican Revolution: Missionaries, Ministers, and Social Change*. Urbana, Ill.: University of Illinois Press, 1990.

Brackenridge, R. Douglas, and Francisco O. Garcia-Treto, *Iglesia Presbiteriana: A History of Presbyterians and Mexican-Americans in the Southwest*. 2d ed. San Antonio: Trinity University Press, 1987.

Hofman, J. Samuel. *Mission Work in Today's World: Insights and Outlooks*. Pasadena, Calif.: William Carey Library, 1993.

Iglesia Nacional Presbiteriana de Mexico. *1872–1972: Centenario Iglesia Nacional Presbiteriana de Mexico*. Monterey, Mexico: Comité Pro-Centenario, 1973.

McClelland, Alice J. *Mission to Mexico*. Nashville, Tenn.: PCUS Board of World Missions, 1960.

McGavran, Donald A. *Church Growth in Mexico*. Grand Rapids, Mich.: Eerdmans, 1963.

Mitchell, James E. *The Emergence of a Mexican Church: The Associate Reformed Presbyterian Church of Mexico*. South Pasadena, Calif.: William Carey Library, 1970.

Wheeler, William R. *Modern Missions in Mexico*. Philadelphia: Westminster Press, 1925.

5b. Mesoamerica and South America, Mexico: Biography

Dale, James G. *Katherine Neel Dale, Medical Missionary*. Grand Rapids, Mich.: Eerdmans, 1943.

Rankin, Melinda. *Twenty Years among the Mexicans: A Narrative of Missionary Labor*. St. Louis: Christian Publishing, 1875.

6a. Mesoamerica and South America, Venezuela

Phillips, C. Arthur. *A History of the Presbyterian Church in Venezuela*. Caracas: Presbyterian Mission Press, 1958.

Wheeler, William R. *Modern Missions on the Spanish Main: Impressions of Protestant Work in Colombia and Venezuela*. Philadelphia: Westminster Press, 1925.

Middle East

1a. Middle East, Middle East Region: Bibliographies

Silverburg, Sanford R. *Middle East Bibliography*. Metuchen, N.J.: Scarecrow Press, 1992.

1b. Middle East, Middle East Region: Reference Works

Bosworth, C. E., et al., eds. *The Encyclopedia of Islam*. New ed. Leiden: E. J. Brill, 1986–. CD-ROM version, 1998.

Esposito, John L. *The Oxford Encyclopedia of the Modern Islamic World*. New York: Oxford, 1995.

Simon, Reeva S., et al., eds. *Encyclopedia of the Modern Middle East*. New York: Macmillan, 1996.

1c. Middle East, Middle East Region: Histories and Studies

Anderson, Rufus. *History of the Missions of the American Board of Commissioners for Foreign Missions to the Oriental Churches*. Boston: Congregational Publishing Society, 1873.

Betts, Robert B. *Christians in the Arab East*. Rev. ed. Atlanta: John Knox Press, 1978.

Coubage, Youssef, and Philippe Fargues. *Christians and Jews under Islam*. London: I. B. Tauris, 1997.

Crabill, Joseph L. "Protestant Diplomacy and Arab Nationalism, 1914–1948." *American Presbyterians* 64 (1986): 113–124.

———. *Protestant Diplomacy and the Near East: Missionary Influence on American Policy, 1810–1927*. Minneapolis: University of Minnesota Press, 1971.

Cragg, Kenneth. *The Arab Christian: A History in the Middle East*. Louisville, Ky.: Westminster John Knox, 1991.

Haines, Byron, and Frank L. Cooley. *Christians and Muslims Together: An Exploration by Presbyterians*. Philadelphia: Geneva Press, 1987.

Hopkins, Paul. "American Presbyterians and the Middle East Conflict." *American Presbyterians* 68 (1990): 143–65.

Horner, Norman A. *A Guide to Christian Churches in the Middle East: Present-Day Christianity in the Middle East and North Africa*. Elkhart, Ind.: Mission Focus, 1989.

Kerr, David A. "Mission and Proselytism: A Middle East Perspective." *International Bulletin of Missionary Research* 20 (1996): 12–22.

McBride, S. Dean, and W. Sibley Towner, eds. "Middle East Perspectives." *Affirmation* 3 (Spring 1990).

Richter, Julius. *A History of Protestant Missions in the Near East*. 1910. Reprint, New York: AMS, 1970.

Sabra, George. "Protestantism in the Middle East." *Theological Review* 14 (1993): 22–39.

Valognes, Jean-Pierre. *Vie et mort des chrétiens d'Orient: Des origines à nos jours*. Paris: Fayard, 1994.

Wessels, Antonie. *Arab and Christian? Christians in the Arab East*. Kampen: Pharos, 1995.

1d. Middle East, Middle East Region: Biographies

Allison, Mary Bruins. *Doctor Mary in Arabia: Memoirs*. Austin, Tex.: University of Texas Press, 1994.

Boersma, Jeanette. *Grace in the Gulf: The Autobiography of Jeanette Boersma, Missionary Nurse in Iraq and the Sultanate of Oman*. Grand Rapids, Mich.: Eerdmans, 1991.

Bond, Alvan, ed. *Memoir of the Rev. Pliny Fisk, A.M.: Late Missionary to Palestine*. 1828. Reprint, New York: Arno Press, 1977.

Morton, Daniel Oliver, ed. *Memoir of the Rev. Levi Parsons*. 1824. Reprint, New York: Arno Press, 1977.

Van Ess, Dorothy F. *Pioneers in the Arab World.* Grand Rapids, Mich.: Eerdmans, 1974.

2a. Middle East, Egypt: Histories and Studies

Dye, Marjorie J. *The CEOSS Story.* Al-Qahirah, Egypt: Dar al-Thaqafah al-Masihiyah, 1979.

Elder, Earl E. *Vindicating a Vision: The Story of the American Mission in Egypt, 1854–1954.* Philadelphia: United Presbyterian Board of Publication, 1958.

Istafanokus, Abdel Masih. "The Church in Egypt Today." *Reformed Review* 50 (1996): 99–117.

Skreslet, Stanley H. "The American Presbyterian Mission in Egypt: Significant Factors in Its Establishment." *American Presbyterians* 64 (1986): 83–95.

Stephanous, Andrea Zaki. "The Coptic Evangelical Organization for Social Services, Egypt." *Transformation* 11 (1994): 18–20.

Watson, Andrew. *The American Mission in Egypt, 1854–1896.* Pittsburgh: United Presbyterian Board of Publication, 1898.

Watson, Charles R. *In the Valley of the Nile: A Survey of the Missionary Movement in Egypt.* New York: Fleming H. Revell, 1908.

2b. Middle East, Egypt: Biographies

Hogg, Rena L. *A Master Builder on the Nile: Being a Record of the Life and Aims of John Hogg.* Chicago: Fleming H. Revell, 1914.

Milligan, Anna A. *Dr. Henry of Assiut.* Philadelphia: United Presbyterian Board of Foreign Missions, 1945.

Wissa, Hanna F. *Assiout: The Saga of An Egyptian Family.* Sussex, U.K.: The Book Guild, 1994.

3a. Middle East, Iran: Histories and Studies

Heuser, Frederick J., Jr. "Women's Work for Women: Belle Sherwood Hawks and the East Persia Presbyterian Women." *American Presbyterians* 65 (1987): 7–17.

Hultvall, John. *Mission och vision i Orienten: Svenska Missionsförbundets mission i Transkaukasien-Persian, 1882–1921.* Stockholm, Sweden: Verbum, 1991.

Iran Mission. *A Century of Mission Work in Iran (Persia), 1834–1934.* Beirut, Syria: American Mission Press, 1936.

Soleimani, Mansoor. "The Educational Impact of American Church Missionaries on the Educational Programs of Iran, 1834–1925." Ed.D. thesis, University of the Pacific, 1980.

Waterfield, Robin E. *Christians in Persia: Assyrians, Armenians, Roman Catholics, and Protestants.* London: Allen & Unwin, 1973.

Zirinsky, Michael P. "Harbingers of Change: Presbyterian Women in Iran, 1883–1949." *American Presbyterians* 70 (1992): 173–86.

3b. Middle East, Iran: Biography

Voorhees, Elizabeth C. Kay. *Is Love Lost? Mosaics in the Life of Jane Doolittle: "Angel Mother" in a Muslim Land.* Pasadena, Calif.: William Carey Library, 1988.

4a. Middle East, Israel

Chambers, D. "Prelude to the Last Things: The Church of Scotland's Mission to the Jews." *Record of Scottish Church History Society* 19 (1977): 43–58.

Hopkins, Paul A. "American Presbyterians and the Middle East Conflict." *American Presbyterians* 68 (1990): 143–65.

McDougall, David. *In Search of Israel: A Chronicle of the Jewish Missions of the Church of Scotland.* London: T. Nelson, 1941.

Wilson, J. H., and James Wells. *The Sea of Galilee Mission of the Free Church of Scotland.* Edinburgh: T. Nelson, 1895.

5a. Middle East, Lebanon and Syria: Histories and Studies

Antakly, Waheeb George. "American Protestant Educational Missions: Their Influence on Syria and Arab Nationalism, 1820–1923." Ph.D. diss., American University, 1975.

Badr, Habib. "Mission to 'Nominal Christians': The Policy and Practice of the American Board of Commissioners for Foreign Missions and Its Missionaries concerning Eastern Churches Which Led to the Organization of a Protestant Church in Beirut (1819–1848)." Ph.D. diss., Princeton Theological Seminary, 1992.

Haddad, Robert M. *Syrian Christians in Muslim Society: An Interpretation.* Princeton: Princeton University Press, 1970.

Jessup, Henry Harris. *Fifty-Three Years in Syria.* New York: F. H. Revell, 1910.

Semaan, Wanis A. *Aliens at Home: A Socio-Religious Analysis of the Protestant Church in Lebanon and Its Background.* Beirut: Longman, 1986.

Tibawi, Abdul Latif. *American Interests in Syria, 1800–1901: A Study of Educational, Literary and Religious Work.* Oxford: Clarendon Press, 1966.

5b. Middle East, Lebanon and Syria: Biographies

Weir, Benjamin, and Carol S. Weir. *Hostage Bound; Hostage Free.* Philadelphia: Westminster Press, 1987.

North America and Caribbean

1a. North America and Caribbean, General Region: Reference Works

America: History and Life. Santa Barbara, Calif.: American Bibliographical Center of ABC-Clio, 1964–. Periodical index covers the United States and Canada.

Melton, J. Gordon, ed. *The Encyclopedia of American Religions: A Comprehensive Study of the Major Religious Groups in the United States and Canada.* 2 vols. 3d ed. Detroit: Gale Research, 1989.

Piepkorn, Arthur C. *Profiles in Belief: The Religious Bodies of the United States and Canada,* 4 vols. in 3. New York: Harper & Row, 1977–1979.

1b. North America and Caribbean, General Region: Histories and Studies

Handy, Robert T. *A History of the Churches in the United States and Canada.* New York: Oxford University Press, 1977.

Hoezee, Scott, and Christopher H. Meehan. *Flourishing in the Land: A Hundred-Year History of Christian Reformed Missions in North America.* Grand Rapids: Eerdmans, 1996.

Noll, Mark A. *A History of Christianity in the United States and Canada.* Grand Rapids, Mich.: Eerdmans, 1992.

2a. North America and Caribbean, Canada: Bibliography

American Theological Library Association. *Bibliography of Church Union in Canada.* Toronto: ATLA, 1959.

2b. North America and Caribbean, Canada: General Histories

Bibby, Reginald W. *Fragmented Gods: The Poverty and Potential of Religion in Canada.* Toronto: Irwin Publishing, 1987.

Murphy, Terence, and Roberto Perin, eds. *A Concise History of Christianity in Canada.* Toronto: Oxford University Press, 1996.

Walsh, H. H., J. S. Moir, and J. W. Grant. *The Church in the British Era.* Toronto: Ryerson; New York: McGraw-Hill, 1972.

———. *The Church in the Canadian Era.* Toronto: Ryerson; New York: McGraw-Hill, 1972.

———. *The Church in the French Era.* Toronto: Ryerson Press, 1966.

2c. North America and Caribbean, Canada: The Presbyterian and Reformed Churches

Fraser, Brian J. *Church, College, and Clergy: A History of Theological Education at Knox College, Toronto, 1844–1994.* Montreal: McGill-Queen's University Press, 1995.

Gregg, William. *History of the Presbyterian Church in the Dominion of Canada from the Earliest Times to 1834.* Toronto: Presbyterian Printing and Publishing, 1885.

Klempa, William, ed. *The Burning Bush and a Few Acres of Snow: The Presbyterian Contribution to Canadian Life and Culture.* Ottawa: Carleton University Press, 1994.

MacBeth, R. G. *The Burning Bush in Canada*. Toronto: The Westminster, 1926.

Marshall, David B. *Secularizing the Faith: Canadian Protestant Clergy and the Crisis of Belief, 1850–1940*. Toronto: University of Toronto Press, 1992.

McNeill, John T. *The Presbyterian Church in Canada, 1875–1925*. Toronto: General Board, 1925.

Moir, John S. *Enduring Witness: A History of the Presbyterian Church in Canada*. N.p.: Bryant Press, 1975.

Ransom, R. Malcolm, ed. *The Lively Acts: The Centennial Year Account of the Missionary Outreach of the Presbyterian Church in Canada*. Toronto: General Board of Missions, 1967.

Smith, Neil G. "The Presbyterian Tradition in Canada." In *The Churches and the Canadian Experience*, edited by John Webster Grant, 38–52. Toronto: Ryerson Press, 1963.

Smith, Neil G., A. L. Farris, and H. K. Markell. *A Short History of the Presbyterian Church in Canada*. Toronto: Centennial Commitee, Committee on History, Presbyterian Church in Canada, 1966.

Vanoene, W. W. J. *Inheritance Preserved: The Canadian Reformed Churches in Historical Perspective*. Winnipeg: Premier Printing, 1975.

Vaudry, Richard W. *The Free Church in Victorian Canada, 1844–1861*. Waterloo, Ont.: Wilfrid Laurier University Press, 1989.

2d. North America and Caribbean, Canada: The United Church of Canada

Clifford, N. Keith. *Resistance to Church Union in Canada, 1904–1939*. Vancouver: University of British Columbia, 1985.

Grant, John Webster. *The Canadian Experience of Church Union*. Richmond, Va.: John Knox Press, 1967.

Pidgeon, George. *The United Church of Canada: The Story of the Union*. Toronto: Ryerson Press, 1950.

Silcox, Claris Edwin. *Church Union in Canada: Its Causes and Consequences*. New York: Institute of Social and Religious Research, 1933.

Wright, Robert A. *A World Mission: Canadian Protestants and the Quest for a New International Order, 1918–1939*. Montreal: McGill-Queen's University Press, 1991.

2e. North America and Caribbean, Canada: Biographies

Craig, T. L. *The Missionary Lives: A Study in Canadian Missionary Biography and Autobiography*. Leiden: E. J. Brill, 1997.

Gill, Stewart D. *The Reverend William Proudfoot and the United Secession Mission in Canada*. Lewiston, N.Y.: Mellen Press, 1991.

Grant, John Webster. *George Pidgeon: A Biography*. Toronto: Ryerson, 1962.

Presbyterian Church in Canada. *Enkindled by the Word: Essays on Presbyterianism in Canada.* Toronto: Presbyterian Publications, 1966.

Reid, W. Stanford, ed. *Called to Witness: Profiles of Canadian Presbyterians, A Supplement to Enduring Witness.* Vol. 1. N.p.: Presbyterian Publications, 1975.

————. *Called to Witness: Profiles of Canadian Presbyterians, A Supplement to Enduring Witness.* Vol. 2. Hamilton, Ont.: Presbyterian Church of Canada, 1980.

Wilson, Keith. *Charles William Gordon.* Winnipeg: Peguis, 1981.

2f. North America and Caribbean, Canada: Theology, Culture, and Society

Allen, Richard. *The Social Passion: Religion and Social Reform in Canada, 1914–1928.* Toronto: University Press, 1971.

Chalmers, Randolph Carleton. *See the Christ Stand! A Study in Doctrine in the United Church of Canada.* Toronto: Ryerson, 1945.

Dow, John. *This Is Our Faith: An Exposition of the Statement of Faith of the United Church of Canada.* Toronto: United Church of Canada, 1943.

Fraser, Brian J. *The Social Uplifters: Presbyterian Progressives and the Social Gospel in Canada, 1875–1915.* Waterloo, Ont.: Wilfrid Laurier University Press, 1988.

Gauvreau, Michael. *The Evangelical Century: College and Creed in English Canada from the Great Revival to the Great Depression.* Montreal: McGill-Queen's University Press, 1991.

VanderVennen, Robert E. *Church and Canadian Culture.* Lanham, Md.: University Press of America, 1991.

3a. North America and Caribbean, Caribbean Region: Reference Works

Bessil-Watson, Lisa. *Handbook of the Churches of the Caribbean.* Bridgetown, Barbados: Cedar Press, 1982.

3b. North America and Caribbean, Caribbean Region: Histories and Studies

Bolioli, Oscar L., ed. *The Caribbean: Culture of Resistance, Spirit of Hope.* New York: Friendship Press, 1993.

Coomans, Henry E., et al., eds. *Building Up the Future from the Past: Studies on the Architecture and Historic Monuments in the Dutch Caribbean.* Curaçao: Universidat Nashonal de Antia, 1990.

González, Justo L. *The Development of Christianity in the Latin Caribbean.* Grand Rapids, Mich.: Eerdmans, 1969.

Goslinga, Cornelis Ch. *The Dutch in the Caribbean and in the Guianas, 1680–1791.* Assen, Netherlands: Van Gorcum, 1985.

————. *The Dutch in the Caribbean and in Surinam, 1791/5–1942.* Assen, Netherlands: Van Gorcum, 1990.

————. *The Dutch in the Caribbean and on the Wild Coast, 1580–1618.* Assen, Netherlands: Van Gorcum, 1971.

Hamid, Idris, ed. *Out of the Depths: A Collection of Papers Presented at Four Missionary Conferences held in Antigua, Guyana, Jamaica, and Trinidad in 1975.* San Fernando, Trinidad: St. Andrew's Theological College, 1977.

Hoornaert, Eduardo, ed. *História da igreja na América Latina e no Caribe, 1945–1995: O debate metodológico.* Petrópolis, Brazil: Editora Vozes, 1995.

Meier, Johannes, et al., eds. *Historia general de la Iglesia en América Latina, IV: Caribe.* México: Universidad de Quintana Roo, 1995.

Mitchell, David I., ed. *New Mission for a New People: Voices from the Caribbean.* New York: Friendship, 1977.

Osborne, F. J., and G. Johnston. *Coastlands and Islands: First Thoughts on Caribbean Church History.* N.p.: UTCWI, 1972.

Williams, Lewin. *Caribbean Theology.* New York: Peter Lang, 1992.

3c. North America and Caribbean, Caribbean Region: Cuba, Grenada, Guyana, Jamaica, Trinidad and Tobago

Gómez Treto, Raúl. *The Church and Socialism in Cuba.* Maryknoll, N.Y.: Orbis Books, 1988.

Davidson, Lewis. *First Things First: A Study of the Presbyterian Church in Jamaica.* Edinburgh: William Blackwood, 1945.

Hamid, Idris. *A History of the Presbyterian Church in Trinidad, 1868–1968: The Struggles of a Church in Colonial Captivity.* San Fernando, Trinidad: St. Andrew's Theological College, 1980.

Ramos, Marcos A. *Protestantism and Revolution in Cuba.* Miami, Fla.: University of Miami, 1989.

Robson, George. *Missions of the United Presbyterian Church: The Story of Our Jamaica Mission with a Sketch of Our Trinidad Mission.* Edinburgh: Office of United Presbyterian Church, 1894.

4a. North America and Caribbean, United States of America: Atlases

Gaustad, Edwin S. *Historical Atlas of Religion in America.* Rev. ed. New York: Harper & Row, 1976.

Goddard, Carolyn E. *On the Trail of the UCC: A Historical Atlas of the United Church of Christ.* New York: United Church Press, 1981.

Halvorson, Peter L., and William M. Newman. *Atlas of Religious Change in America.* Washington, D.C.: Glenmary Research Center, 1978.

4b. North America and Caribbean, United States of America: General Works in Religion

Bass, Dorothy C., and Sandra H. Boyd. *Women in American Religious History: An Annotated Bibliography and Guide to Sources.* Boston: G. K. Hall, 1986.

Burr, Nelson R., ed. *A Critical Bibliography of Religion in America.* 2 vols. Princeton: Princeton University Press, 1961.

———. *Religion in American Life: Goldentree Bibliography.* New York: Appleton-Century-Crofts, 1971.

Fraker, Anne T., ed. *Religion and American Life: Resources.* Urbana: University of Illinois Press, 1989.

Lippy, Charles H. *Bibliography of Religion in the South.* Macon, Ga.: Mercer University Press, 1985.

Religious Books, 1876–1982. 4 vols. New York: R. R. Bowker, 1983.

Sandeen, Ernest R., and Frederick Hale, eds. *American Religion and Philosophy: A Guide to Information Sources.* Detroit: Gale Research, 1978. Continues Burr.

Wilson, John F., ed. *Church and State in America: A Bibliographical Guide.* 2 vols. New York: Greenwood Press, 1986–1987.

Young, Arthur P., and E. Jens Holley, with Annette Blum. *Religion and the American Experience, 1620–1900: A Bibliography of Doctoral Dissertations.* Westport, Conn.: Greenwood Press, 1992.

4c. North America and Caribbean, United States of America: Reformed Tradition

Aycock, Martha B., and Gerald W. Gillette. "A Checklist of Doctoral Dissertations on American Presbyterian and Reformed Subjects, 1912–1982." *Journal of Presbyterian History* 61 (1983): 257–298.

DeKlerk, Peter. *Bibliography of the Writings of the Professors of Calvin Theological Seminary.* Grand Rapids, Mich.: Calvin Theological Seminary, 1980.

Gallagher, Edward J., and Thomas Werge. *Early Puritan Writers: A Reference Guide.* Boston: G. K. Hall, 1976.

Montgomery, Michael S. *American Puritan Studies: An Annotated Bibliography of Dissertations, 1882–1981.* Westport, Conn.: Greenwood Press, 1984.

Parker, Harold M., Jr. *Bibliography of Published Articles on American Presbyterianism, 1901–1980.* Westport, Conn.: Greenwood Press, 1985.

Prince, Harold B. *A Presbyterian Bibliography: The Published Writings of Ministers Who Served in the Presbyterian Church in the United States . . . 1861–1961.* Metuchen, N.J.: Scarecrow Press, 1983.

Trinterud, Leonard J. *A Bibliography of American Presbyterianism during the Colonial Period.* Philadelphia: Presbyterian Historical Society, 1968.

4d. North America and Caribbean, United States of America: Manuscript Guides

Benedetto, Robert. *Guide to the Manuscript Collections of the Presbyterian Church, U.S.A.* Westport, Conn.: Greenwood Press, 1990.

Heuser, Frederick J., Jr. *A Guide to the Foreign Missionary Manuscripts in the Presbyterian Historical Society.* Westport, Conn.: Greenwood Press, 1988.

Selement, George. "A Check List of Manuscript Materials Relating to Seventeenth-Century New England Printed in Historical Collections." *Bulletin of the New York Public Library* 79 (1976): 416–447.

Worthley, Harold Field. *An Inventory of the Records of the Particular (Congregational) Churches of Massachusetts Gathered, 1620–1805.* Proceedings of the Unitarian Historical Society, vol. 16. Cambridge, Mass.: Harvard University Press, 1970.

4e. North America and Caribbean, United States of America: Biographical Reference Works

Balmer, Randall, and John R. Fitzmier. *The Presbyterians.* Denominations in America, no. 5. Westport, Conn.: Greenwood Press, 1993.

Beecher, Willis J. *Index of Presbyterian Ministers . . . From A.D. 1706 to A.D. 1881.* Philadelphia: Presbyterian Board of Publication, 1883.

Bowden, Henry Warner. *Dictionary of Religious Biography.* 2d ed. Westport, Conn.: Greenwood Press, 1993.

Byers, Arthur M., Jr., ed. *Biographical Catalogue of Princeton Theological Seminary, 1900–1976.* Princeton, N.J.: Princeton Theological Seminary, 1977.

Crane, Sophie Montgomery. *Missionary Directory: Presbyterian Church in the United States, 1867–1983; Presbyterian Church (U.S.A.), 1983–1987.* Atlanta, Ga.: General Assembly Mission Board, 1987.

Dennison, James T. *A Ministerial Register of the Orthodox Presbyterian Church, 1936–1991.* Philadelphia: Orthodox Presbyterian Church, 1992.

Gasero, Russell L., ed. *Historical Directory of the Reformed Church in America, 1628–1992.* Grand Rapids, Mich.: Eerdmans, 1992.

Glasgow, William Melanchthon. *Cyclopedic Manual of the United Presbyterian Church.* Pittsburgh: United Presbyterian Board of Publication, 1903.

Hopper, Orion C., ed. *Biographical Catalogue of Princeton Theological Seminary, 1815–1954.* Princeton, N.J.: Princeton Theological Seminary, 1955.

James, Edward T., ed. *Notable American Women, 1607–1950: A Biographical Dictionary.* 3 vols. Cambridge, Mass.: Belknap Press, Harvard University Press, 1971. Supplemented by Barbara Sicherman and Carol Hurd Green et al., eds. *Notable American Women: The Modern Period: A Biographical Dictionary.* Cambridge, Mass.: Belknap Press, Harvard University Press, 1980.

Kelsey, Hugh A., ed. *The United Presbyterian Directory: A Half Century Survey, 1903–1958.* Pittsburgh, Pa.: Pickwick Press, 1958. Supplement to Glasgow.

Scott, E. C., and E. D. Witherspoon Jr. *Ministerial Directory of the Presbyterian Church, U.S., 1861–1983.* 5 vols. The General Assembly of the Presbyterian Church in the United States, 1942–1986.

Smylie, James H., Dean K. Thompson, and Cary Patrick. *Go Therefore: 150 Years of Presbyterians in Global Mission.* Atlanta: Presbyterian Publishing House, 1987.

Sprague, William B. *Annals of the American Pulpit.* 9 vols. 1859–1969. Reprint, New York: Arno Press, 1969. Includes Congregational, Presbyterian, and Reformed ministers.

Youngs, J. William. *The Congregationalists.* Denominations in America, no. 4. Westport, Conn.: Greenwood Press, 1990.

4f. North America and Caribbean, United States of America: Dictionaries and Encyclopedias, General

Ferris, William, and Charles Wilson. *The Encyclopedia of Southern Culture.* Chapel Hill: University of North Carolina Press, 1989.

Hill, Samuel S., ed. *Encyclopedia of Religion in the South.* Macon, Ga.: Mercer, 1984.

Lippy, Charles H., and Peter W. Williams, eds. *Encyclopedia of the American Religious Experience: Studies of Traditions and Movements.* 3 vols. New York: Scribner's, 1988.

Melton, J. Gordon, ed. *The Encyclopedia of American Religions.* 4th ed. Detroit: Gale Research, 1993.

Reid, Daniel G., Robert D. Linder, Bruce L. Shelley, and Harry S. Stout, eds. *Dictionary of Christianity in America.* Downers Grove, Ill.: InterVarsity Press, 1990.

Williamson, William B. *An Encyclopedia of Religions in the United States: 100 Religious Groups Speak for Themselves.* New York: Crossroad/Continuum, 1993.

4g. North America and Caribbean, United States of America: The Reformed Tradition

Nevin, Alfred. *Encyclopedia of the Presbyterian Church in the United States of America: Including the Northern and Southern Assemblies.* Philadelphia: Presbyterian Publishing Company, 1884.

Noll, Mark, and D. G. Hart, eds. *Dictionary of the Presbyterian and Reformed Tradition in America.* Downers Grove, Ill.: InterVarsity Press, forthcoming.

4h. North America and Caribbean, United States of America: Historical Surveys

Ahlstrom, Sydney E. *A Religious History of the American People*. 2 vols. Reprint, Garden City, N.Y.: Image Books, 1975.

Brauer, Jerald C., ed. *Reinterpretation in American Church History*. Essays in Divinity, vol. 5. Chicago: University of Chicago Press, 1968.

Gaustad, Edwin S. *A Religious History of America*. New rev. ed. San Francisco: Harper & Row, 1990.

Hudson, Winthrop S., and John Corrigan. *Religion in America: An Historical Account of the Development of American Religious Life*. 5th ed. New York: Macmillan, 1992.

Lacy, Creighton. *The Word-Carrying Giant: The Growth of the American Bible Society, 1816–1966*. South Pasadena, Calif.: William Carey Library, 1977.

Marty, Martin. *Pilgrims in Their Own Land: 500 Years of Religion in America*. Boston: Little, Brown, 1984.

Melton, Julius. *Presbyterian Worship in America: Changing Patterns since 1787*. Richmond, Va.: John Knox Press, 1967.

Mulder, John M., and John F. Wilson, eds. *Religion in American History: Interpretive Essays*. Englewood Cliffs, N.J.: Prentice-Hall, 1978.

Williams, Peter W. *America's Religions: Traditions and Cultures*. New York: Macmillan, 1990.

4i. North America and Caribbean, United States of America: Congregational Tradition

Atkins, Gaius G., and Frederick L. Fagley. *History of American Congregationalism*. Boston: Pilgrim Press, 1942.

Bacon, Leonard. *The Story of the Churches: The Congregationalists*. New York: Baker & Taylor, 1904.

Bass, Dorothy C., and Kenneth B. Smith, eds. *The United Church of Christ: Studies in Identity and Polity*. Chicago: Exploration Press, 1987.

Gunnemann, Louis H. *The Shaping of the United Church of Christ: An Essay in the History of American Christianity*. New York: United Church, 1977.

Horton, Douglas. *The United Church of Christ: Its Origin, Organization, and Role in the World Today*. New York: Thomas Nelson, 1962.

Johnson, Daniel L., and Charles Hambrick-Stowe, eds. *Theology and Identity: Traditions, Movements, and Polity in the United Church of Christ*. New York: Pilgrim Press, 1990.

Paul, Robert S. *Freedom with Order: The Doctrine of the Church in the United Church of Christ*. New York: United Church Press, 1987.

Starkey, Marion. *The Congregational Way: The Role of the Pilgrims and Their Heirs in Shaping America.* Garden City, N.Y.: Doubleday, 1966.

Walker, Williston. *A History of the Congregational Churches in the United States.* New York: Christian Literature, 1894.

Zikmund, Barbara Brown, ed. *Hidden Histories in the United Church of Christ.* New York: United Church Press, 1984.

4j. North America and Caribbean, United States of America: Presbyterian Tradition

Barrus, Ben M., et al., eds. *A People Called Cumberland Presbyterians.* Memphis: Frontier Press, 1972.

Boyd, Lois A., and R. Douglas Brackenridge. *Presbyterian Women in America: Two Centuries of a Quest for Status.* Presbyterian Historical Society Publications, vol. 22. Westport, Conn.: Greenwood Press, 1983.

Brackenridge, R. Douglas and Francisco O. Garcia-Treto. *Iglesia Presbiteriana: A History of Presbyterians and Mexican-Americans in the Southwest.* 2d ed. San Antonio: Trinity University Press, 1987.

Dennison, Charles G. *The Orthodox Presbyterian Church, 1936–1986.* Philadelphia: Committee for the Historian of the OPC, 1986.

Dennison, Charles G., and Richard C. Gamble, eds. *Pressing toward the Mark: Essays Commemorating Fifty Years of the Orthodox Presbyterian Church.* Philadelphia: Committee for the Historian of the OPC, 1986.

King, Ray A. *A History of the Associate Reformed Presbyterian Church.* Charlotte, N.C.: Board of Christian Education, 1966.

Loetscher, Lefferts A. *A Brief History of the Presbyterians.* 4th ed. Philadelphia: Westminster Press, 1983.

Murray, Andrew E. *Presbyterians and the Negro: A History.* Philadelphia: Presbyterian Historical Society, 1966.

Smylie, James H. *American Presbyterians: A Pictorial History.* Philadelphia: Presbyterian Historical Society, 1985.

———. *A Brief History of the Presbyterians.* Louisville, Ky.: Geneva Press, 1997.

Thompson, Ernest Trice. *Presbyterians in the South.* 3 vols. Richmond, Va.: John Knox, 1963–1973.

Thompson, Robert E. *A History of the Presbyterian Churches in the United States.* American Church History Series, vol. 6. New York: Christian Literature, 1895.

Wilmore, Gayraud S. *Black and Presbyterian: The Heritage and the Hope.* Philadelphia: Geneva Press, 1983.

4k. North America and Caribbean, United States of America: Reformed Churches

Bratt, James D. *Dutch Calvinism in Modern America*. Grand Rapids, Mich.: Eerdmans, 1984.

Cook, James I., ed. *The Church Speaks: Papers of the Commission on Theology, Reformed Church in America*. Grand Rapids, Mich.: Eerdmans, 1985.

DeJong, Peter Y. *The Christian Reformed Church: A Study Manual*. Grand Rapids, Mich.: Baker Book House, 1967.

DeKlerk, Peter, and Richard R. DeRidder, eds. *Perspectives on the Christian Reformed Church*. Grand Rapids, Mich.: Baker Book House, 1983.

Dubbs, Joseph. *A History of the Reformed Church, German*. New York: Christian Literature, 1895.

Dunn, David, ed. *A History of the Evangelical and Reformed Church*. 1961. Reprint, New York: Pilgrim, 1990.

Hutchison, George P. *The History behind the Reformed Presbyterian Church, Evangelical Synod*. Cherry Hill, N.J.: Mack Publishing, 1974.

Kromminga, John H. *The Christian Reformed Church*. Grand Rapids, Mich.: Baker Book House, 1949.

Van Hoeven, James W., ed. *Piety and Patriotism: Bicentennial Studies of the Reformed Church in America, 1776–1976*. Grand Rapids, Mich.: Eerdmans, 1976.

Ware, Lowry, and James W. Gettys. *The Second Century: A History of the Associate Reformed Presbyterians, 1882–1892*. Greenville, S.C.: Associate Reformed Presbyterian Church, 1982.

Williams, Daniel Jenkins. *One Hundred Years of Welsh Calvinistic Methodism in America*. Philadelphia: Westminster Press, 1937.

41. North America and Caribbean, United States of America: Mission

Andrew, John A., III. *Rebuilding the Christian Commonwealth: New England Congregationalists and Foreign Missions, 1800–1830*. Lexington: University of Kentucky Press, 1976.

Beaver, Robert Pierce. *American Protestant Women in World Mission: History of the First Feminist Movement in North America*. Rev. ed. Reprint, Grand Rapids, Mich.: Eerdmans, 1984.

Brown, Arthur Judson. *One Hundred Years: A History of the Foreign Missionary Work of the Presbyterian Church in the U. S. A.* 2d ed. New York: Revell, 1936.

Drury, Clifford M. *Presbyterian Panorama: One Hundred and Fifty Years of National Missions History*. Philadelphia: Board of Christian Education, 1952.

Hutchison, William R. *Errand into the World: American Protestant Thought and Foreign Missions*. Chicago: University of Chicago Press, 1987.

Perry, Alan F. "The American Board of Commissioners for Foreign Missions and the London Missionary Society in the Nineteenth Century: A Study of Ideas." Ph.D. thesis, Washington University, 1974.

Phillips, Clifton Jackson. *Protestant America and the Pagan World: The First Half-Century of the American Board of Commissioners for Foreign Missions, 1810–1860.* Cambridge, Mass.: Harvard University Press, 1969.

Robert, Dana. *American Women in Mission: A Social History of Their Thought and Practice.* Macon, Ga.: Mercer University Press, 1996.

Strong, William E. *The Story of the American Board: An Account of the First Hundred Years of the American Board of Commissioners for Foreign Missions.* Boston: Pilgrim Press, 1910.

Thompson, Ernest Trice. *Presbyterian Missions in the Southern United States.* Richmond, Va.: Presbyterian Committee of Publication, 1934.

4m. North America and Caribbean, United States of America: Colonial Period

Balmer, Randall. *A Perfect Babel of Confusion: Dutch Religion & English Culture in the Middle Colonies.* New York: Oxford University Press, 1989.

Bercovitch, Sacvan. *The Puritan Origins of the American Self.* Reprint, New Haven, Conn.: Yale University Press, 1976.

Bozeman, Theodore Dwight. *To Live Ancient Lives: The Primitivist Dimension in Puritanism.* Chapel Hill: University of North Carolina Press, 1988.

Butler, Jon. *The Huguenots in America: A Refugee People in New World Society.* Cambridge, Mass.: Harvard University Press, 1983.

De Jong, Gerald F. *The Dutch Reformed Church in the American Colonies.* Grand Rapids, Mich.: Eerdmans, 1978.

Hatch, Nathan O., and Harry S. Stout, eds. *Jonathan Edwards and the American Experience.* New York: Oxford University Press, 1989.

McDermott, Gerald R. *One, Holy and Happy Society: The Public Theology of Jonathan Edwards.* University Park: Pennsylvania State University, 1993.

Porterfield, Amanda. *Female Piety in Puritan New England: The Emergence of Religious Humanism.* New York: Oxford University Press, 1991.

Tanis, James. *Dutch Calvinistic Pietism in the Middle Colonies.* The Hague: M. Nijhoff, 1967.

Trinterud, Leonard J. *The Forming of an American Tradition: A Re-examination of Colonial Presbyterianism.* Philadelphia: Westminster Press, 1949.

Westerkamp, Marilyn. *Triumph of the Laity: Scots-Irish Piety and the Great Awakening, 1625–1760.* New York: Oxford University Press, 1988.

4n. North America and Caribbean, United States of America: American Revolution

Bailyn, Bernard. *The Ideological Origins of the American Revolution*. Cambridge, Mass.: Harvard University Press, 1967.

Baldwin, Alice M. *The New England Clergy in the American Revolution*. Durham, N.C.: Duke University Press, 1928.

Griffin, Keith L. *Revolution and Religion: American Revolutionary War and the Reformed Clergy*. New York: Paragon House, 1994.

Hatch, Nathan. *The Sacred Cause of Liberty: Republican Thought and the Millennium in Revolutionary New England*. New Haven, Conn.: Yale University Press, 1977.

Miller, William Lee. *The First Liberty: Religion and the American Republic*. New York: Knopf, 1986.

Smith, Page, ed. *Religious Origins of the American Revolution*. Missoula, Mont.: Scholars, 1976.

Smylie, James H., ed. "Presbyterians and the American Revolution: A Documentary Account," *Journal of Presbyterian History* 52, no. 4 (Winter 1974).

————. "Presbyterians and the American Revolution: An Interpretative Account," *Journal of Presbyterian History* 54, no. 2 (Spring 1976).

4o. North America and Caribbean, United States of America: Early National and Antebellum

Bozeman, Theodore Dwight. *Protestants in an Age of Science: The Baconian Ideal and Antebellum American Religious Thought*. Chapel Hill: University of North Carolina Press, 1977.

Butler, Jon. *Awash in a Sea of Faith: Christianizing of the American People*. Cambridge, Mass.: Harvard University Press, 1990.

Conkin, Paul K. *The Uneasy Center: Reformed Christianity in Antebellum America*. Chapel Hill: University of North Carolina Press, 1995.

Des Champs, Margaret B. "The Presbyterian Church in the South Atlantic States, 1801–1861." Ph.D. diss., Emory University, 1952.

Goen, C. C. *Broken Churches, Broken Nation: Denominational Schisms and the Coming of the American Civil War*. Macon, Ga.: Mercer University Press, 1985.

Harding, Vincent. *A Certain Magnificence: Lyman Beecher and the Transformation of American Protestantism, 1775–1863*. Brooklyn: Carlson Publishing, 1991.

Hatch, Nathan O. *The Democratization of American Christianity*. New Haven, Conn.: Yale University Press, 1989.

Hollis, Daniel W., and Julien, Carl. *Look to the Rock: One Hundred Ante-*

bellum Presbyterian Churches of the South. Richmond, Va.: John Knox Press, 1961.

Hood, Fred J. *Reformed America: The Middle and Southern States, 1783–1837.* University, Ala.: University of Alabama Press, 1980.

Kuykendall, John W. *Southern Enterprise: The Work of National Evangelical Societies in the Antebellum South.* Westport, Conn: Greenwood Press, 1982.

Marsden, George M. *The Evangelical Mind and the New School Presbyterian Experience: A Case Study of Thought and Theology in Nineteenth-Century America.* New Haven, Conn.: Yale University Press, 1970.

McKivigan, John R. *The War against Proslavery Religion: Abolitionism and the Northern Churches, 1830–1865.* Ithaca, N.Y.: Cornell University Press, 1984.

McLoughlin, William. *Modern Revivalism: Charles Grandison Finney to Billy Graham.* New York: Ronald Press, 1959.

Moorhead, James H. *American Apocalypse: Yankee Protestants and the Civil War, 1860–1869.* New Haven, Conn.: Yale University Press, 1978.

Noll, Mark A. *Princeton and the Republic, 1768–1822.* Princeton: Princeton University Press, 1989.

Pearson, Samuel C. "From Church to Denomination: American Congregationalism in the Nineteenth Century." *Church History* 38 (1969): 67–87.

Posey, Walter Brownlow. *Frontier Mission: A History of Religion West of the Southern Appalachians to 1861.* Lexington: University of Kentucky Press, 1966.

Wilson, Charles R. *Baptized in Blood: The Religion of the Lost Cause, 1865–1920.* Reprint, Athens, Ga.: University of Georgia Press, 1983.

4p. North America and Caribbean, United States of America: Post–Civil War

Guarneri, Carl, and David Alvarez, eds. *Religion and Society in the American West: Historical Essays.* Lanham, Md.: University Press of America, 1988.

Gusfield, Joseph R. *Symbolic Crusade: Status Politics and the American Temperance Movement.* 2d ed. Urbana: University of Illinois Press, 1986.

Hardesty, Nancy. *Women Called to Witness: Evangelical Feminism in the Nineteenth Century.* Nashville, Tenn.: Abingdon Press, 1984.

May, Henry F. *Protestant Churches and Industrial America.* 2d ed. New York: Octagon Books, 1977.

Parker, Harold M. *Studies in Southern Presbyterian History.* Gunnison, Colo.: B & B Printers, 1979.

Szasz, Ferenc M. *The Protestant Clergy in the Great Plains and Mountain*

West, 1865–1915. Albuquerque, N.Mex.: University of New Mexico Press, 1988.

4q. North America and Caribbean, United States of America: Twentieth Century

Cavert, Samuel McC. *The American Churches in the Ecumenical Movement, 1900–1968.* New York: Association Press, 1968.

————. *Church Cooperation and Unity in America: A Historical Review, 1900–1970.* New York: Association Press, 1970.

Coalter, Milton J., John M. Mulder, and Louis B. Weeks, eds. *The Presbyterian Presence: The Twentieth-Century Experience.* 7 vols. Louisville, Ky.: Westminster John Knox, 1990–1992.

Hunter, James D. *American Evangelicalism: Conservative Religion and the Quandary of Modernity.* New Brunswick, N.J.: Rutgers University Press, 1983.

Hutchison, William R., ed. *Between the Times: The Travail of the Protestant Establishment in America, 1900–1960.* Cambridge Studies in Religion and American Public Life. Cambridge: Cambridge University Press, 1989.

Lotz, David W., Donald W. Shriver, and John F. Wilson, eds. *Altered Landscapes: Christianity in America, 1935–1985: Essays in Honor of Robert T. Handy.* Grand Rapids, Mich.: Eerdmans, 1989.

Marty, Martin E. *Modern American Religions.* Vol. 1, *The Irony of It All, 1893–1919.* Chicago: University of Chicago Press, 1986.

————. *Modern American Religions.* Vol. 2, *The Noise of Conflict, 1919–1941.* Chicago: University of Chicago Press, 1991.

————. *Modern American Religions.* Vol. 3. *Under God, Indivisible, 1941–1960.* Chicago: University of Chicago Press, 1996.

McKinney, William, and Dean R. Hoge. "Community and Congregational Factors in the Growth and Decline of Protestant Churches." *Journal for the Scientific Study of Religion* 22 (1983): 51–66.

Meyer, Donald B. *The Protestant Search for Political Realism, 1919–1941.* 2d ed. Middletown, Conn.: Wesleyan University Press, 1988.

Roof, Wade Clark, and William McKinney. *American Mainline Religion.* New Brunswick, N.J.: Rutgers University Press, 1987.

Sochen, June. *Movers and Shakers: Women Thinkers and Activists, 1900–1970.* New York: Quadrangle, 1973.

Stelt, John C. Vander. *Philosophy and Scripture: A Study in Old Princeton and Westminster Theology.* Marlton, N.J.: Mack Publishing, 1978.

Wells, David F., and John D. Woodbridge, eds. *The Evangelicals: What They Believe, Who They Are, Where They Are Changing.* Rev. ed. Grand Rapids, Mich.: Baker Book House, 1977.

Wuthnow, Robert. *The Restructuring of American Religion: Society and Faith since World War II.* Studies in Church and State. Princeton: Princeton University Press, 1988.

Zwaanstra, H. *Reformed Thought and Experience in a New World: A Study of the Christian Reformed Church and Its American Environment, 1890–1918.* Kampen: Kok, 1973.

4r. North America and Caribbean, United States of America: Biography

Barkley, John Montieth. *Francis Makemie of Ramelton: Father of American Presbyterianism.* Belfast: Presbyterian Historical Society of Ireland, 1981.

Bender, Norman J. *Winning the West For Christ: Sheldon Jackson and Presbyterianism on the Rocky Mountain Frontier, 1869–1880.* Albuquerque, N.Mex.: University of New Mexico Press, 1996.

Brackenridge, R. D. *Eugene Carson Blake: Prophet with Portfolio.* New York: Seabury, 1978.

Brown, Ira V. *Lyman Abbott: Christian Evolutionist.* Reprint, Westport, Conn.: Greenwood Press, 1970.

Coalter, Milton J., Jr. *Gilbert Tennent, Son of Thunder: A Case Study of Continental Pietism's Impact on the First Great Awakening in the Middle Colonies.* Westport, Conn.: Greenwood Press, 1986.

Collins, Varnum L. *President Witherspoon: A Biography.* 2 vols. 1925. Reprint, New York: Arno, 1969.

Cross, Barbara M. *Horace Bushnell: Minister to a Changing America.* Chicago: University of Chicago Press, 1958.

Dorn, Jacob H. *Washington Gladden: Prophet of the Social Gospel.* Columbus, Ohio: Ohio State University, 1966.

Flory, Margaret. *Moments in Time: One Woman's Ecumenical Journey.* New York: Friendship Press, 1995.

Fox, Richard W. *Reinhold Niebuhr: A Biography.* Reprint, San Francisco: Harper & Row, 1987.

Gaustad, Edwin S. *Liberty of Conscience: Roger Williams in America.* Grand Rapids, Mich.: Eerdmans, 1991.

Giltner, John H. *Moses Stuart.* Atlanta: Scholars Press, 1988.

Griffin, Edward M. *Old Brick: Charles Chauncy of Boston, 1705–1787.* Minneapolis: University of Minnesota, 1980.

Grissen, Lillian, ed. *For Such a Time as This: Twenty-Six Women of Vision and Faith Tell Their Stories.* Grand Rapids, Mich.: Eerdmans, 1991.

Gustafson, Robert K. *James Woodrow (1828–1907): Scientist, Theologian, Intellectual Leader.* Lewiston, N.Y.: Mellen Press, 1995.

Hardman, Keith J. *Charles Grandison Finney, 1792–1875: Revivalist and Reformer.* Grand Rapids, Mich.: Baker Book House, 1990.

Henry, Stuart C. *Unvanquished Puritan: A Portrait of Lyman Beecher.* Grand Rapids, Mich.: Eerdmans, 1973.

Hodge, Archibald A. *The Life of Charles Hodge.* Religion in America. Reprint, New York: Arno, 1969.

Hoeveler, J. David. *James McCosh and the Scottish Intellectual Tradition: From Glasgow to Princeton.* Princeton: Princeton University Press, 1981.

Jeffrey, Julie Roy. *Converting the West: A Biography of Narcissa Whitman.* Norman: University of Oklahoma Press, 1991.

Lazell, J. A. *Alaskan Apostle: The Life Story of Sheldon Jackson.* New York: Harper, 1960.

Longfield, B. J. *The Presbyterian Controversy: Fundamentalists, Modernists, and Moderates.* New York: Oxford University Press, 1991.

McLoughlin, William G. *Billy Sunday Was His Real Name.* Chicago: University of Chicago Press, 1955.

Mead, Sidney E. *Nathaniel William Taylor, 1786–1858: A Connecticut Liberal.* Chicago: University of Chicago Press, 1942.

Middlekauff, Robert. *The Mathers: Three Generations of Puritan Intellectuals, 1596–1728.* Reprint, New York: Oxford University Press, 1976.

Miller, Perry. *Jonathan Edwards.* New England Writers Series. Reprint, Amherst: University of Massachusetts Press, 1981.

Minus, Paul M. *Walter Rauschenbusch, American Reformer.* New York: Macmillan, 1988.

Morgan, Edmund S. *The Puritan Dilemma: The Story of John Winthrop.* The Library of American Biography. Boston: Little, Brown, 1958.

Nichols, James H. *Romanticism in American Theology: Nevin and Schaff at Mercersburg.* 1961. Reprint, Ann Arbor, Mich.: University Microfilms, 1980.

Pilcher, George W. *Samuel Davies, Apostle of Dissent in Colonial Virginia.* Knoxville: University of Tennessee Press, 1971.

Rugoff, Milton. *The Beechers: An American Family in the Nineteenth Century.* New York: Harper & Row, 1981.

Schlenther, Boyd S. *The Life and Writings of Francis Makemie.* Philadelphia: Presbyterian Historical Society, 1971.

Shriver, George H. *Philip Schaff: Christian Scholar and Ecumenical Prophet.* Macon, Ga.: Mercer, 1987.

Silverman, Kenneth. *The Life and Times of Cotton Mather.* New York: Harper & Row, 1984.

Smith, John E. *Jonathan Edwards: Puritan, Preacher, Philosopher.* Notre Dame, Ind.: University of Notre Dame Press, 1992.

Stonehouse, Ned B. *J. Gresham Machen: A Biographical Memoir.* 3d ed. Carlisle, Pa.: Banner of Truth Trust, 1987.

Thompson, Dean K. "Henry Pitney Van Dusen: Ecumenical Statesman." Ph.D. diss., Union Theological Seminary in Virginia, 1974.

Van Dyken, Seymour. *Samuel Willard, 1640–1707: Preacher of Orthodoxy in an Era of Change.* Grand Rapids, Mich.: Eerdmans, 1972.

Walworth, Arthur. *Woodrow Wilson.* 3d ed. 2 vols. Library of the Presidents. New York: Longmans, Green, 1958. Reprint, Norwalk, Conn.: Easton, 1985.

Wentz, Richard E. *John Williamson Nevin, American Theologian.* New York: Oxford University Press, 1997.

Wenzke, A. "Timothy Dwight: The Enlightened Puritan." Ph.D. diss., Pennsylvania State University, 1983.

Williams, Selma R. *Divine Rebel: The Life of Anne Marbury Hutchinson.* New York: Holt, Rinehart, and Winston, 1981.

Ziff, Larzer. *The Career of John Cotton: Puritanism and the American Experience.* Princeton, N.J.: Princeton University Press, 1962.

4s. North America and Caribbean, United States of America: Theology and Culture

Bercovitch, Sacvan. *The American Jeremiad.* Madison: University of Wisconsin Press, 1978.

Guder, Darrell, ed. *Missional Church: A Theological Vision for the Sending of the Church in North America.* Grand Rapids, Mich.: Eerdmans, 1998.

Hamstra, Sam, Jr., and Arie J. Griffioen, eds. *Reformed Confessionalism in Nineteenth-Century America: Essays on the Thought of John Williamson Nevin.* Lanham, Md.: Scarecrow Press, 1995.

Heimert, Alan. *Religion and the American Mind: From the Great Awakening to the Revolution.* Reprint, Cambridge, Mass.: Harvard University Press, 1985.

Hill, Samuel S. *The South and the North in American Religion.* Athens, Ga.: University of Georgia Press, 1980.

Holifield, E. Brooks. *The Gentlemen Theologians: American Theology in Southern Culture, 1759–1860.* Durham, N.C.: Duke University Press, 1978.

Hutchison, William F. *The Modernist Impulse in American Protestantism.* Reprint, New York: Oxford University Press, 1982.

Kuklick, Bruce. *Churchmen and Philosophers.* New Haven, Conn.: Yale University Press, 1985.

Loetscher, Lefferts A. *The Broadening Church: A Study of Theological Issues in the Presbyterian Church since 1869.* 1954. Reprint, Philadelphia: University of Pennsylvania Press, 1964.

Marsden, George M. *Fundamentalism and American Culture: The Shap-*

ing of Twentieth Century Evangelicalism, 1870–1925. New York: Oxford University Press, 1982.

May, Henry F. *The Enlightenment in America.* Reprint, New York: Oxford University Press, 1978.

McLoughlin, W. G. *Revivals, Awakenings, and Reforms.* Chicago: University of Chicago Press, 1978.

Miller, Perry. *The Life of the Mind in America: From the Revolution to the Civil War.* Reprint, New York: Harcourt, Brace & World, 1966.

————. *The New England Mind: From Colony to Province.* Reprint, Cambridge, Mass.: Harvard University Press, 1983.

————. *The New England Mind: The Seventeenth Century.* Reprint, Cambridge, Mass.: Harvard University Press, 1983.

Murdock, Kenneth B. *Literature and Theology in Colonial New England.* Cambridge, Mass.: Harvard University Press, 1949.

Sandeen, Ernest R. *The Roots of Fundamentalism: British and American Millenarianism, 1800–1930.* Chicago: University of Chicago Press, 1970.

Schneider, Herbert W. *The Puritan Mind.* 1930. Reprint, Ann Arbor, Mich.: University of Michigan, 1961.

Smith, Elwyn Allen. *The Presbyterian Ministry in American Culture.* Philadelphia: Presbyterian Historical Society, 1962.

Stout, Harry S. *The New England Soul: Preaching and Religious Culture in Colonial New England.* New Haven, Conn.: Yale University Press, 1986.

Valeri, Mark R. *Law and Providence in Joseph Bellamy's New England: The Origins of the New Divinity in Revolutionary America.* New York: Oxford University Press, 1994.

Wells, David F., ed. *Reformed Theology in America: A History of Its Modern Development.* Reprint, Grand Rapids, Mich.: Baker Book House, 1997.

Ziff, Larzar. *Puritanism in America: New Culture in a New World.* New York: Viking, 1973.

Oceania

1a. Oceania, Pacific Region: Reference Works

Australasian Religion Index. Wagga Wagga, N.S.W.: Riverina-Murray Institute of Higher Education, Center for Information Studies, 1988–.

Day, A. Grove. *Pacific Islands Literature: One Hundred Basic Books.* Honolulu: University of Hawaii Press, 1971.

Douglas, Leonora Misende, ed. *World Christianity: Oceania.* Monrovia, Calif.: Missions Advanced Research and Communications, 1986.

Stratigos, Susan, ed. *Pacific Island Theses and Dissertations: A Bibliography.* New York: Elsevier, 1996.

Streit, P. Robert, and P. Johannes Dindinger. *Missionsliteratur von Australien und Ozeanium, 1525–1950*. Bibliotheca Missionum. Vol 21. Freiburg: Verlag Herder, 1955.

Turner, Harold W. *Bibliography of New Religious Movements in Primal Societies*. Vol 3, *Oceania*. Boston: G. K. Hall, 1990.

1b. Oceania, Pacific Region: Histories and Studies

Afeaki, Emiliana, Ron Crocombe, and John McClaren, eds. *Religious Cooperation in the Pacific Islands*. Suva, Fiji: University of the South Pacific, 1983.

Barker, John, ed. *Christianity in Oceania: Ethnographic Perspectives*. Lanham, Md.: University Press of America, 1990.

Boutilier, James A., Daniel T. Hughes and Sharon Tiffany, eds. *Mission, Church, and Sect in Oceania*. Ann Arbor, Mich.: University of Michigan Press, 1978.

Coop, William L., ed. *Pacific People Sing Out Strong*. New York: Friendship, 1982.

Forman, Charles W. *The Island Churches of the South Pacific: Emergence in the Twentieth Century*. Maryknoll, N.Y.: Orbis Books, 1982.

———. *The Voice of Many Waters: The Story of the Life and Ministry of the Pacific Conference of Churches in the last 25 Years*. Suva, Fiji: Lotu Pasifika, 1986.

Garrett, John. *Footsteps in the Sea: Christianity in Oceania to World War.* Vol. 2, *Suva*. Institute for Pacific Studies, 1992.

———. *To Live among the Stars: Christian Origins in Oceania*. Geneva: World Council of Churches; Suva, Fiji: Institute of Pacific Studies, 1982.

Garrett, John, and John Mavor. *Worship the Pacific Way*. Suva, Fiji: Lotu Pacifika Productions, 1973.

Gunson, W. Niel. *Messengers of Grace: Evangelical Missionaries in the South Seas, 1797–1860*. Melbourne: Oxford University Press, 1978.

Miller, Char, ed. *Missions and Missionaries in the Pacific*. New York: Mellen Press, 1985.

Munro, Doug, and Andrew Thornley, eds. *The Covenant Makers: Islander Missionaries in the Pacific*. Suva, Fiji: Pacific Theological College, 1996.

Tippett, Alan R. *People Movements in Southern Polynesia: Studies in the Dynamics of Church-Planting and Growth in Tahiti, New Zealand, Tonga, and Samoa*. Chicago: Moody Press, 1971.

1c. Oceania, Pacific Region: Biographies

Gutch, John. *Beyond the Reefs: The Life of John Williams, Missionary*. London: Macdonald & Jane's, 1974.

———. *Martyr of the Islands: The Life and Death of John Coleridge Patteson*. London: Hodder & Stoughton, 1971.

Tippett, Alan R. *Deep Sea Canoe: The Story of Third World Missionaries in the South Pacific*. Pasadena, Calif.: William Carey Library, 1977.

2a. Oceania, Australia: Reference Works

The Basis of Union: 1992 Edition. Melbourne: Uniting Church Press, 1992.

Gillman, Ian, ed. *Many Faiths One Nation: A Guide to the Major Faiths and Denominations in Australia*. Sydney, N.S.W.: Collins Australia, 1988.

Hynd, Douglas. *Australian Christianity in Outline: A Statistical Survey and Directory*. Australia: Lancer Books, 1984.

Jenkin, Coralie E. J. *Collections of Religion and Theology in Australia and New Zealand*. Adelaide: Auslib Press, 1992.

McCaughey, J. Davis. *Commentary on the Basis of Union of the Uniting Church*. Melbourne: Uniting Church Press, 1980.

2b. Oceania, Australia: Histories and Studies

Bardon, Richard. *The Centenary History of the Presbyterian Church of Queensland*. Brisbane: Presbyterian Church of Queensland, 1949.

Bowes, Keith, ed. *Partners: One Hundred Years of Mission Overseas by Churches of Christ in Australia, 1891–1991*. Adelaide: Vital Publications, 1990.

Dutney, Andrew. *Manifesto for Renewal: The Shaping of a New Church*. Melbourne: Uniting Church Press, 1986.

Garrett, John. *A Way in the Sea: Aspects of Pacific Christian History with Reference to Australia*. Melbourne: Spectrum Publications, 1982.

Harrison, J. *Baptism of Fire*. Melbourne: Uniting Church Press, 1986.

Kiek, Edward S. *Our First Hundred Years: The Centenary Record of the South Australian Congregational Union*. Adelaide: South Australian Congregational Union, 1950.

Lockley, A. Lindsay. "The Foundation, Development, and Influence of Congregationalism in Australia with Emphasis on the Nineteenth Century." Ph.D. diss., University of Queensland, 1969.

Macdonald, Aeneas. *One Hundred Years of Presbyterianism in Victoria*. Melbourne: Robertson & Mullens, 1937.

Phillips, Walter. *Defending "A Christian Country" : Churchmen and Society in New South Wales in the 1880s and After*. St. Lucia, Queensland: University of Queensland Press, 1981.

Scrimgeour, Robert J. *Some Scots Were Here: A History of the Presbyterian Church in South Australia, 1839–1977*. Adelaide: Lutheran Publishing House, 1986.

Thompson, Roger C. *Religion in Australia: A History*. New York: Oxford University Press, 1994.

White, C. A. *The Challenge of the Years: A History of the Presbyterian*

Church of Australia in the State of New South Wales. Sydney: Angus & Robertson, 1951.

2c. Oceania, Australia: Biographies

Baker, Donald W.A. *Days of Wrath: A Life of John Dunmore Lang.* Carlton, Vic.: Melbourne University Press, 1985.

Cameron, Peter S. *Heretic.* Sydney: Doubleday, 1994.

Emilsen, Susan E. *A Whiff of Heresy: Samuel Angus and the Presbyterian Church in New South Wales.* Kensington, N.S.W.: New South Wales University Press, 1991.

McKenzie, Maisie. *Fred McKay: Successor to Flynn of the Inland.* Brisbane, Qld.: Boolarong Publications, 1990.

Miller, R. S. *Thomas Dove and the Tasmanian Aborigines.* Melbourne: Spectrum Publications, 1985.

Phillips, Walter. *James Jefferis: Prophet of Federation.* Kew, Vic.: Australian Scholarly Publications, 1993.

Ruldolph, Ivan. *John Flynn: Of Flying Doctors and Frontier Faith.* North Blackburn, Vic.: Dove, 1996.

3a. Oceania, New Zealand: Reference Works

Fraser, I. W., ed. *Register of Ministers 1840–1989* [of Presbyterian Church of New Zealand]. Lower Hutt: n.p., 1990.

Lineham, P. J., and A. R. Grigg. *Religious History of New Zealand: A Bibliography.* Palmerston North, N.Z.: Department of History, Massey University, 1984.

McLauchlan, Gordon, ed. *New Zealand Encyclopedia.* Auckland: David Bateman, 1984.

3b. Oceania, New Zealand: Histories and Studies

Booth, Ken, and John Broadbent, et al., eds. *The Farthest Jerusalem: Four Lectures on the Origins of Christianity in Otago.* Dunedin, N.Z.: University of Otago, 1993.

Breward, Ian. *Grace and Truth.* Dunedin: Presbyterian Church, 1975. History of Knox Theological College.

Chambers, J. B. *"A Peculiar People": Congregationalism in New Zealand, 1840–1984.* n.p.: Congregational Union, 1984.

Colless, Brian, and Peter Donovan, eds. *Religion in New Zealand Society.* 2d ed. Palmerston North, N.Z.: Dunmore Press, 1985.

Collie, John. *The Story of the Otago Free Church Settlement, 1848–1948: A Century's Growth by a Southern Sea.* Christchurch: Presbyterian Bookroom, 1948.

Davidson, Allan K. *Christianity in Aotearoa: A History of Church and Society in New Zealand.* Wellington: Education for Ministry, 1991.

Davidson, Allan K., and Peter J. Lineham, eds. *Transplanted Christianity:*

Documents Illustrating Aspects of New Zealand Church History. 2d ed. Palmerston North, N.Z.: Dunmore Press, 1989.

Dickson, John. *History of the Presbyterian Church of New Zealand.* Dunedin: J. Wilkie, 1899.

Elder, John Rawson. *The History of the Presbyterian Church of New Zealand, 1840–1940.* Christchurch: Presbyterian Book Room, 1940.

Grigg, A. R., and Peter J. Lineham. *The Religious History of New Zealand.* 3d ed. Palmerston North, N.Z.: Dept. of History, Massey University, 1984.

Jackson, H. R. *Churches and People in Australia and New Zealand.* Wellington, N.Z.: Allen & Unwin, 1987.

Laughton, J. G. *From Forest Trail to City Street: The Story of the Presbyterian Church among the Maori People.* Christchurch: Presbyterian Book Room, 1961.

Matheson, Peter. *The Finger of God in the Disruption: Scottish Principles and New Zealand Realities.* Alexandria, N.Z.: Presbyterian Church of Aotearoa New Zealand, 1993.

McEldowney, Dennis, ed. *Presbyterians in Aotearoa, 1840–1990.* Wellington: Presbyterian Church of New Zealand, 1990.

McKean, J. *The Church in a Special Colony: A History of the Presbyterian Synod of Otago and Southland.* Dunedin: n.p., 1994.

Murray, J. S. *A Century of Growth: Presbyterian Overseas Mission Work, 1869–1969.* Christchurch, N. Z.: Presbyterian Book Room, n.d.

Oliver, W. H., and B. R. Williams, eds. *Oxford History of New Zealand.* Wellington: Oxford University Press, 1981.

Nichol, Christopher, and James Veitch, eds. *Religion in New Zealand.* Wellington, N.Z.: Christopher Nichol, 1983.

Rae, Simon. *From Relief to Social Service. A History of the Presbyterian Social Service Association of Otago, 1905–1981.* Dunedin: n.p., 1981.

3c. Oceania, New Zealand: Biographies

Belmer, Roy. *Hewn from the Rock: A Memoir of the Very Reverend J. D. Salmond . . . of Queenstown and Dunedin.* Dunedin, N.Z.: Otogo Church Bookstore, [1976?].

MacPherson, M. *The Life and Labours of a Native African Missionary* [J. B. Radasi]. Gisborne, N.Z.: Gisborne Herald, 1966.

New Zealand Department of Internal Affairs. *The Dictionary of New Zealand Biography.* Vol. 1, *1769–1869.* Wellington: Allen & Unwin, 1990.

O'Grady, Alison. *Alan Brash: Voice for Unity.* Auckland, N.Z.: Pace Publications, 1991.

Scholefield, Guy H., ed. *A Dictionary of New Zealand Biography.* 2 vols. Wellington: Dept. of Internal Affairs, 1940.

4. Oceania, Pacific Ocean Islands: Cook Islands
Concise Dictionary of the Christian World Mission: Cyclopaedia of Samoa, Tonga, Tahiti, and the Cook Islands. Sydney: McCarron, Stewart, 1907. Reprint, Papakura, N.Z.: Mcmillan, 1983.

Coppell, William. *Bibliography of the Cook Islands.* Canberra: Australian National University, 1970.

Williams, John. *A Narrative of Missionary Enterprises in the South Seas.* London: John Snow, 1837.

5a. Oceania, Pacific Ocean Islands: French Polynesia: Reference Works
Concise Dictionary of the Christian World Mission: Cyclopaedia of Samoa, Tonga, Tahiti, and the Cook Islands. 1907. Reprint, Papakura, N.Z.: Mcmillan, 1983.

5b. Oceania, Pacific Ocean Islands: French Polynesia: Primary Sources
Williams, John. *A Narrative of Missionary Enterprises in the South Seas.* London: John Snow, 1837.

5c. Oceania, Pacific Ocean Islands: French Polynesia: Histories and Studies
Aldrich, Robert. *The French Presence in the South Pacific, 1842–1940.* London: Macmillan, 1990.

Davies, John. *History of the Tahitian Mission, 1799–1830.* Edited by Colin Newbury. Cambridge: Hakluyt Society, 1961.

Hoiore, Joel. "Soteriologie et Theologie de l'inter-religieux culturel Polynesien Oceanien." Ph.D. diss., Montpellier, France, 1992.

Miles, J., and E. Shaw. *The French Presence in the South Pacific, 1938–1990.* Auckland: Greenpeace New Zealand, 1990.

Newbury, Colin. *Tahiti Nui: Change and Survival in French Polynesia, 1767–1945.* Honolulu: University of Hawaii Press, 1980.

Saura, Bruno. *Politique et Religion a Tahiti.* Pirae, Tahiti: Polymages-Scoop, 1993.

Vernier, Henri. *Au vent des Cyclones: Puai noa mai te vero.* Papeete, Tahiti: Eglise évangélique de Polynésie française, 1985.

6a. Oceania, Pacific Ocean Islands: Hawaii: Primary Sources
Benedetto, Robert. *The Hawaii Journals of the New England Missionaries, 1813–1894: A Guide to the Hawaiian Mission Children's Society Library.* Honolulu: Hawaiian Mission Children's Society, 1982.

Bingham, Hiram. *A Residence of Twenty-One Years in the Sandwich Islands.* Reprint, Rutland, Vt.: Charles E. Tuttle, 1981.

Miller, Char. *Selected Writings of Hiram Bingham (1814–1869), Missionary to the Hawaiian Islands.* Lewiston, N.Y.: Mellen Press, 1988.

6b. Oceania, Pacific Ocean Islands: Hawaii: Histories and Studies

Daws, Gavan. *Shoal of Time: A History of the Hawaiian Islands.* Honolulu: University of Hawaii Press, 1968.

Gallagher, Mark E. "No More a Christian Nation: The Protestant Church in Territorial Hawaii, 1898–1919." Ph.D. diss., University of Hawaii, 1983.

Kuykendall, Ralph S. *The Hawaiian Kingdom.* 3 vols. Honolulu: University Press of Hawaii, 1938, 1953, 1967.

Loomis, Albertine. *To All People: A History of the Hawaii Conference of the United Church of Christ.* Honolulu: Hawaii Conference of the United Church of Christ, 1970.

Morris, Nancy Jane. "Hawaiian Missionaries Abroad, 1852–1909." Ph.D. diss., University of Hawaii, 1987.

Wagner, Sandra E. "Mission and Motivation: The Theology of the Early American Mission in Hawaii." *Hawaiian Journal of History* 19 (1985): 62–70.

Wagner-Wright, Sandra. *Sojourners among Strangers: The Structure of the Missionary Call to the Sandwich Islands, 1790–1830.* San Francisco: Mellen Press, 1991.

Zwiep, Mary. *Pilgrim Path: The First Company of Women Missionaries to Hawaii.* Madison: The University of Wisconsin Press, 1991.

6c. Oceania, Pacific Ocean Islands: Hawaii: Biographies

Hawaiian Mission Children's Society. *Missionary Album: Portraits and Biographical Sketches of the American Protestant Missionaries to the Hawaiian Islands.* Honolulu: Hawaiian Mission Children's Society, 1969.

Miller, Char. *Fathers and Sons: The Bingham Family and the American Mission.* Philadelphia: Temple University, 1982.

Nakano, Jiro. *Samurai Missionary: The Reverend Shiro Sokabe.* Honolulu: Hawaii Conference of the United Church of Christ, 1984.

7. Oceania, Pacific Ocean Islands: Micronesia

Bliss, Theodora Crosby. *Micronesia, Fifty Years in the Island World: A History of the American Board.* Boston: American Board of Commissioners for Foreign Missions, 1906.

Hanlon, David. *Upon a Stone Altar: A History of the Island of Pohnpei to 1890.* Honolulu: University of Hawaii Press, 1988.

Price, Francis M. *Guam: A Sketch of the Mission of the American Board.* Boston: The American Board, 1904.

8. Oceania, Pacific Ocean Islands: Niue

Chapman, Terry. *Niue: A History of the Island.* Translated by Leslie Rex. Suva, Fiji: Government of Niue, 1982.

McEwen, J. M. *Niue Dictionary.* Wellington: Department of Maori and Island Affairs, 1970.

9a. Oceania, Pacific Ocean Islands: Papua New Guinea: Histories and Studies

Crocombe, Ron, and Marjorie Crocombe, eds. *Polynesian Missions in Melanesia: From Samoa, Cook Islands and Tonga to Papua New Guinea and New Caledonia.* Suva, Fiji: University of the South Pacific, 1982.

Flannery, Wendy, ed. *Religious Movements in Melanesia Today.* 3 vols. Goroka Papua, New Guinea: Melanesian Institute, 1983–1984.

Fugmann, Gernot, ed. *The Birth of an Indigenous Church.* Goroka, Papua New Guinea: Melanesian Institute, 1986.

Hilliard, David. *God's Gentlemen: A History of the Melanesian Mission, 1849–1942.* St. Lucia, Queensland: University of Queensland Press, 1978.

O'Brien, Helen, ed. *Christian Worship and Melanesia.* Papua New Guinea: Melanesian Institute, 1980.

Tippett, Alan R. *Solomon Islands Christianity: A Study in Growth and Obstruction.* London: Lutterworth Press, 1967.

Whiteman, Darrell L. *Melanesians and Missionaries.* Padadena, Calif.: William Carey Library, 1983.

Williams, Ronald G. *The United Church in Papua New Guinea and the Solomon Islands.* Rabaul: Trinity Press, 1972.

9b. Oceania, Pacific Ocean Islands: Papua New Guinea: Biographies

Langmore, Diane. *Missionary Lives, Papua, 1874–1914.* Honolulu: University of Hawaii Press, 1989.

———. *Tamate—A King: James Chalmers in New Guinea, 1877–1901.* Carlton, Vic.: Melbourne University Press, 1974.

10a. Oceania, Pacific Ocean Islands: Samoa: Reference Works

Concise Dictionary of the Christian World Mission: Cyclopaedia of Samoa, Tonga, Tahiti, and the Cook Islands. 1907. Reprint, Papakura, N.Z.: Mcmillan, 1983.

Holmes, Lowell D., ed. *Samoan Islands Bibliography.* Wichita, Kans.: Poly Concepts, 1984.

Milner, G. B. *Samoan Dictionary.* Auckland: Auckland University Press, 1992.

10b. Oceania, Pacific Ocean Islands: Samoa: Primary Sources

Moyle, Richard, ed. *The Samoan Journals of John Williams, 1830 and 1832.* Canberra: Australian National University Press, 1984.

Williams, John. *A Narrative of Missionary Enterprises in the South Seas.* London: John Snow, 1837.

10c. Oceania, Pacific Ocean Islands: Samoa: Histories and Studies

Falatoese, K. T. *Tala Faasaolopito o le Ekalesia Samoa (L.M.S.): A History of the Samoan Church.* Pia: Malua Printing Press, 1961.

Setu, Fa atulituili. *The Ministry in the Making: A History of the Church in Samoa, 1830–1900.* Suva, Fiji: Pacific Theological College, 1988.

11. Oceania, Pacific Ocean Islands: Tuvalu

Laracy, Hugh, ed. *Tuvalu: A History.* Suva, Fiji: Institute of Pacific Studies, 1983.

Noricks, Jay S. *A Tuvalu Dictionary.* 2 vols. New Haven, Conn.: Human Area Relations Files, 1981.

12a. Oceania, Pacific Ocean Islands: Vanuatu: Histories and Studies

Flannery, Wendy, ed. *Religious Movements in Melanesia Today.* 3 vols. Goroka Papua, New Guinea: Melanesian Institute, 1983–1984.

Gillan, Helen R. *Vanuatu Victory: Four Generations of Sharing Christian Faith in the Pacific.* Richmond, Vic.: Spectrum Publications, 1988.

Miller, J. Graham. *Live: A History of Church Planting in Vanuatu.* 7 vols. Sydney: Committees on Christian Education and Overseas Missions, Presbyterian Church of Australia, 1978–1990.

Natosansan, Masia. "The Presbyterian Church of Vanuatu: Mission to Church: An Independent or Dependent Church? 1848–1980." B.D. thesis, Pacific Theological College, Suva, 1989.

Parsonson, G. S. "La Mission Presbytérienne des Nouvelles-Hébrides, son histoire et son rôle politique et social." *Journal de la Société des Océanistes* 12 (Décembre 1956): 107–137.

12b. Oceania, Pacific Ocean Islands: Vanuatu: Biography

Miller, R. S. *Misi Gete: John Geddie: Pioneer Missionary to the New Hebrides.* Launceston, Australia: Presbyterian Church of Tasmania, 1975.

Paton, Frank Hume L. *The Triumph of the Gospel in the New Hebrides: The Life Story of Lomai of Lenakel.* London: Hodder & Stoughton, 1903.

Paton, James, ed. *John G. Paton, DD, Missionary to the New Hebrides: An Autobiography.* 2 vols. New York: Fleming H. Revell, 1889.

Appendix 1
The General Councils of the Presbyterian World Alliance and the General Assemblies of the International Congregational Council

ALLIANCE OF REFORMED CHURCHES

1. 1877 Edinburgh, Scotland
2. 1880 Philadelphia, Pa., USA
3. 1884 Belfast, Northern Ireland
4. 1888 London, England
5. 1892 Toronto, Canada
6. 1896 Glasgow, Scotland
7. 1899 Washington, D.C., USA
8. 1904 Liverpool, England
9. 1909 New York, N.Y., USA
10. 1913 Aberdeen, Scotland
11. 1921 Pittsburgh, Pa., USA
12. 1925 Cardiff, Wales
13. 1929 Boston, Mass., USA
14. 1933 Belfast, Northern Ireland
15. 1937 Montreal, Canada
16. 1948 Geneva, Switzerland
17. 1954 Princeton, N.J., USA
18. 1959 Sao Paulo, Brazil
19. 1964 Frankfurt am Main, FRG

WORLD ALLIANCE OF REFORMED CHURCHES (PRESBYTERIAN AND CONGREGATIONAL)

20. 1970 Nairobi, Kenya (Uniting General Council)
21. 1977 St. Andrews, Scotland (Centennial Consultation)
22. 1982 Ottawa, Canada
23. 1989 Seoul, Korea
24. 1997 Debrecen, Hungary

INTERNATIONAL CONGREGATIONAL COUNCIL

1. 1891 London, England
2. 1899 Boston, Mass., USA
3. 1908 Edinburgh, Scotland
4. 1920 Boston, Mass., USA
5. 1930 Bournemouth, England
6. 1949 Wellesley, Mass., USA
7. 1953 St. Andrews, Scotland
8. 1958 Hartford, Conn., USA
9. 1962 Rotterdam, Netherlands

Appendix 2   Theological Comparison of Major Reformed Confessions

Topic	SECOND HELVETIC CONFESSION _Chapter_	SCOTS CONFESSION _Chapter_	HEIDELBERG CATECHISM _Question_	WESTMINSTER CONFESSION _Chapter_	SHORTER CATECHISM _Question_	BARMEN DECLARATION _Thesis_
Scripture	I–II	XVIII–XX	21	I	2–3, 88–90	1
Trinity	III	I	25	II	6	
Creation	VII	II	26	IV	(1), 9–10	
Providence	VI	I	1, 27–28	V	11–12	
Covenant	XX	IV–V	19, 74	VII, XIX	20	
Sin	VIII–IX	III	3–11	VI, IX	12–20, 82–85	
Election	X	VII–VIII	26, 31, 52, 54	III, X	7–8, 20	
Jesus Christ	XI	V–XI	29–52	VIII	21–28	1–2
Holy Spirit	III, etc.	XII	53–64	XXXIV		
Law	XII	XIV–XV	3–4, 92–115	XIX, (VII, XIII)	39–81	
Gospel	XIII	IV–V	19, etc.	VII, XXXV		
Repentance	XIV	(XII)		XV	87	
Justification	XV	(XV)	31–34, 60–64	XI	32–33	
Faith	XVI	XII	1–2, 21, 32, 53, 60–61, 74	XIV	86, (30–38)	2
Christian Life	XVI	XII–XIV	Part III	XIII, XVI, XIX–XX	35, 39–82	2–3
Church	XVII–XVIII	V, XVI, XVIII, XX to XXII	54, 85	XXV–XXVI, XXX–XXXI		3–4
Mission				XXXV		6
Sacraments	XIX	XXI–XXIII	65–68	XXVII	88, 91–93	
Baptism	XX	XXI–XXIII	69–74	XXVIII	94, 95	
Lord's Supper	XXI	XXI–XXIII	75–85	XXIX	96–97	
Worship	IV–V, XX–XXVII			XXI–XX	45–62	
Marriage	XXIX			XXIV		
State	XXX	XXIV		XXIII		
Consummation	(XI)	XVII, XXV	57–58	XXXII	37–38	5

Source: Edward A. Dowey Jr., _A Commentary on the Confession of 1967 and an Introduction to "The Book of Confessions"_ (Philadelphia: Westminster Press, 1968), 280–81. Used by permission.

Appendix 3
Member Churches of the World Alliance of Reformed Churches*

AFRICA

Algeria

Protestant Church in Algeria (Église protestante d'Algérie)

Angola

Evangelical Congregational Church in Angola (Igreja Evangélica Congregacional em Angola)
Evangelical Pentecostal Mission of Angola (Missao Evangelica Pentecostal de Angola)
Evangelical Reformed Church in Angola (Igreja Evangélica Reformada de Angola)

Botswana

Dutch Reformed Church in Botswana

Burkina Faso

Association of Reformed Evangelical Churches of Burkina Faso (Association des Églises évangéliques réformées du Burkina Faso)

Cameroon

Native Baptist Church of Cameroon (Église Baptiste Camerounaise)
Presbyterian Church in Cameroon
Presbyterian Church of Cameroon (Église presbytérriene camerounaise)

---

*Churches marked with an asterisk are selected nonmember churches, several of which are discussed in the dictionary.

Central African Republic

Protestant Church of Christ the King (Église protestante du Christ-roi)

Democratic Republic of Congo

Evangelical Community in Congo (Communauté évangélique du Congo)
Presbyterian Community in Congo (Communauté presbytérienne au Congo)
Presbyterian Community of East Kasai (Communauté presbytérienne au Kasai oriental)
Presbyterian Community of Kinshasa (Communauté presbytérienne de Kinshasa)
Presbyterian Community of West Kasai (Communauté presbytérienne au Kasai occidental)
Protestant Community of Shaba (Communauté protestante du Shaba)
Reformed Community of Presbyterians (Communauté réformée des presbytériens)

Republic of Congo

Evangelical Church of Congo (Église évangelique du Congo)

Egypt

Synod of the Nile of the Evangelical Church

Equatorial Guinea

Reformed Church of Equatorial Guinea (Iglesia Reformada de Guinea Ecuatorial)

Ethiopia

Ethiopian Evangelical Church Makane Yesus*
Reformed Bethel Synod*

Ghana

Evangelical Presbyterian Church, Ghana
Presbyterian Church of Ghana

Kenya

Kenya Evangelical Lutheran Church
Presbyterian Church of East Africa
Reformed Church of East Africa

Lesotho

Lesotho Evangelical Church (Kereke Ea Evangeli Lesotho)

Liberia

Presbytery of Liberia in West Africa

Madagascar

Church of Jesus Christ in Madagascar (Église de Jésus-Christ à Madagascar)

Malawi

Church of Central Africa Presbyterian

Mauritius

Presbyterian Church of Mauritius (Église presbytérienne de l'Ile Maurice)

Morocco

Evangelical Church in Morocco (Église évangélique du Maroc)

Mozambique

Evangelical Church of Christ in Mozambique (Igreja Evangélica de Cristo em Moçambique)
Presbyterian Church of Mozambique (Igreja Presbiteriana de Moçambique)
United Church of Christ in Mozambique (Igreja de Cristo Unida em Moçambique)

Niger

Evangelical Church of the Republic of Niger (Église évangélique de la République du Niger)

Nigeria

Christian Reformed Church of Nigeria
Evangelical Reformed Church of Christ
Presbyterian Church of Nigeria
Reformed Church of Christ in Nigeria (Ekklesiyar Kristi a Nigeria)
The Church of Christ in the Sudan among the Tiv
United Church of Christ in Nigeria (Hadaddiyar Ekklesiyar Kristi a Nigeria)

Reunion

Protestant Church of Reunion Island (Église protestante de la Réunion)

Rwanda

Presbyterian Church in Rwanda (Église presbytérienne au Rwanda)

Senegal

Protestant Church of Senegal (Église protestante du Sénégal)

South Africa (Republic of)

Dutch Reformed Church (Neuderduitse Gereformeede Kerk)
Dutch Reformed Mission Church in South Africa (Nederduitse Gereformeerde Sendingkerk in Suid Afrika)*
Evangelical Presbyterian Church in South Africa
Presbyterian Church of Africa
Presbyterian Church of Southern Africa
Reformed Church in Africa
Reformed Church in Southern Africa*
Reformed Presbyterian Church in Southern Africa
United Congregational Church of Southern Africa
Uniting Reformed Church in Southern Africa
Volkskerk van Afrika

Sudan

Presbyterian Church of the Sudan

Togo

Evangelical Presbyterian Church of Togo (Église évangélique presbytérienne du Togo)

Uganda

Reformed Presbyterian Church in Uganda

Zambia

Presbyterian Church of Southern Africa*
Reformed Church in Zambia
United Church of Zambia

Zimbabwe

Church of Central Africa Presbyterian*
Dutch Reformed Church Synod of Central Africa*
Reformed Church in Zimbabwe
Presbyterian Church of Southern Africa*

ASIA

China

The Church of Christ in China
The Hong Kong Council of the Church of Christ in China

India

Church of North India
Church of South India
Evangelical Church of Maraland
Presbyterian Church of India
Reformed Presbyterian Church, North-East India
The Church of Christ in China (Isua Krista Kohhran)

Indonesia

Christian Church in Central Sulawesi (Gereja Kristen Sulawesi Tengah)
Christian Church in East Timor (Gereja Kristen di Timor Timur)

Christian Church in Luwuk Banggai (Gereja Kristen di Luwuk Banggai)
Christian Church in South Sulawesi (Gereja Kristen di Sulawesi Selatan)
Christian Churches in the Southern Part of Sumatra (Gereja-Gereja Kristen Sumatera Bagian Selatan)
Christian Churches of Java (Gereja Kristen Jawa)
Christian Church of Sumba (Gereja Kristen Sumba)
Christian Evangelical Church in Bolaang Mongondow (Gereja Masehi Injili di Bolaang Mongondow)
Christian Evangelical Church in Minahasa (Gereja Masehi Injili di Minahasa)
Christian Evangelical Church in Sangir-Talaud (Gereja Masehi Injili Sangir-Talaud)
Church of Toraja Mamasa (Gereja Toraja Mamasa)
East Java Christian Church (Gereja Kristen Jawol Wetan)
Evangelical Christian Church in Halmahera (Gereja Masehi Injili Halmahera)
Evangelical Christian Church in Irian Jaya (Gereja Kristen Injili di Irian Jaya)
Evangelical Church in Kalimantan (Gereja Kalimantan Evangelis)
Indonesian Christian Church (Gereja Kristen Indonesia)
Indonesian Protestant Church in Buol Tolitoli (Gereja Protestan Indonesia di Buol Tolitoli)
Indonesian Protestant Church in Gorontalo (Gereja Protestan Indonesia di Gorontalo)
Indonesian Protestant Church of Donggala (Gereja Protestan Indonesia Donggala)
Karo Batak Protestant Church (Gereja Batak Karo Protestan)
Pasundan Christian Church (Gereja Kristen Pasundan)
Protestant Christian Church in Bali (Gereja Kristen Protestan di Bali)
Protestant Church in Indonesia (Gereja Protestan di Indonesia)
Protestant Church in South East Sulawesi (Gereja Protestan di Sulawesi Tenggara)
Protestant Church in the Moluccas (Gereja Protestan Maluku)
Protestant Church in the Western Part of Indonesia (Gereja Protestan di Indonesia Bagian Barat)
Protestant Evangelical Church in Timor (Gereja Masehi Injili di Timor)
Toraja Church (Gereja Toraja)

Japan

Church of Christ in Japan (Nippon Kirisuto Kyoukai)

Korean Christian Church in Japan
The United Church of Christ in Japan*

Korea

Presbyterian Church in Korea (Daeshin)
Presbyterian Church in Korea (Hap Dong Chung Tong)
Presbyterian Church in the Republic of Korea
Presbyterian Church of Korea

Malaysia

Presbyterian Church in Malaysia (Gereja Presbyterian Malaysia)
Protestant Church in Sabah, Malaysia

Myanmar

Independent Church of Myanmar
Mara Evangelical Church
Presbyterian Church of Myanmar
St. Gabriel's Church Union (Congregational)*

Pakistan

Church of Pakistan
Presbyterian Church of Pakistan

Philippines

United Church of Christ in the Philippines
United Evangelical Church of Christ (Iglesia Evangélica Unida de Cristo)

Singapore

Presbyterian Church in Singapore

Sri Lanka

Dutch Reformed Church in Sri Lanka
Presbytery of Lanka

Taiwan

Presbyterian Church in Taiwan

Thailand

Church of Christ in Thailand

CARIBBEAN AND NORTH AMERICA

Canada

Presbyterian Church in America (Canadian Section)*
Presbyterian Church in Canada
Reformed Church in Canada*
United Church of Canada

Cuba

Presbyterian-Reformed Church in Cuba (Iglesia Presbiteriana-Reformada en Cuba)

Dominican Republic

Dominican Evangelical Church (Iglesia Evangélica Dominicana)

Grenada

The Presbyterian Church in Grenada

Guyana

Guyana Congregational Union
Guyana Presbyterian Church
Presbyterian Church of Guyana

Jamaica

Jamaica Baptist Union
United Church in Jamaica & the Cayman Islands

Trinidad and Tobago

Presbyterian Church in Trinidad and Tobago

United States of America

Associate Reformed Presbyterian Church (General Synod)*
Christian Reformed Church in North America*
Conservative Congregational Christian Conference*
Cumberland Presbyterian Church
Cumberland Presbyterian Church in America
The Evangelical Congregational Church*
Evangelical Presbyterian Church
Hungarian Reformed Church in America
Lithuanian Evangelical Reformed Church
Netherlands Reformed Congregations*
Presbyterian Church in America*
Presbyterian Church (U.S.A.)
Protestant Reformed Churches in America*
Reformed Church in America
Reformed Church in the United States*
Reformed Presbyterian Church of North America*
Second Cumberland Presbyterian Church*
The Korean Presbyterian Church in America
United Church of Christ

MESOAMERICA AND SOUTH AMERICA

Argentina

Anglican Province of the Southern Cone
Evangelical Congregational Church (Iglesia Evangélica Congregacional)
Evangelical Church of the River Plate (Iglesia Evangélica del Rio de la Plata)
Reformed Churches in Argentina (Iglesias Reformadas en la Argentina)

Bolivia

Anglican Province of the Southern Cone
Evangelical Presbyterian Church in Bolivia (Iglesia Evangélica Presbiteriana en Bolivia)

Brazil

Arab Evangelical Church of São Paulo (Igreja Evangélica Àrabe de São
  Paulo)
Christian Reformed Church in Brazil (Igreja Crist Reformada do Brasil)
Evangelical Reformed Church in Brazil (Igreja Evangélica Reformada do
  Brasil)
Independent Presbyterian Church of Brazil (Igreja Presbiteriana
  Independente do Brasil)
Presbyterian Church of Brazil (Igreja Presbiteriana do Brasil)
United Presbyterian Church of Brazil (Igreja Presbiteriana Unida do Brasil)

Chile

Anglican Province of the Southern Cone
Evangelical Presbyterian Church in Chile (Iglesia Evangélica Presbiteriana
  en Chile)
National Presbyterian Church (Iglesia Presbiteriana Nacional)
Presbyterian Church of Chile (Iglesia Presbiteriana de Chile)

Colombia

Presbyterian Church of Colombia (Iglesia Presbiteriana de Colombia)

Costa Rica

Fraternity of Evangelical Churches of Costa Rica (Fraternidad de Iglesias
  Evangélicas Costarricenses

Ecuador

United Evangelical Church of Ecuador*

El Salvador

Reformed Church of El Salvador (Iglesia Reformada de El Salvador)

Guatemala

National Evangelical Presbyterian Church of Guatemala (Iglesia Evangélica
  Nacional Presbiteriana de Guatemala)

Mexico

Association of Presbyterian and Reformed Churches in Latin America*
Associate Reformed Presbyterian Church of Mexico (Iglesia Presbiteriana
   Asociado Reformada de Mexico)
Congregational Church of Mexico*
Independent Presbyterian Church of Mexico*
National Presbyterian Church of Mexico (Iglesia Nacional Presbiteriana de
   Mexico)
Presbyterian Reformed Church of Mexico (Iglesia Presbiteriana Reformada
   de Mexico)

Paraguay

Anglican Province of the Southern Cone

Peru

Anglican Province of the Southern Cone
Evangelical Presbyterian and Reformed Church in Peru*

Uruguay

Anglican Province of the Southern Cone
Waldensian Evangelical Church of the River Plate (Iglesia Evangélica
   Valdense del Rio de la Plata)

Venezuela

Presbyterian Church of Venezuela (Iglesia Presbiteriana de Venezuela)

EUROPE

Austria

Reformed Church in Austria (Evangelische Kirche HB in Österreich)

Belgium

United Protestant Church of Belgium (Église protestante unie de Belgique)

Bulgaria

Union of Evangelical Congregational Churches in Bulgaria

Croatia

Reformed Christian Church in Croatia

Czech Republic

Church of the Brethren (Cirkev Brairská)
Evangelical Church of Czech Brethren (Ceskobratrská Cirkev Evangelická)

Denmark

Reformed Church of Denmark (Reformierte Synode in Dänemark)

Finland

Free Church of Finland*

France

Reformed Church of Alsace and Lorraine (Église réformée d'Alsace et de Lorraine)
Reformed Church of France (Église réformée de France)

Germany

Evangelical-Reformed Church—Synod of the Ev.-Ref. Churches in Bavaria and Northwest Germany (Evangelisch-reformierte Kirche—Synode evangelisch-reformierter Kirchen in Bayern und Nordwestdeutschland)
National Church of Lippe (Lippische Landeskirche)
Reformed Alliance (Reformierter Bund)

Great Britain

Church of Scotland
Congregational Union of Scotland*
Presbyterian Church of Wales
Scottish Congregational Church

The Congregational Federation
Union of Welsh Independents (Undeb Yt Annibwynwyr Cymraeg)
United Free Church of Scotland
United Reformed Church

Greece

Greek Evangelical Church (Helleniki Evangeliki Ekklesia)

Hungary

Reformed Church in Hungary (Magyarországi Reformatus Egyház)

Ireland

Presbyterian Church in Ireland

Italy

Waldensian Evangelical Church (Chiesa Evangelica Valdese)

Latvia

Reformed Church in Latvia

Lithuania

Reformed Church in Lithuania

Luxembourg

Evangelical Protestant Church of the Grand Duchy of Luxembourg (Église
protestante réformée du Grand-Duché de Luxembourg)

Netherlands

Reformed Churches in The Netherlands (Gereformeerde Kerken in
Nederland)
Remonstrant Brotherhood (Nederlandse Hervormde Kerk)
The Netherlands Reformed Church (Nederlandse Hervormde Kerk)

Poland

Reformed Evangelical Church in Poland (Kósciól Ewangelicko-Reformowany)

Portugal

Evangelical Presbyterian Church of Portugal (Igreja Evangélica Presbiteriana de Portugal)

Romania

Reformed Church in Romania (Eparhia Reformata, Cluj)
Reformed Church in Romania (Eparhia Reformata, Oradea)

Slovakia

Church of the Brethren in the Slovak Republic (Rada Cirkvj Bratakej V Slovenskej Republike)
Reformed Christian Church in Slovakia (Reformovaná Krest. Cirkev na Slovensku)

Slovenia

Reformed Christian Church in Slovenia

Spain

Spanish Evangelical Church (Iglesia Evangélica Española)

Sweden

The Mission Covenant Church of Sweden (Svenska Missionsforbundet)

Switzerland

Federation of Swiss Protestant Churches (Schweizer Evangelischer Kirchenbund/Fédération des Églises protestante de la Suisse)

Ukraine

Reformed Church in Carpatho-Ukraine

Yugoslavia

Reformed Christian Church in Yugoslavia (Reformatske Hriscanske Crkve U SRJ)

MIDDLE EAST

Iran

Synod of the Evangelical Church of Iran

Lebanon

National Evangelical Synod of Syria and Lebanon
National Evangelical Union of Lebanon
Union of Armenian Evangelical Churches in the Near East

PACIFIC

American Samoa

Congregational Christian Church in American Samoa

Australia

Presbyterian Church of Australia*
Queensland Congregational*
Uniting Church in Australia

Cook Islands

Cook Islands Christian Church*

French Polynesia

Evangelical Church of French Polynesia (Église évangélique de Polynésie française)

Kiribati

Kiribati Protestant Church

Marshall Islands

Reformed Congregational Churches
United Church of Christ-Congregational in the Marshall Islands

Micronesia

Protestant Church of East Truk*
United Church of Christ in Pohnpei*

New Caledonia

Evangelical Church of New Caledonia and the Loyalty Islands (Église évangelique en Nouvelle Calédonie et aux Iles Loyauté)

New Zealand

Congregational Union of New Zealand*
Presbyterian Church of Aotearoa New Zealand
Presbyterian Church of New Zealand*
Reformed Churches of New Zealand*

Niue

Niue Church (Ekalesia Niue)

Solomon Islands

United Church in the Solomon Islands
United Church of Christ in the Solomon Islands
United Church of Papua New Guinea and the Solomon Islands*

Tuvalu

Tuvalu Christian Church (Te Ekatesia Kelisiano Tuvalu)

Vanuatu

Presbyterian Church of Vanuatu

Western Samoa

Congregational Christian Church in Samoa

Appendix 4
List of United Churches with Reformed Heritage*

1820 Evangelical Church of Kurhessen-Waldeck
1821 Evangelical Church in Baden
1891 Evangelical Church of the Augsburg and Helvetic Confessions (Austria)
1918 Evangelical Church of Czech Brethren; Evangelical Church of the Palatinate
1920 Bremen Evangelical Church
1925 United Church of Canada
1927 Church of Christ in China [Hong Kong Council]
1934 Church of Christ in Thailand
1938 Reformed Church of France
1941 United Church of Christ in Japan
1947 Evangelical Church in Hessen und Nassau; Church of South India
1948 United Church of Christ in the Philippines
1954 Evangelical Church of the Union (Old Prussian Union)
1957 United Church of Christ [USA]
1965 United Church of Zambia
1968 United Church of Papua New Guinea and the Solomon Islands; Church of Jesus Christ in Madagascar
1970 Church of North India; Church of Pakistan
1971 Church of Christ in Zaire; Church of Bangladesh
1972 United Congregational Church of Southern Africa
1977 Uniting Church in Australia
1979 United Protestant Church of Belgium; Waldensian Church/Evangelical Methodist Church in Italy
1981 United Reformed Church in the United Kingdom
1983 Presbyterian Church (U.S.A.)
1992 United Church in Jamaica and the Cayman Islands
1994 Uniting Reformed Church in Southern Africa

---

*Selected from a list compiled by Thomas Best, World Council of Churches.

Appendix 5
Research Centers, Publishers, and Online Bookstores

RESEARCH CENTERS

Centers for Reformation Research

Center for Reformation and Renaissance Studies, 71 Queen's Park Crescent East, Toronto, Ontario M5S 1K7 Canada. citd.scar.utoronto.ca/CRRS/ Index.html; University of Toronto Libraries. www.library.utoronto.ca/ Center for Reformation Research, 6477 San Bonita Ave, St. Louis, MO 63105.

Herzog August Bibliothek, Postfach 13 46, 38299 Wolfenbüttel, Deutchland. www.hab.de/

H. Henry Meeter Center for Calvin Studies, Calvin College and Seminary, 3207 Burton St. SE, Grand Rapids, MI 49546. www.calvin.edu/meeter_cr/

Universität Zürich, Institut für Schweizerische Reformationgeschichte, Kirchgasse 9, CH-8001 Zürich. www.unizh.ch/irg/

Université de Genève, Institut d'Histoire de la Reformation, 3 place de l'Université, 1211 Geneva 4–Suisse. www.unige.ch/ihr/index.htm

University of St. Andrews Library, North Street, St. Andrews, Fife KY16 9AL Scotland. www-library.st-and.ac.uk/; St. Andrews Reformation Studies Institute, St. John's House, 69 South Street, St. Andrews, Fife KY16 9AL Scotland. www.st-and.ac.uk/institutes/reformation/rsiew.htm

Centers of World Reformed Heritage

Presbyterian Tradition

Graduate Theological Union, Flora Lamson Hewlett Library, 2400 Ridge Road, Berkeley, CA 94709. www.gtu.edu/library/lib.html

McCormick Theological Seminary, Jesuit-Krauss-McCormick Library, 1100 East 55th Street, Chicago, IL 60615.

Presbyterian Historical Society, 435 Lombard Street, Philadelphia, PA 19147; P.O. Box 849, Montreat, NC 28757.

Princeton Theological Seminary, Speer Library, Mercer St. and Library Place, P.O. Box 111, Princeton, NJ 08542.

Union Theological Seminary and Presbyterian School of Christian Education, William Smith Morton Library, 3401 Brook Road, Richmond, VA 23227. www.utsva.edu/copy/library/index2.html

Union Theological Seminary in New York, Burke Library, 3041 Broadway, New York, NY 10027. www.128.59.143.18/

University of Edinburgh, New College Library/University Library, Mound Place, Edinburgh, Scotland EH1 2LU. www.lib.ed.ac.uk/

University of Toronto, Knox College Library, 59 St. George Street, Toronto, Ontario M5S 2E6. www.library.utoronto.ca:8002/

Congregational Tradition

American Congregational Association, Congregational Library, 14 Beacon Street, Boston, MA 02108. www.14beacon.org

Andover-Newton Theological School, 169 Herrick Road, Newton Centre, MA 02159. www.library.ants.edu/

Chicago Theological Seminary, 5757 University Avenue, Chicago, IL 60637.

Harvard University Libraries, Cambridge, MA 02138. www.hul.harvard.edu/libinfo/faculty/

United Kingdom Research Libraries (copac). www.copac.ac.uk/copac/

Yale University, Yale Divinity Library, New Haven, CT 06520. www.library.yale.edu/htmldocs/col_idx.htm

Reformed Tradition

Calvin College and Seminary, The Hekman Library, 3207 Burton St. SE, Grand Rapids, MI 49546. www.calvin.edu/library/

Dutch Universities, the Netherlands. www.mit.edu:8001/people/cdemello/nl.html

New Brunswick Theological Seminary, Gardner A. Sage Library, 21 Seminary Place, New Brunswick, NJ 18901–1159.

University of Stellenbosch, Theological Library, 171 Dorp Street, 7600 Stellenbosch, South Africa. lib.sun.ac.za/Telnet/

National Libraries

Australian National University Library, Canberra, Australia. www.library.anu.edu.au/screens/opacmenu.html

Library of Congress, Washington, D.C. lcweb2.loc.gov/catalog/
National Library Catalogues Worldwide. www.library.uq.edu.au/ssah/jeast/
National Library of Canada. www.amicus.nlc-bnc.ca/waap/resanet/
searche.htm
National Library of New Zealand. www.natlib.govt.nz/online/ils/
United Kingdom Research Libraries. www.copac.ac.uk/copac/

SELECTED PUBLISHERS

Baker Book House (est. 1939), Box 6287, Grand Rapids, MI 49516–6287.
www.bakerbooks.com
Banner of Truth Trust (est. 1973), 3 Murrayfield Rd., Edinburgh, EH12 6EL,
Scotland. www.banneroftruth.co.uk/Books/banner_of_truth_books.htm
E. J. Brill (est. 1683), Postbus 9000, 2300 PA, Leiden, Netherlands.
ejbrill.infor.com:4900/11/
Claudianna (est. 1855), Via Principe Tommaso 1, 10125 Turin, Italy.
William B. Eerdmans Publishing Co. (est. 1911), 255 Jefferson Ave, SE,
Grand Rapids, MI 49503.
Kok Publishing House (est. 1896), P.O. Box 5018, 8260 GA, Kampen,
Netherlands. www.kok.nl/pharos.htm
Librairie Droz (est.), 11 rue Massot, B.P. 389, CH-1211, Geneve 12.
www.librairie-droz.ch
Pickwick Publications (est. 1982), 215 Incline Way, San Jose, CA 95139.
Pilgrim Press/United Church Press (est. 1895), 700 Prospect Ave E., Cleve-
land OH 44115-1100. www.ucpress.com
Presbyterian & Reformed Publishing Company (est. 1931), Box 817,
Phillipsburg, NJ 08865.
Presbyterian Historical Society, 425 Lombard Street, Philadelphia, PA
19147.
Rutherford House (est. 1983), 17 Claremont Park, Edinburgh, EH6 7PJ,
Scotland. www.rutherfordhouse.org.uk/booksmain.htm
Soli Deo Gloria Publications (est. 1988), Box 451, Morgan, PA 15064.
members.aol.com/SDGbooks/
St. Andrew Press (est. 1954), 121 George St., Edinburgh, EH2 4YN,
Scotland. www.ucsm.ac.uk/church.net.uk/home/sap/
T. & T. Clark (est. 1821), 59 George St., Edinburgh, EH2 2LQ, Scotland.
Westminster John Knox Press/Presbyterian Publishing Corporation
(est. 1838), 100 Witherspoon Street, Louisville, KY 40202–1396.
www.pcusa.org/ppc/homepage.htm

World Alliance of Reformed Churches (est. 1875), P.O. Box 2100, 150 Route de Ferney, CH-1211 Geneva 2, Switzerland. wccx.wcc-coe.org/ warc/

ONLINE BOOKSTORES

Amazon Books. www.amazon.com
The Association of American University Presses—Combined Online Catalog of Books. aaup.princeton.edu/

About the Authors

ROBERT BENEDETTO (B.A., San Francisco State University; M.A., Pittsburgh Theological Seminary; M.L.S., University of Hawaii) is associate librarian and associate professor of bibliography at Union Theological Seminary and Presbyterian School of Christian Education in Richmond, Virginia. He previously served as deputy director of the Presbyterian Church (U.S.A.) Department of History in Montreat, North Carolina. He is the editor of *Presbyterian Reformers in Central Africa* (Brill, 1997) and *Interpreting John Calvin* (Baker, 1996) and has published several bibliographies and research guides, including *P. T. Forsyth Bibliography and Index* (Greenwood Press, 1993).

DARRELL L. GUDER (University of Southern California; Ph.D., University of Hamburg) is professor of evangelism and church growth at Columbia Theological Seminary in Decator, Georgia. He previously served as vice president of academic affairs and dean of the faculty at Whitworth College in Spokane, Washington, and professor of evangelism and global mission at Louisville Presbyterian Theological Seminary in Louisville, Kentucky. His publications include translations of Otto Weber's two-volume *Foundations of Dogmatics* (Eerdmans, 1981, 1883) and Eberhard Jüngel's *God as the Mystery of the World* (Eerdmans, 1983) and *Be My Witnesses: The Church's Mission, Message, and Messengers* (Eerdmans, 1985). He edited *Missional Church: A Vision for the Sending of the Church in North America* (Eerdmans, 1998).

DONALD K. McKIM (B.A., Westminster College; M.Div., Pittsburgh Theological Seminary; Ph.D., University of Pittsburgh) is academic dean and professor of theology at Memphis Theological Seminary. He previously served as professor of theology at the University of Dubuque Theological Seminary in Dubuque, Iowa. His publications include *Encyclopedia of the Reformed Faith* (Westminster John Knox, 1992) and *Major Themes in the Reformed Tradition* (Eerdmans, 1992). He has written *The Bible and Theology in Preaching* (Abingdon, 1993) and *Westminster Dictionary of Theological Terms* (Westminster John Knox, 1996).

508